Wings of Valor, Wings of Gold

Amy Waters Yarsinske

Flying Machines Press

For my naval aviator
Lieutenant Raymond J. Yarsinske Jr., United States Navy
and children, Ashley Nicole, Allyson Emily, and Raymond III

Dedication

I raise the aviator's toast to those we have lost so young, so full of life and the thrill of flying, and to those who have yet to be accounted for. To your glory, to your memory this book is dedicated. To your glory. You will forever be remembered, as in the timeless verse of poet Laurence Binyon (1869–1943) from *For the Fallen* (1917):

> They shall not grow old, as we that are left grow old:
> Age shall not weary them, nor the years condemn.
> At the going down of the sun and in the morning—
> We will remember them.

Published in the United States by Flying Machines Press, 35 Chelsea Street, Stratford, Connecticut 06497.

Book and cover design, layout, and typesetting by John W. Herris.

Digital scanning and image editing by Gretchen H. Herris and John W. Herris.

Text edited by Diana L. Bailey.

Printed and Bound in Korea.

Library of Congress Cataloging-in-Publication Data
Yarsinske, Amy Waters, 1963–
Wings of valor, wings of gold / Amy Waters Yarsinske.
p. cm.
Includes bibliographical references and index.
ISBN 0-9637110-5-9 (hardcover)
1. United States. Navy—Aviation—History. I. Title.
VG93.Y37 1998
359.9'4'0973—dc21 98-34646
CIP

Flying Machines Press

Tel: (203) 378-9344
Fax: (203) 380-1849

For the latest information on our books and posters, visit our web page at:
www.flying-machines.com

Table of Contents

Acknowledgments

First and foremost, I wish to thank all of the Navy and Marine Corps aviators, past and present, who cooperated with me over the past ten years as I compiled their story. With their trust and friendship, I was able to research thoroughly and cull invaluable information from personal and official records, interview key historical and contemporary figures, and experience flight operations, ceremonies, and events firsthand.

I owe an equal debt to my editor and best friend, Diana L. Bailey. Her contributions to the book were extraordinarily important. The day her hand turned the first page of the manuscript, she was captivated by the human story in *Wings of Valor, Wings of Gold,* and from that day onward, Diana devoted so many hours to the project, we have since lost count. Her editing talents will be appreciated by the book's readers who unknowingly leaf through its pages, not realizing how skillfully and seamlessly Diana pared down my long, scholarly paragraphs to reader-friendly passages. In the end, Diana and I experienced one of the true joys of life's work: "Success is a journey not a destination." The joy of painstakingly researching and writing the book came from the people and personalities who comprise United States naval aviation, and in the discovery and telling of that linkage of human events called "history."

I cannot find enough words of thanks for the archivists, curators, librarians, and registrars who conscientiously assisted me and provided critical information, photographs and illustrations: Frederick W. Biddenstadt, photographer and photographic archivist, History of Aviation Collection at the University of Texas at Dallas Library; Chester Browning, director, Quonset Point Air Museum; Gordon Calhoun, publications editor, Joseph M. Judge, curator, and Elizabeth Poulliot, executive director, Hampton Roads Naval Museum; Darryl Collins, archivist, National Park Service, First Flight Museum and Archives, Kitty Hawk, North Carolina; Mark Chambers, External Affairs Office, National Aeronautics and Space Administration, Langley, Virginia; Robert J. "Bob" Cressman, Roy A. Grossnick, Stephen D. Hill (retired) and Gwendolyn Rich, Aviation History Section, Naval Historical Center of the Navy Department, Washington Navy Yard, Washington, D.C.; Thomas D. Crouch, Chief of Aeronautics, National Air and Space Museum; Phil Edwards, Technical Information Specialist, National Air and Space Museum Branch Library, Smithsonian Institution Libraries; Samantha Warden of the Glenn H. Curtiss Museum, Hammondsport, New York; M. Hill Goodspeed, historian and library director, Emil Buehler Naval Aviation Library, National Museum of Naval Aviation; the staff of the Grafl. von Zeppelin'sches Schlossmuseum, Federal Republic of Germany; Dee Anna Grimsrud, reference archivist, State Historical Society of Wisconsin; Peggy A. Haile, Sargeant Memorial Room, Norfolk Public Library; Alice Haines, archivist, Norfolk Naval Shipyard Museum, Portsmouth, Virginia; David W. Hopson, editorial assistant, Columbia University Oral History Research Office; Margaret Hrabe, Special Collections Department, Alderman Library, University of Virginia; the staff of the Hugh M. Morris Library, University of Delaware; Carol A. Leadenham, assistant archivist for reference, Hoover Institution on War, Revolution and Peace, Stanford University; the staff of the Library of Congress Manuscript Division; Jennifer Locke, curator, Armed Forces Collection, National Museum of American History, Smithsonian Institution; Lois Lovisolo, Library Department, Grumman Aerospace Corporation; Margaret Macdonald and Karen Whitehair, Archives Division, and Peter Jacob, Early Flight Department, National Air and Space Museum, Smithsonian Institution; William Massa, chief reference archivist, Sterling Memorial Library, Yale University; Margaret Moseley, chief archivist, Virginiana Room, Newport News Public Library; Dennis Mroczkowski, executive director, and David Johnson, curator and archivist, the Casemate Museum, Fortress Monroe, Virginia; the staff of the National Archives at College Park; Mary Louise O'Brien, acquisitions librarian, Armed Forces Staff College Library; Virginia H. Smith, reference librarian, Massachusetts Historical Society; the staff of the United States Army Intelligence and Security Command; and Richard Van Dearoff, Military Reference, Library of Congress.

Among the hundreds of Navy and Marine Corps personnel who worked with me, I must single out Commander Kevin M. Wensing, Commander Naval Air Force Atlantic Fleet public affairs officer (1993–1996), who went to great lengths to secure access to naval aviation commands, arrange interviews and provide conduits to invaluable research material. Without Kevin's diligence and conscientiousness, fired by his belief in the book and my ability, *Wings of Valor, Wings of Gold* might never have come to fruition. Kevin's enthusiasm and commitment to the project carried me through intense periods of research and writing and I cannot thank him enough.

In the publishing business, I am blessed to have superb legal counsel and guidance from my attorney, Ross C. Reeves, and his associate, Michelle Glover-Foy. They are as dedicated to the successful outcome of my work as I am and their patience with me is extraordinary. I deeply appreciate their friendship and professionalism as they navigate the world of publishing, television and film on my behalf.

So many other people contributed so variously to this work that I can only list their names in alphabetical order, with deepest thanks to all: Petty Officer Corey Ahola and Michael Maus, Commander Naval Air Force Atlantic Fleet Public Affairs Office; Commander Martin R. "Marty" Allard; Vice Admiral Richard C. "Sweetpea" Allen, Commander Naval Air Force Atlantic Fleet (1993–1996, retired) and his wife, Peggy; Lieutenant Colonel David Alley and Major Derek Hoxey of the United States Air Force, members of the Order of Daedalions, Samuel P. Langley Flight No. 34; Harry A. "Andy" Andrews, former photographer, Naval Aviation Depot Norfolk; Frank Ault, founder of the Fighter Weapons School, better known as "Top Gun," and a Golden Eagle; William J. Armstrong, Ph.D., Naval Air Systems Command; Admiral Stanley R. Arthur, former Vice Chief of Naval Operations and Gray Eagle (retired); Virginia Massenburg Barnes; Commander David Barron, former public affairs officer, and Beth Baker, assistant public affairs officer, Commander Naval Base Norfolk; Bruce Barry, reporter, WTKR-TV 3; Chief of Naval Operations Admiral Jeremy "Mike" Boorda (1994–1996) and his staff; Commander Martin P. "Marty" Bricker; Joseph "Bolo" Cavanaugh; Stephen D. Chalker, historian of Naval Air Station Weeksville, North Carolina; Commander Rudy R. Costanzo; Bill Crimmins, photographer; Herbert Davenport; Nannette Davis and Brice Maccubbin, public affairs officers, Naval Aviation Depot Norfolk; Gerry Dickseski (christenings and commissionings), Rear Admiral Jack A. Garrow (retired) (former vice president of public relations and marketing), Lyn Lyon (public affairs officer and archivist), and Jack Schnaeder (retired) (former public affairs officer), Newport News Shipbuilding and Drydock Company; Walter C. Diehl; Captains E. Lee Duckworth (1990–1993) and Daniel J. Franken (1993–1996), former commanding officers, Naval Air Station Norfolk; Vice Admiral Robert F. Dunn (retired); Vice Admiral Richard M. Dunleavy, Commander Naval Air Force

Atlantic Fleet (1986–1989, retired); Stephen Ewing, author and historian, Patriot's Point Carrier Museum; Dorothy Flatley; Rear Admiral James H. Flatley III (retired), president and chief executive officer, Patriot's Point Carrier Museum, and Jim's wife, Nancy; Lieutenant Commander James H. "Seamus" Flatley IV and Seamus' wife, Christine; Lieutenant Commander Joseph Flatley; Rear Admiral Edward L. "Whitey" Fleightner (retired); Janie Forbes, daughter of Lieutenant Robert F. "Red" Barber, who along with Commander L.F. "Mike" Vogt, became the first A-6A Intruder combat fatalities; William W. Gough, M.D.; John Griffiths and Wes Moseman, Norfolk Office, Northrop-Grumman Aerospace Corporation; Lyle and Mary Kay Heldenbrand; Reon G. Hillegass; Thomas C. Hise, Virginia State Vice Commander, Veterans of Under Age Military Service, and owner, Tom's Military Museum; Rear Admiral Alfred C. "Bud" Holmes (retired); Lawrence Jackson, photographer, *The Virginian-Pilot;* Gerald Jean and John Parker, Decal Shop, Naval Aviation Depot Norfolk; Chief of Naval Operations Admiral Jay L. Johnson (1996–) and his staff; Ken Johnson, producer and host, and Tony Macrini, host, WNIS-AM 790; Rear Admiral John T. Kavanaugh, SC, USN (retired); Captain Robert C. Klosterman (retired), first commanding officer of the USS *John C. Stennis* (1993–1997) and his wife, Becky; Gail Lemieux, former public affairs officer, Naval Air Station Norfolk; Vice Admiral Anthony A. Less, Commander Naval Air Force Atlantic Fleet (1990–1993, retired); George H. Loeb Jr., member, Experimental Aircraft Association; Lieutenant Commander Jeffrey Manor, Navy Casualty Office, Pentagon; Linda and Joseph Mathias; Captain David McCampbell (retired and deceased), the Navy's all-time leading ace; Captain J.B. McKamey (retired), former prisoner of war, Republic of Vietnam, and public affairs officer, Naval Air Station Pensacola, Florida; Dennis McCurdy, WFOS-FM 88.7 and WCTV, Chesapeake, Virginia; Rear Admiral Jim Miller (retired), president and chief executive officer, Navy Memorial, Washington, D.C.; Melody Miller, deputy press secretary to United States Senator Edward M. Kennedy, and the Kennedy family liaison; Steven Milner, congressional and public affairs officer, Norfolk Naval Shipyard; Samuel B. Murphey, World War II naval aviator; Lieutenant General Dennis J. Murphy, USMC (retired), chairman, Hampton Roads Naval Museum Foundation; Floyd C. Nugent, former Navy test pilot (deceased); Matthew "Mick" Nussbaum; Commanders Gerald C. Peebles (retired) and Thomas J. "Sparky" Sparks, former commanding officers, United States Atlantic Command, Cruise Missile Support Activity; Lieutenant Dawn T. Peters, Judge Advocate General (retired), legal officer, Naval Safety Center; Colonel Theodore Argyres "Pete" Petras, USMC (retired); Captain Bruce Pieper, former commanding officer, Naval Aviation Depot Norfolk; Captain Nicholas J. Pope (retired); Henry Proescher; Vice Admiral John K. Ready, Commander Naval Air Force Atlantic Fleet (1989–1991, retired); Captain Kenneth S. Reightler Jr., astronaut; Kenneth S. Reightler Sr.; Richard Salzberg, my friend and true believer in the project; Caroline Kennedy Schlossberg; Captain Robert "Whiskey Bob" Schmidt (retired) and Captain Dale O. "Snort" Snodgrass, former Commanders Fighter Wing Atlantic; Nancy Schwartz, assistant editor, *Fly By* and *Foundation,* Naval Aviation Museum Foundation; William L. Skliar, president, United States Air Racing Association; George M. Skurla, former president and chief executive officer, Grumman Aerospace Corporation; Troy Snead, public affairs officer, Naval Air Station Oceana; Lieutenant Commander Greta von Sothen (retired); Commander Alexander Vraciu (retired); Major John Walsh, USMC, Marine Air Group Forty-Six; William B. Waters Jr.; David White; and Alice Williams.

Finally, I wish to thank my husband, Raymond, who encouraged me when I became overwhelmed, discouraged and tired in the process of working on *Wings of Valor, Wings of Gold.* This volume is dedicated to him and to our precious children.

Introduction

"...These are the wings of which I will forever be proud."

On the eve of the Coral Sea engagement an American task force, of which the USS *Lexington* (CV-2) was a part, caught up with the end of the main Japanese invasion force near Tulagi and destroyed three enemy aircraft carriers—the pride of the Japanese Imperial Navy. In the fierce fighting that ensued, a young Navy pilot by the name of Lieutenant (junior grade) Paul G. Baker shot down five carrier attack aircraft from the Japanese carrier *Zuikaku*. Around dusk he was circling above the *Lexington,* the last of his flight waiting to land. Baker was low on fuel and exhausted from battle when, suddenly, ten Japanese aircraft approached above him. The chances of Japanese planes making a suicide run at the *Lexington* were great, and Baker was ordered to shut down his landing lights and hold in the pattern. Baker knew the Japanese would close in on his radio transmissions with the *Lexington.* Without hesitation, Lieutenant Baker turned his aircraft away from the ship, flying into the darkness so enemy planes would give chase. Sailors and aviators aboard the *Lexington* saw Baker's aircraft disappear into the night, to his certain death.

The story of Paul G. Baker touches a cord in all of us. Baker was the last of his breed, the final chief aviation pilot to fly with Fighting Two *Flying Chiefs* squadron. The crowning achievement of his naval career, aside from being winged in 1935, was being commissioned to lieutenant junior grade in March of 1942. Baker's career had begun in 1929, and ended on May 7, 1942, when his plane collided with a Japanese Mitsubishi Zero fighter high in the clouds above the Coral Sea.

Pierre-Anne Towers, widow of Vice Admiral John Henry "Jack" Towers, USN, Naval Aviator No. 3, once remarked that

Early in World War I, sometime in June of 1917, a flying boat was catapulted from the cruiser USS *Huntington,* then underway in a crosswind. This photograph was taken from a kite balloon and constitutes an interesting study compared with aerial photographs today. On August 11, 1915, the Naval Observatory requested that the Eastman Kodak Company develop an aerial camera with a high-speed lens suitable for photography at 3,000 to 6,000 feet altitude, and constructed such that the pressure of air during flight would not distort the image. The first production order for aerial photographic equipment was initiated when the Naval Observatory issued requisitions for twenty cameras and accessories to be manufactured by the Eastman Kodak Company, January 10, 1917, a little less than two years later. The first Navy aerial photographer was Walter Leroy "Dick" Richardson, designated Naval Aviator No. 582 on April 12, 1918. Known as the "daddy of all naval aerial photographers," Richardson founded the photographic section in the Bureau of Aeronautics, and established photographic schools at several naval air stations including, of course, Hampton Roads. The first oblique camera for aerial photography was designed by Richardson. At the time of his death on June 14, 1945, Richardson held the title of senior scientist, photographic inspector for the Bureau of Aeronautics. (Official United States Navy Photograph.)

her husband's life reflected the spirit of early naval aviation. The qualities we would like to admire, even the foibles, of naval aviators like Towers are woven into the texture of their life and times. She would say that it was a felicitous and curious chance of fate that Jack Towers happened to be young, fearless, and stubborn when flying was a daily discovery, and he and his friends had to forge their wings before they could try them.

Naval aviators have been forging their wings and trying them since Eugene B. Ely showed them the way on a dreary day in November 1910, and young Lieutenant Paul Baker gave his life for his country thousands of miles from home in a time and place called the Battle of the Coral Sea. Naval aviation is the embodiment of who we are as a country. Though the profession can be defined by its traditions and the parameters of its sacrifice of life and machine, naval aviation can also be delineated by the voices of the men and women who have established naval aviation from the early ballooning attempts of John La Mountain; the breathtaking flight of a frail aircraft from the deck of the USS *Birmingham* by Ely in 1910; to the fantastic journey of Theodore Gordon "Spuds" Ellyson, our first naval aviator, and his modern-day counterparts flying from the decks of American aircraft carriers deployed around the world who daily shield us from littoral threats and insurrections.

The task of establishing people and places and the impact they have had on their profession is one part of the greater mosaic of naval aviation. Events of national and international importance have surely shaped naval aviation but it is naval aviation, though tasked to uphold the policies and posture of a nation, which has often exposed weak decisions and rewritten the course of events and, consequently, our national history.

There would be challenges to be faced and demons to conquer in the course of naval aviation history. American naval aviators experimented quietly with aircraft until their quiet world exploded into war in 1914. Though the United States was not immediately and officially drawn into the war in Europe until 1917, naval aviators watched from a distance and waited their turn while some even participated in the flying services of America's allies. "A terrible beauty was born," penned poet William Butler Yeats (1865–1939) during the war, a conflict which was grotesquely cruel and hardly the expectation of chivalrous combat so many envisaged before they arrived in Europe or waged the close-in battle to protect America's shores from German submarines and possible invasion. The First World War redefined combat on the ground and introduced the military to the airplane.

World war revisited American naval aviators in 1939, and, once again, the nation remained neutral until drawn into the war by the Japanese attack on Pearl Harbor, December 7, 1941. If the Great War of 1914–1918 was dehumanizing, the Second World War could be characterized as a morally twisted act of destruction which drew upon human suffering for its pleasure and death for its sustenance. Naval aviators fought courageously in all theaters of the war, and in every conflict since.

John Gillespie Magee Jr., wrote in *High Flight:*

Oh, I have slipped the surly bonds of earth,
And danced the skies on laughter-silvered wings;
Sunward I've climbed and joined the tumbling mirth
Of sun-split clouds — and done a hundred things
You have not dreamed of — wheeled and soared and swung
High in the sunlit silence. Hov'ring there,
I've chased the shouting wind along and flung
My eager craft through footless halls of air.
Up, up the long delirious, burning blue
I've topped the wind-swept heights with easy grace,
Where never lark, or even eagle, flew;
And, white with silent, lifting mind I've trod
The high untrespassed sanctity of space,
Put out my hand, and touched the face of God.

Perhaps the most important lesson learned by any writer worth their salt is sticking with the job through good and bad, when time and circumstance dictate less than a favorable outcome, and the most memorable moment takes your breath away and you know you have just experienced one of the greatest thrills of your life, a compelling event etched forever in your soul. This meant covering the high points, which is always a pleasure, but it also meant having the absolute worst day of your life when friends died in aviation crashes. Compelled by the bonds of friendship and honor, you feel nothing but the numbing, solemn silence as grief envelopes the faces of family, friends and naval aviators. The memory of those faces is secreted away in my mind, my heart and my soul inasmuch as the clutching of hands and the memory of holding fast to naval aviators who in their grief for lost friends, clung to me for comfort during memorial services which were too frequent and painful to fathom. I never knew there could be so much grief in my soul as those longest days when young men died and we gathered to say good-bye.

Writing this book meant going back again and again to the flight line and seeing very determined young men climb into the cockpit and head out on training or fleet exercises in the wee hours of the morning when most of us are numb with sleep, and staying to watch night flight operations and struggle to stay awake. It meant bantering with pilots and naval flight officers, learning their interests, their greatest moments and memories, and fears. Some would have no fond memories, at least none which survived trying times, their lives shaped by an endless string of tragic events, while others would painfully note the camaraderie they would miss when the right-sized Navy gave them a pink slip. The memories will remain with me forever. The gallant moments, those spent with retired naval aviators who had in common their proud service and experiences, and who oft reminded me, "once a naval aviator, always a naval aviator," and my own experiences at grand and nostalgic ceremonies like the passing of the Gray Eagle Trophy given "in recognition of a clear eye, a stout heart, a steady hand, and a daring defiance of gravity and the law of averages," made a lasting impression.

The Gray Eagle Trophy passed hands six times in the course of compiling this history, the first occuring on March 1, 1991, when Admiral Jerome L. Johnson, USN, Naval Aviator No. V9523, took the Gray Eagle designation from Admiral Huntington Hardisty, USN, Naval Aviator No. T3919. The crowning of the Navy's senior aviator is an important yet often overlooked right of passage in the annals of naval aviation history and tradition. The awarding of the Gray Eagle Trophy goes back in time to the first determination of the naval aviator bearing the title, "Naval Aviator No. 1," and that name, of course, was determined to be Commander Theodore G. "Spuds" Ellyson. In late 1959, Admiral Charles R. "Cat" Brown, USN, Naval Aviator No. 3159, communicated to former Chief of Naval Operations Admiral George W. Anderson, who was at the time serving as commander of the United States Sixth Fleet, in correspondence dated October 29, 1959, suggest-

Two Grumman F-14B Tomcats from Fighter Squadron 143, Naval Air Station Oceana, Virginia, fly over the USS *George Washington* (CVN-73) somewhere in the Caribbean, 1993. Today's aerial photography, in evidence throughout latter portions of the book, bears a stark contrast to the work of a lone photographer in a kite balloon. (Lieutenant Stephen P. Davis, photographer; Official United States Navy Photograph.)

ing that "it be determined from official records who, at all times, is the senior aviator in point of service in flying; that a baton or similar token be awarded him and that, with due ceremony, this symbol be handed down to the next man with the passing years." By studying the precedence list, Brown and his supporters determined that in spirit and by right, the first name on the Gray Eagle list should be Commander Ellyson even though he had been deceased since February 27, 1928. Ellyson's name is listed as the first Gray Eagle, dated June 2, 1911, through the date of his untimely and tragic passing. He was followed by Vice Admiral John H. "Jack" Towers. The list of Gray Eagles preceding the first formal presentation of the trophy to Brown on the occasion of the Golden Anniversary of Naval Aviation Ball held at the Sheraton Park Hotel, Washington, D.C., on January 25, 1961, included some of the greatest names in naval aviation history.

Events as steeped in nostalgia and remembrance as the Gray Eagle ceremony give us pause to reflect on the fact that we never arrive at our own time and place without a chain of events preceding us. The Gray Eagle ceremony provides naval aviation with the opportunity to stand still and look back. One of the most important lessons to be taken away from the Gray Eagle is how much naval aviation has become, indeed as Pierre-Anne Towers noted, "woven into the texture of those days," of time and place, and of fate. The cyclical nature of history, of life itself, bears its truths every day, and on the momentous occasion of the Gray Eagle ceremony, the dignity and tradition of naval aviation springs to life. Naval Aviator No. 1, "Spuds" Ellyson, lived his life for naval aviation. He took his responsibilities seriously, so seriously that Ellyson hoped his every act, be it routine or experimental in nature, contribute to the technological development of naval aviation and to its dignity and traditions.

It is next to impossible to forget the caveat of all aviation, "safety first," in the context of history. Naval aviation is a dangerous profession, perhaps hard to accept for family and friends of military airmen, but nevertheless true. The 1990s may well be remembered as the decade which heightened our collective awareness of the inherent dangers of flying military and civilian aircraft. United States naval aviators are high on the list of the most courageous people one may

Vice Chief of Naval Operations and Gray Eagle, Admiral Stanley R. Arthur passes the Gray Eagle trophy to Rear Admiral David R. Morris in a ceremony held aboard the Norfolk-based aircraft carrier USS *America* (CV-66) on March 21, 1995.

ever meet. Landing a high-speed jet fighter on the pitching deck of an aircraft carrier morning, noon or night takes more than a keen eye and steady hand, some might say it requires the grace of God and a love of living on the edge. Naval aviators are not a group of professionals we talk about everyday unless their news is spread across a dramatic headline in the newspaper yet because they lay their lives on the line every day in some corner of the world, we breathe easier, sleep more soundly and enjoy our families, livelihoods and jobs in large measure because naval aviators are standing the watch and fighting the fight. Accidents afix themselves to our conscience and remind us of the importance of education and training, and assessment of skill. Naval aviators are required to meet the highest standards of qualification in all facets of tactical concepts including visual responsibility, weapons employment, safety-of-flight, communications, maneuvering, mutual support, and fundamental positioning of the aircraft on and off the deck of an aircraft carrier. Aviation accidents have been taking the lives of young naval aviators since the earliest days of Navy flying. Every aircraft accepted by the United States Navy in the twentieth century has had its flaws. Regardless of the level of technology, aircraft are machines which depend on the thinking processes of the men and women who fly them. As the naval aviation profession has evolved since 1910, every mishap represented a growing pain, a learning experience to be recorded in memory and put back in the classroom and cockpit as an instruction on proper procedure. The Naval Air and Training Operating (NATOPS) Program was established by the Chief of Naval Operations and is administered through the Naval Air Systems Command to keep aviators abreast of the latest operations and safety procedures per their aircraft type. These emergency procedures can and do save lives everyday.

Naval aviation started with less than a handful of daring souls willing to place themselves at great risk to lead the profession into what it has become today. History, at least in the author's view, is a chain of events focused on people and people's actions within the construct of environment, technology, and human circumstance. The historic trust runs deep and true, translating into the story of the people who have made naval aviation so engaging and fascinating to research. The commitment to tell this story was bound by obligation, honor, and forthrightness to the enlisted and officer naval aviation active duty personnel, retirees, and those only in our hearts and memories, and the charge to do so was a weighty one. In the end, you, the naval aviation community, have told your own story, written your own history in action, in deeds, and in the volumes of words you have shared with me.

You have read about San Diego's claim to training the first naval aviator; Annapolis' claim to purchasing the first naval aircraft; and Pensacola's legitimate claim as the "cradle of naval aviation." Now read about Hampton Roads, the birthplace of naval aviation, and see naval aviation history from a new perspective, a view that takes the reader from a tentative perch in the gondola of John La Mountain's balloon high above Hampton Roads to takeoff from the deck of a modern-day Navy aircraft carrier. This book takes a look at where United States naval aviation really began, documenting the people, places, and events which have helped shape the past, present, and future of the profession. The history is dramatic and complex, the story human. If history is, indeed, a compilation of our collective human experience set within a given time and place, it should be written that way. History should enrich our perspective of people and events of the past, be relevant to where we are today, and help us chart the course of the future.

You will be taken into the past of naval aviation with this volume and some of the stories will make you laugh; others, cry. Some of the stories included in the book were naval aviators' remembrances of experiences in Hampton Roads, while so many others carry the reader overseas. Hampton Roads has been at the center of naval aviation history for nearly ninety years, longer if you include the Civil War period, and it is this history which began so long ago on the shores of Hampton Roads that wound its way across America, only to play a significant role in course of world events—and history.

The story of naval aviation in Norfolk and vicinity begins in 1861, ending in the present. This story has never before been told despite the fact that aviation archivists at the Smithsonian Institution National Air and Space Museum and National Aeronautics and Space Administration can document that Hampton Roads is at the center of a Mid-Atlantic region which has contributed the most to the furtherance of naval aviation, and aviation in general, moreso than any other area of the country. The list of firsts in naval aviation at Hampton Roads is daunting, and there was obviously a limit to how much could be included in this volume.

The one regret I carry away from this research is that I could not know all the famous and not-so-famous naval aviators of the past who made the research such a joy, but in the process I grew close to them and to those who knew them best. Telling their story is the greatest honor I will ever have and as you leaf through the pages of *Wings of Valor, Wings of Gold,* I think you will find the collective spirit of naval aviation as compelling and wonderful a story of man and machine, time and place as I did.

Amy Waters Yarsinske
Vincit Amor Patriae

"Andy Aileron" will be on standby throughout the book to point out the basics of aircraft, should anyone need it. Andy was the creation of Navy artist T. Hill who created this delightful caricature during World War II. The cartoon appeared in the Aircraft Recognition Manual prepared by the Recognition Department of the Fighter Direction and Combat Information Center Advanced Training School, a unit of the Fleet Training Center Oahu, Territory of Hawaii. Andy Aileron's "definitions" are highlighted in black and he is normally pointing to the part of the aircraft indicated in each of the line drawings by name. For the uninitiated, Andy is an excellent guide.

Chapter 1: Prelude to Sustained Flight

A little over forty years before Wilbur and Orville Wright went aloft in their flying machine over the dunes of Kitty Hawk, North Carolina, Confederate and Union forces had an air presence. Though balloons made of silk or, in some cases cotton, were used for reconnaissance, there was also an "airplane." An aircraft model was designed between 1862 and 1863 by Confederate architectural engineer and mechanic William C. Powers, a respected designer even before the Civil War. Powers came to the United States shortly before secession and became a citizen, marrying and living the rest of his life in Mobile, Alabama.

Thomas D. Crouch, a recognized authority on early flight and Chief of Aeronautics at the National Air and Space Museum, has remarked, "we know little of Powers' life, where he came from nor what became of him other than the contribution of his model and drawings from Clara McDermott and William V. McDermott, grandchildren of Powers, to Paul E. Garber, founder of the museum." Powers' model and eighteen pages of drawings were turned over to the Smithsonian Institution in 1940 and subsequently to Garber for evaluation. Garber's notations on Powers rank the Confederate architectural engineer's invention amongst the four most remarkable developments to impact the course of modern warfare. The first was the ironclads followed by submarines and then aerial observation.

Powers figured the Confederacy could break the Union blockade through air power. His design was a bomber which looks like a helicopter. Powers was ahead of his time in many regards, this project being no exception. When the Confederacy offered $100,000 to any individual who could devise a means of breaking the Northern blockade, Powers knew his aircraft design was a contender. The money never figured prominently in his plans.

There is little doubt that Powers was a brilliant individual. He intended to use the steam engine to power his aircraft. Documentation describing the craft notes in particular a steam engine to rotate the shafting and gears and drive two pairs of rotors, otherwise called airscrews. There was one pair of airscrews to raise the shaft vertically and another pair to power it horizontally. A rudder was provided for steering and a rolling weight was included to balance the aircraft fore and aft. In 1862, when Powers began tinkering with his drawings and model, the very thought of a flying machine of the magnitude proposed by Powers was beyond any of his contemporaries' imaginations. Perhaps even more interesting is the fact that his revolutionary design called for a crisscross slatting framework used much later in the construction of British-built Wellington bombers. English designers figured Powers' early slatting pattern provided strength to the airframe and would shield the plane from heavy damage as a result of antiaircraft guns.

In the midst of what he should have considered a great achievement worth further development, Powers was overcome by the gravity of the discovery and hid his design and model in a barn. The dilemma for Powers was twofold. On one hand, he was so confident that his aircraft could fly, the engineer and scientist in him wished to pursue further testing of the vehicle. On the other hand, Powers the Confederate patriot was afraid Union forces might discover his work and perfect the design, a task certainly within their material means and creative ability.

Powers never pursued his invention again. His aircraft would never have flown as designed, but it did exhibit a number of features successful in early helicopters of this century. Though the airplane would have to wait forty years, aeronauts flourished in the nineteenth century.

The greatest naval air work during the Civil War would be conducted by balloonists John Wise, Thaddeus Constantine Sobieski Lowe, Chief Aeronaut of the Army of the Potomac, and, of course, John La Mountain. Balloonists dominated the aeronautical world, casting a great shadow over the work of inventors like William C. Powers. The first time in history that aeronautics was successfully utilized by the armed forces of the United States was July 31, 1861, when John La Mountain ascended to 1,400 feet over Fortress Monroe on a reconnaissance mission to spot Confederate forces on the Peninsula and the southside of Hampton Roads.

Confederate architectural engineer and mechanic William C. Powers crafted the aircraft model shown here between 1862 and 1863. This is a three-quarter right rear view of the original experimental model of a helicopter invented by Powers. He intended his invention, if it were capable of being built and flown, to provide the Confederate defenders of Mobile, Alabama, with a means for aerial bombing of the Federal blockading fleet. The model fell into disrepair and was removed from the permanent collection of the National Air and Space Museum in the 1970s. (Courtesy of the National Air and Space Museum, Smithsonian Institution.)

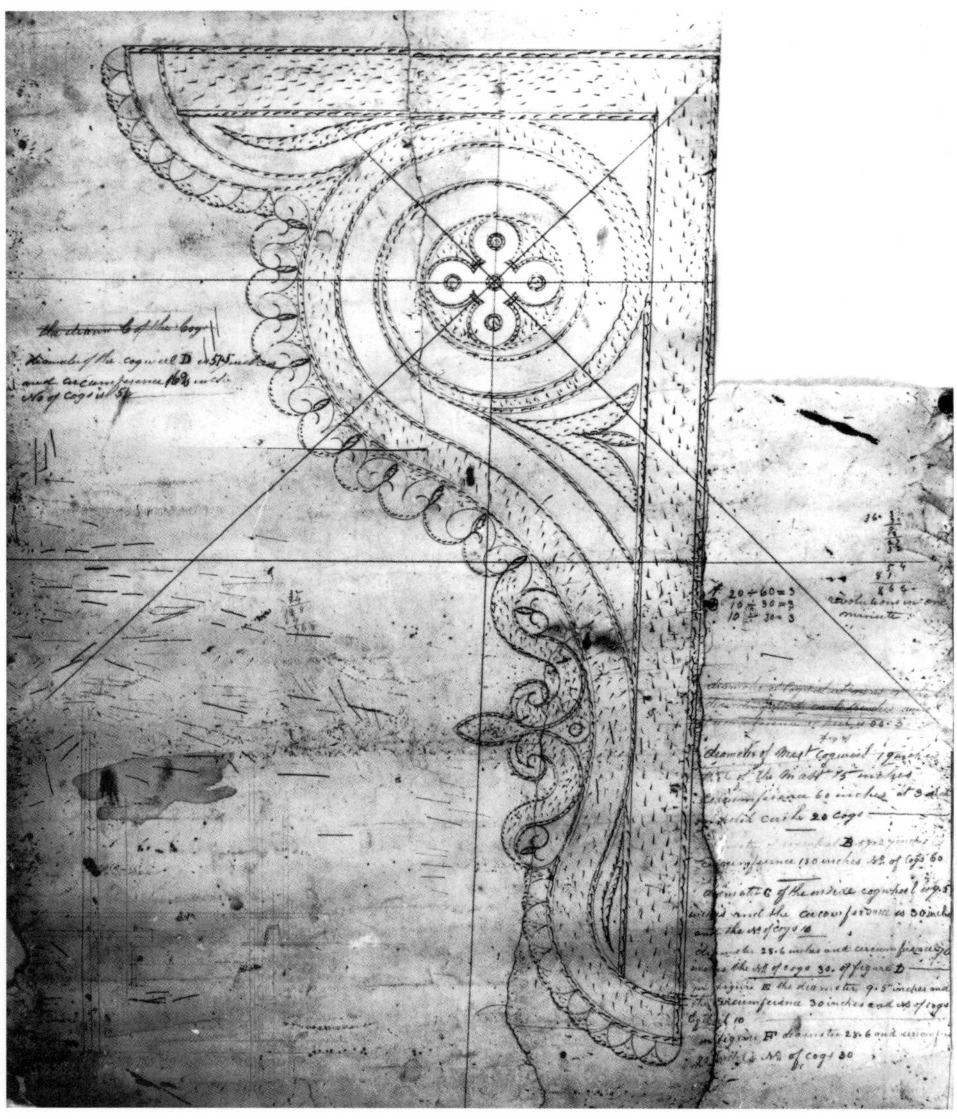

This is one of Powers' renderings of the mast cogwheel of the aircraft, of which there were five. The drawing demonstrated diameter and circumference requirements of the masts. (Courtesy of the National Air and Space Museum, Smithsonian Institution.)

John La Mountain had been summoned to Fortress Monroe shortly before his historic flight by Major General Benjamin Franklin Butler of the United States Army, commanding officer of all Union troops in southeastern Virginia. Butler was convinced the fort was surrounded by Confederate forces. His command consisted of Fortress Monroe with its garrison of approximately two thousand men; the Rip Raps, later called Fort Wool; Camp Hamilton at present-day Phoebus; and Camp Butler at Newport News. Butler's forces were desperate for help. As the lone Union outpost in Confederate-held territory, Butler had plenty of reason to be concerned. La Mountain's balloons seemed the best answer to the general's mounting troubles.

Butler summoned La Mountain to Fortress Monroe by way of a letter dated June 5, 1861. According to accounts of that period, Butler could not promise the balloonist that the Lincoln War Department would agree to, much less fund, the idea of lighter-than-air craft as a tool of war. Though La Mountain ended up with a commission in the United States Army as an aerial observer, he was immediately confronted with fierce competition to prove the balloon's value. The rivalry between La Mountain and Thaddeus C.S. Lowe, his counterpart in northern Virginia, centered around the vision both men shared to cross the Atlantic Ocean by balloon, beating out their European contemporaries and besting one another's ingenuity. The Civil War was their proving ground.

The brash, self-confident La Mountain arrived at Fortress Monroe on July 23, 1861. At the time of his first flight two days later, the balloonist encountered excessive winds and could not gain altitude. His fortune changed on July 31, 1861, when La Mountain made his landmark flight. He reported being able to see at least thirty miles in every direction, including Norfolk,

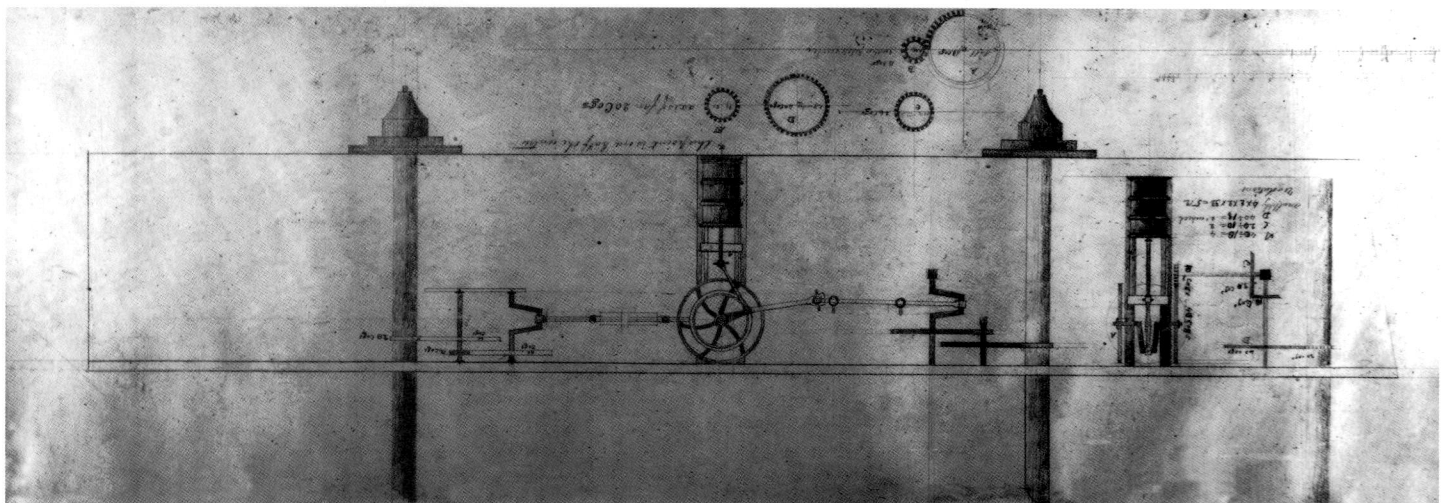

On another page of his drawings, Powers sketched the mid-point of his aircraft, showing what he called the point "one half the centre," and "the axis fan 20 Cogs." (Courtesy of the National Air and Space Museum, Smithsonian Institution.)

John La Mountain, circa 1862. (Courtesy of the Casemate Museum.)

Newport News and Yorktown. Once airborne, balloonist La Mountain could see beyond the Confederate shore battery at Sewell's Point and, in the process, found a hidden rebel encampment of several hundred men. Perhaps the best outcome of his initial flight was La Mountain's ability to dispel Butler's fears of being surrounded. Norfolk did not have the large number of troops along Tanner's Creek suspected by Union informers. Further, there were no camps beyond Newport News.

On August 3, 1861, La Mountain ascended from the deck of the gunboat USS *Fanny* which was operating as the first aircraft carrier in American history, and she did so in Hampton Roads. The USS *Fanny* moved across the channel from Sewell's Point, and La Mountain was able to achieve an altitude of two thousand feet. During repeated ascensions he would spot as many as four to five thousand Confederate troops at Denbigh, or Young's Mill as it was known at the time, and a camp of 150 to 200 tents on the bank of the James River north of Newport News or Watt's Creek, now the site of the Mariners' Museum. La Mountain concluded from his flight that Norfolk should be attacked by air. He actually wrote General Butler that he was convinced "that at an expense not to exceed eight or nine thousand dollars, I can build a balloon in a month's time and with it shell, burn or destroy Norfolk or any city near our camps. Ballooning can be made a very useful implement in warfare. All depends on the encouragement it receives."

During the First World War, English cities were bombed via dirigible balloons designed by Count Ferdinand von Zeppelin. Zeppelin had been a young German officer attached to the Union Army during the Civil War. The German made his first balloon ascension in the United States. Aeronautical research and development by Wise, La Mountain, and Lowe laid the foundation for ghastly twentieth century warfare, war perpetuated in the mind's eye of men like Zeppelin who forty years earlier gazed into the skies over Hampton Roads and saw aeronauts do what no man had ever done before in the history of aviation employed against men on the ground.

The Zeppelins of the twentieth century were a far cry from Jesuit priest Francesco deLana-Terzi's flying boat of 1670, the first definitive design of a lighter-than-air craft. DeLana-Terzi felt balloonships had their limitations and could not really fly through the heavens.

The naval gunboat USS *Fanny,* used for a time as a United States Army transport, was the first vessel fitted to launch an airborne craft, in this case John La Mountain and his famous balloons. The USS *Fanny* has often been called the first aircraft carrier. She certainly beat the competition by nearly fifty years. In this engraving, the *Fanny* is about to be captured by Confederate steamers CSS *Curlew,* CSS *Raleigh,* and CSS *Junaluska* near Chickamacomico in Pamlico Sound, North Carolina, on October 1, 1861. The *Fanny* served in the Confederate States Navy until February of 1862. (Engraving from *Frank Leslie's Illustrated,* 1861. Courtesy of the Hampton Roads Naval Museum.)

This balloon was anchored to the tugboat, USS *Fanny*. The print originated in *Frank Leslie's Illustrated,* August 31, 1861, and shows Professor La Mountain reconnoitering Confederate positions near Fortress Monroe. (Courtesy of the Casemate Museum.)

After all, he surmised, God would never let a creation with such destructive potential succeed. Men of deLana-Terzi's time, men of learning and creativity, came from the church and held allegiance to God over furtherance of flying machines. Men of La Mountain's period lived and breathed to forge ahead, building airships and aircraft.

By the middle of August of 1861, La Mountain's balloons the *Atlantic* and *Saratoga,* were out of sulfuric acid and iron filings which comprise hydrogen gas. He needed to go back north for more supplies. When La Mountain returned to Fortress Monroe in the middle of September, he found Butler had been replaced by Major General John E. Wool, then seventy-seven years of age and a diehard student of the War of 1812 and Mexican War of 1846–1848. Wool was hardly interested in lighter-than-air flight and La Mountain's reception upon returning to the fort could be described as cold at best. Butler ordered La Mountain to the Army of the Potomac in short order, straight into rival Thaddeus C.S. Lowe's camp. The situation became intolerable, Lowe and La Mountain quarreling bitterly and so often publicly, each had to be disciplined.

Historians know little about La Mountain. His transfer to the Army of the Potomac no doubt sealed his fate. Thaddeus C.S. Lowe, his competition, commanded the Union Army's balloon corps under General George B. McClellan, USA, leader of the Army of the Potomac. After battling fiercely with Lowe, La Mountain was dismissed from the United States Army on February 19, 1862, in the shadow of great controversy. Lowe and La Mountain quarreled bitterly one last time over the use of a new balloon. To settle the dispute, La Mountain was let go.

The first great American military aeronaut accomplished his pioneering feet over the waters of Hampton Roads. Though not the first to put the balloon to military use, he certainly brought them to the United States, a nation unfamiliar with their domestic use and warfare applications. And little did he realize his title as the first official aeronaut of the Union Army. La Mountain was employed by General Butler in July of 1861, whereas Thaddeus Lowe was not employed until August 2, 1861. History records tell us that La Mountain holds perhaps the most important title, particularly for Hampton Roads, as the first to ascend from the deck of a Navy vessel. Lowe did not make his first ascent from the deck of the balloon boat *George Washington Parke Custis* until November 12, 1861.

By the age of thirty-two, John La Mountain was despondent, wounded by his untimely dismissal from the Army of the Potomac. He died of what some would say was a broken spirit at the age of forty years in South Bend, Indiana, on February 14, 1870.

The USS *Fanny* holds as much importance for United States Navy history in Hampton Roads waters as La Mountain's flight. The *Fanny* is the direct antecedent of the great aircraft carriers of the modern nuclear Navy. The most important difference between the *Fanny* and the *George Washington Parke Custis* was the fact the former was a steamer with an iron hull and propellor. The *George Washington Parke Custis* happened to be a wooden vessel without motive power; in other words, she had to be

John La Mountain sketched the Confederate batteries at Sewell's Point from his balloon. (Courtesy of the Hampton Roads Naval Museum.)

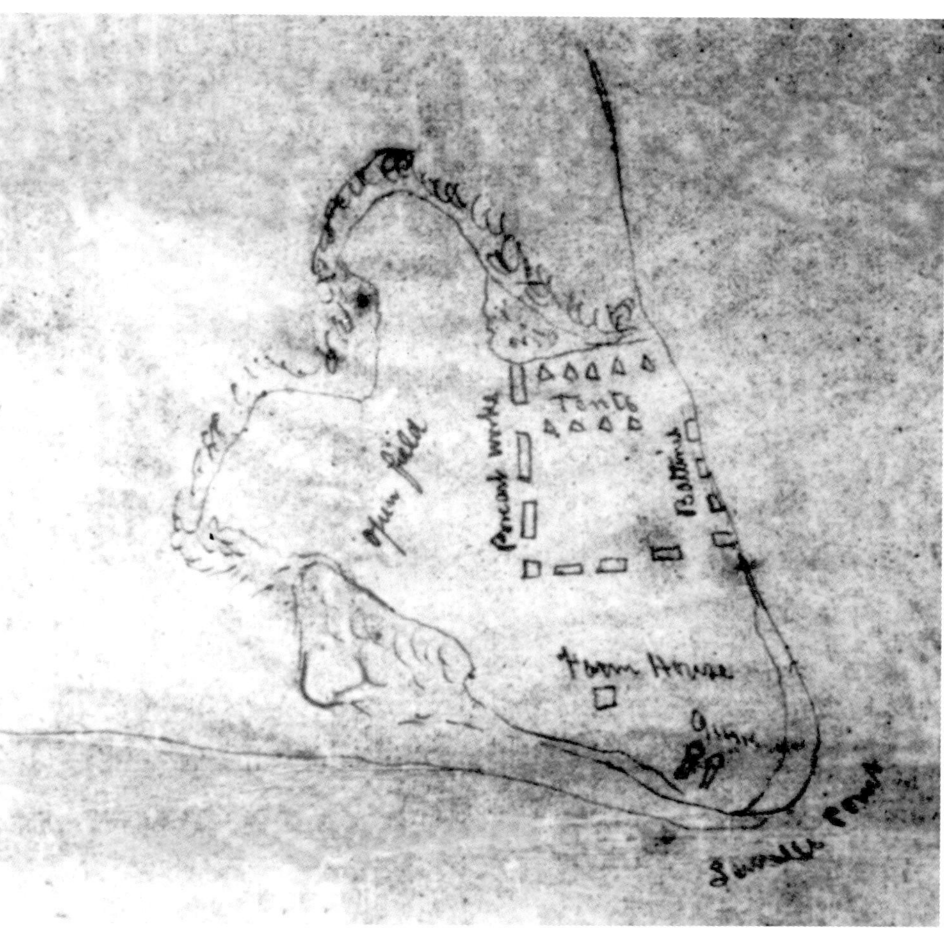

The Confederate batteries at Sewell's Point, sketched by La Mountain from his balloon, came under fire several times, but were never captured nor taken out of action by enemy bombardment. Confederate troops abandoned the battery on May 10, 1862, the day Norfolk, Virginia, fell to Union forces. The batteries, depicted in the bottom image of a page from *Frank Leslie's Illustrated,* 1862, provided only a modicum of protection for the northern approach to Norfolk. As La Mountain drew and the sketch illustrates, the Sewell's Point batteries mounted three 32-pounders and two rifled guns, and had been manned by the likes of American poet and critic Sidney Lanier (1842–1881), part of the Georgia unit which defended the breastwork under heavy fire from the USS *Monticello,* commanded by Captain Henry Eagle, during the Battle of Sewell's Point, May 18–19, 1861. (Courtesy of the Hampton Roads Naval Museum.)

REBEL BATTERIES AT CRANEY ISLAND, mouth of Elizabeth River Va.

REBEL BATTERIES at SEWALL'S POINT. Opposite Fortress Monroe.

***Harper's Weekly,* September 6, 1862, depicts "the last reconnaissance of the war balloon on the James River." (Courtesy of the Casemate Museum.)**

towed. The *Fanny* was also armed, whereas her counterpart was not. The *Fanny* possessed the basic qualities found in the modern aircraft carrier.

The USS *Fanny* reverted to a gunboat after La Mountain's famous flight. She departed for North Carolina waters on August 26, 1861, with General Butler's amphibious expedition to Hatteras Inlet. Unfortunately, the *Fanny* was overtaken and captured by Confederate gunboats at Loggerhead Inlet on October 1, 1861. The Confederates used the *Fanny* against the Union until the rebel fleet was beaten to submission at Elizabeth City, North Carolina, on February 10, 1862. As a consequence, the Confederate commanding officer of the *Fanny* ran the boat aground and set her ablaze. So ended a significant chapter in the annals of naval aviation history.

In 1898, five years prior to the Wright Brothers' successful ascent at Kitty Hawk, then Secretary of the Navy Theodore Roosevelt first entertained the notion of "naval" aviation. He was interested in the work of Dr. Samuel Pierpont Langley, a gentleman whose exploits in early aviation did much to fuel the race to launch an aircraft and sustain flight. Langley was the first to launch a steam-powered airplane from a houseboat in the Potomac River on October 8, 1903, and, though the flight failed, it succeeded in keeping the Navy's interest in aviation.

The Navy continued to have a difficult time seeing the value of aircraft but, by the same token, Navy leaders could not allow the concept of flight to escape their grasp even if aeronautics and its applications within the fleet had yet to be fully understood. By 1910, the Department of the Navy had appointed its aviation champion, Captain Washington Irving Chambers, USN, to the task of responding to public requests for information about aircraft, effectively making him the father of naval aviation.

All military personnel will be treated as regular United States Navy (USN) unless indicated otherwise.

Chapter 2: First Wings Over the Bay

The United States Navy took its first plunge into aeronautics with a fixed-wing aircraft on November 14, 1910, when aviator Eugene Barton Ely, in the Curtiss biplane *Hudson Flyer,* made his way into the Chesapeake Bay aboard the scout cruiser USS *Birmingham* (CL-2) and took flight, effectively giving birth to naval aviation at Hampton Roads, Virginia. Though the flight lasted only a few minutes, it became not only the first successful aircraft launched from a ship but the first flight from ship to shore.

Ely's feat was not only the first in America but also the first in the world. After Ely's flight, Royal Navy aviators began experimenting with the marriage of ships and airplanes. More importantly, Ely's return flight aboard the USS *Pennsylvania* in San Francisco Bay in January of 1911 was also a world first. British Lieutenant Charles Samson did not complete a similar takeoff to Ely's *Birmingham* launch until January 10, 1912, in his Short S.27 from the deck of a makeshift platform aboard the HMS *Africa*.

The brilliant and impatient Eugene Barton "Gene" Ely had a wonderfully logical sense of flying and a deep, abiding interest in how aircraft worked. He gravitated toward Glenn Hammond Curtiss in early 1910 because both men wanted to construct useful as well as sporting aircraft for Captain Washington Irving Chambers at the Navy Department. As a Curtiss exhibition pilot, Ely flew company aircraft in demonstrations all over the country, showing the public—and the Army and Navy—what airplanes could do.

Born in Davenport, Iowa, on October 21, 1886, Ely attended public schools and eventually graduated from Iowa State University. Ely fell in love first with automobiles, progressed to auto racing, and eventually airplanes. As his interest in cars grew, Ely moved from Davenport to San Francisco, California, and Portland, Oregon. The move to Portland provided his first exposure to a Curtiss biplane.

In February of 1910, E. Harry Wemme, an auto dealer in Portland, bought one of the first Curtiss biplanes and subsequently became the Northwest sales agent for the Curtiss Aeroplane Company of Hammondsport, New York, but Wemme was afraid to fly it, so Eugene Ely offered to give it a whirl. The result was Ely's first crash. Ely felt so badly about the crash that he purchased the wreckage from Wemme and repaired it, then actually taught himself to fly the biplane. He aviated with the ease of a bird, and less than two months after his initial accident on April 1, 1910, Ely was able to fly short straight-away hops.

Flying was intoxicating to a twenty-three-year-old from Iowa. Though he would continue to fly in the Portland area, Ely had already decided that exhibition flying was his calling. In early June of 1910, Eugene Ely flew his first exhibition engagement at Winnipeg, Canada. He made two successful flights in Winnipeg then moved on to Minnesota on June 22, 1910, where he met three of the most experienced and renowned aviators of the period, Glenn Hammond Curtiss, Charles Willard, and Bud Mars. The Minnesota meet proved to be the first major turning point in Ely's career.

Glenn H. Curtiss liked what he saw in Eugene Ely, both in his personality and flying ability. Curtiss hired Ely to fly exhibitions for his company on the spot. Still flying his four-cylinder Curtiss biplane, Ely flew his first exhibition as a Curtiss Exhibition Company pilot between June 29 and July 1, 1910, at Sioux City, Iowa, in the company of Bud Mars. Ely traveled with the show to Creighton Field, Omaha, Nebraska, July 23 through 27, 1910; Rochester, New York, August 5 through 7, 1910; and

Eugene Barton Ely, circa 1909. (Courtesy of the Hampton Roads Naval Museum.)

Eugene and Mabel Ely and the famous Curtiss *Hudson Flyer,* Birmingham, Alabama, circa 1910. (Courtesy of the Hampton Roads Naval Museum.)

then Sheepshead Bay Meet, Long Island, New York, August 19 through 28, 1910. During these meets, Ely would again fly with Curtiss, Mars, and Willard, among others. He was flying at Kalamazoo, Michigan, by September 5 through 6, 1910; Rock Island, Illinois, with Curtiss, Willard, and aviatrix Blanche Scott from October 1 through 7, 1910. Ely obtained his *Fédération Aéronautique Internationale* Pilot's License No. 17 on October 5, 1910, at the Rock Island event held on Hawthorne Race Track.

Ely was still considered a new pilot when he flew Youngstown, Ohio, on October 12, 1910, and one of the world's great meets at Belmont Park International Meet in New York from October 22 through 30, 1910. As a participant at Belmont, Eugene Ely flew alongside some of the greatest aviators in the world but made a significant impression on all of them with his fantastic feats in the air. In November, Ely flew in an aviation meet at Halethrope, near Baltimore, Maryland, between November 2 and 12, 1910. This meet would prove to be the second major turning point in his career, leading to a highly successful association with Captain Washington Irving Chambers of the United States Navy, a captivated spectator at Ely's Halethrope exhibition.

Captain Washington Irving Chambers originally met Ely in Baltimore, Maryland, on November 3, 1910, after an airshow in which Ely had once again demonstrated the potential of the airplane before a spellbound crowd of thousands. Chambers had seen enough. He asked the aviator if he might be interested in attempting a shipboard takeoff at Hampton Roads. Ely leapt at the opportunity, promising to bring his Curtiss biplane, accept no fee and make the flight if only to prove it could be done. Captain Chambers could not have been more pleased with Ely's enthusiastic response.

Ely had had enough of bureaucratic prorogues, time wasted, and opportunities lost. President William Howard Taft would not permit the Navy to experiment with aircraft in the first two years of his presidency, and his predecessor, Theodore Roosevelt, though interested in the possibilities of aircraft in the fleet, became a lame duck in Washington.

Ely's daring flight from the *Birmingham* should have signaled a new era in aviation, but it did not, at least not at the time. There is some suggestion that the Wright Brothers, Grover Loening, and even Glenn Curtiss himself did not truly want Ely or anyone else to make the flight for fear it would detract from, if not kill, the use of flying boats or seaplanes. Loening, Curtiss and the Wrights were gearing up to produce hydroaeroplanes, not landplanes launched from a ship. The bane of hydroaeroplanes was perched on the deck of the *Birmingham* and his name was Eugene Ely.

The United States Secretary of the Navy in 1910 was George von L. Meyer, a man set against Ely's plan to fly off a ship. He refused to fund it. Most of those in decision making positions at that time had profound distrust and limited knowledge of aviation. Secretary Meyer

Eugene B. Ely and his famous Curtiss *Hudson Flyer,* circa 1910. (Courtesy of the Hampton Roads Naval Museum.)

was no exception. Aviation in its infancy needed people with vision but also those with enough technical expertise and courage to forge ahead. Few met these requirements. Ely endured great insult to make history in Hampton Roads harbor and give naval aviation its wings. If it was not Navy Secretary Meyer trivalizing the aviator's aircraft, effectively calling it a toy, it was a battleship admiral politely asking the aviator to get off his ship and never come back.

Ely persevered and eventually was able to bring Curtiss around to his way of thinking, the latter finally mustering enough hope of a successful flight to take part in the history-making flight. Fortunate for both men, John Barry Ryan, a millionaire publisher and politician, entered the fray on their behalf. Ryan had the money of investors in the scientific community behind him, and the vision in aeronautics to convince Navy Secretary Meyer from a political standpoint that his failure to back the aviators could affect his future in Washington, D.C. In the end, Meyer agreed to modify and furnish the ship only. Ely and Curtiss would make their landmark flight free of charge. This was probably the first and only time Curtiss would not collect his fee for service since he had always made it quite clear he was in aviation to make his living as well as to pioneer aviation.

The USS *Birmingham* was provided for the flight, forcing Captain W.B. Fletcher to hurry his vessel to Norfolk Navy Yard for deck modifications to accommodate Ely's Curtiss *Hudson Flyer.* The *Hudson Flyer* belonged to the *Golden Flyer* series. Ely chose an historic aircraft for his own historic flight. The name *Hudson Flyer* was given the aircraft after Glenn Curtiss flew it through the channels of the Hudson River Valley from Albany, New York, to New York City. The biplane had likewise been through two previous cross-water flights: one over

Ely was racing an automobile at an unknown locale when this photograph was taken, circa 1910. (Courtesy of the Hampton Roads Naval Museum.)

Ely's Curtiss *Hudson Flyer* was being readied for hoisting aboard the cruiser *Birmingham* when this photograph was snapped the morning of November 14, 1910, at the Norfolk Navy Yard, Portsmouth, Virginia. (Courtesy of the Hampton Roads Naval Museum.)

Lake Erie from Euclid Beach to Cedar Point, Michigan, and back, about seventy miles round trip; the second Curtiss flew over the Atlantic Ocean off Atlantic City, New Jersey, for about fifty miles.

The ramp built aboard the USS *Birmingham* was designed by Naval Constructor William McEntee, a young engineer attached to the Bureau of Construction and Repair in Washington, D.C. For McEntee, the aviation bug had bitten two years earlier when he and Lieutenant George C. Sweet, later the first naval officer to fly in an airplane, were official Navy observers at the first United States Army demonstration trials of the Wright Brothers flying machine at Fort Myer, Virginia, on September 17, 1908. Fresh from Washington and encouraged by what he had seen of flying machines, McEntee was keenly aware the Navy Department was tentatively holding adoption of an aircraft budget pending the success or failure of Ely's flight. The budget would be based on a loose interpretation of the law which qualified airplanes as part of equipment on battleships. McEntee reasoned, as did many others who wanted to see planes used in the fleet, that the Navy was after biplane designs. Once Ely proved the use of airplanes aboard ship, naval constructors could think ahead to retrieval systems, flotation devices, catapults—the work would be leading edge, exciting.

McEntee had been at the shipyard several days before the flight to oversee construction of the makeshift flight deck, an eighty-three-foot platform. McEntee's work on Ely's platform was the first flight deck designed for use on an American naval vessel.

Ely and his wife, Mabel, stayed at the old Monticello Hotel on the corner of City Hall Avenue and Granby Street in downtown Norfolk while the *Birmingham* was being prepared for the flight. Mabel Ely might well have been the first wife of a naval aviator had Ely worn the uniform. She will forever be remembered as her husband's constant companion and spokesperson. Mabel Ely was oft quoted in the newspapers of her day, the trip to Norfolk being no exception. Ely himself noted Mabel would not let him fly if conditions did not look good. "A wife in the hangar is worth several in the hospital," he would say. She settled any and all issues to do with his flying.

The day before Ely made his famous flight, Mabel Ely remarked, "I can't say just exactly when he will go up," she continued, "for at this time of the year there are many different weather conditions that are unfavorable for flying. Mr. Ely will take his machine on the cruiser *Birmingham* and will put to sea on Monday afternoon. I will go along on another government vessel and we will try to keep up with Gene as he flies over the water. I have personally seen to it that he will be properly equipped with life buoys and he will wear them, too. The machine will have pontoons attached so that in case anything should happen to it, it will float until it and Mr. Ely can be rescued. I have the greatest confidence in Mr. Ely and am sure that he will complete the flight all right."

Ely was a modest soul, and, when prompted, he added that his wife did the family talking for him. "What she says is all right, so there you are." What Eugene and Mabel Ely could not hide from the crowd was their obvious affection for one another. The two were inseparable, and it was readily apparent even during their Norfolk stay that the relationship was sustained by their unwavering reliance on one another, and, dare one say in a history, their love.

The *Birmingham* was a scout cruiser with four stacks. It was on the forecastle that sailors built the eighty-three-foot ramp which sloped five degrees from the bridge rail to the main deck at the bow. The ramp's forward leading edge was only thirty-seven feet above the water. Ely's mechanics, fellows by the name of Henning and John Lansing "Lanny" Callan,(1) had to work at Pine Beach, site of the future Hampton Roads Naval Base, to construct the biplane from parts sent from Hammondsport, New York, and Baltimore, Maryland.

From newspaper accounts of the day and Mabel's meticulously kept scrapbooks of her husband's brief but great career, Ely arrived on that Sunday, November 13, 1910, amidst some of Hampton Roads' infamous November rain. He was of a mind to fit the aircraft, sans engine, with cigar-shaped aluminum floats under the wings and a splashboard on the landing gear. Ely's plane had already been seen in Norfolk once before—as it was the same *Hudson Flyer* used by Bud Mars a week prior to the Baltimore airshow to race horses at Norfolk's old fairgrounds.

The plane was transported to Norfolk Navy Yard from Pine Beach aboard the naval tug *Nice*. The evening of November 13, 1910, Ely would be quoted in the Norfolk newspapers, "Everything is ready. If weather is favorable, I expect to make the flight tomorrow without difficulty." Of course, Ely had not even taken the first look at the ship and its new platform nor flight-tested his plane. Mabel Ely had great faith in her "Gene"—he could do it. Her account of this time has proven invaluable in reconstructing the course of events, Ely's state of mind and ultimately, the birth of naval aviation.

In November 1910, a temporary platform or makeshift flight deck was erected aboard the USS *Birmingham* and Ely's Curtiss aircraft was hoisted aboard in preparation for the first flight of a fixed-wing plane from a ship's deck. (Official United States Navy Photograph.)

She would recall his focus on the task at hand and the natural nervousness which accompanied it. Anticipation of possible success, making history in the process, drove Ely to go the farthest, to be the best, to be the one to lead his generation into the forefront of aviation.

Ely had never been much on patience. The plane's engine was due to arrive on an evening boat from Baltimore. By the time it arrived, Ely was already on the ferry to Portsmouth to find his mechanics. The *Hudson Flyer* was craned aboard the ship and secured aft on the platform. Securing the plane required nothing fancy. The tail was tied just up over the ship's wheel, leaving only fifty-seven feet of platform for takeoff.

The *Birmingham* left its berth at Norfolk Navy Yard about half past eleven in the morning, and steamed past in full view of the Norfolk waterfront. The scout cruiser was accompanied downriver by one destroyer while another stopped on the Norfolk side to fetch Mabel and a growing number of anxious Norfolk reporters. Ely, ever the consummate perfectionist, helped install the plane engine, a task which was completed by the time the *Birmingham* passed Pine Beach and headed into the harbor. Neysayers, chiefly his Washington political observers, waited aboard the destroyers USS *Bailey* and USS *Stringham* for Ely's entourage to arrive.

A special board, appointed to study airplanes for the government several weeks prior to Ely's attempt, had followed the goings on at aviation meets up and down the East Coast prior to their arrival in Hampton Roads. Members of the board included Assistant Secretary of the Navy Beckman Winthrop; Captain Washington Irving Chambers, committee chair; Lieutenant N.H. Wright; and Constructor William McEntee. Aboard the *Birmingham* was, of course, Ely's greatest supporter, Captain Chambers. Aside from the destroyers and the very important committee from Washington, the scout cruiser was also accompanied by two torpedo craft, the USS *Rowe* and USS *Terry*. The *Rowe,* the fastest craft on station, was poised closest to the *Birmingham* in the event Ely was unsuccessful and needed plucking from the bay, and it also served as the press boat. Ely's original destination was the marine barracks parade ground at the Norfolk Navy Yard in Portsmouth, Virginia. A fast ship would be needed if Ely encountered trouble anywhere along his planned thirty mile route to the shipyard. Had the weather been propitious, Ely intended to begin his route beyond the Rip Raps, rounding Sewell's Point, Lambert's Point and following the center of the Elizabeth River over the inner harbor, turning to the south then above the ferry wharf and going directly to the Norfolk Navy Yard. The flight would take forty minutes. If the weather remained favorable, Ely planned to take to the air again, fly across to Norfolk and circle the city to fulfill an agreement made between Glenn H. Curtiss and the *Ledger-Dispatch* newspaper.

Captain Fletcher anchored the *Birmingham* approximately a quarter mile off Old Point Comfort. A squall on the water was so bad, hail made it virtually impossible to see the stately Chamberlin Hotel. By anyone else's standard this was a bad day, but Eugene Ely remained undaunted. He was determined to show members of the aeronautic committee the versatility of the airplane. When the weather moved off around two o'clock in the afternoon, Ely immediately climbed aboard the *Hudson Flyer.* His ground crew completed preflight checks and Henning propped the plane. The weather was still very bad, but this was Ely's big chance and he had no choice; the weather was not going to improve.

The wireless operator aboard the *Birmingham* recorded the events as they quickly unfolded. At half past two the afternoon of November 14, the sky lightened ever so slightly. Perhaps caught in the spirit of the event about to take place, Fletcher and Chambers let Ely proceed toward takeoff. Ely was a man of contradictions. Here he was in the middle of the bay, with poor weather and about to take flight over water. Yet Ely hated water, not to mention heights, could not swim, and got seasick at the drop of a hat. It is no small wonder the aviator failed miserably to get along with "black shoes."(2) He knew as little about ships as they did about airplanes, a fact that became all the more apparent when he was ready to launch and the ship was not.

The *Birmingham* needed about half an hour to pull anchor and make way. Ely had another stormfront rapidly making its way across the bay and could not wait. Once again he ordered Henning to prop the plane, only this time he opened the throttle and was poised for takeoff. While Ely set about checking his control surfaces, no one on the bridge seemed to realize he was really set to go.

The squall grew worse as Ely completed his final checks and motioned his ground crew to back away from the airplane. By the time Captain Chambers realized what Ely was up to, it was too late and nothing further could be done to hurry the *Birmingham.*

The first fixed-wing airplane flight from the deck of a Navy ship, the USS *Birmingham,* with Eugene B. Ely at the controls, took place November 14, 1910, at Hampton Roads. A photographer aboard one of the escort ships captured the moment Ely and the *Hudson Flyer* left the flight deck aboard the *Birmingham.* Ely dipped below the deck seconds later, skimming the water before regaining altitude. The USS *Rowe* is in the background. (Courtesy of the Hampton Roads Naval Museum.)

Crewmen had just begun to weigh anchor. In essence, the only choice Ely had was to take off and hope for the best. He could not wait for the ship to steam into the wind as planned. Within moments, Ely gave the release signal which he had to repeat before mechanic Harrington acknowledged the order. No one ever imagined Ely would alight from the ship amidst such pure drama: a squall blowing in and the *Birmingham* without motive power. At precisely 3:16 in the afternoon, the wireless operator aboard ship would send the message, "Ely just gone."

Ely and his *Hudson Flyer* dropped out of sight over the side of the *Birmingham.* When water splashed high in front of the ship and splattered the aviator's makeshift platform, a great gasp could be heard on the deck of the cruiser. The outcry was tempered only by the sight of Ely climbing to a safe altitude. Ely had essentially averted a certain crash through his knowledge of how Curtiss planes worked. In this case, the *Hudson Flyer* required the pilot to steer with the rudder, balanced by ailerons and an elevator set either on climb, level or glide. Ely needed to pick up speed by dipping so he set the elevator on glide. His only real mistake was a split second hesitation before shifting to the climb setting.

Ely's flight into history lasted only four minutes but, as Ely would later recount, it was a gripping four minutes. He was caught in inclement weather over unfamiliar territory. His visibility was hampered by freezing spray and horrific weather. Given his fear of water and bad conditions, Ely determined to land the plane as soon as possible. He spotted Willoughby Spit in Ocean View. He landed on a strip of beach between the home of Julia Smith and the old Hampton Roads Yacht Club.

By the time reporters caught up to him, Chambers, Ryan and Fletcher were already on hand and offering the aviator their praises. Ely could not understand the congratulations since he had failed to reach his destination, the Norfolk Navy Yard. The young aviator had far from failed but it took considerable convincing to change Ely's thinking. He actually returned to Norfolk soon after the flight to rest because he still wanted to fly over the city the next day, weather permitting.

An interesting aside to Ely's post-flight interview involved the millionaire Ryan and his purchase of the propeller off the *Hudson Flyer.* The propeller had been splintered on impact with the water when Ely dipped upon takeoff. Ryan was determined to own a marvelous piece of history and offered Ely five hundred dollars for it on the spot. Ely accepted and later bought Mabel a diamond ring with the money.

Eugene Ely's flight had several important ramifications, not the least of which was the realization that a fixed-wing airplane could take off from a ship. Also, the Navy could not ignore the strategic worth of aircraft on ships. The consensus of the day on all sides of the argument for naval aviation was that flying machines must be taken seriously in the naval warfare plans of the future.

Captain Chambers was the first to step up to Ely and offer him the chance to make history once again by landing a plane on board a ship. Ely would achieve this end in San Francisco Bay on January 18, 1911, when he successfully landed his airplane aboard the USS *Pennsylvania*. When interviewed shortly after the flight at Hampton Roads, Chambers would remark that the flight was much greater than he had anticipated and he issued assurances to reporters on hand that scout cruisers would most certainly carry airplanes in the near future. He continued, "When Mr. Ely flew with such ease from a standing ship, it showed beyond a doubt that his task would have been much simpler if the *Birmingham* had been moving."

By next morning, November 15, the whole world awoke to hear of Ely's colossal success. Chambers continued to fight hard for aeronautical research backed by the National Aeronautical Society and the Smithsonian Institution, the latter's own Dr. Samuel Pierpont Langley already a recognized aviation pioneer with his aerodrome experiments of the 1890s. Contrary to the belief of a number of credible historians, Eugene Barton Ely never joined nor belonged to the armed forces of the United States. He did, however, give aviation to the United States Navy because he thought it would, at least in his time, provide air supremacy to his country. Forward deployment of our modern-day nuclear-powered aircraft carriers in all corners of the world was strategically what a young aviator named Eugene Barton Ely dreamt for naval aviation when he struck out from the deck of a motionless scout cruiser to make history over the waters of the Chesapeake Bay. Ely's wings were fragile, his wings over the bay.

Less than a year after his flight in Hampton Roads on October 19, 1911, Eugene B. Ely, age 24, was killed flying an exhibition in Macon, Georgia. A crowd of 8,000 spectators mistakenly applauded, not realizing until they saw him leap from the plane that he was in trouble. Ely, who had literally crushed every bone in his body on impact, was tenderly removed from the wreckage which covered him. Though he appeared a broken, bloody inert mass to onlookers, between bouts of brief and agonizing consciousness, Ely managed to acknowledge his impending death. His last words were for his beloved Mabel who was unable to be with him for the Georgia exhibition. She had returned to New York two weeks prior to the Georgia State Fair to open a house for the couple. On April 16, 1933, over twenty years after his untimely passing, President Franklin Delano Roosevelt awarded Eugene Ely the Distinguished Flying Cross for, as the citation read, "his extraordinary achievement as a pioneer civilian aviator and for his significant contribution to the development of aviation in the United States Navy."

Ely originally planned to land on the parade ground of the Marine Barracks, Norfolk Navy Yard (shown here). He had wanted to fly over downtown Norfolk and show off his *Hudson Flyer* to the people of the city. Inclement weather prevented his going any further than Willoughby Spit in Ocean View.

Eugene B. Ely would make landfall on his historic flight next to the Hampton Roads Yacht Club built in 1904, and shown here on the left as it appeared about the time of Ely's flight in 1910. The building complex to the right was the boathouse for the club. Private residences were down the beach to the left of the Hampton Roads Yacht Club. This hand-colored photograph is one of the few historically accurate images of the area where Ely came ashore. (Courtesy of the Kirn Library.)

An aviation exhibition by Eugene Ely was held at the Jamestown Exposition grounds, later site of the Norfolk Naval Station, on November 15, 1910. (Courtesy of the Hampton Roads Naval Museum.)

Eugene B. Ely is shown here (second from left) after his safe arrival aboard the USS *Pennsylvania,* January 18, 1911. Mabel Ely is to his left. (Courtesy of the Hampton Roads Naval Museum.)

Chapter 3: Milestones of Flight

Ely's benchmark flight at Hampton Roads, Virginia, lit the fire of aviation technology and milestones of flight. Week to week, technological advancements and record-breaking flights gradually worked their way to the front page of newspapers nationwide. On October 25, 1911, Lieutenant Theodore Gordon "Spuds" Ellyson, Naval Aviator No. 1, and Lieutenant John Henry "Jack" Towers, Naval Aviator No. 3, set out from Greenbury Point, Annapolis, Maryland, to Buckroe Beach in proximity of Newport News, Virginia, a distance of 145 miles in 2 hours, 27 minutes, in a Curtiss A-1 Triad. The famous A-1 flight began on a cold October afternoon in 1911 and proved to be another milestone in naval aviation history.

Ellyson, popularly called the "naval wizard of the air," was officer-in-charge of the aeronautic school at Annapolis. He and copilot Jack Towers landed near Buckroe Beach in Newport News in a hydroaeroplane after what has been described, at least in their time, as the most remarkable and successful flight in the history of naval aviation. These landmark flights quickly eclipsed one another, each building on the other, the technology advancing almost more rapidly than headlines and historians could keep up.

Getting to Newport News by air was not without its difficulties for Ellyson and Towers. Their successful flight of October 25 followed two unsuccessful attempts in a two-week period by the aviators to clear the Potomac River region and make their way south. Even on this successful flight, Towers was forced to climb out of the plane seat and make in-flight repairs to a leaking radiator. Ellyson did most of the flying, while Towers tightened bolts and looked after the engine. Ellyson and Towers made their first stop in the flight after covering 120 miles and in dire need of oil. They walked five miles before finding it.

By the evening of October 25, the A-1 had been pulled up far onto the sand at Buckroe and secured. The landing at Buckroe Beach, about seven miles from Old Point Comfort, was selected because the beachhead at the point further away was unfamiliar to both pilots. Their point of landing—in the water—made landfall at a site void of inhabitants and, of course, all means of communication

At 6:50 p.m. on July 1, 1911, Glenn Hammond Curtiss demonstrated the A-1 Triad, the first aircraft constructed for the Navy, taking off from and alighting on Lake Keuka at Hammondsport, New York. The flight was five minutes in duration, and went to an altitude of twenty-five feet. Three other flights were made the same evening, one by Curtiss with Lieutenant Ellyson as a passenger, and two by Ellyson alone. Ellyson flew the A-1 from Keuka to Hammondsport on the first night flight by a naval aviator on July 3, 1911, landing successfully on the water in the second attempt without the assistance of lights. The crowd posing with the the A-1 Triad after its initial acceptance trials are: (left to right) Curtiss exhibition pilots C.C. Witmer and John D. Cooper; Dr. A. Francis Zahm, Smithsonian Institution; Marine Lieutenant John McClaskey; mechanic Jim Lamont; Glenn Curtiss; Lieutenant Spuds Ellyson; Captain Washington Irving Chambers; Lieutenant (junior grade) Jack Towers; Curtiss publicity man Bill Pickens; and another mechanic. Towers' crutches are hidden from view behind Chambers. (Courtesy of the National Museum of Naval Aviation.)

Lieutenant Spuds Ellyson (left) and Glenn H. Curtiss (right) taxi the A-1 on Lake Keuka, 1911. (Courtesy of the National Museum of Naval Aviation.)

Lieutenant John Henry "Jack" Towers, Naval Aviator No. 3, (left) and Lieutenant Theodore Gordon "Spuds" Ellyson, Naval Aviator No. 1, are posed at the controls of a Curtiss pusher, possibly the A-1, circa summer 1911, at Hammondsport, New York. (Courtesy of the National Museum of Naval Aviation.)

Lieutenant Ellyson and Glenn Curtiss conceived a novel way of launching an aircraft from shore. Their experiment was intended to test the feasibility of using the same device to launch aircraft from ships. Ellyson and Curtiss devised a sixteen-foot tripod and platform from which they strung a 250-foot heavily greased wire cable which ran at a ten degree incline into a piling sunk in Lake Keuka. The A-1 was run up the main wire and fastened by a toggle. The aircraft's lower wings were supported and balanced by two wires running parallel to the main line. On September 7, 1911, Lieutenant Ellyson was ready to test his invention. Ellyson opened up the throttle on the A-1, then gave the signal to release the aircraft. He held the Triad on the wire as long as possible, and when sure of enough headwind to rise, he made his takeoff, rising smoothly and rapidly into the air. A similar device would later be used to launch liaison aircraft from Landing Ships, Tank (LST) during World War II. Ellyson's report contained the following description of the run: "Everything happened so quickly and went off so smoothly that I hardly knew what happened except that I did have to use the ailerons, and that the machine was sensitive to their action." The picture shown here was taken on September 7. While Ellyson is securely poised at the controls of the Triad waiting for the moment to launch, Lieutenant Towers holds the right wing wire (left in the photograph). (Courtesy of the National Museum of Naval Aviation.)

with Washington, D.C., more an inconvenience than a danger.

The Navy Department was being pressed by Washington politicians for news of the A-1 flight. To get to the nearest inhabited stretch of Newport News meant a trek of seven miles, at least four on foot to reach a telephone or wire service. Ellyson and Towers had walked about two miles when they came upon a boy and his horse. The pilots mounted the bareback horse and rode, with the boy walking alongside. Near the populated end of Buckroe Beach, the aviators secured a car and reached the Chamberlin Hotel by seven in the evening.

The two aviators gave a number of interviews from the Chamberlin Hotel after they had rested and eaten. Ellyson said that the start from Annapolis was made in a strong east wind which continued throughout the trip and which grew stronger toward the end. Ellyson also noted that the plane had little difficulty keeping its course and they (he and Towers) steered a straight course down the west shore of the Chesapeake Bay. The speed of their machine varied from fifty to seventy miles an hour and averaged a speed of nearly sixty miles per hour. He and Towers took turns steering by means of shift control, thereby relieving both from the stress of having to be sole pilot for the entire trip.

Aviator Ellyson, son of H. Theodore Ellyson of Richmond, Virginia, and a nephew of Lieutenant Governor J. Taylor Ellyson, noted three world records in the flight from Annapolis to Buckroe Beach. The first was the distance in a hydroaeroplane with two men; the second, the distance record over water; and lastly, the time record of 2 hours, 27 minutes. The distance was roughly 150 miles. The two aviators made it in 147 minutes of real flying time.

On the morning of October 26, 1911, Ellyson and Towers flew their plane to a preselected site at Old Point Comfort and from there they were expected to depart for Annapolis. The two aviators had a reason or two not to leave Hampton Roads right away, though. That same day, a Thursday, Ellyson surprised and thrilled a crowd of 2,000 at the Lafayette Race Track, site of the Curtiss Aviation Meet in Norfolk, when he leapt into a Curtiss biplane and performed a series of spectacular aeronautical maneuvers.

Ellyson was not on the program for the opening day of the Curtiss meet, lasting from October 26 to 28. Norfolk promoters had contracted with the Curtiss Exhibition Company and featured acts of flying by the world-renowned Lincoln Beachey, a daredevil extraordinaire and some would say the best pilot of his day; C.C. Witmer, born June 16, 1882, who later enrolled in the

The A-1 was destroyed on July 31, 1912, during the Navy's first attempt to launch an airplane by catapult at Annapolis, Maryland. The aircraft, flown by Lieutenant Ellyson, was not secured to the catapult, reared about mid-stroke, and was caught in a crosswind and subsequently thrown into the water. Ellyson was not injured. The catapult being tested was powered by compressed air and had been designed at the Naval Gun Factory, Washington Navy Yard, from a plan proposed by Captain Chambers. Crewmen tried to raise portions of the A-1 from the Severn River. (Courtesy of the National Museum of Naval Aviation.)

Naval Reserve Flying Corps on March 6, 1917, to fight for his country; Charles K. Hamilton; and, of course, Eugene Godet, a Frenchman who had visited Norfolk frequently in his flying days. Ellyson and Towers dropped by to see Beachey and Godet do some of their wondrous stunt flying.

On impulse, Ellyson jumped into the seat of Godet's plane and took to the air. The plane was not unfamiliar to him, though. The Curtiss A-1 hydrobiplane he and Towers had landed at Buckroe Beach was identical to those at the meet in Norfolk except exhibition aircraft were the landplane version. Just before sunset, at five minutes past five, Naval Aviator No. 1 soared into Norfolk skies and glided gracefully through a series of maneuvers for approximately nine minutes. During this time, Ellyson dove within twenty-five feet of the ground, but some of the greatest crowd thrills came from the race between Ellyson and the famed motorcyclist Billy Feuerstein.

Feuerstein leapt on his seven-horse-power motorcycle and started a race no one on hand was soon to forget. Eight laps around a half-mile racetrack, Ellyson left Feuerstein a good quarter-mile behind. The airplane prevailed over the motorcycle. Norfolk had been the site of many thrilling aircraft demonstrations but Ellyson's spectacular show eclipsed all others. Ellyson had arrived on the grounds in civilian attire and he was not easy to recognize. Ellyson's exhibition almost cost the Navy its first official aviator. On the second or third lap of the racetrack he nearly became entangled with the wire stretched from the judges' stand to the grandstand. Within fifteen feet of the wire a yell came up from the crowd, "He is going to hit it!" Ellyson saw the wire at the last moment and nosed the plane up sharply, missing the wire by two feet.

Ellyson flew with Towers at the meet again the following day, thrilling them once more with his feats in the air. As for Lincoln Beachey, he gave an outstanding performance in Norfolk. Having Spuds Ellyson around hardly detracted from Beachey's drawing card: it raised exhibition attendance.

By November 2, 1911, Ellyson and Towers had expected to be back in Annapolis. They did not make it. They were forced to land shortly after takeoff from Old Point Comfort at Crab Neck, Gloucester Point, Virginia. The fishing boat *Bena* towed the plane to shore after its landing at Crab Neck. The A-1 had to be refitted with new batteries and test flights were done to ensure the plane was ready to make the trip home. Rumors circulated up and down communities on the Chesapeake Bay as to the aviators' troubles. Not a few thought the plane would have to be shipped to Annapolis from Oriana, while others were sure the plane was leaking and ready to sink.

Ellyson, Towers and their famous Triad finally reached Annapolis on November 3, coming in from Point No

Lieutenant John H. Towers was photographed in 1912 sitting at the controls of what appears to be the Curtiss A-2 landplane. This aircraft was dubbed the "Bat" boat for its snubby fuselage design. The aircraft was initially constructed as a landplane, but rebuilt as a hydroaeroplane. Subsequently, Curtiss rebuilt it again in what has been variously described as an over-water-land (OWL) or "Bat" boat that was fitted with wheels for use as an amphibian. The designation of this aircraft was changed to E-1 by order of Captain Chambers on November 25, 1913, to reflect the aircraft's type: a Curtiss amphibian flying boat. Towers took off from the water at Annapolis, Maryland, in the A-2 at 6:50 a.m. on October 6, 1912, and while flying at an average altitude of 600 hundred feet, remained in the air for 6 hours, 10 minutes and 35 seconds, setting a new American endurance record for aircraft of any type.

Point, Maryland, seventy miles south, in 1 hour, 20 minutes, a little after five o'clock in afternoon. Though the flyers began at Point No Point at 700 feet altitude, intense cold forced them to drop to 150 feet, which they maintained throughout the flight. Ellyson and Towers were nearly frozen by the time they made landfall. The Triad made excellent time from the area near Fortress Monroe en route to Annapolis before its batteries burned out and it was forced down at the mouth of the York River.

Ellyson and Towers would be followed into history by Lieutenant Patrick Neison Lynch "Pat" Bellinger, Naval Aviator No. 8, who, flying a tailless Burgess-Dunne AH-10 to Hampton Roads, spotted mortar fire from Army shore batteries at Fortress Monroe, Virginia, over a span of two days—August 5–6, 1915. This was the first time ground fire was observed from an aircraft. Watchers on the ground registered Bellinger's observations when he signaled his spots with Very pistol flares. The plane had no radio. Bellinger later reported that though the weather was bad, he could see mortar splashes quite well from an altitude of eight thousand feet.

Rapid advances in aviation at Hampton Roads were soon to eclipse early records. Perhaps the first significant records to fall were those of Ellyson and Towers from 1911. By the fall of 1915, Glenn Curtiss had established the Atlantic Coast Aeronautical Station at Newport News, Virginia, under contract with the government to develop and manufacture aircraft for the military. The station was the place to be in terms of "hot" pilots and airplanes.

During Curtiss Field's heyday there was a pilot by the name of Theodore C. Macaulay. On May 4, 1916, Macaulay, departing the Newport News air station flying a Curtiss H-10 hydroaeroplane equipped with two 160-horsepower engines, established eleven new world records and one new American altitude record for a plane carrying a pilot and five passengers. Macaulay's flight was the greatest event to happen to the Curtiss station and came on the heels of the last great period for the famed Newport News experimental ground before World War I. Macaulay set new marks for duration; distance, closed circuit; distance, straight line; speeds from 10 to 200 kilometers; and for greatest speed per hour for a flight of 5 kilometers. The objective was to reach Baltimore, Maryland, but the plane encountered a severe thunderstorm off Point Lookout, eighty-five miles from Newport News on the Chesapeake Bay. Macaulay did manage to cover 170 miles in two hours, 23 minutes, leaving on May 4, 1916, at 1:35 in the afternoon and returning at 3:58 the same day.

Macaulay was accompanied on the flight by Alessandro Pomilio, Italian Royal Flying Corps; Lieutenant Norman

B. Hall, United States Coast Guard; Chief Mechanic Phillip Utter of the Curtiss Aeroplane Company; Frank J. Conway, official photographer of the Curtiss Aeroplane Company; and a reporter from the Norfolk newspapers. Hall was conducting tests for the military services of a new drift compass designed for navigating aircraft. By his assistance with the compass, Hall was able to aid course accuracy from Newport News up the Chesapeake Bay and back. An improved version of Hall's drift compass was used on the famous Navy/Curtiss NC-4 transatlantic flight in 1919.

Top speed of the Curtiss H-10, a fifteen-ton flying boat, was about 130 kilometers per hour. The British government had purchased twenty H-10s from the Curtiss factory in 1916. The wingspan of the plane was seventy-six feet across and the aircraft itself forty-five feet long. The H-10 came equipped with twin 160-horsepower engines that had the capacity to run at about 1,500 revolutions per minute. The airframe was the largest ever flight-tested at that time. Macaulay maintained an altitude of about 1,000 feet, perfect for passengers trying to get a bird's-eye view of Hampton Roads and the Chesapeake Bay. All shipping activities were dwarfed by comparison.

The danger of in-flight repair was a fact of life in early aviation. On Macaulay's first attempt to fly the H-10 to Fort McHenry on May 4, as with Towers' perilous repairs to the A-1 flown to Buckroe Beach, if anything broke, the fix required taking your life in your hands, literally. During the H-10 flight, Utter had to fix a leaking feed pipe that could not be reached from the cockpit. To exact repairs, Utter fished out a roll of adhesive tape, put it between his teeth and climbed out of the safety of his cockpit. As Macaulay's chief mechanic edged himself onto the wing, the wind tore his overalls with such force they were in tatters. By all accounts, Utter's only option was to brace himself carefully against the wing supports, catch the piano wire stay, and wriggle out from the body of the flying boat to get beneath the crippled motor. Nothing was between Utter and the Chesapeake Bay but a thin wing and a thousand feet of sky. Utter braced himself anew with his feet, took the tape from his mouth, reached up with both hands to wind the feed pipe, and waited to see the result of his handiwork. He was successful. Slowly Utter made his way back to the cockpit and the motor gradually picked up its regular 1,400 revolutions per minute.

Macaulay had the opportunity to make Baltimore on May 6, 1916. He scrambled his five-passenger crew and left Newport News bound north for Fort McHenry, a distance of 178 miles. The behemoth flying boat made the Newport News to Fort McHenry run in three hours, three minutes despite gale-force winds. Macaulay noted had it not been for Lieutenant Hall, maintaining a fix on their course and direction, the trip would have been a failure. The weary crew landed at Fort McHenry at 10:51 in the morning. The return trip to Newport News was delayed when Coast Guard officers wanted ample time to look over the H-10 and see how it had endured the trip. As the largest flying boat in the world in its day, the Curtiss H-10 was under careful scrutiny. Despite thorough inspection, the H-10 met with tragedy on its return trip from the Washington, D.C., area when the flying boat plunged 100 feet into the Potomac River and killed two crew in the process.

The ill-fated return trip of the H-10 to Newport News did little to deter growing international interest in the aircraft. The week following his record breaking flights from Hampton Roads, on May 8, 1916, Macaulay departed for Russia whose government had consigned planes from the Curtiss Aeroplane Company. Fascinating fellow that he was, Macaulay would delight in teaching Czar Nicholas II's airmen to fly.

The Atlantic Coast Aeronautical Station, popularly called the Curtiss Flying School or Curtiss Field, was an exciting place to be in the mid-1910s. Run by Captain Thomas Scott Baldwin, renowned for much of the great balloon racing that took place in the latter nineteenth century and early 1910s, the school would eventually have at least a half-dozen instructors under his watchful eye teaching Americans, British, French, Finns, Italians, and Russians to fly. Macaulay was, in fact, one of Baldwin's instructor pilots. Visitors of the period included Russian generals and government representatives, Rear Admiral Robert E. Peary of North Pole fame and an aviation enthusiast, and quite a few Japanese who were interested in purchasing Curtiss planes.

The H-10 with its forty-five-foot hull and great wingspan was the star attraction. Its engines were fastened between the upper and lower wing sections but, without a doubt, the most visually impressive feature of the aircraft was its big, copper-tipped mahogany propellers mounted in front with aluminum shafts braced away aft to withstand thrust from the motors. The hull itself was divided into three compartments: aft, amidship and forward. Aft, located behind the motors and wings, was the pilot's cockpit where Curtiss engineers placed the throttles, motors, and steering devices for the rudder and planes. Aside from crew compartments amidship, there were also two gasoline tanks with 1,200 pounds of fuel to feed the engines. On Macaulay's record breaking flight to Fort McHenry, Phillip Utter, chief mechanic, and Lieutenant Norman B. Hall sat amidship. Forward in the observer's compartment were Frank J. Conway, who took pictures with his cameras and plates, his trusty field glasses strapped over his shoulders, and Charley Good, a student aviator, who later died when the H-10 crashed in the Potomac River on its return trip.

Numbers appearing after the names of selected naval aviators are part of the precedence list which existed between January 1918 and an undetermined date in 1973 when the maintenance of such military precedence rosters was discontinued. John "Jang" Rodgers was Naval Aviator No. 2. The number assigned by the Bureau of Personnel to each naval aviator will be used behind his name the first time the aviator's name appears in the text if his number is known.

the 'fuselage' –

Chapter 4: Naval Aviation Grows

Two years after Eugene Barton Ely successfully flew from the deck of the USS *Birmingham* at Hampton Roads, Captain Washington Irving Chambers of the Navy looked upon Ely's progeny with understandable reservations. His job was an uphill battle to acquire funding, equipment, training grounds, and most importantly, pilots. Though convinced aircraft had a vital role to play in the naval warfare mission, his provisos, caveats and praises for naval aviation could be capsulized in one phrase, "airplanes...could extend the eyes of the fleet."

A little more than a year into their first year of operation in the fleet, aircraft had proved themselves easily carried, stowed and used by ships. In the age of nuclear aircraft carriers, it is easy to forget the trials and tribulations of aviation in its infancy. Vision was the buzz word. In the November 1912 issue of Naval Institute *Proceedings,* Chambers noted four areas in which naval aircraft could be used in the strategic warfare mission at sea. The first was to scout enemy ports, search out enemy advance bases, and to assist the blockade of hostile forces. The second, and perhaps most important to naval aviation's role in the First World War, was to locate and destroy mines, submarines, and dirigibles, and to participate in operations with submarines and torpedo boats. In Chambers' view, the third mission of airplanes was to damage enemy installations, magazines, ships in repair or under construction, dirigible hangars, and any number of enemy assets vulnerable to attack by air. The final, and equally significant future role of airplanes fell square in the middle of the tremendous, almost daily advances in communication technology. If aircraft could carry communications capability to link fleet and shore commanders, naval forces would have the upper hand in battle.

Captain Chambers shared the view of many of his early aviation counterparts, clearly favoring semirigid dirigibles, bombers, observation and photographic reconnoiter aircraft over fighters. Since Chambers had been allocated very little money to launch his plans for naval aviation, progress on the heels of Ely's accomplishments in 1910 and again in early 1911, was plodding at best. By his own account, Chambers had only twenty-five thousand dollars to train

Captain Washington Irving Chambers was in charge of aviation correspondence in the Office of the Secretary of the Navy. He became deeply interested in the possibilities of naval aviation and worked tirelessly toward demonstrating to the Navy the value of aircraft within the fleet, and in encouraging manufacturers to design aerodynamically efficient flying machines. It was Captain Chambers who, convinced that an airplane could be launched from the deck of a ship, provided the ship and the means for Eugene Barton Ely, a Curtiss Aeroplane Company pilot, to make the first attempt on November 14, 1910, from the deck of the USS *Birmingham* anchored at Hampton Roads, Virginia. Chambers Field at Naval Air Station Norfolk is named in honor of the father of naval aviation. The photograph shown here was taken in 1910, the year naval aviation was truly born. (Official United States Navy Photograph.)

Ensign Godfrey deCourcelles "Chevy" Chevalier, Naval Aviator No. 7, sitting on the left, and Lieutenant John Henry "Jack" Towers, Naval Aviator No. 3, on the right facing the cameraman, are pictured in the Navy's first flying boat, the Curtiss C-1. The precise location of the picture is unknown, but the date of the image would have been sometime in the summer of 1913. The C-1 was redesignated the AB-1 in accordance with General Order No. 88 of March 27, 1914. The C-1 was first tested at Hammondsport, New York, by Lieutenant Theodore Gordon "Spuds" Ellyson, Naval Aviator No. 1, on November 30, 1912. Ellyson informally reported his findings as the following: "Circular climb, only one complete circle, 1,575 feet in 14 minutes 30 seconds fully loaded. On glide approximately 5.3 to 1. Speed, eight runs over measured mile, 59.4 miles per hour fully loaded. The endurance test was not made, owing to the fact that the weather has not been favorable, and I did not like to delay any longer." (Courtesy of the Hampton Roads Naval Museum.)

three naval officers and buy less than a handful of planes—three to be exact. Seaplanes were being researched and developed, flight-tested, and evaluated for naval aviation at a rapid pace by aircraft designers and manufacturers. Glenn Curtiss was becoming increasingly influential with Chambers and his seaplane designs were far superior to those of his competition.

As one of Chambers' confidantes, Curtiss cautioned the captain to be careful in his development and training of naval aviators. The year Eugene Ely made his famed flight from the *Birmingham*—1910—thirty aviators in Europe and the United States lost their lives. Aviation was getting a bad reputation as its detractors scoffed at the carnage and touted better means of travel and warfare. Airplanes were not to blame. Aviators became increasingly daring with their stunts at exhibitions all over the world, pushing their aircraft beyond design capability. Many of the world's best pilots died as a result. When Ely himself was killed at Macon, Georgia, in the fall of 1911, he had only been flying for eighteen months prior to his death. His final stunt was a rare departure for Ely's normally controlled, conservative style. Glenn Curtiss had been an overly cautious, safety-oriented mentor to Ely, and the latter's death shattered Chambers and stunned Curtiss. By 1911, the world public, including throngs of Americans, knew aircraft could fly straight and level but what they wanted to watch were stunts. The flying circus, the barnstormer, and the speed king were born.

Ely's two famous flights in 1910 and 1911 were studied repeatedly by early naval aviation students. Lieutenant Theodore Gordon "Spuds" Ellyson, future Naval Aviator No. 1, met Ely while attending Curtiss' flying school located at North Island, California, after Ely's remarkable landing and takeoff from the USS *Pennsylvania*. For a brief time, both Ely and Curtiss instructed three Army students, one civilian student and Ellyson before Ely went back to flying exhibitions. Even after Ely's death, his work and accomplishments established the benchmark for subsequent advancement of naval aviation. Research and development of landplanes, hydroaeroplanes, airships and even helicopters were being investigated. Interest was demonstrated, as early as March 3, 1912, in a helicopter by the Navy Department. The budget for 1912 alloted the sum of fifty dollars to develop models from plans proposed by Chief Machinist's Mate F.E. Nelson of the USS *West Virginia*. Nelson was the first American designer to attract so much attention with a helicopter design since William C. Powers of Civil War fame.

Hampton Roads entered the aviation picture very early with its warm natural harbors, steady currents and vast land tracts for aircraft experimental grounds. Hampton Roads' juxtaposition on the East Coast near the port, transportation lines, manufacturing and industry, yet far enough removed with space for research and experimentation, made the area ideally suited for aviation, most especially naval aviation. By the spring of 1912, the longest continuous flight made with a passenger was that of Lieutenants Ellyson and Towers from Greenbury Point, Annapolis, Maryland, to Hampton Roads, Virginia, and back. The purpose of their flight was clearly to argue the use of a hydroaeroplane for long flights, to demonstrate Curtiss' new dual control system, and to show the need for constant research and development to improve aircraft motors.

Greenbury Point was placed in operation as an air base in the first year of naval aviation to conduct aircraft experimentation which, at least at that time, meant test flights to Hampton Roads. Test flights to the lower Chesapeake Bay in and around Hampton Roads would involve some of the best "seat-of-your-pants" flying ever done in naval aviation history. Though many aviation pioneers,

The first commissioned officers of the Navy's new aviation corps were photographed together at Pensacola Naval Aeronautic Station, Florida, in March of 1914. The picture is a classic, laying the foundation for those amongst their ranks who had already been to or would soon make the trek to Hampton Roads. (Left to right) Lieutenant Victor Daniel "Vic" Herbster, Naval Aviator No. 4; First Lieutenant William Maitland "Mac" McIlvain, USMC, Naval Aviator No. 12 and Marine Corps Aviator No. 3; Lieutenant Patrick Neison Lynch "Pat" Bellinger, Naval Aviator No. 8; Lieutenant Richard Caswell "Caswell" Saufley, Naval Aviator No. 14; Lieutenant John Henry "Jack" Towers, Naval Aviator No. 3; Lieutenant Commander Henry Croskey "Rum" Mustin, Naval Aviator No. 11; First Lieutenant Bernard Lewis "Barney" Smith, USMC, Naval Aviator No. 6 and Marine Corps Aviator No. 2; Ensign Godfrey deCourcelles "Chevy" Chevalier, Naval Aviator No. 7; and, Ensign Melvin L. Stolz, student naval aviator. Towers, Bellinger, Mustin, and Chevalier would become well-known names and familiar faces in Hampton Roads. Herbster tested the new Burgess-Dunne tailless biplane aboard the USS *North Carolina* then came into Hampton Roads for a short period in 1914 prior to his official appointment as Navy Air Pilot No. 5, not to be confused with his designation as Naval Aviator No. 4, shortly thereafter. The Navy Department changed the title "Navy Air Pilot" to "Naval Aviator" on March 22, 1915. Stolz was killed as a student naval aviator on May 8, 1915, in the crash of an AH-9 at Pensacola. Although Lieutenant (junior grade) Stolz died as a student, he had already qualified for Aero Club Hydroaeroplane Certificate Nineteen, according to Navy records. (Official United States Navy Photograph.)

Godfrey deCourcelles Chevalier, Naval Aviator No. 7, (right) was photographed circa 1914 with an unidentified passenger at Naval Air Station Pensacola, Florida. The passenger (left) might be Robert Rudolph "Rip" Paunack, Naval Aviator No. 27, both a heavier-than-air and lighter-than-air pilot. Paunack received a Distinguished Flying Cross for heroism in actual flight for his prompt and courageous action that saved the dirigible *C-8* from destruction, and the lives of its crew of six on June 3, 1919. (Courtesy of the National Museum of Naval Aviation.)

Lieutenant Commander Godfrey deCourcelles "Chevy" Chevalier, Naval Aviator No. 7, circa 1914. (Courtesy of the International News Service.)

(Left to right) Lieutenant John H. "Jack" Towers, Naval Aviator No. 3, and Lieutenant Commander Henry C. "Rum" Mustin, Naval Aviator No. 11, Naval Air Station Pensacola, circa 1914. (Courtesy of the National Museum of Naval Aviation.)

even aviators themselves, were steadfastly opposed to trial and error test flights, there was often no other way to find out how the aircraft would perform under service conditions.

Student naval aviators (SNAs) were hampered in training by lack of funding and support personnel. Aviation service was so new it had yet to spin and weave rates for aviation carpenters, aviation mechanics, aircrew and the innumerable enlisted aviation support professions which were just around the corner. Ellyson, Lieutenant John "Jang" Rodgers, Naval Aviator No. 2, and Towers, were trained to fly in a few short weeks. According to a disgruntled Chambers, the system of instruction should have been, at bare minimum, four months, and should have included the fundamentals of aerodynamics and meteorology. Much of what was being plotted in aviation instruction in Chambers' day evolved from the Massachusetts Institute of Technology(1) which emphasized theory as well as practical application. The first three naval aviators learned their flying trial-and-error style. By the time Chambers was finished evaluating the first year or so of naval aviation, he was bent on establishing a school for aviators.

Given what he had witnessed of aircraft development in his lifetime, Chambers was hopeful though cautious in his expectations for naval aviation. He was knowledgeable of discussions between Glenn Curtiss and a representative of the Bureau of Equipment regarding flying boats as early as 1905. Curtiss had previously shown great interest in the work of France's Jacques Schneider to develop seaplanes. By 1909, Schneider had initiated the first International Schneider Cup Trophy Race, a seaplane race held every year, and in which the United States would eventually compete and win on several occasions. Chambers was aboard the USS *Birmingham* at Hampton Roads when Eugene B. Ely gave birth to naval aviation. He was there when it counted, when he was needed for his wealth of experience and steady guidance.

As naval aviation grew, so did standards imposed on aviation candidates and procurement of aircraft. On October 8, 1912, physical requirements for prospective naval aviators were prescribed by the Bureau of Medicine to set standards for vision, hearing, equilibrium, and the organs of the respiratory and circulatory systems above those demanded of other naval officers.

The origin of flight pay as we know it today began with the Navy Appropriations Bill of March 4, 1913, which granted a modest increase of thirty-five cents a day and allowances to

Sailors carried pilots out to their seaplanes to avoid the flyers getting their feet wet. The pilot being carried in the foreground is John H. Towers. The picture was taken at Pensacola about 1914. (Courtesy of the International News Service.)

not more than thirty officers below the rank of commander who were active heavier-than-air flyers and who had been designated by the Secretary of the Navy. The good news for naval aviation, along with the addition of flight pay, was the replacement of Navy Secretary George von L. Meyer by Josephus Daniels, a man much more intrigued by aviation than his predecessor. Two other acts are worth mention here since both would so strongly impact the course of naval aviation in Hampton Roads, Virginia. The first and most critical to the continuum of naval aviation occurred on October 7, 1913, when the Secretary of the Navy appointed a board, with Chambers once again its head, to draft "a comprehensive plan for the organization of a Naval Aeronautic Service," precursor of the Bureau of Aeronautics. The board's report was submitted to Navy Secretary Daniels in twelve days and stressed the importance

The cruiser USS *North Carolina* was the first ship equipped with a catapult and in 1915 carried N-9 seaplanes with as much pride as the modern aircraft carrier does its jet fighters. (Official United States Navy Photograph.)

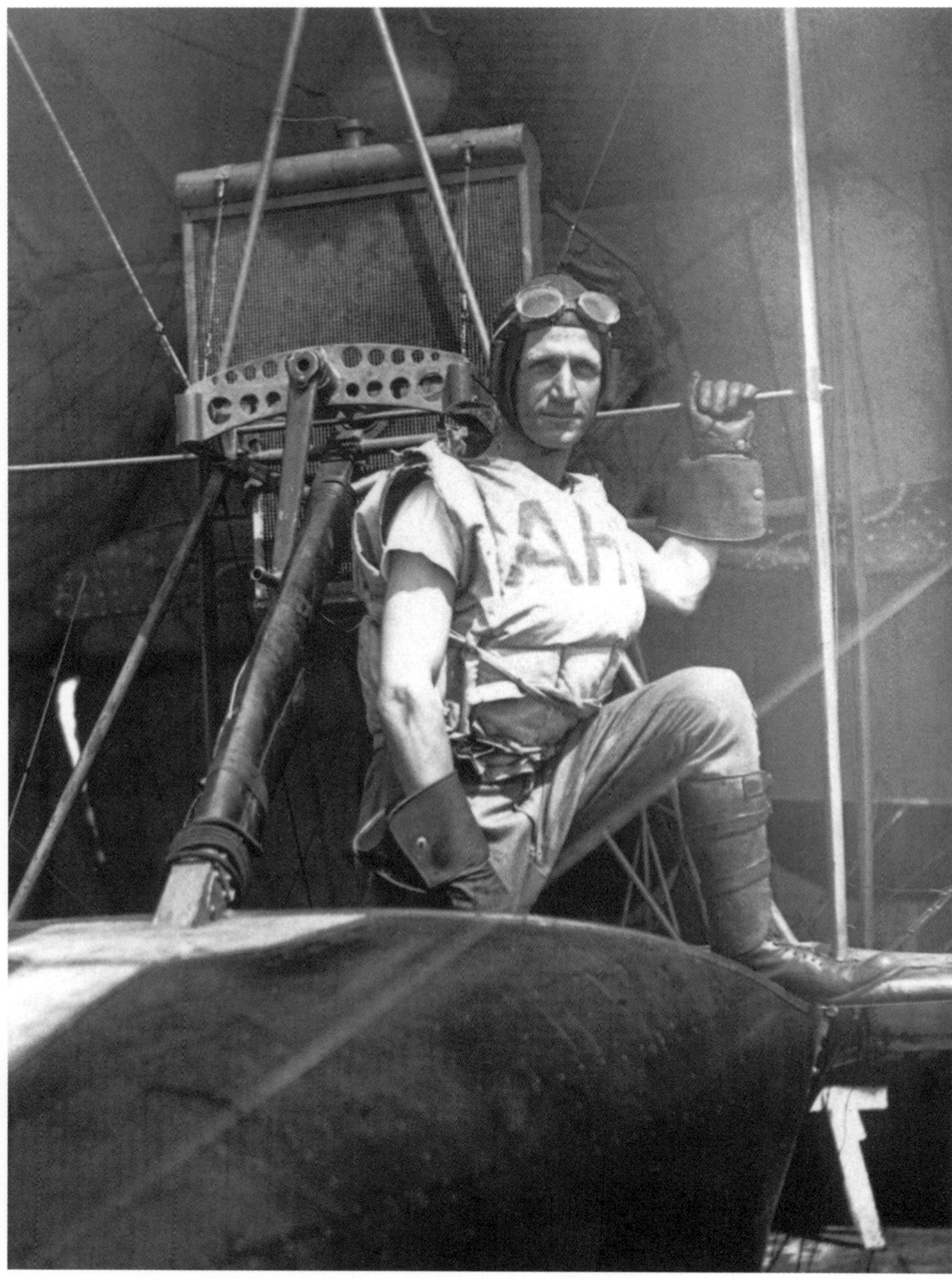

Lieutenant Albert Cushing "Putty" Read, Naval Aviator No. 24, pictured at Naval Air Station Pensacola, circa 1915. (Courtesy of the National Museum of Naval Aviation.)

of expansion and integration of aviation in the fleet—in essence, the first call was issued for creation of an official naval aviation service within the United States Navy. The board recommended, among other items, establishment of an aeronautic center at Pensacola, Florida, for ground and flight training and rigorous lessons in advanced aeronautical engineering; establishment of a centralized aviation office under the Navy Secretary to oversee aviation business within existing bureaus; assignment of a training ship; practical test of equipment for fleet use; and assignment of at least one airplane to every surface combatant in the American fleet. The last item was perhaps the most important, at least to Chambers who had labored with so little for too long, and was near retirement: the expenditure of over $1.25 million to jumpstart the program. Subsequent budgets would include requests to fund an experimental station and, later, an advanced training base at Norfolk: Naval Air Station Hampton Roads.

Despite Chambers' success as officer-in-charge of aviation, the pervasive lack of interest in aviation amongst the Navy's senior officers left the father of naval aviation fighting private skirmishes behind closed doors. With his health failing and retirement looming, Chambers tried to find an officer suitable for his job. The first round of searching yielded no one and Chambers remained on active duty until the Navy Department could broaden the search and locate someone to fill his post. When Captain Mark L. Bristol was named officer-in-charge of aviation on December 13, 1913, Chambers[2] stayed on to smooth Bristol's transition in his challenging new role. Bristol soon proved he, too, had a vision for naval aviation. Bristol's vision went so far as his proposal, the first of its kind, for conversion of a merchant ship for aircraft use as early as October of 1915. The collier *Jupiter* would not be converted to the first aircraft carrier, USS *Langley* (CV-1) until 1922 at Norfolk, Virginia. Captain Bristol would later become the first "Director of Naval Aeronautics" on November 23, 1914, laying the foundation for the Bureau of Aeronautics which was just around the corner.

The summer of 1914 saw the first naval vessel to carry airplanes emerge from Newport News Shipbuilding and Drydock Company, the USS *North Carolina,* an armored cruiser refitted in the very yard which has sinceforth laid the keel of the majority of conventional and every modern nuclear-powered aircraft carrier in the service of the United States Navy. Captain Henry Croskey "Rum" Mustin, Naval Aviator No. 11, and first commandant of Naval Air Station Pensacola, Florida, was ordered to pick up the *North Carolina* to replace the USS *Mississippi* for use in aviation training. The *North Carolina* was perfect for Mustin's use as it was newer and had a quarter-deck large enough to be fitted with a catapult. The cruiser also had adequate berthing spaces for his aviators and ground crew. Mustin was ordered to make the switch at Hampton Roads and take the ship back to Pensacola.

Best laid plans are often foiled by outside forces, and the situation with the *North Carolina* was certainly no exception. World events would soon trigger an American response which denied Mustin taking the *North Carolina* home to Florida. Austria declared war on Serbia on July 28, 1914. The flames of the First World War began to lick American shores, and most immediately affected was the USS *North Carolina,* Captain Mustin and his men. The Navy held the *North Carolina* at anchorage off the Virginia Capes, and, by August 1, 1914, Germany had declared war on Russia.

Upon arrival in Hampton Roads, Mustin and his officer contingent expected to be back in Pensacola within the month, holding fast to the belief that tensions in the Balkans would pass, and,

The Municipal Small Boat Harbor in Newport News developed quickly with the arrival of Glenn H. Curtiss' Atlantic Coast Aeronautical Station. The placid, recreational inlet shown in the first photograph soon became home to aircraft and new industries which developed along the road to the aviation field. Wooded areas and wetlands gave way to pier and building construction (aerial photograph) which would forever change the waterfront of Newport News. (Frank J. Conway, photographer.)

by the end of July, he and his officers would be conducting routine training flights from the deck of their new ship. Those aboard the *North Carolina* with Mustin were quite familiar with Hampton Roads social life, particularly in and around Newport News and Norfolk, cities with well-established social rosters and cultural pursuits. Early naval aviators of society had many friends to call upon on their arrival in "The Roads." Among naval aviation's earliest and most socially prominent officers was Lieutenant Godfrey de Courcelles "Chevy" Chevalier, Naval Aviator No. 7, appointed a pilot on July 1, 1914. Chevalier kept numerous friends in Hampton Roads. In Norfolk, "Chevy" would enjoy the heyday of the city's cultural life and entertainment in the earliest decades of the century. Chevalier would likewise speak highly of meeting acquaintances at the Chamberlin Hotel at Old Point Comfort, one of his favorite points of destination. As was the case with he and most of his brother aviators, they could not wait to escape the tedium of Pensacola, then not much to speak of in terms of built environment and culture. They looked forward to being in Hampton Roads. The spoiler to Chevalier's plans to show friends and colleagues the nightlife of Norfolk and Newport News and, of course, Mustin's to return with a bigger and better training ship to Pensacola, would be greater than any of them ever imagined. Just as the crew of the USS *Mississippi* had set sail from Pensacola to Newport News, Austrian Archduke Franz Ferdinand was assassinated, and Europe hung on the precipice of war. None of the aviators aboard the *Mississippi* could know, nor care, what this would mean until news of the assassination reached them upon arrival at Newport News. In Newport News on July 8, 1914, Captain Henry C. Mustin relieved Commander William Adger Moffett (later to become the first chief of the Bureau of Aeronautics) of his command of the USS *North Carolina*.

Three weeks would pass before all the aircraft gear aboard the USS *Mississippi* could be shifted to the *North Carolina*, and the *Mississippi* turned over to the government of Greece. The situation in Europe was heating up as world war edged closer and eventually gave way to battle. A young lieutenant by the name of Wadleigh Capehart, later Naval Aviator No. 19, boarded the *North Carolina* for aero instruction on July 27, 1914, off the Virginia Capes just one day prior to official declarations of war overseas. Capehart had come from the Burgess Company at Marblehead, Massachusetts, where he had been receiving aviation training since the end of May. Initial plans called for him to return with the ship to Pensacola to begin actual flying instruction; however, as circumstances unraveled, this was not to be until January of 1915. Once Capehart and his fellow officers were aboard, the *North Carolina* remained anchored at Lynnhaven Roads, conducted a few flight operations and hoped to proceed to Florida. This did not happen.

When Germany declared war on Russia, the USS *North Carolina* was dispatched to Boston, Massachusetts, to unload her airplanes and all aeronautical equipment, pick up extra crew and, of course, be coaled. The Germans invaded Belgium, at which time England declared war on Germany. This chain of events rocked the world and touched the lives and careers of those in early naval aviation in untold ways. On August 7, 1914, Captain Joseph W. Oman assumed command of the USS *North Carolina* and Mustin was demoted to executive officer, but retained command of Naval Air Station Pensacola.(3) The cruiser was then sent on her way to retrieve Americans caught in the cross fire of war in Europe.

Curtiss Flying School, part of the Atlantic Coast Aeronautical Station, was opened late in 1915, and, as evident by this photograph by Frank J. Conway, key buildings were not finished. Construction of one wing of the main hangar was just getting underway. A Curtiss Flying Boat (F-boat) sits at left, its tail section resting on a sawhorse. The other two aircraft are early version Curtiss JN-4 Jennies. Notice the rear landing gear of the Jenny to the far right (foreground) is designed like a ski rather than the more common tail-dragger type. (Frank J. Conway, photographer.)

First Lieutenant William Maitland "Mac" McIlvain, USMC, Naval Aviator No. 12 and Marine Corps Aviator No. 3, was charged with getting planes and gear back to Pensacola. So ended the first experience with a ship dedicated to carry aircraft. A little over six months after Mustin's band of aviators returned to Pensacola, on March 22, 1915, the term "Naval Aviator" officially replaced "Navy Air Pilot" in reference to Navy personnel in flying billets—the same term used today.

Hampton Roads continued to play a pivotal role in the training of aviation pilots. Aviation pioneer Glenn Hammond Curtiss had begun his flying school, the Atlantic Coast Aeronautical Station, on a 220-acre tract of land east of Newport News Municipal Small Boat Harbor in the fall of 1915 with Captain Thomas Scott Baldwin as its director. Baldwin, who at the age of sixty-four in 1916 had forty years of aeronautical experience to his credit, engaged as many as thirty young men in flight training at any given time. Many civilian students joined military counterparts, including Canadians, learning to fly at the station. Several of Baldwin's early students later became famous World War I flyers, namely Victor Vernon, Vernon Castle, Edward "Eddie" Stinson, and the infamous Brigadier General Billy Mitchell. Other names and famous faces would ring familiar in later years: the Harvard Flying Unit, Henry Barton "H.B." Cecil, Naval Aviator No. 42, Bert Acosta, and H.M. "Buck" Gallop (the school's first graduate later to become a top fighter pilot in France). Gallop would also become as famous on the silver screen as in the air. His personage was the main character in the 1930 Oscar-winning movie *Dawn Patrol*. Gallop's role was played by silent movie star Richard Barthelmess, himself a frequent visitor to Hampton Roads.

Hampton Roads trained more foreign and American flyers prior to the First World War than any other place in the United States. Curtiss flying schools predated the official start of Navy and Army flight schools. Both the Navy and Army contracted with Curtiss, the Wright Brothers at Dayton, Ohio, and Burgess Company of Marblehead, Massachusetts, to train pilots prior to establishment of the Naval Aviation Camp at Greenbury Point, Annapolis, Maryland, in 1911. Even after the camp was begun, naval aviators rotated through private aircraft companies to fine tune their skills and learn more about how their flying machines functioned. Baldwin's impeccable organization put him ahead of Pensacola, which was stunned by the rapid turn of world events and left scrambling to structure its flight training program. The number of foreign and American young men seeking flight instruction far exceeded military flight schools' capacity both abroad and in the United States. Several major World War I aces and innumerable Navy pilots were trained at Newport News, Virginia, not to mention hundreds of Canadian, British, French, Finnish, Russian, Japanese, and Baltic aviators, all of them young and eager to fly for their country in the first world war to utilize the airplane. The impact of civilian training facilities on the preparedness and competency of early naval aviators has been lost with time, but, in their day, these schools, operated by the likes of Glenn Hammond Curtiss and Orville Wright, were indispensable.

The Curtiss airfield at Newport News stretched from the apex of Jefferson Avenue at the ferry docks for a mile or so before looping northward to Salter's Creek. Landplanes and seaplanes could

Weekend crowds (first photograph) flocked to the Atlantic Coast Aeronautical Station to watch Curtiss instructor/test pilots take off and land (second photograph). The great attraction the weekend this photograph was taken was the Curtiss L-type triplane, visible just left of the large hangar building. This aircraft never saw action in the First World War, but it was prototyped for the Navy which made limited test flights with the aircraft just before war's end. Many of the visitors who came every Sunday to watch the goings on around Curtiss Field had boarded the ferry in Norfolk and alighted at the boat harbor to see the airplanes on the ground and watch Baldwin's instructors fly the diverse assortment of Curtiss aircraft on the field. (Frank J. Conway, photographer.)

use the field and its dock facilities, respectively. When Europe went to war in 1914, Canadian volunteers wanted to fly with the early Royal Flying Corps, precursor of the Royal Air Force (RAF) but most Canadian and British aviation schools were crowded. Upon hearing of the Curtiss school in Buffalo, New York, aspiring Canadian pilots crossed the border and enrolled in the program. The large number of trainees and unfavorable weather and location soon set Curtiss thinking about alternative sites for his flying school. Curtiss made the decision to move the school out of New York to Hampton Roads, Virginia, in order to accommodate his students and, perhaps more importantly, capitalize on a location more favorable to seaplanes.

The renowned aviation pioneer first wanted to move the school to Norfolk since he quickly ascertained the southside was the hub of activity in "The Roads." He initially came to Norfolk with Baldwin, his old friend and famous aeronaut, in 1910 to scout sites. The two found a number of outstanding locations but no cooperation in Norfolk for their work. When Curtiss realized he needed to procure actual service conditions to test his seaplanes, he looked for a prime location in Newport News to conduct his experimental work. Curtiss' objective was to develop a seaplane that could weather the strongest winds aloft and come down and rest on the surface of a turbulent sea. Baldwin helped Curtiss develop perhaps one of the most important features of flying boats—the type of pontoon used on the underside of the wing tips.

Since Baldwin was going to be testing Curtiss aircraft as part of his Newport News operation, he also initially investigated the possibility of establishing an airplane factory in conjunction with the experimental station and school. The factory idea was impeded by the lack of skilled workers to build airplanes, especially in the southeastern United States, and the cost of using such highly skilled labor. In Baldwin's day, aviation mechanics received fifty to sixty dollars a week and had to be of the highest quality to work in the factories, the distinction which must be made being between the men who constructed the aircraft and the fair number of aviation mechanics employed to maintain aircraft already in service. When Curtiss arrived on New Year's Day 1916 to spend several days inspecting his testing plant at the Municipal Small Boat Harbor, he was reportedly quite satisfied with the plant and school. The famed aviation pioneer evaluated Baldwin's operation as "first rate."

The Atlantic Coast Aeronautical Station at Newport News had three instructors when it opened: the famous Victor Carlstrom, Vernon Castle, and a fellow by the name of Walter Edwin Lees, Curtiss' most conservative pilot but also one of his best. Baldwin once remarked of Lees, "Some men simply never could learn to fly," he continued, "while others take to it at once." Of Vernon Castle, one of the first students to take instruction at the station, Baldwin stated unequivocably, "He is a born airman, for he has the *touch* in his hands. That is essential, and he is one of the most apt pupils I have ever seen." The "touch" in airplane lingo means a pilot who knows just how to manipulate his plane to its best performance capability.

Vernon Castle, a stage personality

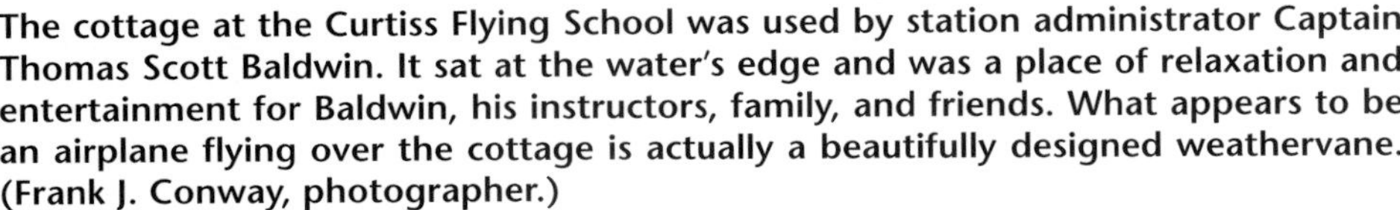

The cottage at the Curtiss Flying School was used by station administrator Captain Thomas Scott Baldwin. It sat at the water's edge and was a place of relaxation and entertainment for Baldwin, his instructors, family, and friends. What appears to be an airplane flying over the cottage is actually a beautifully designed weathervane. (Frank J. Conway, photographer.)

Captain Thomas Scott Baldwin (circa 1916) was Glenn Hammond Curtiss' personal choice to operate the flying school and flight test facility in Newport News, Virginia. At the age of sixty-four Baldwin already had more than forty years of aeronautical experience, primarily as an aeronaut or balloonist. He had, in fact, built and alighted in the first American dirigible. Baldwin was a favorite subject for Curtiss Aeroplane Company photographer, Frank J. Conway, who caught the aging aviation pioneer taking a flight himself from time to time. (Frank J. Conway, photographer.)

who danced with his wife Irene at theatres and dance halls across the nation, was a prize pilot. Irene lived on the Peninsula while he trained, and on weekends Vernon would accompany her to theatrical engagements in Washington, D.C., New York City, and major cities up and down the East Coast. Their specialties were the foxtrot, turkey trot, and wildly daring cheek-to-cheek steps. Castle graduated from the school in February of 1916 at which time he departed the United States via New York for English shores and the Royal Flying Corps. When the United States entered the First World War, Castle resigned from the Royal Flying Corps and returned home to Texas as a flight instructor. He was killed in a training crash, and Irene later married a Chicago millionaire.

Though not one of the first three instructors trained and retained by Baldwin at Newport News, Bert Acosta was one of the most important instructors to work at the Curtiss school. Acosta later served as a pilot for Rear Admiral Richard Evelyn Byrd's polar expeditions, and shares his association with Byrd's string of Antarctic expeditions with the likes of Naval Aviation Pilot Floyd Bennett; Naval Aviation Pilot Harold I. June; Norwegian Bernt Balchen; and Theodore Argyres Petras, one of the Marine Corps' famous "flying sergeants" and now a retired colonel.

The first students to attend Curtiss' school in 1915 at Hampton Roads were Canadians, twenty-eight of them to be precise. With a cap of thirty students at any given time and a wait list of over one hundred, the Canadians were fortunate to receive flight training at the new Curtiss facility. Each of the Canadians received their Aero Club of America certificates, making them licensed pilots, not military pilots until, of course, they joined the service, and most did join the Royal Flying Corps.

Vernon Castle (in cockpit), Curtiss Flying School instructor pilot, Newport News, Virginia, 1916. (Frank J. Conway, photographer.)

Victor Carlstrom, Curtiss Flying School chief pilot and instructor, Newport News, Virginia, 1916. (Frank J. Conway, photographer.)

Below right: Andrew "Stuart" Cogswell, Curtiss Flying School instructor pilot, Newport News, Virginia, 1916. (Frank J. Conway, photographer.)

Baldwin would have truly great students come and go during the few short years the school was in operation. Then Major William "Billy" Mitchell, an Army officer from Washington, D.C., traveled to Hampton Roads every Friday aboard an Old Bay Line steamer, trained at the school all day Saturday and Sunday, then sailed back to the nation's capitol on Sunday evenings. He had taken his first flight on September 4, 1916, at the age of thirty-six. Tuition for Curtiss' students was a dollar an hour for flying instruction but legend has it Mitchell's flying cost him much more than the standard fee. At the end of his first solo flight, Major Mitchell crashed his Curtiss Jenny, totaling the aircraft. He walked away uninjured even though the plane flipped on its back and he was left hanging in the wreckage upside down before being cut out by his ground crew. Curtiss was purportedly quite angry with the future general and sent him a bill for one thousand dollars for services rendered after Mitchell had been sent to France in 1917 to take charge of the American Flying Corps. There are no records to indicate whether the bill was paid but, more than likely, Curtiss received every penny due him. The high price tag most certainly reflected damages to the Jenny. Mitchell would eventually become a general but his persistant, if not mordacious, argument for an independent air force and his vehement criticism of the USS *Shenandoah* disaster so enraged his superiors he was demoted in 1927 to colonel after a lengthy court-martial. He would later resign.

Curtiss instructors had their choice of a Curtiss seaplane or flying boat, five Curtiss landplanes, primarily Jennys, and occasional experimental aircraft to flight test. Victor Carlstrom, Curtiss' chief test pilot, flew speed and endurance flights between Newport News and Fisherman's Island at Cape Charles in 1916 using a twin-engine Curtiss hydroconvertible land and seaplane. Carlstrom's record-breaking speed test at Newport News was acclaimed by the Aero Club of America as "the most important aviation event of the year." The result for Curtiss was worldwide recognition and seven million dollars of Curtiss planes ordered by Great Britain and Russia, but fame and fortune would be tempered by tragedy.

Glenn Curtiss had always feared that pilot and passenger deaths as a result of airplane accidents would place the entire future of aircraft research and development in jeopardy. Though accidents, some quite serious, had occurred at the Atlantic Coast Aeronautical Station between its December 1915 inception and May 9, 1917, the latter date proved particularly tragic for the Curtiss school. Victor Carlstrom, then thirty-two years old, was killed in a crash at the Municipal Small Boat Harbor with student pilot Cary B. Epes, twenty-five, of Newport News, on a training flight when the right wing of the plane suddenly crumpled like a piece of paper. The flight was Cary Epes' first and last. Carlstrom's younger brother, Carl, who had just finished flight training himself, would witness the accident. Sadly, both Victor Carlstrom and Epes were engaged to be married—Epes to Margaret Temple of Danville, Virginia, and Carlstrom to Sallie Blassingham of Newport News.

Walter Lees shared his love of flying with Loa as much as possible. Here, she and Walter pose after a flight in 1916. (Frank J. Conway, photographer.)

Loa Betty Lees, baby daughter of Curtiss instructor pilot Walter Edwin Lees and his wife, Loa, was photographed at the Atlantic Coast Aeronautical Station in 1917. Born at Buxton Hospital, now part of Mary Immaculate Hospital, on March 9, 1916, Betty was a playful, happy child, and obviously a favorite subject of photographer Conway. Walter E. Lees came to Newport News at the end of 1915, and joined Victor Carlstrom as the first two Curtiss instructors to take flights from the field. Carlstrom and Lees would be joined by instructor pilots Victor Vernon, Steven McGordon, Ted Hequembourg, Lawrence Leon, Carl Batts, Jimmy Johnson, Bert Acosta, and Andrew "Stuart" Cogswell. (Frank J. Conway, photographer.)

Charlotte Jane Kennan Lloyd, Loa's mother, was never far from granddaughter Betty, evidenced in this 1917 photograph. Josephine Cooper, Lees' biographer, noted that Walter and Loa's children, Loa Betty, Aerial Burt, and Charlotte Jane affectionately called their grandmother "Danny" rather than "Granny." (Frank J. Conway, photographer.)

The accident occurred a week prior to the Navy contracting Curtiss Aeroplane Company to train twenty men of the Naval Reserve Flying Corps (NRFC) at the field. Though the incident did little to deter the flying corps from its training mission, the Carlstrom-Epes tragedy lingered as a poignant reminder to all of Baldwin's military and civilian instructors and student pilots of the fragility of human beings and flying machines.

All the airplanes at the Curtiss school were designed to carry two people with the exception of the 120-horsepower flyer used by Carlstrom on his Toronto, Canada, to New York flight prior to his untimely death. Each aircraft also had a dual system of controls. The pilot and passenger sat side by side. Curtiss aircraft were controlled by a steering wheel mounted on the right front seat like that in an automobile of the same period. The foot rest was a wooden bar with a pin through the center so when one end was pushed forward the other moved backward, somewhat like the steering arrangement on a bobsled. The steering wheel not only revolved but could be pulled toward the pilot or pushed away. When the pilot pulled it, the elevator tilted so

Socop THE CUB REPORTER

An early version of the Curtiss F-boat met an unfortunate end near the Boat Harbor, Newport News, Virginia, 1916. Crews from Curtiss' Atlantic Coast Aeronautical Station are pictured trying to salvage the aircraft, using a tow line to shore pulled by a horse. (Frank J. Conway, photographer.)

the nose pointed upward; when pushed, the nose angled downward. Airplanes used at Curtiss Field were military tractor type, the same design the Curtiss Aeroplane Company was selling the British and Russians. The motor was placed beneath the bonnet with a radiator in front of it and the propeller in front of the machine, pulling it through the air like a tractor. The pilot sat just behind the motor on the same level, the passenger or student aft of him. The hulls of the great flying boats were mahogany with a V-bottom underboat.

When the United States declared war on April 6, 1917, Newport News witnessed not only the rapid growth of naval installations but also the Curtiss school at Hampton Roads. The school helped give birth to naval aviation unfortunately sometimes at the sacrifice of men and machines. The war also heralded yet another era of aviation experimentation and would not be the last to cost pilots their lives and livelihood. Accidents happened. Each time a pilot crashed, Curtiss and his engineers studied the problems and made corrections in aircraft design. Aside from pilot error, there were crashes easily attributed to flaws in airframe design and construction. Perhaps Captain Baldwin said it best: "Flying is a dangerous business. Aviators are going to be killed from time to time." He would utter this phrase on more than one occasion, his words ringing true time and again. Victor Vernon and his mechanic, Percy Kirkman, crashed their twin-engine hydroconvertible land and water machine into Hampton Roads harbor with so much force of impact, the pontoons smashed and the aircraft turned turtle. Within the first year of the school's existence, June 1916, instructor Steven McGordon was mortally burned in the crash of a Curtiss Jenny. The front engine broke loose from the mount, driving the propeller into the ground and shoving the hot engine into the gas tank. McGordon died two days later. Student naval aviator Donald Barnum "Doc" Alvord, later designated Naval Aviator No. 225, nearly took out a trolley full of passengers flying too low over Jefferson Avenue in the fall of 1917. Though he managed to pull up in time, Alvord crash landed across the street, his aircraft sliding into a popular diner. Miraculously, no one was seriously hurt, particularly since his propeller ended up wedged in the lunch counter.

Several world records for speed and stunt flying were set while the Curtiss school resided at the Municipal Small Boat Harbor. Instructor Eddie Stinson, later manufacturer of the Stinson plane, set a record by looping-the-loop two times in rapid succession in a two-ton flying boat on August 3, 1917, before training regulations forbade these often fatal feats. By August 7, Stinson had broken all American records by looping twenty-two times in rapid succession.

Despite the hazards of flying, attendance at the school peaked with the tide of war. By 1917, Italy, France and Sweden had sent young men for two to three months of flight instruction at Newport News. More importantly, the Curtiss school was perhaps the greatest and largest center of American aviation training, particularly for United States Army flyers. Virtually hundreds of young Army men were taught the basics of flying before departing for France to complete a course in advanced flight and aerial tactics overseas, while fortunate student naval aviators did most of their advanced work stateside before ending up in Europe. Naval Air Station Hampton Roads would be the primary advance camp for these student naval aviators.

Captain Baldwin, in charge of the school and, more specifically, its military contract to train pilots, developed a program for fundamental flight training

By "Hop"

The Newport News *Daily Press* picked up the cartoon Scoop—The Cub Reporter by "Hop" in the August 17, 1916, edition primarily due to local interest in Glenn Hammond Curtiss' Atlantic Coast Aeronautical Station, located in the city's old boat harbor. Note the misprint of "Scoop" in this issue. The Curtiss School at Newport News conducted extensive experiments with hydroaeroplanes and trained—even in 1916—military pilots from European and Asian countries. The skepticism of the times rings loud and clear in the cartoonist's sarcasm for hydroaeroplanes. The Navy had not yet opened its operation at the site of the former Jamestown Exposition grounds on the southside of Hampton Roads. Navy pilots were trained, instead, at Newport News. (Courtesy of the Virginiana Room, Newport News Public Library.)

Witness to History: Neta Snook

The woman who taught Amelia Earhart to fly started her flying career in Hampton Roads amidst the great excitement created by preparations for war in Europe. Naval aviators, and military pilots in general, have many civilians to thank for their training. More often than not, civilian instructors or schools under contract to the Army and Navy have historically been least recognized for their contribution to military aviation. Such was the case of the Atlantic Coast Aeronautical Station, Glenn Hammond Curtiss' flight operation at Newport News, Virginia, where civilian instructor pilots, engineers, and ground crewmen left a lasting legacy to naval aviation.

Neta Snook had an insider's perspective of early naval aviation history, a first-person, thrilling ride through her own flying career that touched upon the lives of more than a dozen American naval aviators and countless Canadians, British, Finnish, Russian, and French student aviators who flocked to the airfield in the hopes of receiving enough training to fight for their respective countries in the First World War. Neta Snook (later Southern) was a familiar face in Hampton Roads between 1915 and 1917. Born in 1896, Snook dreamed of flying airplanes from the time she was a little girl. She discovered the Atlantic Coast Aeronautical Station or Curtiss Flying Field at Newport News, Virginia, about the time she turned twenty, and somehow charmed Captain Thomas S. Baldwin, field operator, to let her take flying instruction. In those days, women were considered a tremendous liability to aviation. A woman killed in an airplane crash would have branded aviation as unsafe, tentative transportation at best. Neta Snook could have counted the number of American female aviators on one hand in 1915; worldwide, maybe only a dozen others were trying to make a name for themselves in the air.

Andrew "Stuart" Cogswell, one of Baldwin's best instructor-test pilots, consented to teach Snook how to fly. She had gone about as far as she could in the training syllabus and was about to make her solo flight when the United States entered the First World War, thus ending civilian flying lessons. Disappointed, Snook remained at Curtiss Flying Field, giving pointers to some of the first student naval aviators to receive training in Hampton Roads. She would converse with Army students and those from foreign governments as well. Neta Snook later, in fact, tried to join the Army Air Service but was turned down because of gender—indicative, of course, of the times in which she lived.

Snook moved away from Hampton Roads in 1917 to become an expeditor for the British War Mission in Canada, inspecting the assembly of Curtiss OX-5 engines. When the war ended in 1918, she bought a wrecked Canuck, the Canadian version of a Curtiss JN-4 Jenny aircraft, rebuilt it, and in the spring of 1920, trailered the plane to a level pasture and flew the Canuck solo—her first solo flight. Neta Snook's adeptness at machinery and aeronautical engineering were clearly indicative of someone who had studied both disciplines in higher education, yet she never studied either formally.

Neta Snook was photographed at the Atlantic Coast Aeronautical Station, circa 1916, standing in front of a Curtiss JN-4 Jenny, a tractor-type trainer used by Curtiss at his flying schools and by Army and Navy flight schools. (Frank J. Conway, photographer.)

By the summer of 1920, she was flying exhibitions and pleasing crowds from coast to coast. During the fall of the same year, Snook moved to Los Angeles and opened her own business at Bert Kinner's new field (Kinner Field) in the South Gate area of the city. Kinner designed small, fixed-wing aircraft. He had just completed his first, the Kinner Airster, when Snook opened for business as a nationally-known exhibition pilot. In return for tie-down fees and a percentage of her promising commercial enterprise, Snook became Kinner's test pilot. From time to time, Snook flew exhibitions with Kinner aircraft, and it was during one of those shows in December of 1920 she met Earhart. In her own book, *I Taught Amelia To Fly* (Vantage, 1974), the first time Earhart met Neta Snook, her first words to Snook were, "I'm Amelia Earhart and this is my father...I want to learn to fly

A few moments after Neta Snook posed with the Jenny, she donned her flight coat, head gear, and goggles to go flying, circa 1916. (Frank J. Conway, photographer.)

Mugging for the camera, Neta Snook dressed up and jumped into the cockpit of a JN-4. Andrew "Stuart" Cogswell, her Curtiss instructor pilot, is shown perched in the rear cockpit behind Snook, circa 1916. (Frank J. Conway, photographer.)

and I understand you teach students... Will you teach me?" Her fee for instructing Earhart was one dollar a minute. Snook liked the shy Earhart right away. The two would become not only instructor and student, but friends, double-dating often as Snook attempted to draw Earhart out of her shy, retiring persona. Snook, quite ambitious, well traveled, and socially skilled, was perhaps the first person to bring out those qualities in Earhart.

Neta Snook never held Earhart's flying in high regard. Earhart's history of crashes started during her instruction with Snook. Determined to buy an airplane, Earhart made a play for Kinner's Airster, an aircraft Snook repeatedly warned Earhart was too much airplane for a beginner. Despite the warnings, Earhart purchased the plane but promptly crashed it. Snook chastised Earhart, "you have to learn to fly by feel." Earhart was not an intuitive pilot and never quite mastered taking off and landing, the two most basic, important elements of flying.

In the golden era of aviation, the 1920s and 1930s, Hampton Roads would be visited by some of the greatest aviatrixes of all time, including those as well-renowned as Amelia Earhart Putnam and Louise Thaden. As more than a couple of longtime Norfolk residents have recalled, it was Thaden who flew her aircraft under the arch in the Grand Basin at the former Jamestown Exposition site during that colorful era in aviation history. On September 23, 1933, residents of Hampton Roads were assembled to meet some of the best female aviators in the world at the Women's Air Derby, then held at the State Rifle Range Airport in Virginia Beach. Many came out to meet Amelia Earhart Putnam, Helen McClosky, Carolyn Jamieson, and Tiny Goddard, all nationally and internationally known female flyers. "Lady Lindy," as Earhart was called in the press, arrived from New York City via an aircraft flown by her friend and fellow aviator, Goddard.

"Women have a definite place in aviation," Earhart told the admiring crowd, as she noted, "your field is very attractive. The last time I was here, I rolled my plane over at your Naval Air Station [Hampton Roads], so this time I thought I'd be safe with a woman to pilot me." The reference was to a landing mishap two years before in which her aircraft overturned on the runway and Earhart suffered a few bruises. Earhart would not fly herself back to New York, opting instead for a Ludington Air Line flight which departed from the company terminal off Granby Street near what is now the Naval Air Station Norfolk cargo terminal.

Neta Snook was one of those rare individuals who was close enough to Earhart the aviator to assess her ability, and her fears. When the public realized Amelia Earhart Putnam had flown herself neither to nor from Virginia Beach for the derby, questions were raised, people talked. Most remarked that Earhart did not fly herself because of several flying mishaps, especially in the two to three years previous to her appearance at the meet. Mishaps had shaken Earhart's confidence and tested her resolve to continue flying. The famed "Lady Lindy" eventually eased back into flying, though her career ended tragically with Earhart's disappearance in July of 1937 near Howland Island in the Pacific. Snook, on the other hand, continued to have a rich, fulfilling aviation career, though often in the shadow of her student and friend, Amelia Earhart Putnam.

Neta Snook struck this striking pose in the cockpit of her Jenny in 1916. (Frank J. Conway, photographer.)

Curtiss Flying School instructors, test pilots, plane crews, and students pose with Captain Thomas Scott Baldwin in the winter of 1916. Baldwin (11) stands to the far left. Others notable in the photograph are Jimmy Johnson (3), Major Billy Mitchell's instructor pilot; Walter Lees (4) who sent Mitchell aloft on his first solo; Carl Batts (26); and Andrew "Stuart" Cogswell (44), the instructor who taught Neta Snook, Amelia Earhart's future flying instructor, to fly. (Frank J. Conway, photographer.)

Glenn H. Curtiss sponsored aircraft in aviation exhibitions all over the United States, particularly the East Coast. In this 1921 photograph, a Curtiss 1911 period aircraft was on display near the grandstand. Curtiss is on the grandstand (second man from the flag leaning forward, facing the camera) with Captain Thomas S. Baldwin (the large man with the fedora hat facing the camera and standing next to the little boy). (Photographer unknown.)

A Curtiss Aeroplane Company "Bat" boat (named for its unique wing shape and short-hull) or floatplane, was designed by Glenn Curtiss for the United States Navy's use. The aircraft was tested at Curtiss' Newport News airfield where this picture was taken about 1916. Although the plane was deemed a success, the military never picked it up for use. (Courtesy of the Hampton Roads Naval Museum.)

which turned out solid Army and Navy pilots within the few days afforded by wartime. The Army, for example, screened its pool of pilot candidates for flight acuity before Baldwin received them at the station. Experienced Curtiss flight instructors made the decision whether an aspiring aviator would work out or not. Candidates arrived at the Newport News field prior to eight o'clock in the morning, each taken by an instructor who explained the operation of the Curtiss JN-4 Jenny tractor and provided him his flight gear—a coat, helmet, and goggles. The student sat forward in the cockpit of a dual control training plane, the instructor pilot in the rear. Instructors spent about a half hour to forty-five minutes taking the student aviator through a few cycles of vertical diving, banking and slipping, all the while keeping a close eye on the young student in the front cockpit for signs of composure. Failures were spotted quickly. Those who passed muster the first time went up again to learn simple signals to converse aloft, at which time the instructor turned the aircraft over to the student to fly. Instructors could easily correct the novice's mistake with dual controls. The third flight usually lasted about one-and-a-half hours. If the student aviator was adjudged favorably, he went to advanced training.

Some comment regarding the contribution of the college programs and facilities like the Atlantic Coast Aeronautical Station to the evolution of naval aviation should be noted here. Though Secretary of the Navy Daniels had dominion over a three-and-a-half million dollar appropriation for aviation as part of the Naval Appropriations Act of 1916, he had failed to establish a Naval Flying Corps until the United States entered the war. When war in Europe closed in, student groups such as those at Yale, Harvard, Massachusetts Institute of Technology, and volunteers being trained in private schools like Curtiss' operation in Newport News, made up the future of naval aviation. Their combined efforts sparked the rapid growth of naval aviation, aviation technology, and, ultimately, creation of an official Naval Flying Corps.

Curtiss Field at Newport News was sustained both voluntarily and, much later, under contract, until naval aviation service could establish air bases in coastal areas of the United States. Lieutenant Henry Barton Cecil, Naval Aviator No. 42, managed the Navy's contract with the Curtiss Aeroplane Company at

By America's entry into World War I, airplanes had found a niche in popular culture. This colorful Christmas postcard from the 1910s captures a little boy's fascination with a toy Curtiss Jenny. The postcard was produced by the GL Company and obtained in Hampton Roads from the original owner.

Newport News from May 19, 1917, up to the time Naval Air Detachment Hampton Roads came into being August 28, 1917. As an aside, the chief of the Naval Reserve Flying Corps at the time was Lieutenant Commander John Henry "Jack" Towers, Naval Aviator No. 3, a proponent of Hampton Roads as a prime location for a master air base.

Though training at Curtiss Field was satisfactory, the outbreak of the First World War finally convinced Navy Secretary Daniels of the need to establish a major naval facility on the East Coast. Naval Operating Base Norfolk was born in 1917, a direct outcome of the Navy Appropriations Act dated August 21, 1916, which called for the appointment of a Commission on Navy Yards and Naval Stations or Helm Board, so named for its chairman, Rear Admiral James M. Helm. Captain Mark L. Bristol, director of naval aeronautics, had given his highest recommendation to creation of coastal air bases in his annual report of 1916. Unfortunately, the Helm Board did not comment on naval aviation in its first round of reports and ended up looking for guidance from those directly involved in the air service. Bristol was in total agreement an air base should be located on the lower Chesapeake Bay.

Commission files indicate Bristol initially proposed Cape Henry or Lynnhaven Inlet as a location for a naval aviation complex. The Joint Army and Navy Board on Aeronautic Cognizance was appointed to focus on aviation and educate the Helm Board to the value of tactical air bases. Before the cognizance board could make headway, the Chief of Naval Operations circumvented their proceedings and asked Secretary Daniels for patrol stations up and down the East Coast, Gulf Coast and Canal Zone. Hampton Roads made his list, effectively pushing Army/Navy cooperative ventures out of the picture. As part of his comprehensive plan to eventually build a master naval facility at Norfolk, Secretary Daniels added a proviso creating the Naval Reserve Flying Corps (NRFC), a group of student naval aviators, primarily from Harvard University, who had begun their training at the old Curtiss Field on May 19, 1917, and who would comprise the nucleus of seven students designated as Naval Air Detachment Hampton Roads.

With Daniels' instruction came the end of Navy pilot training at Curtiss Field on August 28, 1917, and the construction of a newer, better aviation camp at Pine Beach on lands adjoining the naval base. Sadly, there would be one student naval aviator denied his pilot certification as a result of yet another horrific accident at Newport News. Curtiss instructor Ted Hequembourg and his naval student, Lawrence Curtis of Boston, Massachusetts, crashed in an F-2—a new Curtiss aircraft—six days after the fatal accident which killed Carlstrom and Epes. Curtis would have his leg amputated, and Hequembourg, a New York native, later died of his injuries.

Norfolk businessmen, who had earlier paid no mind to Curtiss' and Baldwin's overtures to place the school on the southside, now attempted on more than one occasion to draw the Curtiss school across the water by proffering use of the abandoned tract of the 1907 Jamestown Exposition fronting water on Pine Beach, future site of Naval Air Station Hampton Roads. Newport News fought hard to keep Norfolk at bay but the Municipal Small Boat Harbor quickly became limited by the city's encroaching business and industrial complex which effectively boxed in the school. Baldwin had even attempted to buy a site near Buckroe Beach, his efforts quashed by one important landowner who held out for too much money. The Armistice ending the First World War was signed November 11, 1918, and the school's end was not far off.

The Newport News business community eventually got wind the Navy was planning to build aviation fields in Hampton Roads, Florida, and California. As a result, Peninsula businessmen lobbied hard to convince the Navy to take over the old Curtiss Field but to no avail. The Atlantic Coast Aeronautical Station at Newport News officially closed in 1922. The Helm decision all but killed operations at Curtiss Field by 1919. The Navy decided in August of 1917 to construct its main airfield and seaplane ramps on part of the land tract which once comprised the Jamestown Exposition grounds adjoining, of course, the newly established Naval Operating Base Norfolk.

By the end of May 1917, the Navy had dispatched five officers, eighteen students, twenty mechanics and seven seaplanes to Pine Beach, soon-to-be headquarters of the new naval aeronautic center, for familiarization and training even though Curtiss Field was still under contract with the Navy to train these student naval aviators. Building was already underway on the new aviation school located at the northeastern corner of the original 143 acres of land for the naval station at Norfolk. Though this move had spelled the end of Curtiss Field, it was by no means the end of Glenn Curtiss' efforts pioneering aviation, particularly his tremendous impact on the course of naval aviation.

Frank J. Conway was a Curtiss Aeroplane Company contract photographer who settled in Norfolk about 1915. His home, at least for a brief time, was 1509 Brambleton Avenue. City directories listed him at this address for 1918 and 1919, but he was gone by 1920. Conway maintained a studio at 1419 Brambleton Avenue during the same period. Though little information is available about Conway, he did take photographs for Curtiss at the Atlantic Coast Aeronautical Station between 1915 and 1922, and his freelance work in Norfolk and vicinity represents a respectable body of work.

Chapter 5: Training the Eyes of the Fleet

Nowhere was training acknowledged to be more complete than at the new Hampton Roads air station. When it was formally established as an air detachment in the fall of 1917, the site encompassed perhaps a half mile of waterfront and included the famous lagoon from the 1907 Jamestown Exposition. A few acres were converted to a landing field and, with the meager sum of five hundred dollars, necessary improvements were made to make the site suitable for stowing aircraft and housing men. Great white hangars, temporary wooden structures, were partly concealed by huge canvas tents full of aircraft. This was considered a major improvement over having seaplanes moored in the water where they were subject to all kinds of weather, saltwater damage, and deterioration. The Navy planned to construct permanent hangars of concrete and steel, but, with a war underway, training was top priority. An unknown observer of the period wrote, "...the blue waters of the bay and the blue of the sky seem to meet the great flying boats that swim out a little distance and then mount upward with the freedom of birds, have no suggestion of the grimness of war machines, although they will play so big a part in the present conflict as 'the eyes of the fleet.'"

In the spring of 1917, aviators at Pine Beach had just eight planes to share among dozens of men being trained to fly. Norfolk was originally to have gotten ten heavy Curtiss tractor planes but two were damaged in August prior to the move from Newport News. Several dozen additional aircraft were expected between October and December of 1917.

Despite the fact that much actual flight instruction had taken place in the months prior to establishing the aeronautical center, the "birdmen," as they were officially known, were not able to commence real aviation training at the new Hampton Roads naval base until September 1917. Finally, on the evening of September 2, people in the densely populated areas of Norfolk could see Navy planes circling overhead for the first time. Press reports of the day remarked that student naval aviators were seen, "wearing a uniform that is new to Norfolk, have been the cynosure of many eyes within the past week. They wear a close-fitting khaki uniform, leather boots, khaki cap with a black band and semicircled by a narrow strap of gold. Above the visor is the usual insignia worn by naval officers. Few civilians are familiar with the uniform of the student in the aviation section of the Navy. Its proud wearers have been pointed out on the streets as being everything from Australian reservists to French cavalrymen."

The student body of the aviation school at Hampton Roads would steadily grow by leaps and bounds, numbering some forty-two men and six instructors by the end of the summer of 1917. Lieutenant Edward Orrick "Eddie" McDonnell, Naval Aviator No. 18, was the first commanding officer of the center. Student naval aviators ranged in age from twenty to twenty-four and came primarily from colleges in the northeast. Harvard, Dartmouth, Yale, and Tufts were all well-represented at the naval base. Each of these young men had already passed required physical and mental training and screening. Though many would apply for naval aviation through the college programs, on the average only a few hundred out of two thousand or more would be selected to

Sweptback wings, which characterize today's high-speed aircraft, first appeared on the Navy's Burgess-Dunne seaplane in 1913. The two photographs here show both versions of the aircraft, the first in 1916 (above), and the second (below), taken at Naval Air Station Hampton Roads on February 21, 1918, demonstrate the radical changes in airframe in a relatively short time. The second photograph is of the Burgess-Dunne AH-10 tailless biplane. This very distinctive aircraft had an interesting evolution. The manufacturing rights to the British Dunne tailless aircraft had to be licensed to the Burgess Company of Marblehead, Massachusetts, which built two versions of the aircraft, the AH-7 and AH-10 (shown here), respectively. The extreme swept wings, angled at 30 degrees, were a first. The Navy conducted its first aerial gunnery experiments with these pusher aircraft. The engine was a 100-horsepower Curtiss OXX-2, therefore limiting the aircraft to a top speed of only 69 miles per hour. (Official United States Navy Photographs.)

In the spring of 1917, the Gallaudet Aircraft Corporation reorganized and moved to new headquarters facilities at Greenwich, Rhode Island. Here, the company produced two D-4 aircraft for the Navy, Bureau Numbers A2653 and A2654, the latter of which is shown here at Hampton Roads, Virginia. The aircraft was powered by a Liberty engine and could reach about 90 miles per hour top speed. (Official United States Navy Photograph.)

(Left to right) United States Naval Reserve Ensigns Lyman Stannard Peck, Naval Aviator No. 172, J.J. Finnegan, no record as a naval aviator, and Emory Arthur Stone, Naval Aviator No. 138, had their picture taken in front of a Curtiss R-6L training aircraft at Hampton Roads in 1917. This photograph was taken just prior to these gentlemen being commissioned naval officers and designated naval aviators. (Frank J. Conway, photographer.)

attend ground school at Massachusetts Institute of Technology (MIT). Beginning in October 1917, the naval aviation school at Hampton Roads would not accept those who had not completed MIT's preliminary eight-week course which covered navigation, radio, wireless, seamanship, gunnery and, perhaps most importantly, rudimentary training for practical flying: theory.

Henry Pratt "Hank" Lewis, Naval Aviator No. 493, recounted his experiences at the station in his unpublished memoirs, "The Story of Flight A." Lewis remarked that he and his class from MIT were given a choice of Hampton Roads or Pensacola, and twenty-two of them chose Norfolk. Mostly, as he put it, they "wanted to learn how much truth there was to the rumor that newly arrived students were in fact being used as mechanics." The students of Flight A found a number of newly commissioned ensigns who had comprised a detachment that transitioned from the Curtiss Flying School at Newport News. The new ensigns were qualified aviators and had "first dibs" on aircraft and equipment. Lewis had good cause to figure he would be used as a mechanic. He quickly learned that commanding officer McDonnell was a taskmaster. Shortly after the arrival of Flight A, chief machinist's mates took over and put new students in waders handling seaplanes, working the manual winch, and performing every needed function from pouring gas to changing oil in the R-6 and N-9 aircraft. Those who had opted for Norfolk took longer to get their wings, at least in Lewis' class. Student naval aviators were expected to be ready for the rigors of patrol and test flight duties with only eight to ten hours of solo time spread over a period of weeks. Later, Lewis and his fellow student aviators would rejoice when Lieutenant Commander Patrick N.L. Bellinger, Naval Aviator No. 8, assumed command of Hampton Roads. Training and lifestyle markedly improved.

Flight did come. Lewis would remark: "Actually they hadn't forgotten what you were there for and as a result of the N-9s you helped put together, your first flight and instruction came sooner. My first [flight] came on a beautiful day. I can still see Hampton Roads, the James River and the towns along their edges spread out in a map-like configuration. Though the closest I'd ever been to flying was when I stumbled down a hill with a homemade glider that never carried more than its own weight, I'd dreamt so often of flying that I'd experienced everything from takeoff to landing again

Flight A

The legislature of the Commonwealth of Massachusetts created a committee on public safety on February 10, 1917, as the first step towards mobilization of the state's populace for the eventuality of the United States entering the First World War on the side of her European allies. One part of the program was the creation of a subcommittee on naval forces which, taking advantage of an Act of Congress the previous August that authorized the creation of a Naval Reserve Force, and a school to supply the Navy with a highly qualified group of young men trained to qualify for enrollment and pilot instruction in the Naval Reserve Flying Corps. The school became known as the Massachusetts School for Naval Aviation which, between February and May, constructed a training complex at Squantum, bought two seaplanes and screened close to five hundred candidates for Navy pilot instruction and future commissions. These young men were recruited in New England colleges and universities and from civilian industry which might suggest suitable qualifications for aviation. Upon satisfying a review board with their qualifications, candidates were given physicals at the Charlestown Navy Yard and enrolled as quartermasters, first class, in Class IV, for aviation. The first group of candidates sent through training reported for duty in early May. The recruiting program of the Massachusetts Committee on Naval Forces ended on May 11, 1917, when, by direction of the commandant of the First Naval District, his command assumed administration of the Squantum school, its enrollment activities and the roster of students waiting to be called to active duty. Living in tents, Class IV attended classes in ground school subjects and received flight training from Ensign Doyle "Brad" Bradford, Naval Aviator No. 111½, and Ensign Clifford Lawrence "Cliff" Webster, Naval Aviator No. 112½. Lieutenant Earl Winfield "Duke" Spencer, Naval Aviator No. 20, was the commanding officer of the Squantum base.

Lieutenant Spencer made arrangements with representatives of Massachusetts Institute of Technology (MIT) to provide faculty and facilities for a naval aviation ground school and the group of aviation students called up to make the first class at MIT was extracted from a roster of candidates already enrolled for the Massachusetts School of Naval Aviation. The members of this group constituted Flight A. The story of Flight A officially began on July 23, 1917, when fifty candidates for Navy wings arrived at the Charlestown Navy Yard and, subsequently, reported to the commanding officer of the MIT Aviation School. Lieutenant (junior grade) Edward Hyslop "Mac" McKitterick, Naval Aviator No. 39, oversaw the curriculum and training of Flight A. McKitterick had organized the Naval Aviation Detachment at MIT in Cambridge, Massachusetts, and was the first commanding officer of the ground school. The day candidates in Flight A arrived to begin orientation, McKitterick was experiencing his own case of first day jitters. These young men were the beginning and their spirit and courage casts a lengthened shadow which reaches into the naval aviation of today.

As an aside, Squantum, Massachusetts, was the former air station of the Naval Militia. It was taken under Navy jurisdiction in May 1917 and commissioned a naval air station the same month. The station seems to have ceased operation when its student aviators were transferred to Hampton Roads in October 1917. Squantum later emerged as the first of the post-World War I reserve air stations when commissioned on August 13, 1923, and remained active until decommissioned on January 1, 1954. The first commanding officer at Squantum was Earl Winfield "Duke" Spencer.

and again. My dreams were confirmed." His pilot that day was Henry Pomeroy "Harry" Davison Jr., Naval Aviator No. 72, a member of the First Yale Unit, who became a flight commander at Naval Air Station Hampton Roads in October of 1917 for experiments with bombs, radio apparatus, and machine guns. Davison would be Lewis' instructor and as such, suggested to his student that he "hold the controls lightly to experience their effect on the plane as it banked for turns, glided for the landing and maneuvered on the water."

Training with the Naval Aviation

Ensign Cecil Dunmore "Mike" Murray, USNR, Naval Aviator No. 117, and Ensign Emory Arthur Stone, USNR, Naval Aviator No. 138, posed for the camera in their flight gear standing on the seaplane ramp, Naval Air Detachment Hampton Roads, November of 1917. Both Murray and Stone trained at the Curtiss Flying School, Newport News, Virginia, prior to transferring to the detachment at Hampton Roads in June of 1917 to begin lengthy training as naval aviators. (Frank J. Conway, photographer.)

Ensign Charles Fairchild "Charles" Fuller, USNR, Naval Aviator No. 139, was photographed on the day he and his fellow student aviators were finally designated naval aviators in ceremonies held at Hampton Roads in November 1917. Fuller was officially designated November 7, 1917, and had done all of his flight training at Curtiss Flying Field in Newport News and, of course, Hampton Roads. He was born on January 11, 1897, in New York City, New York, attended Harvard University Class of 1919, and received a wartime degree in 1920. After he left Navy service, Fuller obtained a bachelor's degree in architecture from Columbia University in 1924. Fuller died in January of 1960 at the age of sixty-three. (Frank J. Conway, photographer.)

Ensign Cecil Dunmore "Mike" Murray, USNR, Naval Aviator No. 117, Naval Air Detachment Hampton Roads, November of 1917. (Frank J. Conway, photographer.)

Right: Ensign Cecil Dunmore "Mike" Murray, USNR, Naval Aviator No. 117, (right) poses with an unidentified crewman in November 1917. (Frank J. Conway, photographer.)

First Yale Unit

The First Yale Unit enlisted in the Naval Reserve Flying Corps and four days later left Yale University to begin flight training at West Palm Beach, Florida. This was the first of several college groups to join up as a unit for naval aviation service. The First Yale Unit consisted of twenty-nine young men, four of whom were destined to hold important positions pertaining to the United States military: Assistant Secretary of War, Assistant Secretary of the Navy for Air, Under Secretary of the Navy, Deputy Secretary of Defense and Secretary of Defense. Artemus Lamb "Di" Gates, Naval Aviator No. 65, was appointed September 5, 1941, as Assistant Secretary of the Navy for Air, and on July 3, 1945, Gates assumed the significant role as Under Secretary of the Navy, a post he resigned on December 31, 1945, after successfully demobilizing nearly 3,389,000 uniformed personnel and more than 750,000 civilian employees of the Navy. Robert Abercrombie "Bob" Lovett, Naval Aviator No. 66, was appointed Deputy Secretary of Defense and Chief of Staff to Secretary of Defense George C. Marshall by President Harry S. Truman on September 28, 1950. Lovett succeeded Marshall as Secretary of Defense in 1951. F. Trubee Davison, founder and prime mover of the First Yale Unit, became an Assistant Secretary of War. Due to poor physical condition after a training accident, Trubee Davison could not be designated a naval aviator, but his brother and co-founder of the unit, Henry Pomeroy "Harry" Davison Jr., Naval Aviator No. 72, carried Trubee's spirit with him throughout his career. David Sinton "Dave" Ingalls, Naval Aviator No. 85, the Navy's only ace in World War I, was appointed Assistant Secretary of the Navy for Air by President Herbert H. Hoover on March 16, 1929, and from this position, Ingalls oversaw the advancement of the Naval Aviation Test and Development Program for three years.

Left: Ensign George Walter Shaw, USNR, was a 1917 graduate of the Curtiss Flying School, receiving pilot certificate No. 4. Since he was from Attleboro, Massachusetts, Shaw returned to his home state where he enrolled as a quartermaster first class at Boston. He returned to Newport News later that year, and was later designated Naval Aviator No. 171 on November 13, 1917, and commissioned on the twenty-sixth. The photograph here was taken in November of 1917. Shaw saw action in the First World War and was awarded the Navy Cross as a seaplane pilot on patrol and convoy duty in the vicinity of Wexford, Ireland, and bombing a submarine under minimal flying conditions. Shaw went into partnership with Eddie Stinson in the Stinson Flyers, the first recorded commercial gypsy flying circus in the United States. He barnstormed the country until 1930. (Frank J. Conway, photographer.)

Above: Ensign William Bull "Bill" Atwater, USNR, Naval Aviator No. 112, received part of his ground and flight instruction at the Curtiss Flying School or Atlantic Coast Aeronautical Station, Newport News, Virginia, and was designated a naval aviator at Hampton Roads on October 19, 1917. He was a seasoned flyer, having learned to fly before entering the Navy. (Frank J. Conway, photographer.)

Detachment at Hampton Roads was thorough primarily due to the fact the center had schools for all disciplines related to naval air service. The station had a flight school, mechanics' and quartermasters' school, dirigible and balloon school, radio department, and ordnance department. The aviation school was divided into two sections: the junior and senior departments. A young aviator's day typically started at half past five in the morning with roll call at five minutes to six. By quarter to seven, student aviators and instructors had had breakfast and mustered at the hangars. The day was divided into training periods, each section switching off activities with the other at timed intervals. While the junior section studied Navy regulations, seamanship, theory, flight and navigation and received some flight instruction, the seniors practiced semaphore—a system of signaling with flags—or studied the wireless.

The senior section was distinguished by its members' flight time. Each student naval aviator in the advanced stage of his training had at least five to ten hours with an instructor before being allowed to take a solo flight. He needed twenty-five to forty hours of solo time before he was eligible for a Navy commission. On any given day at the station, flyers broke for lunch by half past eleven and reconvened after their meal for the commanding officer's daily lecture, which covered subjects such as aviation life, including Navy regulations, seamanship, theory of flight, and navigation. After the lectures, the junior section would be in flight training until nightfall. No flights for new student aviators lasted longer than forty-five minutes. The level of enthusiasm and fascination of the men who trained to be naval aviators was not dulled by the rigorous routine nor built-in hazards of the profession. Senses became sharper, excitement parlayed into energy to accomplish the difficult tasks at hand. One aviator remarked on October 13, 1917: "when you first go up you have a feeling that you have never had before of the wonderfulness of the earth. You get a panoramic view of everything below you. Your engine buzzes incessantly and almost deafens you. But you don't feel nervous. When you start on a glide, at first the sensation is a queer one, but you soon get used to it, and the feeling of the marvelousness of it all grips you again. You look down at the big warships and transports and they appear no larger than little rowboats. And you feel as if you were seeing so much that you don't care very much what happens to you—you don't care if there is a chance of getting killed. It's worth it."

Very early on, the Navy Department realized that the Hampton Roads station's climatology and juxtaposition on the East Coast would spawn growth and make the base one of the most important aviation installations in the country. When the weather did become cold, as Henry Lewis noted, "Most of us got pullover sweaters, knit helmets, socks and mittens from the home folks. The helmets were worn under those atrocious crash helmets and the sweaters under the leather flight coats the Navy supplied." In balmy weather, working in waders along the shore was not so terrible. Occasional winters did challenge aviators' pioneer spirits. In the early part of December, Hampton Roads used to ice over. Lewis would remember, "icing was common. Planes returned to the beach with pontoons and brace wires coated with ice. It is a wonder the underpowered N-9s would even fly." Sometimes, the weather would become so cold, the harbor from Norfolk to Old Point Comfort would freeze over, effectively ending flight operations until the bay thawed. The winter of 1917 was one of the coldest winters on record for Hampton Roads, a fact also noted in the writings of the station's future commanding officer, Bellinger. "In the midst of winter," wrote Bellinger, "the coldest winter I had ever heard of in the area, the waters of the roads froze thick and solid, and Hampton Roads was one sheet of thick, solid ice. I was told that a man walked across to the Chamberlin Hotel at Old Point."

Despite bouts of miserable weather, from April of 1917 through November of 1918, Naval Air Station Hampton Roads trained 622 officer pilots and 1,000 mechanics at its schools. As of June 1918, with the exception of the flying station at Naval Air Station Pensacola,

The naval aviator shown in these two Conway photographs, Ensign Phillips Ward Page, USNR, Naval Aviator No. 170, strikes a pose first in the cockpit of a Curtiss N-9H floatplane, and in the second image, in front of the aircraft, crewmen working behind him. Page was a native of Boston, Massachusetts, born November 28, 1885, making him much older than his contemporaries. Accordingly, there were some special aspects to Page's life worth mention. This Harvard graduate found Orville Wright shortly after graduation and earned his "wings" in 1912. From 1912 to 1917, Page performed on the exhibition circuit as both a pilot and instructor for the Burgess Company of Marblehead, Massachusetts, and Curtiss Aeroplane and Motor Company, Hammondsport, and Buffalo, New York. The Army rejected Page's application for service since he was already thirty-one years of age—too old for combat flying. The Navy did not seem to have the same qualms about his age and he came into the service as an ensign May 19, 1917, and immediately went to work as an instructor. He met all qualifications necessary to bear the title "Naval Aviator" by November 13, 1917, at Hampton Roads, where these pictures were taken. Fate was not good to "P.W." Page. He reported to Paris, France, for initial assignment, and was sent to Royal Naval Air Station Felixstowe, England, where he was killed on December 17, 1917, in an airplane crash. His body was never recovered, and his life difficult to trace. Page was a loner, never taking a wife, and leaving not a single relative to mourn his passing. Tracking Page was like tracking someone who never existed. Naval records show no photograph. His life had to be pieced together in time and place from tidbits of information that took years to put in some semblance of order to make "P.W." Page come alive again. (Frank J. Conway, photographer.)

Florida, the air station at Norfolk had become the most important. Without argument, Hampton Roads was the most significant in terms of patrol operations, experimental work and advance training of aviators. Canvas hangars had given way to wood frame barracks, a mess hall, administration building, shops and hangars for aircraft repair and storage, and, a bit later, a permanent dispensary. Naval Air Station Hampton Roads would be commissioned on August 27, 1918, becoming a separate command from Naval Operating Base Norfolk.

The day after flight training got its "official" start at Pine Beach, two additional Navy aircraft were destroyed in separate incidents. The fateful afternoon which claimed two aircraft was Sunday, September 3, 1917. On the brighter side, the two advanced student naval aviators who lost control of their planes at low altitudes were not killed, only shaken up a bit. The first to go down was Charles Fairchild "Charles" Fuller. Fuller's accident happened shortly after three in the afternoon. Not an hour later, Seaman Second Class (Sea2c) Lyman Stannard Peck took off from Pine Beach. He was airborne only a few minutes when he lost control of his plane at one hundred feet and crashed. There were no instructors aboard either aircraft as both Peck and Fuller were qualified for solo flight. In their defense, aircraft power plants were temperamental and Peck and Fuller's N-9 aircraft were reported to have been underpowered for low-altitude recovery. In a tight spot, aviators took a fifty-fifty chance of aircraft engine failure. All in all, Fuller was fortunate to not be injured since he came within fifty feet of the ground as he lost control and the plane pancaked. Peck was taken to Norfolk Protestant Hospital, earliest precursor of Sentara Norfolk General Hospital, where Dr. L.C. Shepherd tended his hip injury. Peck was stabilized

The three student naval aviators shown here were photographed shortly being commissioned as ensigns in the Navy. On the left is Ensign Charles Fairchild "Charles" Fuller, USNR, Naval Aviator No. 139. Ensign J.P. Warburg, USNR, no record as a naval aviator, (center) did not receive his wings. Standing beside Warburg on the far right is Ensign Westmore Willcox, USNR, Naval Aviator No. 136, of Norfolk. Within a five day period between November 5 and 10, 1917, all three were commissioned and, within two weeks, Fuller and Willcox were designated naval aviators. (Frank J. Conway, photographer.)

This fine looking fellow trained as part of the second group of the First Yale Unit. His face appears in a composite photograph of young men of the first and second groups of the First Yale Unit, many of whom ended up receiving their flight training and/or commissions in Hampton Roads. Many of these naval aviators returned after the war to finish their education; others never finished at all, going only two or three years to college before war came and duty called. These photographs were taken in November of 1917 at Hampton Roads, certainly the correct time frame for those who were commissioned ensigns from the First Yale Unit. Even after consultation with the Manuscripts and Archives Department, Sterling Memorial Library, Yale University, no positive identification was made of this naval aviator by name. Though his picture here and in the unit photograph are a positive match, sadly no one has yet been able to match a name and life history with the face. (Frank J. Conway, photographer.)

and moved to Portsmouth Naval Hospital and later released.

Despite their accidents, both Fuller and Peck passed advanced flight training and received commissions in the Naval Reserve Flying Corps. Fuller was commissioned an ensign on November 5, 1917, and subsequently designated Naval Aviator No. 141. Peck would be commissioned an ensign on November 26, 1917, becoming Naval Aviator No. 172. A graduate of Sheffield, Yale University Class of 1914, Peck entered the service as a seaman second class as did all student naval aviators from the college programs at that time. Two months later he would earn the World War I Life Saving Medal for recovering the body of Sea2c R.M. Ensor from his seaplane wreckage on November 16, 1917, at Hampton Roads.

As the site of advanced aviator training as well as experimentation with seaplanes and communications equipment, the new aeronautic center also saw frequent and often tragic operational accidents. When Captain Baldwin remarked that accidents will happen, little did he know how many and under what circumstances. Fuller and Peck were fortunate to have survived their ordeals, while others would not be so lucky. Conditions under which they were injured or killed led to improved flying machines and regulations for aviators, some of which are still in evidence today. As most any naval aviator will attest, aviation rules and regulations are written in blood. Someone paid the ultimate price for progress.

Though they had a first aid facility at the station, if an aviator had the slightest injury or accident, he was taken to either the Naval Base Hospital, a local hospital, or was transferred to Portsmouth Naval Hospital. Transportation to one of these medical facilities took time a severely injured naval aviator did not have to spare. The Navy Department, acknowledging the hazardous nature of flying and the particularly high mishap rate at Norfolk after the Fuller and Peck incidents, thereafter assigned three medical officers to the base, the precursor of flight surgeons at Norfolk. Physicians assigned to the air base in 1917 were not trained as aviators nor were they subjected to the rigorous flight conditions of flight surgeons today.

Lieutenant Commander Patrick

Prior to issuance of the first wings of gold, January 18, 1918, designated naval aviators had no clear form of identification other then their flying clothes. On June 22, 1917, a change in the uniform regulation called for the first uniform solely used by naval aviators: a summer weight uniform similar to Marine Corps khaki. The uniform resembled the pattern of service whites, but could be worn by officers only involved with flying. The new uniform regulation also provided for the first flight suit—a coverall of canvas, moleskin, or khaki the same color as the uniform—to be used as flying dress. The uniforms of naval aviators at Hampton Roads show the various aviator garb quite clearly. This photograph illustrates yet another oddity of naval officer uniforms of the period, the Naval Militia or NNV insignia, a circle around the star on the officer shoulder board device. Naval Militia units were notified on May 28, 1915, that a small number of its aviators could undergo refresher flight training at Naval Air Station Pensacola, Florida. A few weeks later, July 10, 1915, a general order provided for an aeronautic force within the Naval Militia. A limited number of naval aviators belonged to the militia upon America's entry in the war, and were demarcated with the special, yet subtle change to the shoulder board, while others were simply officers with ground duties involving maintenance, administration, supply or ordnance. Taken in November of 1917 at Hampton Roads, the picture here shows Lieutenant William O'Connell, USNR, head of aviation maintenance at Hampton Roads, bearing the Naval Militia designation on his shoulder boards. (Frank J. Conway, photographer.)

Neison Lynch "Pat" Bellinger, Naval Aviator No. 8, was detached November 16, 1917, from Pensacola and ordered to command the aeronautical center at Hampton Roads. His executive officer was Lieutenant George Dominic Murray, Naval Aviator No. 22, a colorful character destined to marry Corinne Mustin, widow of Captain Henry C. Mustin, Naval Aviator No. 11, who died unexpectedly in 1923. Toward the end of Bellinger's tenure as commanding officer, he would grow the station to twelve hundred officers and enlisted personnel and average fifty naval aircraft operating out of Norfolk waters.

Bellinger would remember the inopportune weather and poor working conditions which could have spelled failure had he not had the personnel and pure luck to look past temporary setbacks and expand the air station at every opportunity. The day "Pat" Bellinger came to Norfolk it was cold and rainy, his office on the station hardly what he would have expected of his first major command. Since all the buildings at the air station were temporary, his office floor was dirt, and on the day of his arrival dirt had given way to mud. Since he had no quarters per se, Bellinger checked into the Norfolk Yacht and Country Club. After settling into his role at the station, Bellinger sent his student pilots to Pensacola to complete their training since Norfolk was too cold and all flight operations had been stopped due to ice on the waterways in and around Hampton Roads. While students worked at Pensacola, Bellinger and his staff readied what was to become the Navy's newest air station, completing a number of wooden structures on the piers, laboratories, and hangars for lighter-than-air craft.

The original half mile of waterfront occupied by the air station expanded considerably in less than a year's time. The former site of the Jamestown-Exposition-turned-aeronautic-center was once described as having an incredibly picturesque approach from the water: "with the graceful concrete arch looming in the center, and its pier hangars well grouped on each side, it presents an unusually interesting picture of activity and color." The station was soon to extend over a mile of waterfront and included numerous shops and buildings(1) for construction, repair, launching, and operation of every type of naval aircraft. In short order the station would eventually make use of three beaches as runways for seaplane operations. Pine Beach, a premier resort beach before and during the Jamestown Exposition of 1907, was still intact but divided into three distinct sections by construction of a basin and piers for the exposition. One of the three beaches was located inside the arch in what was a holdover from the Grand Basin of the Jamestown Exposition. The other two were outside, known as the East Pier and West Pier (also from the exposition), and these had been converted for experimental operations. By June of 1918, reclamation of the lagoon had already begun, extending the air base out into the water a thousand feet.(2)

No other department on the naval base experienced more rapid growth and

An early naval aviator joke at Naval Air Station Hampton Roads went something like this:

"Did you know the Pine Beach Ferry sometimes gets lost on foggy days?" said one naval aviator to another.

"You don't mean it?" said his friend, "That sounds like a fairy tale."

"Well, it is a ferry tale, stupid."

Naval Base Norfolk and its adjacent naval air station were constructed on land which had previously been a popular beach resort. The Pine Beach Hotel and Pavilion, and the resort's lovely cabanas, drew large crowds to beautiful beaches. Built in 1902 in an area that was known as "Norfolk-on-the-Roads," the Pine Beach complex would nowadays rival the popularity of the Boardwalk at Virginia Beach, Virginia, or the beaches along the Outer Banks of North Carolina.

The kite balloon shown here was photographed at the United States Naval Training Center, Hampton Roads, Virginia, in 1917. Pennsylvania House on Naval Station Norfolk, once the centerpiece of the state houses on the 1907 Jamestown Exposition grounds, is visible in the background. The pilot is climbing the rope ladder to get aboard. After the First World War, it is interesting to note the Navy used the kite balloon on battleships, and even aboard the USS *Wright* (AV-1), but later discontinued their use in favor of rigid and semirigid airships. Since the Germans had perfected the great rigid airships, the United States would turn her attentions toward purchase of and training crews for rigids and semirigids. Of the four balloon hangars (two of which are visible here) which once stood at Norfolk, two were eventually disassembled and moved to the Navy's air base at Yorktown, Virginia, and one went to Lakehurst, New Jersey, after 1924. The Marine Corps acquired the fourth balloon hangar and rebuilt it at Quantico, Virginia. (Courtesy of the Hampton Roads Naval Museum.)

A winged, fouled anchor was adopted as the official device to be worn on the left breast of all qualified naval aviators on September 7, 1917, but the wings were not issued at that time. Before this design was made standard naval aviator issue, the use of the letters "U.S." which had been incorporated into the pattern was dropped by a general order dated October 12, 1917, and the design adopted was essentially that of the wings worn today (see illustration). The Bureau of Navigation issued solid gold wings with the aviator's name and designation number engraved on the back for the first time on January 18, 1918. Prior to that time naval aviators of the Naval Reserve Flying Corps were known to have worn embroidered gold wings on their uniform shoulder boards, an oft forgotten subtlety to aviator uniforms before the issuance of the wings of gold. The very first wings were issued as they appeared on the original list of 282 names prepared by the Office of Aviation, Navy Department. The assigned numbers were the beginning of the official precedence list of naval aviators, a practice discontinued in its alphanumeric form by 1973. Engraved gold wings crafted by Bailey, Banks and Biddle were presented to every new naval aviator until April of 1924, when the Secretary of the Navy ordered the practice stopped. In 1924, a little over three thousand wings of gold had been issued.

"For Distinguished and Heroic Service..."

Many Hampton Roads-born aviators would distinguish themselves overseas in World War I, but only two—Emory Arthur Stone and Robert Maury Stocker—would be awarded the Navy Cross for duty above and beyond the call. Emory Arthur Stone, Ensign, Naval Reserve Flying Corps, Naval Aviator No. 138, born in Norfolk on July 19, 1891, was a young man, full of life and all its adventures when he headed off to Yale University. The outbreak of the First World War in Europe would change his direction, his sense of adventure, and his perspective of the world forever.

Prior to his service as a naval aviator, Stone was attached to the British military as a veterinarian and travelled back and forth on transports pressed into service to carry horses from the United States to England for war service. In his day, Stone had also been quite well-remembered about Norfolk as a dog fancier. He raised a number of prize winning Dachshunds seen in local shows at the time.

Stone was a British army officer for two years prior to his American naval service. He enlisted in the Naval Reserve Flying Corps when the United States declared war on Germany in the spring of 1917. He was in training at Newport News until he received his commission as a flyer and was later designated an instructor at Hampton Roads. Upon leaving Norfolk at the end of 1917, Stone headed for Calshot, England.

On March 16, 1918, as pilot of a British seaplane, he and an observer were engaged in a convoy patrol. While in pursuit of a supposed submarine, they were forced to alight on the ocean as a result of catastrophic engine failure. Rough seas battered the aircraft beyond all hope of repair. As Stone and his observer clung to the aircraft for their lives, Stone released a carrier pigeon which brought a message from the flyer saying he had been forced down and needed help. Though a search was launched at once, the two men were at sea for eighty-two hours without food or water, and suffering from severe exposure when a trawler picked them up off the coast of Portland, England, on March 20, 1918, and carried them to a hospital in the city. Stone's parents, Mr. and Mrs. A.J. Stone, lived in a modest flat at the Redgate Apartments in the Ghent section of Norfolk. They were telegrammed by the Navy Department that their son was rescued by a trawler completely exhausted but not lost and feared dead as previously cabled. Stone won the Navy Cross for his bravery, courage and fortitude while in pursuit of the enemy and for his survival at sea.

Lieutenant Robert Maury "Bob" Stocker, Naval Aviator No. 141, was born on September 20, 1897, at Hampton, Virginia. He would attend Adelphi University, Garden City, Long Island, New York, before enlisting at Norfolk on May 25, 1917, for aviation service. Stocker received all of his ground and flight training at Hampton Roads, and was commissioned on the ninth of November. His Navy Cross was awarded posthumously for bombing enemy bases from September to November 1918 while attached to the famous Northern Bombing Group. The citation read, in part:

"For distinguished and heroic service as an aviator of land planes attached to the Northern Bombing Group in active operations cooperating with the Allied Armies on the Belgian front during September, October and November 1918, bombing enemy bases, aerodromes, submarine bases, ammunition dumps, railroad junctions..."

Sadly, Stocker was killed the afternoon of November 24, 1919, in the crash of his flying boat near Chester, Pennsylvania. He would never know of his Navy Cross.

Ensign Emory Arthur Stone of the Naval Reserve Flying Corps, 1917.

permanent development than the soon-to-be-commissioned air station. To demarcate the naval air station from the naval operating base, a line of sentries was posted on the road running between the two and, as one early observer noted, "Its secrets are closely and jealously guarded, and movements of visitors on the station are rigidly restricted to those having special passes." Besides seaplanes, there would also be dirigibles and balloons. Kite balloons were supplied to special battleships in Hampton Roads. There were buildings on the pier and more going up as months went by and wartime conditions led to bigger and better facilities. In addition to buildings on the piers and promenades, along the

A Boeing Aeromarine seaplane, February 14, 1918, Naval Air Detachment Hampton Roads, sits in the foreground of what aviators of the period dubbed "Tent City." Pennsylvania House, a landmark structure from the 1907 Jamestown Exposition, can be seen in the background. Note the canvas tents and wood-frame structure draped with canvas tarps. These tents housed repair facilities for the aircraft, and sometimes doubled as barracks for enlisted and officer personnel. (Official United States Navy Photograph.)

Right: Just for fun, airmen from Naval Air Station Hampton Roads and corpsmen from the Naval Base Hospital Unit A competed at tug-of-war on Field Day, March 1, 1918, Old Chambers Field. (Official United States Navy Photograph.)

Below right: The eastern section of Naval Air Station Hampton Roads was rung with bulkheads during the process of land reclamation started in 1918, when this picture was taken. (Official United States Navy Photograph.)

road passing through the station there was a series of shops for blacksmiths, carpenters, machinists, and riggers who wore rates of seaman (aviation). Civilian experts were enlisted to work on motor construction, wing and fabric manufacture, aerial bomb releases and special air armament. Scientific gas engineers had to be brought in to supervise motor and machine shops. Master carpenters and smiths oversaw intricate wire and joiner work. Not until many years later would anyone outside the military know the extent to which major inventors—creative geniuses—were brought in and out of the new air station to conduct research and experiments in aviation communication, chiefly radio telegraphy and radio telephony, under the guise of the communication department. Bellinger recruited the best administrators he could find to keep squadrons together, so they were prepared to provide patrols, pilots and planes anytime, anywhere.

Every naval aviation service specialty took instruction at the Navy's Hampton Roads flight facility which had student officers training in elementary flying but also those training for large flying boat duty in addition to commissioned officers under instruction for administrative tasks. The air base's role was threefold: to provide a base for experimental work, to conduct much-needed antisubmarine patrols, and to train pilots and instruct enlisted personnel in the construction and maintenance of seaplanes. After the war, Naval Air Station Hampton Roads would also be tasked with enlisted flight training as the

The condition of the ground outside the bulkheads at the air station was photographed by an unknown photographer on Saturday, October 29, 1919. This perspective shows the airship hangar at the air station to the far left (looming above some of the barracks buildings). (Official United States Navy Photograph. Courtesy of the Hampton Roads Naval Museum.)

The United States naval air base at Killingholme, located on the east coast of England, was home to two thousand men and fifty seaplanes during the First World War. It was also the site of the first loop of a twin-engine Curtiss flying boat flown by a Curtiss school pilot. Patrols flown by Navy pilots from this base totalled approximately one hundred thousand miles. Killingholme was a former British seaplane patrol station turned over to the United States and commissioned as a naval air station on July 20, 1918. The air base was closed on February 22, 1919. Killingholme's first United States Navy commanding officer was Kenneth Whiting, Naval Aviator No. 17. The photograph here was taken sometime in 1918. (Official United States Navy Photograph.)

direct result of Rear Admiral William Adger Moffett's directive to maintain enlisted pilots in both Navy and Marine Corps service. Enlisted pilots were known well in Hampton Roads. "Naval Aviation Pilot" (NAP) was the formal title given enlisted aviators between 1919 and 1973, with the exception being a short period in the 1920s lasting until 1933 when NAPs were called "Chief Aviation Pilots" (CAPs). The term "Chief Aviation Pilot" proved too confusing since enlisted pilots were already "chiefs."

February 1, 1918, saw the arrival of the first H-16 flying boat assigned to operational service delivered to Hampton Roads. A twin-engine tractor biplane built by Curtiss and the Naval Aircraft Factory, the H-16 was used on antisubmarine patrol from stations on the East Coast and in Europe and, as a consequence, was equipped to carry two 230-pound bombs and five Lewis machine guns, one forward, two aft, and two amidship. The H-16 made its first flight on March 27, 1918, and a few days later the plane and another shipped from the factory were sent overseas.(3)

The personal resolve and professional commitment of Hampton Roads naval aviators was tested time and again in the period between 1917 and 1919. The hazards of their relatively new profession would become all the more apparent as training and testing intensified in the last year of America's involvement in the First World War. On March 13, 1918, Ensign Malcolm Leslie "Les" MacNaughton, Naval Aviator No. 330, of Fort Edwards, New York, and his copilot, Ensign Malcolm "Mike" Stevenson, Naval Aviator No. 499, were part of a group of five seaplane crews who left Norfolk for a flight over Hampton Roads. MacNaughton, only twenty-three years old, had enlisted in naval aviation service while an undergraduate at Yale University Class of 1918. He was assigned to the naval base and had been flying in the aviation program at Hampton Roads. MacNaughton had married and brought his bride to Norfolk only ten days before the accident. Stevenson was a well-known and respected horseman in Virginia for years prior to his naval service, frequently showing horses at shows throughout the Old Dominion. In trouble within minutes of takeoff, MacNaughton's seaplane plunged five hundred feet into Chesapeake Bay. Ensign MacNaughton drowned after being rendered unconscious from the fall. His body was

The Beating Wings of Peerless Pilots

On December 21, 1929, the administration of Naval Air Station Hampton Roads discharged its last 75 carrier pigeons from the naval service. The beating wings of these intelligent birds carried calls for help from aviators forced down at sea and in other places far from the paths of civilization.

Early naval aviators normally carried four pigeons with them on each flight to relay messages or SOSs. Wireless communications aboard naval aircraft were not perfected until the 1920s. Carrier pigeons remained in use until at least 1929 because not every Navy plane carried its own sending set until 1930. The sending set could, in the space of a few minutes, flash out a message that it would have taken the pigeons hours to deliver.

When the carrier pigeons' services were no longer needed, they were not the only ones out of a job. The title "Pigeon Handler" began as an enlisted quartermasters' role as early as 1883. Prior to 1886, what is known today as a specialty mark—an enlisted sailor's occupational specialty and an essential part of the rating badge of petty officers and above—was not part of the rating badge. Pigeon handlers remained a specialty until 1929, at which time their services were no longer needed. Less than a month prior to the outbreak of World War II in 1941, the rating of specialist was developed to accommodate all four petty officer grades to cultivate specialties for which there was no existing provision in the naval service. Pigeon trainers fell into this category and were provided the classification "Specialist T" under the broader category of "teacher" for pigeon training. After completion of their training, handlers moved to "Specialist X," a catch-all for specialties that did not conform to any other area. Pigeon handlers were used in naval aviation from 1943 to 1961 to train carrier pigeons for use on blimps and patrol aircraft.

Peerless Pilot is released by a naval aviator, circa 1918. Peerless Pilot delivered over 150 messages during the First World War, and probably saved a few lives, too. When the last seventy-five pigeons were auctioned at Naval Air Station Hampton Roads in December 1929, all the birds were sold for the meager sum of sixty dollars to a man from Norfolk. Another gentleman from Phoebus bought the pigeon loft while a man from Portsmouth purchased the crates and baskets. Neither the farmer from Phoebus or the Portsmouth businessman paid more than a few dollars for the goods. Sadly, the price for the pigeons seemed all too little for the service they rendered. (Official United States Navy Photograph.)

retrieved by flyers in two other seaplanes who swooped down, landed, and dove to the aid of their friends. Stevenson was more in shock than physically injured. Friends would later take him back to his apartment at the Southland Hotel on Granby Street in downtown Norfolk.

By the summer of 1918, just prior to commissioning, there were seven separate departments in the aviation section and each school or unit had an officer-in-charge. The flying school was headed

This was the first class of student naval aviators to make the transition from Curtiss Field at Newport News, Virginia, to become part of Naval Air Detachment Hampton Roads, November of 1917. Shown here (back row, left to right) were Ensign John White Geary Jr., Naval Aviator No. 134; Ensign J.J. Finnegan, no record as a naval aviator; Ensign Benjamin "Ben" Lee II, Naval Aviator No. 137; Ensign Robert "Bob" Maury Stocker, Naval Aviator No. 141; Ensign Lyman Stannard Peck, Naval Aviator No. 172; Ensign Westmore Willcox, Naval Aviator No. 136; Ensign Arthur Lee "Lee" Boorse, Naval Aviator No. 333; Ensign George Walter Shaw, Naval Aviator No. 171; Ensign William Bull "Bill" Atwater, Naval Aviator No. 112; (front row, left to right) Ensign Charles Fairchild Fuller, Naval Aviator No. 139; Ensign Emory Arthur Stone, Naval Aviator No. 138; Ensign Hurd Hutchins, Naval Aviator No. 140; Ensign Cecil Dunmore "Mike" Murray, Naval Aviator No. 117; Ensign John Collier "Jack" Foster, Naval Aviator No. 142; Ensign J.P. Warburg, no record as a naval aviator; and Ensign Royal Winter "Royal" Wetherald, Naval Aviator No. 134½. The class itself consisted of some of the most interesting naval aviators of the period. After graduation, Geary remained at Hampton Roads as a flight instructor, patrol pilot, and test pilot. While assigned to Killingholme, England, Lee, in 1918, was reportedly the first pilot to loop a twin-engine Curtiss flying boat. Ensign Lee was killed shortly thereafter when his seaplane crashed in the Humber River near Killingholme on October 18, 1918. Stocker, born in Hampton, Virginia, died the afternoon of November 12, 1919, in the crash of his flying boat near Chester, Pennsylvania. He was the son of Rear Admiral Robert Stocker. Boorse was killed instantly on August 21, 1918, when an HS-1 flying boat, Bureau Number A1628, crashed into the harbor at Brest, France. Killed with Boorse were Ensign Robert F. Clark, Naval Aviator No. 196, and Machinist's Mate Second Class (MM2c) William F. Redman. Clark was instructing Boorse in the handling of H-boats when the plane fell off the wing, making a steep turn in rough air and entered a spin from which the pilots could not recover. Boorse's only child, a daughter, was born in Milwaukee, Wisconsin, the day he was killed. Shaw went on to win the Navy Cross as a seaplane pilot on patrol and convoy duty near Wexford, Ireland. He bombed a U-boat in very bad weather. The daring Shaw later became a partner with Eddie Stinson in Stinson Flyers, the first commercial gypsy flying circus in the United States. He barnstormed the country until 1930. Atwater had a colorful past before coming to naval aviation. In addition to four states, he flew in Japan, China, the Philippines, Southern Asia, and India prior to Navy duty. He also received his flight training at the Curtiss school in Newport News, eventually resigned from the Navy and owned a restaurant in New York City. Fuller trained with a group of Harvard men at the Curtiss school in Newport News and transferred to the new training field at Hampton Roads in October 1917. He had been there less than a month when this picture was taken. After the war, he went back to being an architect and city planner. Hutchins, also trained at the Curtiss school, moved to Hampton Roads in May of 1917 as part of a Harvard group. He became one of the earlier officers-in-charge of the Mechanics' and Quartermasters' School and a coastal patrol pilot. Murray also trained with the Harvard unit at the Curtiss school and transferred to Hampton Roads in September 1917. He was sent to France, specifically Naval Air Station Moutchic, and eventually flew with the Northern Bombing Group near Calais, France. After the war, Murray graduated from Columbia University's medical school, Class of 1929, and practiced medicine in Mississippi where he died in 1935. Foster went on to become a lawyer after the First World War. Wetherald, assigned a half number to reflect his earlier designation as a naval aviator, trained with the Massachusetts Institute of Technology Unit at the Curtiss school and Hampton Roads. (Frank J. Conway, photographer. Official United States Navy Photograph.)

A Curtiss JN Jenny does a slow roll over Hampton Roads, 1917. (Frank J. Conway, photographer.)

Ensign Emory Arthur Stone, USNR, Naval Aviator No. 138, of Norfolk, 1917. (Frank J. Conway, photographer.)

Ensign Lyman Stannard Peck, USNR, Naval Aviator No. 172, trained at Hampton Roads, was designated here and commissioned an ensign on November 26, 1917, the day this photograph was taken. He received a letter of commendation and World War I Life Saving Medal for the recovery of the body of student naval aviator Seaman Second Class R.M. Ensor from seaplane wreckage on the sixteenth of November, just days prior to receiving his pilot and officer designation. His actions were considered particularly brave as he dove into the frigid waters off present-day Naval Station Norfolk to attempt his rescue of Ensor. Peck served in France during the war. In later years, he would work as an engineer for Pan American Airways. Lyman Stannard Peck was one of those rare breed of naval aviators who had to forge his wings before he could wear them. Quite literally, his class at Hampton Roads did not even have wings to wear the day they were designated. He was issued the wings with his name and designation number some time later. (Frank J. Conway, photographer.)

Lieutenant Commander Patrick Neison Lynch Bellinger, Naval Aviator No. 8, commanding officer of Naval Air Station Hampton Roads, 1918. (Official United States Navy Photograph.)

Experimental triplane, possibly the Curtiss L-type, July 15, 1918. Notice the Grand Basin and stone arch, and the large air station buildings located down the piers and ashore. (Courtesy of the Hampton Roads Naval Museum.)

Fire caused by a hydrogen-filled airship landing across the high-tension wires of a hangar near the administration building of Naval Air Station Hampton Roads, July 24, 1918, destroyed most of the station. (Official United States Navy Photograph.)

A Curtiss H-12 flying boat undergoing maintenance on the ramp, Naval Air Station Hampton Roads, September 18, 1918. (Courtesy of the Hampton Roads Naval Museum.)

by Ensign Robert Livingston "Liv" Ireland, Naval Reserve Flying Corps (NRFC), Naval Aviator No. 84. Ireland would serve in numerous vital roles at Naval Air Station Hampton Roads, first as a flight instructor and progressing to beach master, head of the flight school, squadron commander and division commander of all patrol pilots. As head of the flight program, Ireland covered instruction, eight weeks of ground school which encompassed theory and all textbook materials, and training flights. Every officer in charge of a department was required to be a flyer, even supplemental departments within the flight instruction department, administration, maintenance and operations.

The mechanical school, also called the Mechanics' and Quartermasters' School, was given to Ensign Westmore Willcox, Naval Aviator No. 136, a Norfolk native. There were upwards of one thousand men trained in Willcox's department. Two large buildings on the station had been set up to train seamen in machinist and quartermaster trades. The six-week course was only open to enlisted personnel who had experience working with motors and machinery, or trades close enough to pick up the curriculum and practical lessons taught for the benefit of future aviation rates. Willcox was head of the largest department on the station and he proved more than capable in the role. Perhaps one of the most interesting aspects of Westmore Willcox's career was that he learned to fly at Curtiss Field, Newport News, Virginia, and finished his training at Hampton Roads. He was born in Norfolk on October 23, 1894, and educated at Harvard University, bachelor of arts, 1917. Westmore Willcox was discharged from service in 1921 as a lieutenant.

The Dirigible and Balloon School was also a large department of the air station. Lighter-than-air activities for rigid and nonrigid types continued at Hampton Roads until 1924 when the school moved to Naval Air Station Lakehurst, New Jersey. The main airship hangar at Norfolk was disassembled and relocated to Lakehurst where it still stands.(4) During both the First and Second World Wars, blimps were used for patrol work.

Many of those in machinist or quartermaster school transferred to the balloon school for more training. Dirigibles were inflated constantly, having their own section or plant for generating gas. The great dirigible hangar was the largest on the entire base. The officer-in-charge was Lieutenant Henry Willets "Susie" Hoyt, Naval Aviator No. 545, Lighter-Than-Air (LTA) and Naval Aviator No. 984, Heavier-Than-Air (HTA).(5) While at Hampton Roads, Hoyt was in charge of all dirigible activity in addition to kite balloons and crew supplied to the fleet. A sad footnote: Hoyt was killed in the line of duty by drowning when the dirigible *ZR-2*(6) crashed at Hull, England, on August 24, 1921.

The experimental station at Naval

Right: Two kite balloons carried photographers into the sky over the air center at Hampton Roads August 16, 1918, one of which is visible in the lower center portion of this photograph. (Official United States Navy Photograph.)

Below right: On October 7, 1918, aerial photographs were taken of property to be acquired by the Navy to expand the air station. Norfolk was farm land in those days. The Virginian Railroad had a major line running through the area, visible in the photograph. (Official United States Navy Photograph.)

Air Station Hampton Roads profoundly impacted the course of naval aviation. The radio department fell under this experimental station. Department personnel kept close contact with flyers in their aircraft and interested parties in Washington, D.C. "Many celebrated radio engineers and inventors found their way to us," Bellinger recalled in later years, "especially Lee de Forrest [*sic*]. One day the radio officer came to me and said, 'If you come with me, you can talk to and hear the pilot of a plane in the air.' I went with him, tried the phone and talked to the plane in the air. It seems strange to say so now, but it was then a weird sensation to be talking to a man flying in a plane. The test worked perfectly and I believe it was the first really successful test of the kind."

In addition to daily weather reports, radio department personnel also broadcast all baseball games as a welcome morale booster. The radio laboratory was extensive, boasting radio sets for seaplanes which proved both a tremendous source of discovery and trial and error for naval aircraft. Perhaps one of the highest points for the department came on November 18, 1918, when an H-16 flying boat, assigned to Hampton Roads and equipped with a radio direction finder using the British six-stage amplifier, received signals from an Arlington, Virginia, radio station at a distance of 150 miles.

The three remaining departments

Lee De Forest

Lee De Forest (1873–1961) was one of the most gifted electrical engineers and inventors produced by the United States in the twentieth century. He graduated in 1896 from Yale University's Sheffield Scientific School and completed his doctoral degree, also from Yale, in 1899. He went to Chicago to work for Western Electric Company, researching as time permitted. De Forest would be granted over 300 patents in his lifetime. He patented the audion in 1907. Though a recognized talent in his day, even then, De Forest was so prolific, people often overlooked some of his greatest achievements. In 1910 De Forest made the first radio broadcast of live music with a program featuring Enrico Caruso at the Metropolitan Opera, and six years later, he made the first radio news report. Today, we would not enjoy motion pictures so much if De Forest had not developed a sound system for movies in 1919. He proceeded to establish the De Forest Phonofilm Company to produce his sound system for the burgeoning film industry. De Forest made important contributions to the electric phonograph, long-distance telephony for the United States Navy and civilan application, facsimile transmission diathermy, radar, television, and many other communication mediums.

The Curtiss R-9 was an advanced trainer in the First World War. The aircraft shown here, Bureau Number A958, was photographed at Naval Air Station Hampton Roads on May 17, 1918. One hundred and twenty-one of the R-9 were procured by the Navy and another ten went to the Army. (Official United States Navy Photograph.)

on station—ordnance, repair and supply—functioned as support for station and fleet units. The ordnance department was headed by Ensign Royal Winter "Royal" Wetherald, NRFC, Naval Aviator No. 134½. Wetherald's unit was relatively new on the air station in 1918. Ordnance was in charge of bombs, machine guns and rifles. The repair department at Naval Air Station Hampton Roads was largest in terms of men assigned. Ensign J.M. Hanchett, was officer-in-charge of repair, earliest precursor of the Assembly and Repair Department, known later as Naval Aviation Depot (NADEP) Norfolk (see Chapter 12). The supply department would be charged with all stores and upkeep work. Ensign Richard Sullivan "Dick" Townsend, NRFC, Naval Aviator No. 119, was officer-in-charge of supply as well as all construction.

Not all of the horrific accidents and losses witnessed by the air station were caused by airplanes. Perhaps the earliest colossal accident and a close rival to a later explosion September 17, 1943, which would kill so many, occurred on July 24, 1918. A nonrigid airship landed atop the main hangar building of the naval base where it came in contact with live wires, causing sixty-five thousand dollars in damage and killing an undetermined number of sailors who came from the naval base and air station to help extinguish the fire.

The main braces of the dirigible's great gas bag had buckled, causing the machine, charged to Boatswain Kit Mullenax, Naval Aviator No. 557 (LTA), to become uncontrollable and land on the roof of the hangar. Bellinger, who yearned for just one day to pass without incident, was having a department head meeting in his office when he caught a glimpse of a sailor running across the field. He looked out his window just in time to see sparks pass between the blimp bag and the top of the hangar. He was powerless to do more than yell at sailors and airmen to clear the area as an explosion was imminent. Fortunate for Boatswain Mullenax and his student naval aviator, they had climbed out of the car to assess the damage. As they did so, the big gas bag suddenly exploded and flames shot up over one hundred feet. Mullenax and the student were miraculously unhurt, but, within seconds, the wood frame hangar was on fire, engulfed by intense flame, and they were left scrambling to get far enough away. Mullenax and his student slid down the roof and jumped. To everyone's astonishment, the airmen escaped the fire unscathed, that is if you did not count the singed flight gear and sweaty palms.

Naval base firemen, assisted by thousands of sailors, fought the fire but could not save the main hangar or a number of outbuildings. Since it was war time, reports of the fire were played down, including the number of sailors who died of burns. Queries to Lieutenant Commander Bellinger regarding the extent of damage received vague answers at best. Since station buildings were constructed primarily of wood and canvas, the fire jumped from one to another, devastating anything in its path. Bellinger reported twenty planes in the main hangar as saved but most of those were damaged and needed extensive repair.

His lighter-than-air department later informed Bellinger that the airship in question was the British-built *SSZ-24* and its fabric had rotted from age, thus giving way in places. With the resulting loss of hydrogen and lift, the blimp landed on the hangar. This accident and the eventual loss of the airship *Roma* in 1922 ended the use of hydrogen in American rigid and semirigid gas bags. Helium would become the element of choice.

Bellinger was not without his sense of humor amidst the chaos of the blimp fire. Once circumstances calmed down, his operations officer, Ensign Ganson Goodyear "Gans" Depew, Naval Aviator

Student naval aviators in the First World War were not so different from the young men and women who train today, but their aircraft were vastly different. Here, a Burgess-manufactured N-9 hydroaeroplane, Bureau Number A2429, is being taxied at Naval Air Station Hampton Roads on November 4, 1918. The N-9, an adaptation of the Army JN-4 Jenny aircraft, was the instrument with which many aspiring students won their wings of gold. (Official United States Navy Photograph.)

No. 121, brought him a message to be released to the Navy Department. As Bellinger took it in hand, he could not help but notice Depew's purposeful straight face and mischievous grin. The message read simply, "Station burning down, but Patrol Operations continuing as ordered." Trying very hard not to let on to his handiwork, "Gans" Depew sent the message as he had penned it.

In Bellinger's remembrances of people and events which shaped early Naval Air Station Hampton Roads history, Godfrey Lowell Cabot stood out. Not too long after the airship fire, Bellinger recalled getting a call from the Navy Department informing him Cabot was being sent to Norfolk for flight instruction and qualification as a naval aviator. That would have been fine except Cabot was fifty-seven years old and stood a pretty good chance of getting himself killed if he had undergone standard flight training. Bellinger had his old friend given the designation of naval aviator, No. 1339, and sent to Hampton Roads where Lieutenant Cabot, already a respected physicist and chemist, conducted experiments in which seaplanes picked up weighted materials from the water while in flight. Cabot remained under the watchful eye of his longtime friend Bellinger who was determined to keep "the old man" from meeting a premature end. Cabot, born in Boston, Massachusetts, on February 26, 1861, held the distinction of being the oldest naval aviator ever designated. He had received his bachelor of arts degree from Harvard University in 1882, and attended Harvard Graduate School from 1891 to 1893. Somehow it comes as no surprise that he lived to be 101 years of age.

Commissioned on August 27, 1918, the aeronautical center enjoyed the benefits of recognition which came with its designation as a major naval air station. Aside from training aviators, the most significant duty of the station had already become patrol. The search for enemy submarines and escort for government convoys became the primary functions of the air station in the First World War. It was rather extraordinary that, in this period of submarine chasing and escort, the air station never lost a plane attributable to wartime operations, and had no pilots lost to enemy fire.

At the time Naval Air Station Hampton Roads was formally established, station pilots had previously conducted operations via seaplane patrols covering a sea area of 112 miles north to 125 miles south of Cape Henry and up to 115 miles offshore. It was not exceptional for squadrons on station to cover fifteen thousand nautical miles in a week. Extended patrol areas led to establishment of refueling stations to the north and south of Cape Henry at Assateague, Virginia; Manteo, North Carolina; and Morehead City, North Carolina, in October of 1918, enabling the air station to dispatch patrols covering four hundred miles in length and lasting anywhere from six to eight hours. The time and distance was extremely efficient for the times. Morehead City eventually became an auxiliary air base under the jurisdiction of Hampton Roads as did several other locales. When emergency messages were received at the air station, they would be delivered to the communications officer, and, within five minutes, planes could be on the beach, in the water and airborne—also not bad for the times.

Aircraft used for patrol were N-9 seaplanes, HS-1 flying boats (also used for training), and the quite large H-16 and F-5L twin-engine flying boats. The first F-5L had been delivered to Hampton Roads on September 3, 1918, and was constructed by the Naval Aircraft Factory from a British design.(8) Unfortunately, the F-5L was produced too late to be used in the war in Europe, but it did quite nicely as a coastal patrol plane and saw extended service for years to come.

Chapter 6: "...The Human Wing in the Heavens of the World"

Lighter-than-air ships were the great hope of aviation through most of the nineteenth century. By the turn of the century, lighter-than-air experimentation ballooning had virtually died, primarily due to the Wright Brothers flight in 1903 at Kitty Hawk; Eugene Ely's exploits in 1910 and 1911; and subsequent fixed-wing landplane and hydroaeroplane flights and experiments which proliferated the 1910s and 1920s. Count Ferdinand von Zeppelin of Germany revived lighter-than-air experimentation in the twentieth century. Maneuverable lighter-than-air ships, called dirigibles, came in two types: semirigid and rigid, while the nonrigids, particularly popular during World War II and for a couple of decades thereafter, were called blimps. After the First World War, the United States Navy began to develop an interest in airships and established the Lighter-Than-Air (LTA) program. The United States Navy would not be the first to get an airship, though. The honor of being first went to the Army.

The Navy acquired the *O-1* airship upon completion of its construction by the Halian Company in 1919. The *O-1* was the only semirigid airship to serve in the American Navy and it was Lieutenant Raffe Emerson, Naval Aviator No. 622, who supervised her construction as an engineer attached to the Bureau of Construction and Repair. Emerson went on to qualify as kite balloon pilot and naval aviator lighter-than-air. Though an engineering genius,

The excitement which accompanied the approach of the first Navy dirigible, the *DN-1,* to its floating hangar, is evident in the tense postures of the figures in the foreground of the hangar. *DN-1,* manufactured by the Connecticut Aircraft Company, entered naval service in December of 1916, and was powered by two 140-horsepower Sturtevant engines. This picture was taken April 27, 1917, shortly after the United States declared war against Germany. The *DN-1* airship marked the introduction of lighter-than-air into naval aviation. Although neither the *DN-1* nor its floating dock proved particularly successful, their development heralded important contributions by airships in two world wars. The pilot of the *DN-1* on this famous flight was Lieutenant Commander Frank Robert "Squinch" McCrary, Naval Aviator No. 91, the first naval officer to qualify as a free balloon and lighter-than-air (LTA) pilot on June 3, 1916. He qualified as a heavier-than-air (HTA) pilot on August 22, 1917. Born on October 1, 1879, McCrary was thirty-eight by the time he had been designated a naval aviator, an "old man" to his younger counterparts. (Official United States Navy Photograph.)

Crew of "Blimp" Preparing for Flight

B-series airships were without a doubt among the most unusual to fly in the skies over Naval Air Station Hampton Roads. Powered by a 100-horsepower Curtiss OXX-2 engine, the B-series was distinguished by the absence of a top vertical fin. The Navy bureau numbers on the Goodyear-manufactured B-series were A235–A243. Goodyear manufactured all three of the B-series airships known to have operated in and around Hampton Roads: *B-3, B-4,* and *B-8*. The car hanging below the airbag is actually an aircraft fuselage (lower left photograph) with regular dual cockpit and usually the Curtiss OXX-2 or Hall-Scott water-cooled engine in the nose cowling. Pneumatic flotation bags dangle below the aircraft fuselage. The first photograph of a B-series, taken February 15, 1919, is the *B-8* which first went aloft over Hampton Roads in November of 1918. *B-8* was disassembled at the air station sometime in 1919. The second photograph of a B-series (above right), believed to be *B-4,* was taken circa 1918 while the airship was on maneuvers over Fortress Monroe. (Top and above left: Official United States Navy Photographs; photo above right courtesy of the Casemate Museum.)

his name is often dropped from discussions of early lighter-than-air developments. At the tender age of twelve in 1892, Emerson undertook serious study of aeronautics with a string of sophisticated experiments and models. By the time he became an ensign in the Navy in August of 1917, Emerson had seventeen years of engineering experience and was immediately assigned to the Bureau of Construction and Repair in the Navy Department.

As for the *O-1,* the semirigid made a particularly troubled flight on December 13, 1919, with Lieutenant Harry H. O'Claire, Lieutenant Smith Morris "Smith" Bradford, and Lieutenant Charles Bauch as flight crew. The airship ran into serious trouble and had to be dismantled after making an emergency landing in the countryside around Pennsville, New Jersey. The *O-1* was shipped back to Camden, New Jersey, then site of the Navy scrap yard. The airship was saved when one of her crew chiefs asked to exact repairs on the *O-1* and once again make her flight worthy. By the time the *O-1* was ready for flight, Lieutenant Ralph S. Barnaby, a project engineer at the Naval Aircraft Factory, was ordered to temporary additional duty at Hampton Roads.

O-1 came to Hampton Roads with Barnaby who would use it in test flights of antiaircraft target gliders Barnaby had designed and constructed. The mount and release mechanism for Barnaby's gliders was ensconced just under the control car of the *O-1*. From the sixth to the ninth of July, 1921, Barnaby's gliders were taken up about three thousand feet over the lower Chesapeake Bay off Norfolk and released by less than a handful of test pilots who included Lieutenant Charles E. Erdman, Naval Aviator No. 2159, and Lieutenant Donald James MacCalman, Naval Aviator No. 1747.

Images and information about the *O-1* are considered rare; the fate of this unique airship unknown. The *O-1* made no further appearances in photographs or official Navy records after 1922, leading historians to believe she was completely dismantled sometime that year.

At the great urging of Army Brigadier General William "Billy" Mitchell, the United States purchased the Italian-constructed *Roma,* destined to be the first great airship flown by any branch of the American military, and certainly the only one dependent on hydrogen.

The *Roma* story is an important one in the annals of American military aviation.

Brigadier General Mitchell had received authorization for $475,000 towards purchase of the semirigid dirigible, but exchange rates at point of purchase significantly lowered the price. The United States government purchased the *Roma* from the Italians in March of 1921 for $194,000. America's ambassador to Italy, Robert Underwood Johnson,(1) was instrumental in the United States Army's decision to keep the name *"Roma"* and he would provide

The Navy used its free balloons primarily for training but, on April 2, 1920, records indicate Naval Air Station Hampton Roads had successfully launched candlelit free balloons to measure night weather soundings for at least the first four months of the year. Free balloons were well-suited vehicles for scientific experiments and had been used for such purposes at Hampton Roads. (Official United States Navy Photographs.)

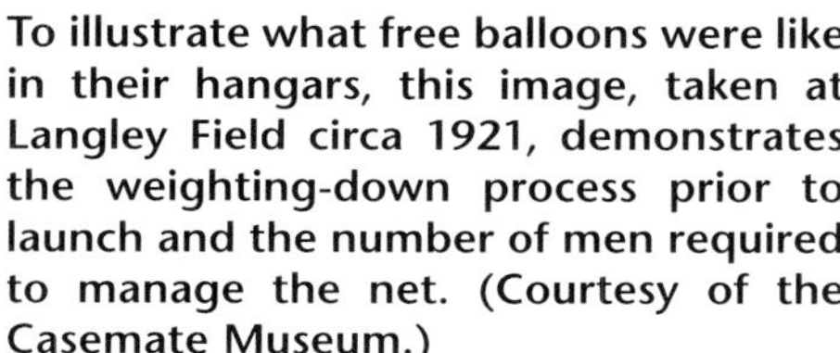

To illustrate what free balloons were like in their hangars, this image, taken at Langley Field circa 1921, demonstrates the weighting-down process prior to launch and the number of men required to manage the net. (Courtesy of the Casemate Museum.)

invaluable observations of *Roma's* activities during its first two Italian familiarization flights during transfer to the Army Air Service. Johnson was enamored with his March 3, 1921, flight aboard the *Roma*, an hour-and-a-half sojourn over Rome and Lake Albano. *Roma* was awaiting the arrival of American experts sent to make a trial run prior to painstakingly dismantling and shipping the dirigible to Langley Field, Virginia, when Johnson got his first flight aboard her. The ambassador could not convince his wife, Kate, to go with him on what he described as "a glorious morning, such as we have had for three weeks, but with a bit of mist along the horizon—that beautiful opal gray which haunts the Alban Hills and sifts into Rome these crisp winter mornings."

As Johnson arrived at the *Roma's* hangar in Campagna, the airship's ground crew of one hundred soldiers and workmen had already guided the dirigible from its berth and held fast to the ropes which bound her to earth. Johnson observed two additional airships in Roma's hangar: an O-type, a much smaller craft, and the colossal German Zeppelin *LZ 120* which had bombed London three times and Paris once during World War I. *LZ 120* had been provided to Italy under the Versailles reparation agreements reached between the Allies, of which Italy was one, and Germany. Though it still had an Iron Cross painted under one side, *LZ 120* had been renamed the *Ansonia*.

The aircrew and passengers of *Roma* ascended at nine in the morning. As some of its passengers seated themselves comfortably, Johnson elected to move about the ship with a crewman, remarking that if he had fallen from a long plank to the bow, holding on to ropes, "I should have tested the strength [of the rubberized cotton envelope] I might have gone through." The frame of *Roma* was aluminum, and silk was used throughout certain points also.

Johnson's only complaint on his first *Roma* voyage seemed to be "the noise of the engines speech," which "pained the ear." The view of the approaching city of Rome was spectacular to the ambassador who later wrote, "St. Peter's rose gray-white in the distance and the whole of the Eternal City lay before us in one comprehensive glance. We had the advantage over Julius Caesar and his contemporaries of seeing their favorite city as they had never seen it—from above." Upon seeing the Piazza, which seemed to them to occupy a third of Rome, "and its noble proportions, the beauty of the dome and lantern were like a revelation. Owen said it made him think that, when it was criticized as being difficult of view to the ordinary

The *O-1* airship, Bureau Number A5587, is shown here releasing a glider over the lower Chesapeake Bay on July 7, 1921. The *O-1* was manufactured by the Italian government and transferred to the American Navy for experiments connected with its airship program. (Courtesy of the Hampton Roads Naval Museum.)

There would be three C-class airships assigned to Naval Air Station Hampton Roads, including *C-3* (Bureau Number A4120), *C-7* (A4127), and *C-9* (A4124). *C-3*, pictured here, was manufactured by Goodyear and delivered to Hampton Roads in February of 1919, when this photograph was taken. The *C-3* was destroyed by fire when a spark from her engine ignited it near Hampton Roads on July 8, 1921. (Official United States Navy Photograph.)

tourist, it must be remembered that Michale Angelo [*sic*] planned it for the eye of the Bon Dieu!"

As a result of his experiences on the first *Roma* flight, Johnson recommended to the Secretary of War that the United States Army retain the name *"Roma"* in honor of its designer, Usuelli; Umberto Nobile, its maker; and the airship's craftsmen. Nobile remarked on April 23, 1921, "the decision taken by the Government of the United States of America to preserve the immortal name of *'Roma'* for the dirigible constructed by this Establishment constitutes the highest honor of the most ambitious satisfaction that the Italian technicians could have expected as the crowning of their work." General A. di Siebert, Superior Commandant of Aeronautics, concluded, "the two aeronautical industries promise to unite in fraternal exchange for the development of the human wing in the heavens of the world." The *Roma* was more than fabric and frame—it represented the exchange of technology and innovation between the United States and Italy, two nations destined to become fierce competitors for aeronautical supremacy for the remainder of the 1920s.

Ambassador Johnson made a second flight on the *Roma* on March 15, 1921, this time in the company of eight American Army crew, the same crewmen who would be among those with *Roma* on her fateful last day less than one year later. The trip from Campagna to Naples on the fifteenth was to enable the Americans, commanded by Major John G. Thornell, a veteran lighter-than-air flyer, Captain Dale Mabry and First Lieutenant Walter J. Reed, to become familiar with the workings of the dirigible. On the flight with Johnson, the American crew, and its Italian instructors were Prince Viggo of Denmark, fourth son of King Christian, and the prince's

WHAT THE NAVY IS DOING

Press, Navy Recruiting Bureau, New York.

"SHE WENT AWAY ONE DAY"

After a successful voyage from Montauk Point, Long Island, to St. Johns, Newfoundland, covering 910 miles, lasting 25 hours and 50 minutes, most of the trip being made in a fog, the Navy Airship C-5, on May 16, 1919, broke her moorings during a severe storm, was blown to sea and lost, and her chances of making an overseas flight destroyed. Another ship is being prepared for the flight. Join the Navy and help finish the job.

THE NAVY TRAINS MEN TO START SOMETHING, AND SEE IT THROUGH

aide; Signor Cortesi of the Associated Press; Signor Usuelli who designed the *Roma;* Nobile who built it; General A. di Siebert, head of the Italian Aviation Force; Kenneth Roberts of the *Saturday Evening Post;* and a Signor Zezi, an expert on the subject of parachute jumping and "who would," as Johnson recorded, "gladly have given us an exhibition of his skills had it not been forbidden." As they passed over Rome that day, Johnson sent the following wireless message to the Secretary of War:

"American Embassy Rome. For Secretary Weeks, Washington, by wireless from airship *Roma* above Naples. Successful trip carrying American Flag for the first time. American Aviation officers and American Military and Naval Attachés and American guests send greetings and congratulations. Robert Underwood Johnson, Ambassador."

Thornell, Mabry and Reed accepted the *Roma* for the United States after the second Italian flight, their lives destined to be linked with the semirigid dirigible to its tragic end.

The *Roma* was fast for its time, able to make forty miles per hour on six Ansaldo-San Giorgio engines turning nearly 3,000-horsepower. During the first flight on March 3, 1921, Johnson remarked that "an interesting feature, and almost the only dangerous one, was the operation of the two men in one of the six projecting motors who, at full speed, transferred the propeller from one motor to another to show that it could be done. They seemed to be in a perilous position, the motor being supported only by fine projecting iron rods, with a narrow path to the airship. Only four of the motors were in operation or we could have had a greater speed. We went at an altitude of from 700 to 850 feet, so that we had no difficulty in making out details below us."

The airship's speed would increase to sixty miles per hour once technicians at Langley swapped the Italian power plants for six American Liberty engines. As a non-military and non-aeronautical observer, Johnson's views of the *Roma* eventually would run up against those of numerous airship detractors and, later, survivors of the *Roma's* disastrous last flight. There would be no delight or wonder the day she met her end.

The semirigid airship was dismantled and shipped to Langley Field in August of 1921, and by November 15, 1921, was ready for its first flight on American soil. The *Roma,* which measured 410 feet in length, was pumped full of 1,167,220 cubic feet of highly flammable hydrogen. She went aloft over

The first flight of an airship inflated with helium was made by the *C-7* (Bureau Number A4127) at Naval Air Station Hampton Roads, Virginia on December 1, 1921. Lieutenant Commander R.F. Wood, Naval Aviator No. 2924, was the pilot. The rest of the crew consisted of Lieutenant Commander Zachary "Zach" Landsdowne, Naval Aviator No. 105, and Lieutenant Charles E. Bauch. It is interesting to note that the gondola of C-class airships could be equipped with a bomb rack. The *C-7* was powered by Hispano-Suiza engines. Landsdowne stands out amongst the crew of the *C-7*. He had been the naval attaché in Berlin, Germany, during negotiations for construction of the dirigible later designated *ZR-3* or the USS *Los Angeles*. Lieutenant Commander Landsdowne would fall to his death from the USS *Shenandoah,* formerly *ZR-1,* when the airship was torn to pieces in a line squall near Caldwell, Ohio, on September 3, 1925. (Official United States Navy Photograph.)

Below: The day after its historic flight, the *C-7* is seen emerging from a hangar at Naval Air Station Hampton Roads, Virginia, December 2, 1921. The *C-7* was manufactured by the Goodyear Corporation and had a short period of naval service: she was deflated in March of 1924. (Official United States Navy Photograph.)

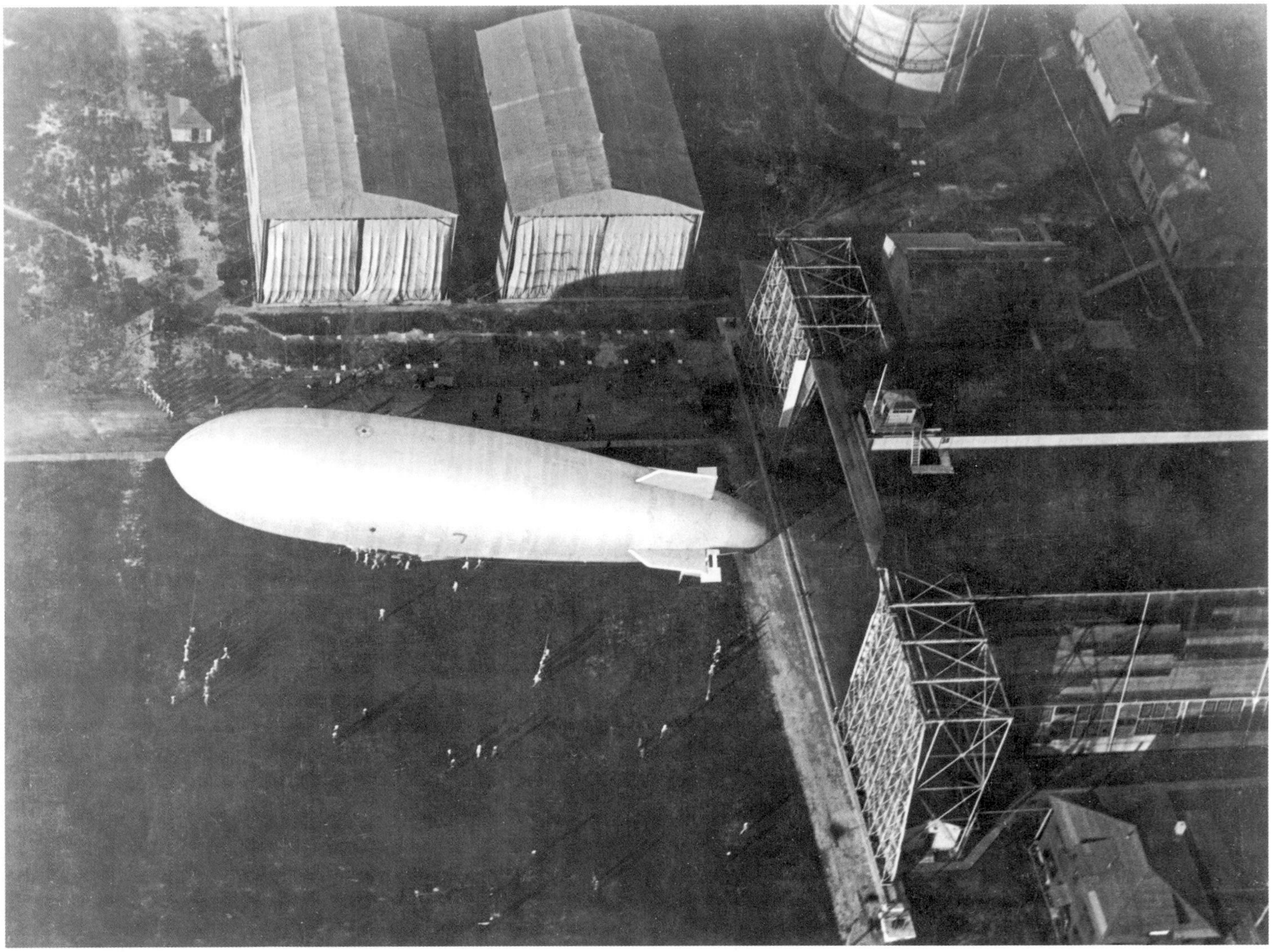

Navy airships were stored in hangars much like the ones employed by the Army at Langley Field, shown here, circa 1920. The airship hangars at the naval air station as well as Langley Field were large enough to accommodate three to four inflatables at once. (Courtesy of the Casemate Museum.)

The *C-9* (Bureau Number A4124) was manufactured by the Goodrich Tire and Rubber Company as a prototype for the Navy. As in the B-series, an aircraft fuselage doubled as the gondola on the C-series as well. Two-hundred-horsepower Hall-Scott L-6s could be found on the majority of C-class airships, favored by their designers over the underpowered 150-horsepower Wright-Hispano power plant. The *C-9* was assigned to Naval Air Station Hampton Roads on December 27, 1921, and stricken from the Navy record on November 9, 1923. The *C-9* had been delivered to the Navy in November of 1919, and Naval Historical Center records indicate she served at Saufley Field, Coco Solo, and, finally, Hampton Roads. Her record of service was brief. Quite often the airbag was deflated, the skeleton dismantled, and the car reused or scrapped. There is no way to be sure if *C-9* met this fate or some other. Records do not indicate details of her demise. (Official United States Navy Photograph.)

Langley Field as scheduled. This flight would be followed by a troubled trip to her christening ceremony in Washington, D.C. On the flight to Washington, three of the airship's six engines failed and on the way home, only one engine worked. Despite the rough flight and increasing doubts about the airship's performance ability, a hangar was constructed at Langley to house the *Roma*. Captain Mabry, an ardent proponent of dirigibles, was certain she could open new avenues in military aviation.

February 21, 1922, was overcast with intermittent rain showers. Despite these unfavorable conditions, *Roma* crew and passengers, numbering forty-five souls, lifted off on the dirigible's fourth flight just as one rainstorm ended and another was expected. The gray pallor of the afternoon boded badly for *Roma* and her human cargo. Captain Mabry was in command. Major Thornell and First Lieutenant Reed were aboard. Contrary to some accounts of the airship's last flight, the *Roma* handled perfectly for Lieutenant Reed, her pilot, as he maneuvered her for forty-five minutes over Newport News, Hampton, and Norfolk. Reed, recovering from the flu, was relieved when Captain Mabry tapped him on the shoulder and replaced him at the controls according to accounts by the few crewmen who would survive the crash. Mabry was a devoted follower of Billy Mitchell and a highly experienced World War I airship officer. He turned the *Roma* on course for Willoughby Spit and headed toward Naval Station Norfolk over which crewmen were to run further tests on the Liberty engines. Mabry had just passed over the United States Army Quartermaster Intermediate Depot(2) when two problems occurred simultaneously, sealing the crew's fate. Onlookers at Naval Air Station Hampton Roads watched in stunned silence as the box-kite elevator on *Roma's* stern went awry, jamming the airship's flight controls. As the *Roma* plummeted earthward, her crew started throwing out equipment in a last desperate attempt to lighten the airship's load. About the same time, a valve controlling air intake into one of the airship's six ballonets had also failed. As a result, air could not be added to the cell, and the upper curve of the gas bag's nose began to flatten. Boatswain's Mate Richard E. Deal, a young sailor, gazed upwards from his work at the air station as the *Roma* nose cap began collapsing, and the great airship pitched nose-first toward the ground beyond the flying field. Deal naively thought the *Roma's* crew would be shaken but otherwise unharmed because the descent appeared to be in slow motion. What Deal and others did not know was the volatility of hydrogen.

Hydrogen is the lightest known gas, which made it most desirable for airship gas bags, but explosive when mixed with air or oxygen. The gas burns with a hot blue flame. Once *Roma's* air bags were breached and air mixed with hydrogen, the coup de grace was high-voltage electrical wires whose sparks instantly ignited the *Roma's* hydrogen in the descent. The hydrogen explosion, in turn, set off the airship's gasoline tanks. The ignited hydrogen became a sea of liquid flame. Deal saw the flash and smoke as the *Roma* became a funeral pyre for her crew.

Lieutenant Reed survived the conflagration by leaping from the airship at the last possible moment; Mabry and Thornell did not make it. Mabry was incinerated at the helm still gripping the

The Army's semirigid airship, *Roma,* the morning of February 21, 1922, Langley Field, Virginia. (Photographer unknown.)

Sailors and soldiers work to extinguish the *Roma.* (Photographer unknown.)

The *Roma,* in flight over the Army base prior to the crash, was the picture of perfection on February 21, 1922. (Photographer unknown.)

The fire which enveloped the *Roma* burned for hours before the last flame could be extinguished. (Photographer unknown.)

controls. Lieutenant William Riley jumped too soon and, in accounts of the Newport News *Daily Press,* "he drove his knee bones through his skin and dashed his brains out against the pavement." Master Sergeant Harry Chapman whipped out his knife and cut a hole in the flaming gas bag but courageously did not escape the inferno until he had helped eight other crewmen out of his emergency exit.

Only the metal skeleton of the *Roma* remained once the flames were extinguished. Inside was a grizzly scene as sailors from Naval Air Station Hampton Roads helped Army investigators sift through wreckage for charred bodies of thirty-four crewmen—and a cause. The flame burned so hot, it shrunk skulls to the size of a man's fist, making identification more difficult. Reed, Sergeant Joseph M. Biedenbach, Chapman and the eight men Chapman saved, survived. A cause for the two primary mechanical malfunctions was never found.

Roma's critics would later state that they perceived her to have been flawed from the start on the basis of her underpowered engines, sluggish handling characteristics and vulnerability to inclement weather conditions. In the airship's defense, however, there are two points which should be made. Firstly, all of the airships constructed by the United States Navy after the *Roma* disaster, commencing with the USS *Shenandoah* in 1923, and followed by the USS *Akron,* USS *Macon,* and USS *Los Angeles,* had brushes with bad weather, and all but the *Los Angeles* ended in tragedy. Secondly, the Italian engines thought to be debilitating to the craft's performance were not a factor a year later when *Roma* plummeted to the earth. That she had problems with the American Liberty engines there is no doubt. Where the Army may truly have failed was in its training syllabus and hands-on instruction to the *Roma's* crew. Anxious to be as successful as the United States Navy in airship development, the Army gave the *Roma's* junior officer and enlisted crew a crash course in handling and troubleshooting. The Army Air Service sacrificed proper engine maintenance and ignored recommended engine replacement, also to keep up the race with the Navy for money to research and develop the airship concept.

The *Roma* crash plunged the Peninsula into mourning. This was, after all, the worst air disaster in American history at that time. What remained of the bodies was taken to Rouse's Undertaking Firm in Newport News where every effort was made to identify them. The dead were shipped to hometowns if requested by family members, but many were unidentifiable. Mabry was buried at Arlington National Cemetery. Sergeant James Murry was laid to rest at National Cemetery in Hampton, Virginia. Private John Thompson, who had no one to claim him, was buried at Greenlawn Cemetery in Newport News.

A public funeral to honor the *Roma* dead was held at St. Paul's Church in downtown Newport News on February 24. Local American Legion posts, civic clubs, and a band from Fortress Monroe marched in the funeral procession, as did troops from Langley Field. Businesses were closed. Virginia Attorney General John P. Saunders delivered the eulogy. At the close of Saunder's oration, the bugler played "Taps," troops saluted, and aircraft from Langley Field swooped low and dropped flowers on the coffin of one unidentified victim of the crash, which served as a symbol of *Roma's* lost crew.

Wreckage of the *Roma's* Liberty engines and metal skeleton littered the Army Intermediate Depot site after the crash. The engines bear witness to the intense heat which permeated the airship as it came to rest on the ground. (Photographer unknown.)

Below right: A crane operator was photographed raising the structure of the *Roma's* basket or control car off telephone poles carried down by the semirigid airship. The devastation and human carnage left by the *Roma* is clearly captured in this scene. (Photographer unknown.)

Captain Mabry, had he lived, would have continued to champion the airship, or so said those who lived to tell the story.

The Army took the *Roma* disaster for what it was—a sign that the service should not pursue airship development—and turned its efforts toward research and development of heavier-than-air craft. The Navy, on the other hand, adopted lighter-than-air, often with disastrous results. Within a few days of the *Roma* crash, Congress decided to continue research and development on helium airships. The Army's experience with the *Roma* would leave a lasting impression on Navy officials.

The Navy eventually constructed four large-class dirigibles (ZRs and ZRSs):(3) USS *Shenandoah* (ZR-1), USS *Los Angeles* (ZR-3), USS *Akron* (ZRS-4), and USS *Macon* (ZRS-5).(4) "ZR" stood for Zeppelin rigid. The airships were not intended to be used in actual combat, but rather as the eyes of the fleet and, later, as an effective platform for carrying aircraft over long distances for scouting and observation.

The *Shenandoah,* built at a cost of $1.5 million, was 682 feet long, 80 feet across, and could make 60 miles per hour. Her crew numbered about thirty, but it was common for the Navy's giant rigid airships to carry additional crewmen and passengers. Completed at the Naval Aircraft Factory in September 1922, the "Daughter of the Stars" was the first rigid airship to be inflated with helium. The *Shenandoah's* length was divided into frames at every five meters, and these frames corresponded with the outer ribs of its skeleton. Frames were

Army and Navy personnel remove the charred remains (center in canvas) of a *Roma* crewman, February 21, 1922. This was a macabre accident; arms, legs, and pieces of flesh were just swept into baskets. (Photographer unknown.)

Naval Air Station Hampton Roads personnel and civilian bystanders look over the wreckage of the *Roma*. Women were not allowed at the scene. (Photographer unknown.)

Individual identification of *Roma's* victims was impossible in a majority of cases. Though every effort was made to identify her crew, in the end, some of the lost would never be properly returned to their families because coroners could not make absolute positive identifications. Members of the Peninsula community attended a public funeral at St. Paul's Church in downtown Newport News. Mourners leave the church, in this photograph, ahead of the caskets. (Photographer unknown.)

Local American Legion posts, civic clubs, and a band from Fortress Monroe marched in the funeral procession as did troops from Langley Field. (Photographer unknown.)

Aviators from Langley Field swooped low and dropped flowers on the coffin of one unidentified victim of the *Roma* disaster. (Photographer unknown.)

numbered consecutively from zero at the base of the rudders to 195 at the tip of the nose. Crewmen spaces could be found amidship between frames 100 and 105, and officer staterooms were fore and aft of the control car which hung below frame 160. Frames aft of zero had no numbers.

The maiden flight on September 4, 1922, from Naval Air Station Lakehurst, New Jersey, was a complete success. Captain Frank Robert "Squinch" McCrary, Naval Aviator No. 91, who commanded the *Shenandoah* on the voyage (and most of the dirigible's initial flights), was also commanding officer of the Lakehurst air station. Though McCrary was one of the most experienced lighter-than-air pilots in the Navy, having operated the *DN-1,* the Navy's first dirigible, from a floating hangar at Naval Air Station Pensacola in April of 1917, he actually went on record after the *Shenandoah* flights as being opposed to huge dirigibles.

The *Shenandoah's* first operational commanding officer was Lieutenant Commander Zachary "Zach" Lansdowne, Naval Aviator No. 105. Like McCrary, Landsdowne, at the age of 35, was one of the few Navy officers with appreciable experience in airships. Despite McCrary's warnings against further construction of huge dirigibles, the Navy continued plans to build more, and regardless of Lansdowne's considerable experience, the *Shenandoah* was destined to fail, lost in a severe line squall over Ohio.

Lansdowne, coincidently an Ohio native, was all too familiar with the line

The bugler played "Taps" and the soldiers saluted. (Photographer unknown.)

squalls produced in his home state that same time of year. However, overly eager Midwest politicians insisted a Navy airship tour their districts during county fair season to show the hometown folks where their tax dollars were being spent. Landsdowne confidentially cautioned his superiors against making the trip

The USS *Wright* (AV-1) was the Navy's first seaplane tender. The Navy had acquired the ship in 1919 as an unfinished merchant vessel and completed its subsequent conversion to a tender by December 16, 1921, at which time it was commissioned into the fleet. Captain A.W. Johnson was the ship's first commanding officer. A kite balloon can be seen in the balloon well of the *Wright,* 1922. (Official United States Navy Photograph. Courtesy of the Hampton Roads Naval Museum.)

because the weather risk was too great. Dismissed by his superiors as overly chary, Lansdowne's recommendations went unanswered.

At 2:52 p.m. on September 2, 1925, Lansdowne and his crew cast off the mooring mast at Lakehurst for what was to be their final flight. The crew of forty-one was joined by two guests, Lieutenant Walter L. Richardson, Naval Aviator No. 582, and Colonel C. G. Hall of the Army Air Corps. Lansdowne turned over the helm of the "Daughter of the Stars" to his executive officer, Lieutenant Commander Lewis Hancock Jr., Naval Aviator No. 3175, at 12:10 a.m. and retired to his quarters. The *Shenandoah* had reached the foothills of the Allegheny Mountains, cruising at 3,000 feet and two-thirds speed, approximately forty miles per hour. There was no reason for Lansdowne to worry when he left the bridge.

At three in the morning, crewmen spotted lightning popping to the west, northwest and east with increasing head-wind. Hancock called Lansdowne and the ship's aerologist, Lieutenant Joseph Anderson, ten minutes later. The town of Cambridge, Ohio, was visible below. Lansdowne ordered an increase in power and steady course at 2,500 hundred feet. By 4:35 a.m., the airship struggled to make headway against winds that were veering abruptly by as much as seventy degrees, at which time Lieutenant Commander Charles Emery Rosendahl, Naval Aviator No. 3174,(5) the airship's mooring officer and navigator, relieved Hancock. Though relieved of his official duties, Hancock insisted on staying in the control car anyway.

What Lansdowne, Hancock, Rosendahl, and Anderson could not see was the line squall forming directly above the airship—their fate was sealed. The "Daughter of the Stars" was moments from being plucked from the sky. What Lansdowne had foreseen was coming true.

At 5:22 a.m. the *Shenandoah* was caught by vertical air currents and lifted from 1,800 feet to 3,150 feet in eight minutes; held at 3,150 feet for six minutes; then pulled to 6,100 feet in less than ten minutes; and dropped rapidly to 3,000 feet in three minutes. The airship rose again, this time sharply up by the nose, to 3,700 feet, at which point the agonizing sounds of the *Shenandoah* splitting apart reached the ears of its crew. As she split on the last rise, the dirigible rotated in a horizontal plane,

The great airship USS *Los Angeles* (ZR-3) was called the "Pride of the Navy" during her reign as America's most successful dirigible. Here, she is shown flying over the lower Chesapeake Bay, circa 1931, a six-masted top-sail schooner making way at sunset beneath her. This image could hardly state more clearly the incredible technological advancement in travel, trade, and military weaponry which had come about since the Wright Brothers took flight at Kitty Hawk in 1903. When Grace Coolidge christened her she said: "Go forth under the open sky and may the winds of Heaven deal gently with thee." (Photographer unknown.)

Lieutenant Commander Charles Emery Rosendahl, Naval Aviator No. 3174, circa 1922. (Courtesy of the University of Texas at Dallas.)

rolling and pitching violently. Stress breaks opened her hull and wires snapped. *Shenandoah* was uncontrollable.

The first break in the main structure occurred between frames 120 and 130, dumping Lieutenant (junior grade) Edgar W. Sheppard and Chief Aviation Rigger (ACR) James W. Cullinan, Naval Aviation Pilot (NAP), to their deaths. While the separation led to the immediate deaths of two men, it also divided the airship into two sections, the control car still attached to the forward section. The lives of the remaining forty-one men now hung in the balance.

Those in the control car were in the most immediate danger. Only a few cables attached the car to the hull, the weight of which was impossible for the cables to hold. Knowing what was coming, Lansdowne told his control car crew that anyone who wanted to leave had his blessings to do so. Hall and Anderson scurried up the ladder and out of the car. Hancock, Lieutenant (junior grade) John B. "Jack" Lawrence, Naval Aviator No. 580, and Lieutenant A. Reginald Houghton, Naval Aviator No. 859, stayed with their commanding officer. Crewmen Aviation Machinist's Mate First Class (AMM1c) James A. Moore, Chief Radioman (CRM) George Schnitzer, Chief Aviation Rigger (ACR) Everett P. Allen and Aviation Rigger First Class (AR1c) Ralph T. Joffray remained at their posts.

As the *Shenandoah* continued breaking up, and less than one minute before he plummeted to his death, Lansdowne purportedly came over the airship's intercom to his men: "Pass the word forward: All men on their toes. We are going through together." The control car and after section of the hull broke free and fell directly to the ground along the edge of a cornfield, 3,700 feet below the now drifting bag of the *Shenandoah*. Lawrence's watch stopped abruptly at 5:47 a.m. As the control car fell, a second break occurred between frames 100 and 110. The mid-section fell quickly but slowed down when power cars four and five wrenched free and carried four more of the enlisted crew to their deaths: Chief Aviation Machinist's Mate (ACMM) Charles H. Broom, Aviation Machinist's Mate First Class (AMM1c) Celestine P. Mazzuco, AMM1c Bart B. O'Sullivan and AMM1c William H. Spratley.

Within moments of the second break, the stern split in two, leaving fourteen men, including Lieutenant Charles Bauch, Lieutenant (junior grade) Thomas Handley, and Richardson trapped in a 425-foot tail section, and four enlisted men in a smaller piece, both gliding to earth somewhere near Caldwell, Ohio. Though it was a rough landing, all fourteen men in the larger stern section survived. The four enlisted men landed in a stand of trees at 6:06 a.m., none the worse for wear.

Meanwhile, the bow section of the *Shenandoah* continued to rise with Rosendahl, 33, and six men aboard. At 10,000 feet, darkness precluded Rosendahl from identifying his companions in what was now a free balloon blowing aimlessly across stormy Ohio skies in a ten-mile circle. Scared, but composed, each of the men called out to one another. Rosendahl ordered Lieutenant Roland Mayer who ordered Colonel Hall to valve the helium. Warrant Officer Shine Halliburton, Naval Aviator No. 346, and mechanic Joseph Shevlowitz drained ballast and slashed the gas cells at the right moments. Unbelievably, by working together, Rosendahl and his men landed safely at 6:44 a.m., twelve miles from the other two sections and control car. To prevent the gas bags from being pulled about the ground by the wind, Halliburton borrowed a shotgun from a farmer and shot holes in the gas cells. They had landed in a field near Ava, Ohio.

The *Shenandoah* disaster was surely an unnecessary waste of men's lives, but

The USS *Los Angeles* accompanied the USS *Patoka* (foreground, below the airship), USS *Lexington* (CV-2) (aircraft carrier in the center of the photograph) and USS *Saratoga* (CV-3) (upper left, above the *Lexington*) during fleet exercises in 1928 off the coast of Virginia. (Courtesy of the Hampton Roads Naval Museum.)

perhaps more shameful was the looting which occurred even before the dead crewmen's bodies could be placed in makeshift wooden coffins. Reporters on the scene were appalled by what they saw. Looters came by the thousands: well-to-do, middle-class, and poor, they came. Farmers, bankers, local politicians, young men, old men, women and children, it did not matter. They came in droves and carted away anything and everything that could be pulled, pried, or loosened from the "Daughter of the Stars." She was stripped bare by the clamoring throngs. Dead crewmen, mouths agape in their last moments of horror, were grotesquely, though unintentionally, part of the public display as their bodies were left in open coffins before being carried away.

As previously noted, Lansdowne had protested the fateful flight. The day after the *Shenandoah* went down, his safe at Lakehurst was opened and documents needed by a court of inquiry to clear his name in the disaster were removed. His personal papers, including Lansdowne's confidential protests against the September 2, 1925, voyage, were gone. Someone with his safe combination had taken the papers within hours after the carnage over Ohio. Lansdowne had anticipated the theft of his papers because his widow, Margaret, would later produce carbon copies that would clear his name of any wrongdoing.

The *Los Angeles* (ZR-3) was the third and last of the rigid airships to be designed and built in Germany. *ZR-3* arrived from Germany on October 15, 1924, and came into service in November of the same year amidst great fanfare. Because of Prohibition, the *Los Angeles* was christened by Grace Coolidge, wife of President of the United States Calvin Coolidge, not with the traditional champagne but with water from the River Jordan in the Holy Land. Further, since Germany could not officially construct the *Los Angeles* as a military aircraft, she was classed by the Navy as the prototype of a commercial aircraft to explore the possibility of regular passenger service.

Regardless of peculiarities of her construction and semantics to describe her mission, the *Los Angeles* spelled new promise for the Navy's lighter-than-air program. She was affectionately called "The Pride of the Navy." Rear Admiral William Adger Moffett (1869–1933), Naval Aviation Observer No. 1,[(6)] heralded the arrival of the *Los Angeles,* convinced that the ship would breathe life into the work of the Bureau of Aeronautics to strengthen the use of airships within the fleet if she was successful in fleet exercises. Moffett was giving airships the opportunity to prove

The USS *Los Angeles* (ZR-3) moored successfully on the USS *Saratoga* (CV-3) at sea off Newport, Rhode Island, on January 27, 1928. The *Los Angeles* remained aboard long enough to transfer passengers and take on fuel, water, and provisions. The photograph shows *Saratoga* crewmen taking the mooring lines of the airship. The behemoth *Los Angeles* expended excess ballast water onto the *Saratoga's* deck just moments after this picture was taken, drenching a number of the ship's crew. (Courtesy of the University of Texas at Dallas.)

their value to the Navy. The *Los Angeles* would serve the latter role faithfully in addition to its use as a training ship for lighter-than-air personnel.

In February 1931, the *Los Angeles* deployed as part of exercise Fleet Problem XII off the west coast of Panama, the first time since 1925 that an airship had been deployed with the fleet. Although the airship was able to locate and spot enemy ships with great ease, it was also quickly spotted and open to attack from enemy aircraft in the exercise. The *Los Angeles* would land successfully on the deck of the aircraft USS *Saratoga* on January 27, 1928, off the coast of Newport, Rhode Island. This feat was tried only once and, perhaps by the grace of the holy water with which she was blessed, the experiment worked. The *Los Angeles* remained aboard the *Saratoga* just long enough to transfer passengers and take on fuel, water, and much-needed supplies.

Lieutenant Commander Rosendahl,(7) by now her commanding officer, could be proud of the "Pride of the Navy." The grand *Los Angeles* amassed 5,366 flight hours in her 331 flights between 1924 and 1932, a record for American Navy airships of her day, but the Great Depression brought a swift and sure end to large dirigibles in the Navy. When the *Los Angeles* was decommissioned on June 30, 1932, the budget for her operation, maintenance, and personnel was down to $270,000, nowhere approaching the budget needed to maintain and operate a large dirigible in the fleet.

The "Pride of the Navy" was nearing the end of its career when the Navy revealed its plans to construct the finest and largest class of rigid dirigibles in the world. The USS *Akron,* dubbed the "Queen of the Skies," was constructed by the Goodyear-Zeppelin Corporation of Akron, Ohio, for $8,000,000. At 785 feet in length, the behemoth airship held 6,850,000 cubic feet of helium. Her Goodyear-Zeppelin designers had created what they believed to be the ultimate in safe airships. *Akron* was designed with three reinforced keels to prevent the same breakup that downed the *Shenandoah,* and her duralumin parts had been treated with aluminized varnish to prevent corrosion. On August 8, 1931, *Akron* was christened by the wife of President of the United States Herbert H. Hoover.

The *Akron* was taken on her maiden voyage, August 23, 1931, by Lieutenant Commander Rosendahl, by now a veteran of the *Shenandoah* and *Los Angeles*. Rosendahl was the officer-in-charge of *Akron's* precommissioning trial flights, a position he assumed on April 21, 1931. The "Queen of the Skies" was commissioned on October 21, 1931, at which time Rosendahl became her commanding officer.[8]

Rosendahl's airship was, to put it simply, the epitomé of sophistication. She had eight inboard engines and could make eighty miles per hour with ease. *Akron's* fighter-observation airplanes were carried in a seventy-by-fifty-eight-foot hangar inside the hull. Aircraft could be picked up and lowered with the assistance of a trapeze device lowered through the bottom of the airship.

Though the *Akron* performed satisfactorily, many Navy officers doubted the airship would be useful in combat. Dirigibles were too easily spotted and targeted for destruction in fleet exercises, *Akron* included. Dirigibles were also fast succumbing to the aircraft carrier, the Navy's fastest growing and most important research and development program. To state that the *Akron* was a wholly unsuccessful aerial platform would belie the fact that she made several flights without incident. Yet despite her accident-proof design, Rosendahl noted a series of problematic incidents which warranted caution.

The evening of April 3, 1933, at 7:28 p.m., *Akron* lifted off from Lakehurst with Commander Frank C. McCord in command and Lieutenant Commander Herbert V. Wiley, Naval Aviator No. 3183, as executive officer. The purpose of the flight was to calibrate radio compass stations in the First Naval District[9] and train junior aviators. Three of naval aviation's most important officers were aboard for the evening, Rear Admiral William Adger Moffett, Chief of the Bureau of Aeronautics; Commander Henry B. Cecil, Naval Aviator No. 42, and head of the Flight Division of the Bureau of Aeronautics; and Commander Fred T. Berry, commanding officer of Naval Air Station Lakehurst.

Weather conditions, marginal when *Akron* lifted off, only deteriorated as the flight progressed. McCord headed west at 7:39 p.m. with six of eight engines turning. Thinking it prudent, McCord kept the airship over coastal reaches until the skies in front of him cleared. The *Akron* headed north to make Newport, Rhode Island, by seven the following morning. At 8 p.m. *Akron* was over Philadelphia, Pennsylvania. Lightning flashed to the south. Lieutenant Herbert M. Wescoat, Naval Aviator No. 3912, reported there were thunderstorms over Washington, D.C., one hour earlier. With this information in hand, McCord decided to reverse direction and, with all eight engines running, turned east through increasingly dense fog. *Akron* transversed the coast near Atlantic City, New Jersey, as lightning flashed closer and heavy rain began pelting the windscreen of the control car. Wiley, more experienced than any other airman on the flight, including Frank McCord, recommended McCord revert to his westerly course, but the *Akron's* commanding officer disagreed with Wiley and ordered the helmsmen to head northeast. McCord's decision proved flawed, the skies the deceptive calm before the storm.

The air was still, but horizontal and vertical lightning intensified as the airship neared the city of Asbury Park, New Jersey. Static fouled radio transmission and an aerial antenna was reeled in to prevent a lightning strike. Wiley reiterated his suggestion they set course due west, but, again, McCord decided to turn east and then south to move in front of the storm center. Hindsight put aside, it would have been safer to move out of the storm's path and plot the airship on a secure course east.

In a desperate attempt to get a weather bulletin over the radio, McCord ordered the aerial lowered just a few feet, risking the threat of lightning all around at 1,600 feet. At 11 p.m., McCord ordered the helmsmen to head back to the coast. This would have given cause for sighs of relief by everyone in the control car except for two things. The navigator had lost *Akron's* position because of veering winds. Secondly, the helmsmen had misunderstood the captain's previous order to make a *fifteen* degree heading change, hearing instead *fifty* degrees, and executed accordingly.

The New Jersey shoreline was spotted before midnight. McCord ordered the course changed to 120 degrees. This did not help. Just after midnight, *Akron* lost altitude quickly in exceptionally strong down currents but was brought back to 1,600 feet, weighed off, and discovered to be about 5,000 pounds heavy. Three minutes elapsed, and by then the *Akron* had come upon more turbulent air. The great airship started down once again. When increasing speed and use of elevators failed to stop the descent, Wiley sounded, "landing stations." *Akron* was falling at fourteen feet per second, up by the nose.

McCord, Wiley and the rest of the crew of seventy-six heard girders snap, which severed both elevator and rudder controls. According to records, there was no confusion in the control car, only the fear and desperation of men listening to the shrieking moans of an airship coming apart. At two hundred feet, Wiley ordered, "stand by for crash." Still falling rapidly up by the nose, the lower tail fin struck the water hard, shearing away the lower rudder and collapsing the tail section. The impact of the tail brought the nose down and carried the entire airship into the sea. *Akron* collapsed and sank in roughly 105 feet of the Atlantic Ocean. The time was 12:26 a.m. on April 4, 1933, about twenty-seven nautical miles and 140 degrees from Barnegat Inlet Light, New Jersey. The safest and most sophisticated airship in the Navy had gone down without one life preserver and just one fourteen-man life raft for seventy-six crew.

The men of the *Akron* who perished did not die from the crash, but of drowning. The three survivors, Lieutenant Commander Wiley, Boatswain's Mate Second Class (BM2c) Richard E. Deal and Aviation Metalsmith Second Class (AMS2c) Moody Irwin had grabbed hold of floating gas tanks and debris. All three later testified they heard the voices of those who could not find flotation and who eventually drowned. The sound of *Akron's* dying crew, including guests Moffett, Cecil, and Berry, began as voices tinged with fear and ended with the gasps and screams of men slipping below dark, stormy seas. Wiley, Deal and Irwin were saved by the German oil tanker *Phoebus* which had to fight twelve-foot seas and a forty-five-mile-hour gale to get

The original Goodyear airship NC-8A *Volunteer* pictured here was procured by the Navy from the company's advertising fleet just prior to the outbreak of World War II. Upon acquisition by the Navy, the *Volunteer* (L-4) and her sister ship, L-5, were actually assigned Bureau Numbers 09801 and 09802, respectively, unlike the remaining L-type airships of her class to follow and serve the Navy. The Navy's designation for the *Volunteer* was ZNN-L, "L" standing for the L-type. This photograph was taken circa 1930 while the *Volunteer* was still part of Goodyear's advertising fleet. Goodyear had begun its blimp program in 1925 with the introduction of its first helium-filled public relations airship, the *Pilgrim*. Most of the blimps which followed the *Pilgrim* were named for winners of the America's Cup yacht race. (Photographer unknown.)

The K-class blimp, built as a training ship in the early 1930s, was the first American lighter-than-air craft constructed to use gaseous instead of liquid fuel and the prototype for patrol airships in the Second World War. The Goodyear designed *K-1* (Bureau Number 9992) was an entirely experimental airship and the first to have an all-metal car attached flush to the 320,000-cubic-foot gas envelope which made it the largest nonrigid airship manufactured for the Navy at that time. Constructed by the Naval Aircraft Factory in 1931, the *K-1* was powered by two 330-horsepower J-6-9 tractor engines. The *K-1* was also known as the blimp which pioneered the use of a mobile mooring mast, critical to forward deployment of airships in World War II. (Official United States Navy Photograph.)

to them. *Akron's* three survivors personally briefed President of the United States Franklin Delano Roosevelt on April 5, 1933, providing the president with detailed descriptions of the tragedy which claimed so many lives.

Included in Rear Admiral Moffett's five-year plan of airship development was *Akron's* sister ship, USS *Macon*. Moffett's plan, approved by Congress in 1926, called for ten *Akron*-class rigid airships to be built. Loss of the *Akron* in 1933 placed increasing pressure and public attention on construction of the *Macon*.

At 859 feet long with a helium capacity of 7,430,000 cubic feet, *Macon* was powered, like the *Akron,* by eight 560-horsepower German Maybach engines. Her engine number was eventually reduced to six. The wife of Rear Admiral Moffett had christened the airship at Goodyear-Zeppelin in Akron, Ohio, less than a month before the admiral would die aboard the *Akron*. She named the *Macon* for the largest city in the congressional district of Carl Vinson, then chairman of the United States House of Representatives Committee on Naval Affairs.

Unlike the ship's predecessors, the Navy decided to base the USS *Macon* on the West Coast after her test flights had been completed. Construction of a new airship base was already underway as *Macon* began her test flights on April 21, 1933. Three additional test flights, the last ending on June 14, 1933, preceded her commissioning on June 23 at Goodyear-Zeppelin. Commander Alger Dresel, Naval Aviator No. 3665, was *Macon's* first commanding officer and Lieutenant Commander Joseph Arnold, Naval Aviator No. 3184, her first executive officer. USS *Macon* departed Lakehurst on October 12, 1933, and headed for her new home at Moffett Field, Naval Air Station Sunnyvale, California.

The last of the Navy's great rigid dirigibles made a series of interesting cross-country excursions as she participated in fleet exercises on both coasts. In April of 1934, *Macon* was in Opa-locka, Florida, taking part in an exercise with the scouting fleet. The trip was punctuated by the wildlife which joined the crew on their voyages around the Caribbean. Owls roosted inside the airship's superstructure and stubbornly refused to give up their new mobile home, even on exercises far from land in the middle of the Caribbean Sea. *Macon* had truly become "the eyes of the fleet" with her fearless owl crew aboard. On the return flight to California in May, crewmen discovered a

Naval Air Station Weeksville, North Carolina, was commissioned on April 1, 1942, with blimp operations commencing June 8. The base was 822 acres and had enough hangar space to accommodate twelve Navy K-class airships. Base barracks, visible in the photograph, could house about 700 enlisted personnel and 150 officers. Airdock No. 1, on the far right, was completed on November 3, 1942. At 960 feet long, 328 feet wide and 190 feet high, Airdock No. 1 is 7.3 acres of steel airship enclosure. The weight of each leaf of the hangar's clamshell-type doors is 420-tons. Construction of Airdock No. 2, located in the upper left of the photograph, was started in July 1942 and finished on July 15, 1943. Airdock No. 2 was 1,080 feet long, approximately 1/5 of a mile, and 298 feet wide. The floor to ceiling height of the hangar was 177 feet though its outside frame reached 192 feet. Airdock No. 2 provided 7.5 acres of blimp storage space, the equivalent of about six football fields. Unlike Airdock No. 1, No. 2 was built with over two million board feet of fire retardant treated Southern yellow pine cut to dimensions of 3" x 8" to 6" x 14". Blimp squadrons at Weeksville were ordered disestablished on May 31, 1957. The last local flights by Weeksville airships occurred on June 12, 1957, during the International Naval Review in the Chesapeake Bay. Naval Air Facility Weeksville was decommissioned on June 30, 1957, and the Navy lighter-than-air program ended in 1961. On August 3, 1995, Airdock No. 2 was destroyed by a pre-dawn fire. Westinghouse Airships' *Sentinel 1000,* the largest airship in the world, was destroyed in the hangar at approximately 12:55 am. Airdock No. 1 was purchased by TCOM, manufacturer of airships and aerostats, in 1996 and its clamshell-type doors restored to working order. The photograph was taken about 1950. (Courtesy of the University of Texas at Dallas.)

two-foot stowaway alligator in one of the water ballast bags. The crew felt obliged to catch their little gator friend and serve him up for dinner.

Like her sister airship *Akron, Macon* was never utilized properly by the fleet, and subsequently proved a liability in tactical combat exercises in 1933 and 1934. Commander-in-Chief of the United States Fleet, Admiral David F. Sellers remarked that *Macon* was not a useful fighting platform, and he denied the six million of funding per airship required for the next round of *Akron*-class airships.

Lieutenant Commander Herbert V. Wiley, former executive officer of the *Akron* and one of her three survivors, took command of the *Macon* on July 11, 1934. Wiley came at a time when his leadership and airship skills were desperately needed. The *Macon* had experienced significant tail damage during a previous flight that had not been fully repaired prior to Wiley taking command. He insisted the damage be repaired properly. The only way Wiley could convince the Navy Department to do a thorough overhaul and repair of the airship's tail section was to guarantee no interruptions in *Macon's* operational schedule. A complete repair could not be achieved while operations continued, but Wiley was left with few equitable options.

Repairs were not complete when *Macon* was ordered out on February 11, 1935, to participate in war games off the coast of Los Angeles. Her crew of eighty-one was joined that day by two guests, Lieutenant Clinton S. Rounds, Naval Aviator No. 3675, and Commander Alfred T. Clay, Naval Aviator No. 3808 and prospective commanding officer of Naval Air Station Sunnyvale. The *Macon* also took aboard five fighter aircraft en route to the operating area.

During the course of the evening, *Macon* encountered rough air currents. At 10:30 a.m. on February 12, the airship was located just west of Los Angeles. Fleet exercises proved very successful for the *Macon* as she deployed her Curtiss F9C-2 Sparrowhawk aircraft to scout "the enemy" in various combat scenarios. *Macon's* fighter aircraft were best used as scouting planes over sweeping areas of the ocean. Her scouting aircraft were capable of covering as much as 130,000 square miles of ocean in one day.

The *Macon* completed participation in the prescribed exercises at 2 p.m. on the twelfth, and Wiley ordered the helmsmen to set course for Moffett Field. With her aircraft recovered and tucked away in their hangar bay, the *Macon* headed for Point Sur at 3:55 p.m. A little after 4 p.m., the *Macon* was struck by a squall which caused her to rise 1,200 feet and drop 1,100 feet in less than ten minutes. By 4:15 p.m., Wiley had brought the *Macon* down to 1,700 feet to pass under a cloud spitting a steady stream of torrential rain over the airship. The navigator advised Wiley the airship would be three miles off Point Sur at 5:05 p.m.

Macon would never get that close. A gust of wind dropped the already vulnerable tail section sharply at 5:03 p.m. as a steady soft rain came over the control car's windscreen. Crewmen in the tail section witnessed the top of the tail fin wrenched away and a number of helium cells ripped open. The mighty airship began to yaw on course. The rudder and elevator wheels were torn from the grip of *Macon's* helmsmen. Three minutes passed. At 5:06 p.m. the remaining tail section had begun to break up and rudder controls were carried away. Nine minutes later Wiley ordered the radioman to issue an SOS. Admiral Sellers was sent a message informing him that the *Macon* was breaking up at sea. Girders began to snap. Officers and enlisted crewmen in the aft section received orders to move forward on the outside chance their doing so might correct the airship's up-nose position. Some of *Macon's* crew seemed little impressed by the gravity of the situation and reportedly joked about their predicament and complained about Navy life.

At 5:18 p.m. Wiley ordered evacuation of the *Macon's* five fighter aircraft. Less than seven minutes later, the dirigible rocketed to five thousand feet, then began plummeting three hundred feet per minute until levelling off at three thousand feet. Wiley ordered a message sent to the crew at 5:36 p.m. to abandon ship as soon as she made contact with the water, then estimated to be about twenty miles from Point Sur or ten miles off the California coast. Forward emergency ballast was released at five hundred feet. Wiley's final order was for everyone to move out of the control car just as the last of *Macon's* emergency tanks had been discharged. *Macon's* tail struck the ocean at 5:40 p.m. and bounced, pitching forty men overboard from a distance of less than ten to one hundred feet above the sea. Forty minutes later, the nose of the Navy's last great rigid airship slipped under the Pacific Ocean. All but two of *Macon's* crew of eighty-three survived because she was equipped with an adequate supply of life rafts and life preservers to go around. The two who perished, a radioman named Dailey and a messboy listed only as "Edquiba" on the *Macon's* crew list, drowned. Most of the eighty-one crew who survived were plucked from the water by 7:30 p.m.

The loss of the USS *Akron* was by far the most devastating blow to the Navy lighter-than-air program. The "Queen of the Skies" had taken with her Rear Admiral Moffett, the man who structured the aviation component of the Navy through the addition of aircraft carriers, seaplanes, rigid dirigibles, and air stations. The champion of airships, and the Navy's chief of the Bureau of Aeronautics (1921–1933), was dead. If the *Akron* had not been a decisive enough loss foreshadowing the end of the rigid airship Navy, the loss of the USS *Macon* on her fifty-fifth flight most certainly was.

The *Macon* tragedy also drew public opinion into the argument against the colossal airships, and the court of public opinion determined the airships were too dangerous. The Navy Department was all too willing to concur, since it had previously adjudged the rigid dirigibles useless. At this critical juncture, the Navy's interest turned to flying boats and dive-bombers. The demise of the German dirigible *Hindenburg* on May 6, 1937, was the final nail in the coffin of airships. As the story goes, German Air Marshal Hermann Göring had Zeppelins melted down and used their valuable duralumin for his warplanes. The Navy was lucky with the USS *Los Angeles,* the only dirigible which never lost one of her crewmen. The *Los Angeles* would become the only airship in United States naval aviation history to be gracefully retired to hangar storage.

Throughout the Second World War, the Navy employed nonrigid blimps for coastal patrol and convoy escort duty. The first blimp to land at Naval Air Station Weeksville, North Carolina, near Elizabeth City, was *K-3* on May 6, 1942. Weeksville was transformed into a major base of operations for airship patrol squadrons on the East Coast during the war. The K-class became the workhorse of the airship Navy. Blimp Patrol Squadron Fourteen (ZP-14)(10) had numerous airships in and out of Weeksville in 1942 alone, including *K-8, K-10, K-12*, and in mid-1943, *K-13* and *K-18*. The scarred earth at Weeksville belies the history of the place. Most of the hangars which housed the great airships are gone. In their place only building footprints remain, cheating history of physical reminders of the the airship Navy. Only one of the original blimp hangars remains at Weeksville, testimony of sorts to the days when Rear Admiral Moffett was so assured airships were the future of naval aviation.

In its impressive record of service to the Navy, only one K-class airship was ever lost to enemy marksmen in the Second World War. Airship *K-74,* on a late night patrol off the coast of Florida July 18, 1943, encountered a surfaced U-boat and in the heat of the fierce gun battle which ensued, was hit and brought down in the Atlantic Ocean. The German submarine *U-134* was damaged enough by the *K-74* to force her speedy return to base, or so thought her crew. After surviving two subsequent attacks on the way, *U-134* was ultimately sunk in the Bay of Biscay by even better British bomber gunners. The Navy would gradually move its blimp squadrons farther south, fanning coverage away from the mid-Atlantic and its bases in close proximity to Hampton Roads. On September 27, 1943, blimps began operating in the South Atlantic out of Fortaleza, Brazil.(11)

The Navy did not end its blimp—not to be confused with the dirigible—program until October 31, 1961, at which time the service disestablished its last lighter-than-air wing and squadrons.(12) Fleet Airship Wing One and Blimp Patrol Squadrons ZP-1 and -3, the last operating units of the lighter-than-air part of United States naval aviation, were disestablished at Naval Air Station Lakehurst.

With their increased use in the Atlantic Fleet, lighter-than-air forces were placed under Fleet Airships, Atlantic Fleet, and the Fleet Airships Groups which had been operating under Fleet Airships Wing Thirty were designated fleet airship wings. Captain George H. Mills, Naval Aviator No. 3925, and a survivor of the famous USS *Macon* disaster, commanded Fleet Airships, Atlantic Fleet, as well as its precursor. Mills' headquarters was located at Naval Air Station Lakehurst, New Jersey.

Chapter 7: Incidents, Accidents, and Flights of Fame

When Lieutenant Murray, the air station's executive officer, left Hampton Roads in late 1918 to become the first commanding officer of Naval Air Station Anacostia,(1) in Washington, D.C., he was replaced by a temporary executive officer, Lieutenant George Samuel "George" Gillespie, Naval Aviator No. 32, and eventually Lieutenant Ganson Goodyear "Gans" Depew, NRFC, Naval Aviator No. 121, of Buffalo, New York, a man described by some in 1919 as "an old timer in naval aviation." Depew had organized and placed himself officer-in-charge of Unit Two of the Aerial Coast Patrol which was in existence before any such unit existed in naval aviation for the reserves. Practically every one of the pilots who trained in this unit would hold important positions in naval aviation at one time or another. Depew eventually went to Pensacola as an instructor, progressing up the chain of command to division commander, squadron commander, operations aide, and finally executive officer, at Naval Air Station Pensacola.

"Gans" Depew was nothing short of brilliant in terms of planning and supervision. Upon leaving his tour at Pensacola, he was sent to the Office of Naval Operations (Aviation) where he fine tuned his organizational skills. Depew came to Norfolk as flight superintendent where he made sweeping administrative and operational changes to the air station. As executive officer, Depew has been credited with making Naval Air Station Hampton Roads the best patrol station in the history of early naval aviation. His organization plan at Hampton Roads was approved by the

The administrative heads of Naval Air Station Hampton Roads, circa late 1918. Front row (left to right): an unidentified lieutenant (nonaviator); Lieutenant Ganson Goodyear "Gans" Depew, USNR, Naval Aviator No. 121; Lieutenant Commander Patrick N.L. Bellinger, Naval Aviator No. 8; an unidentified lieutenant commander (nonaviator); and an unidentified lieutenant (nonaviator). Back row (left to right): an unidentified lieutenant (nonaviator); an unidentified lieutenant (junior grade)(aviator); an unidentified ensign (aviator); Lieutenant (junior grade) Robert Livingston "Liv" Ireland, USNR, Naval Aviator No. 84; Lieutenant John Vorys, Naval Aviator No. 73; Lieutenant Louis Theodore Barin, Naval Aviator No. 56; an unidentified ensign (nonaviator); an unidentified lieutenant (nonaviator); an unidentified lieutenant (nonaviator); an unidentified lieutenant (junior grade)(nonaviator); an unidentified ensign (specialty undetermined); and another unidentified ensign (aviator). Depew was the flight superintendent and executive officer of the air station. Bellinger was commanding officer, Naval Air Station Hampton Roads. Ireland was detailed as officer-in-charge of Naval Air Station Morehead City, North Carolina, in September of 1918, a patrol station under the command of Naval Air Station Hampton Roads. Barin was an experimental and test pilot at Hampton Roads from July 1918 until his assignment with Bellinger in April 1919 when he became copilot of NC-1. Barin was killed at five minutes to ten the morning of June 12, 1920, in an aircraft accident at Rockwell Field, North Island, San Diego, California. (Courtesy of the Hampton Roads Naval Museum.)

A closer view of the famous Curtiss F-boat, Bureau Number A2305, taken at Naval Air Station Hampton Roads in 1918, shows the proximity of the pilots to the engine. This was not a large aircraft, measuring only a little under twenty-eight feet in length and just over eleven feet in height. The wingspan was forty-five feet, one and three-eighths inches. Accidents in an F-boat were nearly always fatal, the pilots either crushed by the impact or burned to death by the engine after being caught in the wreckage. (Official United States Navy Photograph.)

Navy Department and ordered into effect at all other patrol stations stateside and overseas. Depew was perhaps one of the most colorful personalities of early aviation, but one unsung in terms of achievement. As the nephew of Senator Chauncey M. Depew of New York, Ganson was accustomed to public life and driven by accomplishment. Sadly, he would die young—at the age of twenty-eight—on March 21, 1924, of a ruptured appendix, cutting short what promised to be a productive and distinguished career in naval aviation.

Unfortunately, no one, not even "Gans" Depew, could change the beleaguered life of patrol pilots. They reported for work at four o'clock in the morning, often flying before sunrise. Late patrols or emergency calls frequently came in after dark when the only light to guide the pilots was that flickering from the engine. The reality of a crash touched depths of feeling few brotherhoods could ever know. The deep sea patrol experiences of Hampton Roads pilots conveyed much of the character of their service, and commitment to protect the home front. With war's end, flying continued at a feverish pace, most of it focused on experimental aircraft and communications equipment, conditions of flight, and extended distance and altitude testing. The pilots of this period, many of them with experience from the First World War, were as colorful as any before or after them, flying their passion and sometimes their end.

The week of November 11, 1918, Armistice Day, Ensign Rutledge "Irv" Irvine, Naval Aviator No. 1001 (later renowned for his participation on the Schneider Cup Race team of 1923 and his air racing exploits in general), departed on a flight from Hampton Roads neither he nor fellow pilot, Ensign Frederick Lathrop "Fred" Tracy, Naval Aviator No. 724, would ever forget. Irvine was flying seaplane No. 1909, Tracy No. 1207, when they reached a point about thirty miles southeast of Cape Henry, Virginia. The two climbed out of a fog bank at fifteen hundred feet when something snapped on the motor of Irvine's aircraft, severing the gas lead from the gravity tank and setting the engine on fire. Irvine made an emergency landing at sea. Once on the ocean, the whole plane became engulfed in flames. His Pyrene in the front cockpit was not enough to douse the flames that licked closer to the main fuel tank. With the danger of explosion imminent, Irvine and his two crewmen leapt into the Atlantic Ocean. In the meantime, Tracy saw what was happening and landed within a safe distance of No. 1909. After skillful juxtapositioning, Tracy picked up the downed crew and began taxiing thirty miles back to Norfolk. On the way to the naval air station, the crew of No. 1909 was taken off Tracy's plane by a submarine patrol boat, enabling Tracy to fly back to the base. For his skill and daring in the rescue of the three crewmen, Ensign Tracy would receive a letter of commendation from the Secretary of the Navy.

The Curtiss-designed F-boat pictured here, Bureau Number A3331, was manufactured by the American Trans-Oceanic Company for Curtiss Aeroplane and Motor Company of Hammondsport, New York, and Buffalo, New York. The flying boat was a trainer for Navy pilots, shown in the photograph getting ready to take out the aircraft for a flight from Naval Air Station Hampton Roads in 1918. The pilot and instructor sat side by side below a 100-horsepower Curtiss OXX power plant. (Courtesy of the Hampton Roads Naval Museum.)

This British-built Sopwith baby seaplane, Bureau Number A394, was the only one of its make to be acquired by the United States Navy. Its distinctive squadron insignia, the famous hat in a ring, suggests this aircraft was flown by a pilot familiar with the American 94th Pursuit Squadron, Captain Eddie Rickenbacker's squadron, which used this distinctive insignia. Taken at Naval Air Station Hampton Roads on August 10, 1918, the aircraft made its appearance but a few times. Story has it that Rickenbacker popularized the insignia among military pilots. This is evidenced by the photograph from a recruiting poster (below) taken of three Gallaudet-manufactured Curtiss HS-2L flying boats on the levee at Memphis, Tennessee, in the late spring of 1918. An embellished hat in a ring is on two of the aircraft. (Official United States Navy Photograph.)

Further excitement would stir the station on November 27, 1918, when two patrol aircraft in the charge of Ensign Henry Coe "Coe" Lanpher, Naval Aviator No. 1264, and Ensign John Vernon "John" Manners, Naval Aviator No. 923, reached a point well out to sea when difficulties forced Lanpher to land. He signalled Manners to send for a tow at quarter to twelve in the morning. By the time Manners reported it was ten minutes to one in the afternoon and Lanpher's last known position adrift was provided to Ensign Richard Newcomb Stillwell, Naval Aviator No. 00,[(2)] who struck out in search of Lanpher close to two o'clock in the afternoon. Stillwell was able to locate Lanpher in about an

The significance of this photograph lies in the pilots gathered around the Curtiss JN-4HG at Marine Corps Airfield Miami,(3) Florida, in the spring of 1918. The JN-4HG was a gunnery trainer equipped with a 150-horsepower Wright-Hispano engine or "Hisso," a nickname given by aviators to the engine, and the letters "H" for Hispano and "G" for gunnery clarified modifications to the aircraft made in 1918. Captain Bernard Lewis "Barney" Smith, USMC, Naval Aviator No. 6, Marine Corps Aviator No. 2, stands to the immediate right of the aircraft cowling. Smith established, built, and operated a school for aerial gunnery and bomb delivery at Miami, Florida, in late 1917. Third from Smith is Captain William Maitland "Mac" McIlvain, USMC, Naval Aviator No. 12, Marine Corps Aviator No. 3, who was assigned at the time this photograph was taken to the First Marine Aviation Force (FMAF) when it was organized at Miami on April 15, 1918. McIlvain became commanding officer of Squadron B on the sixteenth of June, and took his unit to Brest, France, to train as part of the FMAF contingent with the British and French. Squadron B became Squadron Eight and began flying missions over Oye, France. McIlvain and his squadron went into battle over the skies of Knessalare, Belgium, in October, flying three combat missions against the enemy. The FMAF, including McIlvain, returned to Naval Air Station Hampton Roads in December of 1918, leaving for their homebase at Miami in January of 1919. Among those returning with the FMAF were Second Lieutenant George McCully "Dizzy" Laughlin III, USMCR, Naval Aviator No. 165, assigned No. 790 by the Marine Corps upon transferring from the Navy May 26, 1918, a winner of the Navy Cross; and, Second Lieutenant Chester Julius "Chet" Peters, USMCR, Naval Aviator No. 806. During the Second World War, Peters became the commanding officer of the Marine Corps Air Station at Edenton, North Carolina. He died in the line of duty as a lieutenant colonel, October 4, 1944, in an airplane crash near Plymouth, North Carolina. (Official United States Navy Photograph.)

hour and a half due in large part to his great navigation skill.

Another incident perhaps more dramatic than Lanpher's rescue had occurred before the truce in Europe. The afternoon of October 30, 1918, a message was received by the refueling station at Assateague, Virginia, from the pilot of a patrol seaplane who lost sight of his wingman, an HS-2, Bureau Number A1195, with Ensign Charles Mortimer Sanborn, Naval Aviator No. 953, and Cadet Officer Howard "R" Miller, future Naval Aviator No. 1425, aboard. In all likelihood, the plane had been forced to land a few miles offshore; the accompanying pilot was not sure. With a thick fog bank rolling in and low on fuel, the pilot flying Sanborn's wing was unable to execute a proper search before returning to Assateague.

The wind offshore was blowing about twenty-five knots. Two H-12s and four HS-2s were immediately dispatched from Hampton Roads to search for the missing plane. All United States Coast Guard stations were notified, as was the Fifth Naval District,(4) Fourth Naval District,(5) and Naval Air Station Cape May, New Jersey. Two destroyers got the call, along with six subchasers. The search continued the rest of the day and all the following day using boats, seven seaplanes from Norfolk, and four seaplanes from Cape May with four more en route from same. A total of eight surface craft and fifteen seaplanes would look for the downed aircrew.

No trace was found of the seaplane and no one heard from Sanborn and Miller until the morning of the third day when they called Norfolk from Hoboken, New Jersey. Sanborn and Miller's HS-2 apparently developed problems, and they landed out of fuel and drifted from nearly noon on the thirtieth of October for another twenty-four hours. Near lunchtime on October 31, the seaplane

The two Curtiss H-12 flying boats, Bureau Numbers A781 and A770, were photographed in 1917 at what became Naval Air Station Hampton Roads. These aircraft were the new, improved version of a flying boat ordered in 1914 by Rodman Wanamaker, who planned to use the aircraft he had dubbed *"America"* for transatlantic flight. The Navy ordered the upgraded design in 1916 and the aircraft was designated the H-12, though it was affectionately referred to as a "Large America." There were only nineteen of these aircraft in the H-12 production line, including the two shown here. (Courtesy of the Hampton Roads Naval Museum.)

and its crew were plucked from the Atlantic Ocean by an Army transport tug which was not equipped with a wireless. Though relieved at their rescue, both airmen had had a couple of close calls during the night. Three other vessels had approached the seaplane, but as soon as the pilots fired their Very lights, the ships put out all their lights and hastened retreat. The Fourth Naval District later reported winds upwards of fifty miles per hour and rolling seas, but the seaplane did not break up. Sanborn and Miller had used the plane's sea anchor to ride the waves. The aircraft did not break up until under tow by the tug. Rough seas crumpled the wings and the plane turned over and sank.

Naval Air Station Hampton Roads would see many greats come and go, but one of best was surely an original member of the First Yale Unit, Lieutenant John Martin "John" Vorys, Naval Aviator No. 73. Vorys was a seasoned combat pilot by the time he returned to the United States in March 1918 to train the Whiting Unit at Naval Air Station Hampton Roads. His wartime exploits, not the least of which was his involvement as one of the first two naval aviators (the other being Ensign Albert Dillon "Al" Sturtevant, NRFC, Naval Aviator No. 77, also his roommate) assigned to fly patrols with the infamous British unit known as the Spider Web Patrol, were significant. At his roommate's request, Vorys swapped flights with Sturtevant on February 15, 1918, and, as fate would have it, Sturtevant became the first naval aviator killed in enemy action the same day.

Vorys had come into early naval aviation with Trubee Davison, Ganson Depew (Naval Aviator No. 121), and David Hugh McCulloch (Naval Aviator No. 168 and the pilot of the NC-3 seaplane on the famed transatlantic flight of 1919), who formed the nucleus of naval aviation after the First World War. He was destined to advance naval aviation both by invention and flying skill. He, along with Ensign Leslie Price "Jake" Jacobs, NRFC, Naval Aviator No. 526, invented the Vorys-Jacobs Bombsight, a hardwood bombsight used during the summer of 1918 on nearly all patrol planes at Naval Air Station Hampton Roads.

Vorys was an interesting person who savored every opportunity to fly and thought each flight should be tinged with some kind of adventure even if he had no idea what the adventure was going to be. The very first time he flew to Washington, D.C., he got into an air pocket which caused the plane to abruptly drop four hundred feet. On another occasion, he flew one thousand miles in fourteen hours, visiting every air station on the East Coast. Yet again, Vorys would fly for three hours in a torrential rain storm with high winds which, toward the end of the flight, were gusting at 45 knots. His crewman on that flight needed nerves of steel and extra stomach powders. Every time Vorys momentarily took his eyes off the instruments, the crewman held up a piece of paper on which he had scribbled, "Let's land." Eventually, Vorys gave in and landed, much to his passenger's satisfaction. There would be other times when Vorys tested the winds. He once flew from Chincoteague to Hampton Roads in fifty knot winds. By the time he reached the air station, Vorys was forced to back his plane through the arch at the Grand Basin because the wind was so bad and the sea so rough. Of the nineteen pilots out that night, Vorys was the only one who dared fly home.

Vorys' job as a patrol pilot was a dangerous but exciting one: fly low and look for enemy submarines. He was on patrol within fourteen miles of the spot where the *O.B. Jennings*(6) was torpedoed on August 14, 1918, by a German U-boat just outside the Virginia Capes operating area. At quarter to six the afternoon of August 16, 1918, Vorys again jumped into his plane with emergency orders taking him to Cape Hatteras, North Carolina. His message read, "The *Mirlo*(7) being shelled by sub." Vorys headed down the coast at seventy miles per

A Boeing manufactured HS-2L flying boat (Bureau Number A4236), photographed May 10, 1919, in the New Assembly Building at Naval Air Station Hampton Roads, was quite a grand aircraft. A Curtiss Aeroplane Company design, the HS-2L was powered by one 350-horsepower Liberty twelve-cylinder engine and, during the postwar period, remained the premier patrol and training aircraft both at Norfolk and other naval air stations across the United States. (Official United States Navy Photograph.)

hour, and, by quarter to eight, he came upon the *Mirlo,* broken in two and sending smoke and flames into the air. He circled around in search of the German U-boat, his bombs at the ready, but found nothing. In complete darkness, Vorys started back to Norfolk around half past eight, following the breakers on the coastline because it was too dark to see his compass. About an hour later, he landed at the station.

Though Vorys had fully intended to return to fight in Europe with the Whiting Unit, the war was drawing to a close and his skills were needed at Hampton Roads. He remained on staff at the air station until January of 1919, at which time he retired from active duty. Vorys would later become a four-term United States congressman from Ohio.

Navigation in the early days of naval aviation was, as one observer so aptly put it, "very much a matter of moving in the dark." Aviators were easily thrown off course flying over unfamiliar territory. The perfect example of this occurred during early fall of 1918. Ensign DeLos "Tommy" Thomas, Naval Aviator No. 1023, and Ensign Noel E. "Sandy" Sainsbury, student naval aviator, made a rather historic trip south of Hampton Roads. The two aviators were running out of fuel and decided to try landing on inland waters. Without much knowledge of the locale, both flyers found themselves lost over water with a surface like glass all around as far as the eye could see. Forced to land, Thomas and Sainsbury were almost sure they would be unable to take off again, so the two decided to remain overnight and wait until morning to assess their predicament. After some time had gone by, their patience exhausted, the two aviators were startled by a strange, unfamiliar sound close to them near nine o'clock that night. Turning their flashlight toward the noise, they espied a horse attached to a dog cart plodding through the brine. Thomas and Sainsbury had alighted on Albemarle Sound in shoal water which ran a great distance offshore. The water was no more than three feet deep. The horse and the man with wings stared long and hard at one another, the man annoyed at his machine. Thomas' annoyance reached fever pitch by morning. He was so abraded he made Sainsbury get out and push under the water rudder. The plane was quickly aloft but "Sandy" was left standing waist high in water waiting for his pilot to come back and pick him up. The two never again strayed so far inland nor got lost. Thomas and Sainsbury's decision to land and not waste precious fuel trying to find their way out of Albemarle Sound close to darkness proved wise.

Sainsbury never received his wings. He was probably one of the most unlucky student naval aviators in history. On January 28, 1919, Lieutenant (junior grade) Sainsbury and Ensign James Archie "Jimmy" Clark, Naval Aviator No. 407, pilot, took off from Norfolk in a Curtiss MF flying boat, Bureau Number A2347. Sainsbury had flown for awhile before Clark took over and headed for the Norfolk Yacht and Country Club. As Clark passed over the club about twenty minutes past four in the afternoon, the port wing struck the top of a tree near the water's edge, throwing the plane into an horrific skid. Ensign Clark was unable to control the plane as it lost air speed and banked into the water.

Sainsbury was only slightly injured due in large part to the protective head

The Sopwith 1½ Strutter shown here, Bureau Number 5741, circa 1920, was acquired from the United States Army for use as a scouting aircraft on battleships. This aircraft was among the second lot of 1½ Strutters, Bureau Numbers 5734 to 5750, purchased by the Navy. The Navy accepted a total of twenty-two 1½ Strutters into its inventory, A5660, acquired in Europe during the First World War, being the first. The aircraft, originally of British manufacture, had a Clergêt engine. Notice the hydrovanes extending just beyond the forward landing gear. Hydrovanes were thought to break a hard landing and provide flotation should a pilot ditch his aircraft on the water. Quite the opposite was true. Hydrovanes proved more hazard than help, often cartwheeling the aircraft onto its nose and, consequently, its back.

gear he was wearing. Clark wore no cranial protection and died of massive head injuries. The Navy Department thereafter required aviators wear protective head gear.

The week of July 24, 1918, two seaplanes on patrol found a hazard to coastal navigation about sixty miles at sea off the Virginia Capes. With charts in hand and guided by their navigation instruments, the planes pinpointed the obstruction and reported it to the air station. A Navy ship was shortly dispatched with a seaplane escort. The commanding officer of the ship would later commend the effort and rightly so: aerial navigation was in its infancy and finding the derelict vessel was a major accomplishment at that time.

By the last week of October 1918, Lieutenant Hurd Hutchins, NRFC, Naval Aviator No. 140, would set a new record and add to his growing list of accomplishments while stationed at Norfolk. Hutchins had been part of the original Harvard group trained at the old Curtiss school at Newport News, transferring to Hampton Roads in May of 1917. While on regular patrol, Hutchins established the record for continuous flight over the sea at eight hours and twenty minutes. At the time of his record breaking flight Hutchins was also officer-in-charge of the Mechanics' and Quartermasters' School.

In addition to Hutchins' milestone, Naval Air Station Hampton Roads would set a number of important records in short succession. Ensign Robert Dixon "Bob" Hively, Naval Aviator No. 1358, flew from New London, Connecticut, in an HS-2 seaplane in seven hours, fifty-three minutes on December 19, 1918, landing at Norfolk that afternoon. During the last week of December, Lieutenant Alexander "Alex" Strong, Naval Aviator No. 374, in an F-5 seaplane, flew from Hampton Roads to Rockaway, Long Island, New York, in four hours flat. The same week, two divisions of seaplanes, in battle formation, flew to Baltimore, Maryland, where they maneuvered over the fleet for two hours, returning to Norfolk the next day in fog which at times was so thick it was impossible to see the water clearly at an altitude of fifty feet.

Pilots have always loved to share their experiences, some hair-raising, others comical, but never boring. There was one occasion at Hampton Roads in the summer of 1918 which had the entire station abuzz over two pilots who had gone over 12,300 feet, as high as anyone had ever gone, until their engine quit. The airmen plummeted 12,000 feet in a spin. The pilot on the flight, Lieutenant Louis Theodore Barin, Naval Aviator No. 56, was an experimental and test pilot at Hampton Roads who would later become a pilot on the famed NC-1 transatlantic flight in May of 1919. Barin was never satisfied with anything less than perfection, as his copilot, Ensign Donald B. MacMillan, NRFC, soon

24, when he reached his destination without incident. These pilots performed a lifesaving service to the people of Manteo. Grader's efforts, so the story goes, also kept influenza from spreading or intensifying to more populated areas south of Hampton Roads.

Lieutenant Commander Patrick N.L. Bellinger detached as commanding officer of Naval Air Station Hampton Roads on March 20, 1919, to take part in yet another great chapter of naval aviation history: the famed transatlantic flight of 1919 in which NC-4 emerged triumphant. Bellinger would not return to Norfolk, with the exception of passing through, until 1938.

The months immediately following Bellinger's departure would be filled with high expectations for naval aviation in Hampton Roads. But for one unexpected tragedy, this mood would continue. On June 14, 1919, Ensign Charles Haseltine Hammann, USNR, Naval Aviator No. 1494, winner of the Medal of Honor for the rescue of a brother aviator shot down by enemy fire during the First World War, was killed flying an Italian Macchi M-5 flying boat over Langley Field. Hammann, who was attached to the Naval Air Detachment at Langley at that time, was performing as part of a flying circus sponsored by the Army. At roughly twelve hundred feet his plane suddenly plummeted in a horrific, unrecoverable tailspin. The accident made newspaper headlines. Upon reading of Hammann's tragic death while participating in a flying circus, the American public immediately concluded the accident must have been the result of an aerobatic-maneuver-gone-wrong. Hammann's Macchi M-5 was not involved in an aerobatic maneuver at the time of the accident. A court of inquiry determined that his accident probably occurred when the control cable fitting snapped. The investigation also determined Hammann's accident could also be blamed on the performance limits of the aircraft pertaining to spin recovery on dead center, particularly given the awkward placement of its engine. He died instantly. Hammann never saw his Medal of Honor; it was awarded posthumously for, as the citation read:

"For extraordinary heroism as the pilot of a seaplane on August 21, 1918, when with three other planes he took part in a patrol for dropping propaganda on Pola, they encountered and attacked a superior force of enemy landplanes; in the course of the engagement which followed, the plane of Ensign George Hartwell Ludlow, USNR, Naval Aviator No. 342, was shot down, and fell into the water five miles off Pola. Ensign

Ensign Charles Haseltine Hammann, Naval Aviator No. 1494 and the Navy's only aviator awarded the Medal of Honor for combat during the First World War, posed in front of his flying boat at Naval Air Station Porto Corsini, 1918. Hammann made a permanent place for himself in history on August 21, 1918, when a flight of two bombers and five fighters from Porto Corsini was intercepted by a superior force of Austrian aircraft over the naval base at Pola. Ensign George H. Ludlow's (Naval Aviator No. 342) fighter seaplane was forced down at sea, three miles from the Pola harbor entrance, during the air battle which ensued. Hammann evaded the enemy in his damaged aircraft and landed alongside Ludlow, took him aboard, and flew back to Porto Corsini. Hammann received the Silver Medal for military valor from the King of Italy for the same action which earned him the coveted Medal of Honor from his own country. Photographs of Hammann are rare, his life too short. (Courtesy of the National Museum of Naval Aviation.)

discovered. That day Barin tested the nerves of even MacMillan, a famed Arctic explorer who had gone with Rear Admiral Robert E. Peary on his trip to the North Pole. In all his adventures with the admiral, nothing quite matched dropping 12,000 feet with Barin and recovering, with 300 feet to spare, to a safe landing.

The earliest precedent of naval aviators working in concert with the community in Hampton Roads, indeed for its benefit, came on January 1, 1918, when Bellinger and his officers got wind of a great fire in downtown Norfolk—the famous Monticello Hotel blaze. Many naval aviators from the base worked side by side with Norfolk firemen to douse the flames. Lieutenant (junior grade) Robert Livingston "Liv" Ireland, USNR, Naval Aviator No. 84, actually relieved the city's fire marshall.

During the influenza pandemic which killed nearly twenty-five million people around the globe between 1917 and 1919, naval aviators wore wings of mercy. Naval aviators from Hampton Roads bravely assisted those stricken with influenza at Manteo, North Carolina, and its surrounding areas beginning on January 19, 1919. The Spanish influenza had caught local physicians and medical facilities unprepared. The only local travel from Manteo to mainland North Carolina was a ferry service which at that time took seven to eight hours, time people with the influenza could not afford. Ensign George Wilson "Doc" Grader, NRFC, Naval Aviator No. 1887, organized the relief expedition to Manteo, taking with him doctors and supplies. Pilots in the lead plane included Grader and copilot, Ensign Raymond Joseph "Cush" Cushman, Naval Aviator No. 1415, and in the second plane, Ensign William Earnest "Shorty" Widmer, Naval Aviator No. 1201, pilot, and Ensign Robert Leavitt "Bob" Fuller, Naval Aviator No. 1682, copilot. Grader even stayed for a time, caring for the sick and leaving only when doctors needed more medicine. Naval aviators would make regular return trips to the Outer Banks and, on January 21, Ensign Grader endured terrible weather before realizing he could not make it to Manteo safely. His return to Manteo was not possible until January

The Curtiss H-12, Bureau Number A767, shown in this image was taxiing for takeoff off Naval Air Station Hampton Roads on November 24, 1918. Note the insignia on the nose. The United States Naval Academy mascot, a goat, appears to be butting the letters "R U TUF." This H-12 was manufactured in a lot of nineteen of its type, Bureau Numbers A765–A783, which were accepted by the Navy in 1918. (Courtesy of the Hampton Roads Naval Museum.)

Hammann immediately dove down, landed upon the water close alongside the disabled plane, took Ludlow on board, and though his machine was not designed for a double load, and with threat and danger of attack by Austrian planes, made his way to Porto Corsini."(8)

Hammann was the only naval aviator of the First World War to be awarded this decoration for combat,(9) following in a long line of courageous naval personnel to receive the award. At the time of his death, Hammann was augmenting to regular Navy and held orders to the USS *Oklahoma* for duty as an aviator.

World War I brought to the forefront the need to evaluate the awarding of decorations such as the Medal of Honor, Distinguished Service Medal, Navy Cross and, of course, the need to establish a Distinguished Flying Cross to be awarded for feats of valor in the air. The awarding of medals for heroism goes back many centuries, and some historians would agree that the Chinese originated tokens of valor long before the advent of Christianity. During the Crusades in Europe, the armies of the English crown exchanged prizes of war. The very first individual war medal (a medal as we know it today) was presented by Queen Elizabeth I of England in honor of the British Navy, so naval decorations were the first to be given. There was an American custom dating to the Revolutionary War in which Congress, on the recommendation of General George Washington, accorded John Paulding, David Williams, and Jacob Van Wart (who had captured Major André, the British spy) the honor of being awarded a token of their country's indebtedness for their act of courage and valor. The medals Congress awarded these gentlemen were silver, quite simple in design with but one word on the face, "Fidelity," and on the reverse, the legend, *"Vincit Amor Patriae,"* meaning "the love of country conquers." The Medal of Honor did not come along until December 21, 1861, when the first medal of its kind was struck for the Navy, inaugurating the Navy Medal of Honor. The medal looks the same today as it did then, the only change since its inception being the criteria for its award as a result of war, established by Congress on February 4, 1919.

The earliest attempt to organize fleet aviation units occurred on February 3, 1919, when Captain George W. Steele Jr., Naval Aviator No. 3172, assumed command of Fleet Air Detachment, Atlantic Fleet aboard the USS *Shawmut,* his flagship, in the Boston Navy Yard. The detachment was established for the sole purpose of testing capabilities of aviation to operate in fleet forces. The new command marked the beginning of a permanent provision for aviation in the fleet's organizational plan. Although all elements of the detachment had not been assembled when Steele took the job, prospects for growth looked promising. The Fleet Air Detachment, Atlantic Fleet, aboard the tender *Shawmut* is considered the first formal aviation organization in Navy fleet history.

The Flying Souceks

The very mention of the Soucek name at Naval Air Station Oceana, Virginia Beach, Virginia, should bring a look of recognition to the base's bevy of modern-day jet pilots and radar intercept officers. The airfield at Oceana is named for Vice Admiral Apollo Soucek, pronounced Sō-check. "Soucek" is the final word on takeoff and approach spoken by all aviators coming in and out of Oceana. But if aviators are asked who this venerable gentlemen with the distinctive name is, faces become puzzled.

This account of Vice Admiral Soucek, often called the test pilot admiral, begins with his death. He died(1) on July 22, 1955, just days after retiring from naval service but also a good many years before many of the young naval aviators at present-day Oceana were born. A few days after the admiral's untimely passing, the Chief of Naval Operations received a fervent message from Naval Air Station Oceana asking that its airfield be named in honor of the "late Admiral Apollo Soucek in order to perpetuate most appropriately the memory of this great naval aviator who contributed so much to the advancement of the field of aviation and the growth of naval aviation."

On June 4, 1957, the airfield at Oceana, the East Coast Master Jet Base, was named Soucek Field to honor the man, his accomplishments, and his dignity as a naval aviator. Soucek was one to be remembered as much for his strength of character and personal esprit de corps as his feats in the air.

So, who was this Apollo Soucek? Stories from the past tell us much of the man. Actually, the Navy might just as well have named Oceana's airfield for all the "Flying Souceks." After all there were four—two brothers and their two cousins—with naval aviation ties. The story actually begins in the spring of 1875 when their grandfather, Matthais Soucek, packed all his belongings and fled war-torn Kolin, Bohemia, for America, settling in Baltimore, Maryland, with his wife and four children. The elder Soucek ended up in Grant County, Oklahoma, a place destined to sow the seeds of great naval aviators but he would settle first in Crete, Nebraska, where he bought land and cattle. His family did not prosper well in Nebraska, so Matthais moved them to Caldwell, Kansas. Matthais had two sons, John and Charles. John later became the father of Apollo and Zeus, and Charles, the father of Victor and Archie.

John and Charles were nearly grown men when the family relocated to Caldwell. The two young Souceks helped their father on the farm, but Matthais made certain both attended the country school nearby. John, in fact, studied so hard he qualified for advanced schooling at the state normal school in Emporia, Kansas. When the United States government opened Cherokee land for settlement, the Souceks—Matthais, John, and Charles—all staked out claims on 160-acre farms, built homes, and the younger Souceks started their own families around the town of Lamont. John, the most learned of Matthais' two sons, loved the classics but was even more taken by Greek mythology, so much so, he named his six children Apollo, Zeus, Romus, Ormus, Myrrha, and Venus.

John Soucek moved to Medford, Oklahoma, in 1897, the year Apollo was born, and opened a blacksmith shop. Zeus was born two years later, in 1899. The children received their early education in Medford public schools. John was a particularly successful businessman, becoming quite prominent in the town of Medford, a small agricultural center in the state. His wife, Lydia Pishny Soucek died in 1907, and shortly thereafter, his youngest daughter Venus followed. The loss of his wife and daughter struck a severe blow to John Soucek, but he continued forward, sending Apollo and Zeus to the home of a neighbor to ensure their proper upbringing.

Apollo and Zeus attended high school at Medford and simultaneously had their first exposure to aeronautics. The two built many model airplanes and, finally, a real glider. The glider was truly the talk of small-town Medford, particularly when Apollo and Zeus decided to see if it really worked and launched the aircraft and themselves from the top of a two-story building. Well, neither was hurt because their creation really did work. This event foreshadowed the Souceks' future role in naval aviation—test piloting.

Apollo Soucek graduated from Medford High School in 1915, and taught school in Grant County for about a year. His father had by that time become mayor of Medford, a position that put him in perfect position to persuade Congressman Richard Morgan to appoint Apollo to the United States Naval Academy in 1917, and Senator Robert L. Owen to appoint Zeus two years later. Apollo graduated from the Naval Academy June 3, 1921, was commissioned an ensign, and immediately assigned to the USS *Mississippi,* operating first with Division Eight, Battleship Squadron Four, Pacific, and later with Division Four, Battle Fleet. He obtained a transfer to aviation in February 1924, and was sent to Pensacola where he earned his wings and was designated Naval Aviator No. 3145 on August 1 of the same year. On November seventeenth, Apollo Soucek joined the USS *Langley* as assistant flight officer, Observation Squadron Two, Battle Fleet. After two months, in January of 1925, he received orders to report to Lieutenant Commander R.C. Davis, as junior aviation officer aboard the USS *Maryland* with Observation Squadron One, and later, for six months as assistant navigator.

While Apollo was serving aboard the *Maryland,* Zeus Soucek(2) cruised the West Indies and Atlantic Ocean. Two years later, Zeus ended up at the Naval Aircraft Factory in Philadelphia as superintendent of the aeronautical engine laboratory. When the Navy acquired the new Douglas PN-12 flying boat, Zeus was given the job of testing the aircraft. On May 3, 1926, along with Lieutenant Art Gavin, Naval Aviator No. 1242, as copilot, he took one of the PN-12s aloft and stayed in the air thirty-six hours and one minute, establishing a world's endurance record for seaplanes. Gavin would become renowned as winner of the 1927 Schiff Memorial Trophy, and also as a premier Navy test pilot akin to Apollo and Zeus Soucek and the great Carleton C. Champion. Zeus Soucek would later, with Lieutenant Lisle J. Maxson as copilot, take the same aircraft to an altitude of 19,000 feet with a dead load of 3,204 pounds, thus breaking the altitude record for seaplanes at that time.

Apollo Soucek was not to be outdone by his younger brother. By the time Zeus had set records with the PN-12, Apollo was attached to the Bureau of Aeronautics as assistant in the power plant design section under Rear Admiral William Adger Moffett, Naval Observer No. 1. Apollo volunteered to attempt a new landplane altitude record, a record held at that time by Lieutenant Carleton C. Champion, who reached 38,418 feet in 1927. Apollo took off from Naval Air Station Anacostia, part of the Washington, D.C., area, on May 8, 1929, flying a Wright Apache powered by a 425-horsepower Pratt & Whitney Wasp engine fitted with supercharged Scintilla magnetos, special Stromberg carburetor and BG-brand spark plugs. A high grade Gulf oil called Gulfpride was used for

Lieutenant Apollo Soucek walks away from his Wright Apache after establishing a new world altitude mark for Class C seaplanes at 38,560 feet, June 4, 1929. (Official United States Navy Photograph. Courtesy of the National Museum of Naval Aviation.)

lubrication. The supercharger was known as a roots type as manufactured by the Allison Engineering Company. He got up to 39,140 feet on this attempt. His success was due in part to careful preflight preparations and study. Over a period of time, Apollo familiarized himself with engines, particularly the Wasp configuration, superchargers, flight clothing, and oxygen apparatus.

Test pilots in Soucek's day donned fur-lined leather flight suits and fur-lined boots, mittens, and head gear complete with face mask. After his 1930 flight, Soucek would remark in an NBC radio broadcast, "you see, aviators do not wear woolen or silken underwear and they manage to stay warm in a wrap of bear or caribou skin." Very few people are aware of the fact that Apollo's brother, Zeus, had been experimenting with goggles with a defogging feature. The goggles would have come in handy had Zeus made it to the airfield in time to hand them to Apollo before the flight. As a result, Apollo confronted numerous problems that marred his vision and impacted his breathing. In retrospect, he would note:

"While low temperature may not be troublesome to one's comfort, it does cause the pilot much difficulty. In fact, the extreme cold and low barometric pressure are the only two conditions that do cause difficulty. When the altitude experiments were conducted [1929], my first record flight came near being a failure because of frost on my goggles. Moisture collected on the inside surface of the lens, and froze there when the cold zones were reached, just as moisture freezes inside window panes on a cold winter morning. Never had I had such a hard time flying an airplane as I did on that occasion; I couldn't see with the goggles on, and it was too painful to remove them."

By the next year, though, they had found a solution. Zeus, who was assigned to the Naval Aircraft Factory in 1929, had left the Navy and was working for Eclipse Aviation Corporation of East Orange, New Jersey, by the time of Apollo's 1930 flight. Electrically heated goggles had been used by the Army Air Corps, so Zeus Soucek built a pair of electrically heated goggles by winding the electric element across the lens and heating this element with a battery. Apollo used these goggles in his record-setting flight on June 4, 1930.

Apollo Soucek's first record in 1929 would be broken about a month later by Herr Willi Neuenhofen of Germany who flew a Junkers monoplane 41,797 feet to garner the record for his homeland. Apollo Soucek answered the German's challenge by making another flight on June 4, 1930, this time to 43,166 feet, establishing a mark that remained unbroken for many years. For his efforts, Apollo Soucek was awarded the

Lieutenant Apollo Soucek stands in the cockpit of his Wright Apache landplane after establishing a world altitude record, June 4, 1930, a year to the day from his last record-setting flight. (Official United States Navy Photograph. Courtesy of the National Museum of Naval Aviation.)

Distinguished Flying Cross for "extraordinary achievements while participating in duly authorized aerial flights...carrying on high altitude experiments in connection with the development of aviation (he) established on June 4, 1929, a world's altitude record for seaplanes, and on June 4, 1930, established a world's altitude record for heavier-than-air [aircraft]..." The citation further stated, "These experiments are considered to be of the very highest importance in the proper development of engines, propellers, oxygen equipment, and flying equipment for high altitudes..."

It has been said that out of ignorance of the facts of history, the accomplishments of early naval aviators like Soucek are discounted, perhaps even belittled and lost in the age of high-tech aircraft, moon shots, and space shuttles. Essentially, pioneers like Soucek took the leap of faith and advanced naval aviation to the precipice of the jet age. He hung on and took his chances because that was all he could do. In 1930, Apollo Soucek's altitude was every bit as exciting as man's walk on the moon. During the NBC radio address of 1930, Soucek said:

"Naturally, I think [flight test] is valuable. It seems to me that something was gained. In the Navy we enter research work for a definite purpose. Actually records are secondary matters, they are useful only as goals for which we strive. Ever since the airplane industry began, men have strived to build craft that are strong and light. In the Apache the efforts of many men were coordinated to cut down weight, to develop greater horsepower, and to improve material. The Apache is a flying laboratory wherein experiments are tried; the height attained is the test proving that experiments were based on correct formulas. The equipment in some parts of the airplane and its power plant is just a step in everyday flying; surely it must follow that this advanced material will appear as everyday equipment on standard aircraft in the near future."

Between June of 1930 and 1932, Apollo Soucek served successively as squadron flight officer, Fighting Squadron Three, based on the USS *Lexington,* and as gunnery officer and executive officer of Fighting Squadron One aboard the USS *Saratoga*. He then returned to the Naval Aircraft Factory where he had a three year tour of duty as assistant to the superintendent of the aeronautical engineering laboratory. Soucek detached in June of 1935, and joined the USS *Ranger* (CV-4) as hangar deck officer, flight deck officer, and finally, senior watch officer.

Apollo and Zeus Soucek were only half of Matthais' legacy. The other two were Charles' sons, Victor and Archie, both of whom also attended the United States Naval Academy. Victor entered the academy in 1927, graduating in 1931, and Archie began studies there in 1932, graduating in 1936. Victor would serve a year on the USS *Saratoga* before going to Pensacola to earn his wings.(3) He became quite famous as a result of events that occurred the night of February 10, 1934, while serving as an aviator on the West Coast. While flying in a four-aircraft formation off the coast of southern California, headed from San Clemente to San Pedro, the planes in his section ran out of fuel over open water. Luckily the aircraft, originally landplanes, had been fitted with a single pontoon for flotation. Unfortunately the weather was extremely bad and the aircraft, repeatedly pelted with waves, threatened to sink. Unable to see more than a few feet in front of them, the aviators' situation appeared grim. Without hesitation, Victor Soucek removed his flying gear and dove into the ocean, striking out in the general direction of the California coastline. He had no idea how far out the aircraft had strayed from shore but, after swimming perhaps a half mile, his feet touched bottom and Soucek waded ashore. Reporting the plight of his brother aviators, two Navy ships were dispatched to their rescue. The spotlight of fame cast on Victor Soucek brought national and international attention to Apollo and Zeus as well, hence the trio was dubbed "The Flying Souceks" by the press.

Zeus retired from the Navy in 1930 to pursue commercial aviation. Victor remained in the Navy and was flying combat aircraft in the 1930s. Archie finished at the Naval Academy and pursued naval aviation upon graduation. Romus, another son of John Soucek, did not attend the Naval Academy but he did join the ranks of pioneers in private aviation. Romus worked for the experimental department of the Wright Brothers Aeronautical Corporation located in Patterson, New Jersey.

As for Apollo Soucek, he returned to the USS *Lexington* in June 1937 as commanding officer of Fighting Squadron Two and, in May of the following year, was ordered to the Navy Department where he had two years of duty as assistant to the chief of the personnel division, Bureau of Aeronautics. From May of 1940 through June of 1941, Soucek served as navigator of the USS *Yorktown* (CV-5) and, from her commissioning October 20, 1941, until June of 1942, served as air officer of the USS *Hornet* (CV-8). He was on duty as her executive officer when the *Hornet* was lost in the Battle of Santa Cruz Islands on October 26, 1942.

During the time Apollo Soucek was aboard the *Hornet,* the carrier transported Lieutenant Colonel (later Major General) Jimmy Doolittle's B-25C Mitchell bombers toward Japan, and launched them from her decks for the famous raid on Tokyo on April 18, 1942. Continuing her extended cruise in enemy waters without making contact with the Japanese, the *Hornet* was ordered in May 1942 to carry her squadrons to the vicinity of Midway as part of Rear Admiral Raymond A. Spruance's Task Force Sixteen consisting not only of CV-8 but also the USS *Enterprise* (CV-6), five heavy cruisers, one antiaircraft cruiser, and nine destroyers. The part played by the *Hornet* and Carrier Air Group Eight in the Battle of Midway in June 1942, when the Japanese Navy suffered its first decisive defeat in 350 years, is one of the epics of American naval history.

In a fitting epilogue, the *Hornet* continued her destruction of the enemy in the Battle of Santa Cruz Islands before she was finally lost as a result of consecutive enemy aircraft attacks by Japanese Zeroes and Kates at quarter past one in the afternoon, and the coup de grace, a final strike by four Val dive-bombers and Zeroes from the *Junyo* at five o'clock on October 26, 1942. To keep the *Hornet* from being declared sunk by enemy fire, and to prevent her from falling into enemy hands, an American destroyer tried to finish off the *Hornet* but was unsuccessful. The carrier was so well constructed by workers at Newport News Shipbuilding and Drydock Company, it refused to go down. The *Hornet* did not sink until a couple of enemy destroyers hit her with additional torpedoes in the early morning hours of October 27, 1942.

For his part in the *Hornet* saga, Apollo Soucek was awarded the Silver Star Medal and the Legion of Merit with Combat "V." His Silver Star citation read:

"For conspicuous gallantry and intrepidity as executive officer of the USS *Hornet* during action against Japanese forces near Santa Cruz Islands, October 26, 1942. With utter disregard for his own personal safety, Captain Soucek skillfully directed difficult operations, including handling of the heavy towing cable and anchor chain, which enabled the aircraft carrier to be taken in tow after she suffered serious damage. His courageous leadership in this action and during his earlier direction of the control of fires aboard the carrier served as an inspiring example to the *Hornet's* crew."

He would also be awarded the Bronze Star Medal, which read:

"For meritorious achievement as executive officer of the USS *Hornet,* prior to and during the attack by Task Force Seventeen on enemy Japanese shipping in the Faisi-Tonolei area of the Solomon Islands on October 5, 1942. Responsible for developing and maintaining the personnel and material of the *Hornet* at a high degree of efficiency, during a protracted period of operations at sea, (he) contributed directly to the success of his vessel in delivering a highly successful attack against the enemy without disruption of plans and without damage to the *Hornet.*"

Following the loss of the *Hornet,* Captain Soucek served from January through June of 1943 as assistant chief of staff for operations on the staff of Commander Aircraft United States Pacific Fleet, and for outstanding services during that period was awarded a gold star in lieu of the second Legion of Merit. In July 1943, he returned to Naval Air Station Pensacola, Florida, to serve first as chief of staff and aide to the chief of Naval Air Intermediate Training Command, and later as deputy chief of Naval Air Training in the Naval Air Training Command, Pensacola.

Reporting in March of 1945 to the New York Navy Yard, Apollo Soucek was in charge of fitting out the USS *Franklin D. Roosevelt* (CVB-42), and on October 27, 1945, he became the *Roosevelt's* first commanding officer at commissioning ceremonies held at Naval Station Norfolk, Virginia. By January of 1946, he was relieved from his duties aboard the *Roosevelt* to become Commander Carrier Division Fourteen. And, in August of the same year, Soucek became Commander Fleet Air Wing One. Soucek would become commanding officer of the Naval Air Test Center, Patuxent River, Maryland, on July 15, 1947, where he remained for two years. Being in charge of the test facility at Patuxent River had to have been akin to returning to his roots in naval aviation.

In April of 1949, Apollo Soucek became director of the Aviation Plans and Program Division in the Office of the Deputy Chief of Naval Operations for Air, and on June 10, 1949, reported as Assistant Chief of Naval Operations for Aviation Plans. January of 1951 expanded Soucek's horizons. He was designated as the United States Naval Attaché to London, England, and later United States Naval Attaché for Air, also in London. Soucek remained in London until his wife, the former Agnes Eleanor O'Connor of Wellsville, New York, died on November 13, 1951. Following a brief tour of duty in the Office of the Chief of Naval Operations, he reported in February of 1952 as Commander Carrier Division Three. His crowning achievement came on June 18, 1953, when Vice Admiral Soucek was appointed Chief of the Bureau of Aeronautics, Navy Department, for a term of four years. Unfortunately, the admiral fell ill in February of 1955 and was hospitalized at the Bethesda Naval Hospital. This action resulted in his transfer to the retired list on July 1, 1955. He died on July 19, 1955, and was buried at Arlington National Cemetery with full military honors on the twenty-sixth of the month. Soucek Field at Naval Air Station Oceana is intended as a lasting memorial to this great pioneer of naval aviation, a man who gave his all to a profession he genuinely loved and worked so hard to perpetuate.

1. Rear Admiral Soucek was hospitalized for an undisclosed illness at Bethesda Naval Hospital in February 1955 and was removed from active duty to the retired list with the rank of vice admiral shortly thereafter. His retirement was made final only eighteen days before his death.
2. Zeus Soucek earned his wings on April 24, 1926, and was subsequently designated Naval Aviator No. 3287.
3. Victor Soucek was designated Naval Aviator No. 3987, effective upon earning his wings on April 17, 1933.

This Curtiss L-2 triplane, Bureau Number A292, was one of three L-2 types bought by the Navy. This photograph, taken November 3, 1918, shows the L-2 taxiing away from the beach at Naval Air Station Hampton Roads on a training flight. (Official United States Navy Photograph. Courtesy of the Hampton Roads Naval Museum.)

Chapter 8: Gobs, Hogs, and Ground Pounders

Aside from pilots and observers, there were ground crew, communications specialists, radio telephone operators, and others who did not wear wings but gave of their considerable talents and ideas to further naval aviation at Hampton Roads. As early as 1910, it took roughly ten men to keep a pilot in the air. This ground crew became known as "gobs,"[1] a nickname which stuck a good number of years around the air station. These early plane captains would patch wings, grease wires, repair wooden hulls, maintain engines, even sew leather flight suits back together and attend to any other task their pilot needed.

John J. Hill, Machinist's Mate First Class (Aviation) (MM1c-A), was one such plane captain said to have gone above and beyond the call of duty on behalf of

"Gobs" move two Curtiss R-9 aircraft into the waters of the Grand Basin area at Hampton Roads. This photograph was taken in the summer of 1918 when Navy pilots were still assigned to the naval air detachment and the designation "air station" had not yet been approved. The tents to the left were being used to house everything from repair operations to men and machines. (Courtesy of the Hampton Roads Naval Museum.)

This image, taken at Hampton Roads on May 29, 1918, shows an H-12 flying boat, Bureau No. A769, with a damaged upper wing and engine problems. There are numerous enlisted ground crew and officers assessing the H-12's condition and repair requirements. (Courtesy of the Hampton Roads Naval Museum.)

A Curtiss H-16 flying boat sunk at Hampton Roads on July 30, 1918. Sailors on boats to the left and right in the photograph attempted to tie on lines to keep the H-16 above water, but the battle was not one they were going to win. Sea water had already begun to come over the crew compartments and flood the plane's interior. The weight of the water soon carried the H-16 under. (Courtesy of the Hampton Roads Naval Museum.)

In order to check the depth of the water and the draft of the R-9 aircraft in this photograph, taken August 8, 1918, a sailor took draft readings. These tests were conducted at the aircraft's full-load capacity, hence the need to have two "gobs" sitting in the cockpit while the measurements were taken. The setting for the picture was the naval air detachment at Hampton Roads. (Courtesy of the Hampton Roads Naval Museum.)

Naval Air Station Hampton Roads, Virginia, was growing steadily when this photograph was taken in 1918. The HS-2 flying boat seen next to Hangar I, Bureau Number A1173, was manufactured by Lowe, Willard and Fowler under a special contract with the Navy to produce two hundred such aircraft, one hundred and fifty of which were actually built. The HS-2 was a bigger and better version of the original Curtiss HS-1 aircraft. Powered by a twelve-cylinder, 400-horsepower Liberty engine, the HS-2 was the signature aircraft of the period. The photograph is dated not so much by the aircraft as by the two Mustin sea sleds sitting near the water's edge. These surface craft were used during experiments in November of 1918 to launch seaplanes and were dubbed Mustin sea sleds for their inventor, Captain Henry Crosky "Rum" Mustin, Naval Aviator No. 11, and one of the true pioneers of naval aviation. (Official United States Navy Photograph.)

his pilot. On September 18, 1918, a big, twin-engine seaplane broke free of its mooring lines under eighty-knot gale force winds. The plane would have been totally destroyed except Hill, who donned his rain gear and sea boots, dove over the seawall, carried a line through incredibly rough seas and fastened it to the plane, essentially keeping it from being battered to pieces.

Today, we hardly think these enlisted men of yesteryear did so much flying but, truth is, they did. They tested engines, and it was not at all uncommon for enlisted mechanics to be assigned as flight engineers on large twin-engine flying boats. These men were as much daredevils as their pilots, climbing out on wings to repair engine spark plugs at two hundred feet, snuffing out fires in proximity to gas tanks while the pilot kept the aircraft gliding at two thousand feet or, as in the case of one chief, flying only on planes he knew were highly experimental at best. Of course, the dean of all flight engineers and one of the first in his profession was Chief Machinist's Mate (CMM) E.S. "Smoke" Rhodes who went with Commander Patrick N.L. Bellinger aboard the NC-1 flying boat across the Atlantic Ocean in 1919.

"Groundhogs,"[(2)] or "hogs" for short, was the term used to describe all naval aviation officers who did not wear wings, though they certainly played a critical role in keeping aircraft and pilots in the air. Among their ranks could be found engineering officers who supervised repairs, and maintenance officers responsible for the wings and hulls. Lieutenant William O'Connell, former naval militia (NNV), for instance, was the maintenance officer in charge of keeping the big flying boats flight ready. There were communications officers to plot U-boat patrols, and men like Lieutenant William M. Fellers, later Naval Aviator No. 2474, who, with the aid of his facts, figures and calculations for experimental planes, could tell pilots what might go wrong. Navigation, radio, and ordnance officers were joined by their administrative counterparts in the effort to keep the station's planes and men ready to go on a moment's notice. Many times the "hogs" and "gobs" would bravely serve as observers on test flights.

There would be many touch-and-go moments for those known today as

An Italian-built Caproni Ca-44 bomber is shown here on a Mustin sea sled on November 15, 1918. The sea sled essentially provided the aircraft a double set of floats: one for cruising which remained on the water after launch of the plane, and the other set permanently attached to the plane for landing and flotation only. These motor-driven sleds were designed to transport bombers close to their targets and launch them to the attack. Both the aircraft and sea sleds were in use at the end of the First World War. A Curtiss F-5L flying boat rests in the water behind the Caproni Ca-44 aircraft. (Official United States Navy Photograph.)

"ground pounders." Lieutenant Fellers would be commended by the Secretary of the Navy for his daring flying as an observer in an H-16 piloted by Lieutenant Louis T. Barin, a top experimental pilot of his day. The H-16 had been fitted with a stabilizing device which proved to be overbalanced, causing the plane to sideslip five times in a matter of minutes and at very low altitude. Fellers was a cool customer, seemingly unphased by the experience and eager to complete testing of the device.

In November of 1918, Naval Aviator No. 1096, Ensign Frank Milton "Ben" Johnson, pilot, and Lieutenant Howard Greenley, a communications officer sitting in the copilot's seat, flew from Washington, D.C., to Hampton Roads in an aircraft under constant risk of catching fire from a leak in the gravity gasoline feed tank which, in turn, trailed fuel too close to the flame of the exhaust ports. Johnson was no stranger to the dangers and challenges of flying. He had been the first pilot to launch an N-9 training plane from the deck of a sea sled at Hampton Roads on March 7, 1919, effectively testing an idea of Captain Henry C. Mustin, Naval Aviator No. 11.

Captain Henry C. Mustin's sea sled project continued into 1919. In this photograph, a Caproni Ca-44 bomber is underway for launch. (Official United States Navy Photograph.)

The Navy Department approved the expansion of its aviation pilot training program on May 1, 1917. The first provision for training enlisted men as aviation mechanics and for selection of a few for pilot training and qualification as quartermaster was included in the Navy directive. The Navy's participation in the war slowed the inclusion of qualified enlisted men in this program, but a few made it through the training process and were designated among the first 2,000 naval aviators. The men pictured here, circa 1922, are Naval Aviation Pilots (NAPs) and Navy chiefs. From their bullion eagle rating badges with the eagle volant and head turned to the right, these men are wearing the eagle of the World War I period. None of these gentlemen is wearing the Aviation Pilot specialty mark promulgated in 1924 for enlisted pilots.

The sea sled was still being tested at war's end, its practical use still in question. As Mustin envisioned his creation, the sea sled would have ideally carried a three-engine Caproni landplane bomber. Once in the waters of the English Channel, the sea sled was to launch the Caproni fully armed and fueled for bombing runs on German targets. The aircraft with its great store of fuel could then return to England. Bellinger oversaw sea sled testing at Hampton Roads, and both he and Mustin were actually present for the first tests, albeit unsuccessful, with the Caproni. The test was called a failure since the sled never reached the flying speed needed by the Caproni to launch the aircraft. Johnson's successful test using an N-9, a smaller and much lighter plane, was achieved with the sea sled making fifty knots.

By the summer of 1918, with war still raging in Europe and patrols stepped up along the Atlantic coastline, there would be much opportunity for experimentation, not all of it intended. During this time, Lieutenant Irving "Tish" Paris, Naval Aviator No. 317, pilot, and Cadet Officer (later Ensign) Thomas Woods, copilot, were on an antisubmarine patrol. The patrol called for a massive search for enemy submarines over an area covering 150 miles of open sea. The aircraft was between 1,500 to 2,000 feet and about seventy to eighty miles out when Paris smelled trouble. The fastening on the hatch over the main gas tank had sheared off, allowing the hatch to fall open. In this position, the hatch could easily tear from the rear fastening and blow into the propeller, meaning that any change in airflow with the level of the plane spelled serious danger. At that time there were intercommunicating telephones attached to the pilots' helmets but, in this case, the phones did not work. In what can only be described as an incredible scene, Paris gave Woods the controls while writing him a message to climb out of the main cockpit and repair the hatch. This, mind you, was the cadet's first patrol. Woods hardly knew how to handle himself with the controls, much less climb out on the wing, but climb he did. Once out of the cockpit, the wind rush knocked him spread-eagle to the wing. He hung on to the wing's edge for his life before struggling to regain his footing. As Woods tried to crawl back to the hatch, he risked his life between the lesser of two deaths: the fan propeller was between Woods and the hatch cover, and behind him was the propeller of the main engine. His head was blown against the fan pump blade as Woods tried to inch closer to the hatch and had he not been wearing his heavy leather helmet, the encounter with the blade might have been fatal. As the story was retold, the wind whipped under his clothes, stripping him to the waist, his leather belt ending up caught in the blades of the fan pump. Hanging on and hard at work to release the belt, Woods was cut repeatedly across his arm and

A Curtiss H-16 flying boat, Bureau Number A3512, was being secured to a towing sled when this picture was taken in the winter of 1918. Though a Curtiss design, this particular aircraft was manufactured by the Naval Aircraft Factory, Philadelphia, Pennsylvania, which built aircraft A1049 to A1098 and A3459 to A3558. The aircraft carried a crew of four and was powered by two 400-horsepower Liberty twelve-cylinder engines. (Official United States Navy Photograph.)

hand by the fan pump blade. Once he got his clothes out of the blades, he made a quick return to the cockpit before trying again. Since he could not fix the hatch cover on the second attempt, the young cadet decided to sit on the hatch. He stayed there for the hour and a half it took Paris to get the plane back to Hampton Roads.

When war was declared, radio work on aircraft was far from sophisticated. A prime example was Paris and his cadet, unable to communicate between themselves on their troubled flight, which occurred well into 1918. The Navy had not succeeded with the spark-type telegraph sets because they were too large and heavy on airplanes. The very first successful radio telegraph transmitter developed by the Navy was contained in a small box which mounted to the wing and was controlled by a key at the pilot's seat. The set gave the pilots a means of signalling from planes making patrols not more than seventy-five miles from their receiving station, but this was primarily a device with limited success on small aircraft. With the development of larger seaplanes, the Navy needed a more powerful means of signalling and wasted no further time establishing a small experimental laboratory at Pensacola. It stayed there only a short period, given its time and distance from business, industry and the politics of Washington, D.C. The Experimental and Test Department was transferred to Naval Air Station Hampton Roads on January 1, 1918. Once at Norfolk, the experimental station had three officers detailed to radio experimentation. The Radio Division, as they became known, conducted all experimental work in radio and associated patrol work. The Radio Division patrol work passed to Ensign P.D. Naugle (later Naval Aviator No. 2894) in August of 1918, and research work to one of the communications "hogs." The officers were ably assisted by twelve enlisted personnel. Valuable research work was done at Norfolk, so much so that new radio sets were developed almost weekly. The greatest of the early developments to come out of Naval Air Station Hampton Roads was a radio telephone conversation over a distance of fifty miles between a seaplane and the base.

Perhaps worth mention, and important to what was to come later, spark sets mounted to the wing were still being fine tuned by radio manufacturers. Up until early 1918, telegraphic communication between an aircraft and shore at two hundred miles, also considered the longest seaplane patrol at the time, was news. With the coming of larger seaplanes in late 1918 and, of course the grand NC-1 to NC-4 Nancies, telephonic communication was more important than old telegraphic methods. Telephonic communication had been achieved to seventy-five miles at that time and, if using telegraphic on the same set, could reach up to 150 miles. In February of 1918, the first radio telephone set for seaplanes, larger than any ever used, was placed on an aircraft, and the pilot was able to maintain telephonic communication with shore, give reports and receive orders at 125 miles. During the same time frame, communications specialists immediately set to work to get the distance to 175 miles, and, by June of 1918, the device was ready for larger seaplanes. Technology was moving at such a rapid pace, nearly every week new sets passed laboratory tests and were taken out for service tests aboard patrol seaplanes for five or six hours. The feasibility of using voice radio and telephone relay for air-to-ground communications was first demonstrated on March 12, 1919, when Lieutenant Harry Sadenwater, in an airborne flying boat, carried on a conversation with the Secretary of the Navy seated at his desk in the Navy Department roughly sixty-five miles from the aircraft. Through all the radio testing emerged perhaps the earliest precursor of today's Naval Flight Officer, a second pilot whose sole role in those early days of experimental flight was navigation, observation and communication.

Chapter 9: Arresting Developments

Following World War I, peacetime demands limited naval aviation activities, but the Navy made every effort to continue experimental testing, equal amounts of which would take place at Langley and Norfolk, with instruction in navigation, gunnery, and aerial bombing at Naval Air Station Hampton Roads. An officier-in-charge was assigned to the Navy detachment under instruction in landplanes at the Army Air Service School, Langley Field, Virginia.(1) Training at Langley was in preparation for operation of landplanes from battleship turrets, the first successful flight from a turret having been made by Lieutenant Commander Edward O. McDonnell, piloting a Sopwith Camel from a platform atop Turret No. 2 on the USS *Texas* at Guantanamo Bay, Cuba, on March 9, 1919. Record-setting flights occurred in rapid succession. An F-5L flying boat, equipped with two 400-horsepower Liberty engines and piloted by Lieutenant Harold B. Grow, Naval Aviator No. 2354, out of Hampton Roads, completed a flight of twenty hours, nineteen minutes in which he managed to cover 1,250 nautical miles, April 26, 1919. Although the flight was not made under *Fédération Aéronautique Internationale* (FAI) supervision and took place prior to the date on which seaplanes were recognized as a separate class for record purposes, an exception was made and the record was accepted

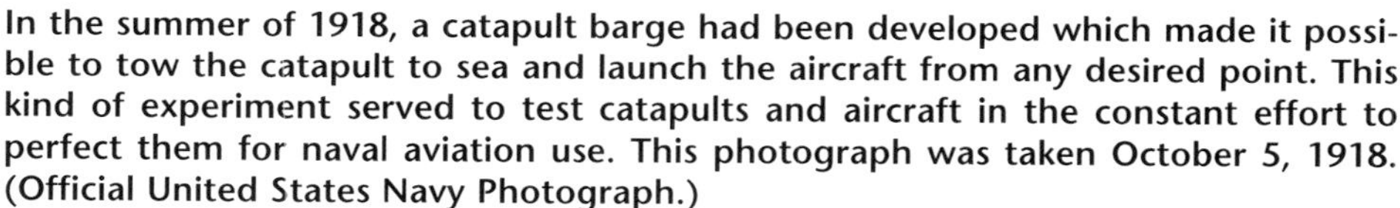

In the summer of 1918, a catapult barge had been developed which made it possible to tow the catapult to sea and launch the aircraft from any desired point. This kind of experiment served to test catapults and aircraft in the constant effort to perfect them for naval aviation use. This photograph was taken October 5, 1918. (Official United States Navy Photograph.)

Spectators and sailors watch an early parachutist float to earth at the site of Old Chambers Field, August 6, 1919. The 'chute is not yet fully deployed. (Official United States Navy Photograph.)

Catapults: "The Most Important Achievement..."

Captain Washington Irving Chambers first head of naval aviation, never favored catapult launches on pitching and rolling decks. Little did he know what lay ahead. Catapults developed in Chambers' time occupied very little space and were designed as temporary pieces of equipment, folded and stowed between uses. These earliest precursors to our modern-day catapults could be mounted to the top of the gun turret on a cruiser, were easily transported to any location on the ship, and could be readily dismounted and kept clear of the guns. Compressed air powered catapults because all naval vessels carrying planes also carried torpedoes supplied with air compressors. The airplane itself rested on a car. The catapult was prepped for aircraft launch as air was pumped into a receiver connected to a small cylinder conveniently located on deck. The stroke of the cylinder's piston was about forty inches. The piston rod was connected to a small wooden car by a wire rope purchase, which multiplied the travel of the piston to any desired extent, or to any limit fixed by the travel of the car on its tracks. The car simply dropped off into the water and was retrieved after the launch.

The catapult could be dismantled to fit into a box about eight feet square. Large ships, battleships in the 1910s, were able to carry airplanes with relative ease. Glenn H. Curtiss would be quoted

as saying the catapult was, "the most important achievement since wheels were put on land machines." Captain Chambers did much to facilitate early research and development of catapult technology.

AERIAL ACROBATICS

PARACHUTE JUMP FROM A NAVY PLANE

The Navy has Always Been Among the Leaders in Aviation

The parachutist captured on film in this photograph is Lieutenant Jackson R. Tate, a naval aviator. Parachuting, even in the mid-1920s, was still highly experimental as new parachutes and jump techniques were perfected. Tate jumped from the one and only Douglas DT-5 aircraft, Bureau Number A6428, an upgrade of the Naval Aircraft Factory DT-2. Tate conducted his parachute experiments over Hawaii for the most part but later gravitated back to Hampton Roads where he eventually became an admiral and resided in Virginia Beach. Tate's daredevil days were not limited to parachute tests. As a naval aviator, the story goes he once crashed an airplane into the side of a hangar at Norfolk and, none the worse for wear, continued to fly for many years thereafter. Friends remembered his exploits with a smile many years after Tate retired from active duty. (Official United States Navy Photograph.)

by the FAI as the best until broken in May of 1925.

Given the increasing closure of technology on paper and practical testing, it came as no surprise that the Sperry gyrostabilized automatic pilot system was tested in an F-5L aircraft at Hampton Roads on March 27, 1920, nor when, on the twelfth of July, a test of the radio compass as an aid to navigation was successfully made in an F-5L which left Hampton Roads and flew directly to the USS *Ohio,* ninety-four miles at sea in a position unknown to the pilot. Without landing, the pilot turned the aircraft toward home at Naval Air Station Hampton Roads, this time navigating via signals from Norfolk.

As development of the air station at Norfolk continued, the Navy added new facilities, and the base's population increased. Education and training of naval aviators remained one of the air station's primary functions. Research and testing of arresting and catapult equipment linked closely to development of aircraft carriers (the *Langley* and all to follow) also began to unfold. A contract was issued by the Navy on June 12, 1919, to construct a revolving plat-

The Curtiss HA-1 Dunkirk fighter shown here, circa 1919, at Hampton Roads was a two-seat escort and air superiority aircraft of which only two were built for the Navy: Bureau Numbers A4110 and A4111. The Dunkirk fighter was originally test flown by Roland Rholfs, who took the aircraft to the unheard of altitude of 35,000 feet. This aircraft proved itself to the Navy and became the parent of the RC-1, the first of Curtiss' famous racing aircraft. The A4110 had a 400-horsepower Liberty engine and had been modified to include parts from the aircraft's prototype. The Dunkirk fighter was equipped with dual synchronized machine guns forward and dual flexible machine guns in the rear cockpit. The HA-1 was tested at the naval air station after the First World War. (Official United States Navy Photograph.)

The postwar version of the F-5L aircraft was fitted with a much larger vertical tail. The aircraft shown here in 1919 belonged to Patrol Squadron Fourteen (VP-14). Powered by two 400-horsepower Liberty twelve-cylinder engines, the F-5L could carry a crew of four. (Official United States Navy Photograph.)

form at Hampton Roads for use in experimentation related to landing aircraft aboard ships.

The British Navy first developed arresting gear aboard an aircraft carrier in 1918. The HMS *Furious* was equipped with a device described, in simplest terms, as a system of wires drawn taut fore and aft high enough for an airplane axle with a hook to snag wires and not bounce the plane. Fatalities were frequent with this system: pilots coming in too fast, coupled with air turbulance over the aft flight deck proved a deadly combination, one the British were unable to improve upon. The United States Navy was planning to use the same gear on the *Langley* while she was being readied at Norfolk Navy Yard in 1920. Fortunately they tested it first via a large wooden turntable built at Old Chambers Field, Naval Air Station Hampton Roads.

On August 11, 1921, Lieutenant Alfred Melville "Mel" Pride, Naval Aviator No. 1119, conducted the first practical application of carrier arresting

Lieutenant Commander Newton H. White, Naval Aviator No. 2281, was commanding officer of Naval Air Station Hampton Roads from May 1919 to December 1920, following the station's primary architect, Lieutenant Commander Patrick N.L. Bellinger, in the post. (Official United States Navy Photograph.)

This three-quarter view of the Curtiss MF flying boat was taken at Naval Air Station Hampton Roads, on April 28, 1919. The "MF" stood for military flying boat, a larger version of the Curtiss F-boat. (Official United States Navy Photograph.)

The Martin MBT ("B" for bomber and "T" for torpedo) aircraft was primarily an Army plane purchased by the Navy. The Navy bought two of the aircraft identical to Army specifications in 1920, when the photograph here was taken, and eventually designated them A5711 and A5712. The appearance of the aircraft in Hampton Roads occurred the same year in which they were purchased. (Official United States Navy Photograph.)

The Morane-Saulnier AR-1 trainer shown here at Naval Air Station Hampton Roads in 1921 was one of six such aircraft purchased by the Navy the same year. Powered by an eighty horsepower Le Rhône rotary engine, this was indeed an unusual aircraft to see even then on an American Navy flight line. Two F-5L flying boats are moored in the water behind the AR-1 aircraft. The aircraft next to the hangar, Bureau Number A5665, is a Lewis and Vought VE-7 aircraft of which there were nineteen of the model built for the Navy. (Official United States Navy Photograph.)

gear at Hampton Roads when he landed an Aeromarine onto a dummy deck and successfully caught the arresting wires. The results of his testing would eventually lead to development of arresting gear for the USS *Langley,* then in the process of conversion to the Navy's first aircraft carrier. Arresting gear used on the *Langley* consisted essentially of both athwartship wires attached to weights, and fore and aft wires.

Both Lieutenant Commander Godfrey de Courcelles Chevalier, Naval Aviator No. 7, and Commander Kenneth Whiting, Naval Aviator No. 16, worked to develop arresting gear and landing techniques for what these aviators envisioned as an aircraft "carrier," but it was Whiting who did more to develop America's first carriers. He would work tirelessly between 1916 and 1919 to have the *Langley* conversion approved through Congress, and he continued to work even after approval to help congressional leadership overcome its great opposition to a fleet led by aircraft carriers. Whiting envisioned the carrier as a floating laboratory for naval aviators. On March 20, 1922, naval aviation, naval warfare, and naval history were revolutionized when Commander Whiting, often referred to as the father of the aircraft carrier,

A Lewis and Vought VE-7GF, distinguished by the hydrovanes between the landing gear, makes a landing on the USS *Langley* (CV-1) in 1922. The aircraft was equipped with the British designed hydrovane purportedly to prevent nosing over in the water if the pilot was forced down at sea. According to pilot recollections of the period, the device did not quite live up to expectation. (Official United States Navy Photograph.)

The Curtiss HS-3 (Bureau Number A5459) was one of five constructed by the manufacturer, and one of only seven ever built. The other two were built by the Naval Aircraft Factory. Pictured on its cradle outside a hangar at Naval Air Station Hampton Roads in 1921, this HS-3 shows the much-improved hull design which bettered the aircraft over its predecessor, the HS-2L. The HS-3 design never made it to mass production because it was introduced too late in the First World War to be useful to the Navy. (Official United States Navy Photograph.)

commissioned the USS *Langley* (CV-1) in Norfolk, Virginia.

Once the Navy had its first aircraft carrier, it had to have pilots and aircraft to outfit the first naval aviation squadron, in this case an air detachment. The first fifteen carrier qualified naval aviators assigned to an aircraft carrier as a group was formed in the spring of 1922 at Naval Air Station Hampton Roads, Virginia, and included Whiting and Chevalier; Lieutenant Commander Virgil Childers "Squash" Griffin, Naval Aviator No. 41; Lieutenant Alfred Melville "Al" Pride, Naval Aviator No. 1119; Lieutenant Braxton "Blackie" Rhodes, Naval Aviator No. 2916; Lieutenant (junior grade) Carlton David "Cal" Palmer, Naval Aviator No. 116; Lieutenant Stanton Hall Wooster, Naval Aviator No. 2731; Ensign Delbart Lawrence Conley, Naval Aviator No. 1166; Chief Boatswain's Mate Anthony "Tony" Feher, Naval Aviator No. 95 (who had been an officer but reverted back to chief boatswain's mate in January of

Famous "Felix the Cat" has been a naval aviation icon since 1921 when an outfit known as Combat Squadron Four used this feisty feline for the first time. When the squadron was disestablished in 1922, Felix was adopted by a continuous string of fighter and bombing squadrons, all meeting their end well before lucky Felix. For those too young to remember, Felix was adapted in his present form from the Pat Sullivan cartoon character by Emil Chourré to suit the purposes of these earliest fighter and bombing squadrons. On July 1, 1935, VF-1B was established and picked up on the Felix insignia. Fighting One (B) would be redesignated on several occasions, the first occurring on July 1, 1937, when the unit became known as Fighter Squadron Six (VF-6). VF-6 was redesignated Fighter Squadron Three (VF-3) on July 15, 1943, and, subsequently, VF-3B on November 15, 1946. Felix followed his lucky lot of naval aviators through one more redesignation on August 7, 1948, when VF-3B became known as Fighter Squadron Thirty-One (VF-31), now the famous *Tomcatter* squadron.

On September 27, 1922, eighteen Naval Aircraft Factory PT-1 aircraft from Torpedo and Bombing Squadron One (VT-1) hit a formation of three battleships and their escorts maneuvering at full-speed. Squadron pilots dropped seventeen Mk VII One "A" torpedoes at five hundred to one thousand yards, scoring eight direct "hits" in what can only be described as the first practical test of torpedo runs on live targets. The torpedoes were, of course, dummy ordnance and not intended to achieve anything more than to demonstrate the capability of a coordinated air attack on a formation of naval vessels. The test proved perhaps once and for all the ability of torpedoes to make a straight run at their designated targets. Torpedo trails are visible in both photographs. The large ship in the photograph is the battleship USS *Arkansas*. (Photographer unknown.)

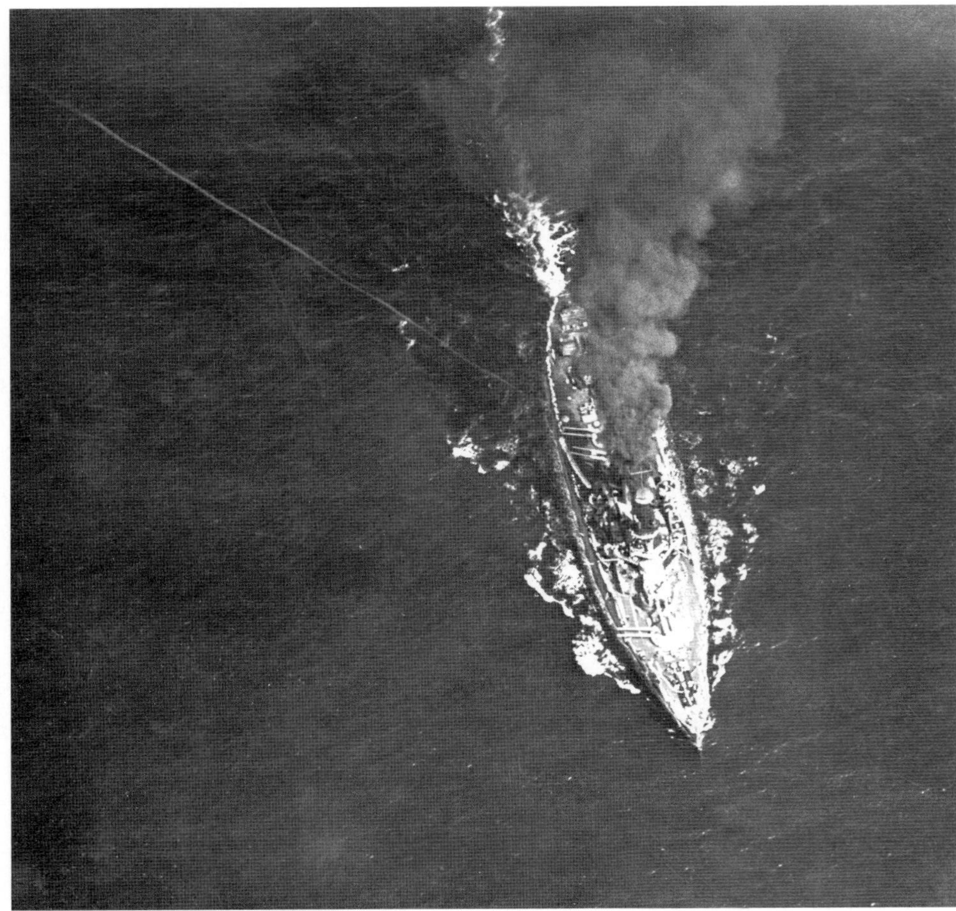

1922), and a Lieutenant (no first name) Dillon and Chief (no first name) Darling. There were initially fifteen total pilots in this squadron. In the spring of 1922, no one had ever landed nor taken off from the deck of an aircraft carrier. These men burned a trail for all to follow, gradually building the framework for naval air squadrons to come. Of the pilots named here, Palmer, Rhodes and Feher would contribute as much as their famed counterparts, Griffin, Chevalier, and Pride, to naval aviation, fundamentally changing, in some cases, the course of research and development of aircraft, aircraft equipment, and organizational structure of fleet squadrons.

Feher was the epitomé of the American success story. Born in Budapest, Hungary, on October 22, 1883,

The Infamous Billy Mitchell

Brigadier General William "Billy" Mitchell, assistant chief of the United States Army Air Service, learned back in his days of flight training at Glenn Curtiss' Flying School that aviators in the 1910s and 1920s—Army or Navy—had to stick together to advance one another's military service. Mitchell had angered many government officials, even his Navy counterparts, with his unrelenting insistence that aircraft could be used for more than subchasing, coastal watching, and routine patrol. As soon as Mitchell put the First World War behind him, he began a crusade for dirigibles, aircraft carriers, and all the necessary personnel and support equipment to establish aviation in all branches of American military service. The most he could get out of Washington were scowls and skepticism. He wrote in 1906 in the *Cavalry Journal,* "conflicts no doubt will be carried on in the future in the air, on the surface of the earth and water and under the water."

Mitchell was born in 1879 at Nice, France, on the famed Riviera. As the son of a Wisconsin United States Senator, young Mitchell's upbringing in a demanding household would have great bearing on the "can do" personality he exhibited in his adult life. When naval aviators dropped dummy bombs on the USS *Indiana* in 1920, a report issued afterward remarked it was doubtful a battleship could be sunk from the air, a challenge Mitchell was not going to fast overlook. Ever anxious to prove his point, Mitchell sat patiently before a congressional committee and calmly pronounced he could most assuredly "destroy or sink any ship in existence." His plan was to have Navy and Army aircraft alternate attacks on captured German warships, starting with a submarine, destroyer, cruiser and, finally, the battleship *Ostfriesland,* a twenty-seven-thousand-ton vessel built in 1911. The mighty *Ostfriesland* had taken eighteen hits at the Battle of Jutland during the First World War, struck a mine, and still made way to a port for repairs. If he could sink the *Ostfriesland,* Mitchell might be able to get somewhere with Washington.

Mitchell's original plans called for targets to be set thirty miles east of Cape Hatteras, but that arrangement was rejected and the ships were anchored seventy miles east of Cape Charles lightship, almost one hundred miles from Langley Field, Virginia. Navy and Army aircraft, led by Mitchell, dropped seven one-ton bombs on the *Ostfriesland,* scoring two direct hits. The other five bombs were not wasted. The concussion of the blast from five near-misses was enough to pop the hull plates of the German juggernaut and send her to the bottom of the sea twenty-one-and-one-half minutes after the first explosion. The night the *Ostfriesland* was sunk in July 1921, there was a tremendous celebration at Langley with huge bonfires that lit up the Peninsula skies, and the merry sounds of victorious Army and Navy aviators echoing in the darkness. Reportedly even a few snake dances were known to have taken place.

Mitchell's early success with the *Ostfriesland* revolutionized the military's perception of warfare and gave the airplane a new mission. This was particularly true for naval aircraft because the Navy was less inclined to and, in fact, did not lay the keel of another battleship like the ones in service in 1921. Instead Navy visionaries began to think long and hard about an "aircraft carrier" built from the keel up. The fight, however, had just begun since the Navy was still driven at its highest level by stalwart, unbending battleship admirals.

By March of 1922, the Navy's first twentieth century carrier, the USS *Langley* (CV-1), was commissioned at Norfolk, Virginia. During the late summer of 1923, the Navy struck the USS *Virginia* and USS *New Jersey,* sister ships weighing fifteen thousand tons, from the Navy record, anchored them off the coast of Cape Hatteras where Mitchell had originally wanted to conduct his tests in 1921, and used the ships for targets. Throughout the summer, construction of a makeshift airstrip was underway on the Outer Banks. Reporters from local and national newspaper services were expected to be ferried to the site aboard a couple of mine layers, and accompanied by dignitaries aboard a Navy transport ship to observe the bombing of the *Virginia* and *New Jersey* on September 23, 1923.

Mitchell arrived at Hampton Roads on September fourth, and proceeded to Hatteras to relieve the officer-in-charge because the airstrip and base were in such an unacceptable state. With Mitchell's arrival, much work lay ahead for everyone on the base. The first order he barked resounded loud and clear, "get the airstrip in shape." Mitchell's stan-

The German submarine *U-117,* one of America's great World War I prizes of war, was photographed at the foot of Commerce Street in Norfolk, Virginia, on May 11, 1919. A little over two years later, on June 21, 1921, the Army, at the invitation of the Navy, participated in bombing tests off the Virginia Capes in which the *U-117* was sunk that day. Twelve bombs were dropped from Navy F-5L aircraft at 1,100 feet. The twenty-first of June marked the first day of month-long tests to determine the effectiveness of aerial bombing of combatant ships and, of course, the best means by which ships could be constructed to counter such destructive power from the air.

dards were high, his way of dictating to subordinates totally in keeping with his reputation for quality and control. His brilliance was often masked by an impetuosity, his unquestionable position as the nation's leader in air tactics and development of the Army Air Service marred by borderline bouts of insubordination with superior officers and Washington politicians.

It is interesting to note that the Hatteras tests included the first use of Alexander de Severeky's new automatic bombsight. In addition, completely new superchargers were installed in Mitchell's aircraft to enable them to get above the eight-thousand-foot ceiling required of large bomb loads. Mitchell actually flew one of the planes.

A direct hit from a six-hundred-pound bomb from 10,000 feet was the coup de grace for the *Virginia*. She was sunk in less than twenty-six minutes by fourteen aerial bomb strikes. The *New Jersey* would share her fate. Despite Mitchell's great success with naval and army air forces off Cape Hatteras, military leadership in Washington remained doubtful planes could be used as bombers. Mitchell remained critical of his superiors in the nation's capitol for the rest of his career, such that it was given what lay ahead.

Any account of Mitchell should include the fact he went on a tour of the Pacific not a month after his bombing tests at Cape Hatteras and he predicted, having seen the enormous sea and air power buildup of the Japanese, that they were sure to attack in the future at Ford Island, Hawaii. Ford Island is in the middle of Pearl Harbor. His 323-page document for the Army which Mitchell completed in October of 1924 included his predication that the Japanese would send one hundred aircraft to hit Ford Island, the aerodrome, hangars, ammunition dumps, fuel tanks, barracks and other areas of military importance. He even estimated the attack would occur at half past seven in the morning, twenty-five minutes earlier than the actual attack time on December 7, 1941, at Pearl Harbor. The United States would lose three battleships, one capsized and four damaged by the force of 360 carrier-based bombing and torpedo planes which had positioned themselves off the Hawaiian coast undetected by American intelligence. Mitchell never knew his predilections would come true. United States involvement at the onset of the Second World War was predicted by Mitchell in 1924 when he noted, among other events, Clark Field in the Philippines would be attacked, as would Corregidor. Mitchell's report was discounted as another of his diatribes and filed away. The document was not declassified until 1958.

The eventual court-martial of Billy Mitchell centered not on his disagreements with his military superiors and politicos in 1921 and 1923 but, rather, on comments he made in 1925 regarding the Navy dirigible USS *Shenandoah* which had crashed in a storm near Sharon, Ohio, killing fourteen of her crew including Lieutenant Commander Zachary Lansdowne, a close personal friend of Mitchell's. In strong language, Mitchell remarked that the disaster of September 3, 1925, was the direct result of incompetence and almost treasonable negligence on the part of Navy admirals and Washington politicians bent on pushing aviation too far, too fast, skipping over critical considerations for the safety of aircrewmen and rigorous training syllabi. Mitchell took his case to the press which translated his words into damning headlines and front page diatribes. Of course, not a month later, Mitchell was charged with contemptuous and insubordinate criticism of his superiors and found guilty on all counts. He was demoted, stripped of his command, and had his pay suspended as a result. The Army eventually amended its original punishment to provide Mitchell with living expenses and half his pay but he resigned anyway, retiring to his home in Virginia and dying there in 1936.

The Douglas DT-2 torpedo plane in this photograph, Bureau Number A6569, belonged to Torpedo Squadron Two (VT-2). The aircraft was down for repairs in a farmer's field, location unknown, about 1924. This landplane version of the DT-2 was one of a group of twenty aircraft, Bureau Numbers A6563 to A6582, built by Douglas for the Navy. The landplane DT-2 was powered by a 400-horsepower Liberty 12 engine, which gave the aircraft a top speed of 101 miles per hour and a service ceiling of 7,800 feet, some 400 feet higher than its seaplane cousin. (Courtesy of the Hampton Roads Naval Museum.)

Lieutenant Alfred Melville "Al" Pride, Naval Aviatior No. 1119, makes a pass in a War Department DH-4B (Bureau Number A5983) at the large flight deck gear turntable constructed at Naval Air Station Hampton Roads. Pride was first attached to the USS *Langley* (CV-1) for development and testing of flight deck gear in April of 1922, and this photograph was taken some time after tests by this pioneer naval aviator were well underway. The DH-4B flown by Pride was acquired from the Army by the War Department and turned over to the Navy along with forty-one others just like it. (Courtesy of the National Museum of Naval Aviation.)

he came to the United States and enlisted in the American Navy on September 27, 1904. Feher would become a naturalized American citizen on February 9, 1914, ten years after his enlistment. He was designated Naval Aviator No. 95 on September 18, 1917, and made a temporary ensign or Ensign(T) Anthony Feher. Though he made it to lieutenant (junior grade)(T), Feher reverted back to boatswain in January of 1922 and served in the first squadron aboard an aircraft carrier on the USS *Langley* (CV-1). Feher made chief boatswain's mate in September of 1926 and went on to serve with Fighter Squadron Five, Scouting Fleet, in June 1927 and, later, Bombing Squadron One (B)[(2)] aboard the USS *Lexington* (CV-2) in January of the following year. Before leaving Hampton Roads to become a test pilot for the Naval Aircraft Factory in Philadelphia, Pennsylvania, Feher served with Utility Squadron One (B) or VJ-1B on the USS *Aroostook* (CM-3) in October 1928. His experience with a wide array of squadrons in the Atlantic Fleet gave Feher great insight into what would be expected of him at the Naval Aircraft Factory, a position he held from July 1930 until his return to the fleet in 1934. His later assignments included tours with Utility Squadron Two (F)[(3)] or VJ-2F on the USS *Wright* in June 1934, and again, with VJ-2F aboard the USS *Wright* and USS *Riegel* in 1937. By the time he finished as a test pilot at the Naval Aircraft Factory, Feher was once again an officer. He would retire as a commander in 1947, having provided practical insights into squadron composition and aircraft development which might have been sorely missed had a young Hungarian not immigrated to America at the turn of the century and given forty-three years of his life to the United States Navy.

As for his squadron mate at Hampton Roads, Lieutenant (junior grade) Carlton D. Palmer, his remembrances of Hampton Roads remain a priceless piece of naval aviation history. Palmer enlisted in the Navy in 1911. He was designated a naval aviator at Naval Air Station Hampton Roads on August 15, 1918, just days before the official declaration of the detachment as a full-fledged air station. This designation was predated to August 11, 1917, to reflect his earlier qualification as an enlisted man. Palmer was one of the first to fly a landplane from the turret platform of a battleship, the USS *Texas* in March of 1919, and among those elite first naval aviators to operate an aircraft from the deck of the USS *Langley,* America's first

The Boeing PB-1, Bureau Number A6881, is a one-of-a-kind aircraft. The Navy acquired the aircraft August 5, 1923. It had two 800-horsepower Packard engines. (Official United States Navy Photograph.)

aircraft carrier, in October of 1922. Prior to his first retirement from naval aviation on September 1, 1934, Palmer had been responsible for considerable flight test of aircraft radio, and for pioneering the use of a radio compass and radio telephone. He came out of retirement on August 1, 1941, to supervise the installation of aircraft radios at Naval Air Station Norfolk, and remained on active duty until the end of World War II.

Lieutenant Braxton Rhodes would have much to do with furthering research and development of catapults. He is most famous for his tests regarding the feasibility of flush-deck catapults to launch landplanes in 1925, at which time he and Lieutenant Commander Charles Perry "Charlie" Mason, Naval Aviator No. 52, demonstrated such a launch in a Douglas DT-2 from the carrier *Langley,* then moored to her berth at San Diego, California.

Specifications of arresting gear of the type later installed aboard the USS *Lexington* (CV-2) and USS *Saratoga* (CV-3) were sent to several design engineers, including Carl L. Norden and Warren Noble, on April 1, 1922. The memoranda read, in part, that "arresting gear will consist of two or more transverse wires stretched across the fore and aft wires [and which] lead around sheaves placed outboard to hydraulic brakes. The plane, after engaging the transverse wire, is guided down the [flight] deck by the action of the transverse wire working with the hydraulic brakes." Of course shortly thereafter, on May 24, 1922, at least launching via catapults aboard ship commenced successfully with the launching of a Vought VE-7 piloted by Lieutenant Andrew C. McFall, Naval Aviator No. 2891, with Lieutenant DeWitt Clinton "Duke" Ramsey, Naval Aviator No. 45, as passenger, from the USS *Maryland,* positioned off Yorktown, Virginia. A compressed air catapult was used, the same catapults installed on other battleships and cruisers of the fleet at that time. It was not until 1923 that a project of far reaching importance materialized on the air station to further enhance aviators' knowledge of the carrier: construction of an arresting device to train pilots for deck landing aboard the fleet's first aircraft carrier, USS *Langley,* a converted collier. Simultaneously, the air station at Norfolk carried on equally important work on the catapult, a role previously played by aircraft from Yorktown and those in the fleet.

Fortunately for aviators on the *Langley,* Whiting and Chevalier, officer-in-charge of flight operations on the carrier, did not approve installation of British engineered arresting gear on the ship. Instead, Whiting and Chevalier gave the testing process to Lieutenant Alfred Melville Pride, Naval Aviator No. 1119, test pilot and later officer-in-charge of the Experimental Detachment, Naval Air Station Hampton Roads, in 1926. The only guidance given Lieutenant Pride was "do better," and that is what he did. Pride landed on the turntable, which had already been constructed at the air station, but he felt axle friction on the wires made it impossible to safely stop his aircraft. He needed to find a way to attach a hook to the plane so it did not turtle. His solution was a cross-deck wire. In what has proven a fascinating story in itself, Pride dispensed with the turntable, strung a wire between two wooden sawhorses, and made passes at it with an Aeromarine aircraft, a plane already so plodding it drifted backward across an open field flying in mild wind. Ultimately, Pride replaced Ely's sandbag principle with weights that could be lifted and lowered to absorb the pressure of the landing. His weights were thirteen-inch shells for obsolete guns, held in check so only a few were picked up in succession as the cross-deck line ran out. The arresting gear developed by Pride in April of 1922 was used on the *Langley* but, in the end, it turned out to be more a combination of British fore and aft wires and Eugene Ely's cross-deck cables

Naval Air Station Hampton Roads was still in its infancy when this photograph was taken on February 23, 1923. The landing field and lagoon area are still under construction. Jamestown Exposition houses are demarcated by the Pennsylvania House tower (upper left, looking above the two hangars on the left), and the Grand Arch, a gift of the government of Japan in 1907, can be seen to the right below the two buildings at the edge of the airfield on the water. Directly north of the airfield are the Naval Station Norfolk submarine pens, now the site of the Navy tugboat facility. There are a number of submarines visible in their berths. The area to the south was landfill, white patches indicating areas not quite finished. (Official United States Navy Photograph.)

This aerial view of Naval Air Station Hampton Roads, taken about 1923, clearly demarcates development of the naval installation on lands acquired for expansion in 1918 and 1919. (Official United States Navy Photograph.)

The seaplane area shown in this aerial view of the naval air station was constructed at the mouth of Boush Creek. The angle of the picture shows East Camp to the left above the hangars. The original Chambers Field would have been off to the right (out of the photograph). The Virginian Railroad line ran straight across the upper half of the image. Further landfill obliterated what was Boush Creek to complete the area once occupied by the Naval Aviation Depot side of the air station, 1923. (Official United States Navy Photograph.)

connected to lifting weights. To land, the airplane's hook caught the wire cross-deck, the plane stopped immediately and was bridled by the fore and aft wires, essentially keeping the aircraft from turtling and killing the aircrew.

L.C. Stevens, a naval constructor as well as aviator, later proved Pride's system was slow. By then, Pride's arresting gear system was on the USS *Lexington* and the USS *Saratoga* but had been removed by 1929. Ever since that time, the concept of arresting gear has been built on Eugene Ely's original cross-deck wire design. Heavy steel cables still stretch across the decks of modern day aircraft carriers.

Following on the heels of Billy Mitchell's successful bombing demonstrations off the Virginia Capes in the summer of 1921, the Navy conducted its first mass torpedo practice against a live target in the same area on September 27, 1922. Eighteen Naval Aircraft Factory PT-1 aircraft of Torpedo and Bombing Squadron One (VT-1) attacked their designated target, the USS *Arkansas,* which was one of a formation of three battleships maneuvering at full speed. The attack lasted more than twenty-five minutes during which time the aircraft approached the ships from port to starboard and discharged seventeen Mk VII Mode One "A" torpedoes(4) at distances of five hundred to one thousand yards, and made eight hits on their designated target. Subsequent naval analysis emphasized the artificialities of the test which rendered the practice unreliable as a combat indicator. The Navy did discover, however, that torpedoes could be successfully launched from aircraft and run straight to a target.

Many firsts of carrier aviation and naval aviation in general would occur at Hampton Roads in the 1920s, particularly after Lieutenant Pride's important work with arresting gear. Lieutenant Commander Virgil Childers "Squash" Griffin, Naval Aviator No. 41, executed the first aircraft carrier takeoff in Navy history in a Vought VE-7SF from the deck of the *Langley* on October 17, 1922, while the ship was anchored in the York River. A few days later, of course, on October 26, Lieutenant Commander Chevalier, flying an Aeromarine, made the first landing aboard an aircraft carrier, again the *Langley,* while the ship made way at six-knots off the Virginia Capes.

The excitement of Griffin and Chevalier's feats would be marred in short order when Chevalier was fatally injured while stunting over the Lochhaven section of Norfolk. Lieutenant Commander Chevalier was one of the most widely known naval aviators in the world, keeping friends around the globe, some of the closest being in Hampton Roads. Chevalier, whose home was Baltimore, Maryland, graduated from the Naval Academy in 1910. While still a midshipman, he was known to all in the Navy for having

The pilot of this Lewis & Vought VE-7SF, Bureau Number A5937, landed his aircraft on the waters of the Dismal Swamp Canal on July 17, 1925, to participate in the celebration of the opening of the George Washington Highway which winds its way parallel to the canal. The fighter plane was attached to the USS *Arkansas* as part of Observation Squadron Six (VO-6), Aircraft Squadrons, Scouting Fleet. VO-6's squadron insignia is visible on the side of the aircraft. Established in 1924 as VO-6, the squadron's existence was short-lived. By 1927, VO-6 had been redesignated VO-5S and was no longer flying the VE-7SF, and in 1930, the squadron was disestablished.

Commander John "Jang" Rodgers (center), Naval Aviator No. 2, who won his pilot's wings in 1911, is shown fifteen years later, February of 1926, in the flight uniform worn by naval aviators of that period. With him are Lieutenant L.W. Curtain (left) and Naval Aviation Pilot Harold I. June. Rodgers was appointed Assistant Chief of the Bureau of Aeronautics in January of 1926, a position he held until his death on August 27, 1926, from injuries sustained in an airplane crash. This pioneer aviator came from a long line of distinguished naval officers, starting with Commodore John Rodgers of War of 1812 fame; Admiral John Rodgers, Civil War; Rear Admiral Frederick Rodgers, Naval Academy Class of 1861; Rear Admiral John A. Rodgers, his father, Naval Academy Class of 1868; Rear Admiral Raymond P. Rodgers, Naval Academy Class of 1868; Admiral William L. Rodgers, Naval Academy Class of 1879, and Captain Christopher R.P. Rodgers, Naval Academy Class of 1904. Rodgers himself was a graduate of the Naval Academy, 1903, and the first Navy pilot trained by the Wright Brothers. As for Naval Aviation Pilot June, he later accompanied Commander Richard E. Byrd on the first flight over the South Pole in the Ford trimotor named the *Floyd Bennett* on November 29, 1929. Bernt Balchen was Byrd's chief pilot, June his copilot. (Official United States Navy Photograph.)

Dr. Edward P. Warner, aeronautical engineer from the Massachusetts Institute of Technology, was appointed July 2, 1926, as the first Assistant Secretary of the Navy for Air. He served in this capacity until March 1929. (Official United States Navy Photograph.)

The arresting gear and four Boeing Pursuits are clearly visible on the deck of the nation's first aircraft carrier, USS *Langley*, in 1926.

Experiments with aircraft and submarines took place at Hampton Roads in 1926. The Bureau of Aeronautics had issued a contract to the Cox-Klemin Company of College Point, Long Island, New York, to build what amounted to six aircraft, Bureau Numbers A6515 to A6520. The XS-1 (A6515) was a twin floatplane of wood and canvas construction. Aircraft bearing the XS-1 designation were powered by a sixty-horsepower Lawrence engine but, of the XS-1s, one was redesignated XS-2 (Bureau Number A6519) and fitted with a Kinner three-cylinder engine (the same aircraft shown in the second or center photograph). The Navy also contracted the Glenn L. Martin Company to build a handful of the same type aircraft known as MS-1s. The MS-1s were all-aluminum construction. On July 28, 1926, the submarine *S-1*, commanded by Lieutenant C.B. Momsen, surfaced and launched a Cox-Klemin XS-2 seaplane—called a submarine scout—flown by Lieutenant Dolph Chadwick "Dick" Allen, Naval Aviator No. 1639. The *S-1* later recovered and stored the XS-2, then submerged with the aircraft under its protective tank. Allen was a well-known experimental pilot who not only assisted in the development and test flights of the XS-2 seaplane, but was also renowned for his participation in the International Air Races of 1923. Lieutenant Allen is shown here in the first photograph posing aboard the *S-1*, the XS-2 still in its storage tank. The second image shows the *S-1* preparing to leave the pier at Norfolk for flight test, the XS-2 out of its cylinder and fully assembled. The third photograph was taken on July 28, 1926, during the actual test of the XS-2 at Hampton Roads. (Official United States Navy Photographs. Courtesy of the National Museum of Naval Aviation.)

Crewmen of the USS *Langley* recover an amphibian. Side nets off the carrier's wooden decks are in the foreground, 1926.

The Boeing NB-1 aircraft was used as a pilot and gunnery trainer, the aft cockpit being fitted with a Scarff ring for a gun. Navy training squadron VN-6D5 at Naval Air Station Hampton Roads received a mix of NB-1s and NB-2s to use as trainers. The photograph shown here was taken July 28, 1925, and clearly shows the 200-horsepower Lawrence J-1 engine, and characteristic N-strut configuration. (Official United States Navy Photograph.)

Lieutenant Commander Harold Terry "Cueless" Bartlett, Naval Aviator No. 21, flight commander of the famous PN-10 nonstop flight from Naval Air Station Hampton Roads to the Canal Zone, is shown here in 1926. The flight covered a distance of 2,060.9 miles. Bartlett was a member of the Naval Academy Class of 1911, and a winner of the Navy Cross as an aviator in active operations with Allied armies on the Belgian Front while attached to the Northern Bombing Group from September to December 1918. He had a fascinating naval career from his time as White House Junior Naval Aide to President Woodrow Wilson in 1914 to the end of his rich and record setting aviation service. Bartlett would be in Hampton Roads many times in his naval aviation career, the most remarkable as officer-in-charge of Fleet Torpedo Plane Division, Hampton Roads, in 1920, and as commanding officer of VT-1 in 1922, the Navy's first torpedo plane squadron. He did, in fact, direct the construction of VT-1's base at Yorktown, Virginia, in 1921. Aside from his flight in 1926, Lieutenant Commander Bartlett returned to Naval Air Station Hampton Roads in 1929, two years before he retired the first time in 1931 as a commander. He would be recalled to service in World War II, retiring a second time in 1943. (Official United States Navy Photograph. Courtesy of the Hampton Roads Naval Museum.)

rescued twenty men from drowning in the North River. He was in a small liberty boat going from ship to shore when the boat capsized. Most of the men were unable to swim so one by one Chevalier swam for them and carried each back to the boat, which he had already righted. He advanced to Lieutenant Commander, serving the major portion of his time in France where he was decorated by the French with the Legion of Honor, Order of Chevalier and the *Croix de Guerre* with palm, as well as awards from the English and American governments. His landing aboard the *Langley* in October was more than just a first. Chevalier had also accomplished by this act one of the most hazardous feats ever witnessed at that time in naval aviation—landing on a moving aircraft carrier. Chevalier would also become the first American to take off in a plane from the deck of an aircraft carrier without the use of a catapult. He played a part in many other experiments of naval aviation, adding immeasurably to the technological advancement of the service.

The most senior flight officer of the

The Boeing FB-1 was primarily a Marine Corps aircraft, though two FB-2s were modified for Navy use on aircraft carriers. Nine of the ten aircraft, 1925 production models, were eventually assigned to the Marine Expeditionary Force in China in 1927 and 1928, then manned by Marine Fighter Squadron Ten (VF-10M), later redesignated VF-3M. The aircraft was powered by a 435-horsepower Curtiss D-12 engine and had wooden wings. Bureau numbers of the planes, of which the FB-1 shown here was one, were A6884–A6893. This photograph shows an FB-1 on the squadron's landing field at Tientsin, China, in 1927. Squadrons from Hampton Roads regularly deployed to faraway ports and, as is the case in this photograph, Near East and Far East locales. (Official United States Marine Corps Photograph.)

A Boeing TB-1 landplane, Bureau Number A7024, was photographed in a hangar at Naval Air Station Hampton Roads, April 15, 1927. This was the first of three constructed for the Navy. The three-seat, 730-horsepower Packard 3A-2500 engine aircraft could be used as either a seaplane or, in the case shown here, a landplane. (Official United States Navy Photograph.)

aircraft carrier USS *Langley* and regarded as one of the most daring Navy airmen of his day, Chevalier crashed just after eight o'clock the morning of November 12, 1922. He wrecked negotiating a forced landing in a marsh at the rear of William Sloane's home in Lochhaven on the bank of the Lafayette River. Chevalier was purportedly speeding back to duty aboard the Langley from Naval Air Station Hampton Roads when he detoured his flight over the river to stunt for friends. In reality, Chevalier had done a significant bit of backtracking to be over the Lafayette River because the *Langley* was anchored off Yorktown, Virginia, far north of where Chevalier's fatal accident occurred. Residents of Lochhaven saw the plane overhead about eight that morning stunting, now and again darting close to the ground, swooping up again for safety. The engine stopped several times then raced with increased speed. Spectators realized Chevalier was in trouble and, though he had been performing thrilling feats in the air, his distress quickly became apparent to all those who watched helplessly.

Dr. W.E. Driver who lived near the crash site, reported to naval authorities he thought at one time the plane, in its swooping, would strike his home. It came so close, he said, it threw a big shadow across the window from which he was watching. Driver would further

Andy Aileron demonstrates the "wings" of an airplane.

This handsome dog was the mascot of VT-1, the Navy's very first torpedo squadron, formed at Yorktown, Virginia, in early 1919. The squadron would eventually come under the administration of Lieutenant Harold Terry Bartlett, Naval Aviator No. 21, in 1922. This photograph was taken about 1929. Notice the naval aviator's wings pinned to his coat.

VT-1's mascot is ready to go flying, circa 1929. Note the VT-1 squadron insignia on the fuselage. This squadron's rather distinguished history appears to go back to the days when the Navy conducted extensive torpedo tests at Hampton Roads using Curtiss R-6s. VT-1 would evolve from part of Air Detachment, Atlantic Fleet, organized February 3, 1919. The Atlantic Fleet Torpedo Plane Squadron was officially established in May of 1920, a little over a month before its counterpart, Torpedo Squadron Five, on the West Coast. An Air Detachment, Pacific Fleet (parent of VT-5) was not formed until September of 1919, several months, of course, after its Atlantic Fleet equivalent. On August 1, 1921, a World War I high-altitude bombsight mounted on a gyroscopically stabilized base was tested by Torpedo Squadron One, Atlantic Fleet, at Yorktown, Virginia, thus marking the successful completion of the first phase of Carl L. Norden's development of an effective high-altitude bombsight for the Bureau of Ordnance.

This world-renowned insignia of Fighting Fourteen was originally adopted in June 1927, though the squadron had been established about eight years prior to its use. According to squadron lore, one of Fighting One's pilots donned a beat up top hat, thus giving birth to the famous *"High Hat"* name. There was not too much aforethought to choosing the hat symbol but, it is has stuck with the squadron for over seventy years of their unprecedented continuous history. When Ensign James Arbes, Naval Aviator No. 5713, was a member of the squadron, then designated VB-3, the squadron was still called the *High Hats.* Arbes commented, "I recall we were all very proud of our insignia. We had it on folding matches and our Christmas cards. I believe we felt we had a tradition to uphold and were a cut above the other squadrons."

remark, "the plane must have been less than one hundred feet in the air." The second time the fated plane dipped down, it crashed into the marsh. Dr. Driver expressed his belief that the steering gear of the aircraft went awry. The plane, a Lewis and Vought VE-7SF, Bureau Number A5932, was demolished.

William Sloane Jr. was the first to reach the wrecked plane. Sloane would later tell naval investigators all he knew of the crash and would provide them the only eyewitness testimony of the incident. Dr. Driver was on the scene immediately after the accident and assisted Sloane in dragging Chevalier from under the wreckage. He did what he could to make the aviator comfortable while waiting for an ambulance from the base. Chevalier was conscious when rescuers reached him. He smiled when Dr. Driver offered him hot coffee but could not speak or drink. Driver and Sloane wrapped Chevalier in heavy blankets, talking all the while with the famed aviator and friend of many who now lay

On May 9, 1926, a trimotor Fokker named the *Josephine Ford* (first photograph) made the first flight over the North Pole, circled the pole and returned to base at King's Bay, Spitzbergen. The flight was completed in 15 ½ hours, Naval Aviation Pilot No. 9 Floyd Bennett at the controls, Lieutenant Commander (later Rear Admiral) Richard Evelyn Byrd sitting right seat. Upon return to the United States, Bennett caught pneumonia and died in 1928 at the age of 38. This great American explorer and adventurer thirsted to chart the unknown expanses of the world as much as he loved to fly. Stationed at Naval Air Station Hampton Roads for duty between 1922 and 1924, just prior to his polar exploration, the strikingly handsome and gentle Bennett lived at 816 West 42nd Street in Norfolk where he lent neighborhood children his garage to transform into whatever they wished—a fort, playhouse, or quiet retreat. Byrd chose a Ford trimotor (second photograph) for his 1929 expedition to the South Pole and named it the *Floyd Bennett*. Piloted by Bernt Balchen, the *Floyd Bennett* flew into the history books during that winter. Byrd had set up a base at the Bay of Whales and named it Little America. The Ford trimotor was designed for antarctic conditions but exhibited problems lifting its total fuel capacity, equipment and supplies. A refueling stop was plotted 440 miles south of Little America. Byrd gathered his crew for its first attempt at flight over the South Pole at 10:29 the evening of November 28, 1929, New York time. Takeoff from McMurdo Sound occurred moments later, and the South Pole was reached at 8:55 the morning of the twenty-ninth. Bernt Balchen would pilot the *Floyd Bennett* on its historic flight. The rest of the crew consisted of Naval Aviation Pilot Harold I. June (radioman); Byrd (navigator and copilot); Captain Ashley C. McKinley of the United States Army (surveyor and photographer). As the *Floyd Bennett* winged over the South Pole, Byrd took an American flag weighted with a stone from the grave of Naval Aviation Pilot Floyd Bennett and dropped it over the South Polar plateau. When Bennett died in 1928, he was buried in Arlington National Cemetery with the honors and fanfare accorded full admirals of the United States Navy. In his memoirs, Byrd would write, "it seemed fitting that something connected with the spirit of this noble friend...rest as long as stone endures at the bottom of the world." The *Floyd Bennett, Josephine Ford,* and *Stars and Stripes* (third photograph) are shown here on a tour through Naval Air Station Hampton Roads in the summer of 1928 to promote Byrd's efforts to return to the South Pole. Each aircraft bore the "Byrd Antarctic Expedition" name down the fuselage. The *Stars and Stripes* was a Fairchild aircraft and one of three planes Byrd took with him to the Antarctic in November of 1928. Byrd wanted to return to the Antarctic in 1930 but the nation had just slipped into the Great Depression, and financing another expedition took three more years. Jacob Ruppert, owner of the New York Yankees, would be the esteemed Rear Admiral Byrd's major benefactor for the 1933 Antarctic Expedition.

Chinook: "Man Never Had a Truer Friend..."

Rear Admiral Richard E. Byrd's expeditions to the polar reaches were about more than men and their flying machines, ships and science. The dogs who went with Rear Admiral Byrd on his Arctic and Antarctic explorations were Eskimo dogs, otherwise known as huskies. In teams of half-dozen or more, huskies drew the sledges which transported most the equipment and provisions for Byrd's men across two polar regions. An unknown writer of the 1920s wrote:

"Is a pole to be discovered? Man stands powerless before the ice and snow without the dogs of the North. Is an expedition to reach the interior of a bleak region in dead of winter to rescue some hapless explorer or pioneer, or to help an ice-besieged population fight an epidemic of fever or smallpox? Then the sleds and dogs make the trip possible."

This story is not about airplanes and it is not about people. This story is about Chinook, the most famous of Byrd's huskies and "boss dog" of the first Antarctic expedition. Arthur T. Walden, veteran musher of Byrd's 1928 expedition to the Antarctic, was Chinook's master. But the relationship went further than dog and master: Chinook and Walden were friend and pal.

Chinook was the the grandson of Admiral Peary's lead dog and, as Walden recalled in 1930, "a personality if ever there was one." Walden operated Chinook Kennels, his 1,400-acre property in New Hampshire, where Chinook was reared, but not where he died. Walden's grief was visible as he spoke to a Norfolk reporter in 1930 regarding details of Chinook's death.

"Chinook was whipped, all right," Walden recounted, his eyes welling with tears. As Walden continued, his lips trembled:

"He was put down once or twice by his own dogs, the dogs he had never allowed to fight. That night, although it wasn't right at all, but just sleeping time in the long, long Antarctic day, he awakened me twice by patting me with his paw. I knew he felt badly, for he'd never done that before."

The next day, January 17, 1929, Chinook's twelfth birthday, he worked with Walden, breaking in another leader. Some distance from camp, Walden thought he would unharness Chinook, as he and the team were traveling light, and let him follow them into camp.

Chinook followed for awhile, and then Walden and his team met up with another sledge and the dogs mixed up. Though he did not notice right away, Walden turned around and realized Chinook was not following anymore. At first, Walden figured Chinook had turned and gone with one of the other

Two of the puppies from the 1939–1941 expedition rest in the arms of one of the crewmen aboard the USS *Bear*. Byrd had many men on his third exploration of the Antarctic who were veterans of one or both of the previous South Pole expeditions. Among these men were Jack Bursey, dog driver, who had been a member of the First Byrd Antarctic Expedition, and Joseph D. Healy, dog driver, a veteran of the Second Byrd Antarctic Expedition. It is unclear from Larson's notations whether the crewman holding the puppies is either Bursey or Healy. (R.K.T. Larson, photographer. Courtesy of the Kirn Library.)

teams. "But he hadn't at all. He had gone out by himself to die. Almost any animal will do that when he realizes the time has come, and Chinook realized that, and the end must have come—out there somewhere on the ice." One of the men in the camp later told Walden that he had seen Chinook a long way off on the ice barrier, headed away from the pack and his master.

Chinook's grandson, Karluk, fought for leadership of the pack upon Chinook's death. Six of Walden's dogs were killed in fierce fighting for the honor of "boss dog." Karluk, though a powerful dog, was not the winner and though he proved to be a leader, he was never the noble dog his grandfather had been. Walden remarked with deep sorrow:

"Most of the friends I have in this world have come to me as the result of Chinook or some other dog. For never did man have a truer friend. I glory in the way he died and shall cherish his memory. He was more of a man than I will ever be."

Wolflike in appearance, the huskies of the 1939–1941 expedition were devoted hard-working animals who played a noteworthy part in Antarctic expeditions. Byrd took 160 sled dogs to the Antarctic in 1939. Some of them were veterans of the Second Byrd Antarctic Expedition, and seven of those had been born in the Antarctic. The dogs were divided between East and West Bases; seventy went to West Base, the rest to East Base. This photograph depicts a sailor holding onto one of the dogs prior to the expedition's departure from Norfolk on November 25, 1939. The picture was taken by R.K.T. Larson of the Norfolk newspapers. (Courtesy of the Kirn Library.)

Vought O2U-1 Corsairs of VO-2S, off the battleship USS *Florida,* are from the last series of the O2U-1s, indicated by their Bureau Numbers A7912 and A79??, respectively. The squadron was assigned to Battleship Division Two, circa 1928. The O2U-1 aircraft was a proven record-setter. Lieutenant Steven W. Callaway, Naval Aviator No. 2138, flying the O2U-1 Corsair at Hampton Roads on April 23, 1927, had set a new 100-kilometer world speed record for Class C seaplanes with a 500-kilogram useful load at 147.263 miles per hour. Lieutenant J.D. Barner broke the 500-kilometer world speed record for Class C seaplanes at Hampton Roads on April 30, 1927, carrying a useful load of 500 kilograms with a speed of 136.023 miles per hour, and on May 21, 1927, Lieutenant Rutledge "Irv" Irvine, Naval Aviator No. 1001, took a Corsair equipped with a Pratt & Whitney Wasp engine into the skies over Norfolk to establish yet another record for 1,000 kilometers at a speed of 130.932 miles per hour. (Official United States Navy Photograph.)

This photograph is a rare view of the Loening ambulance, built by the Keystone-Loening Company of Bristol, Pennsylvania. The Loening Amphibian Ambulance was one of two ever built, both for the United States Navy. One was sent to Naval Air Station Hampton Roads in 1928 for the purpose of medical evacuations. The Navy designation of the aircraft was XHL-1. Here, the ambulance climbs ashore at Norfolk after a flight to Hatteras, North Carolina, to get Desmond Austin. (Courtesy of the Hampton Roads Naval Museum.)

before them dying. An examination of Chevalier's injuries was not made until he arrived at the Portsmouth Naval Hospital. "It was a privilege," Dr. Driver would later recall, "to see how plucky this man was." The absence of fire in the wreckage led some observers to believe the engine had stopped running before the plane hit the ground. Flyers who inspected the scene said the marsh would have appeared from the air as a safe landing place. At the rear of it, however, was a sand pile which the wheels of the aircraft struck in the descent. It is believed the pile of sand caused the problem; otherwise Chevalier would have made a safe landing. Flyers noted the sand was not visible from the air, and it was equally apparent to them that Lieutenant Commander Chevalier's engine had stopped and landing was his only option.

News of his accident spread quickly through the naval aviation community. As if Chevalier's accident were not enough, his wife would figure prominently in another accident when the airplane in which she was speeding from Washington, D.C., to her husband's bedside made a forced landing in the Chesapeake Bay. One wing of the plane was torn away by rough waves but the passengers were rescued uninjured by naval launches, the wreck towed to the naval base. Aviators paced hospital corridors waiting for news of their beloved "Chevy." He would expire the morning of November 14, 1922, as the result of massive internal injuries. Commander Kenneth "Ken" Whiting, Chevalier's commanding officer and best friend, as well as the aviator's wife and brother, Grosvenor Chevalier, were with him when he died.

The list of firsts would fire in rapid succession as Commander Kenneth Whiting, commanding officer of the *Langley,* made the first catapult launching from his ship piloting a Naval Aircraft Factory PT torpedo plane on November 18, 1922. As Whiting would later comment, he made this landmark flight in honor of his friend and brother aviator, Lieutenant Commander Chevalier. Less than a year later, November 5, 1923, a series of tests demonstrating the feasibility of stowing, assembling, and launching a seaplane from a submarine were completed off Hampton Roads using a Martin MS-1 and submarine *S-1,* commanded by Lieutenant P.M. Rhea. A crew from the USS *Langley* supervised by Lieutenant Commander "Squash" Griffin, cooperated with the submarine crew. The idea was to launch the seaplane by submerging the submarine. This test was not attempted again, though a submarine did not only successfully deploy but also recover a seaplane during experiments off Norfolk shores a little over three years later on July 28, 1926, using a Cox-Klemin XS-2 aircraft flown by Lieutenant Dolph Chadwick "Dick" Allen, Naval Aviator No. 1639. The submarine *S-1,* then commanded by Lieutenant C.B. Momsen, surfaced and launched the XS-2, recovered the aircraft and submerged with it, thus completing the first cycle of operations in a series of tests investigating the use of airplanes on submarines.

Fighter Squadron Two (VF-2) became the first organization of pilots to operate as a squadron from an aircraft carrier when its pilots began coordinated landing practice aboard the USS *Langley,* on manuevers just off San Diego,

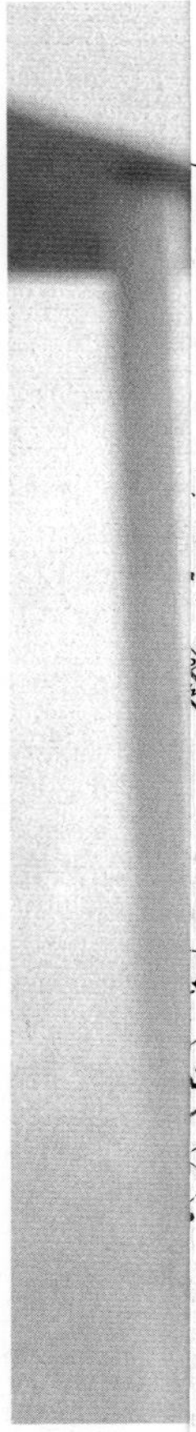

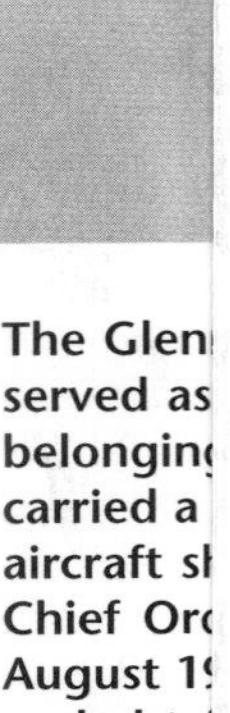

The Glen
served as
belongin
carried a
aircraft s
Chief Or
August 1
and obta

CEL ④
ACRES
PARCEL ⑦
FAYER REALTY CORP ET ALS
ACRES
ROAD
P. ET ALS.
PARCEL ⑥
85 ACRES
PARCEL ⑨
80 ACRES
POINT ROAD
S 0° 28' E
ARE TRUE NORTH.
LINES PLOTTED FROM SURVEYS
BLIC WORKS OFFICER BETWEEN
D MARCH 1, 1940.
ED FROM SURVEYS AND
OF NORFOLK REAL ESTATE
d Virginian R.R. R/w added.
Tract "C"
ngs added
cted
"B"
BRIEF
BY
ERATING BASE, NORFOLK, VA.
DS APPRAISED
FOR
ATION EXPANSION
Y 28, 1940

Californi
date also
Langley's
of Aircr
Fighter S
would op
ing Ham
carrier ar
Atlantic
did a lot
would lat
pilots i
January
naval av
pilots (e
Lieutena
Shoemak
was com
time.

If h
lesson i
summari
was neve
the case
Herbert
who ma

Boeing F4B-1 aircraft of VF-5B *Striking Eagles* appear on the flight line at Naval Air Station Hampton Roads, May 7, 1930. The squadron was stationed aboard the USS *Lexington.* Section leaders' aircraft are demarcated with a vertical band around the fuselage centered around the squadron designation letter and full-colored cowlings. The top wing of these aircraft was also painted with the section color. Interestingly, on January 19, 1937, then-Lieutenant James H. "Jimmy" Flatley Jr. would become a centurion (one hundred aircraft carrier traps) with VF-5B aboard the *Lexington.* (Charles S. Borjes, photographer. Courtesy of the Kirn Library.)

into the propeller arc of his aircraft the afternoon of July 11, 1924. Official Navy accounts of the accident note the engines of his H-16 flying boat, Bureau Number A3515, were being warmed up on the apron at Norfolk awaiting the impending arrival of Rear Admiral William Adger Moffett for his return flight to Anacostia. Schiff, the second pilot, started aft of the port side of the pilots' cockpit to talk with the mechanic standing between the engines. He was struck by the prop and died instantly. The Schiff Memorial Trophy, founded in his memory that year, was for a time given annually to the pilot or command with the best safety record, but it was later retired.

Naval aviators would learn from Schiff's demise, but one, in particular, put the experience to good use. Lieutenant Alford Joseph "Al" Williams, Naval Aviator No. 1820, assigned to Naval Air Station Hampton Roads as a test pilot and destined to become one of the greatest aviators of all time, was purportedly the first Navy pilot to paint his propeller tips for the safety of pilots and ground crew—the same year of Schiff's death. The Navy's first directive requiring painted wing tips is dated June 1, 1931.

In a relatively short period of time, night landings aboard aircraft carriers were made possible by the daring of a handful of aviators. Lieutenant John Dale Price, Naval Aviator No. 2730, made the first night landing aboard the *Langley,* on April 1, 1925. Price would later make a number of experimental night landings aboard the USS *Lexington* in 1933. He would be followed in his record-making endeavor aboard the *Langley* by Lieutenants Delbert Lawrence Conley, Naval Aviator No. 1166, and Adolphus W. Gorton, and Lieutenant Commander Rossmore Denman "Sox" Lyon, Naval Aviator No. 968, who made his flight on April 8, 1925. Lyon became the commanding officer of Scouting Squadron One (B) (VS-1B) on the *Langley* in January of 1932. As for the low rank and aviator designation number of Conley not going hand in hand, he augmented from the reserves to regular Navy in 1920 as an ensign. Conley had been designated a naval aviator heavier-than-air on September 12, 1918, in Pensacola, Florida, with subsequent assignments to Anacostia and Hampton Roads. As Naval Aviator No. 1166, Conley should have shared rank with Lieutenant Commander Lyon because he certainly shared the distinction of being in the elite group of naval aviators to conquer the first nighttime landings

Pilots of the United States Naval Reserve Aviation Unit pose in front of a Consolidated NY-2 seaplane at Naval Air Station Hampton Roads circa 1930. The officer third from the left, standing, is Melvin N. Gough. A Marine Corps pilot stands on the end of Gough's row. Kneeling on the first row are officer pilots with the exception of the fellow on the end, right, a "flying chief." (Courtesy of the National Museum of Naval Aviation.)

aboard an aircraft carrier. When experimental flights in night carrier landings were made aboard the USS *Lexington* in 1933, it would be Delbert Conley who made the feat look easy.

While so many milestones were taking place in training, education, research and development at Hampton Roads, the Morrow Board, created by President Calvin Coolidge to study aircraft in national defense and headed by Dwight W. Morrow, convened on November 30, 1925, to recommend a five-year construction program for fleet air bases to Congress. The program was approved and officially well underway by 1926, bringing with it a new position at the Navy Department, an Assistant Secretary of the Navy for Air. One of the most important men to occupy this office would be David Sinton Ingalls, Naval Aviator No. 85, who was appointed by President Herbert Hoover on March 16, 1929. In his duties as overseer of the test and development program, Ingalls directed plenty of appropriations to Hampton Roads, funds which no doubt sustained the air base between the wars and resulted in some of the most critical research and development in naval aviation history.

There is no doubt that one of the events to galvanize the world's attention on Naval Air Station Hampton Roads and its growing aviation complex was the International Schneider Cup Seaplane Trophy Race of 1926, an event which drew tens of thousands of visitors to the air station and its surrounding vistas in November of that year. When Eugene Ely made his benchmark flight in November of 1910, hardly a soul witnessed his great feat and those who did see him launch from the USS *Birmingham* were among the few who were obligated to observe the event on behalf of the Navy Department. Ely created barely three-inch headlines. The Schneider Cup Race of 1926 was proof of how important aviation had become to the world public. Headlines and hysteria swept around the world as *Il Duce's* Major Mario de Benardi won the contest for Italy. The air race brought spectators from Europe, South America, and the Orient to Norfolk to watch the United States Navy team and Italian military pilots go head to head for the coveted trophy.(7)

Following on the heels of excitement generated by the Schneider Cup race in November, the spring of 1927 would be dictated by the perils of mother nature and the superhuman feats of America's most daring naval aviators. April and May of 1927 were eventful in the great number of speed records set by naval aviators at Hampton Roads. On April 23, 1927, Lieutenant Steven W. Callaway, Naval Aviator No. 2138, pushed the world's speed record for Class C-2 airplanes with a 1,102.31 pound

Dr. Claude Dornier's world-renowned DO-X flying boat, a monstrosity, flew over Naval Operating Base Norfolk in 1931. The DO-X had twelve engines mounted back-to-back in what is referred to as six nacelles, each with one tractor and one pusher propreller. Dornier replaced the aircraft's original engines, 550-horsepower Siemens (Bristol) Jupiter radial engines, with 600-horsepower Curtiss Conqueror liquid-cooled engines which could get the DO-X up to 134 miles per hour. The flying boat had a wing span of 157 feet, 5 inches and was three decks high. The aircraft even had a dining room and dance floor that measured sixty feet long. The Dornier DO-X would make three transatlantic flights, the first completed between November 2, 1930, and August 5, 1931, but not without exacting a high price, namely onboard fires. The crew ended up making the flight in legs, hopping the continent of Europe and skirting the Atlantic, and stopping at other ports like Norfolk until it reached New York in August 27, 1931.

load to 147.263 miles per hour for 100 kilometers in a Vought O2U-1 Corsair with the Pratt & Whitney Wasp engine, a nine-cylinder radial motor capable of 425-horsepower, surpassing records previously set by the French. At the time of Callaway's record-setting flight, the O2U-1 was the only one of its kind being used by the Navy, but within a couple of weeks, thirty-three of the aircraft would be delivered to naval air stations for assignment as scout planes shot from catapults aboard light cruisers.

Callaway would enjoy his achievement less than a week when, on April 13, 1927, Lieutenant J.D. Barner, flying the Vought O2U-1, also equipped with the Pratt & Whitney 425-horsepower Wasp engine, set the world's speed record for Class C-2 aircraft with a useful load of 1,102.31 pounds at 136.023 miles per hour for 500 kilometers. Renowned air racer Lieutenant Rutledge Irvine, Naval Aviator No. 1001, would reappear at Norfolk on May 21, 1927, to set yet another time and distance record with the O2U-1 model equipped with the Pratt & Whitney Wasp engine. Irvine would take the aircraft 1000 kilometers at a constant speed of 130.932 miles per hour, breaking previously set world's records for the C-2 class at equal distance. Irvine was a dedicated career naval aviator whose parting remembrance of his service stated, "only the planes change. Once a naval aviator, always a naval aviator." Naval aircraft epitomized the rapid convergence of technology: modifications to existing aircraft coupled with new airframe and engine designs would revolutionize flight. Irvine was on the leading edge of experimental testing of naval aircraft until his retirement in 1939.

the engine 'nacelles'

A topside view of the German Dornier DO-X flying boat was taken as the aircraft made its way over the lower Chesapeake Bay in the vicinity of Naval Operating Base Norfolk, 1931.

The Pitcairn XOP-1 Autogiro (experimental), photographed September 10, 1931, at Naval Air Station Hampton Roads, foreshadowed the arrival of rotary-wing aircraft on Navy carrier decks. The aircraft underwent carrier evaluation on September 23, 1931, aboard the USS *Langley* in the Chesapeake Bay. The Navy only purchased three of the underpowered OP-1s, one of which was sent to Nicaragua to help the Marines fight the "Banana Wars" in June 1932. (Charles S. Borjes, photographer. Courtesy of the Kirn Library.)

the 'Inline' engine (liquid cooled)

The Curtiss-Wright Condor, NR12384, painted for Byrd's Second Antarctic Expedition, was photographed departing Naval Air Station Norfolk in October 1933. The Condor, named the *William Horlick,* was new when Byrd took it to the Antarctic on his second expedition in 1933. The twin-engined, long-range biplane used either skis or floats (as seen here). Later, Byrd selected two twin-engined United States Navy Curtiss-Wright R4C-1 Condors with him in 1939. Both of these aircraft had seen five years of service with the United States Marine Corps before being picked for the Byrd expedition. The USS *Bear* picked up the twin-engined Barkley-Grow seaplane during its stop in Norfolk in late November 1939, and carried it to the Antarctic, leaving the Condors behind. The Condor was neither an efficient nor well-conditioned aircraft for Byrd's 1939–1941 expedition. Though the Condors were expected to be the primary exploratory aircraft of the expedition, their age and fuel consumption precluded them from going on the trip. Byrd chose to use the Beech D17A. The Barkley-Grow operated off the USS *Bear.* (Charles S. Borjes, photographer. Courtesy of the Kirn Library.)

Aside from revolutionary flight performance, Mother Nature was also to have a say in naval aviation. Though it seems almost unimaginable today, the first naval aircraft believed struck by lightning occurred at Hampton Roads one fateful afternoon in April of 1927. Lieutenant Victor Francis "Vic" Marinelli, Naval Aviator No. 1223, of Washington, D.C., was pilot of an H-16 flying boat, Bureau Number A3533, one of five such aircraft to leave the Naval Aircraft Factory at Philadelphia, Pennsylvania, for Naval Air Station Hampton Roads on April 29, 1927. As news reports of the time indicate, the five planes departed shortly after lunchtime. Marinelli and his crew, consisting of Lieutenant George W. Lehman, Naval Aviator No. 3272, Chief Aviation Machinist's Mate (ACMM) Loren Edward Poyner, and Aviation Machinist's Mate Second Class (AMM2c) George Martin Michaels, were one of two planes which pressed on to Hampton Roads. The other three smartly turned back at Hog Island, south of Philadelphia, because of inclement weather conditions. The other plane, piloted by Naval Aviation Pilot Patrick J. "Pappy" Byrne, an enlisted aviator, continued the flight behind Marinelli because he could not let the officer proceed alone. Byrne was accompanied

The Navy flight tested the Boeing XF7B-1, Bureau Number 9378, shown here as it appeared November 8, 1933. This low-wing monoplane prototype with its all metal airframe joined the Boeing P-26A in revolutionary aircraft designs of the late 1920s and early 1930s, designs which carried military aviation out of the golden era of fabric and wood biplanes to sleek metal skinned aircraft. (Official United States Navy Photograph.)

C.C. Champion Sets Seaplane Record

On May 5, 1927, flying from Langley Field, Virginia, Lieutenant Carleton C. Champion Jr. established a world's altitude record for seaplanes. His altitude-setting 33,405 feet was part of the National Advisory Committee for Aeronautics (NACA) flight evaluation of the Navy's Wright Apache aircraft. Champion, a well known air racing and test pilot in his day, would later become commanding officer of Naval Air Station Norfolk from February 22, 1943, through May 24, 1943. His feats in the Wright Apache, both seaplane and landplane versions, are shown here. His record for the Wright Apache seaplane would be broken by Lieutenant Apollo Soucek, on May 8, 1929, as he climbed to the height of 39,140 feet.

In this photograph, Lieutenant C.C. Champion suits up for the flight. Note the full leather flight gear replete with fur collar and, of course, the parachute.

Champion is shown "raring to go," as he left the hangar and headed for his aircraft.

The Wright Apache was warming up when this photograph was snapped.

Champion was finally ready to go, his NACA ground crew pushing the Apache into Little Back River.

The flight over, Champion alighted the aircraft into a waiting boat, and the Apache was pulled to shore.

The Wasp engine, clearly shown in this photograph, had a standard steel propeller and an engine that ran 425-horsepower at 1,800 revolutions. This was a supercharged engine capable of climbing 2,500 feet per minute in this aircraft.

The Wright Apache flown by Champion underwent extensive cowling tests at NACA. The aircraft came to NACA with its factory propeller spinner mounted over the hub, a metal case enclosing the crankcase and inner parts of the engine cylinders. NACA engineers experimented with different cowling configurations. In the photograph here, Melvin N. Gough, a NACA mechanical engineer, shows off the Navy's Apache landplane and its Wasp 425-horsepower engine. Note the variety of propellers along the hangar wall behind the aircraft.

Champion stands in front of the Wright Apache landplane, Langley Field, Virginia, July 4, 1927, just prior to making high altitude tests in the aircraft.

Champion climbed into the cockpit of the Wright Apache, dressed in the garb of high altitude testing, on a hot July day at Langley Field to set the altitude record, 38,418 feet, for the landplane Apache. But, again, Lieutenant Apollo Soucek broke the record for the Apache landplane with his 1929 climb to 40,366 feet.

After development of the Norden bombsight, bombing from high altitudes attained a fair degree of accuracy. The photograph shown here was taken May 17, 1932, and shows Douglas PD-1 patrol aircraft dropping 500-pound bombs from an altitude of ten thousand feet. There were only twenty-five aircraft of this configuration built by the Douglas Aircraft Company. The plane was unique: its seventy-two foot, ten-inch wing span covered entirely with fabric might be considered a bit unusual since most aircraft manufacturers were moving toward the use of metals, not linens. PD-1s were powered by two 525-horsepower R-1750 Wright Cyclone engines. The PD-1 was developed in the late twenties and was stricken from service in 1936. The first PD-1 was delivered to Patrol Squadron Seven (VP-7) on June 6, 1929, but Patrol Squadrons Four (VP-4), Six (VP-6), and Ten (VP-10) also used the aircraft. (Official United States Navy Photograph.)

Sailor Orbie William "Zoomie" White stands on the pontoon of a VS-10S Vought OU3-1 Corsair aircraft on the treaty cruiser USS *Salt Lake City,* part of Cruiser Division Four, in December 1931. White was born September 26, 1912, in Newport, Arkansas, and enlisted in the Navy at the age of seventeen. When he retired on September 1, 1953, Orbie White had served his country for nearly twenty-three years. He died on March 4, 1980. According to his son, David, Orbie White got the nickname "Zoomie" after having had some association with flying duty. At the time this photograph was taken, Orbie White was a Seaman Second Class (Sea2c). Records of enlisted naval aviation pilots are difficult to track because recordkeeping was so poor when it came to enlisted naval aviators. Orbie White would eventually attain the designation ACM(PA), a chief aviation metalsmith, permanent appointment. It is uncertain how much flying he did as part of his duties. The Silver Eagle Association welcomes additions to its roster of enlisted personnel who can prove a legitimate designation as a Naval Aviation Pilot. Time will tell whether there are more names to be added to the elite of the fleet, the "white hat" pilots of naval aviation.

in his H-16 flying boat, Bureau Number A3474, by Lieutenant Joseph J. Rooney.

By the time Marinelli and Byrne reached Mathews, Virginia, they had caught wind of a severe thunderstorm fast approaching at twelve hundred feet. It was at this point Byrne observed a tremendous bolt of lightning above Marinelli's H-16, which was flying about a mile and a half ahead of him. "In about two seconds a puff of white smoke enveloped the plane," Byrne stated. "It must have hit the oil tank, for had it been the gas tank that exploded, the smoke would have been black. The ship immediately nosed down slightly, then came up on a straight course. I thought this was a signal that the machine was going to turn back instead of running on into the storm, which we had not reached." He watched helplessly as the aircraft spun out of control, tumbling into the turbulent waters of the Chesapeake Bay at New Point Comfort, Virginia. At about six hundred feet above the bay, the aircraft nosed in, the wings and superstructure folded back, and the craft, in Byrne's words, "hit the water with such force that it looked like a big bomb exploding." Since it was half past three in the afternoon, there were plenty of fishermen at work harvesting their catch and making way to their fishing base. Many of them saw lightning strike the plane, and word of the incident spread quickly through many of the communities ringing the bay.

Though Byrne landed almost immediately at the location Marinelli's aircraft struck the water, his hour-long search yielded nothing. The flight from Philadelphia to New Point, near Mathews, Virginia, had taken two and a half hours; the fatal flight from New Point to Hampton Roads, only a half hour. When Byrne arrived at Hampton Roads, Commander Albert C. Read, Naval Aviator No. 24, commanding officer of the air station, dispatched a minesweeper, the USS *Teal,* which successfully found the wreckage and drug it to shallow waters within a couple of days. Byrne later explained that Marinelli's aircraft sank in only eighteen feet of water and not more than five hundred yards from where Lieutenant Frank H. Conant II was killed in a crash a few days before the start of the Schneider Cup seaplane race in 1926.

Rear Admiral William Adger Moffett was the first chief of the Bureau of Aeronautics and one of the great figures of American aviation. Appointed chief in 1921, Rear Admiral Moffett accomplished miracles in the first six years of his administration. Among the numerous important items developed under his supervision and direction were the first successful radial engines, the Norden bombsight, metal hulls for seaplanes, and a series of racing aircraft, which in 1923 enabled the Navy to hold twenty-three world records. Perhaps one distinction held by Rear Admiral Moffett, and least mentioned on his list of accomplishments, was the fact he had been designated Naval Observer No. 1. Rear Admiral Moffett lost his life on April 4, 1933, while making a test flight aboard the dirigible USS *Akron* which crashed off Barnegat Light, New Jersey, during an electrical storm. (Official United States Navy Photograph.)

The Consolidated XBY-1, Bureau No. A8921, dubbed the "Horizontal Bomber," crashed at Naval Air Station Norfolk on November 24, 1933. According to hearsay the crash occurred during a landing on the simulated USS *Langley* deck at the air station. In Navy lingo, the XBY-1 experienced a "hard landing." This was an interesting aircraft for its period. The aircraft was a single-engine monoplane, highly streamlined in its design. The aircraft had gone through a series of flight tests at Naval Air Station Anacostia and the Naval Proving Ground, Dahlgren, Virginia, prior to its arrival in Norfolk on March 13, 1933. Consolidated Aircraft Corporation controlled the aircraft's testing until it was accepted by the Navy in May. The aircraft was sent to the Naval Aircraft Factory on June 15, for static tests (S.O. No. 981) and subsequently returned to Norfolk. Its "hard landing" at Norfolk was too extensive for repairs. The aircraft had only logged 41.90 flight hours at the time it was stricken, on January 31, 1934, from the Navy record. The "Horizontal Bomber" was sent to Dahlgren for target practice in April 1934. The Navy did not invest in production of any high-wing, single-engine monoplanes like the XBY-1. Consolidated did convince the Navy to experiment with the XB2Y-1. (Courtesy of General Dynamics.)

And, in the irony of ironies, it was Byrne who had gingerly lifted the body of Conant from the wreckage of his seaplane when it was recovered.

A fisherman named C. Biggs, of Horn Harbor, Mathews County, recovered Poyner's body not long after the crash. The body of Michaels was recovered with the wreckage, Marinelli and Lehman's about two weeks later. Byrne, accompanied by Lieutenant Commander J.F. Moloney, Naval Aviator No. 2692,

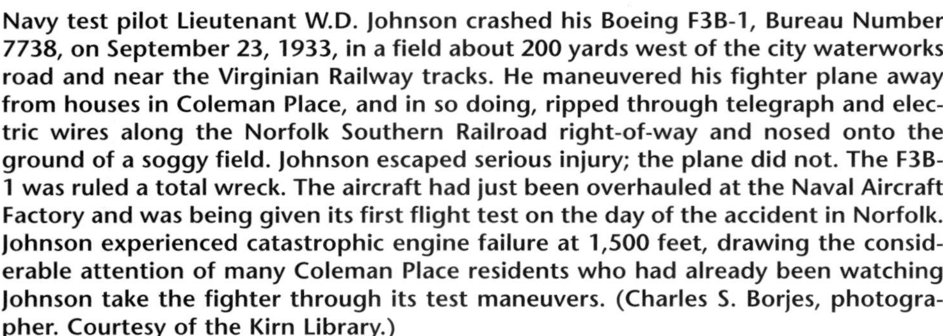

Navy test pilot Lieutenant W.D. Johnson crashed his Boeing F3B-1, Bureau Number 7738, on September 23, 1933, in a field about 200 yards west of the city waterworks road and near the Virginian Railway tracks. He maneuvered his fighter plane away from houses in Coleman Place, and in so doing, ripped through telegraph and electric wires along the Norfolk Southern Railroad right-of-way and nosed onto the ground of a soggy field. Johnson escaped serious injury; the plane did not. The F3B-1 was ruled a total wreck. The aircraft had just been overhauled at the Naval Aircraft Factory and was being given its first flight test on the day of the accident in Norfolk. Johnson experienced catastrophic engine failure at 1,500 feet, drawing the considerable attention of many Coleman Place residents who had already been watching Johnson take the fighter through its test maneuvers. (Charles S. Borjes, photographer. Courtesy of the Kirn Library.)

Experimentation with devices to launch aircraft from battleships and cruisers continued in the 1920s and 1930s. Aircraft were released via a structural steel platform foundation designed, as shown here on December 5, 1933, with a tension bar release and tail wheel for landplane catapulting. (Official United States Navy Photograph.)

Extensive experimentation in the 1930s led to advancement of the catapult, and a great deal of this work would be performed at Naval Air Station Norfolk. The landplane catapult dead load with axle hooks and safety hook (close up) were photographed on March 15, 1934. (Official United States Navy Photograph.)

had helped search for the downed aircraft. Flying the F-5L flying boat, Bureau Number A3575, the two men searched from Hampton Roads to New Point and back to locate the wreckage. In a sad footnote to the story, each of the four men killed in the H-16 left behind families. Marinelli's wife, Mary Annette, and their two-year-old-son, Victor Francis Marinelli Jr.; Margaret Lehman and the couple's eleven-month-old daughter; Beulah Louise Poyner; and Lillian Gladys Michaels, all resided in Norfolk or South Norfolk. It is not known how many children, if any, Poyner and Michaels had at the time of the accident.

Perhaps the words of Samuel Taylor Coleridge (1772–1834) from *The Rime of the Ancient Mariner,* composed in

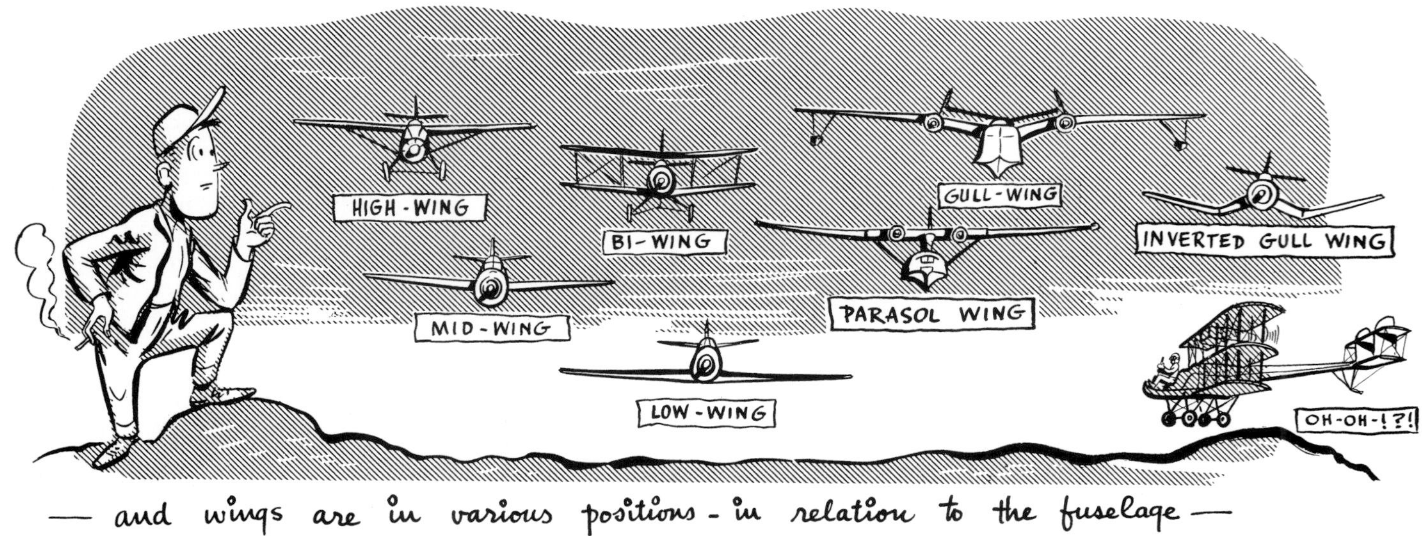

Andy Aileron shows the reader all the different wing positions in relation to the fuselage.

The Vought OJ-2 floatplane was photographed at Naval Air Station Norfolk while perched atop its moving cradle, January 25, 1934. (Official United States Navy Photograph.)

1797–1798, never wrung quite so true as in the case of these fated aviators who are now but a memory. Coleridge wrote:

> And the bay was white with silent
> light,
> Till rising from the same,
> Full many shapes, that shadows were,
> In crimson colours came.
>
> A little distance from the prow
> Those crimson shadows were:
> I turned my eyes upon the deck—
> Oh, Christ! what saw I there!

The 1920s are synonymous with great events and tragedies in the history of naval aviation in Hampton Roads, perhaps due in part to the trial and error of flight testing but also flight procedures. Since naval aviation in general was still in its formative stage, the accident which killed the nation's first naval aviator, "Spuds" Ellyson, can be attributed as much to lack of procedure as good judgment.

Theodore Gordon "Spuds" Ellyson came into naval aviation at a time when few of the ground rules had been established. In 1912, the Secretary of the Navy George von L. Meyer issued a memorandum to require all those in aviation service to have at least two years of sea duty in grade to qualify for promotion. As Helen Glenn Ellyson, the aviator's wife, would later remark, "a good aviator must first be a good naval officer." Ellyson's first tour at sea since his midshipman days was as first lieutenant aboard the battleship USS *South Carolina* in April of 1913. After a long stretch of duty stations—some involved directly with flying and aviation experimental work and others not—Ellyson was returned to aviation duty as executive officer of Naval Air Station Hampton Roads on January 10, 1921. From about 1925 until the time of his death, Ellyson was not in a flying billet. Refresher training was not done in his time; aviators were assumed to be just as proficient flying as they would have been two or three years previous to serving at sea. The point to be made is that Ellyson's death on his forty-third birthday, February 27, 1928, was as much a precedent-setting event as it became a tragedy of portentious proportions.

At the time of his death, Commander Ellyson was executive officer of the Navy's second aircraft carrier, the USS *Lexington,* and had done little flying of his own because the billet called for sea duty as second in command of the ship, not flying. On Saturday, February 26, 1928, the *Lexington* was in Hampton Roads with planes ashore at the naval air station. Ellyson got permission to fly a plane from Norfolk to Annapolis, Maryland, to visit his sick daughter. While at the station, however, the aviator called his wife who told him their daughter was hospitalized but resting comfortably. Not until later in the evening was Ellyson called away from a party by urgent telegram telling him his daughter had taken a turn for the worse and needed an operation, scheduled for the morning of February 28. With two pilots, Lieutenant Commander Hugo Schmidt, Naval Aviator No. 2897, and Lieutenant Rogers S. Ransehousen, Naval Aviator No. 3340, Ellyson called his friend, Commander Albert Cushing "Putty" Read, Naval Aviator No. 24, at his quarters informing the commander of Naval Air Station Hampton Roads he intended to depart immediately for Annapolis. Ellyson had no problem with permission to take the plane. He

A photographer caught two unusual aircraft over Naval Air Station Norfolk in 1934: a Boeing YIP-26, later designated a P-26A monoplane fighter (above), and a Boeing YB-9 or B-9 bomber (below, foreground). The P-26A Peashooter, equipped with a Pratt & Whitney SR-1340G engine, first flew on March 20, 1932, and was tested at the National Advisory Committee on Aeronautics (NACA) in June 1934. The aircraft's all metal construction and open cockpit were revolutionary in its day. The B-9, with its two GIV-1570C Curtiss engines and retractable landing gear, became the focus of intense controversy regarding the patent on its cowling design, a dispute which pitted NACA against Boeing. Through extensive testing under NACA's cowling program, the Martin B-10 bomber was fitted with a high-performance NACA cowling which increased the aircraft's speed. The B-9 was fitted with Townend ring cowlings in 1933, a decision which resulted in Boeing losing a production contract to the Army. The Army Air Corps favored the faster Martin B-10 bomber with its maximum speed of 225 miles per hour. Boeing was angered by the loss. The aircraft shown here helped revolutionize aircraft design in the 1930s. Though the Navy bought neither aircraft, the air station was often frequented in those days by manufacturer prototypes and Army visitors from Langley Field. (Official United States Navy Photograph.)

outranked Read and, after all, was the Navy's first aviator; no one questioned his judgment. Commander Read ordered the officer of the day, Lieutenant Clyde Smith, to help in any way possible to get Ellyson and his aircrew ready for departure. A Loening amphibian was prepped at midnight, by all accounts a cold and blustery February night. The aircraft had no running lights and no radio, but it was not out of the ordinary for aviators of that period to fly a plane without either. Ransehousen, the junior officer aboard, knew the most about Loening amphibians and was chosen as pilot for the flight north. The plane was last seen lifting off Willoughby Bay.

Without the benefit of adequate air-to-ground communications, various locations of the aircraft were reported by ships over a radio net. It would be noon of February 28 before anyone at the air station discovered Ellyson's plane never arrived in Annapolis. An immediate search was ordered. Three days later, wreckage was found floating near Cape Charles, Virginia, and more than a month later, on April 11, 1928, Ellyson's body washed ashore at Willoughby Spit near Norfolk. The body, found by civilian C.D. Surber, was identifiable only by personal papers in his clothing, a driver's license and perhaps most telling, his Naval Academy ring and watch engraved with the initials "TGE." The watch hands had stopped at 2:56:28. An inquest at Portsmouth Naval Hospital determined Ellyson had drowned. Schmidt's body was presumed trapped in the wreckage of the aircraft fuselage, which was never found, and Ransehousen's body was also not recovered, but naval authorities believed the body separated from the wreckage and was taken away by the sea.

Though no one was willing to venture a guess as to the cause of the crash, Navy officials held Ellyson, Ransehousen and Schmidt responsible. Interestingly enough, it would be one admiral, Rear Admiral Richard H. Leigh, Chief of the Bureau of Navigation, who pointed the finger of blame elsewhere. Leigh criticized Commander Read and his officer of the day, Lieutenant Smith, for ever allowing the flight to take off under night conditions in freezing cold weather. Dr. Edward P. Warner, Assistant Secretary of the Navy for Air, noted that the air station commander had no authority over fleet aircraft movements. Warner proposed a General Order permitting flights from naval air stations only in accordance with approved operating schedules or with the station commander's specific authority. Leigh would, in time, formally reprimand Read and Smith, but no General Order was approved. If anything positive came of Ellyson's tragic passing, it would be the

the 'landing gear'—

"The Greatest Air Race of All Time"

There was a chill in the air, a crisp November breeze as it were over Willoughby on race day. The world had descended on Norfolk, and it was the start of a glorious day for the likes of de Bernardi, Schilt, Tomlinson, Bacula, Cuddihy and all those who came to see the greatest air race of all time. At its finish, the Schneider Cup Trophy Race of 1926 would become perhaps the penultimate air race—sea or land—for air supremacy in the years from 1913 through the latter 1930s and leading up to the start of the Second World War.

The 1926 race was held at Willoughby in Ocean View before a crowd numbering in excess of thirty thousand captivated onlookers. Reporters of the period noted it was doubtful if such a crowd had ever assembled in one place in Norfolk prior to this event. There was more than an acre of close-parked automobiles on the site of what was intended to be an observation area for spectators. Anyone with a car not from Virginia was said to have a "foreign" license plate. In addition to cars parked in the acre site, there were another five thousand or so on the naval air station. Though the great race did not begin until half past two in the afternoon, the crowds surged, overrunning the reservations made for them by their Navy hosts. People watched from any vantage point possible. Throughout the race people poured into Ocean View to watch the planes speed low over the water, virtually skirting the heads of those pushed off the beach into Willoughby Bay as the crowd built up behind them. Some of those forced into the water were fearful of drowning.

Norfolkians were used to seeing aircraft, given the close proximity of populated areas to the naval air station and army base, but the Schneider Cup Trophy Race brought more airplanes into the skies above the city and county than anyone had ever seen. By November 13, race day, the Navy had roped off a field ten to fifteen acres near the home pylon marked, "Visiting Planes." Planes came from as far away as Buffalo, New York, and equal points south and west. Prior to race time, over one hundred planes were counted in the visiting plane area. There was also a significant number of seaplanes which had landed in Little Bay and were towed up the slipways to shore. Though aircraft above Norfolk had become commonplace, everyone was completely entertained by the variety of airplanes and seaplanes, and by the enormity of the event about to take place. One observer remarked that the world was about to embark on a "glorious adventure." The same individual continued, "the camaraderie of the air is something apart from the ordinary rules of military service." Indeed, the camaraderie was never put to the test moreso than in the weeks just prior to the race and, of course, race day itself.

In its historical context, the air race at Ocean View came near the end of the 1920s, a period of rapid building of air power worldwide. The publication *Aeronautical Chronology* declared that, due to its historical importance and international aspect, as well as the almost phenomenal speeds achieved, the 1926 race for the Jacques Schneider Trophy may well be regarded as the greatest air race ever held. Jacques Schneider, donor of the trophy and originator of the contest, initiated his race to

The 1926 International Schneider Cup Trophy Race brought some of the fastest aircraft in the world to Hampton Roads, including the Curtiss/Packard R3C-3 with its 700-horsepower Packard 2A-1500 engine flown by Lieutenant William Gosnell "Red" Tomlinson. This aircraft was clocked at over 258 miles per hour on practice runs preceding the race on Saturday, November 13. Unfortunately, Tomlinson would crash the Curtiss/Packard aircraft in Willoughby Bay the day before the race in speed trials, and, though he was unhurt, the accident was a devastating blow to the Navy team. This special aircraft, denoted as A7054 by the Bureau of Aeronautics, would surely have been the most competitive American entry in the contest. (Official United States Navy Photograph.)

The Curtiss F6C-3 Hawk, Bureau Number A6970, Navy seaplane was converted from an F6C-1, and is shown in this photograph as it appeared on September 16, 1925. Bureau Number A6970 was one of two aircraft prototyped as upgraded F6C-1s. Powered by a 520-horsepower Curtiss D-12 engine, the Curtiss Hawk was the aircraft flown by Lieutenant Tomlinson in the 1926 contest when his Curtiss/Packard racer was lost in a practice heat.

The Navy/Curtiss R3C-2, Bureau Number A6978 and the same aircraft flown by Lieutenant Alford J. Williams in the 1925 Pulitzer Race, was re-engined with the more powerful Packard 650-horsepower 2A-1550 engine and, after modification to a seaplane, redesignated the R3C-3 for the 1926 Schneider Cup Trophy Race at Hampton Roads. The aircraft, shown here, was photographed on October 26, 1926, while taking practice runs at Hampton Roads. Lieutenant Frank H. Conant is in the cockpit. He was killed four days later. (Courtesy of the National Museum of Naval Aviation.)

counter landplane races which had been held since 1909 as the Gordon Bennett Aviation Cup and the *Coupe Deutsch de la Meurthe,* the Bennett's European counterpart. Schneider was the son of the wealthy owner of the Schneider armament factory at Le Creusot, France. He was drawn to aviation the instant he saw Wilbur Wright demonstrate his Model A plane in France in 1908. This event profoundly affected the life of a relatively young Schneider. He rationalized that since seventy percent of the world was covered by water, there should be some use of water to operate aircraft. He was not alone in his thinking. Schneider's fascination with water and planes touched off a series of experiments in the period around 1910 which saw the birth of seaplanes. Even Glenn Hammond Curtiss, winner of the first Bennett Cup in 1909, followed Schneider's lead and began designing seaplanes.

The evolution of the Schneider Cup Trophy Race (1913–1931) from its inception in 1913 to the race at Ocean View in 1926 gives some indication of how far aviation had progressed in little over a decade. When the first race was won at Monaco by Maurice Prévost in April 1913, the winning speed was just forty-four miles per hour. His little Deperdussin seaplane had a 160-horsepower Gnome engine and covered only 150 miles in three hours, forty-eight minutes and twenty-two seconds. He averaged about forty-five miles per hour in the straightaway. When de Bernardi won the 1926 contest, the average speed of his Macchi-Fiat monoplane was clocked at 248.189 miles per hour at one hundred kilometers and 248 over two hundred kilometers—the fastest man had ever traveled in a seaplane at that time. De Bernardi covered 4.10 miles per minute and hit a top speed of 264 miles per hour on the straightaway.

The year preceding the race in Hampton Roads would be marked by a number of important events which ultimately determined the winner of the cup. First and foremost, the United States government made the decision after the 1925 win at Baltimore by Army Lieutenant James H. Doolittle to end the funding of its military race team and consequently, research and development of new planes for the 1926 contest in Norfolk. There would be no new planes for the race. The all-Navy team was also some indication that America was ready to move its wealth of racing experience into development of fighter planes for future military applications. Lieutenant Al Williams of the United States Navy, on hand in Norfolk for the 1926 race, observed that cessation of government funded research and development would take America out of contention for the trophy. His observation would, of course, prove correct.

The 1926 race would further bring out another important concept, one not readily accepted by the Italian and American teams. British and French teams had wanted to put at least two years between trophy races to allow more time to develop competitive aircraft and aircrew. Both the British and French withdrew from the race in Hampton Roads because they perceived one year insufficient time to design and build aircraft to challenge the American hold on the cup. Interestingly enough, the British experience at Schneider Cup races from 1927 onward led to their

The Curtiss R3C-1 racer shown here, Bureau Number A6979, was the winner of the 1925 Schneider Cup Race at Baltimore, Maryland, on October 26, but it also raced at Hampton Roads in 1926. After it was re-engined with a 685-horsepower Curtiss V-1550, the R3C-2 was redesignated R3C-4. In the photograph, Lieutenant James H. "Jimmy" Doolittle, of the United States Army, winner of the 1925 International Schneider Cup Trophy Race, stands on the pontoon of his winning aircraft.

successful design of the Supermarine Spitfire which, as history tells it, saved the day in the 1940 Battle of Britain. The American team, winners at Cowes in 1923 and Baltimore in 1925, was anxious to capture its third Schneider Cup Trophy in five years, thereby retiring, according to contest rules, the competition with the United States. *Il Duce,* Benito Mussolini, had determined after the 1925 race to win the contest in Hampton Roads at all cost. Mussolini would furnish the Macchi and Fiat companies with the funding and encouragement needed to take the trophy home to Italy. The Italians designed and built what became known as their "little red devils"—Macchi-Fiat monoplanes—in five months' time to compete in the November race. British and French requests for postponement fell on deaf ears.

The American team never anticipated the heavy losses it would take in the weeks preceding the race. The confidence of the Navy team would be badly shaken by the loss of three airplanes and two pilots, one of whom was team leader Frank H. Conant. Lieutenant Frank Hersey Conant II was killed when his practice plane struck a fishnet pole and cartwheeled into the water at Winter Harbor, located about thirty miles north of Norfolk, on October 30, 1926. Conant, a 1920 graduate of the Naval Academy and one of the finest air race pilots of his day, was laid to rest with full military honors at Arlington National Cemetery while two airplanes, one each from the Navy and Army circled like soaring eagles overhead.

A little over a month prior to Conant's untimely death, the Americans lost First Lieutenant Harmon John Norton, USMC, Naval Aviator No. 1675, who was killed September 13 while practicing in his CR-3, Bureau Number A6081, the 1923 Schneider Cup winning aircraft, near Naval Air Station Anacostia. His aircraft went into the Potomac River off Haines Point in a full power dive from an altitude of two thousand feet.

By the planned start of the race in early November, the Navy team had experienced some critical changes both in aircrew and strategy. First Lieutenant Christian Frank Schilt, USMC, Naval Aviator No. 2741, was brought on board to replace Norton, and Lieutenant Carleton C. Champion became the team's reserve pilot. When Champion later became ill, a dashing red-haired pilot by the name of Lieutenant William Gosnell "Red" Tomlinson, became a fixed member of the team. Tomlinson would nearly be killed himself the day before the race as he practiced over Willoughby Bay. His plane turned bottom side up after it crashed. Tomlinson was strapped to the fuselage as the aircraft settled to the bay's bottom. Though he managed to extricate himself and survive an otherwise harrowing incident, his great seven-hundred-horsepower blue and gold Curtiss/Packard R3C-3 aircraft was lost. The Packard seaplane would likely have proved the strongest contender in the 1926 race. Rear Admiral William Adger Moffett, who witnessed preliminary speed trials with the Packard, remarked to reporters that the aircraft had been the fastest one in two recent tests. Tomlinson's Packard backers and manufacturer's representative, in this case the Naval Aircraft Factory, were understandably disappointed. In unofficial tests, the Curtiss designed racer with its new Packard engine clocked 258 miles per hour over a two-and-one-quarter mile course just days before the race. Since the fuselage and engine were not badly damaged, Moffett had the aircraft salvaged and sent for repairs. In the end, Tomlinson would be relegated to flying the Curtiss F6C-3 Hawk.

The Italians experienced their own devastating blow just prior to Conant's

The Curtiss aircraft (A6979), shown here during an engine test at its proving grounds near Winter Harbor, was piloted by Lieutenant Frank Hersey Conant (in the cockpit), and it was Conant who was to have flown the aircraft in the 1926 International Schneider Cup Trophy Race at Norfolk on November 11. The aircraft, designated the R3C-4, had a 650-horsepower Curtiss V-1550 motor and could top 250 miles per hour. Conant was killed on October 30, 1926, in another aircraft. The Curtiss racer was later sent to Hampton Roads for the air race and flown in speed trials prior to the race by Lieutenant "Red" Tomlinson. Tomlinson crashed the aircraft in Willoughby Bay and, though it was salvaged, the plane was lost for race day.

death at Winter Harbor. Their team leader, Marchese Vittorio Centurione, stalled his Macchi M.39 into Lake Varese, the team's home base, and was killed instantly. At the Italian team's request, the Schneider Cup Trophy Race was postponed two weeks and rescheduled for Saturday, November 13, 1926.

Planes and pilots set to race in Norfolk were as impressive as the crowd gathered to watch them. The Navy team flew three Curtiss R3C-2s from 1925, two of which had been re-engined. The third Curtiss plane, perhaps the most competitive American entry left by racetime, was fitted with a 650-horsepower Curtiss V-1550, a twelve-cylinder water-cooled inline V-engine. This aircraft was designated R3C-4. Schilt was placed in Doolittle's 1925 R3C-2, and Tomlinson in the reserve Curtiss Hawk aircraft. Rear Admiral William A. Moffett, Chief of the Bureau of Aeronautics, stepped in as team captain when Commander Homer C. Wick fell ill just prior to the big race. It was Moffett who put Lieutenant George T. Cuddihy, Naval Aviator No. 2956, in the R3C-4, thereby making the young pilot the first choice of the American team to win the race. Cuddihy, the best hope of an American victory, did not climb into the cockpit of his formidable racer until minutes before the race began. Preflight strategy dictated that no one but Moffett and the team would know who America's top contender would be prior to November racetime. Newspapers from around the world tried very hard to discover the identity of the Navy's lead pilot but to no avail. Intrigue surrounding the race was certainly fed by the Italians but reached its peak when Cuddihy mounted the cockpit of his racer.

The Italians were confident they would take the trophy back to *Il Duce* and throngs of their wildly patriotic countrymen. To avoid Prohibition in Virginia, the team smuggled Chianti wine in the floats of their seaplanes so they could celebrate an expected victory in the proper fashion. During preparation for the race, the Italians experienced chronic engine troubles which they, in turn, attributed to sabotage by the Americans. At the behest of Commander Silvio Scaroni, the leading surviving Italian ace of World War I and air attaché at the Italian Embassy in Washington, D.C., the team's Macchi-Fiat planes were switched to American spark plugs and fueled with the same gasoline used by the Navy team.

Race day was replete with electrifying, death-defying excitement. As entertainment, one Navy pilot went up and did stunts to put the crowd in the right mood for the race. A Navy band played as the lone pilot performed his aerobatics high above the crowd milling about the air station. This was, after all, the age of daredevils and speed kings. As the start of the race drew closer, one American and one Italian plane were wheeled out to the ramp from nearby seaplane hangars. The planes' propellers whirled, their motors coughed and came to a steady roar, creating a tremendous

The Curtiss R3C-4 aircraft was kept at Winter Harbor, thirty miles north of Norfolk. When the photograph was taken, Conant was piloting the racer on a practice run.

rush of spectators to the seawall and seaplane hangars to watch the race. Lieutenant Adriano Bacula of the Italian team started off the contest when his little but powerful red Macchi monoplane slipped off the water over Willoughby followed by Tomlinson in the Curtiss Hawk. The crowd was enthralled. Due to a last minute change in the wind, the pilots were given a new start point. Rather than start the race at the air station, pilots continued in the straight from the slipway on the first leg, taking off after crossing the finish line.(1) Though this rerouting obscured the start from a good many in the crowd on the naval air station, it failed to dampen their enthusiasm on what turned out to be a picture-perfect day for flying. An easterly breeze and bright sun would make memories of the day all the more vivid for onlookers. The 31.06-mile course began near Naval Air Station Hampton Roads at Ocean View and ran northwest to a pylon in the Chesapeake Bay in close proximity to Old Point Comfort before cutting back over Newport News and heading back to the start line at Willoughby. Crowds also massed at Old Point Comfort and Newport News to catch a glimpse of the competitors as they streaked by at speeds of 240 miles per hour or better.

The Schneider Cup Trophy Race of 1926 was hard fought. Cuddihy went down as he started for the home pylon on his last lap—the seventh—due to a failed gasoline tank pump. Major Mario de Bernardi sped past him to become the champion seaplane speed pilot of the world, depriving the United States the chance to retain the coveted international trophy permanently. As he edged his Macchi into the shallows at Willoughby, de Bernardi was met by Mario Castoldi, the aircraft designer, and Ettore Ferretti, a Fiat engineer, along with de Bernardi's mechanics who carried their victorious pilot from his aircraft to shore. De Bernardi's victory was in sharp contrast to Cuddihy's defeat. Cuddihy climbed out of his Curtiss R3C-4 with a crippled right arm and a hand so blistered and swollen from pumping the manual gasoline tank pump, he could not exit the aircraft without assistance from his ground crew. This was a tremendous victory for Italy and an end to American dominance of the Schneider Cup Trophy Race. Schilt finished the race in second and Tomlinson fourth. Italian Captain Arturo Ferrarin finished third in his Macchi M.39.

Porter Adams of Boston, president of the National Aeronautic Association, presented the trophy to de Bernardi at a fine banquet held in Norfolk the evening after the race. Adams would praise the Italians for their ability, courage, and spirit, and he issued a challenge to the Navy team to bring back the cup in 1927. Little did he realize that the United States would never again race for the Schneider Cup trophy. The Italians were highly complimentary of their American counterparts.

The Navy team was gracious in defeat, and its members received a victor's welcome at the White House hosted by President Calvin Coolidge days after the race. Rear Admiral Moffett set up a straightaway course for the Italians to test their speed capability postliminary to the actual competition. The straightaway record set in 1925 by Doolittle was shattered by de Bernardi who achieved a speed of 258.874 miles per hour over Hampton Roads.

Norfolk was besieged with famous personalities who came to witness the trophy race. In addition to Rear Admiral Moffett, Commander Scaroni, Doolittle, and Williams, there was Secretary of the Navy Curtis D. Wilbur; Assistant Secretary of the Navy for Air Edward P. Warner, Ph.D.; Major General Mason M. Patrick, Chief of the Army Air Corps and a familiar face in Norfolk during that time; General Augusta Villa, the Italian military attaché; Attorney General of the United States John G. Sargeant; Commander Georges Thenault, French naval attaché and former commanding officer of the world-renowned Lafayette Escadrille; Commander Albert Cushing "Putty" Read, Naval Aviator No. 24, commanding officer of Naval Air Station Hampton Roads and the first man to fly across the Atlantic as part of a Navy

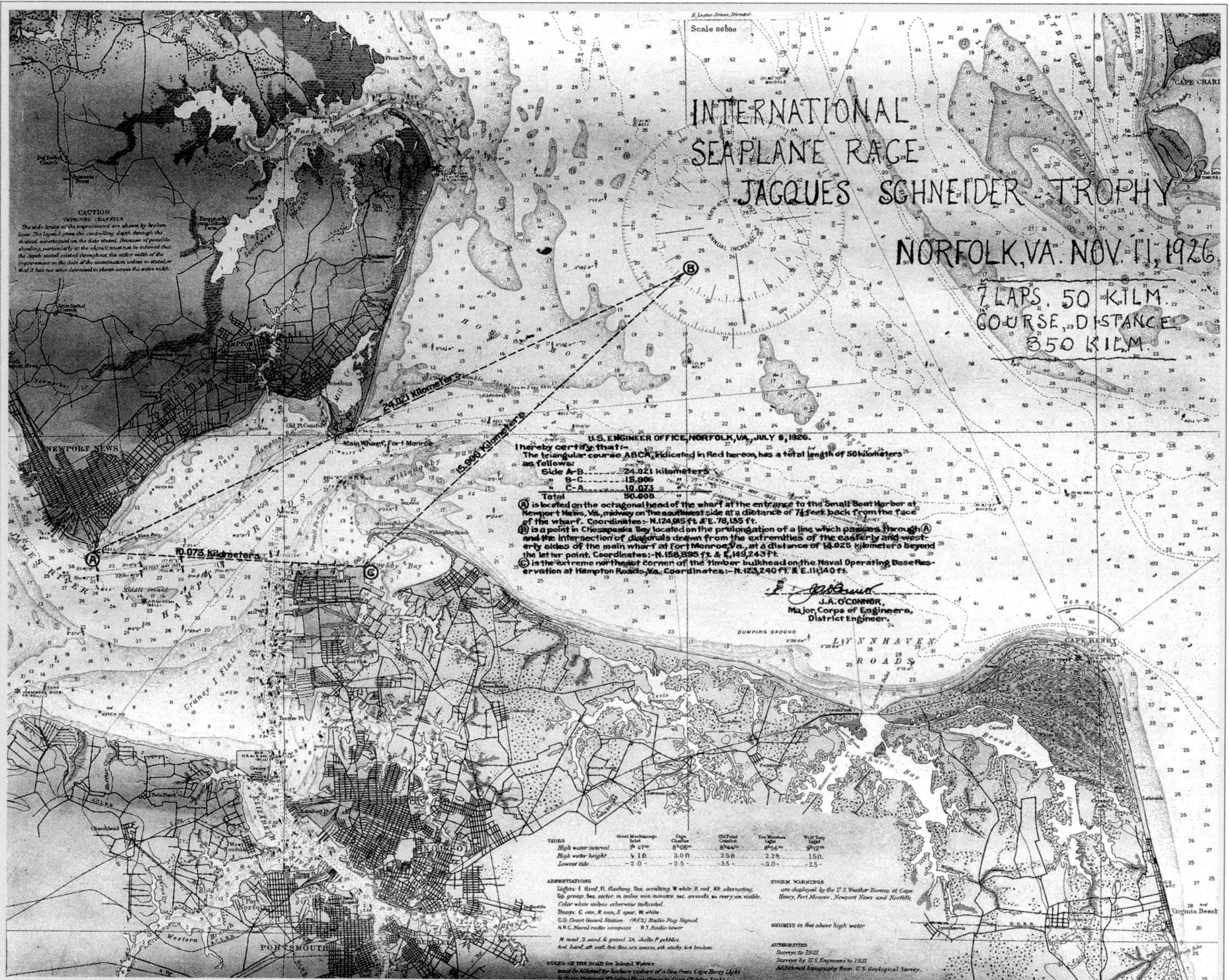

A course map was drawn for the Schneider Cup Trophy Race by the Navy and United States Army Corps of Engineers, Norfolk District.

team; Glenn Martin, airplane manufacturer from Cleveland, Ohio; Dr. G. W. Lewis, research director of the National Advisory Committee for Aeronautics; Venerio di' Annunzio of New York, son of the famous Italian poet and soldier; Henry Berliner, inventor and manufacturer of airplanes; Casey Jones of the Curtiss Aeroplane and Motor Company; and many leading airplane experts from around the world.

There were three attendees who hold particular significance beyond their contribution to the list of colorful personalities on hand for the race in Norfolk. Lieutenant Alford Joseph "Al" Williams, Naval Aviator No. 1820, was on his way to becoming perhaps the best air racer in the world and a pioneer in aircraft research and development (See page 138). Lieutenant Isoroku Yamamoto would go on to become the same Admiral Yamamoto in charge of the Imperial Japanese naval air force commencing with his appointment by Emperor Hirohito in the late 1930s and ending with his death during the Second World War at the hands of American pilots over Bougainville in the North Solomons. In 1926, Yamamoto was the assistant Japanese naval attaché to Washington, D.C. Orville Wright was also on hand. Wright had flown the first airplane down the sand dunes of Kill Devil Hills, North Carolina, twenty-three years before the race in Norfolk. It is incredibly ironic that Wright would be present at the last race attended by Jacques Schneider, then forty-seven and in poor health. Schneider, so inspired in his own work by the Wright Brothers, was soon to fade from the public spotlight forever. He died at Beaulieu-sur-Mer, France, two years later. His trophy race was retired with Great Britain after the September 13, 1931, win of Lieutenant John N. Boothman, Royal Air Force, at Calshot, England. Boothman cleared the rest of the field in that race at a remarkable speed of 340.08 miles per hour in his Vickers S.6B Supermarine seaplane.

As a final postscript, Lieutenant Cuddihy was killed in an aircraft crash in 1929, bringing an abrupt end to the glorious career of a consummate naval aviator.

1. The race course was originally supposed to begin at the air station's start-line, but due to the wind shift, racers took off on an alternative run from station, crossing the original finish line (also at the air station) in the first leg.

Fleet aircraft at Naval Air Station Norfolk in September 1934 included Vought SU-1, SU-2, and SU-3 Corsairs of VS-2B, then assigned to the USS *Saratoga;* Grumman SF-1s of VS-3B from the USS *Lexington;* and Great Lakes TG-2s belonging to VT-2B aboard the *Saratoga.* In the foreground are aircraft marked 4•M•2 and 4•M•4 belonging to that unusual category of "Miscellaneous Squadron," referred to as VMs and, in this case, VM-4, shown here at Norfolk. (Official United States Navy Photograph.)

establishment of a system of flight releases and faster plane movement reports. Without adequate communications with aircraft nor an established tracking system for planes, no one could have known Ellyson was in trouble.

The early 1930s continued the pattern of rapid technological advancement seen in the twenties. Hydropneumatic arresting gear, a type which eventually proved unable to absorb the incredible energy generated by heavy aircraft landing at high speeds, was reported to be beyond research and into actual development at Naval Air Station Hampton Roads on January 29, 1930. Perhaps among the most memorable turn of events occurred on September 23, 1931, when Lieutenant Pride landed an XOP-1, the Navy's first rotary wing aircraft or autogiro, aboard the *Langley* while the ship was positioned off Hampton Roads.

Captain Ernest J. King, later admiral, was commanding officer of the air station from May 4, 1929, to June 20, 1930. He would go on to become Commander-in-Chief, United States Fleet, his tenure as head of the Hampton Roads air facility good background for later decisions he would make regarding naval aviation. King was followed as commanding officer of Naval Air Station Hampton Roads by Captain Kenneth "Ken" Whiting, who proved a dynamic force in naval aviation and an outstanding leader while in Norfolk between June of 1930 and 1932.

A Vought O2U-3 landplane, Bureau Number A8210, shows the towing details and release mechanism used for landplane catapult shots (side view) from an aircraft carrier deck. The two tension bars depicted in this October 3, 1934, photograph held four thousand pounds of pressure. (Official United States Navy Photograph.)

New tenants would come and go in the 1930s, including Marine Corps squadrons VS-14M and VS-15M flying the Vought SU-1, -2, and -3 Corsairs, which embarked on the USS *Saratoga* and USS *Lexington,* respectively, to operate as an integral part of Aircraft, Battle Force, from November 2, 1931. Marine Scouting Squadron Fourteen and Marine Scouting Squadron Fifteen were the first Marine Corps squadrons to be assigned to aircraft carriers, and remained as such until November 14, 1934, at which time other Marine Corps squadrons maintained some carrier proficiency through periodic operations aboard ship. Though VS-15M remained aboard the *Lexington* in its carrier assignment, the squadron shifted from Aircraft, Battle Force, to Aircraft, Scouting Force, in 1932.

By August of 1932, the nomenclature had changed and Naval Air Station Hampton Roads had become Naval Air Station Norfolk. Two world records were set shortly thereafter when, on September 7 and 8, 1933, six Consolidated P2Y-1 flying boats belonging to Patrol Squadron Five (F) flew nonstop from Norfolk to Coco Solo, Canal Zone, establishing the world's formation, nonstop, and distance record at 2,059 statute miles. The aircraft made the flight in twenty-five hours, nineteen minutes. Two years later, an XP3Y-1, in connection with its delivery, transversed from Naval Air Station Norfolk, Virginia, to Coco Solo nonstop and, from Coco Solo to San Francisco, California. The latter leg of the flight established two new international distance records for seaplanes: an airline distance of 3,281.402 statute miles and a broken line distance of 3,443.23 statute miles.

Aviation Division One, VN7RD5, was officially established at Norfolk on January 4, 1934. As early as 1930, reserve pilots operated within squadrons at Norfolk, and these are the very same pilots who became part of the VN7RD5. Not too many people in Hampton Roads, even in 1934, realized Naval Air Station Norfolk had its own naval reserve aviation division. Comprised entirely of officers and enlisted men from Norfolk and South Hampton Roads, Aviation Division One of the naval reserve made its headquarters in Hangar V-3 at the station. Commanding officer of the division was Lieutenant Arthur "Art" Laverents, USNR, Naval Aviator No. 1154, who had returned to active duty in 1929. Laverents was one of four Navy participants in the first Pulitzer Trophy Race at Mitchel Field, Long Island, New York, in 1920 in which he finished fifth. By the end of the Second World War he retired as a captain.

As for Laverents' pilots, all were graduates of Pensacola and commissioned into the naval reserve. Dr. John Quincy Adams, head of the medical department, was a local practicing physician, while Levi J. Roberts, a Norfolk merchant, ran the supply department. Aviation Division One was directly supervised by Captain Aubrey W. Fitch, commanding officer of Naval Air Station Norfolk from June of 1932 to June of 1935.

The story of Aviation Division One carries great importance. Its creation in

Great Lakes BG-1 biplanes of VB-3B *Black Panthers* (left) and Curtiss BF2C-1 biplanes of VB-5B *Bellerophons* (right), both USS *Ranger* bombing squadrons, were quartered at Naval Air Station Norfolk, shown here, when not aboard ship. This photograph shows the flight line, March 23, 1935. The *Bellerophons* of VB-5B took their insignia from Greek mythology, specifically the myth of Bellerophon and Pegasus. Bellerophon captured the winged stallion, Pegasus, and set out to slay the three-headed chimera. By diving three times over the monster, Bellerophon was able to strike off one of its heads on each attack. This myth seemed to suit the mission of the squadron: dive-bombing. The motto, faintly visible over the insignia, translated from its correct Greek, is "First to Attack." (Charles S. Borjes, photographer. Courtesy of the Kirn Library.)

the early 1930s indicated the Navy Department recognized the importance of reserve aviation in a strategic locality. Even at that time, some reserves were used on active duty to supervise and direct training at the air station.

Laverents was a veteran pilot of the First World War and spent six years as an instructor at Naval Air Station Pensacola, Florida. His duties in Norfolk were twofold: keep his reserves up-to-speed in event they were called to active service and provide training opportunities to active duty aviators and students as needed. In 1934 the division was provided hangar spaces, workshops, an armory, instruction rooms, and six airplanes: three Helldivers and three Curtiss Fledglings. During weekly drills, pilots and enlisted men went through each phase of flying and ground operations, tactics, and maneuvers. In addition to weekly duty, reservists also had fifteen days of active duty every year which entailed intensive training in aerial gunnery, bombing practice, navigation, night flying, and blind flying. One of the reserve officers in the unit was Lieutenant (junior grade) Melvin N. Gough, an engineer at the National Advisory Committee for Aeronautics (NACA), later known as the National Aeronautics and Space Administration (NASA). Gough was the only member of the complement of Aviation Division One not selected for active duty at the start of the World War II because his services as chief test pilot and engineer at NACA were already too valuable.

By April 6, 1936, Aviation Division One had become known as the United States Naval Reserve Aviation Unit, VN7RD5. There were two active duty officers joined by six active duty enlisted reservists for support. Though reservist Gough was division commander in 1936, active duty personnel were needed to ensure smooth daily operations.

While experimental work with catapult and arresting gear continued at Hampton Roads, significant strides were made on April 18, 1933, when Lieutenant George Alfred Ott, Naval Aviator No. 133, senior aviator aboard the USS *Maryland,* piloted a Vought O2U seaplane, with Lieutenant (junior grade) B.A. Van Voorhis as passenger, made the first operational test of a device, later called a plane trap, installed on the stern of the *Maryland.* This device had been proposed by Lieutenant Lisle J. Maxson and was a V-shaped float attached to the stern of a ship by a system of struts which allowed it to ride at an even depth in the water. In operation, the seaplane taxied toward the float, pushing a knobbed probe on the nose of the pontoon into the V-float which engaged the probe and held the seaplane in position for hoisting aboard. The plane trap was an immediate success, and preparations were made to install Maxson's invention on five other battleships.

During the years leading up to overtures of war in Europe, Naval Air Station Norfolk continued to bustle with activity. On December 20, 1933, Fleet Marine Force, Aircraft Squadrons East Coast Expeditionary Forces was redesignated Aircraft One, Fleet Marine Force, and, on the West Coast, Aircraft Two, Fleet Marine Force. A little over a year later, squadrons assigned to the USS *Ranger* (CV-4) and quartered at Naval Air Station Norfolk, made the first of a series of cross-country flights from the air station to Hartford, Connecticut, and Buffalo, New York, to test the functioning of carrier aircraft, various special equipment, and flight gear under exacting conditions encountered in cold weather flying. When the tests were completed on February 2, 1935, many valuable and practical lessons had been learned and subsequently taken back to the *Ranger.* When the aircraft carrier did deploy to Cook Inlet, Alaska, on January 22, 1936, for cold weather operations, its squadrons were prepared.

Norfolk had played host to the Navy's elite Ship Experimental Unit since 1921, but on July 15, 1937, this activity was moved to the Naval Aircraft Factory in Pennsylvania. The unit had spent sixteen years at the naval air station developing and testing equipment and techniques for carrier landings and launchings. Despite the unit's move to Philadelphia, Norfolk still held on to significant pieces of naval aviation research and development. On November 11, 1938, the USS *Yorktown* (CV-5), berthed at Pier 7, Naval Station Norfolk, launched a Vought O3U-3 Corsair, Bureau Number A9329, from its hangar deck catapult in the first practical demonstration of launching aircraft

Major Al Williams Jr.: An Airman's Pilot

Lieutenant Alford Joseph "Al" Williams Jr. won the 1923 Pultizer event at the National Air Races at St. Louis on October sixth with this Curtiss R2C aircraft, Bureau Number A6692. His winning speed was 243.68 miles per hour. (Courtesy of the Hampton Roads Naval Museum.)

One could not chronicle the history of naval aviation, particularly in Hampton Roads, and forget perhaps the greatest naval aviator of all time: Major Alford Joseph "Al" Williams Jr., Naval Aviator No. 1820, whom Captain Eddie Rickenbacker, former First World War Army Air Corps ace and later president and general manager of Eastern Air Lines, wrote in 1940, "an airman's pilot, and with true contempt for armchair goggles, Al Williams, whose enlistment dates back to America's World War I, was an outstanding Navy aviator, whose pioneering flying research, study of practical flight, and world speed records brought many vital improvements to fighting aircraft and many radical innovations in aerial maneuvers."

The youth in this country once beamed from ear to ear at the mention of Williams' name, his achievements having inspired a generation of young people to fly. This matter-of-fact, no nonsense naval aviator knew his profession and knew it well. Even today, those who recall the famous Major Al Williams talk about his natural flying ability, his aerobatic maneuvering (which most note they have never seen done quite so well as when Williams was in the cockpit), his patriotism for his country, and, of course, devotion to both the Navy and Marine Corps which can equally lay claim to his legacy of outstanding accomplishments. Considerable research from New York to Pensacola, Florida, culminated in this retelling of what can only be called a glimpse into the life of the greatest naval aviator of all time. In aviation when you hear the words "hot pilot," think of Major Al Williams—he defined the term.

Alford Joseph Williams Jr. was born in New York City, New York, on July 26, 1896, and grew up in the Bronx borough of the city. In 1915, Al Williams graduated from Fordham University where he had excelled in baseball, football, and basketball. Upon graduation, he was signed by the New York Giants baseball team as a pitcher. He began in the minor league, pitching for the farm club with every intention of moving up to the majors, but along came the First World War and, of course, naval aviation. Williams wanted to fly. Enrolling as a Seaman Second Class student naval aviator at New York City on November 10, 1917, young Williams was sent first to ground school at the Massachusetts Institute of Technology (MIT) and eventually to Pensacola, Florida, for actual flight instruction. Al Williams was winged and commissioned an ensign in the United States Navy on December 10, 1918. His innate flying ability and outstanding airmanship earned him an instructor's billet at Pensacola and, later, a position as squadron commander and test pilot. He was that good.

Aviators typically had a strict career track to follow, but Williams was the exception. He was never bound to ship duty, a desk, nor, for that matter, convention. Still in Pensacola, he made the first Navy inverted flight tests in April 1919 in a modified N-9 to determine and perfect correct control handling for recovery from different flight attitudes. Exhaustive tests of tailspin recovery were conducted by Williams in an HS-2L flying boat in March of 1921, which air station logs reveal he did at Naval Air Station Hampton Roads, Virginia.

Williams would spend considerable time at Naval Air Station Hampton Roads from 1921 through 1926. He transferred from the Naval Reserve Flying Corps (NRFC) to regular Navy on February 18, 1922, losing his rank of lieutenant and once again becoming an ensign. Assigned initially to duty with the Atlantic Fleet Torpedo Squadron, he was shortly thereafter given orders to report to Naval Air Station Hampton Roads as a test pilot in May 1922, where he quickly regained the rank of lieutenant. Log books of the air station for March 1921 through May 1922, and January to February 1925, show Lieutenant Williams was conducting flight tests in 1921 and 1922 in the HS-2L flying boat, R-6L, HS-1, HS-2, F-5L, and the N-9 aircraft.

His contemporaries at the time were Lieutenant Webster Matting "Web" Wright, Naval Aviator No. 322; Lieutenant Felix B. Stump, Naval Aviator No. 2734, later Commander Naval Air Force Atlantic Fleet as vice admiral from December 1948 to April 1951; Lieutenant Robert Leavitt "Bob" Fuller, Naval Aviator No. 1682; and, Lieutenant Frederick Harrison "Fred" Becker, Naval Aviator No. 309. Becker was the first to make terminal velocity dives in an aircraft, the first to launch torpedoes from an aircraft, and first to test a fully automatic pilot device—all at Hampton Roads. Fuller was yet another pioneer in aviation as he helped to plan the Navy's first aircraft carrier, the USS *Langley* (CV-1), and remained a Navy test pilot for nearly ten years. During 1925, log entries indicated numerous training flights.

As a test pilot at Hampton Roads, Al Williams made numerous suggestions for improvements in equipment for Curtiss racers competing in the Pulitzer Trophy. He won the Pulitzer Trophy in his Curtiss R2C on October 6, 1923, competing against the best of Navy, Army, and Marine Corps pilots. His win set world records for 100 and 200 kilometers at a little over 243.68 miles per hour, both faster times than the previous year. Navy planes swept the Pulitzer race that year at St. Louis, taking both first and second place, thanks to Williams' suggestions.

On November 4, 1923, Lieutenant Al Williams, flying a Navy/Curtiss R3C-1 racer, raised the world's absolute straightaway speed record to 266.59 miles per hour at Mitchel Field, Long Island, bettering the record set by Lieutenant Harold James "Hap" Brow, Naval Aviator No. 571, his friend and fellow air racer, only two days before, on November second. This second speed record was the last official speed record held by the Navy until 1947, an absence of nearly a quarter-century. During this period at Hampton Roads, Williams and

Lieutenant Al Williams, speed record holder, stands beside his Curtiss R3C-1 racer, October 1925. The R3C-1 produced 610-horsepower from its enlarged 1,400-cubic-inch engine, also called a V-1400. The aircraft flown by Williams in the 1925 Pulitzer race was Bureau Number A6978. (Courtesy of the Hampton Roads Naval Museum.)

Fuller would give numerous public exhibitions of vertical dive bombing tactics later used successfully by Navy and Marine Corps pilots in the Second World War, a contribution which would have its long-term effects on the success or failure, life or death, of many pilots from both services in time of war.

Al Williams wrote the book on precautions for safety in violent maneuvers and inverted flight in 1924. He is credited with the first recommendation to the Navy Department to adopt parachutes for all Navy pilots that year, perhaps reinforcing previous Navy directives to that effect of August 23, 1919, December 22, 1919, January 16, 1922, and the final order of July 1, 1922, requiring the use of parachutes. Williams used his matter-of-fact manner to convince the Navy of the absolute necessity of parachutes; otherwise the service may have taken longer to enforce the order for its pilots.

In 1923, Williams conducted initial flight tests for recovery of aircraft from flat spins, flying his aircraft to total destruction on one occasion because he had the weight of an extra passenger sitting in the backseat. The same tenacity that brought forth his directive calling for parachutes made Williams work equally hard to have propeller tips on aircraft painted for the safety of aircrew and ground personnel, many of whom had already lost their lives and limbs to propellers. Lieutenant Al Williams was the first to paint his propeller tips, a practice he began in 1924. The Navy's first directive requiring painted tips was dated June 1, 1931. Williams could bear witness to the horrific accidents at Naval Air Station Hampton Roads as a direct result of personnel being struck by moving propellers, the most prominent of these being Lieutenant (junior grade) Herbert "Herb" Schiff, a contemporary of Williams, who was killed on July 11, 1924, when he walked into the propeller arc of an H-16 flying boat warming up on the apron at the air station. (See Chapter 9, page 118).

Upon completion of his official duties at Naval Air Station Hampton Roads in 1925, Al Williams was detailed to the Curtiss Aeroplane and Motor Company in New York to work with company engineers trying to improve visibility in high speed, high performance aircraft. Most of Williams' suggestions could be found in Navy and Army planes in production by Curtiss in 1926 and 1927, no doubt laying the foundation for the direction of aircraft configurations well beyond that time frame.

The year 1925 would culminate in some of Williams' greatest personal accomplishments. While a test pilot at Norfolk, he had begun law school at Georgetown University, somehow fitting in a demanding flying schedule with classes and legal briefs; he earned his LLD in 1925. Williams was also a man not without artistic talent. History records him as a great naval aviator and athlete, but he was also a naturally gifted pianist. The well-rounded nature of his achievements is reflected in his undergraduate degree in liberal arts where he excelled in his studies as much as the playing field. Perhaps one of the greatest qualities about Al Williams was his constant thirst for knowledge. A voracious reader who took an interest in politics and foreign policy, he had, in the words of Eddie Rickenbacker, "no haven for sympathies, no tempering of unpleasant fact, no compromise with truth to be found." When he set the unofficial speed record of 302 miles per hour in a Navy racer, also in 1925, it was the first recorded speed greater than three hundred miles per hour in history. He broke his own record in 1927 with a 322.6-mile-per-hour mark set in his own Mercury racer.

Throughout the 1920s, Williams competed in the Pulitzer and Schneider Cup races. He was quite well known for his work with the Schneider Cup International Seaplane Trophy races, particularly those held at Norfolk in 1926, and in Italy in 1927. After the races he attended at Norfolk in 1926, Williams became highly critical of the United States government's failure to financially support research and development of racing aircraft. His criticisms came from one basic understanding which the British, French, and Italians seemed to grasp well: information gained in the research and development of racing aircraft such as airframe and engines (power plant) were reflected in the development of new and improved military aircraft, the best example of which was the British Supermarine Spitfire S.6B. With the Italian win in 1926, the United States never again competed in the Schneider Cup races. The secret to European domination of the cup after 1925 was capitalization on Williams' 1923 Pulitzer winning Curtiss aircraft engine, and aerodynamic innovations akin to those found in Williams' Mercury racer such as flush-mounted radiators. Al Williams promoted development of a 24-cylinder X-type Packard engine of 1,200-horsepower for use in the 1927 International Schneider Cup Trophy Race, but the engine was not developed in time for the event. He did not drop the idea, however, and the aircraft he had in mind was redesigned in 1929 as a four-hundred-plus-horsepower monoplane with 24-cylinder Packard engine increased to 550-horsepower.

Williams would do a considerable amount of testing in 1927 with hook-on and launch of aircraft to and from dirigibles in flight, adding to the volume of

Lieutenant Al Williams steps out of the cockpit of his Curtiss F6C-4 racer at the National Air Races in 1929. Williams developed inverted flight with this aircraft in early 1928 and reported the first comprehensive Navy inverted flight research. He was awarded the Distinguished Flying Cross on May 10, 1929, for this work. Williams designed inverted flight fuel and oil systems for continuous inverted flight research and promoted development and use of the shoulder safety harness for pilots. The harnesses are visible in the photograph. The F6C-4 had an air-cooled R-1300 Pratt & Whitney engine. Near the end of 1926, beginning of 1927, military aircraft manufacturers began designing and building their aircraft with air-cooled rather than liquid-cooled engines. The aircraft shown in this photograph has the naval air station where it was assigned, Anacostia, painted on its fuselage. (Courtesy of the National Museum of Naval Aviation.)

information on the subject that began in December 1918 when Lieutenant (junior grade) George Crompton, Naval Aviator No. 100, made the first launch from the Navy dirigible *C-1* above Rockaway, New York, in an Army JN-4 Jenny aircraft. By early 1928, Al Williams had developed inverted flight with the F6C-4, and reported the first comprehensive Navy inverted flight research. He flight-tested and recorded every known and conceivable normal and inverted aerobatic maneuver for load factors, including the very first demonstrated outside loop, inverted tailspin, inverted falling leaf and inverted snap barrel roll. The impact of G-forces on pilots, especially those related to redouts and blackouts in sharp maneuvers, were recorded by Williams. His research of inverted flight culminated in his being awarded the Distinguished Flying Cross on May 17, 1929, for extraordinary achievement in projecting the general knowledge of flight through extended study of inverted flight.

As the Navy's chief test pilot, Williams was on the cutting edge of aviation. The American Society of Mechanical Engineers awarded him their trophy for his flight research, thereby recognizing Williams as one of the twelve men contributing the most to aviation in the United States. Awards aside, Al Williams kept developing and perfecting such concerns as inverted flight fuel and oil systems for continuous inverted flight research, and he promoted the development and use of a shoulder safety harness for pilots but did not claim his invention since he referred to harnesses used in World War I Spads in his study.

On May 15, 1930, Lieutenant Al Williams resigned his Navy commission, put off by the sad state of research and development in naval aviation, and his sense that the powers-that-be lacked direction. His first act as a civilian aviator was to buy a Curtiss Hawk, later called *Gulfhawk I.*(1) He struck out on the airshow circuit, quickly becoming one of the most sought-after performers in the world. On July 21, 1932, he was appointed a captain in the Marine Corps Reserve but remained a civilian except for reserve drills. With the Great Depression a fact of life, Williams joined the legal department of Gulf Oil Corporation in 1933 but clearly itched to fly. He had himself transferred to the aviation division of Gulf Oil. During the 1930s, Al Williams became a syndicated columnist for the Scripps-Howard newspaper service appropriately called, *Airpower,* and was read by nearly ten million people in three hundred newspapers across the country. He even became commander-in-chief of Scripps-Howard Junior Aviators, a youth movement of five hundred thousand strong interested in aviation. In the 1930s it was particularly important to have a real-life great like Williams to inspire youth beyond the doldrums of the Great Depression.

As part of the aviation division of Gulf Oil, the company purchased a Grumman F3F aerobatic biplane for Williams right off the factory line. Williams took delivery of the aircraft he dubbed *Gulfhawk 2* on December 6, 1936. Williams described it in his 1940 book *Airpower* as, "a single-seater Grumman fighter biplane with a thousand horsepower Wright Cyclone engine and is identical to the fighting ship standardized by the United States Navy and the United States Marine Corps." The F3F had a 1,000-horsepower Wright engine and a few other special features suited to high-G aerobatic performance, including an inverted fuel and oil system and aerodynamic airframe customized to Williams' needs. Because he worked for Gulf, all company or company-associated aircraft were painted in company colors: orange, blue and white. *Gulfhawk 2* would be flown by Al Williams until 1948 when he replaced it with the *Gulfhawk 4th,* a Grumman F8F Bearcat. In 1938, Williams took *Gulfhawk 2* on a tour of Europe. He would write in *Airpower* (1940), "It [*Gulfhawk 2*] is admirably adapted to aerobatics and from the day it was rolled on the field at the Grumman Factory at Farmingdale, Long Island [New York], no one had ever flown it but myself. It had only one pilot—and one mechanic—Frank Tye."

Gulfhawk 2 was loaded aboard the *Queen Mary,* whose first destination was England. Making his way from England through Europe, Williams would renew his friendships with most of the great airmen of the world. When he arrived in Berlin, he found Germany's famous ace, Ernst Udet, by then a major general in the German *Luftwaffe.* He wrote of Udet, "this man of rare ability and many parts is one of the finest airmen I have ever known. And when I say 'airman,' I mean not only that he can pilot a ship in a superior fashion, that he knows his aerodynamics and is possessed of indomitable courage, but that he symbolizes the finest traditions of air sportsmanship." He concluded of Udet and other great airmen he had known, "There's a man, who once having assumed a job will see it through or won't live to make his own excuses—and win or lose, he'll top it off with a grin." Udet would become the only person other than Williams himself to fly the *Gulfhawk 2*. Letting go of his prized airplane was emotionally difficult for Williams, who loved that aircraft as much as anyone can love an inanimate object. He did not doubt Udet's ability for a moment but, as he put it, "What a beautiful little ship, thought I, as I watched her grow smaller in the distance. At the end of the field he turned into the wind, waited a few seconds, and then I heard the loud roar of the Cyclone engine. After what seemed like a ground run of only a few feet, the plane leaped into the air. For the first time, I was watching the *Gulfhawk* fly," he continued, "affection and love for an airplane—yes, I imagine you ground dwellers are smiling—smiling indulgently. An airplane is made of steel and fabric and all that, but when a flying machine and you have been through lots of tight places, where a single slip or faltering response to the controls would have meant the end—and she has never failed you—you have, 'a brave and gallant little ship.'" In return for Udet's flight in the *Gulfhawk 2,* Williams was given the opportunity to fly the Messerschmitt Me 109, Germany's premier single-seater fighter. *Gulfhawk 2* was briefly joined by *Gulfhawk 3,* a two-seat aircraft, in 1938. Williams made little use of *Gulfhawk 3* before the company sold it.

America came to know Williams quite well in the 1930s during his weekly national radio broadcasts, none of which was quite as pointed as the address on neutrality, printed in the *Congressional Record* of October 16, 1939. In this particular address, Williams said:

"The most devastating recent shock to the nerves of Americans was the President's [Franklin Delano Roosevelt's] report to his press conference that two submarines had been sighted near the American coasts. That report should have come from the United States Navy. Coming from the President, it scared the country—and his jocular comments, after refusing to identify the subs: 'They might have been Swiss submarines'—did not reduce the scare effect. I have disagreed with other administrations and other Presidents in the past. That's my right. I expect to disagree with other administrations and other Presidents in the future. But this is the first time I have ever feared a President or an administration. And now this same administration is seeking full and complete authority to handle our neutrality policy while a war is on in Europe. Looking over that record, I say, 'Don't give them that authority.'"

Williams' book, *Airpower*, a Coward-McCann publication, was a tremendous success and brought much focus to America's airpower crisis prior to the formal outbreak of world war. Al Williams resigned from the Marine Corps Reserve on July 8, 1940, as a major. He continued to work for Gulf Oil Company, promoting the Miami Air Maneuvers between 1937 and 1941 with an offer of free oil and fuel to those who flew their small privately owned aircraft to the races. Pilots needed only to write Williams for a free coupon book good for the promotion, and information on Gulf Oil.

When the Japanese attacked Pearl Harbor on December 7, 1941, Williams, forty-five years of age, reactivated his Marine Corps Reserve commission but did not join the front lines. He was ultimately more valuable to the war effort working with Gulf Oil, and, of course, instructing. Major Al Williams was appointed a special technical consultant to the Chief of the Army Air Corps in 1943 to demonstrate fighter tactics and build combat morale. His aerobatic routines in the *Gulfhawk 2* at twelve Army Air Corps fighter pilot schools were described as beyond impressive. No one could fly a plane like Al Williams, no one could make it snap and roll, dance in the air with the same finesse and grace as this great airman.

After World War II ended, Gulf Oil and Williams decided it was time to retire the aged F3F for a new aircraft. Parting with *Gulfhawk 2* was difficult for Williams, who had grown so very attached to the aircraft that had served him faithfully since 1936. Paul E. Garber of the Smithsonian Institution said in 1956:

"Al Williams' expert piloting of the high performance airplane *Gulfhawk 2* was a feature of air meets in America and abroad for more than a decade. His flying was superb airmanship, which advertised progressive aviation, thrilled thousands, and inspired countless youth to take up flying. This plane in his hands became also a flying laboratory for testing special aviation fuels and lubricants. Following his final impressive flight demonstration at Washington National Airport on October 11, 1948, the *Gulfhawk 2* was formally presented to the National Air [and Space] Museum by the Gulf Oil Corporation."

Williams picked the Grumman F8F Bearcat to replace the F3F, and he would be the first citizen to have a Bearcat released for private use. He established numerous climb and takeoff records with the Navy aircraft, and, as was true of Williams' other *Gulfhawks,* this was no ordinary Bearcat. Grumman manufactured the F8F specifically for Al Williams, dispensing with its usual military armament and carrier tailhook, thus shedding the aircraft of nearly 1,300 pounds. Generally, everything else about the aircraft remained the same as in standard Navy versions. The F8F was a fighter class single-place, folding low-wing fighter powered by a Pratt & Whitney R-2800-34W single-stage, two-speed supercharged engine equipped with a water injection system. The main self-sealing fuel cell, located beneath the cockpit floor, had a capacity of 185 gallons. Navy versions of the Bearcat could carry three additional drop tanks. Williams took possession of the aircraft July 23, 1947, and immediately began a little over a year of test flights and experimentation to measure the Bearcat's flight performance. Alice Williams christened her husband's plane *Gulfhawk 4th* at Washington National Airport on October 11, 1948, at which time Al Williams began officially flying the Bearcat in exhibitions and air shows.

Few realize how far Williams took his experimentation, case in point his fitting the Bearcat with jet assisted takeoff (JATO) rockets. This was one hot aircraft but, unlike its predecessor, *Gulfhawk 2,* which ended up in the National Air (and Space) Museum, *Gulfhawk 4th* met its end early. On January 18, 1949, Al Williams was

the 'Radial' engine (air-cooled)

returning from the Miami Air Maneuvers to his home outside Elizabeth City, North Carolina. On approach to the field at Weeksville, his landing gear would not come down, so he took the plane south to New Bern, North Carolina, to Simmons-Knott Airport to make an emergency landing. His left main gear did not engage and the Bearcat came in belly down, its extra fifty-gallon drop tank trailing aviation fuel down the runway as it skidded to a stop. The gas ignited almost immediately. Williams leapt from the cockpit to watch from a reasonably safe distance as the flames caught up to the Bearcat and set her ablaze. His decision to shoot for Simmons-Knott was made under the assumption the airport had better facilities and emergency gear available on the airfield to combat accidents and fires. No one even had a fire extinguisher in hand as he ran from the aircraft, much to his chagrin.

Al Williams semi-retired from Gulf Oil Corporation in 1949, offering his services as a consultant until his final retirement in 1951, at which time he also retired from exhibition flying. Williams lived the life of a gentleman farmer on his beloved Eyrie Farm located in Weeksville, North Carolina, his home beginning in 1941, growing soybeans, and raising cattle and hogs. His land spread far and wide around the old blimp station at Weeksville, the place he kept his aircraft for many years. In his retirement from one profession, Williams found another in farming and, of course, the lecture circuit. He lectured to the National War College, National Advisory Committee on Aeronautics, colleges and universities around the country, and the aircraft industry. With a pen in hand, he spun leading edge articles for national periodicals and technical journals related to aviation. Al Williams died of cancer on June 15, 1958, at Albemarle Hospital in Elizabeth City, North Carolina. He would be buried with full military honors in Arlington National Cemetery in the uniform of a major of the United States Marine Corps, his cherished naval aviator wings and Distinguished Flying Cross, symbols of his life accomplishments, rightfully buried with this greatest of naval aviators.

When many of today's naval aviators were asked if they knew of Al Williams, sadly, the response was, "no." This great airman should be immortalized for his tremendous contribution to high-speed research, fighter developments, sustained inverted flight, outstanding airmanship and air racing performance, and asundry other accomplishments too many to mention. But, perhaps it is even more important for generation after generation of naval aviator to remember his inspirations, his patriotism, his devotion to the Navy and Marine Corps, and his words, written so eloquently and with such fire. His own characterization of great airmen said it best, "they all share one characteristic in their self-reliance. In thought, expression, and action, they fairly exude self-sufficient confidence without the faintest trace of [conceit]."

1. Williams actually named his *Gulfhawks I, 2, 3,* and *4th.*

A BM-2 aircraft of Torpedo Squadron One (VT-1S) skirts the Chesapeake Bay on a flight. This aircraft carries the section leader's band around the "T" and is marked with the numeral "1" to the right of the band, indicating not only a section leader but the squadron commanding officer, 1932. There were only sixteen BM-2 aircraft produced by the Glenn L. Martin Company of Baltimore, Maryland, for the Navy, Bureau Numbers A9170 through A9185, of which this is A9178. The original contract for the BM-2 was issued to Martin on October 17, 1931, and the first aircraft made their appearance the next year. Powered by a 625-horsepower Pratt & Whitney engine, the BM-2 remained in service for a short period of time. The BM-2 was retired from fleet squadrons in 1937. Torpedo Squadron One flew its BM-2 aircraft from the USS *Lexington* in 1932, when the photograph here was taken. The squadron was redesignated Bombing Squadron One (B) (VB-1B) on July 1, 1934. (Official United States Navy Photograph.)

Captain J.H. Hoover was commanding officer of Naval Air Station Norfolk from June 1937 through October 1938. (Official United States Navy Photograph.)

The position of Assistant Secretary of the Navy for Air was established by an Act of Congress on June 24, 1926, with the title Assistant Secretary of the Navy for Aeronautics. The office was vacant from June 1, 1932, to September 5, 1941. The office was retitled Assistant Secretary of the Navy for Air on September 11, 1941. The position was abolished on February 5, 1959.

from carriers by means of hydraulic flush-deck catapults, this one in the hangar bay. The event was also the first demonstration of catapulting aircraft from the hangar deck. The O3U-3 was one of two such aircraft attached for utility duties aboard the USS *Yorktown*.

Aviation Division One, VN7RD5, of the United States Naval Reserve Unit, Naval Air Station Norfolk, was photographed in front of hangar V-3 in April 1936. Lieutenant (junior grade) Melvin N. Gough, USNR, Naval Aviator No. 4474, division commander, is seated in the front row (sixth from left).

The Quest for Glory

Taken in 1918, this photograph shows Rear Admiral Joseph Strauss and his staff on board the admiral's flagship, USS *Black Hawk.* Left to right: Lieutenant Commander (then a lieutenant) Noel Davis, Rear Admiral Joseph Strauss, Lieutenant W.K. Harrill, and Ensign K.C. Richmond. (Photographer unknown.)

As Charles A. Lindbergh touched down in Paris after his world record, non-stop transatlantic flight from New York, he triumphed where others had failed or perished in the attempt. The deaths of naval aviators Lieutenant Commander Noel Davis and his copilot, Lieutenant Stanton Hall Wooster, occurred during one of the most significant, yet by far most tragic, decades in aviation history. Death would end Davis' and Wooster's plans to make the first non-stop flight from New York to Paris by a single aircraft, and their opportunity to collect the $25,000 prize offered by Raymond Orteig, a New York hotelier, for the achievement. Though Lindbergh successfully flew the transatlantic flight, he was conscious, if not painfully so, of the military and civilian aviators who flew their last mission in the quest for fame and fortune. The story of Davis and Wooster is in large measure the story of a by-gone era and of two men's lives forever changed by one mistake.

Noel Davis was raised on the plains of Utah. In his early school days, Davis demonstrated an aptitude for mathematics and a strong interest in the Navy. He was appointed to the United States Naval Academy in Annapolis in 1910, and, once graduated, served as aide to Admiral William Snowden Sims (1858–1936), later a champion of naval aviation, and Rear Admiral Joseph Strauss. When the United States entered the war against Germany, Davis went abroad as chief of staff in charge of mine laying to Strauss. Davis was largely responsible for planning and subsequent operations to lay out the United States Navy's 56,611 of the over 70,000 mines in a field that ran 240 miles from the coastline of Scotland to the shores of Norway. Known as the North Sea mine barrage, the Navy's laying of these mines eventually ended German submarines from using that route to the high seas. When the war ended, Davis was part of the crew assigned to remove the mines he had earlier laid. His ship struck one of the mines and Davis was thrown overboard and nearly drowned. After this experience and his own long-term interest in aviation, Davis entered naval aviation training in Pensacola, where he was subsequently designated a naval aviator. Davis possessed a natural aptitude for aerodynamics, so much so that he wrote several books on the subject which were used by Navy pilots as study guides. Before entering the Orteig competition and coming to Langley, Davis had been officer-in-charge of the reserve field at Squantum, Massachusetts, and had served for three years as head of Naval Reserve aviation, headquartered in Washington, D.C., immediately prior to the crash.

Lieutenant Stanton H. Wooster was a 32-year-old native of New Haven, Connecticut, with a fiancée he planned to marry prior to his departure on the actual transatlantic flight. His career in naval aviation had been punctuated by a series of significant flights, including the May 2, 1924, flight in which a Davis Douglas DT aircraft, carrying a dummy torpedo, catapulted from the deck of the USS *Langley* at anchor in Pensacola Bay. The plane was piloted by Lieutenant W.M. Dillon, but carried Wooster as the gunnery officer.

Lieutenant Commander Davis had announced in March of 1927 that he would take off from Mitchel Field, Long Island, New York, in early June in an all-American aircraft, including its engines and crew, in the race to be the first to make the nonstop transatlantic flight. His aircraft derived its name from Davis' desire to make the flight an all-American endeavor. Lieutenant Stanton H. Wooster, a naval aviator like Davis, would be his copilot. The *American Legion* was paraded before a curious media and public over a three-day period from April 16–18, and christened by Lieutenant Commander Davis' wife at Curtiss Field in Bristol, Pennsylvania. Davis, accompanied by his wife, and copilot Wooster, boarded the Keystone-Pathfinder trimotor and flew it to Langley Field on April 19. Davis opted to bring the plane to Langley to put it through a series of tests because he doubted as to whether the Pathfinder, designed by C. Talbot Porter, chief engineer of Keystone Aircraft Corporation, could take off fully loaded at nearly 17,000 pounds for the transatlantic crossing. He was quoted at the time:

"It is by no means certain that I will attempt a New York to Paris flight. My purpose in going to Langley Field is to determine whether the plane has the initial capacity to make the flight. If the consumption and other tests do not show a reasonable margin of safety, we will not make the attempt. I have always stated, and I repeat, that this is a scientific effort and not a stunt."

Davis' wife had come along on the trek from Bristol via Washington, D.C., to Langley to prepare her husband's and Wooster's rations of food which they would carry with them on their test flights and, in the end, the transatlantic flight. When asked about her role in an interview before the accident she stated, "I always look after my husband's rations. I came here to make final preparations for supplying my husband and his assistants with the food for their long flight." She had faced squarely the possibility of a disastrous outcome as well. "If my husband is compelled to descend at sea," she said, "I have planned eight days' emergency rations, which should suffice until the radio of the *American Legion* picks up a ship to rescue them." Like Eugene Ely's wife, Mabel, nearly twenty years earlier, Davis' wife exhibited the utmost confidence in her husband's success. She had accompanied him on many of his flights, and though unwavering in her comments, would

Is Another Nonstop Record to Be Shattered?

This cartoon, drawn by J.M. Davis, ran in the *Norfolk Landmark* on Wednesday, April 20, 1927, six days before Davis and Wooster lost their lives in the crash of the *American Legion.* The pilot of this whimsically drawn piece is a caricature of President Calvin Coolidge dumping gasoline into the tank of an airplane which closely resembled the kind to be used by the likes of Bert Acosta and Clarence D. Chamberlain, or Davis and Wooster. Newspapers around the country ran syndicated political cartoons such as this one, but the pervasive sentiment among reporters was that the notion of flying nonstop across the Atlantic Ocean had suicide written all over it. Imagine their surprise when Lindbergh touched down in Paris.

Two naval aviators lost their lives on April 26, 1927, over Hampton, Virginia, in the crash of the transatlantic aircraft, *American Legion,* a Keystone-Pathfinder Army bomber, tail code N-X179. Lieutenant Commander Noel Davis, Naval Aviator No. 2944, and Lieutenant Stanton Hall Wooster, Naval Aviator No. 2731, were engaged in the great transatlantic race for the Orteig prize of twenty-five thousand dollars to the aviator who made the crossing first. Davis and Wooster were racing against Charles A. Lindbergh and Navy Commander Richard Evelyn Byrd for the purse. Lindbergh emerged victorious with the *Spirit of St. Louis* in a race that had been called suicide by international media. Davis and Wooster crashed in a marsh area in Hampton which submerged the cockpit of the aircraft, trapping them in the twisted wreckage. They suffocated from gasoline fumes. The *American Legion* was equipped with three J-5 engines. The first photograph gives a portside view of the aircraft; the second a three-quarter portside perspective. Both ground shots were taken at Langley Field. The third picture is the remains of the pilot seats after the fatal crash on the Back River.

plunge into deep shock upon learning of her husband's death moments after take-off from Langley.

At 6:20 a.m. the morning of April 26, 1927, Davis and Wooster rolled their Keystone-Pathfinder plane, *American Legion,* out of a Langley airfield hangar belonging to Aerial Squadron Fifty-Nine. The first reveille had just been sounded by Army buglers as Lieutenant J.K. Nissley, assistant operations officer of Langley Field, glanced out his window half-dressed and saw the *American Legion* taxi past the operations shack. Nissley continued to watch as the plane took off to the northeast at low altitude, made a sharp turn to the right and went down. He sounded the station alarm.

Others were watching, too. In the barracks of Aerial Squadron Fifty-Nine, some of the men stared out their windows at Davis' and Wooster's aircraft. Most had been roused from their sleep by a combination of the first bugle call and the roar of the *American Legion's* three motors turning at such an early hour of the morning. Two of the airmen saw the plane make its slow banking turn over the Langley hangar built to house the ill-fated airship *Roma* five years before and fall from the sky into the marshes on the fringe of the Back River. One of them yelled, "Crash!" as the others scrambled to get dressed and down to the field.

Within moments of the crash, Captain C.P. Clark, commanding officer of Langley's Nineteenth Airship Company, formed a rescue party composed of himself, Lieutenant Nissley, Captain R.C. Cocke, and Lieutenant E.R. McReynolds. They crossed the Back River in a fast boat, but soon realized they were too late to save Davis and Wooster.

Davis and Wooster had previously conducted load tests with the Keystone-Pathfinder at 13,500 and 15,000 pounds, respectively, and the aircraft performed well. The morning of April 26, Davis planned a full-load test preparatory to the flight from New York to Paris. This was to be the *American Legion's* first full-load test and its last. Davis and Wooster had great difficulty getting the plane, fully-loaded at 16,480 pounds, into the air. The *American Legion* went three-quarters of a mile over the ground before it lifted off over the Back River and its marsh. At about fifty feet in the air, Davis began circling back in an apparent attempt to climb. One turn was executed without a problem, but on the second, the *American Legion* sideslipped. Davis got it under control and glided to the marsh. The aircraft, loaded beyond its performance capacity, ploughed through the mud and water for a distance of approximately 125 feet when it nosed over into a duck pond, burying the cockpit and its crew in the mud. It started to sink nose first. At the point of impact, the *American Legion* was a mile from Langley Field and less than a quarter mile from Messick, Virginia, a fishing settlement on the Back River.

Davis and Wooster lived only a short time after the crash. Contrary to the speculation of media at that time, they did not die on impact. There were a few cuts and bruises on both naval aviators, but more compelling evidence of suffocation from gasoline fumes and of suffocation due to the depth the two pilots, submerged in the cockpit, were imbedded. The *American Legion* was carrying 1,500 gallons of gasoline at the time of impact, some of which broke free from its storage and flooded the cockpit. Mute testimony to the frantic efforts of two men in their last moments of life to avert tragedy was documented by rescuers who arrived on the scene about twenty minutes after the crash. The switch of the engines to starboard and port of the center engine had been shut off, but the switch to the main engine had not been disconnected. But, speculation as to cause of death began almost as soon as the cockpit was raised. One newspaperman claimed Davis' face was crushed and Wooster's neck was broken. Neither proved true. Fate was not kind to the aviators. Their deaths were not quick, but wrought with agony, and because investigators would later refuse to discuss the subject and no autopsies were ever performed, the press theorized even more about their deaths.

The only person to witness the crash from the Back River was W.J. Forrest, a Messick fisherman. Forrest was sitting in his bateau about 500 yards away as the *American Legion* careened across the river and nosed into the duck pond. Unable to reach the crew in the quagmire, Forrest frantically stood up and waved his arms at rescuers making their way across the river in their fast boat He was not telling them anything they did not already know. Even if help had arrived five minutes after the crash, the *American Legion* was so heavy and its angle of impact so great, there would have been precious little time to pull Davis and Wooster from the cockpit because the aircraft was pulled under so rapidly. When rescuers arrived barely twenty minutes after impact, airmen from Langley had to pull ropes over the tail section and use it as a lever to bring the forward portion of the plane to the surface.

The gold-colored *American Legion* with its smart read trim once again glistened in the morning light as its cockpit peeked above a watery grave, but instead of being described as a magnificent flying machine, observers called it "a grotesque beetle caught in a trap." The wife of Colonel C.C. Culver, commanding officer of Langley, flew to the scene by way of the Army dirigible *TC-5*. She was checking the tragic scene for her friend, Davis' wife, and Lieutenant Wooster's fiancée, Sallie Finney, who had flown with Davis and Wooster on the Washington, D.C., to Langley leg of their journey from Bristol. Accompanying Culver's wife were several officers and photographers. Colonel Culver was himself quoted as saying, "I believe if there had been no duck pond where the plane fell, Commander Davis would have made a safe landing, and the plane would now be back in its hangar here and both the officers alive." Davis' wife and eighteen-month-old son, Noel Davis Jr., were anxiously awaiting word at Langley Field. No one had the heart to tell young Noel that his father was dead.

Soon after the aviators' bodies were removed from the wreckage, investigators went to work. Colonel Culver initiated an Army inquiry with support from a Navy board. The Navy was more focused on the cause of the crash than the way in which Davis and Wooster met their end. The Navy figured their manner of death would come to light as the investigation progressed. Lieutenant Kenneth Boedecker, assigned as a field engineer with the Wright Airplane Corporation which engined the plane, inspected the wreck. Though the investigative panel convened to uncover the cause of the crash never offered conclusive findings, Boedecker thought the crash was not due to overloading but the fact Davis turned the tail of the *American Legion* into the wind. His opinion would be in the minority. Most flying officers of the Army and Navy felt strongly that the crash was caused by more load than the aircraft was capable of handling, particularly at low altitudes. Boedecker also observed that he thought the gas tanks did not break free of their moorings in the rear compartment until the plane turned over, but he would not hazard a guess as to how much gasoline then flooded the cockpit. After investigators left the scene, taking with them the aircraft's valuable technical instruments, the Army allowed the public to siphon gasoline from the wreckage. They carted away about 900 gallons. But, the Army never counted on the souvenir hunters who followed. Unscrupulous scavengers wasted little time getting to the plane and taking everything that could easily be carried away, including the plane's fabric. The once-beautiful gold and red plane, the symbol of one man's pride in an all-American endeavor, was stripped bare.

The competition for the transatlantic flight was formidable, but the race was also characterized by the number of accidents which eliminated several planes and pilots before it began. On Sunday, April 24, two days before Davis' and Wooster's fatal crash, a Bellanca monoplane, scheduled to be in the transatlantic race and which had recently set a world endurance record over Mineola, Long Island, with Bert Acosta and Clarence D. Chamberlin as its pilots, was the center of attention at Curtiss Field, also on Long Island. Chamberlin, this time with two little girls as passengers, landed safely after the Bellanca suffered a broken strut as it left the ground on its first flight after its formal christening. Chamberlin held the crowd of five thousand in breathless suspense for an hour before he negotiated the landing. The Bellanca would undergo repairs, but did not re-enter the competition. Charles A. Levine, chairman of the board of directors of the Columbia Aircraft Corporation, sponsors of the proposed flight of the Bellanca monoplane for the Orteig Prize, when informed of Lieutenant Commander Davis' death, said: "A tragic fate has eliminated another gallant attempt to cross the Atlantic. While the plans will proceed with the Bellanca plane, the sporting spirit has been removed because of the fact that we have lost Davis. And Commander Byrd's plane, the *America,* has been practically eliminated."

Davis' mother, Lena B. Price, lived far from the tragedy which unfolded on Virginia's Back River. Price and her husband resided on a ranch six miles outside of Oakley, Utah, an area roughly 150 miles from Salt Lake City. As she was handed the message bearing news of her son's death, she faltered for a moment, then exclaimed: "My boy, my only boy," her agony readily apparent to those who surrounded her and tried desperately to comfort a mother who was struggling to comprehend the loss of her child. After a few moments, Price steadied herself and made one official statement regarding the death of her thirty-five-year-old son: "It is terrible, the death of my boy, but I have the knowledge that at least he died as he lived, in the service of his country."

Commander Richard E. Byrd and his pilot, Floyd Bennett, and radio operator George O. Noville, were injured when their aircraft turtled on the runway at Hasbrough Heights, New Jersey, on April 16. Bennett and Noville were hospitalized. The plane underwent repair.

Chapter 10: War, Peace, and Whirlybirds

Captain Patrick N.L. Bellinger detached from his five-month tenure as Admiral Ernest J. King's chief of staff in Washington, D.C., on June 23, 1938, and headed for Naval Air Station Norfolk, still part of the Naval Operating Base. Nearly twenty years had passed since Bellinger commanded Norfolk's naval air station. In that time, the air station had become more an overhaul and assembly plant than active airstrip. Planes in need of overhaul were sent to Norfolk, the aircraft rebuilt and returned to the fleet. Throughout the 1930s between twelve and sixteen aircraft engines were being overhauled monthly. Productivity was obviously not meeting Bureau of Aeronautics standards and the administrative arm of naval aviation threatened to suspend air station overhauls and close the base. Due to Norfolk civic leaders' efforts in Washington, D.C., Naval Air Station Norfolk remained open, increasing its share of aircraft overhauls. By the time Bellinger arrived, efforts to restrict the air station's growth were beginning to give way. Bellinger proved the final catalyst, the one person who pushed hard enough to grow the base in size and importance much as he had done in the air station's infancy.

At first, the base was occasional home to a patrol wing and squadrons assigned to aircraft carriers. Few aircraft were permanently attached to Norfolk and those that found refuge there consisted of transport and utility types. By 1939, Rear Admiral J.K. Taussig had become the commandant of the Fifth Naval District, also making him overseer of Naval Air Station Norfolk. Taussig had

Planes were lined up on the first airfield at Naval Air Station Norfolk to bear the name Chambers Field, July 29, 1939. The ferry from Hampton was arriving at Willoughby (above the field on the left). Chambers Field was named on June 1, 1938, in honor of Captain Washington Irving Chambers, the first officer-in-charge of aviation and director of early efforts to find a home for naval aviation in the Navy. (Official United States Navy Photograph.)

Mel Gough and NACA: Engineers in Charge

Melvin Neilson "Mel" Gough was born in 1906 at Anacostia, Washington, D.C. He started his career at the National Advisory Committee for Aeronautics (NACA), Langley Field, on July 23, 1926, as a junior mechanical engineer. The Navy had more of an investment in NACA than any other branch of the service in those early years. Some historians jokingly acknowledge the Navy's influence over the facility, calling NACA the "Naval" Advisory Committee for Aeronautics. Members of the original Advisory Committee of the Langley Aerodynamical Laboratory in 1913 were Orville Wright, Glenn H. Curtiss, Captain Washington Irving Chambers of the United States Navy, Samuel W. Stratton, and General George P. Scriven of the United States Army. The marrying of military personnel and civilian scientists served to harness knowledge on all fronts.

Educated at Johns Hopkins University, Gough was perfectly suited to the environs at Langley, a place clamoring with aeronautical engineers joined by some of the most outstanding physicists in the world. He started in the Propeller Research Tunnel (PRT) but learned to fly via the United States Navy, going through flight training at Naval Air Station Pensacola, Florida, and joining the reserves. Gough was a student naval aviator in class P-4-28, Squadron Eight VN8RD8 and, upon graduation, became Naval Aviator No. 4474, recorded as of July 18, 1929. An order sent to the fleet on July 1, 1927, required that Naval Reserve aviation officers go through one year of training duty with an active duty squadron after graduation from Pensacola. The first class to complete this requirement was a class of fifty new ensigns that year. By earning his wings of gold in 1928, Gough not only completed a NACA requirement of all prospective test pilots that they be engineers as well as qualified pilots, but he also fulfilled a boyhood dream to fly. He would also record some fabulous naval aviation history of his own in the process. Mel Gough became an official NACA Experimental Engineer and Test Pilot in 1929 while continuing to fly for the Navy. As part of his active duty training, Gough became a member of VF-1(B), otherwise known as the *High Hatters*. His friend, Ensign George C. Helebrandt, USNR, wrote in Gough's USS *Saratoga* (CV-3) log album dated May 19, 1930, "God's gift to VF-1(B), the *High Hat* '6'—This is written hoping you'll respect the inexperienced—and remember my pointers." Gough would regard his status as a *High Hatter* aboard the USS *Saratoga,* and a member of the Navy stunt team called the *Hell Divers,* high on his extraordinary list of accomplishments.

On September 23, 1933, Lieutenants Melvin N. Gough, Robert Sanders, and Charles G. Ironmonger of Reserve Squadron VN7RD5 stationed at Naval Air Station Hampton Roads, and former members of the famous *High Hat* squadron, attended the Women's Air Derby at the State Rifle Range Airport at Virginia Beach to meet Amelia Earhart Putnam, Helen McClosky, Carolyn Jamieson, and Tiny Goddard, all nationally and internationally known aviatrixes, and observe the flying. "Lady Lindy," as Amelia Earhart Putnam was sometimes called in the press, arrived via an aircraft flown by her friend Tiny Goddard. Earhart gave a speech to the admiring crowd, noting "Your field is very attractive. The last time I was here, I rolled my own plane over at your Naval Air Station (Hampton Roads), so this time I thought I'd be safe with a woman to pilot me." The reference was to a mishap in landing some two years before in which her aircraft overturned and Earhart suffered a few bruises, and to the fact she flew down from New York City with Goddard.

By October 27, 1933, Gough and his famous *Hell Diver* stunt team were performing in Richmond, Virginia, for the city's Navy Day celebration. The pilots that day aside from Gough were Lieutenant Arthur "Art" Laverents, USNR, Naval Aviator No. 1154, (formerly a Navy participant in the first Pulitzer Trophy Race at Mitchel Field, Long Island, New York, in 1920, finishing fifth); and Lieutenant Robert Sanders, USNR. The team arrived from Naval Air Station Hampton Roads at Byrd Field, and was immediately welcomed by Mayor J. Fulmer Bright, Adjutant General S. Gardner Waller, and Lieutenant Commander R.H. Maury, officer-in-charge of the Navy recruiting office in Richmond. Lieutenant Laverents commanded the formation. Lieutenant Gough was, even at that time, already recognized as a stunt flyer and engineer. As for Sanders, he was regarded as a specialist in Navy wind tunnel aircraft testing. *Hell Diver* aircraft, painted gray with red tails and sectional markings, were F4Bs powered by 500-horsepower engines. The F4B was truly the classic aircraft of the period, used both as a fighter and bomber.

Melvin Neilson Gough, designer, at his drafting table, 1926.

The Variable Density Tunnel at NACA, made operational on October 19, 1922, is shown here as it appeared in 1926. The eighty-five-ton pressure shell was constructed at Newport News Shipbuilding of steel plate lapped and riveted according to standard steam-boiler construction of the period. When in use, the tunnel enabled engineers to conduct their aerodynamic tests at high Reynolds numbers.

Gough once called this "the hobby," perhaps expressing his boyhood dream to fly—a dream that was destined to come true. Here, a little fellow by the name of "Eb" holds a Curtiss JN4D-2 model, as much a classic as the picture, 1926.

Mel Gough was destined to become one of the United States' most successful experimental test pilots and aeronautical engineers, working in concert with the likes of Fred E. Weick, Elton W.

A Navy/Curtiss F4C-1 fighter, all metal construction, was fitted with a Wright Whirlwind motor and tested at NACA, Langley Field, Virginia, 1927. The bureau number of the aircraft was 6690.

A Vought UO-1 being hoisted aboard ship was a test bed for NACA in 1926. The diagram (shown below) pertains to water pressure effects on the UO-1 pontoon. The aircraft was taken out for flight evaluation of a pontoon design engineered at the facility.

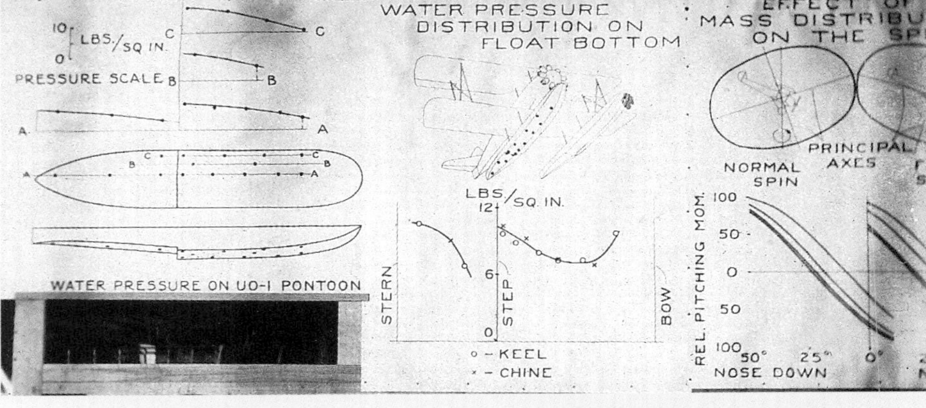

Civilian test pilot Paul B. King, wearing a seat or pack type parachute, climbs into a Wright Apache, 1926. King tested aircraft at NACA between 1922 and 1927, the year he resigned. As for the Wright Apache, it was borrowed from the Navy to test the effects of different cowlings on aircraft and engine performance.

Vought UO-1 in the hangar at NACA, 1926.

Addison Rothrock, NACA physicist, 1927. Rothrock, called "Rothy" by his co-workers, would become a good friend to Gough. He worked at NACA from 1926 to 1942, transferring to the Aircraft Engine Research Laboratory in 1934—a facility he helped design, along with Carlton Kemper and Oscar W. Schey. The engine laboratory studied methods to increase the power and efficacy of aircraft engines as well as improve upon start mechanisms, radial cooling, and fuel economy.

This Sperry M-1 Messenger (AS 68473) is seen here mounted on the balance in the Propeller Research Tunnel, early 1927. On the left is a Mr. Poe, and on the right is Fred E. Weick, formerly of the Navy's Bureau of Aeronautics and instrumental in setting up the Propeller Research Tunnel at NACA. Weick came to NACA specifically driven by his own desire to further testing on naval aircraft and the offer of first-class facilities to do so. He would be employed at NACA from 1925 to 1929, and again from 1930 through 1936.

Miller, Donald H. Wood, Lieutenant Commander (later Captain) Walter S. Diehl of the Bureau of Aeronautics, Navy Department, and the famous Max M. Munk. When the rest of Aviation Division One, his reserve command, was called to active duty at the start of the Second World War, Gough was left behind at Langley where he was considered essential in the research and development of America's fighter and bomber aircraft. During the 1940s, Gough was one of only four research pilots at the Langley Research Center, a prestigious group that included John P. "Jack" Reeder and Herbert H. Hoover. In 1941, Mel Gough received the Octave Chanute Award given by the Institute of the Aeronautical Sciences for "outstanding contributions by a test pilot in the field of aeronautics." By 1943, Mel Gough was already a world-renowned aeronautical engineer and scientist. He was appointed chief of the Flight Research Division the same year, and in this role, helped establish NACA's High

Donald H. Wood, mechanical engineer, stands at the entrance to the Propeller Research Tunnel, August 20, 1926. He worked at NACA from 1924 through 1941. Wood, whom Gough fondly called the "comedian," worked side-by-side with Gough, another mechanical engineer, in the Propeller Research Tunnel section.

Fred E. Weick, mechanical engineer and head, Propeller Research Tunnel section, 1925 to 1929.

There was not a generating plant on the entire Peninsula of Hampton Roads powerful enough to supply electricity to drive the new Propeller Research Tunnel at NACA. As a result, the facility acquired two 1,000-horsepower diesel engines from a Navy T-2 submarine, shown here. Langley engineers designed the configuration of this innovative power source by placing the engines end-to-end, their crankshafts joined by a large sheave running between them. Belts connected their sheave to yet another sheave nearly fifty-five feet away. As a result, this assemblage (shown protruding from the backside of the building in this 1927 photograph, above right) drove the shaft of a gigantic propeller fan which forced the air through the tunnel.

Workers continue to put finishing touches on the new engine assemblage at the Propeller Research Tunnel, April 1, 1927. The tunnel was operational by July 1927. Once in use, the tunnel enabled NACA engineers to exact full-scale tests on aircraft propellers, seaplane pontoons, and airframes in general.

Speed Flight Station at Edwards Air Force Base, California, a program in which Gough would make significant contributions toward better understanding of faster-than-sound research aircraft. Flying labs were put into play to study flight hazards.

After the war, Gough and Captain Walter S. Diehl of the United States Navy would be instrumental in research and flight test of German wartime aircraft. It was Mel Gough who coordinated the interrogation of Karl Baur, former chief test pilot of the Messerschmitt Company, at Naval Air Station Patuxent River, Maryland. Questioning of Baur was done at the suggestion of Diehl, and the group from Langley's Flight Test Division, aside from Gough, included Joseph W. Wetmore, William H. Phillips, Walter C. Williams, John P. Reeder, W.E. Gray, Thomas A. Harris of the Stability Research Division, and G.G. Kayten of the Full Scale Research Division.

Before meeting with Baur, Langley personnel inspected the German airplanes in the Flight Test hangar. There was a completely assembled Messerschmitt 262 (Me 262) and an Arado 234. There was also an Me 262 complete except for the engines. Both the Me 262 and the Arado 234 had adjustable stabilizer and very narrow-chord elevators with no tabs of any sort. The elevators on both aircraft were mass overbalanced. The ailerons on the Me 262 had a plain overhang aerodynamic balance with an elliptical shape. The Arado 234 had a very sharp-nosed Frise-type aileron. Control surfaces on both airplanes were metal-covered and the aileron and rudder tabs on each were mass balanced. Both German aircraft were equipped with leading edge slots which apparently opened and closed in a manner similar to the slots on the SC-1 airplane. American aircraft types of interest previewed at the Flight Test Center at that time were the Lockheed P-80 Shooting Star, Ryan FR-1 Fireball, and XF15C-1. The XF15C-1 had a thick horizontal tail, fixed or adjustable.

Many Navy officers, mostly aviation type, witnessed the interrogation. Much was learned of German aircraft engineering and test pilot practices. Gough and his fellow NACA engineers and test pilots were particularly interested in Mach capability.

The highest reliable Mach number which Baur knew had been obtained was about 0.86. This speed had been attained with both the Me 163 and Me 262. The Me 163 was apparently in serious trouble at this speed, although both the 163 and 262 experienced a nose down trim change at about Mach 0.83. There was considerable noise and buffeting of the pilot's canopy at Mach 0.75. Baur noted that the Me 262 had not been higher than 0.86 because there was insufficient

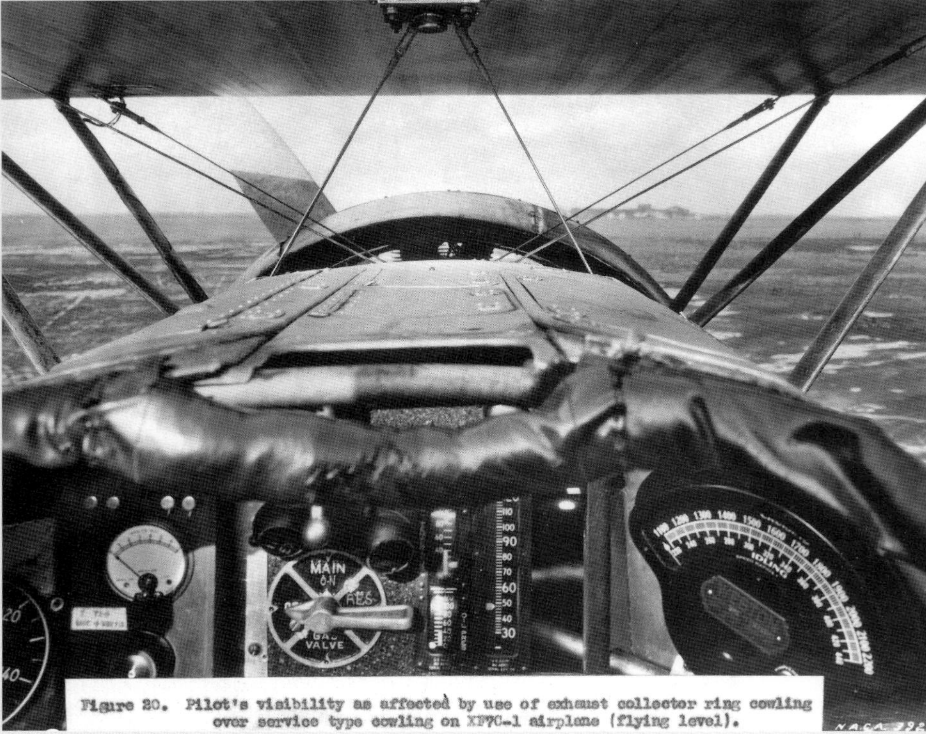

Navy Bureau Number A7653 was the XF7C-1, a prototype for the Curtiss F7C-1 Seahawk fighter aircraft. The NACA evaluated the aircraft as part of the cowling research program. The Navy wanted an air-cooled radial engine design, and as a result of work at NACA in 1927 and 1928, the XF7C-1 was produced with the 450-horsepower Pratt & Whitney R-1340B Wasp engine. The XF7C-1 was first flown on February 28, 1927, and eighteen production F7C-1s were delivered to Marine Fighter Squadron Five (VF-5M). The Marines were the only branch of service to fly the aircraft. Interestingly, eighteen-plane squadrons were the standard in the 1920s and 1930s. In the second photograph, NACA modified the XF7C-1 with an exhaust collector ring cowling over the service type cowling on the aircraft. The experimental cowling reduced the pilot's visibility, clearly evidenced by the angle of the photograph. (Official National Advisory Committee for Aeronautics Photographs.)

Melvin N. Gough, reserve naval aviator and NACA test pilot, 1929.

altitude available for the dive as the jet engines available at the time of the tests cut out at thirty thousand feet. The more precise reasoning for the Germans backing off further Mach experimentation was due to the fact the aircraft had already been released to the *Luftwaffe*. If trouble were to develop and the aircraft grounded, both manufacturers and test pilots paid the price. The *Luftwaffe*, particularly so late in the war, could not afford to have aircraft grounded.

Interestingly, Baur remarked that the Germans saw most of the American technical reports issued during the war. The people at Messerschmitt were quite pleased with the United States Army's evaluation of the Me 110, which rated the aircraft high. The German Air Force Test Center at Rechlin flight tested and reported on most Allied airplanes. The pilots at Rechlin preferred the North American P-51 Mustang. The only Allied aircraft Baur had flown during the war was a British Spitfire, perhaps as early as 1941. He believed the Spitfire was superior to anything the Germans had at that time.

America's race into space in 1958 spelled the end of NACA as it had existed for more than forty years. The creation of the National Aeronautics and Space Administration (NASA) meant ever changing roles for all who survived the reorganization, Mel Gough included. He would be sent to open Cape Canaveral for the new regime at NASA, and he did so with great excitement. Upon his retirement from NASA on December 30, 1963, Gough went to work for the Civil Aeronautics Board and, later, the Federal Aviation Agency, Bureau of Aircraft Development, precursor of the Federal Aviation Administration (FAA).

When Gough passed away in March 1994, he left behind a rich legacy of early aviation—particularly naval aviation—history. His son, William W. Gough, M.D., remembers the wonderful cast of characters who came to dinner, who always seemed to be present in

Melvin N. Gough was photographed with other student naval aviators in Advanced Flight Training, Squadron Eight, United States Naval Reserve, Class P-4-28, VN8RD8, at Naval Air Station Pensacola, Florida, 1928-1929. Those standing in the back row (left to right) were B.F. Jones; W.W. Jones; M.L. Hoblit; W. Burke, whom Gough noted had his arm cut off in an accident on the USS *Saratoga* (CV-3); E.T. Mooney, later killed; C.J. Schlapkohl; D.L. Marshall; T.S. Smith; N.S. Clifford; M.F. Heaway; E.L. Borlick; A. Borchers, later killed; J.H. Baldwin; and D.G. Jackson; middle row (left to right) R.W. LaFore; E.G. Whitney; Ensign Melvin N. Gough; C.P. Kerschner; L. Schreuder, later killed; A. Brink, later killed; E.S. Gilmore, later killed; B.Z. Redfield; E.E. Bard; J.V. Kipp; G.D. Omer; D.L. Grover; P.T.W. Scott, later killed in a commercial airline accident; G.M. Elliott; G.G. Calhoun; and, E.S. Spangler; bottom row (left to right) Chief Aviation Pilot William A. Cluthe (Naval Aviation Pilot No. 12); Chief Aviation Pilot Edward A. Heinz (Naval Aviation Pilot No. 63); Chief Aviation Pilot Chief Ralph W. Ritchie; Chief Aviation Pilot Skiles R. Pope; Lieutenant Robert Dixon "Bob" Hively, USNR, Naval Aviator No. 1358, squadron commander; Lieutenant Elmer Lawrence "Joe" Johansen, USN, Naval Aviator No. 325, squadron executive officer; Second Lieutenant E.T. Taylor, of the Eagle Squadron, England; Ensign Samuel F.S. Patterson, USNR, Naval Aviator No. 4412; Ensign Donald R. Terry, USNR, Naval Aviator No. 4410; and Ensign Malcolm M. Cloukey, USNR, Naval Aviator No. 4300.

some respect in the Gough household. "Dad would call Mother just before he was due to come home and announce eight guests for supper," he continued, "among them Jimmy Doolittle and his wife, Curtis LeMay and his wife, and about all the truly famous aviators of his day. As a boy, even a teenager, I hardly appreciated the significance nor opportunity to be had in these visits, they seemed so much a routine occurrence." Doolittle would be the last chairman of the National Advisory Committee for Aeronautics. Today, Dr. Gough recalls these events vividly, sharing his recollections of his father, a pilot of the first order whose contributions to the rich fabric of naval aviation history in Hampton Roads, and the nation, have been immeasurable. As Dr. Gough remarked, "My dad was a pilot through and through, full of life, energy, and a bit of mischief."

A modified Ford Model A was used as a starter truck for aircraft at Langley Field. Here, the truck props a Vought VE-7, 1929.

A small boy on his tricycle peddles along the flight line at NACA, Langley Field, Virginia, circa 1929. The boy was beginning his childhood, aviation its golden era.

This Stearman three-place biplane was photographed at NACA in 1929. The aircraft, with its supercharged Wasp engine, led Mel Gough to comment, "a fast fighting plane." Though never used by the Navy, it was a project on which Gough not only worked but also one he clearly enjoyed.

Mel Gough (center) was one of less than a handful of pilots to fly the famous North American XP-51 Mustang fighter at Langley Field during the Second World War. The XP-51 was the fourth Mustang off the assembly line when it was given to NACA for evaluation in 1941. There were four pilots who flew the famous fighter, John P. "Jack" Reeder, Mel Gough, Herbert H. Hoover, and William E. Grey. Gough was chief test pilot at NACA during that time. Pictured with Gough in front of a North American P-51D Mustang in October of 1945 were Raymond Braig (left of Gough) and George Bulifant, ground crew.

The Sikorsky S-42, *Bermuda Clipper,* tail code NC6736, belonging to Pan American Airways System, made a stop at Naval Air Station Norfolk in 1940. There were ten S-42 transoceanic models built by Sikorsky. (Courtesy of the Kirn Library.)

Below left: The Walt Disney Company designed and produced much of the great World War II insignia artwork for the United States military. Navy commands, especially aviation units, were proliferated with Disney artists' renderings of cartoon caricatures, serpents smashing Axis submarines, and eight-legged creatures handling vital communications. The insignia shown here is an original Disney cartoon cell designed for the United States Naval Communication Station Norfolk shortly after the United States entered the war. This colorful, somewhat whimsical octopus sounds the alarm, answers the phone, takes dictation and messages, sends message traffic, and even types—quite a job for a seagoing creature. A modified version of this insignia is used today by the Naval Computer and Telecommunications Area Master Station LANT Message Center.

known Bellinger for a very long time, their working rapport proving critical to the growth of naval aviation in Hampton Roads.

With the threat of war on Norfolk's doorstep, the Navy had only the air station at Norfolk and two grass auxiliary fields for aviation practice work. Naval Air Station Norfolk and her two auxiliary landing practice fields would be insufficient to take on the number of carrier squadrons expected to be headquartered at Norfolk. Bellinger received orders from the Bureau of Aeronautics to locate four additional fields around Norfolk. Since sound grass airstrips could not be found, Bellinger and his staff pinpointed desired locations on a map and determined to prepare proper runway surfaces. The Bureau of Aeronautics hesitated to go along with the idea but became convinced that the added cost would be worth the effort in the end. One of these fields was, of course, what became Naval Air Station Oceana in Virginia Beach, Virginia. An auxiliary landing field had been planned for Norfolk in Princess Anne County, Virginia, present day Virginia Beach, as early as 1938. On November 25, 1940, the United States government initiated purchase of the original 328.95 acres to begin a small airfield accommodating 32 officers and 172 enlisted men. Asphalt runways were begun December 31, 1940, and completed in November of 1941. These runways at Oceana were only twenty-five hundred feet long.

Plans were executed under Bellinger's command to expand Naval Air Station Norfolk but not without much difficulty. When the Hepburn Board visited Norfolk to inspect the air station and make recommendations for enlarging the base for seaplanes and carrier based aircraft, its membership—at least while in Norfolk—agreed to the purchase of more land and construction of hangars as needed. By the time the board issued its final evaluation upon return to Washington, D.C., however, Norfolk was denied further expansion, a completely different outcome than Taussig and Bellinger expected.

Pete and the Penguins

Theodore Argyres Petras was born May 16, 1911, in Birmingham, Alabama, roughly a year prior to the birth of Marine Corps aviation on May 22, 1912. At the age of sixteen Petras obtained permission from his parents to enlist in the United States Marine Corps and, on November 1, 1929, he put in his paperwork and was subsequently sent to boot camp at Parris Island, South Carolina. As a private, he was told he was being sent down to Nicaragua. He did not go. Instead, Petras explained to his sergeant that he had applied for aviation and was waiting for orders. Ted Petras, "Pete" to his friends, wanted to fly airplanes. Pete came home to begin flight training after a brief tour of duty in Haiti.

Enlisted Naval Aviation Pilots (NAPs) typically completed their course of flight instruction at Naval Air Station Pensacola, Florida, but many received their first taste of aviation instruction at Norfolk, Virginia. Petras received ten hours of instruction and two hours of soloing in seaplanes at Naval Air Station Hampton Roads and, interestingly enough, it would be James McCoy, then a chief, who gave him his first flight. McCoy would meet up with Petras again on the United States Antarctic Service Expedition.

Private Theodore A. Petras, USMC, at the United States Navy Flight School, Pensacola, Florida, 1932.

During his tour of duty in Haiti, Petras owned a couple of nice polo ponies. "One cost me twenty-five dollars, and the other about thirty," he noted. The year was about 1932.

NAPs, "flying sergeants" if they were in the United States Marine Corps, acted as copilots in many larger aircraft as the Second World War began to unfold, though this was not their only role. A squadron aboard the USS *Lexington,* the famed *White Hat* squadron (VF-2) commanded by Jimmy Flatley, was comprised of all enlisted pilots. The NAPs of Flatley's squadron had a safety record and gunnery performance rated outstanding in the fleet. Perhaps wisely, enlisted pilots were chosen from among those with a background in aviation, such as mechanics, radiomen, ordnancemen, and other specialties. Only a small number of them made it to piloting aircraft, and nearly all who did not become pilots were offered a chance to be aircrew. Back in Petras' day, of his class of twenty-eight in Norfolk, only eleven graduated. Of the eleven, all were enlisted. He was sent from Norfolk to flight school at Naval Air Station Pensacola, Florida.

Pensacola instructors weeded out many student naval aviators, Pete's class was no exception. Of the fourteen who made up his class in 1932, only seven received the coveted wings of gold.

The infamous Snow Cruiser ended up best serving the men on the expedition as a living quarters. The behemoth cruiser took eighteen days to drive from its manufacturer in Chicago, Illinois, to Boston, Massachusetts, in 1939, and backed up 70,000 cars for ninety miles.

Petras poses next to his Staggerwing Beech with its specially fitted ski landing gear. The boots Petras is wearing in the photograph are dogskin like the Alaskans would wear. "They'd put grass inside and seal it. The grass absorbed the moisture, keeping your feet nice and warm," he explained.

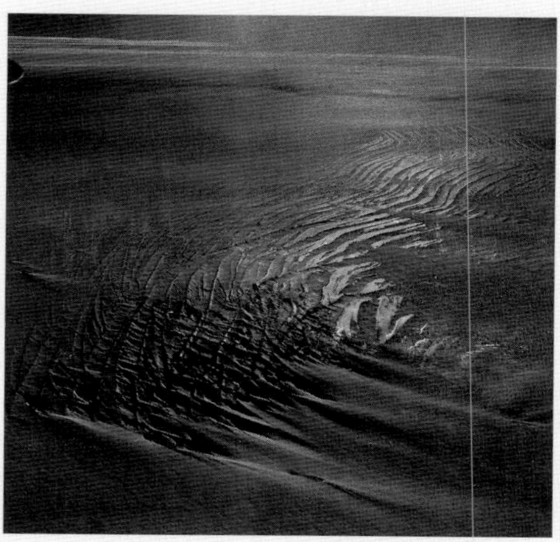

"This was the area we were supposed to traverse with the Snow Cruiser with the Beechcraft on top," recalled Petras. "We would have ended up under a 2,000-foot crevasse."

When the mercury dropped to minus fifty-one degrees, Petras could not do any flying. The Antarctic "night" as it is called, lasted nearly three-and-a-half months. Petras lost his flight pay during this time.

Designated a heavier-than-air pilot, he was detailed for duty involving actual flying in aircraft, "including dirigibles, balloons, and airplanes, in accordance with the Acts of Congress approved 3 March, 1915, and 2 July, 1926." The Marine Corps did not have any dirigibles, so he got airplanes and was assigned to Haiti during the infamous "Banana Wars." Following his duties in Haiti, Pete returned to Quantico, Virginia, and later became a member of the famous VF-9M Stunt and Fighter Squadron touring the United States and Canada. Petras was still a private when he returned from Haiti. Upon receiving his wings, he and other enlisted pilots like him were supposed to be promoted to sergeant but, as Pete noted, the Great Depression was a fact of life that kept even the federal government from paying more money to servicemen. Promotions were slow. By 1934, two years after obtaining his wings, Petras was promoted to staff sergeant and, in 1935 while assigned to VF-9M, to technical sergeant.

In 1936, Pete married Josephine Albis of Richmond, Virginia, and the newlyweds were sent to St. Thomas, Virgin Islands, with squadron VO-9M where Pete would serve for twenty-eight months as pilot and radio communications officer. With the formation of the United States Antarctic Service Expedition 1939–1941,(1) he was selected as chief pilot serving under Rear Admiral Richard Evelyn Byrd. Petras was chosen from nearly one thousand Marine Corps volunteers. This was to be the most highly technological expedition to the Antarctic and an ambitious one by any stretch of the imagination. Byrd, as Pete pointed out, "always picked enlisted pilots. He never had an officer pilot because he knew an enlisted pilot could work on his own engines, fly and navigate. So he was smart." A long line of famous pilots had already worked with Byrd, including Floyd Bennett and Bernt Balchen.

On a visit with his wife, Josephine, and daughter, Betty, in Richmond, Virginia, prior to departure on the expedition, Pete would explain some of the finer points of extreme Southern navigation, primarily discarding the magnetic compass due to the convergence of magnetic fields close to the South Pole. A sun compass and radio beams would be used instead. Radio stations were set up at the base camps at Little America, located on the Bay of Whales in the Ross

Sea, and at Hearst Land, which is near the Antarctic Archipelago.

Pete picked up his custom Staggerwing Beech from the factory at Wichita, Kansas, on November 1, 1939. This most historic of aircraft was a Beech Model D17A with a 350-horsepower Wright R-760-E2 engine, serial number 357. Upon reaching the Naval Aircraft Factory at Philadelphia, Pennsylvania, the Staggerwing was fitted with skis. The aircraft had to fit atop the Snow Cruiser, a behemoth forty-eight ton, fifty-five-foot-nine-inch long giant snowmobile. The cruiser's designer, Dr. Thomas C. Poulter, Scientific Director of the Armour Institute of Technology in Chicago, Illinois, had envisioned a mobile base for polar exploration. Poulter commanded the Snow Cruiser on the expedition, his crew consisting of Technical Sergeant Petras; Dr. Alton F. Wade, chief scientist of the United States Antarctic Service; Corporal Felix L. Ferrano, USMC, radio operator; and Machinist's Mate Second Class Clyde W. "Griff" Griffith, serving as mechanic for both the Cruiser and the Staggerwing Beech, Petras' aircraft.

"The Snow Cruiser failed to live up to expectation," as Petras vividly recollected when interviewed in 1994. The cruiser acted more like a snow plow than snowmobile as it was too heavy to glide over snow. As he described it, the cruiser "had four wheels [ten feet in diameter] and two extra to get double wheels up front. Each wheel was independently powered by a seventy-five-horsepower electric motor, but this was still not enough to propel it on top of the ice. We even gave the cruiser the supreme test—76 below zero—but she was not much improved. Finally, we left the cruiser to come home. It is probably on the bottom of the ocean."

The Snow Cruiser was delivered to Little America III from the *North Star,*(2) a 1,434-ton wooden ice ship on loan from the Department of the Interior and one of two vessels on the expedition. As the leviathan was unloaded, with Dr. Poulter at the controls, it collapsed a sixty-foot steel and wood ramp, splintering a dozen three-by-twelve support beams. Aside from the cruiser, there were two Navy/Curtiss R4C-1 Condors, and a Barkley-Grow twin-engine seaplane, brought along by Admiral Byrd aboard the USS *Bear of Oakland,*(3) known simply as "the *Bear,*" once the Navy acquired the ship, to explore the coastal reaches of Antarctica. One Condor was sent to East Base, Pete's camp, and the other to West Base.

Petras poses in front of his custom Staggerwing Beech at Little America.

The USS *Bear* with a dog team in the foreground were photographed near the Bay of Whales, Little America, about 1940.

These are the marvelous emperor penguins which so delighted Petras while in the Antarctic. "They'd come up and talk, put their heads on my chest and just stand there," Petras fondly remembered.

An emperor penguin looks over the USS *Bear* as the ship was preparing to unload its cargo and supplies in 1939. The penguins were curious observers of the expedition, often getting very close to Petras and his friends.

Petras and the rest of the expedition remained icebound for twenty-two months—nearly two years. Pete recounted the time the Condor lost an engine two hundred miles from Little America:

"We left the plane there because it was too late in the season. So we picked up the crew and put their load on my plane, but the dog team got away from my guide and disappeared and, about a week later, one dog came back. So, Dr. [Paul Allman] Siple and I got in the plane and followed her tracks, finally arriving where they [the tracks] stopped. Of course, all we found was where she went to sleep and rested before she came all the way back again. So we went out another fifty or sixty miles until we ran into a bunch of crevasses. We figured the other dogs ended up in the crevasse, but the one dog made it back somehow. These crevasses could be anywhere from fifty to eighty miles across and two to three thousand feet deep. Crevasses are impossible to detect at ground level. Only flying over could you see just what you might be getting into. I am kind of glad the Snow Cruiser failed, as we could have ended up like the dogs."

Flying was what Pete was there to do, despite the intense cold and poor living conditions. During one of his many flights over unmapped areas, he discovered an unknown and unnamed mountain peak 12,500 feet high. It was aptly named Mount Josephine Petras for Pete's wife. A smaller adjacent peak, 8,500 feet high, was named for his daughter, Betty, by Dr. Paul Siple, leader

Above left: In Petras' own words, "this was a warm day," at Little America with the temperature holding at 40 degrees above zero and very dry. James McCoy (standing), Condor pilot, and Ted Petras (shovel in hand), Staggerwing pilot, were digging fuel from a depot, December 7, 1940. Fuel cans had originally been stacked in the open, but winter storms buried them.

Left: At 57 degrees below zero, team members built a hangar of ice for the Beech and Condor aircraft. Petras is the one lifting the ice block on the right.

and scientist of the expedition. As Pete recalled, "We were flying over taking pictures and I told Dr. Siple, 'Remember, I saw it first,' to which Dr. Siple said, 'Yes, you did, and we are going to name it [the large peak] for your wife.'" Petras thought highly of Dr. Paul Allman Siple. Siple was the Boy Scout who went with Admiral Byrd in 1928 to the Antarctic. Between the first expedition and 1939, Siple received his master's and doctoral degrees.

Perhaps one of Pete's best memories of the Antarctic is that of the marvelous emperor penguins which, at least for a time, brought him great enjoyment. Emperor penguins, *Antenodytes sp.*, are the most colorful of the penguin family, possessing vibrant orange and yellow patches on the sides of their necks. Penguins, in general, are the most marine of all birds, and can swim beneath the water as fast as any seal. Though it has been over fifty years since the expedition, he has kept his fascination, perhaps understandable affection, for penguins.

"Three of us decided we were going fishing. We got out three-and-a-half miles from Little America, and we came upon 170 penguins sitting by the bay ice. They were about three-and-a-half feet tall, weighing maybe eighty-five pounds. Curious like a kid, I walked right into the middle of them. They'd come up and talk, put their heads on my chest and just stand there. Griff [Clyde Griffith] said, 'Let's try to herd these things back to base.' Every time we came to a crevasse, they wouldn't go across it, so we had to tie up one of their buddies, and drag him across the crevasse, tie him on the other side, and sit and wait ten or fifteen minutes until the others got curious and saw a penguin on the other side. Only then would the rest come across to investigate. It was grand watching them. It took seven hours to get back three-and-a-half miles to camp. We ended up with thirty-seven as the rest scattered."

Petras adored the emperors. He had one of his own that he was going to bring back, but the camp radioed the Smithsonian Institution and told them they had thirty-seven emperors and no food. "We did not know what to do and, most regrettably, we were going to have to kill them all," Petras recalled. "Dr. Fraser showed us how to hit the spinal cord and we killed all thirty-seven, putting them in the hold on ice." These thirty-seven penguins are the emperors on display at the Smithsonian Institution in Washington, D.C.

The USS *North Star* unloaded near Little America. The USS *Bear* is in the background. Expedition personnel were snowbound for twenty-two months in the Antarctic.

Ted Petras first discovered this mountain, so it was named in honor of his wife, Josephine. Mount Josephine Petras stands 12,500 feet.

An emperor penguin visits the Snow Cruiser. The Snow Cruiser was used as Petras' living quarters a good portion of the twenty-two months spent in the Antarctic.

The First Provisional Observation Squadron, First Marine Division, lined up in front of their Piper Cubs for inspection by Major General W.H. Rupertus, USMC. The unit was on New Britain, Cape Gloucester at the time.

As horrible as euthanizing the penguins sounded, the expedition members had more serious matters to consider. "We had thirty-three men at our base, Little America, and twenty-six at East Base. The camps were roughly 1,700 miles apart," explained Petras. By December of 1940, ice was building up. An iceberg half a mile wide and one mile long was spotted by the Condor. The Condor flew to the iceberg to pick up half the crew of East Base, and then return for the rest. "Then we realized we'd better hurry because the ice was moving in and we could be caught there. So, anyway, someone asked what we were going to do with all the dogs,(4) and, of course, the answer was we were going to have to kill them so we set up all the explosives we had and tied the dogs on a great big platform, setting it for six hours in case we could not get back to the iceberg and unload, at least we would be back in time to save the dogs." Since no one wanted to stay another year at the South Pole, the plane made it, the dogs did not.

By January 31, 1941, the USS *Bear* and USS *North Star* started the return trip home. Members of the 1939-1941 expedition received the United States Antarctic Expeditionary Medal from Secretary of the Navy James V. Forrestal for their courageous pioneering in polar exploration which resulted in important geographical and scientific discoveries.

Being on the cutting edge of exploration was rough by any stretch of the imagination, methods and preparations a learning experience. Petras was on that cutting edge, his remembrances of this period of history providing a window to often brutal facts of life and death, grand exploration, and scientific accomplishment. "There would be another expedition in 1947 by Admiral George Dufek [called Operation Highjump]. He asked me to go with him but at the time I was flying the Marine Corps Commandant around, and I turned him down. Once was enough for me."

Upon his return to Quantico, Virginia, by then Lieutenant Petras was assigned as pilot for Major General Alexander A. Vandegrift, First Marine Division Commander. As events unfolded in the Pacific theater, he proceeded with General Vandegrift to New Zealand, followed by the Guadalcanal campaign and later, Australia, in preparation for the Battle of New Britain under General Douglas A. MacArthur, theater commander. He formed the first Provisional Air Observation Unit with twelve Cubs at Cape Gloucester, New Britain,during the summer of 1943. Pete would recall:

"One day I noticed the Army had these Piper Cubs, eight of them. I went to General Vandegrift and asked if he thought we could get any of them. General Vandegrift says, 'Pete, let's go see.' And so we flew to Brisbane [Australia] which was General Douglas MacArthur's headquarters. That's how MacArthur came into things. General Vandegrift met with MacArthur who approved the loan of twelve Cubs, the eight I saw and four more in crates. We asked for volunteers and, wouldn't you know, one guy [PFC R.J. Remicks] had been a plant foreman at the Piper Cub factory, so he put together the ones in the crates. That's how we formed the observation squadron."

Pete's observation squadron flew reconnaissance and reprovisioning missions. Pilots and crew carried hand grenades and mortar shells to bomb enemy positions but had no means to defend the tiny Cub from Japanese ground fire and aircraft. "We supported all the trail parties, even [Lieutenant Colonel] Chesty [Lewis Burwell] Puller's five-hundred-man outfit," stated Petras. When the Marines secured New Britain, Pete was the first to land an Allied aircraft on its makeshift airfield. "That was near the beginning of 1944," he noted.

There would be many close calls for Petras, by then a captain. He had occasion while scouting landing beaches to save the lives of untold numbers of fellow Marines. As invasion barges headed for Japanese positions in Talasea Harbor, east of Willaumez Peninsula and Talasea Village, this daredevil pilot spotted trouble. Skimming low over the beach, he could see strong enemy emplacements directly where the Marines were supposed to land. In his tiny Piper Cub, Petras flew out to sea to intercept Marine barges and dropped a note, wrapped in a weighted handkerchief, warning them of the danger ahead. In his note he told the Marines of the Japanese fortifications and recommended they land farther to the left on a clear beach. Following his instructions, Marine ground forces made a successful landing.

Petras' unit on New Britain was later integrated into VMO-3 Marine Observation Squadron, a newly formed air group within the Corps. In the course of his time in the South Pacific, Petras would have many adventures, some of them hair-raising, and some shared with the likes of Vandegrift, Brigadier Generals W.H. Rupertus and Roy S. Geiger, and Brigadier General David A. Ogden, United States Army. When General Vandegrift was appointed Commandant of the Marine Corps after the war, Petras was called to Anacostia with the rank of major to be staff pilot for the general. He would also double as officer-in-charge of the Headquarters Flight Section for three years. Following the appointment of General Clifton B. Cates as commandant, Pete spent another three years as staff pilot.

By 1950, Petras was assigned to Marine Corps Air Station El Toro, California, as air operations officer, followed by service in the Korean Conflict with tours of duty in 1951 and 1952. As officer-in-charge of Flight Marine Air Wing, he was assigned twenty-two planes providing service for ten thousand air troops, and five-and-a-half million pounds of air cargo per month to forward battle zone areas. During the years that immediately followed Korea, 1953 to 1955, he headed up the Marine Air Repair Squadron out of Miami, Florida. Other commands would follow, his last as operations officer at Marine Corps Air Station Beaufort, South Carolina.

Petras retired on November 1, 1959, as a colonel. His personal decorations include two Distinguished Flying Crosses, eight Air Medals, the Congressional Medal of Antarctic Expedition, and three presidential citations. For a young private, this would have seemed impossible to imagine but, to Colonel Theodore Argyres Petras, his success was reality. His boyhood dream to fly blossomed into one of the most outstanding careers in naval aviation history: the first to aerially explore the Antarctic, winner of the Medal of Antarctic Exploration, tours of duty in World War II, homecoming and the Korean Conflict, and finally, enshrinement in the Alabama Aviation Hall of Fame. History will record him as a Marine Corps aviator, pioneer polar explorer, and man of extraordinary accomplishment, character, and bravery.

Colonel Theodore Argyres Petras, USMC, pioneer pilot, retired from the Marine Corps in 1959 after thirty continuous years of service. The man who once feared retiring as a private had become one of the greats of naval aviation.

1. Byrd led two Antarctic expeditions prior to formation of the United States Antarctic Service by approval of the United States Congress in two acts in 1939, and on the order of President Franklin Delano Roosevelt to Admiral Byrd dated November 25, 1939. Unlike the First and Second Antarctic Expeditions, privately funded explorations, the United States Antarctic Service Expedition of 1939–1941 was a quasi-government funded scientific exploration which also incorporated considerable private funding. The Secretaries of State, Treasury, Navy and Interior formed the nucleus of the committee established to oversee the expedition. With the exception of the participation of scientific societies in formulating experiments and scientific regimens, and a smattering of civilian scientists, the United States Antarctic Service Expedition was organized and operated by the United States Navy as were the two previous Byrd exploratory ventures. The United States Antarctic Service Expedition of 1939–1941 was the largest expedition at that time. There were 125 men from the United States aboard the expedition's two ships, the third Antarctic and the first government expedition to be commanded by Rear Admiral Byrd.
2. The *North Star* was manned by its regular officers and crew and commanded by Captain Isak Lystad.
3. The *Bear of Oakland* was used on the Second Byrd Antarctic Expedition. The barkentine was chartered by the Navy for one dollar a year and reconditioned for the purposes of the third expedition. The ship was commanded by Lieutenant Commander Richard H. Cruzen and Bendik Johansen was ice pilot.
4. There were still as many as eighty-five dogs with the expedition at that time.

"Big Boats"

During America's pre-World War II neutrality period, patrol wings such as Patrol Wing Five out of Norfolk, for instance, operated as tactical units, scouting flights making up the majority of missions. Twelve aircraft comprised a unit assigned to search and patrol. Each aircraft fanned out on a scouting line over several hundred miles of sea, all planes maintaining the line, but not within sight of one another. Pilots relied solely on the quality of their, or the navigator's, navigation. The big flying boats had navigators whose job it was to make rendezvous points whether in practice or real attack scenarios. The navigator measured his drift precisely, often by float lights and drift observations. This officer had to keep the bubble octant working well to give him plenty of confirming lines of position crossed by radio bearings on shore stations, if available. Other than the commanding officer of the plane, the pilot who was not flying navigated while the duty pilot watched the instruments and saw to it that the aviator sitting copilot kept track of the mission. The plane captain, an off-duty radio operator or mechanic, would often slip into the other pilot's seat to keep the pilot company. Big flying boats, like the Consolidated PBY-1 patrol bomber or the Vought-Sikorsky four-engine patrol bomber typically had the pilots, a radioman, and a flight engineer to watch the power plant. The aircraft were even furnished with cooking accoutrements and actually produced some excellent flying cooks. Each aircraft had a two-burner electric stove.

Today, we seldom think of the fact the crews of those grandiose flying boats had to be as good at their seamanship as airmanship. Landings were the best opportunity to practice good seamanship for flying boat crews. If the aircraft taxiied into the wind, the landing was fairly straightforward as long as the chop did not drench the windshield and the pilot. On the other hand, if the pilot taxiied across wind, the pilot full-throttled the engines. The aircrew would do what was called "make buoy" as one aircrewman would take the buoy from the nose of the flying boat with a boat hook. The buoy would be snubbed close to the plane, and the aircrewman secured the pendant. There was no perfect mooring technique developed for flying boats, large or small. This is evidenced in accounts of the flying boats as early as the 1910s.

Takeoffs in big flying boats did improve with increased horsepower and improved hull lines. With extensive model basin experiments, takeoff trim investigations by the National Advisory Committee for Aeronautics at Hampton Roads, and other tests done with experimental and squadron pilots, the aeronautical community concurred that takeoff worked better if control adjustments were set to allow the big boats to be flown out of the water rather than being abruptly pulled up from the water.

Of all the rather interesting aspects of the great flying boats, the elaborate radio equipment found aboard was far ahead of what early pilots at Naval Air Station Hampton Roads tested in 1917. Even further from their wildest envisionings was the fact most of the time the flying boats of the late-1930s and 1940s would frequently be flown on automatic pilot to free up the pilots to observe the oceans and air space for the "enemy"—even though there would be no enemy until December 7, 1941.

A Curtiss SO3C-1 landplane was photographed in January of 1942, a snow-covered landscape behind the aircraft giving away the dead of winter. The SO3C-1 was used by scouting squadrons at Norfolk for training purposes in the first half of 1943. Scouting Squadron Thirty-Five (VS-35), formerly VS-5D4,[1] flew the aircraft from May 22, 1943, through October 11, 1943, before transitioning to the more popular Douglas SBD-5 Dauntless. Lieutenant Alex D. Walker, USNR, was commanding officer of the squadron during its SO3C training at Naval Air Station Norfolk. (Official United States Navy Photograph.)

A Curtiss SB2C-1 Helldiver (Bureau Number 00018), eighteenth of the first production lot of two hundred -1s, was photographed on a flight out of Naval Air Station Norfolk in September 1942, just months after the first production aircraft had taken to the air. Navy censors had done a pretty good job of removing aircraft designation numbers, bureau numbers, and squadron markings but, fortunately, someone chalked in the bureau number on the tail of the aircraft, thus making it easier to identify in years to come. (Official United States Navy Photograph.)

Hangar Queen

When Rear Admiral Patrick N.L. Bellinger became Commander Air Force, Atlantic Fleet on March 20, 1943, he nosed around Naval Air Station Norfolk quite a bit, refamiliarizing himself with the station he had helped to establish during the First World War. This was no easy task since the air station had burgeoned with wartime activity, its men, materials, buildings, aircraft, and the like focused on the supply and demand of war with Germany and Japan. One day, Bellinger happened upon an aircraft he knew all too well, the Navy/Curtiss NC-4. It was the plane, along with NC-1 and NC-3, that took part in the famed transatlantic crossing of 1919.

Allied ships had paid a heavy price to cross the Atlantic during the First World War. German submarines attacked shipping and passenger liners without hesitation, sending most of their prey to the bottom of the ocean. On August 25, 1917, Rear Admiral D.W. Taylor, Chief Constructor of the Navy, wrote to his aeronautics assistant, "the United States motor (referring to the Liberty engine) gives good promise of being a success, and if we can push ahead on the aeroplane end, it seems to me the submarine menace could be abated, if not destroyed, from the air." Taylor continued, "the ideal solution would be big flying boats, or the equivalent, that could be able to keep the sea (not air) in any weather, and also be able to fly across the Atlantic to avoid difficulties of delivery."

Aircraft manufacturer Glenn Hammond Curtiss was the leading aircraft builder of his day, and it was Curtiss whom Taylor called upon to construct the now famous NC or Nancy aircraft. Curtiss was a brilliant aircraft designer but in the case of this aircraft series, the Navy needed his building expertise. When the time came for designating this marvelous collaborative flying machine, they named it "N" for Navy and "C" for Curtiss. The NC aircraft was by far the largest aircraft Curtiss Aeroplane and Motor Company, Garden City, Long Island, New York, or the Naval Aircraft Factory, located in Philadelphia, Pennsylvania, developed in the late 1910s and early 1920s. The Nancy's linen-covered upper wing measured 126 feet across from wing tip to wing tip with a lower wing stretching yet another ninety-four feet. From stem to stern, the aircraft was a little over sixty-eight feet long. The NCs were originally powered by three Liberty water-cooled engines, two nacelles mounted between the wings and the third, a pusher-puller power plant, mounted directly above the hull. The "boat" part of the flying boat was a hull forty-five feet long and ten feet wide with six water-tight compartments. Two of these compartments housed the lookout and navigator cockpits, while another contained flight controls for the pilot and his copilot. The three remaining

The first aircraft to fly the Atlantic, NC-4 was one of three Nancies which started the trip in May of 1919 for Europe. She was the only one to make it. Piloted by Lieutenant Commander Albert Cushing "Putty" Read, NC-4 successfully completed the crossing. The flight began at Trepassey, Newfoundland, on May 16, 1919, and after seventeen hours, the NC-4 arrived at Horta, Azores. Ten days later, on May 28, 1919, the aircraft and her crew refueled at Lisbon, left on May 30, 1919, and completed the flight. Read and his aircrew arrived at Plymouth, England, their ultimate destination, on May 31, 1919. (Official United States Navy Photograph.)

The NC-4 refueled at Lisbon, Portugal, on May 28, 1919, before taking off for England. It had a fuel capacity of 1,800 gallons in the main tanks which gave the flying ship a 1,200-mile range. Powered by four 400-horsepower Liberty V-12 engines, the NC-4 could still make 74 miles per hour fully loaded at 28,000 pounds. The NC-4 had an upper wing span of 126 feet, a lower wing span of 94 feet, and was 68 feet, 5½ inches bow to stern. Each of the Nancies carried a crew of six.

The crews of the three NC flying boats were congratulated officially by officials of the Navy following their flights in May of 1919. This photograph was taken July 2, 1919, and shows seated, left to right, Secretary of the Navy Josephus Daniels; Assistant Secretary of the Navy Franklin Delano Roosevelt; Representative Lemuel P. Padgett; and, Rear Admiral J.S. McKean, Assistant for Material in the Office of the Chief of Naval Operations. McKean was a great proponent of Liberty engine development for naval aircraft, the very engines aboard all NC aircraft. Standing, left to right, are Ensign Herbert C. Rodd (standing closest to the wall); Lieutenant Commander Albert Cushing "Putty" Read, Naval Aviator No. 24; Commander John Henry "Jack" Towers, Naval Aviator No. 3; Lieutenant Richard Evelyn "Dick" Byrd Jr., Naval Aviator No. 608, who assisted in navigation preparations for the NC flight and invented, interestingly enough, numerous aerial navigation instruments used on the flight; Commander Holden Chester "Dick" Richardson, Naval Aviator No. 13; Lieutenant Commander Marc A. Mitscher, Naval Aviator No. 33, and first pilot of NC-1 commanded by Bellinger; Lieutenant (junior grade) Walter Hinton; Lieutenant (junior grade) Harry Sadenwater; Lieutenant Louis Theodore Barin; Lieutenant Elmer Fowler Stone, of the United States Coast Guard (USCG); and, Chief Machinist's Mate (Aviation)(CMM(A)) E.S. "Smoke" Rhodes. (Official United States Navy Photograph.)

compartments were devoted to storage and sleeping quarters. This fourteen-ton aircraft was intelligently designed and built with the center of gravity of all weight factors falling in the center of lift on all surfaces.

The Naval Aircraft Factory initially constructed just four of the Curtiss NC long-range flying boats though more were to come. Because of storm damage to the wings of NC-1 coupled with the fact NC-2's engine configuration was adjudged unsatisfactory for the transatlantic crossing, NC-2's wings were removed and installed on NC-1. The Navy/Curtiss transatlantic flight set off from Naval Air Station Rockaway Beach, Long Island, New York, on May 8, 1919, for the purpose of establishing air routes across the Atlantic Ocean for passenger airlines and cargo planes. The NC-1 was commanded by then-Lieutenant Commander Patrick Bellinger, NC-3 by Commander John Henry "Jack" Towers, and the legendary NC-4 by Lieutenant Commander Albert Cushing "Putty" Read. Both Bellinger and Read spent time as commanding officers of Naval Air Station Hampton Roads. All three of the Nancies destined to make the flight were redesignated NC-TA ("TA" for transatlantic) prior to their departure from Trepassy Bay, Newfoundland, on May 16, 1919. From Trepassy, the aircraft set a course over the 1,400 miles of ocean to the Azores. Along their route were sixty-eight destroyers and five battleships serving as navigational aids and emergency rescue vessels.

Hindered by clouds and fog, NC-1 and NC-3 were forced down at sea short of Lajes, Azores. NC-1's aircrew was picked up by a Greek freighter before the aircraft sank in thirty-foot swells. NC-3, under Towers' command, spent sixty-eight hours taxiing the two hundred miles to the Azores, making it to the Azores in such battered condition the aircraft was nearly unrecognizable. It only took Read and his crew aboard the NC-4 fifteen hours and thirteen minutes to make the harbor at Lisbon, Portugal, then onward to Plymouth,

England, where the aircraft alighted on May 31, 1919. The crew of NC-4 had made the flight of flights: the one that paved the way for transatlantic passenger travel which came to fruition nearly twenty years later. This flight literally established naval aviation, proving once and for all that the airplane could be the eyes of the fleet.

The NC-4 made an extensive publicity tour of coastal cities along the eastern seaboard, eventually ending up in Norfolk to be tucked away and forgotten in an old air station storage building until Bellinger stumbled on it twenty-four years later. He had the NC-4 sent to Cheatham Annex, a Navy warehouse facility on the Peninsula side of Hampton Roads, for safekeeping until World War II ended and the aircraft could be properly turned over to the Smithsonian Institution. Had it not been for Bellinger's quick thinking, the world renowned Paul E. Garber, primary architect of the National Air (later Air and Space) Museum in Washington, D.C., may never have gotten the opportunity to painstakingly restore the aircraft. It seems only fitting that Bellinger, himself an important figure in the aircraft's history, would be the one to rediscover perhaps the greatest symbol of naval aviation success in this century: the Navy/Curtiss NC-4 flying boat, harbinger of history and legacy of the founding fathers of naval aviation.

Crews of the NC flying boats after their famous transatlantic flight of May of 1919, pose on the steps of the Department of the Navy, Washington, D.C., July 2, 1919. (First row, left to right) Lieutenant Commander Albert Cushing "Putty" Read, commanding officer and navigator, NC-4; Josephus Daniels, Secretary of the Navy; Commander John Henry "Jack" Towers, flight commander and commanding officer of NC-3; Franklin Delano Roosevelt, Assistant Secretary of the Navy; and, Lieutenant Commander Patrick N.L. "Pat" Bellinger, Naval Aviator No. 8, commanding officer of NC-1. (Second row, left to right) Ensign Herbert C. Rodd (later Naval Aviator No. 2917), radio operator of NC-4; Lieutenant (junior grade) Harry Sadenwater, radio officer, NC-1; Lieutenant Louis Theodore Barin, Naval Aviator No. 56, copilot, NC-1; and Commander Holden Chester "Dick" Richardson. Richardson, aside from being an excellent Navy pilot, had a brilliant mind for aircraft design. One of the roles for which he is best remembered was as superintendent to the Office of the Constructor of Aircraft, Curtiss Aeroplane Company, Buffalo, New York, in 1918. Richardson designed the NC hulls then supervised their construction and inspection prior to the transatlantic flight. He was pilot of NC-3, Towers' flagship. The last fellow on the row is Lieutenant David Hugh "Dave" McCulloch, Naval Aviator No. 168, first pilot of NC-3. (Third row, left to right) Lieutenant James L. Breese, engineering officer, NC-4; and Lieutenant Commander Robert A. Lavender (face shielded), radio officer, NC-3. (Fourth row, left to right) CMM(A) Eugene S. "Smoke" Rhodes, mechanic, NC-4; Chief Machinist's Mate (Aviation)(CMM(A)) Rasmus "Chris" Christensen, reported to NC division, April 21, 1919, as engineer and reserve pilot (enlisted), NC-1. Christensen later became Naval Aviator No. 1885. Finishing the row are Lieutenant Elmer Fowler Stone, USCG, Naval Aviator No. 38, first pilot of NC-4; and, Lieutenant (junior grade) Walter Hinton, Naval Aviator No. 135, second pilot, NC-4. (Official United States Navy Photograph.)

NC-8 (A5635) was photographed at Naval Air Station Hampton Roads, 1921. Information on the NC-8 placed the aircraft at Norfolk in service with the Atlantic Fleet Air Detachment within three months of its delivery from the Naval Aircraft Factory on June 25, 1920. Interestingly, naval records note the aircraft might have had three or four Liberty twelve-cylinder engines, presuming modifications took place at Norfolk or the factory. In the spring of 1921, NC-8 was assigned at Hampton Roads and the USS *Wright* (AV-1) during an Atlantic Fleet exercise at Guantanamo Bay, Cuba. By 1922, the aircraft was returned to the factory for engine work before being sent back to Norfolk. Unfortunately, in a matter of ten days, from June 6 to June 16, 1922, the Navy would order the grand flying boat stricken from the record. (Official United States Navy Photograph.)

There were ten Nancies constucted for the United States Navy. While the emphasis has been the great transatlantic crossing and the triumph of NC-4 (Bureau Number A2294), Hampton Roads was to play an important role in the history of all the Nancy aircraft. The hull numbers of NC-1 through NC-4, manufactured by the Curtiss Aeroplane Company under contract to the Navy, were A2291 to A2294. The "N" stood for Navy and "C" for Curtiss. Few know that, aside from the famous quartet of aircraft there were six more constructed and delivered to the Navy. NC-5 to NC-8 carried Bureau Numbers A5632 to A5635, while NC-9 and NC-10 were catalogued as A5885 and A5886, respectively, by the Bureau of Aeronautics. This picture shows NC-2T coming up on the old air station, Norfolk. NC-2T was built at the Curtiss Engineering Corporation at Garden City, Long Island, New York. She had three 330-horsepower Liberty engines—two tractors and one pusher engine. The aircraft was received at Hampton Roads in early August of 1920, and kept in hangar V-4, thus indicating the photograph was taken sometime between then and July of 1921. On July 20, 1921, trouble reports show the NC-2T was damaged beyond repair and unfit for further use. The wreck of the NC-2T is also shown here. The bottom was rotten and, while the aircraft was taking off in smooth water, a section of it carried away. The plane was recommended stricken from the Navy record and this had been carried out on October 18, 1921. (Official United States Navy Photograph.)

NC-9 (A5885) pictured here was photographed at Naval Air Station Hampton Roads about 1922. By far one of the most interesting of the Nancy flying boats, the NC-9 was built at the Naval Aircraft Factory and delivered to Norfolk in the spring of 1921 for service with the Atlantic Fleet Air Detachment. Though there would be periods in which the aircraft was sent to the factory for repairs and testing, its assignment to Hampton Roads was permanent. Trouble reports on the aircraft were extensive, noting in particular three incidents which led to its removal from Navy inventory on May 20, 1924. The first occurred on June 13, 1921, at Hampton Roads when one blade of a four-blade pusher propeller flew off from the hub, causing excessive vibration before the pilot could land the aircraft. The center member of the propellers' lamination was cross grain, thus it was recommended the propellers be given a whirling test and, of course, be replaced. A little over a month later, July 11, 1921, the copper tip of a propeller cracked. Flight engineers determined that the tip's construction was not sufficiently rigid. Henceforth, these were replaced with four blade oak Paragon propellers with overlapping copper stockings. By November of 1922, NC-9's hull was very soft in spots and in dire need of complete overhaul; all surfaces required recovering. In view of the fact that the overhaul was expected to be very costly, the recommendation was made to strike the seaplane from the record, its motors, instruments, and salvageable equipment removed and used as spares for other aircraft. (Official United States Navy Photograph.)

The Vought OS2U-3 Kingfisher pictured here, Bureau Number 5909, at Naval Air Station Norfolk, was welcomed by its pilot and observer aircrew as it proffered thick armor-plating and better protected its human passengers from antiaircraft fire. Built by the Vought-Sikorsky Division of United Aircraft Corporation, this aircraft was produced for the Navy between 1941 (shortly before America's entry in the Second World War) and 1942 when production of the -3 ended. (Official United States Navy Photograph.)

The original *Jolly Rogers* of Fighter Squadron Seventeen (VF-17) were established at Naval Air Station Norfolk with Lieutenant Commander John T. "Tom" Blackburn, as the squadron's first commanding officer. In January 1943, the squadron adopted the Jolly Roger insignia. The skull and bones were actually painted on the cowl of Blackburn's F4U-1 Corsair, named *Big Hog,* by the end of that February. The selection of the pirate Jolly Roger was symbolic of Fighting Seventeen's penchant for getting into trouble but, of course, in fine fashion. The insignia used to illustrate the skull and bones belonged to VF-84, an F-14 Tomcat squadron at Oceana.

Many of naval aviation's earliest aviators returned to serve the United States Navy or foreign governments during the war. Bruce Gardner "Bruce" Leighton, Naval Aviator No. 40, commanded a seaplane squadron of six H-16 flying boats in 1919 as part of Fleet Air Detachment, Atlantic Fleet, and in this capacity he pioneered the concept of joint surface and aviation operations at sea. Leighton retired to private life between the wars and became an executive with Intercontinent Corporation and Central Aircraft Manufacturing Company in 1937. In this capacity, Leighton engaged directly in training Chinese engineers and factory personnel in Hankow, China. Later, he operated mobile repair and maintenance units for the Chinese Air Force while remaining in personal charge of the firm's operation in-country until 1939. Leighton made a formal request to the Secretary of the Navy in 1941 asking that he be permitted to recruit United States Navy and Naval Reserve pilots and mechanics for service with General Claire Chennault's *Flying Tigers* in China.

Both men were determined to acquire more land for the air station and proceeded with plans to do so without the consent of the Hepburn Board. As good fortune would have it, Naval Air Station Norfolk owes its land acquisition of 1940 to Congressman Colgate Whitehead Darden, formerly Naval Aviator No. 871, of Norfolk, for listening to Bellinger's plan and sponsoring a bill in Congress to buy the additional property. Without the Hepburn Board ever knowing about the plan concocted between Bellinger and Darden, Darden's bill passed without comment and the growth of the air station began.

The first construction at Naval Air Station Norfolk under the World War II base upgrade and expansion program consisted of three 4,000-foot concrete runways, three steel landplane hangars, three seaplane ramps, a combination of barracks and messing facilities for 1,288 men, an operations building, dispensary, aviation storage facilities, aviation gasoline structures, and extensions to existing shops at the station. Congress authorized the original plan, of course, in mid-1940. Under Hepburn Board requirements which still applied to Norfolk, the air station was to have facilities for at least two carrier groups with room for expansion to four groups; facilities for four patrol plane squadrons with room for expansion to six; facilities for two utility squadrons; and facilities for complete engine and plane overhaul. By August of 1945, facilities included quarters for 29,000 personnel, nine hangars, and storage for 3,430,000 gallons of gasoline.

Norfolk's auxiliary fields were included in upgrades, and by May of 1942, barracks for 132 men were ordered for each of the five outlying fields under Norfolk's administration: Fentress, Pungo, Monogram, Creeds, and Oceana. At Fentress and Pungo, concrete runways were built. Later, in November, fuller development of Norfolk's auxiliary facilities provided for construction of four additional fields. Harvey Point seaplane base was provided with barracks for two thousand men, a timber hangar, and two seaplane ramps. Chincoteague was alloted funds to build quarters for four hundred men and a storehouse.

Captain Bellinger detached as commanding officer of Naval Air Station Norfolk on October 15, 1940, and proceeded to his new assignment in command of Patrol Wing Two based at Naval Air Station Pearl Harbor, Hawaii. Before leaving the states, Bellinger

—there are land and float types—

A Martin PBM-3 Mariner is shown anchored in the water off Naval Air Station Norfolk in late summer of 1942. The -3 Mariner differed from early versions of the aircraft with its extended engine nacelles and strut-girded wing floats, not visible in the photograph. This great flying boat was powered by two 1,700-horsepower Wright R-2600-12 engines. (Courtesy of the Hampton Roads Naval Museum.)

Lieutenant Commander John Thomas "Tom" Blackburn, later famous as the leader of the infamous *Jolly Rogers* squadron, first commanded Escort Fighting Squadron Twenty-Nine (VGF-29) at Naval Auxiliary Air Station Pungo, fifteen miles due south of Norfolk. Blackburn's executive officer was Lieutenant (junior grade) Harry Brinkley "Brink" Bass, a former dive-bomber pilot who earned a Navy Cross for contributing to the sinking of the Japanese light carrier *Shoho* at the Battle of the Coral Sea. Flying the Grumman F4F-3 Wildcat, VGF-29 trained at Pungo.

Blackburn's VGF-29 *Shillelaghs* were assigned to the USS *Santee* (CVE-29) which eventually took the *Shillelaghs* into combat over the skies of North Africa in support of the Operation Torch invasion.

dropped in on his old friend, Vice Admiral "Jack" Towers who, in turn, invited him to visit newly appointed Assistant Secretary of the Navy James Vincent "Vince" Forrestal, formerly Naval Aviator No. 154 and an old acquaintance of Bellinger. According to Bellinger's memoirs, Forrestal served under him at Naval Air Station Hampton Roads during the First World War. Bellinger, architect of the new and improved Naval Air Station Norfolk, would have to wait until his return in 1943 as the second Commander Air Force Atlantic Fleet to see the fruits of his labor.

Naval Air Station Norfolk experienced tremendous growth at the onset of the Second World War, growth which did not end until the station eventually encompassed some 1,847 acres. The air station would have seven commanding officers during the war starting with

When Artemus Lamb "Di" Gates accepted his appointment as Assistant Secretary of the Navy for Air on September 5, 1941, the Navy had 5,200 aircraft, 3,900 pilots and seven aircraft carriers. By the time Gates left his post on July 1, 1945, the Navy had 70,000 aircraft, 59,600 pilots and about one hundred aircraft carriers. Gates was Naval Aviator No. 65.

– with various 'enclosures' or 'greenhouses' –

Patrick Bellinger: Air Boss

Vice Admiral Patrick Neison Lynch Bellinger, Naval Aviator No. 8 ("Pat" to his brother aviators), served as Commander Air Force, Atlantic Fleet during all but two-and-one-half months of the command's existence(1) in its infancy, born in the tumultuous days of January of 1943. Born in Cheraw, South Carolina, on October 8, 1885, young Bellinger entered the United States Naval Academy in 1903 after a short stint at Clemson College. He graduated with the rank of "passed midshipman" in 1907, proceeding aboard the USS *Vermont* which accompanied the Great White Fleet on its cruise around the world, begun on December 16, 1907. On May 12, 1908, he was transferred to the USS *Wisconsin* and completed the world cruise on that ship. He was commissioned in the rank of ensign on June 7, 1909, after the required two years of sea duty.

Upon the completion of the world cruise in 1909, Ensign Bellinger was given torpedo instruction aboard the USS *Montgomery* and in October of that year was assigned to duty aboard the USS *South Carolina*. While serving aboard the *South Carolina*, he was promoted to the rank of lieutenant (junior grade), and in April 1912, was transferred to the USS *Severn* where he served until September of that year, when he was given command of the submarine *C-4*. Not two months later he was assigned to aviation duty at the United States Naval Academy, Greenbury Point, and served in naval aviation from that time to the day of his retirement.

Bellinger followed his Greenbury Point tour with duty at Guantanamo Bay, Cuba, where he was ordered in January 1913 for duty in connection with the aviation camp established there. This tour of duty coincided with the first occasion on which naval aviation accompanied the fleet in winter maneuvers, and during these maneuvers, aviation had an opportunity to clearly demonstrate its value in scouting for and locating minefields and submarines. Bellinger's previous tour as commanding officer of *C-4* proved invaluable.

Upon completion of his tour of duty in March 1913, Lieutenant (junior grade) Bellinger returned to the Naval Aviation Camp, Greenbury Point, during the same month he was designated a heavier-than-air pilot. Bellinger was issued Aero Club of America Seaplane Certificate No. 4, on May 3, 1913. A little over a month later, on June 13, he established a new American altitude record for seaplanes—6,200 feet—piloting an AH-3.

In January 1914, Bellinger was assigned duty aboard the USS *Orion* which was engaged in ferrying aircraft equipment to the newly established aviation training station at Pensacola, Florida. In April 1914, he proceeded to Vera Cruz, Mexico, on the USS *Mississippi* as officer-in-charge of the Navy's aviation detachment in connection with the United States occupation forces located in country. While serving at Vera Cruz, Bellinger was engaged in flights over enemy territory during which his plane was under fire by enemy ground troops who made several hits on his plane by rifle fire. This constituted the first attack on a United States naval aircraft by hostile gunfire. He left Vera Cruz in June 1914, returning to Pensacola, Florida. Here he was appointed Navy Air Pilot No. 4, as of June 1, 1914. Shortly afterward, he reported aboard the armored cruiser USS *North Carolina* for aviation duty, and served in this capacity until December of that year when he was reassigned to Pensacola, Naval Aeronautics Section. It was at Pensacola that Bellinger would achieve a series of outstanding feats in the development of naval aviation. In February of 1915, he launched an aircraft from a catapult mounted on a coal barge, the first catapult launch from a surface craft. The catapult was a redesigned version of the one from which Lieutenant Theodore Gordon "Spuds" Ellyson, Naval Aviator No. 1, had made the first successful catapult launch at the Washington Navy Yard in 1912. By the middle of February, under instructions from the Secretary of the Navy, Bellinger made the first extended seaplane flight from Pensacola, Florida, to Mobile, Alabama, to demonstrate the AH-3 at the Mardi Gras carnival.

Designated Naval Aviator No. 8 on March 4, 1915, he continued to test aircraft, establishing a new American altitude record for seaplanes by piloting a Burgess-Dunne AH-10 to an altitude of ten thousand feet on a flight of one hour and nineteen minutes' duration. From July 25 to August 25, 1915, Bellinger had

Bellinger was part of the aviation contingent en route to Vera Cruz, Mexico, in April 1914, when this photograph was taken of naval aircraft aboard the USS *Mississippi*. The aircraft if one of the original five Navy F-boats procured from the Curtiss Aeroplane and Motor Company of Hammondsport, New York. These F-boats were designated AB-1 through AB-5, and it was AB-3 (shown here), that was flown by Lieutenant Bellinger in the first operation of an American military aircraft against a foreign country. AB-3 was powered by a single 100-horsepower Curtiss OXX engine, and sat a pilot and observer, or pilot and instructor as the case may be, side by side. (Official United States Navy Photograph.)

The Lockheed (Vega) PV-1 Ventura, a Navy patrol bomber, entered the war early in 1943. It operated in both oceans and the Aleutians, assisting in the recapture of Attu, driving the Japanese out of Kiska. Later, the aircraft was used to attack the Kuriles. The photograph here was taken June 1, 1943. (Official United States Navy Photograph.)

charge of a special aviation section which conducted the first tests of use of aircraft for spotting experimental gun and mortar fire at Fortress Monroe, Virginia. During these tests, Lieutenant (junior grade) Bellinger soloed a Burgess-Dunne AH-10 over Fortress Monroe as the first Navy aircraft to spot gunfire, a feat that had not been achieved by a military pilot at that time. Bellinger singlehandedly had to pilot the aircraft, spot the gunfire and signal its position to firing ground forces—no small achievement given the precarious perch of the pilot in an AH-10 compounded by the distraction of observing ground fire.

Bellinger continued to establish many firsts, among them (and related of course to his tests at Fortress Monroe) conducting the first aircraft spotting of target gunfire from battleships at sea off Guantanamo Bay, Cuba, in March 1916. That April, he also conducted what is believed to be the first operational test of airborne radio, using a Curtiss pusher type seaplane, an AH-18.

By May of 1916, Lieutenant Bellinger was detached from Naval Air Station Pensacola, promoted to the rank of lieutenant, and ordered to rejoin the USS *North Carolina* for aviation duty. Here he carried on the first machine-gun firing tests to be made from a naval aircraft. The firing tests took place in January of 1917, and after his return to Pensacola in April, he made the first night seaplane flight in which floodlights were used for illuminating the landing area. This exploit marked the beginning of night flying and night flying instruction within the naval aeronautical establishment.

Promoted to lieutenant commander in October 1917, Bellinger was given command of the fledgling naval air detachment at Hampton Roads, Virginia, soon to become a naval air station. Bellinger retained command of Naval Air Station Hampton Roads until March of 1919, at which time he departed his duties to participate in preparations for the first transatlantic flight in May. He signed on as commander of NC-1. Bellinger would win the Navy Cross with the following citation: "For distinguished service in the line of his profession as commanding officer of the seaplane NC-1 which made a long overseas flight from Newfoundland to the vicinity of the Azores in May 1919."

Lieutenant Commander Bellinger was next assigned duty with the Bureau of Aeronautics when it was organized in August 1921. The Navy Department eventually assigned him to duty with Aircraft Squadrons, Pacific Fleet, until December 1923, when he was ordered as executive officer of the aircraft tender USS *Wright* (AV-1). He would attend the Naval War College at Newport, Rhode Island, and it was there, in November 1924, Bellinger was promoted to full commander. From Newport, where he had become staff for a few months, Bellinger reported as aide and fleet aviation officer to Admiral C.F. Hughes, then Commander-in-Chief, Battle Fleet, and later, as of September 4, 1926, Commander-in-Chief, United States Fleet. As aide to Admiral Hughes, Bellinger learned a great deal, taking with him inestimable knowledge as assistant naval attaché to the American

These Martin PBM-3 Mariners bear the white paint scheme of squadrons which patrolled the South Atlantic looking for German submarines from bases in Brazil, 1944. Mariners carried radar equipment and depth charges to combat the submarine menace. Fleet Air Wing Sixteen was established on February 16, 1943, and spent its first two months training its Mariner squadrons in antisubmarine warfare at Norfolk, Virginia, before heading to Natal, Brazil, forming a headquarters for the giant flying boats on April 14, 1943. The wing reported to Commander Fourth Fleet for operational control. Air wing headquarters was moved to Recife, Brazil, on July 13, 1943, to provide a better base of operations for the Mariners. (Official United States Navy Photograph.)

Embassy at Rome, Italy, until a change of orders called him home in May 1931. He assumed command of the *Wright* until July 1932 at which time he was relieved of command and assigned command of the USS *Langley* (CV-1), which he retained until June 1933 when he was placed in charge of the Plans Division of the Bureau of Aeronautics. Eventually, Commander Bellinger moved up to the Administration Division at the bureau, and in June 1935 he was appointed to the rank of captain, becoming commanding officer of the USS *Ranger* until 1937. When Captain Bellinger relinquished command of the *Ranger,* he was assigned duty as Chief of Staff and aide to Vice Admiral F.J. Horne, Commander Aircraft Battle Force, and Carrier Division One, United States Fleet. This assignment would last only a short time, as Bellinger was sent in July 1938 to once again command Naval Air Station Norfolk, Virginia, a command which he held until November 1940, when he reported as commanding officer of Patrol Wing Two (COMPATWINGTWO), based at Pearl Harbor, Hawaii, and promoted to the rank of rear admiral. On completion of his tour as COMPATWINGTWO, he reported for duty as Commander Patrol Wings, Pacific Fleet, in May 1942, and three months later he was appointed Deputy Chief of Staff, United States Fleet under Admiral Ernest J. King. This was his last assignment before being designated Commander Air Force, Atlantic Fleet, on March 10, 1943.(2) In his role as King's right hand, Bellinger was responsible for assigned aircraft and ships in the Atlantic Fleet, particularly those engaged in antisubmarine warfare, a task right in line with his future role as commander of all Atlantic Fleet naval air forces. Bellinger observed on numerous occasions that Admiral King was the first naval aviator to make flag rank and that John Towers was the first of the early naval aviators to reach flag. He found the lack of naval aviators at flag rank abhorrent, but naval aviators were never promoted then as quickly as they are today. Though the Navy's leadership was gradually embracing its naval aviators and aviation officers during the 1930s and 1940s, guaranteeing them critical—and permanent—leadership positions in the postwar Navy regime, Bellinger was impatient. He was quite literally thrilled to detach from King's staff and head for Norfolk, a station bustling with as much activity and excitement as it did in his youth when he was commanding officer of Naval Air Station Hampton Roads. The air station complex was still growing in land mass and aircraft, the result of Bellinger's second tour as commanding officer of the air base in the late 1930s.

As Commander Air Force, Atlantic Fleet, Bellinger was tasked as type commander of all fleet aircraft and any surface vessels assigned to the naval air force. His responsibility for allocation and distribution of officer personnel, other than commanding officers, assigned to the air force, except those attached to surface vessels, would come at a crucial period of American naval aviation history—World War II.

The Consolidated Vultee PB4Y-2 Privateer, photographed in June of 1944, entered combat in 1945 with VP-24, later nicknamed the *Batmen* because of ASM-N-2 Bat anti-shipping missile mounted under the wings of the aircraft. This land-based patrol bomber was powered by four 1,350-horsepower Pratt & Whitney R-1830-94 engines. The Privateer was a variant of the Navy Liberator. (Official United States Navy Photograph.)

Bellinger was also accountable for the allocation and distribution of enlisted personnel; the maintenance of all aircraft squadrons at home and abroad which were attributable to the Atlantic Fleet; distribution of aircraft and airships to the fleet; coordination of overhaul and repair; preparation of tactical instruction and doctrine in all aircraft types and ultimately, assignment of all facilities ashore for fleet use. The conditions of Bellinger's service, though rigorous and at times frought with the frenetic pace of war, were met above and beyond the call of duty. As Bellinger later observed of his new command, the Air Force, Atlantic Fleet, was a very comprehensive administrative, or type, command. By the time Bellinger came to this position—and observation—the Air Force, Atlantic Fleet, also consisted of large aircraft carriers from the time of their commissioning until, as he duly noted in his own words, "the carriers and crews were trained and considered ready to proceed to the Pacific."

The Air Force, Atlantic Fleet, had been established during a time when the Axis submarine menace in the Atlantic was enjoying its greatest success. With sinkings increasing steadily, they reached their all time peak in March 1943, the month Bellinger assumed his new command. His experience not only with positioning but fashioning American antisubmarine warfare response on King's staff parlayed into perhaps one of the most successful battle outcomes of the Second World War—winning the prolonged Battle of the Atlantic, hands down.

American production of the materials of war had just begun to hit its stride, to borrow a colloquialism, but the threat to their safe arrival to the battlefront was a major consideration, one which had to be resolved quickly. Had German U-boats continued their successful pattern of Allied merchant and military ship destruction, the flow of American manpower, weapons, food, and other materials of war would have been significantly reduced, the war's end unforeseeable.

German and Italian forces were very much aware of their strengths and weaknesses in the fight for the Atlantic. Since their surface vessels were outnumbered and outgunned from the start of the war, the best remaining combatant in the Axis arsenal was the U-boat. Seasoned U-boat captains patrolled the Atlantic, picking off merchant ships with relative ease. The United States needed to confront the threat with one of its own. In the end, it was up to Bellinger and his force commanders to devise a strategy to shut down Axis submarine action against Allied convoys. Until Bellinger became Commander Air Force, Atlantic Fleet (COMAIRLANT), new planes, armor and armament to fight the U-boat had been tested with little success. Pilots and crews had to be trained in the operation of each new weapon, and then be trained all over again when subsequent changes were made in the aircraft. This lapse in training protocol, as well as flaws found in particular aircraft being sent to the fleet, fell in Bellinger's lap. He had to find the solution.

Bellinger inherited many of the problems which would later be considered as part of a master strategy to defeat the Axis in the Battle of the Atlantic. First and foremost, the Navy had placed considerable reliance in its newest and largest patrol bomber—the Martin PBM-3C Mariner. Obvious deficiencies of the aircraft and others like it presented the first of many vexing problems for Bernhard, Bellinger's predecessor, and, later, Bellinger himself. COMAIRLANT's battle with the Bureau of Aeronautics and the Martin Company are well documented. Eight days after Air Force, Atlantic Fleet, was formed, it was obligated to report to the bureau an accumulated list of major and minor defects in the PBM-3C, the latest model being used in the fleet. Sixty-four of these aircraft were available to fit out nine patrol squadrons, one of which was operating in the Caribbean Sea, VP-32, while the other eight, sent to VP-201 and VP-208 (inclusive), were being delayed in their deployment cycle by deficiencies encountered in the aircraft.

Two major steps were taken during January 1943 to remedy the situation. The first occurred on January 10, when Admiral King ordered the formation of eight medium bombing squadrons to be fitted with twelve PV-1 Venturas each. The first of these squadrons was established by February 1, and became operational on May 9 at Natal, Brazil. The Ventura proved a difficult aircraft to fly, resulting in a number of fatal accidents. In the meantime, two Consolidated PBY-5A Catalina squadrons, VP-82 and VP-93, had been equipped with PV-1s and redesignated VB-125 and VB-126, continuing their operations from Argentina. Twelve additional PV-1 squadrons were formed during 1943, all of which became operational before the end of the year.

The second step taken to overcome problems readying squadrons for deployment was modification of the PBM-3C to make it suitable for combat operations. The first round of modifications was ordered on January 30, 1943, when certain squadrons operating PBM-3Cs and the older model, PBM-3, were ordered to eliminate waist guns, oxygen equipment, bombsight and stabilizer, armor, mattresses and so on in order to relieve the overloaded condition of the planes. While this was only a temporary fix, it expedited the deployment of aircraft, at the same time making the aircraft safe for flight. Aviators still thought this quick fix left a lot to be desired as the Martin Mariner continued to be inefficient and cumbersome.

When the Transitional Training Squadron, Atlantic, a subordinate unit of Air Force, Atlantic Fleet, was established on February 1, 1943, a detachment for modification and testing of PBMs was sent to Annapolis, Maryland, with instructions to work in cooperation with the manufacturer on required modifications to the plane. This detachment was ultimately moved to Middle River, Maryland, the location of the Martin factory, and after necessary modifications were decided upon, a similar detachment was established at Elizabeth City, North Carolina. On April 6, 1943, Bellinger recommended the immediate cancellation of the existing contract with Martin for production of the PBM-3C to the Bureau of Aeronautics. His recommendation was based on the fact the past history and future prospects, as he put it, "would not perform effectively the work for which it was intended." Along with this recommendation, Bellinger notified the bureau, specifically Vice Admiral John S. McCain, that the Air Force, Atlantic Fleet, would not accept further deliveries of PBM-3C aircraft until reasonably adequate squadron kits of spares were made available.

Rear Admiral Bellinger directed that seven PBM-3Cs be completely stripped and the essential parts replaced and relocated in an effort to reduce the weight of the planes and make them more satisfactory for the conduct of antisubmarine warfare operations in the Atlantic. This was done at Naval Air Station Norfolk and the planes, as stripped, became the prototype of the PBM-3S(3) model.

Bellinger wrote to Commander-in-Chief of the Atlantic Fleet, Admiral Royal E. Ingersoll, on April 8, 1943, proposing that squadrons VP-201, VP-202, and VP-203 be re-equipped with Consolidated PBY-5s. Bellinger followed up this request with another letter dated April 10, reviewing the continuing difficulties encountered in the PBM-3C and the drastic modifications necessary to operate them, stating further that the recommendations of April 6 to cancel the Martin contract was made in order to make the best of a bad situation and to prevent the Navy from being overstocked with inefficient aircraft. On April 15, Ingersoll concurred with Bellinger's recommendations but, on April 20, Admiral King's office informed Ingersoll's staff he expected every effort to be made to get PBMs in antisubmarine warfare operations quickly.

Despite King's order, Bellinger found creative ways around relying on PBMs. As if to substantiate all over again Bellinger's stand regarding the troubled Martin aircraft, the next deficiency record in the command logs was a failure of the bomb bay door release mechanism which took thirty days to correct in the planes. It was not until June 1, that the first completely modified PBM-5S came out of the modification center at Elizabeth City. Nearly two months later, on July 27, the first PBM-3S aircraft rolled out of the modification center at Middle River. From that time on no further major deficiencies were noted, but the PBM-3S, as "stripped," left much to be desired. To overcome these deficiencies, a new model—the PBM-3D—was designed by Martin, the first of which was delivered on December 3, 1943. The PBM-3D was only a slight improvement over its predecessor. Bellinger, ever-vigilant, continued to request PBY-5s in correspondence with the Bureau of Aeronautics, hopeful he would eventually have a good aircraft at his disposal. The Martin Mariner was not the only aircraft unable to meet fleet expectations, but the Mariner was perhaps one of the most difficult aircraft to modify. The Mariner was also anticipated to be critical in the antisubmarine warfare campaign in the Atlantic and long-range patrol bombing in the Pacific. The PBM-3S variant was eventually used effectively from Norfolk to the Solomon Islands in the Pacific. The PBM-5, which appeared by late 1944, was the first bug-free patrol aircraft produced by Martin during the Second World War.

Vice Admiral Patrick Neison Lynch Bellinger, Naval Aviator No. 8, Commander Air Force Atlantic Fleet, 1944. (Official United States Navy Photograph.)

While the Mariner was troublesome,

The Navy ordered the Lockheed PV-2 Harpoon on June 30, 1943, a new and improved version of the manufacturer's PV-1 Ventura. Though very similar, the aircraft was also quite different in what could not be seen to the untrained eye. The Harpoon had greater fuel capacity and a larger wing, but also a reconfigured tail section. These changes improved its range and engine-out handling, but reduced its speed. The photograph here was taken on September 22, 1944, six months after Lockheed began delivery of the Harpoon to Navy squadrons. (Official United States Navy Photograph.)

there were aircraft brought into fleet inventory which Bellinger considered important additions, not the least of which was the B-24 Army bomber, designated a PB4Y-1 Liberator by the Navy. This aircraft was furnished to five newly established squadrons and three existing ones which were thereafter designated to reflect their bombing role. The first of these squadrons was outfitted with the Liberator by May 1, and was using them in Argentina by the middle of the month. By the end of 1943, six of the eight Liberator squadrons engaged the Axis in the Atlantic.

One of the most significant force changes under Bellinger's direction was instituted in the first few months of his taking over Air Force, Atlantic Fleet. Escort or "jeep" carriers were assigned to duty in the Atlantic. Bellinger was delegated the task of inspecting all heavy, light and jeep carriers in the purview of the United States Atlantic Fleet by Admiral Ingersoll who had received his orders from Admiral King. The job of inspecting all carrier types and assessing their readiness and personnel requirements was no small task. Bellinger was busy. Of the first four jeep carriers (CVEs) to take up residence at Norfolk, one was the USS *Charger* (CVE-30). The *Charger* began its seagoing life as a C-3 cargo ship from the Moore-Macormick Line named the *Rio de la Plata* before she was converted by the United States Navy to an auxiliary aircraft carrier and floating school for naval aviators in early 1942. Other jeep carriers followed but, none served the same purpose as the *Charger* in the CVE classification.(4) The first combatant jeep carrier appeared on March 28, and although four more arrived by year's end, only three remained operational in the Atlantic. Jeep carriers proved outstanding deterrers to German submarines during their routine convoy escort duty. Grumman TBF-1C Avengers from Composite Squadron Nine (VC-9) aboard the USS *Bogue* (CVE-9) attacked and sank the *U-569* in the middle of the North Atlantic on May 22, scoring the first sinking of the war by an escort carrier on hunter-killer patrol.

The effectiveness of COMAIRLANT forces in the Atlantic became obvious by the middle of 1943, when the tonnage sunk by U-boats started to decrease. The Germans began mounting heavy antiaircraft guns on the decks of their submarines in order to engage Allied aircraft diving from above. This development necessitated a change in American antisubmarine tactics and led to heavier armament and armor on Navy aircraft which, in turn, translated into more forward fire power and armorplating, searchlights, low-altitude bomb sights, LORAN (long-range navigational aid; a device still standard on Navy combatants today), an IFF(5) (Identify Friend or Foe) which was placed in shipboard combat information centers. By the end of 1943, aircraft were also fitted with rockets, still experimental, but, nonetheless effective in runs at German U-boats.

Bellinger's hunter-killer (HUK) antisubmarine strategy was in full operation. As the submarine threat came under control in the Atlantic, Bellinger and his staff focused almost entirely on training, equipping and forming units for the Pacific theater. Five aircraft carrier groups (CVs), seven light carrier groups (CVLs), thirteen carrier air groups (CAGs) including thirty-one squadrons comprised of eight bombing squadrons (VBs), fourteen fighter squadrons (VFs), nine torpedo squadrons (VTs), five patrol squadrons (VPs), five additional composite squadrons (VCs), and fourteen battleship-cruiser aviation units, also known by the acronym AVUNITS, were trained.

Bellinger instituted a specialized training program called the Night Fighter Training Unit, a follow-on to the original Night Fighter Development Unit established April 18, 1942, and the Group Training Center(6) established October 1, 1943, for the sole purpose of

The PBY-5A was the amphibian version of the Catalina, also known as the workhorse of naval aviation. The aircraft was used all over the world by the United States and its allies. The Catalina's versatility is indicated by the many missions it performed—bombing, air/sea rescue, transport, and patrol. In February 1943, the Catalina was fitted with retrorockets designed to fire aft with a velocity equal to the forward velocity of the aircraft, and thus launched vertically. The retro-rocket was designed by a team at the California Institute of Technology and became the weapon most complementary to the Catalina's magnetic airborne detector (MAD) gear. The retro-rocket was first fitted to Patrol Squadron Sixty-Three (VP-63) PBY-5 aircraft and used for the first time in conjunction with MAD gear by VP-63 as well. Patrol Squadron Sixty-Three was stationed at Norfolk when the equipment was added, and late in 1943 the squadron deployed with Fleet Air Wing Sixteen (FAW-16) out of Port Lyautey using MAD capability. The Catalina shown here in a photograph taken January 14, 1945, is equipped with retro rockets in addition to its regular armament. The photograph here was taken January 14, 1945. (Official United States Navy Photograph.)

training newly formed fighter and attack squadrons in fighter direction and radio telephone procedure and discipline. The Marine Corps developed the first active night fighter squadron, VMF(N)-531, established at Marine Corps Air Station Cherry Point, North Carolina, on November 16, 1942. Lieutenant Colonel Frank M. Schwable was VMF(N)-531's first commanding officer. The Marines flew the Lockheed (Vega) PV-1 Ventura aircraft equipped with British Mark IV radar. The Navy did not have its first night fighter squadron until April 1, 1943. Commander William J. Widhelm was the first commanding officer of VF(N)-75. His squadron was outfitted with the Corsair. Lieutenant H.D. O'Neil of VF(N)-75 was the first night fighter pilot to shoot down an enemy aircraft, a Japanese Betty bomber, on October 31, 1943.

On October 8, 1943, his birthday, Bellinger's telephone rang. The caller said only, "'Hello Vice,'" to which Bellinger replied, "Who are you and whom do you want to talk to?" The caller repeated, "'Hello Vice,'" before a surprised Bellinger recognized the voice as that of his old friend, Vice Chief of Naval Operations for Air Vice Admiral John S. McCain. McCain told Bellinger, "'I just want to congratulate you as you have just been made a vice admiral.'" Bellinger's appointment was made official by a letter from President Franklin D. Roosevelt dated October 5, 1943. Bellinger recalled this personal moment in his unpublished manuscript, "Gooney Bird," years later. His promotion to vice admiral during the war gave him little opportunity to pause and reflect on the past. He was pleased to be promoted, but had little time to savor the success.

Not to be overlooked in Bellinger's overall plans to win the Atlantic and secure European shores for future land invasions was Observation Fighter Squadron One (VOF-1), created December 15, 1943, at Naval Air Station Atlantic City, New Jersey, and commanded by Lieutenant Commander William F. Bringle. The squadron was the first to work the spotting function via a Navy fighter. VOF-1 started out flying the Chance-Vought F4U Corsair, but eventually flew the Grumman F6F-3 Hellcat, deploying on the USS *Tulagi* (CVE-72). The squadron was taking on Hitler's *Luftwaffe* in and around the Mediterranean Sea by the end of June 1944. Two additional VOF squadrons, VOF-2, flying the F4U-1D Corsair, and VOF-3, outfitted with the F4U-1 Corsair, were established in March and June 1944, respectively, but never saw action. The pilots of VOF-1 played an important role in close air support and spotting for Operation Anvil Dragoon, the invasion of southern France, under the operational direction of Rear Admiral Calvin T. Durgin, Naval Aviator No. 2725, Task Group 88.2 commander. During Anvil Dragoon, some of VOF-1's pilots flew the

North American P-51 Mustang from land bases. Their Mustangs were painted in Navy colors.

The cooperation of American naval air forces and Soviet pilots left a lasting impression on Bellinger and created a unique page in the annals of naval aviation history. A letter from Admiral King at the beginning of 1944 directed Bellinger to find an air station to house and train Soviet pilots in flying PBN-5 and PBY amphibians. The aircraft were provided to the Soviets on lend lease agreement. It was Bellinger's role to choose a base from which the aircraft's Soviet pilots could receive instruction before ferrying the amphibians back to their country. The Elizabeth City air station was chosen to quarter and train Soviet pilots and ground crew. The Soviets presented numerous challenges for their American instructor pilots, language being far down the list of difficulties. Bellinger's reports revealed that the Soviets did not seem to understand they fell within his chain of command. Bellinger corrected the misunderstanding through his Russian-language interpretor, and followed up with an inspection of the Elizabeth City seaplane base. After this inspection, Bellinger reported no further problems with the Soviets. He extended an invitation to the Soviet colonel and three officers to have lunch at the Norfolk air station which, except for both parties not trusting one another, went well. Bellinger and the Soviet colonel brought their own interpretors to lunch, though the colonel spoke nearly perfect English. Bellinger praised the Soviet mechanics and pilots. "Many were practically engineers," he wrote years later. Unfortunately, the Soviet colonel did not live to tell his side of the Elizabeth City story. He was killed on a ferry flight somewhere over Europe on his return to the Soviet Union. This was the only crash Bellinger remembered the Soviet pilots ever having the entire time the ferry program was underway.

The highlight of Bellinger's command's success in 1944 could be quantified in the number of new units established and trained to operate in the Pacific, thus, extending COMAIRLANT's original mandate to train existing units to fight in diverse Pacific campaigns against the Japanese. During the year, one hundred and forty-two units rotated out of Norfolk to fight in the Pacific theater, among them 16 aircraft carriers, 20 carrier air groups, 67 carrier squadrons, 21 patrol squadrons, and 18 aviation units. All newly constructed aircraft carriers in the United States Navy, in addition to many escort carriers built on the West Coast and ferried to the East Coast, brought their ships and crews to the Atlantic where they were trained by AIRLANT personnel. The full-effect of Vice Admiral Bellinger's training and readiness protocols was felt in every theater of the war.

One month to the day after the D-Day invasion,[7] Bellinger established Navy Special Air Unit One and placed Commander James A. Smith[8] in command. The unit was transferred "without delay" to Captain William H. Hamilton, Commander, Fleet Air Wing Seven, in Europe. The unit was to execute high-level plans designed to eliminate German launching sites associated with the V-1 pilotless aircraft and long-range V-2 rockets using its PB4Y-1 Liberator aircraft, some of which had been converted to assault drones. Upon arrival in England, the unit was under the operational control of Project Aphrodite, an Army Air Corps operation directed by Lieutenant Colonel Roy W. Forrest and based at Fersfield Airdrome in the English countryside.

Navy documents indicate that Consolidated PB4Y-1 aircraft rigged as drones were initially going to be used against Japan, but the German V-1 and V-2 threat to England became too intense to apply the newly developed drone technology anywhere except Europe. Two PB4Y-1 aircraft of Navy Patrol Bombing Squadron 110 (VB-110), based at Dunkeswell,[9] England, were going to be used for this unique and top secret operation. Special Air Unit One arrived at Dunkeswell on July 23, 1944, with PB4Y-1, Bureau Number 32271, and two PV-1s, Bureau Numbers 33429 and 34926. Headquarters Squadron Seven, the maintenance squadron for Fleet Air Wing Seven, carried out modifications to the aircraft. Lieutenant Commander James R. Reedy was commanding officer of VB-110 until April 28, when he turned over squadron command to Commander Page Knight. Knight was in command when the squadron made its first flights with their top secret aircraft in August and September. When the Army Air Corps selected its first target, Mimoyecques,[10] in occupied France, the site was believed to be part of Nazi Germany's V-1 and V-2 program, making it a legitimate strategic mark on the map. When Navy Lieutenants Joseph Patrick Kennedy Jr.[11] and Wilford J. Willy[12] departed Fersfield on August 12, they were headed for Mimoyecques. Kennedy volunteered for the mission as did his copilot, Lieutenant Willy, who was executive officer of the unit. Kennedy was an experienced PB4Y-1 plane commander, but Willy had no previous flying experience in the aircraft.

The mission of Project Aphrodite on August 12 was to destroy German V-2 rocket installations in occupied France via a jury-rigged PB4Y-1 Liberator guided to the target by a remote control apparatus, equipped with a forward-looking television and transmitter, and chocked with twenty-five thousand pounds of torpex. Because there was no time to perfect the mission, the aircraft had to be flown to two thousand feet by Kennedy and Willy at which time both pilots could switch to autopilot and bail out. The flight was monitored by two escort aircraft, the PV-1 Ventura control aircraft and a B-17 Flying Fortress, to monitor television transmissions. Approximately twenty-eight minutes into the flight, the PB4Y-1 exploded near Beccles, England, killing both pilots. This was not what many people have speculated to be a suicide mission nor did Kennedy or Willy volunteer for publicity-seeking reasons. Flying these drone aircraft laden with thousands of pounds of volatile torpex was dangerous business. Previous tests utilizing the aircraft and VB-110 pilots proved successful on three out of four tests about eight days prior to Kennedy and Willy's tragic outcome. Four Liberator drones had been used on dry runs without incident. Of the four drones, one crashed with its pilot after he lost flight control and the other three PB4Y-1 aircrews bailed out successfully. Two of the three test drones struck close to V-1 and V-2 target sites. On August 6, drone tests continued with mixed success. Flight control, bailing out, and, later, premature detonation, were acknowledged hazards of drone aircraft.

Premature detonation was not a proven problem prior to Kennedy and Willy's flight. Pre-flight checks revealed no evidence of interference with the aircraft's electrical circuits. American and British ground stations monitored the airwaves for interference and found none before August 12. The aircraft's electrical system was grounded to prevent static electricity from prematurely detonating the plane. The aircraft flown by Kennedy and Willy was checked daily and guarded round-the-clock. There is no way to be assured whether Kennedy or Willy may have removed critical safety devices from the electrical arming circuits. Ordnance experts at that time knew more about what did not cause the accident of August 12 than what did. Since the firing keys were intact in the control aircraft, it did not cause Kennedy and Willy's plane to detonate mid-air. Commander Smith's report of the accident, also conveyed to Bellinger, dated August 14, 1944, stated with emphasis that among the most probable causes named, the most likely was a stray radio signal which energized the electrical circuits and blew up the PB4Y-1 aircraft.

Undaunted by the tragic loss of Kennedy and Willy, VB-110 pressed on and near the end of August 1944, a second PB4Y-1 was test flown. This aircraft was equipped with a mechanical rather than electrical fuzing system to prevent stray radio signals from prematurely detonating the aircraft. Since France had been liberated by that time, the target shifted to German submarine pens at Heligoland Island, Holland. Lieutenant Ralph Spaulding, USNR, flew the second Liberator drone from Fersfield on September 3, set the aircraft on radio control and parachuted safely to the ground. Ensign J.M. Simpson, controlling the Liberator's flight over the North Sea from a PV-1 Ventura, attempted to guide the drone to the target at Heligoland Island. An engineer attached to VB-110 monitored the drone's movements over the Dutch countryside from his perch in a B-17 Flying Fortress. Simpson lost view of the drone in a driving rain during final alignment with the target. He had to rely on the drone's television picture of the terrain to hit the barracks and industrial center of an airfield on nearby Dune Island, located approximately one mile from the intended target. The Liberator drone may not have hit its intended target but, it certainly made history as the first and only guided bomb used in the European theater of World War II by Allied forces.

Stateside, Bellinger aggressively pursued two important areas: establishment of an Aircraft Safety Board, precursor of the Naval Safety Center, and disposition of his subordinate commands upon cessation of hostilities in the European and Pacific theaters. In September 1944, an Aircraft Safety Board was established to inquire into causes of and institute measures for prevention of aircraft accidents pertaining to COMAIRLANT units. This board was the forerunner of the Aircraft Safety Division created in early 1945, and, of course, the center in later years.

With the demise of Germany close at hand, Bellinger began laying the groundwork for the disposition of his subordinate commands. By September 24, 1944, he recommended to Admiral King that upon cessation of hostilities in Europe, the Atlantic Fleet air wings be reassigned to the Pacific, as needed, and consolidated in purpose and manpower. In a Navy document dated November 18, Bellinger recommended to Admiral Jonas Ingram, his Naval Academy classmate and Ingersoll's successor as Commander-in-Chief, Atlantic Fleet, that the plan to have operational control of all aircraft squadrons in the Atlantic revert to Ingram should take place immediately following the end of the war in Europe.

By January 1945, Bellinger had already begun the laborious task of regrouping, reassigning, and disestablishing aviation units, and decommissioning facilities. In the nine months leading up to victory over Japan, the needs of the Air Force, Atlantic Fleet, had been considerably reduced. Victory in Europe came on May 8, 1945. Bellinger's command was getting smaller with the exception of one new unit—the Fleet Airborne Electronics Training Unit—established on July 20, 1945. The role of this unit was to provide more effective training of aircrews in the use of new electronic equipment.

Despite victory in Europe, there was still a war raging in the Pacific. While German U-boats were the menace in the Battle of the Atlantic, the greatest enemy to Allied naval forces in the Pacific was the Japanese kamikaze pilot. Bellinger was tapped to assist in an important program to combat this threat. Experimental Squadrons XVF-200 and XVJ-25 were established on June 15, 1945, at Naval Air Station Brunswick, Maine, to provide, under operational control of Admiral King, flight facilities for evaluating and testing tactics, procedure, and equipment for use in defense tasks, particularly those dealing with kamikazes. A considerable portion of what XVF-200 and XVJ-25 learned regarding kamikazes came from experienced fleet pilots and flight test personnel located at naval air stations up and down the East Coast, but most especially Norfolk. Flight test engineers at Naval Air Station Norfolk's Assembly and Repair Department maintained in their inventory a captured Japanese human-guided missile called a Baka.

On February 2, 1946, a beleaguered Bellinger realized his naval career of forty years was drawing to a close. He relinquished command of the Air Force, Atlantic Fleet, and headed for his last duty, as a member of the General Board of the Navy Department. Bellinger was not removed from flying duty until poor health forced then chairman of the General Board, Admiral John Henry "Jack" Towers, Naval Aviator No. 3, to detach his friend of thirty-five years from flight status. On October 1, 1947, Vice Admiral Patrick N.L. Bellinger gracefully departed Washington, D.C., for his retirement at Earlehurst, his country estate near Covington, Virginia.

Even in retirement, Bellinger kept active. In April 1955, he was honored by having the two-mile stretch of road running between gates three and four at Naval Air Station Norfolk changed from East Field Boulevard to Bellinger Boulevard, thereby recognizing him as one of the pioneers of Navy history, particularly naval aviation history. Early

The effects of Vice Admiral Patrick Bellinger's changes and additions to his command structure of Air Force, Atlantic Fleet in its infancy have left their mark today. Atlantic Fleet Weather Central was created by Admiral Royal E. Ingersoll, acting on Bellinger's recommendation, on April 15, 1944, at Norfolk under the command of Air Force, Atlantic Fleet. Establishment of this unit took place on April 29, and provided a central agency for the preparation and dissemination of weather data throughout the fleet. Timely and accurate forecasts of the hurricane which occurred September 14 that year, known as the "Great Atlantic Hurricane," played a great part in carrying out a successful evacuation of aircraft which saved countless thousands, translated today into millions, of dollars of potential damage to aircraft in the path of a devastating hurricane. Norfolk was near the primary path of the hurricane of 1944, a storm which previously held the record as the most violent in history. The central pressure of the hurricane as it approached the Bahamas was below twenty-seven inches, a storm of large diameter. Although its center passed about fifty miles east of Norfolk, the force of the hurricane was tremendous. Fleet Weather Central reported six stacks blown down at the Naval Base and heavy damage from high water. The bureau noted that Seaside Park at Virginia Beach reported winds estimated at eighty-three miles per hour with gusts to one hundred miles per hour while Cape Henry had winds in excess of 135 miles per hour for thirty seconds. The extreme velocity of the storm was ninety miles per hour with a maximum at seventy-three miles per hour.

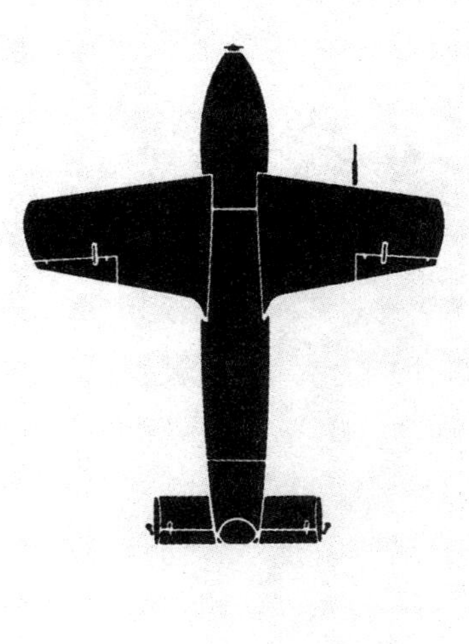

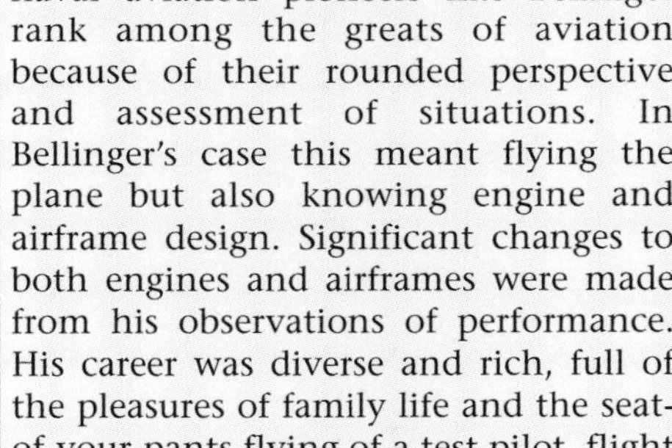

The silhouette and caricature of the Japanese Baka suicide aircraft bomb appeared in the Fleet Training Center Oahu Aircraft Identification Manual. The Baka, whose name means "fool" in Japanese, looked something like a flying torpedo. The aerial bomb attached under the fuselage of a parent aircraft such as Betty, Peggy, or Helen bombers. From its time of release, the Baka was guided by its suicide pilot into a high-speed dive directed toward the target.

naval aviation pioneers like Bellinger rank among the greats of aviation because of their rounded perspective and assessment of situations. In Bellinger's case this meant flying the plane but also knowing engine and airframe design. Significant changes to both engines and airframes were made from his observations of performance. His career was diverse and rich, full of the pleasures of family life and the seat-of-your-pants flying of a test pilot, flight instructor and naval aviator. From frail Curtiss flying boats to Navy jet aircraft, Bellinger saw his progeny—a United States Navy with the most powerful air force in the world—deployed on magnificent aircraft carriers. He died of a heart attack at the age of seventy-six on May 26, 1962.

1. Once the United States entered the war, consolidation of commands took place. The most significant changes for naval air occurred in late 1942 and early 1943. The creation of the United States Naval Air Forces, Pacific, and, later, the switch to a simpler title, Air Force, Pacific Fleet took place on September 1, 1942. A similar command structure was instituted on the East Coast on January 1, 1943. It was called Air Force, Atlantic Fleet. Commander Air Force, Atlantic Fleet would then gain control of Carrier, Atlantic Fleet; Carrier Replacement Squadrons, Atlantic Fleet; and Fleet Air Wings, Atlantic, all of which ceased to exist as independent commands as of January 1. The naval air station at Norfolk, Virginia, was designated as the headquarters for the Commander Air Force, Altantic Fleet. Rear Admiral Alva D. Bernhard, former commanding officer of Fleet Air Wings, Atlantic, was the first Commander Naval Air Force, Atlantic Fleet.
2. Bellinger remained Commander Air Force, Atlantic Fleet, until the end of the Second World War.
3. The "S" in the model type stood for "stripped."
4. The USS *Wolverine* (IX-64) was commissioned at Buffalo, New York, on August 12, 1942, with Commander G.R. Fairlamb commanding. This vessel, as well as the USS *Sable,* commissioned in May 1943, were former Great Lakes excursion ships converted for aviation training and, as such, they operated for the remainder of the war on the inland waters of Lake Michigan. The *Wolverine* and *Sable* provided flight decks upon which hundreds of student naval aviators qualified for carrier landings and many flight deck crews received their first practical experience in landing aircraft aboard ship.
5. The IFF installation was one of Bellinger's ideas. It remains a vital tool to aviators and surface sailors today.
6. An outgrowth of the Group Training Center was the Combat Information Center (CIC) school at Brigantine, New Jersey, which trained CIC teams for surface vessels while also providing a twenty-four-hour radar and radio watch for lost or distressed aircraft.
7. Operation Overlord began on June 6, 1944.
8. Commander Smith was commanding officer of Patrol Air Group One, part of Fleet Air Wing Seven, at the time of his selection to run Navy Special Air Unit One.
9. The Navy had three patrol bombing squadrons at Dunkeswell which flew the PB4Y-1: VB-103, VB-105 and, of course, VB-110. In a gesture of thanks for the townspeople's support during the war, members of these squadrons purchased a new organ for the town church because the original organ had been destroyed in a German bombing. The town of Dunkeswell, in return, placed memorial plaques to all the Navy's dead PB4Y-1 pilots and aircrew in the church as solemn remembrance for those who gave their lives in the service of the United States Navy and the British people.
10. Mimoyecques was captured late in the war by Allied troops who discovered the site was not, as suspected, a V-1 or V-2 rocket station but a storage facility for long-range experimental guns.
11. Kennedy had been assigned to VB-110 since July 1943 and was an experienced plane commander in the PB4Y-1 aircraft. VB-110 was the only PB4Y-1 squadron at Dunkeswell directly attached in support of Special Air Unit One. Squadron support entailed supplying enough pilots and aircrews to fly drone aircraft.
12. Willy had been a participant in the Navy drone program for three years prior to August 12, 1944, but, as duly noted in Navy records from the period, he had no previous flying experience in the PB4Y-1 aircraft.

The TDN-1 in this photograph was a prototype built by the Naval Aircraft Factory in 1943 as a radio-controlled, television-directed assault drone. This one-of-a-kind aircraft had two 220-horsepower Lycoming engines, and an open cockpit provision for one check pilot. The TDN-1 was the designation given this particular Navy prototype for testing, the "D" standing for drone, and the "N" for Naval Aircraft Factory. The drone was tested quite a bit in its short-lived existence, partly here, of course, in Hampton Roads. (Courtesy of the Hampton Roads Naval Museum.)

Captain C.A. "Baldy" Pownall (April 14, 1941-May 2, 1942); Captain Elliot Buckmaster (July 8, 1942-October 2, 1942); Captain James M. Shoemaker, Naval Aviator No. 2951 (November 2-14, 1942; May 24, 1943-November 30, 1943); Captain J.R. Tague (November 14, 1942-February 22, 1943); Captain C.C. Champion (February 22, 1943-May 24, 1943); Captain M.R. Greer, Naval Aviator No. 2981 (November 30, 1943-August 5, 1944), and Captain George L. Compo, Naval Aviator No. 201 (August 5, 1944-July 17, 1947).

Under Pownall's command the air station began offering important services, some of which would have greater impact beyond his tenure as commanding officer. An Aircraft Armament Unit (AAU) was formed at Naval Air Station Norfolk, with Lieutenant Commander W.V. Davis as officer-in-charge, on June 11, 1941. The sole purpose of the AAU was to test and evaluate armament installations which, at least in 1941, had grown more complex. Less than a month later, on July 1, 1941, the Test, Acceptance and Indoctrination Unit, established at Norfolk and San Diego in May to outfit new patrol aircraft and indoctrinate new aircrews in their use, was expanded and stood up as a separate command. The Norfolk unit became the Operational Training Squadron under Commander Patrol Wings Atlantic with facilities located on the naval air station.

To provide aviation maintenance men with special training required to support diverse and fast paced air operations at advanced bases, Aircraft Repair Units One and Two (Atlantic and Pacific, respectively) were merged to form the Advanced Base Aviation Training Unit (ABATU) at Naval Air Station Norfolk on April 7, 1942. The ABATU melded with activities of the Assembly and Repair Department which had been in its various forms, part of the naval air station since its inception in 1918.

Advanced carrier training, an indoctrination school for naval aviators, was established at Naval Air Station Norfolk to teach operation of the latest carrier aircraft, advanced gunnery, and tactical training of new flight crews on July 28, 1941. As a result of new training edicts issued from the Bureau of Aeronautics, the Operational Training Squadron of the Atlantic Fleet was redesignated the Transition Training Squadron, Atlantic, on the same day. In the fall of 1941, Patrol Squadron Eighty-Two (VP-82), later redesignated Patrol Bombing Squadron One Hundred Twenty-Five (VB-125) on March 1, 1943, received the first of its complement of Lockheed PBO-1 Hudsons at Naval Air Station Norfolk. Assignment of these first PBO-1s was not intended to be permanent for VP-82 because the aircraft were destined for England and had been painted in British markings. The squadron later received PBO-1s for its own purposes, but the arrival on October 29, 1941, of those first Hudsons was the beginning of what became an extensive use of landplanes by patrol squadrons during the Second World War. Although it was not yet apparent, this was the first move toward eventual elimination of flying boats from patrol aviation. VP-82 would eventually become the first patrol squadron to receive the Lockheed (Vega) PV-1 Ventura patrol bomber, the Hudson's successor, in December of 1942.

The Naval Air Transport Service established operations from Norfolk on January 1, 1942, when its first aircraft, a Douglas R4D-1 Skytrain, otherwise known as a C-47 Dakota, was received. The Skytrain took its inaugural flight

The formation of Commander Air Force Atlantic Fleet (COMAIRLANT) was still several months off when the Navy began many of the great research and development projects later taken over by COMAIRLANT, headquartered at Norfolk. A Night Fighter Development Unit was formed at Naval Air Station Quonset Point, Rhode Island, on April 18, 1942, originally under the name Project Argus. The name "Project Argus" was changed to Project Affirm to avoid confusion with an electronic device known as an Argus unit found at many of the Navy's advanced air installations. The purpose of the night fighter unit was to develop and test night fighter equipment for Navy and Marine Corps aircraft squadrons, develop much-needed tactics, and train officers and enlisted aircrew as early night fighter directors. Another project of equal importance at Quonset was called Project Sail. Project Sail was organized on June 10, 1942, for airborne testing and associated research on what is still known today as the magnetic airborne detector or MAD gear. Long-range navigation equipment or LORAN was given its first airborne test on a K-2 airship on June 13, 1942, at Naval Air Station Lakehurst, New Jersey. Naval Air Station Patuxent River was not established as a test center until November 2, 1942, and most of the research and development typically associated today with the Maryland facility was done at naval air stations such as Lakehurst, Quonset, Squantum, Norfolk and the Naval Aircraft Factory at Philadelphia, all locations close to industries which manufactured naval aircraft and components, or had university and/or government researchers and manufacturer aeronautical engineers close at hand.

The Curtiss SOC Seagull was designed in the early 1930s for use on battleships and heavy cruisers of the fleet by the Curtiss-Wright Corporation and, later, the Naval Aircraft Factory, as a scout-observation aircraft. This was the last biplane of its kind to be used aboard battleships and cruisers, far surpassing its competitors in time of service and completion of mission for the battle and scouting fleets. The Seagull shown here was being launched from a Navy heavy cruiser on April 13, 1943. The venerable Seagull was not retired until the end of World War II. (Official United States Navy Photograph.)

around Norfolk on February 3, 1942. Regularly scheduled flights by the Naval Air Transport Service (NATS) were inaugurated with an R4D-1 flight from Norfolk to Squantum, Massachusetts, on March 2, 1942. One week later, on March 9, 1942, Transport Squadron One (VR-1) became the first NATS operating squadron established at Naval Air Station Norfolk with 27 officers, 150 enlisted men, and 4 R4D-1 aircraft. Transport Squadron One became the first of thirteen VR squadrons established under NATS during World War II. Commander Cyril K. Wildman, Naval Aviator No. 2973, was VR-1's first commanding officer. The Naval Air Transport Service was one of two major flying commands to establish themselves at Naval Air Station Norfolk in early 1942, the other being Carrier Replacement Air Group Nine on March 1, 1942, under the command of Commander William D. Anderson. This was the first numbered air group in the United States Navy and marked the end of the practice of naming air groups for the carriers to which they had been assigned.

Norfolk became the center point of far-reaching experiments conducted on April 19, 1942, to test the feasibility of using drone aircraft as guided missiles. Two tests were conducted in the Chesapeake Bay. In the first, Utility Squadron Five (VJ-5), utilized visual direction and crash-dived a Great Lakes BG-1 drone aircraft into the water beyond its target, the wreck of the *San*

German U-boats learned the dangers of tangling with American patrol bomber aircraft very early in the Second World War. On March 1, 1942, Ensign William Tepuni, USNR, piloting a Lockheed PBO-1 Hudson aircraft of VP-82 based at Argentina, Newfoundland, attacked and sank the *U-656* southwest of Newfound-land: the first German submarine sunk by United States forces in the war. This would be the first of a string of successful patrol bomber attacks on enemy submarines, both German and Japanese, and Axis surface ships.

- Incidentally - this angle is called 'dihedral' -

Margretta von Sothen: Career Officer in World War II

Margretta von Sothen spent five years in Norfolk, from January 1944 through April 1949. Her first assignment was with the Advanced Base Aviation Training Unit (ABATU) at the naval air station. When the unit moved to Lambert Field in St. Louis, Missouri, Ensign von Sothen requested to remain in Norfolk and was, in her own words, "happily assigned to Air Operations as a watch officer." She would work two round-the-clock watches, each stretching in shifts from 3 to 11 p.m., 11 p.m. to 7 a.m., and 7 a.m. to 3 p.m., with forty-eight hours off. Her work entailed signing flight plans of non-instrument flights after checking the weather and field conditions en route and at destination. This also meant checking for the arrivals and, when necessary, alerting search and rescue. During the war years, her unit also alerted planes to investigate enemy submarine sightings. She and her fellow WAVES[1] were given the classification W(A), meaning aviation specialist.

Margretta von Sothen remained on active duty and was among the first 288 women selected for the United States Navy. She would remark, "My duty remained in air operations as a permanent assistant duty officer with the delightful hours of ten o'clock in the morning to six o'clock in the afternoon," she continued, "I had the honor of being the only non-aviator authorized by the Chief of Naval Operations to sign and clear instrument flight plans due to instrument weather conditions."

Upon leaving Norfolk, her next duty was with VR-1, a transport squadron at Naval Air Station Patuxent River, Maryland, in the administration department. As a United States Navy officer, she was no longer classified W(A) and assigned an 1100 designator (line officer).

After a tour at the training station in San Diego, California, von Sothen went to the United States Embassy in Oslo, Norway, as an assistant to the naval attaché. Her primary duty was officer-in-charge, Joint United States Military Communications Center, handling all traffic for the military, "American Eyes Only," for the North Atlantic Treaty Organization (NATO), and military traffic for the ambassador. Because of her aviation background, von Sothen also did the diplomatic clearances for all Navy flights coming into or departing Norway. "Naturally, I had some intelligence training before Oslo and was next assigned to the Pentagon in the collection desk for the Office of Naval Intelligence," von Sothen recalled.

Eventually she would resign her Navy commission and accept a reserve one, joining a ready reserve intelligence unit in San Francisco, California. At the time Margretta von Sothen retired, she was a lieutenant commander.

Ensign Margretta von Sothen, USNR (active), was photographed in the spring of 1944, at Norfolk, Virginia.

1. The acronym WAVES stood for Women Accepted for Voluntary Emergency Service. More than 23,000 of the 86,000 WAVES who served during World War II worked on naval air installations around the United States and Territory of Hawaii. While some of them were trained as navigators, receiving fifty hours or more of flight instruction, none of them were officially used as pilots. Aside from being used as navigators, thousands of WAVES were used to teach instrument flying as well as instruct in celestial navigation, aircraft gunnery, and air traffic control. The WAVE service was initiated in 1942 and ended in 1972.

Devastation from the explosion of September 17, 1943, is readily apparent. An SNJ-4 aircraft (foreground) was totally destroyed by the blast and subsequent fire. The hangar was still ablaze as personnel worked to salvage remaining aircraft from the hangar and fight the flames. (Official United States Navy Photograph.)

Marcos. A live bomb detonator in the drone failed to explode. The second test was more successful. Dubbed "Project Fox," the test was conducted from Civil Aeronautics Administration Intermediate Field, Lively, Virginia, using another BG aircraft drone equipped with a television camera to provide a view of the target. Lieutenant M.B. Taylor flying in a control aircraft eleven miles away, directed the drone's crash-dive into a raft being towed at a speed of eight-knots.

As the center of the largest complex of air bases on the East Coast, Norfolk became the home of Fleet Air Atlantic and, of course, Commander Air Force, Atlantic Fleet (COMAIRLANT). The station harbored its own major overhaul and repair facility for aircraft, and continued to operate such a facility until September of 1996 when Naval Aviation Depot Norfolk shut its doors under the Base Realignment and Closure Committee military drawdown plan (see Chapter 12).

On March 29, 1943, the air station also became home to Air Transport Squadrons, Atlantic, a command formed to supervise and direct operations of Naval Air Transport Service squadrons based along the Atlantic seaboard. Shortly thereafter, on May fifth, Air Transport Squadron VR-1 extended its area of operation with a flight from Norfolk to Prestwick, Scotland, via Reykjavik, Iceland. This was the first Douglas R5D Skymaster or C-54 operation in the history of the Naval Air Transport Service.

The naval air station at Norfolk became the training ground for American allies during the war. French Patrol Squadron One (VFP-1), manned by the "Fighting French," was established at Naval Air Station Norfolk on September 15, 1943. French naval aviators and mechanics trained under United States Navy personnel, but remained under the command of Lieutenant Commander C.H. Mirepoix, French Navy. The squadron flew the Consolidated PBY-5A Catalina aircraft and trained at American naval air fields from Jacksonville, Florida, to Elizabeth City, North Carolina.

The hustle and bustle around the air station and repair facilities would experience only one major tragedy during the war. The homefront was shaken at eleven o'clock the morning of September 17, 1943, by the explosion of twenty-four aerial depth bombs near hangars V-1 and V-2, which at the time were situated where building V-88 stands today. The bombs, which rolled off an overloaded munitions trailer, wreaked massive destruction. As a result of the explosion, thirty Navy personnel, including one woman and a civilian, were killed. Nearly four hundred people were injured by the blast which rocked businessmen in their offices in downtown Norfolk and shattered glass in the base dispensary as well as the entire air station, injuring even more personnel. In addition to lives lost and injuries suffered, fifteen buildings, including the old Public Works Office, six barracks,

The Public Works Department Building (V-35) was virtually destroyed altogether by the explosion. Personnel who surveyed the scene afterwards were appalled by the extent of destruction on the air station. (Official United States Navy Photograph.)

We Died at Hiroshima

Raymond Lloyd Porter was born in Butler, Pennsylvania, on April 22, 1921, and trained at Naval School of Pre-Flight, Iowa City, Iowa; Naval Air Station Lambert Field, St. Louis, Missouri; Naval Air Training Center Pensacola, Florida; and Naval Air Station Deland before joining Bombing Squadron Eighty-Seven (VB-87) at Naval Auxiliary Air Station (NAAS) Oceana in the fall of 1944. Porter grew up in small town America, a culture profoundly touched by the Great Depression. He had small town dreams—dreams which would never be. If there had been no war, Raymond Porter would probably have become an accountant and married a high school sweetheart. When the war finally came that sleepy Sunday morning of December 7, 1941, any expectation young Raymond may have had to live his life in the town of Butler were gone forever—and so was an age of innocence in America.

Porter was a young pilot assigned to VB-87 at NAAS Oceana in the fall of 1944. When Porter first arrived at the squadron, Lieutenant Commander George C. Simmons Jr. was in command. Simmons stayed with the squadron at Naval Air Station Wildwood, New Jersey, until July 15, 1944, when Lieutenant Commander Porter W. Maxwell assumed command of VB-87 and plans were being made to move the squadron to Oceana.

While at Oceana, Porter continued writing his parents on a regular basis, and it is from these letters that so much has been learned about him. On letterhead of United States Naval Auxiliary Air Station Oceana, Virginia, Raymond Porter wrote:

Ensign Raymond Lloyd Porter, USNR, born April 22, 1921, died August 6, 1945. (Courtesy of the National Museum of Naval Aviation.)

Dear Mom and Dad,

I intended to write sooner, but this has been quite an eventful week. First we had night flying Tuesday night, and Wednesday I had to go out to the carrier and practice landings. I didn't get out until late in the afternoon and on my last landing I had a flat tire. By the time they got it changed it was dark and since my radio had gone out of commission after I left the base they wouldn't let me take off. I begged and pleaded with them to let me return to Oceana but to no avail. Consequently, I had to stay aboard all night. The next day, a heavy fog settled over the water and I didn't get off until the following afternoon, so I got a little taste of carrier life aboard this small carrier [USS *Charger*] before going aboard the *Randolf* [*sic*]. So far I have twelve and will probably get the remainder of them tomorrow. This carrier we have to qualify on is the smallest in the fleet. Its flight deck is about 480 ft. long. The *Randolf* [*sic*] is about 880 ft. so if we can land and take off from this small one, we shouldn't have any trouble on our own.

I didn't get to the commissioning ceremonies of the *Randolf* [*sic*]. I could have gone if I had tried hard enough but several of us were scheduled to qualify aboard the carrier that day and some of the fellows had their families here, so I took another fellow's place. I figured I would see plenty of it before its all over. The irony of it all was the fact that we stood by until about two o'clock and then they called up and said we wouldn't have to go out. Of course it was too late then to go to the ceremony.

I didn't want to say too much over the phone about when we were going out. The way it looks now we will probably leave about Nov. 5. The regular shake-down cruize [*sic*] is scheduled for Nov. 15. Ordinarily they go out into the Chesapeake Bay for a trial run before the shake-down, but the skipper [Captain Felix L. Baker] wants to go straight out to sea. He is really an eager person. He wants our ship to break all records for getting into action, so I don't know just how things are going to turn out. It doesn't look as though we are going to get a leave after the cruize [*sic*] though.

I received my coat and shoes yesterday and I wish you could have seen the condition in which they arrived. Your suitcase was smashed into a hundred pieces and my coat looked like it had been buried in the ground. Everything was there though. I will probably send the shoes back because we were issued a pair the day before I got my old ones.

I guess I am going to have to ask you to send me another fifty dollars. I hope this will be the last. There are several things I am going to have to buy before long and with what I am drawing I don't think I will have enough to take care of it.

Glenn told me he expects to get a furlough the first of November, so if he needs any money, draw it from my account and send it to him. He will probably need it.

I think I shall go to town to a movie this afternoon so will close for now.

Love,
Raymond

Porter's first plane crash came in mid-October 1944, shortly after this letter was written. As he put it, "other than a goose egg on my head I wasn't hurt a bit, but the plane was completely demolished." The incident occurred during squadron practice landings aboard the USS *Charger* (CVE-30), the Navy's training carrier in the Chesapeake Bay. On his first landing Porter's tailhook caught a steel plate on the flight deck and broke it away. His aircraft went screaming down the deck and crashed into the barrier, nosing over. As he later wrote his parents: "I was all set to go for a swim but luckily I managed to keep on the deck." The accident was caused by an overly worn flight deck. A steel plate protruding about an eighth-of-an-inch above the flush deck caught Porter's tailhook. There was only one spot on the deck where he could have landed and encountered the protruding plate and he was unlucky enough to hit it dead-on.

In another letter, Porter discussed at some length one the most common fears of naval aviators—landing at night aboard an aircraft carrier. The letter, dated October 30, 1944, was addressed to his father and stepmother. Porter wrote:

"We have been flying from noon until two or three o'clock in the morning every day this last week. We were making night landings aboard the carrier, which is probably the worst thing I have had to do since I started to fly. I don't particularly care about flying fifty feet above the water at night at practically stalling speed and not being able to see where you are going to land until you cut your gun and are ready to land."

Bombing Squadron Eighty-Seven rode piggyback aboard the USS *Bunker Hill* (CV-17) until the ship reached Alameda, California, and squadron proceeded to Hawaii. The squadron eventually picked up the USS *Ticonderoga* (CV-14), where it flew missions from her decks. Pilots aboard the *Ticonderoga* affectionately called the aircraft carrier the "Big T." Commanded by Captain Dixie Kiefer, the "Big T" was fighting her way into position off the coast of Japan as part of Task Force Thirty-Eight's eventual plan to attack the enemy's homeland in the last summer of the war.

On February 19, 1945, Porter wrote home:

"Everyone has been rather disgruntled the last few days, ever since that carrier raid on Tokyo. That is what we were all looking forward to. In fact we were on the operations order for that first strike, but through some ill hand of fate we missed it. If we had been on it we would probably have been back in the states about June, but as it is now we can't even venture a guess on when we will get back. Everything seems to happen to us; I don't know why."

The pilots of VB-87 must have been a pretty boisterous bunch at times. Porter confessed on February 25 that he had been hobbling around the *Ticonderoga* "like an old man" for a couple of days because:

"We were acting the fool here the other night and having a water fight with the fire extinguisher (We do things like that once in awhile.). Someone dropped a Coke bottle and broke it and I stepped on it. I was in my bare feet so naturally I cut a pretty good gash in my foot."

He had some good days and bad days. Porter was not an intuitively gifted pilot and had more than one crash. He had an accident around March 2 of which he wrote: "My engine cut out on the takeoff and I had to make a crash landing at the end of the runway. The plane was completely demolished, but fortunately neither my gunner nor I got so much as a scratch." On a good day, Porter was hopeful. In a letter dated April 11, he told his parents about the forthcoming marriage plans of his friend, Chuck Kurtz: "He says he is not going to get married until after the war. I told him he had better not because I wanted to be around to kiss the bride."

Porter's pride in the uniform he wore, accentuated by the wings of gold, was demonstrated in his correspondence on several occasions. On June 4, he made lieutenant (junior grade) and three days later requested that his father take his good suit of blues which he had previously sent home from Alameda, California, to a tailor to get the quarter-inch gold stripe added to the sleeves. He concluded, "There is no particular hurry about this but I would like to have it done before I get home." In the same letter, Porter also wrote:

"You will probably get a big kick out of what I am going to say next. Anyhow, I have often wondered what I would look like with a mustach, so I have grown one. Now don't get excited because you, or no one else around home is ever going to see it. I am now convinced that it looks horrible."

Humor aside, Porter's letters home, dated July 16 and 21, 1945, would be the last correspondence received by his parents before Raymond was lost. These letters are emotionally moving and foretell Porter's end. On July 16, Porter put closure on his special relationship with Bea, his stepmother, explaining to her, once and for all, what she truly meant to him:

"You mentioned something in your letter about me calling you 'Bea.' I don't know whether I can explain it or not but I will try. In the first place I think you are the best stepmother a person could ever have. I really think you are swell and I admire you, even though at times I may not show it. No one else could have taken the place you did and do so much to be a mother to us kids. Believe me I can't tell you how much I appreciate it and know Merle and Glenn [his brothers] do too. So when I call you 'Bea,' to me that is the same as 'mother,' but as you know there was a long time that I had no one to call 'mother' and I guess I just got out of the habit. I don't know whether this explains it or not, but I hope it does and I know you understand."

And, finally, on July 21, Porter reminisces of the day he joined the Navy:

"Well, it was just three years ago today that I joined the Navy; remember. In a way it doesn't seem that long, but in another way it seems as though I have spent most of my life in the Navy. I am just hoping that I don't have to spend three more years in it. I think I have seen just about all I want to see...Love, Raymond."

Those would be Porter's last words to the people he loved.

An integral component of Air Group Eighty-Seven, VB-87's Helldivers were scheduled to hit Japanese naval surface combatants in Eta Shima Bay, part of a well-defended system of coastal waterways, the morning of July 28, 1945. The mood of the pilots on "Big T's" deck that morning was colored by the loss four days earlier of Commander Maxwell, who at that time was commanding officer of VBF-87, a bombing fighting outfit. Maxwell was downed over the Inland Sea. The target of VB-87's planes on the

Curtiss SB2C Helldivers of VB-3 *Black Panthers* fly over North Field, Naval Auxiliary Air Station Oceana in 1946. On November 15, 1946, VB-3 was redesignated VA-3A. VA-3A was redesignated VA-34 on August 7, 1948, and it was not until February 15, 1950, that the squadron became Attack Squadron Thirty-Five (VA-35) *Black Panthers*. VA-35 was disestablished on January 31, 1995. Raymond Porter flew this aircraft type from the decks of the USS *Ticonderoga*.

twenty-eighth was the Japanese heavy cruiser *Tone,* anchored in the inner bay of Nishinomi Shima, due west of Kure, in Hiroshima Bay.

Maybe the restlessness of "Big T's" pilots had reached Porter in his cockpit, maybe it had not. No one will ever know. As he waited his turn to launch, Porter's thoughts might have drifted to the small town in Pennsylvania where he grew up, maybe even that job he had waiting for him when the war was finally over, the girl next-door, his family, his friends, the mission. The mission would not be an easy one. The day Maxwell was killed the squadron lost eight of its thirteen Helldivers which had been launched against the Japanese carrier-battleship *Hyuga.* The Japanese were digging in, fortifying their mainland and outlying islands as American naval and amphibious forces edged closer to their homeland. Fate was to deal Porter a blow beyond anyone's comprehension.

Porter could not know as he eased his aircraft off the *Ticonderoga's* deck it would be for the last time. Lieutenant (junior grade) Porter and his gunner, Aviation Radioman Third Class (ARM3c) Normand R. Brissette, successfully pressed their attack on the *Tone,* and were returning with their flight back to the *Ticonderoga* when Porter developed engine trouble. As Porter and Brissette's Curtiss SB2C-4E Helldiver lost oil pressure, the plane began falling behind in formation and Porter made the decision to ditch. Squadron mates witnessed the airmen ditch their Helldiver and climb into the liferaft, the last time any of them saw Porter and Brissette alive.

Captured by the Japanese, Porter and Brissette were imprisoned at Chugoku Military Police Headquarters at Hiroshima along with crewmen of two Army Air Force planes shot down that day. Porter and all but two of the prisoners in his camp were killed as a result of the atomic bomb blast on August 6, 1945.

What happened to Porter and Brissette may not have ever been known if Carleton Holden, an Army Air Corps second lieutenant during the war, had not come forward to be interviewed by M. Hill Goodspeed, library director and historian at the National Museum of Naval Aviation in Pensacola, Florida, and document research had not revealed the testimony of a Japanese soldier who had personal contact with both airmen. Holden crossed paths with a dying ARM3c Brissette and another Army Air Corps crewman from the B-24 Liberator *Lonesome Lady,* Staff Sargeant Ralph Neal. Holden's B-29 Superfortress *Nip Clipper* took a hit in the starboard wing near the number three engine as it banked away from a bombing run on the industrial city of Yawata on August 8, just two days after the *Enola Gay* dropped the atomic bomb on Hiroshima. The fire could not be extinguished and began eating away at *Nip Clipper's* wing. The crew bailed out and all but one, the aircraft commander, survived. He parachuted into the burning wreckage of the aircraft.

The crew of the *Nip Clipper* drifted in the sea for several days before being picked up by Japanese fishermen and turned over to military authorities. Blindfolded, the nine surviving crewmembers of *Nip Clipper* were taken to a revetment near a train station in Hiroshima. The terrible sight of Brissette and Neal awaited them in the revetment. Brissette and Neal were in grave condition from severe radiation poisoning, so much so that green pus flowed from their ears and neither could keep any food down. Holden spent time with Brissette maybe because both had in common that they were New Englanders and Brissette wanted to talk about home. Brissette came from Lowell, Massachusetts, and Holden from Maldin, located just a short distance away. Knowing he was going to die, Brissette asked Holden to tell his parents what happened to him if Holden survived whatever the Japanese had in store for he and the other prisoners.

Brissette died on August 19, 1945, just a few days after the end of World War II, while en route to the Fourth Branch of the Hiroshima War Prisoner's Camp. Holden survived and kept his promise to Brissette. Though Holden visited Brissette's parents to tell them exactly what happened to their son soon after his return to the United States, Brissette's mother was so shaken by the news of her son's fate, when she wrote to Porter's stepmother, she related only basic information. She never mentioned the atomic bombing. Porter's family would have to wait almost four years after the war to be told the official cause of their son's death by the Navy.

Raymond Porter's father was informed by the Bureau of Medicine and Surgery, Department of the Navy, on May 27, 1949, that the cremated remains of several American flyers had been recovered from Hiroshima City, Japan, by the American Graves Registration Service. The Navy explained the circumstances of Porter and Brissette's Helldiver going down, their subsequent capture, and the location of the prison in which they were held. After this notification was made, Porter's father was informed the Japanese cremated the remains. A Navy review of all the facts concluded that the ashes recovered by the American Graves Registration Service were, indeed, those of William B. Porter's son, Raymond, and the other prisoners who died on August 6.

Porter and Brissette's families were not made aware of facts taken from Japanese documents which reveal that in Saeki County near Hiroshima Prefecture, Private First Class Masumoto of the First Infantry Reserves, formerly the Eleventh Regiment, was dispatched to the village of Yahata to take into custody Porter and Brissette as well as members of an Army Air Corps bomber crew captured in Kuga County. Masumoto testified after the war that two American Navy airmen from the *Ticonderoga* exlaimed rather fearfully, "A bomb will be dropped soon that will completely destroy Hiroshima."

In the years since the end of World War II, research has led to a better understanding of the fate of the estimated seventeen American servicemen who died in the atomic bombing of Hiroshima. The day that Private Masumoto rounded up Porter and Brissette, there was also one airman from the *Randolph* who had been captured and taken to Yoshiki County in the Yamaguchi Prefecture. This pilot is believed to have been Lieutenant James E. "Buck" Toliver of Fighter Squadron Twelve (VF-12), who ditched off Hokada on February 17. But, if the pilot was Toliver, he died with Porter on August 6, and is not the "big, strong, and handsome pilot" Japanese eyewitnesses testified being taken to the Aloi Bridge in Hiroshima August 7, tied to a post, and stoned and clubbed to death. The identity of this pilot remains a mystery. "The pilot was probably not Raymond Porter," remarked Hill Goodspeed, "Porter was only 5'5" tall and weighed under 150 pounds. The pilot killed on the Aloi Bridge was quite large, some witnesses attesting to the fact the pilot was tall with particularly 'good looks.'"

The deaths of Porter and Brissette attest to the great sacrifice of young life in war. Porter was young, scared, and about to go to war when he started writing home about his experiences. He was going into the thick of a fight which records the unfortunate deaths of many youthful, vibrant, and intelligent men of his generation.

The impacts of war upon generations of young men like Porter are seldom assessed on the basis of their often insightfully written correspondence. Porter's letter of February 2, 1945, stated what no one else could tell us but those who met their end in a war. Of death and separation, Porter penned:

"I am wondering what it will be like going home after this war and not seeing these fellows I once knew. It doesn't seem right that so many young fellows should have their lives cut short like this, but I guess that is war. All we can do is hope and pray that it will soon be over."

Porter would never know.

hangar V-30, and the chief petty officers' club were wrecked. Thirty-three aircraft were totalled and others damaged. Hangars V-1 and V-2 were so far gone the Navy razed them and rebuilt. The heat from the blast was so intense, car tires blew, too. To this day, the explosion of September 17, 1943, remains the worst tragedy in Naval Air Station Norfolk's history. Personnel, male and female, were consumed by events of that day as were people throughout Hampton Roads who offered a helping hand.

It should be noted that throughout World War II, all branches of military service employed women. This is perhaps even more true of aviation components which, across the board, used women in more responsible positions, positions of authority requiring as much intellect as muscle. Naval Air Station Norfolk had an extraordinary number of women on its rolls. In yearbooks for any given year of the war, women's faces outnumber men's in many departments on the air station. The Navy treated women as players in the melodrama of war, and a few would die for their country. Seaman Second Class (Sea2c) Elizabeth Korensky was killed in the great explosion on the air station, September 17, 1943, thus becoming the first WAVE(2) to die in the line of duty during the war.

Women outnumbered men in administration, aviation repair shops, test and experimentation laboratories, flight control, and asundry technical and scientific disciplines. According to statistics of the period between 1942 and 1945, more than one in four WAVES, numbering about twenty-five thousand, worked in naval aviation alone. Their jobs at Norfolk as well as naval air stations around the country ranged from ground crew to instructors in aircraft gunnery, celestial navigation, and navigation. Women would fill critical slots in aviation ordnance, routine maintenance and repair, and aircraft assembly. As women completed college programs,

An aerial perspective of the September 17, 1943, explosion near the V-30 area shows hangar doors blown clear of buildings, fires raging, and structures quite literally obliterated at the blast epicenter. (Official United States Navy Photograph.)

The first squadron to make its home at Naval Auxiliary Landing Field Oceana was Fighter Squadron Nine (VF-9), established at Naval Air Station Norfolk in March 1942. Though the squadron was assigned to the USS *Essex* (CV-9), the *Essex* was still in the yards, so the squadron headed to Oceana to enjoy the open spaces proffered by the base's remote location. Fighting Nine was commanded by Lieutenant Commander John "Jack" Raby, and, at least initially, equipped with the Grumman F4F-3 Wildcat. With the *Essex* still under construction, VF-9 was temporarily attached to VF-41 aboard the USS *Ranger* (CV-4) and deployed as part of Operation Torch in November of that year. The squadron returned home shortly thereafter, and the *Essex* was commissioned on December 31. Fighting Nine's executive officer, Lieutenant Theodore Hugh Winters Jr., ferried VF-9's first Grumman F6F-3 Hellcat from the factory to Oceana on January 16, 1943, the first Hellcats to reach the fleet.

WAVE officers filled billets in aeronautical engineering, research, instrument flight checks, and so forth. The Navy did not allow women to become pilots, at least officially. Some women did manage to make their way into the cockpit, though none of these occasions are recorded for posterity.

Naval Air Station Norfolk was home to many squadrons during the war, ranging from fighters to large patrol bombers and transports. An advance detachment of Patrol Bombing Squadron One Hundred Seven (VB-107) from Norfolk, formerly designated VP-83, and equipped with new PB4Y-1 Liberator aircraft, arrived at Ascension Island to join Army Air Force units on antisubmarine warfare barriers and sweeps across the narrows of the South Atlantic. Commanding officer of VB-107 was Lieutenant Commander Renfro Turner Jr. who assumed command of the squadron from Lieutenant Commander Bertram J. Prueher on August 28, 1943.

The importance of having the Naval Air Transport Service on the Norfolk air station would become increasingly evident under the administrations of Captains Shoemaker and Greer. On November 10, 1943, the Naval Air Ferry Command was established as a wing of the Naval Air Transport Service for the purpose of ferrying new aircraft from contractors' plants and modification centers to embarkation points for ultimate delivery to the fleet. Captain Greer would oversee special emergency flights in connection with the Normandy invasion, "Operation Overlord," between May 15 and 23, 1944, by NATS aircraft. These planes carried 165,250 pounds of cargo across the Atlantic in sixteen trips. The cargo, according to official reports, "was of the most urgent nature and one of the factors upon which the success of the operation hinged."

At war's end, the commanding officer of the station was Captain George

A ground crewman secures the wing of a Curtiss SB2C Helldiver belonging to Bombing Squadron Eight (VB-8) in December of 1943 at Naval Air Station Norfolk. (Official United States Navy Photograph.)

A flight of VB-8 SB2C Helldivers from Norfolk fly in formation over the coastal operating area in December of 1943 just prior to their departure as part of Carrier Air Group Eight assigned to the USS *Intrepid* (CV-11). Bombing Squadron Eight was formerly designated Bombing Squadron Twenty-Eight (VB-28), a squadron established at Naval Air Station Norfolk on June 1, 1943. The designation change came on July 15, 1943, at which time Lieutenant Commander Ralph L. Shifley, was the squadron's commanding officer. Shifley assumed command of the squadron from acting commanding officer Ensign Robert L. Spohn, USNR, on June 2, 1943. The *Intrepid* departed Norfolk for the Pacific theater on December 11, 1943, and according to fleet records at the time of departure, the squadron had also flown the Douglas SBD-5 Dauntless aircraft. (Official United States Navy Photograph.)

The face of naval aviation was young and so full of life. Here, newly commissioned Ensign Falvey McKee "Sandy" Sandidge Jr. of Norfolk is shown shortly after graduating flight school at Naval Air Station Pensacola, Florida, in early 1944. This was still the silk scarf era of flying, and Sandidge truly loved to fly. He was destined to be on the cutting edge of naval aviation after the Second World War, particularly in the organizational development of airborne early warning squadrons on both coasts.

Navy pilots head to their Goodyear FG-1D Corsairs, parked on the flight line at Naval Air Station Norfolk, circa 1944. (Official United States Navy Photograph.)

Leo "Baron" Compo. Compo, a veteran of World War I, held his post at Norfolk from August 1944 to July 1947, thus seeing the air station transition from wartime operations to its new responsibilities as a center for demobilization, and reassignment and relocation of aircraft. During postwar years, Naval Air Station Norfolk continued to operate and expand, increasing and improving services provided the fleet and the many tenant commands cropping up all over the base. In fact, at the end of the Second World War in 1945, the Hepburn Board reviewed naval air stations for additional construction funding. Operational stations were those which the Hepburn Board report, and subsequent studies in support of authorized aircraft expansions, designated as bases for patrol squadrons and carrier group facilities. Large stations such as Norfolk also served the naval air training program in any number of important ways by acting as one of its primary operational training centers, an advanced school for flyers, per se. Norfolk, as a prewar facility, was enlarged well beyond the 1940 plan.

Naval Air Station Norfolk held the distinction of being not only one of the oldest air stations in the country but also the one with the most wartime construction on record. Its prewar landplane and seaplane facilities were augmented by construction of three runways and large seaplane parking areas with adjacent ramps. By 1945, there were six landplane hangars, three seaplane hangars, personnel facilities for 29,000, and 1,012,420 square feet of floor space in the assembly and repair shops. Aviation and other storage at the Norfolk air station covered about a million square feet, equivalent to that provided at a small supply depot.

One of the sites acquired in accordance with Hepburn Board recommendations was located in part of a marshy inlet at Willoughby Bay. Preparation work included constructing a culvert to carry a small amount of flow from the inlet, filling and draining the marsh, and

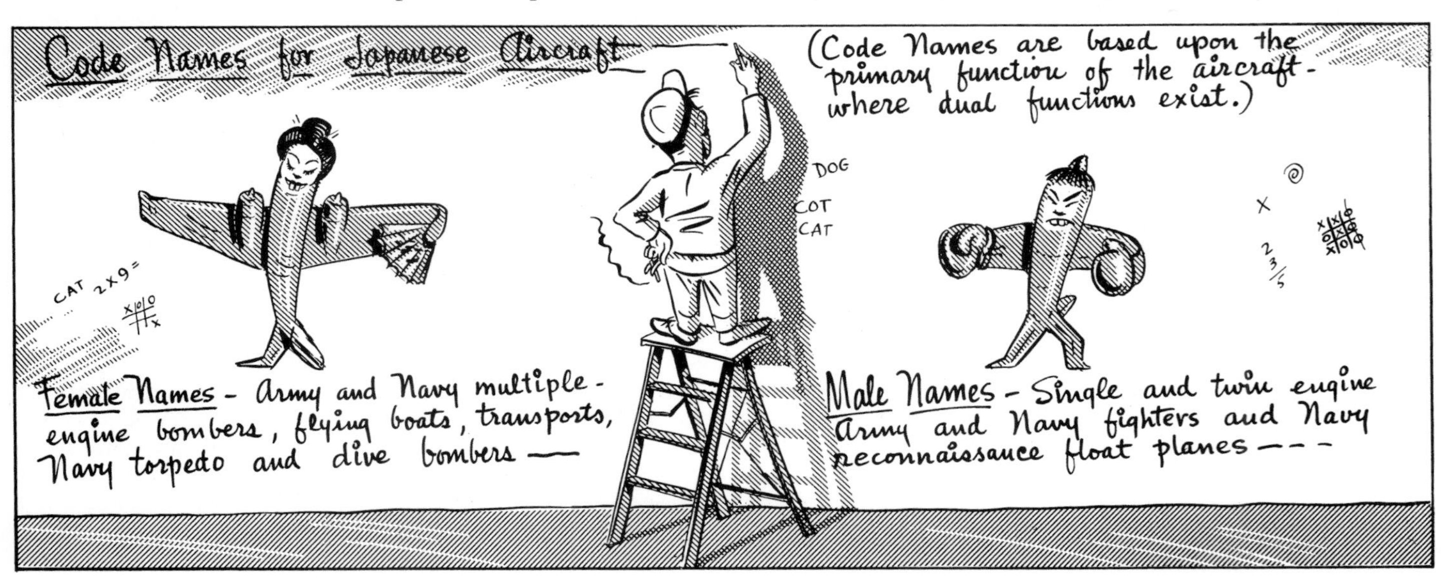

The Culver TD2C-1, Bureau Number 69541, was third in its production lot of Navy radio-controlled drone aircraft. In this three-quarter right front view, the aircraft's retractable landing gear is clearly visible. Powered by a 150-horsepower Franklin 0-300-11 engine, the TD2C-1 was ferried back and forth across the United States by Navy pilots, some of whom, like Nicholas J. Pope, now retired, had been patrol bomber pilots in the war. The photograph here was taken on May 23, 1944, a time when the Navy was near the height of its experimentation with drone aircraft. (Official United States Navy Photograph.)

building sheet pile bulkheads, behind which hydraulic fill could be deposited for land reclamation. More than 22.5 million cubic yards of fill was deposited, providing 352 acres of new land for the air station. The entire reclamation area would end up being about 1,785 acres, considerably more than the original forty-three reclaimed acres in the air station's early history. About thirty miles of drainage ditches had to be built as part of the drainage project. In reclaimed areas, it was necessary to wait for the land to settle before buildings could be constructed, and at various locations strata of quicksand necessitated the use of concrete mat or pile foundations. Most excavations were unwatered either by direct pumping or by the use of well points. Well points were also used to lower the ground water level at proposed building sites, thus hastening the needed ground settlement. Despite precautions, some differential settlement occurred in constructed buildings.

By the end of the 1940s, the Douglas AD-1 Skyraider with its air-cooled radial engine was the primary carrier attack aircraft, and it, serving side-by-side with the Grumman F8F Bearcat and Chance-Vought F4U Corsair rounded out the workhorses of the Navy's fighter-bombers but, jets were beginning to take over and this was never moreso apparent than on the flightline at the air station. Jet aircraft with names like the FD-1 Phantom, Sea Vampire F.20, F6U-1 Pirate, FJ-1 Fury, F9F Panther, F9F-8 Cougar, and F11F Tiger loomed on the horizon; the last three, in particular, were soon to dominate naval air squadrons in the Korean Conflict. In order to cater to jets and jet operations, Naval Air Station Norfolk was designated the support-industrial airfield; Naval Air Station Oceana, a master jet base; and airfields Chincoteague, Virginia, Edenton and Weeksville, North Carolina, and Fentress in Princess Anne County became auxiliaries. Commensurate with these changes, the Naval Air Transport Service (NATS) which had had such a presence at Norfolk, consolidated with the Air Transport Command to form the Military Air Transport Service (MATS) on June 1, 1948, a joint service effort resulting from the unified military establishment doctrine so prevalent at the time. The growth of naval aviation meant growth for Norfolk and, as a direct consequence, the Hampton Roads military complex. Once again in its long history, Naval Air Station Norfolk would become the testing ground for new aircraft, carrier based experimentation, and technological advancement both ashore and at sea, often times despite budgetary cutbacks and unwanted force reduction.

Less than a year after the end of the Second World War, in August of 1946, a Marine Air Reserve Training Detachment (MARTD) was established at Naval Air Station Norfolk in support of Marine Reserve Fighter Squadron Two Hundred Thirty-Three (VMF-233), flying the Chance-Vought F4U Corsair. The association of the Marine Corps Reserve with Norfolk has lasted over fifty years, but their presence is too often overlooked. Historically, the squadron has flown everything from fixed-wing propeller-driven and jet aircraft to helicopters.

In the immediate postwar era, Naval

The Grumman JRF-5 Goose, photograph circa 1946, had two Pratt & Whitney R-985-AN-6 engines rated at 450-horsepower. The aircraft had a forty-nine-foot wingspan, and was thirty-eight feet, six inches, in length. The one shown here was stationed at Naval Air Station Norfolk and, at the time the picture was taken, had just passed over downtown Norfolk heading south on a training flight. (Official United States Navy Photograph.)

Combat-experienced Navy and Marine Corps pilots flooded reserve units after the war. There were 10,229 active duty officer pilots and forty-seven active duty "flying sergeants" in the Marine Corps in 1945. Active duty pilots dropped to 1,948 in 1948, while there was an increase in enlisted Marine Corps aviators whose numbers climbed from forty-seven three years earlier to 352.

The *Truculent Turtle*

Over the years, sundry naval aircraft have been displayed at naval base gates across Hampton Roads. Perhaps the greatest of them all was the famous *Truculent Turtle,* now restored and on display at the National Museum of Naval Aviation, Naval Air Station Pensacola, Florida. For many years, this grandiose Lockheed P2V-1 Neptune sat at the corner of Granby Street and Taussig Boulevard. One of her command pilots, Commander Thomas D. Davies, became commanding officer (as a captain) of Naval Air Station Norfolk in September 1963 and held that post until July 1964. This plane, which sat for so many years silent at the gate, was third in the first production lot of Neptunes, Bureau Number 89082, with its armament removed and nose fairing extended.

The popularly known *Truculent Turtle* set the world long-distance record with its 11,236-mile nonstop flight from Perth, Australia, to Columbus, Ohio, in 1946. The flight took fifty-five hours, seventeen minutes and was manned by Commander (later Rear Admiral) Thomas D. Davies, pilot; Commander (later Captain) Eugene P. Rankin, copilot; and pilots Commander (later Captain) Walter S. Reid and Lieutenant Commander (later Commander) Roy S. Tabeling, copilot on the first leg.

The pilots prepared for six months, working pre-flight strategy. The plane was ready for takeoff at ten minutes past six in the evening (Perth time) on Sunday, September 29, 1946, from the Royal Australian Air Force's Pearce Aerodrome Field. The *Turtle* crew had been given its mandate by the Chief of Naval Operations, Admiral Chester W. Nimitz, who wrote in July 1946 to the Secretary of the Navy that the flight was for: "the purpose of investigating the means of extension of present patrol aircraft ranges, physiological limitations on patrol plane crew endurance and long-range navigation by pressure pattern methods, it is proposed to make a nonstop flight of a P2V-1 aircraft from Perth, Australia, to Washington, D.C. (11,568 statute miles), with the possibility, weather permitting, of extending the flight to Bermuda."

The P2V-1 had a ground run of 4,720 feet, and with its two 2,500-horsepower Wright Duplex Cyclone engines, her pilots pulled the *Turtle* smoothly off the runway—that is, with a little help from four jet assisted takeoff (JATO) units attached to the Neptune's sides. Jet assisted takeoff bottles gave the aircraft another one thousand pounds of static thrust for twelve seconds. Additional thrust was certainly needed; the *Turtle* had an incredible gross weight of 85,575 pounds compared to the plane's empty weight of 29,240 pounds. The Neptune was also carrying 8,467 gallons of gas on board, fifty-nine percent of its gross weight, with a wing loading of 85.5 pounds per square foot, then one of the greatest ever recorded for any aircraft.

The *Turtle* crew had plotted five alternative routes, all converging on Washington, D.C., and Bermuda—the island being almost exactly halfway around the world from their point of origin in Perth, Australia. The crew expected inclement weather, icing, and headwinds, all of which struck at some point in the flight. Davies would ultimately make the decision to land in his home state of Ohio rather than push on to the nation's capitol. The P2V-1 ran into particularly bad weather over Bougainville, a little island off the northeast coast of Australia in the Coral Sea, and again over New Guinea. The aircraft entered an equatorial front that stretched over 250 miles. The pilots climbed to twelve thousand feet as the Neptune droned over Shortland and the Marshall Islands, near Midway Island, where the flyers encountered their second sunrise. The sunrise was spectacular as the *Turtle's* pilots pointed the aircraft for Marco Reef in the Hawaiian Islands.

The flight of the *Truculent Turtle* spawned quite a bit of radio traffic up and down the West Coast as folks coast to coast pulled for the P2V-1 to make its ultimate destination and set the record. The *Turtle* crew established communication with Honolulu, its last radio contact until the aircraft reached the West Coast of the United States fourteen hours later, hitting the California coast near Point Cabrillo, California.

In proximity to Ogden, Utah, the plane encountered more bad weather and an incredible phenomenon known to ancient mariners as St. Elmo's fire. Fireballs formed on the tips of the Turtle's propellers and electrical tongues of flame raced up and down the windscreens. One engine sputtered under the phenomenon and actually stopped for a matter of moments before coming to life with an injection of carburetor heat. The crew had a few tense moments as Mother Nature played with fire.

As the aircraft leapt across the rest of the United States to Omaha, Nebraska; Peoria, Illinois; and finally, Columbus, Ohio, Commander Davies made the decision to end the extraordinary flight and landed at Port Columbus on October 1, 1946, having covered 11,500 ground miles, and due to headwinds, 11,665 statute miles. In true naval aviator fashion, the crew exited the aircraft with a thirty-five pound baby kangaroo which had made the historic trip unscathed—the first kangaroo aircrew—and a history-making one to boot.

The *Turtle's* pilots received the Distinguished Flying Cross for their efforts. They proved above all else that it is physically possible for a four-man crew to endure twelve thousand mile flights.

The famed Lockheed P2V-1 Neptune, known affectionately by her equally famous aircrew as the *Truculent Turtle,* sat at the corner of what was, at least in the 1950s and 1960s, Granby Street and Taussig Boulevard. She remained at the Breezy Point Gate for nearly twenty years before being shipped to the National Museum of Naval Aviation in Pensacola, Florida. (Courtesy of Naval Air Station Norfolk.)

Key members of the *Truculent Turtle* history-making aircrew returned to Naval Air Station Norfolk in 1956 for a ten-year reunion. (Left to right) Captain Eugene Rankin, Assistant for Naval Operations to the Commander-in-Chief, Atlantic Fleet, Naval Base Norfolk; Commander Roy S. Tabeling, Bureau of Aeronautics, Washington, D.C.; and Captain Thomas D. Davies, Commanding Officer, Naval Air Material Center, Philadelphia, Pennsylvania, struck a pose with the wonderful turtle artwork on the nose of their famous aircraft. (Courtesy of Naval Air Station Norfolk.)

Davies, Rankin, and Tabeling posed for one last formal photograph in front of the *Truculent Turtle* in 1956, ten years after their world renowned and record-breaking flight. (Courtesy of Naval Air Station Norfolk.)

Years had passed and visitors become few for the famed *Truculent Turtle* at the corner of Granby Street and Taussig Boulevard. The aircraft had already begun to exhibit signs of wear from exposure to the elements when this picture was taken. (Courtesy of Naval Air Station Norfolk.)

"Daddy's little girl" tries on his cover, circa 1947. "Patty" (Patricia) Sandidge, daughter of Lieutenant Falvey McKee Sandidge Jr. of Norfolk, was just able to walk when she sported Sandidge's khaki cover.

On April 1, 1948, the Navy established Helicopter Utility Squadron One (HU-1) and HU-2 at Naval Air Station Lakehurst, New Jersey, and accepted the HO3S-1 and Bell HTL-2 as the squadrons' first aircraft. Helicopter Utility Squadron One (HU-1) was assigned to the West Coast and HU-2 remained on the East Coast. During the summer of 1948, helicopter utility squadrons began providing plane guards to the aircraft carriers, but only after a rigorous experimental period to test the viability of their service as utility platforms and plane guards to the fleet. The squadrons sent a detachment of two HO3S-1 aircraft to fleet carriers when the helicopter deployed to a carrier. The HO3S-1 made its debut aboard the USSs *Boxer* and *Princeton.* The HO3S-1 aircraft, shown here, was lifting off the USS *Kearsarge* (CV-33) near the coast of Malta during the May to September 1948 Mediterranean Sea deployment.

The insignia formerly worn by the *Sunday Punchers* of Attack Squadron Seventy-Five (VA-75) was a scrappy little boy wearing boxing gloves and riding a bomb. The design was completed after the Second World War, and approved for use on June 25, 1947, for the squadron, then designated VA-7A. This original insignia was intended to project fighting spirit so the boy's facial expression was one of fierce determination. Squadron literature indicated the insignia shown here, a bomb coming through a boxing glove placed over a pair of aviator wings, is symbolic of the haymaker punch, a knockout punch. The design was initially approved by the Bureau of Aeronautics for Bombing Squadron Eighteen (VB-18) but, of course, the boy with boxing gloves replaced it in 1947. The insignia as it is displayed here, the same as the one used in 1945, reappeared with modifications around 1970.

Air Station Norfolk would also become home to a whole new class of flying machine: the helicopter, popularly called a "whirlybird" in its infancy. Helicopters were thought to be a relatively new development in the late 1940s and 1950s when, in truth, the Navy had begun experimenting with the autogiro configuration in the 1930s at Norfolk and the rudimentary drawings of a Navy chief in 1912. Lieutenant Alfred Melville "Al" Pride, famed aviator who later retired as an admiral, landed the XOP-1 autogiro aboard the USS *Langley* on September 23, 1931. At the time of his historic flight, Pride was the officer-in-charge of the Experimental Detachment at the air station. Since no practical application of the autogiro was deemed possible in 1931, the helicopter would have to wait until 1943, and even then, its use would be quite limited. The postwar climate was fueled by intense competition by aircraft manufacturers to build whirlybirds for the military, the Navy included. The helicopter would play a major role in the Korean Conflict where many downed pilots were rescued from behind enemy lines by the newest Navy aircraft. By 1949, the Navy made Norfolk a base of operations for helicopters, causing many local residents to stare skyward, mouth agape, as they darted overhead. At least by the time the Navy stationed helicopters on the base, it was a proven airframe. It is interesting to note that helicopters were used as observation platforms at the Bikini atom bomb tests in late July of 1946, and again on Admiral Richard E. Byrd's "Operation Highjump" expedition to the Antarctic which departed Norfolk on January 2, 1947.

The Second World War had been over less than a year when Marine Air Detachment, Naval Air Station Norfolk was established on July 3, 1946, in support of Marine Reserve Fighter Squadron 233 (VMF-233), reactivated on August 8, 1946, and flying the F4U-4 Corsair. The mission of the reserve detachment was to train Marine reservists to support operations of the Marine Air Reserve Training Program as directed by the Commander of Marine Air Reserve Training.

The first helicopter squadron in Norfolk was actually a detachment of Helicopter Utility Squadron Two (HU-2), homeported at Lakehurst, New Jersey. The squadron's arrival at Norfolk in the summer of 1949 was met with much anticipation as area based ships were gaining a faster means of ship-to-shore transfer of cargo and passengers. The unit was commanded by Lieutenant Commander Alton B. Payne who had been a Navy pilot since 1942. HU-2's Norfolk detachment consisted of Payne, eighteen mechanics, and six pilots including Lieutenant Edward J. Larkin, Lieutenant Clarence Harbour, and Chief Aviation Controlman William J. Price, one of the Navy's few enlisted helicopter pilots. Since there were no hangar spaces set aside for the detachment on their

Fighter Squadron Thirty-Three changed their tactical call sign from the *Tarsiers* to *Starfighters* in early 1981, though the new insignia did not appear until late 1987. The *Tarsier* never quite went away, however, since it held the longest history with the squadron. Both versions are shown here. The *Tarsier* call sign and insignia evolved from the time of the squadron's establishment on October 12, 1948, and continued thus until Fighting Thirty-Three was disestablished in 1993 during an initial drawdown of F-14 Tomcat squadrons at Naval Air Station Oceana. The tarsier, as a matter of explanation, looks somewhat like a monkey-type squirrel with some characteristics so much its own the animal has been assigned to genus *Tarasius.* This small nocturnal East Indian mammal is actually related to the lemur, hence the enormous pair of goggle eyes. The squadron adapted their insignia from this nimble beast, accentuating his teeth as large fangs, and making the little fellow's eyes look quite ferocious.

Santa arrived by helicopter, ferried from the North Pole by Lieutenant Edward J. Larkin of Helicopter Utility Squadron Two's Norfolk detachment. Larkin delivered Santa Claus to the flight deck of the escort carrier USS *Mindoro* (CVE-120), berthed at Naval Station Norfolk, on December 23, 1951. Santa was portrayed by Boatswain's Mate C.L. Jones. He gathered the children about him on a forward elevator. The helicopter is an HO3S-1.

The Navy's Strangest Air Mission

A new chapter in naval aviation and crime history was written in February of 1954 with what observers called "The Navy's Strangest Air Mission." Norfolk's own Lieutenant Falvey McKee Sandidge Jr., a pilot attached to Helicopter Antisubmarine Squadron Three at Weeksville, North Carolina, played the pivotal role in the capture of the Bacardi heir kidnaper. Sandidge's helicopter would turn the tide against Manuel Hecheverria, the sole accomplice in the kidnapping of Facundito Bacardi. As Hecheverria dragged eight-year-old Facundito into Cuba's mountainous terrain, Lieutenant Sandidge and his crew gave chase, their strange looking "whirlybird" creating great fear and panic for the little boy's kidnaper. Hecheverria was so frightened that he fled toward a highway and was apprehended by the police. He would later tell them he needed protection from the "whirlybird."

Manuel Hecheverria was sentenced to four years in prison for his role in the kidnapping. His fate was far better than the mastermind of the ill-fated kidnap plot. Guillermo Rodriquez was killed in a hail of bullets after being cornered by Cuban Army troops. Rodriquez, a chauffeur for Daniel Bacardi—great-grandson of the founder of the famous Bacardi rum distillery—concocted the plot to kidnap Daniel's eldest son while taking him to school the morning of February 19, 1954. Somewhere between school and the Bacardi home, Rodriquez dropped young Facundito with Hecheverria. He then proceeded to deliver a ransom note to the Bacardi family asking for fifty thousand dollars for the boy's safe return. Otherwise, Facundito would be killed. His plans backfired.

The Naval Air Station at Guantanamo Bay, Cuba, was called in to search for the boy and Hecheverria. Though there were no helicopters available at the air station, it just happened that the carrier USS *Antietam* (CVS-36) was in the harbor with four Sikorsky helicopters aboard. Lieutenant Commander Robert E. Hickle, of Jacksonville, Florida, hurriedly briefed his pilots who departed immediately to look for the boy—time was running out. Sandidge remarked during interviews afterward that "we flew forty to fifty miles back into those mountains. The people had never seen a helicopter before, and came out of their mud huts and did one of two things: they stared up in fright, or ran." Fortunately, Hecheverria was so frightened that he gave up and ran. Of course, Sandidge and his crew had no idea they had successfully aborted the kidnapers' plans.

It was not until the Navy helicopters reached an airfield near Santiago, Cuba, that news of Facundito's release reached them. Daniel Bacardi was at the airfield waiting for the heroes when they landed. He was overjoyed to have his son safely returned and, as a gesture of thanks, planned to take the Navy pilots to a hotel in town for an evening of celebration. Sandidge recalled that this turned out to be more of an adventure than the search for young Bacardi. "We really were scared when some Cubans, carrying guns, knives, and cannon, stopped us on the road [to town]." The Cubans were unaware the boy had been recovered, thus they continued searching every car on Cuban highways for him. Ironically, the very helicopter pilots who triggered Facundito Bacardi's release were among those detained until they properly identified themselves.

In the end, Bacardi did take the pilots to the hotel and bought them drinks—Bacardi rum, of course. Daniel Bacardi would credit the Navy helicopter pilots with saving his son's life.

The Bacardi kidnapping case made headlines. Shown on the flight deck of the USS *Antietam*, February 20, 1954, reviewing their actions that resulted in the dramatic rescue of eight-year-old Facundito Bacardi, heir to the Bacardi fortune, were the officers and men of the HS-3 Detachment who participated in the search and rescue. Shown are, front left to right, Lieutenant Falvey McKee Sandidge Jr. of Norfolk, Virginia; Lieutenant Commander Robert E. Hickle of Jacksonville, Illinois, and officer-in-charge of the detachment; (rear left to right) Aviation Machinist's Mate First Class (AD1) Teddie J. Lonski of Jamestown, North Dakota; Lieutenant William W. Loy of Keyser, West Virginia; Lieutenant (junior grade) Richard C. Fowler of Marblehead, Massachusetts; and Aviation Machinist's Mate Second Class (AD2) Richard P. Allen of Baltimore, Maryland. (Official United States Navy Photograph.)

In this picture, dated May 3, 1950, eight Marine Air Reserve pilots had checked out in jet planes with Air Reserve Fighter Squadron 233, Norfolk. They flew the McDonnell FH-1 Phantoms. Shown after a qualifying flight are (left to right) First Lieutenant T.B. Wilson, Norfolk; First Lieutenant Andy Yates, Arlington, Virginia; First Lieutenant W.A. Higgins, Waverly, Virginia; First Lieutenant Forris M. Hollowell, instructor, from the Churchland section of Portsmouth, Virginia; First Lieutenant Robert W. Cole, Richmond; First Lieutenant Russell Friske, Harrellsville; First Lieutenant Jerome Miner, Raleigh, North Carolina; First Lieutenant J.B. Hardy, Norfolk; and First Lieutenant Edward J. Cieszko, Richmond. Of the thirty-eight pilots in the squadron, more than half were flying the FH-1 Phantoms at that time. (Official United States Marine Corps Photograph.)

arrival, they worked out of quonset line shacks in the Breezy Point area of the air station.

Helicopters from HU-2 would account for many of the daring rescues at sea in these early years (much as they do today) as they took gravely ill sailors off ships at sea, saved watermen and pleasure boaters from rough seas, and transported medical supplies aboard ships in dire need of replenishment. Helicopters from HU-2 and HS-3 aboard the USS *Valley Forge* (LPH-8), a converted aircraft carrier, rescued twenty-seven men from the oiler SS *Pine Ridge* as she was breaking up in heavy seas one hundred miles off Cape Hatteras, North Carolina, December 22, 1960, perhaps the best example of daring rescues executed by Navy helicopters from Norfolk.

Naval Air Station Norfolk was the home of two basic types of helicopters during the Korean Conflict period, the older Sikorsky HO3S single rotor, and the newer Piasecki HUP-1. The HO3S had a long skinny afterbody ending in a small vertical propeller used for flight control and the pyramid shaped structure supporting the main rotor amidship. The Piasecki model had the thicker fuselage with very little tapering off forward to aft. The forward rotor sat atop the pilot's cockpit, the aft rotor over a single vertical tail rudder. Another visitor was the Bell HTL. The Bell model had no afterbody, its rotor perched atop a fragile framework over the pilot's bubble. The HTL also landed on skids. Even the original Piasecki "Flying Banana," the first tandem rotor helicopter operated by the military, came to the air station in 1951. The "Flying Banana" was first flown for the Navy in 1945 by its creator, Frank Nicholas Piasecki, an aviation pioneer and one of the fathers of helicopter aviation. Piasecki's famous twin-rotor whirlybird, also the first helicopter designed exclusively for the Navy, is now at the National Air and Space Museum in Washington, D.C.

The air station at Norfolk would play host to quite a number of other types as well, some outright visitors, others on a hop participating in maneuvers from nearby Naval Amphibious Base Little Creek,(3) established August 10, 1945, had been a series of camps prior to its official designation as a naval base. Even after designation, Little Creek made an excellent training ground for Navy and Marine Corps personnel operating from helicopters. It is important to remember that a critical element of the amphibious mission remains helicopter aviation; without it, an essential part of the amphibious ready group would be missing.

Even amidst the intense tempo of training by Navy and Marine Corps servicemen in preparation for tours of duty in Korea, a little humor crept in once in awhile. Local papers reported the

The Convair XFY-1, known as the *Pogo Stick,* was first flown in April 1954. It was powered by twin Allison T-40 turboprop engines and featured vertical takeoff and horizontal flight.

From April 1954 to August the same year, *"Pogo"* only flew anchored down in a hangar. The first free flight with the aircraft occurred in August but this was only vertical. In November 1954, horizontal flight was accomplished after fitting *"Pogo"* with horizontal landing gear. The XFY-1 sat at the Naval Air Station Norfolk Gate Four for many years. The photograph here was taken about 1960. (Official United States Navy Photograph.)

story of a perplexed duty officer at Fleet Aircraft Service Squadron 102, which serviced HU-2's detachment. He had received a phoned request for gasoline from Lieutenant Harbour, unusual since the gas truck was parked within a few feet of the helicopter shack. The duty officer demanded something to the effect: "Why don't you just look out the window and call him yourself [Harbour]?" to which the pilot replied, "I would, only the helicopter is parked in the Ocean View Amusement Park lot, and I'm phoning from the lobby of the Pinecrest Hotel."

The Bureau of Aeronautics authorized the establishment of "Project Arowa" or Applied Research Operational Weather Analysis at Naval Air Station Norfolk on October 2, 1950. The purpose of the facility was to develop basic meterological research data into practical weather forecasting techniques, critical to planning and execution of naval air missions.

Before the end of the decade of the 1950s, Naval Air Station Norfolk stood not just at the forefront of aircraft, maintenance, and personnel achievement. Its flight physiology department made tremendous strides in aircrew flight performance under various degrees of altitude. Lieutenant R.H. Tabor, wearing a Goodrich lightweight full-pressure suit, completed a seventy-two hour simulated flight in the pressure chamber at Naval Air Station Norfolk, September 8, 1958, in which Tabor was subjected to altitude conditions as high as 139,000 feet. He would surpass the record set May 11, 1958, by Lieutenant Commander Jack Neiman, who completed a forty-four hour simulated high altitude flight in the pressure chamber, also at Naval Air Station Norfolk, and under conditions characteristic of eighty to one hundred thousand feet.

A Grumman F8F Bearcat belonging to activated Marine Corps reservists from Norfolk is shown here after a crash near Merit, North Carolina, March 19, 1951. (Official United States Marine Corps Photograph.)

Emily: Aeronautical Marvel Returns to Japan

For thirty-two years, a World War II Japanese seaplane, the largest of all operational Japanese wartime aircraft, was stored at a remote location on Naval Air Station Norfolk. Nicknamed the Emily by Allied forces in the Pacific theater, this one-of-a-kind seaplane was transferred from United States Navy inventory to the Museum of Maritime Science in Tokyo harbor on April 23, 1979, by Vice Admiral Forrest S. Peterson, Commander Naval Air Systems Command, during formal ceremonies on the air station. Emily was far from beautiful when she left Norfolk for Japan. Three decades of prolonged exposure to the elements, including a hurricane, had damaged the aircraft's protective sheath and rust bubbled and scaled off her expansive fuselage.

The Japanese built the Emily seaplane for long-range patrols, transport and reconnaissance missions though the aircraft's crews also participated in limited bombing and torpedo runs during the war. A single Emily actually attacked Oahu, Territory of Hawaii, on March 1, 1942, and albeit unsuccessful, the aircraft displayed remarkable distance capabilities. Advisories published by Fleet Training Center Oahu during the war called the Emily the most successful aircraft designed by the Japanese. Although many Japanese planes had outstanding performance records in one or more respects, performance figures for the Emily indicated the seaplane could move and climb faster and travel much farther than any Allied flying boat while carrying an equal bomb load. American naval forces encountered the Emily in every combat zone in the Pacific. Emilys could carry eight 550-pound bombs or two 1,765-pound torpedoes.

The Emily which found its way to the United States was a prize of war claimed by United States Navy forces at Yokohama, Japan. At war's end, the Emily was ferried across the Pacific aboard a seaplane tender to Naval Air Station Whidbey Island, Washington, where it was quickly determined the aircraft was not in flying condition and should be taken to Naval Air Station Norfolk through the Panama Canal route. With National Advisory Committee for Aeronautics (NACA) scientists, engineers and test pilots at Langley Field and their counterparts at Naval Air Station Norfolk already engaged in evaluation and testing of captured German and Japanese aircraft, Navy evaluators at Whidbey Island were confident Norfolk offered the best environment for further study.

Though a wonderful learning platform, the Emily presented stumbling blocks the Navy had never before encountered with such a complex aircraft. There was no maintenance manual in English for workers at the air station's Overhaul and Repair Department as they sought to rebuild the aircraft, officially known as a Kawanishi H8K-Type 2 aircraft with the Serial Number 426, the last of 167 such aircraft which went into production in Japan in 1940. Without the benefit of good instructions and system diagrams, the facility's engineers and technicians began the laborious task of rebuilding the seaplane. The aircraft supported a wingspan of 124.7 feet and was powered by four 1,850-horsepower Kasei 22 engines. Aircraft weight without any of the frills was 38,096 pounds. Extensive repairs were made to the hull; flight controls; fuel, lubrication, and electrical systems.

By the time all the work was completed, a United States Navy flight crew had been selected from United States Naval Test Flight Center, Patuxent River, Maryland, to fly the Emily from Norfolk to the flight center for further testing and evaluation. The aircrew consisted of Commander Thomas F. Connolly, Lieutenant Commander Jack Shrefer and two chief aviation machinist's mates. The crew encountered serious trouble on the flight to Patuxent River as one by one the Emily's engines began to fail. Connolly and Shrefer landed her with two engines fully func-

Kawanishi H8K-Type 2 Emily flying boat, Naval Air Station Norfolk, Virginia, 1979.

tioning but even they were questionable. The date of this flight was May 23, 1946, the Emily's first and last logged flight in United States territorial waters.

Though her first and last recorded American flight was a disappointment, the Emily continued to be seen taxiing and making short flights on Patuxent River but the flights were nothing akin to real flying time. Her project pilot, Commander J.A. Ferguson, lifted the aircraft off the water and set her down again almost immediately. After nearly fifteen thousand total airframe flight hours, the Navy ended its testing for design and operational information on January 30, 1947. Later that year, Emily came back to Norfolk where she sat in storage for decades. Repeated attempts to restore the Kawanishi H8K-Type 2 failed and the elements did the rest. A hurricane in 1960 tore the aircraft away from her tie-downs, turned the seaplane on its starboard side and displaced the number four engine from its mount. The wing and hull sustained signicant damage as well.

One might wonder why the Emily, considered a majestic marvel of aeronautical engineering, could not be restored by the Navy after the war. Public law at that time prohibited the Navy from restoration of historic aircraft. The same law also demanded that such aircraft could only be donated to a museum operated and maintained for educational purposes with a charter for nonprofit use. This policy was still in effect even in 1979. The Japanese Museum of Maritime Science came to the Navy in 1976 with the requisite credentials and enough funding to get the Emily back to Japan without the United States government incurring any cost. The Japanese plan was sanctioned by the United States Congress and formal transfer discussions began.

Japanese engineers were dispatched to Norfolk to disassemble the Kawanishi and carefully place her fuselage parts, tail section and wings on a Japanese merchant ship bound for the museum in Tokyo harbor in the spring of 1979. The Museum of Maritime Science, built to resemble a sixty-thousand-ton ocean liner and located at a prominent point on the mouth of Tokyo Bay, was designed as an educational facility to instill an appreciation and understanding of the sea to the young people of Japan.

World War II aircraft spotters used the recognition profiles shown here for the Emily. The recognition profiles for the Emily were taken from an original Navy aircraft recognition manual used by the Fleet Training Center at Oahu, Territory of Hawaii.

"EMILY"

- NARROW HULL, POINTED BOW
- GRACEFUL CURVE TO UNDERSIDE OF HULL FROM NOSE TO TAIL
- HIGH WING, SINGLE FIN AND RUDDER
- WINGS SLENDER AND EVENLY TAPERED TIPS, FIXED WING FLOATS
- SMALL TAIL PLANE, ROUNDED TIPS
- FOUR ENGINES

The aircraft recognition manual used at Oahu was conceived in an effort to provide recognition instruction to fighter director officers. The caricature drawings of the airplanes were designed to underline and exaggerate peculiarities of the aircraft that would have made it stand out in memory. The Emily caricature shown here was taken from the manual.

The Emily was taken by the United States Navy as a prize of war off Yokohama, Japan. The Emily was encountered frequently in all combat zones in the Pacific. This drawing was excerpted from the aircraft recognition manual promulgated by the Navy's Fleet Training Center at Oahu.

Chapter 11: Arrivals, Departures, and the Nuclear Age

The patrol community remained the backbone of naval aviation after the Second World War, entering the Cold War period with new aircraft and equipment. Moreso than any other naval aviation community at that time, patrol aviators bore the brunt of Soviet and Chinese aggression in the air. There would be repeated incidents of patrol aircraft lost to enemy fire in the 1950s, fatalities abounded and being a patrol aviator became one of the most dangerous jobs in the Navy. The mainstay of landbased patrol aircraft from roughly 1947 through 1962 was the Lockheed P2V Neptune, capable of carrying a crew of nine to ten men. Patrol squadrons maintained a presence all over the globe. The Neptune was susceptible, however, to heavy losses without the benefit of fighter cover. This proved true on most of the squadrons' routine patrols over international waters during the height of tensions with China and the Soviet Union. To support this point, on November 6, 1951, a Neptune aircraft belonging to Patrol Squadron Six failed to return from a weather reconnaissance mission over international waters off Siberia after Soviet fighters fired on it. Subsequently, a Patrol Squadron Twenty-Two Neptune, conducting routine patrol operations over the Formosa Strait on January 19, 1953, was shot down off Swatowby by Red Chinese antiaircraft fire. Seven of the ten men aboard the VP-22 aircraft were killed. Less than a year later, on September 4, 1954, a Neptune of Patrol Squadron Nineteen on routine reconnaissance over international waters was attacked by two Soviet MiGs and forced down off the Siberian coast. Nine of the Neptune's ten aircrew escaped and were later rescued. A Patrol Squadron Nine (VP-9) P2V-5 Neptune aircraft, a squadron newly established on March 15, 1951, had been operating in the Aleutian area when it was detected by a pair of Soviet MiG-15 fighters which set fire to the Neptune's starboard engine and forced it down. The date was June 1, 1955, and though no one died, this proved a harrowing experience for the crew which was rescued off St. Lawrence Island near Gambell.

The 1960s brought about several changes, including the departure of some tenant commands and the arrival of new ones, but, with few exceptions, most change spawned new growth at the Norfolk air station. During the summer of 1960, Captain G.P. Koch, who was then commanding officer, received more than two million dollars in appropriations from Congress for new construction. Perhaps a sad footnote in its passing, a P-5B Marlin seaplane marked the end of an era when it made the last flight of a seaplane into Willoughby Bay on December 30, 1963. Seaplanes were being replaced by the Lockheed P-3A Orion. Koch's successor as commanding officer of the air station, Captain Thomas D. Davies, of *Truculent Turtle* fame, would have appreciated the significance of the Marlin's last flight: his, too, had been the age of grand aircraft. Davies commanded the station from September 1963 through July 1964.

The early 1960s brought mission essential commands and technologies to the naval air station and the Atlantic Fleet. While the retirement of seaplanes from the fleet was what some aviators have called the closure of a second golden era of naval aviation, the Navy had conducted intense studies of command and control of the air of fleet aviation via an airborne early warning platform was critical to the success of the carrier battle group in an era of Cold War warriors.

Carrier airborne early warning squadrons in today's Navy can trace their origins to Project Cadillac, a

Taken April 2, 1954, at Naval Air Station Oceana, this photograph depicts the reception committee for the record-breaking trio of VF-21 who made national news when they unofficially broke the cross-country speed record in their new Grumman F9F-7 Cougars. Pictured are (left to right) Mrs. F.X. "Gus" Brady; Lieutenant Commander F.X. Brady; Rear Admiral Frederick N. Kivette, Naval Aviator No. 3409, Chief of Staff, Commander Naval Air Force Atlantic Fleet; Lieutenant (junior grade) J.C. Barrow; and Lieutenant W. Rich. The children are Mary Anne, James, and John Brady. Rear Admiral Kivette had recorded quite a bit of naval aviation history himself as a young junior lieutenant aboard the ill-fated USS *Macon* (ZRS-5), the last of the United States Navy's large rigid dirigibles. He survived its deadly crash at sea February 12, 1935, and went on to have a successful naval career. VF-21 was a lineal antecedent of the VF-43 *Challenger* squadron which was disestablished at Oceana in 1994. (Official United States Navy Photograph.)

An AJ-2 Savage is shown about to touch down on USS *Yorktown* (CVA-10) as an AD-5N Skyraider awaits to be deck launched, December 6, 1955. (Official United States Navy Photograph.)

The Navy's S2F-2 Tracker, a twin-engine carrier-based plane, was used in anti-submarine search and attack. The S2F, a Grumman aircraft, was a high-wing monoplane powered by two 1,525-horsepower engines. The Tracker had a retractable radome under the rear fuselage behind a large bomb bay, and carried a crew of four. The Tracker was first produced in 1953. (Official United States Navy Photograph.)

program initiated in 1942 to develop airborne radar relay platforms. By June 1945, the first group of Eastern Aircraft TBM-3 Avengers, modified carrier airborne early warning (AEW) TBM-3s, were conducting trials with the USS *Ranger*. The end of World War II meant these first AEW units never saw action but, following the war, fleet aviation electronics training units (FAETUs) were established on both coasts and continued to train pilots, operators and maintenance personnel on AEW equipment. Carrier Airborne Early Warning Squadron One (VAW-1) on the West Coast and VAW-2 on the East Coast were formed to replace the FAETUs in 1948. Within a year, VAW-2 was redesignated VC-12 and relocated to Naval Air Station Quonset Point, Rhode Island, where the TBM-3W was replaced with the Douglas AD-3W Skyraider. During the Korean Conflict, VC-12 sent detachments to deploy aboard West Coast carriers bound for Korean waters.

Fleet Composite Squadron Twelve (VC-12) continued to operate an improved version of the Skyraider, the AD-5W, until 1960 when the squadron acquired the new Grumman WF-1 Tracer, also called the "Willy Fudd," and later redesignated as the E-1B. VC-12 was redesignated VAW-12 in 1960 and, in

A P2V-3C Neptune of Composite Squadron Five (VC-5) takes off from the deck of the USS *Midway* (CV-41) in 1949. Since existing hydraulic catapults lacked power to launch the Neptunes, the aircraft were fitted with JATO (jet-assisted takeoff) boosters. There is a great deal of history associated with this photograph. The Navy established VC-5 at Norfolk, Virginia, in September of 1948 for the purpose of evaluating a heavy attack aircraft, one that could carry nuclear weapons from a carrier. Commanding Officer of the squadron was Captain John T. Hayward, and his executive officer none other than Commander Frederick Ashworth, the officer who armed the atomic bomb dropped on Nagasaki, Japan. Hayward had been involved in atomic weaponry research during the war, primarily in the area of rocket development, thus his assignment to VC-5 at Norfolk was particularly significant.

VC-5 would take delivery of twelve P2V-3C Neptunes in January of 1949, designated with the "-3C" to reflect special features suited to carrier launch and the aircraft's high-altitude engines. The plane could carry a Mark VIII atomic warhead. The first practical test of the P2V-3C from a carrier deck had taken place off Norfolk on April 28, 1948, aboard the USS *Coral Sea* (CV-43) with Commander Thomas D. Davies at the controls.

The pilots of VC-5 were specially trained to fly the Neptune, and its successor, the AJ-1 Savage. The Savage was designed by North American as a high-wing aircraft with two piston engines and a jet mounted in the after fuselage. Savages would quickly replace the Neptunes, starting with North American's first delivery of the Savage in the fall of 1949. The AJ-1 has the distinction of being the first carrier-based heavy attack aircraft in the Navy inventory. At year's end, VC-5 had six AJ-1s and its flight line of P2V-3C Neptunes. Savages were not used aboard for lengthy operations. Size alone precluded the aircraft from making an extended home for itself aboard ship. Neptunes were kept ashore.

The AJ Savage was kept in service until the early 1960s, having been relegated to the role of aerial tanker and photographic reconnaissance. Frank Ault, founder of the Navy's Fighter Weapons School, popularly known as Top Gun, in 1969, and one of the finest fighter and attack pilots in Navy history, recalled flying the "one turn and burn" Savage at Norfolk in 1950 as a member of VC-5. Ault told the author, "I was there at the end of the silk scarf era when we flew the SB2C, AD-1 Skyraider, then the AJ, the Navy's first atomic bomber. Those were the days." (Courtesy of the Kirn Library.)

An aerial view of a C-47(R4D) Skytrain was photographed in flight over Norfolk, Virginia, November 1954. Naval Air Station Norfolk is in the background. (Official United States Navy Photograph.)

A Lockheed P2V-5F Neptune of Patrol Squadron Eight (VP-8) is shown here at Naval Air Station Norfolk about 1956. This aircraft had undergone some major design changes from its predecessors. The P2V-5s were first delivered to squadrons starting December 29, 1950. An Emerson ball turret with a 20mm cannon was built in the nose, though this addition was removed after the Korean Conflict and is not in evidence here on Bureau Number 131541. Perhaps the most obvious airframe changes in this aircraft are the wing tip tanks, enlarged and centerline on the wing. Aircraft in this series were also modified with 3,400 pounds of static torque and Westinghouse J34-WE-34 turbojet engines under each wing to increase speed and performance over the target. The long protrusion off the tail is a fixed magnetic anomaly detection or MAD boom. Bureau Number 131541 was among the last 144 of the -5F made, and actually qualifies as an -5FS with the addition of its Julie/Jezebel active/passive detection system—the pod under the main fuselage. VP-8, now attached to Patrol Wing Five at Naval Air Station Brunswick, Maine, has a long and distinguished history dating to September 1, 1942, when it was established as Patrol Squadron Two Hundred One (VP-201). Redesignation to Patrol Bombing Squadron Two Hundred One (VPB-201) occurred on October 1, 1944, a designation which lasted less than two years. On May 15, 1946, VPB-201 was redesignated VP-201, and on November 15, 1946, the squadron again changed designations to VP-MS-1.(2) In roughly six months, June 5, 1947, VP-MS-1 was redesignated VP-ML-8, and finally, on September 1, 1948, VP-ML-8 became simply Patrol Squadron Eight (VP-8). The squadron was one of the first two to receive the first Lockheed P-3A Orion aircraft on August 13, 1962. The squadron has a continuous history dating back to the earliest days of World War II. (Official United States Navy Photograph.)

An unidentified naval aviator, a lieutenant (junior grade) in his aviation greens, nuzzles a friend, circa 1957. (Jim Mays, photographer. Courtesy of the Kirn Library.)

Right: A Grumman F9F-5 Panther, Bureau Number 125628, of Fighter Squadron Eighty-Four (VF-84), then nicknamed the *Vagabonds,* not the *Jolly Rogers,* sits in front of the air traffic control tower, Naval Air Station Oceana, circa 1957. The F9F-5 aircraft differed from -2s and -3s with its extra two feet of fuselage and taller fin. VF-84 was a new squadron, having only been established on July 1, 1955, at the air station. (Official United States Navy Photograph.)

The Grumman F11F-1 Tiger was still in production when the above photograph was taken. The Tiger was the first aircraft to be designed and flown with the "area rule" or "pinched waist" fuselage design, pinched waist meaning the area where the wing meets the fuselage. This design reduced the aircraft drag at transonic speeds. The fighter was powered by a Wright J65-W-6 engine of 7,800 pounds thrust, 10,500 in afterburner. The Tiger has the distinction of being one of the few aircraft in history to have shot itself down. On a firing test in 1956, defective bullets fodded the engine in flight, causing a flameout and crash landing of the aircraft. (Official United States Navy Photograph.)

1962, moved from Quonset Point to Naval Air Station Norfolk. In 1966 the East Coast's first Grumman E-2A arrived, and in 1967 the Chief of Naval Operations directed the formation of separate squadrons and a functional air wing for the fleet on both coasts. On April 1, 1967, Carrier Airborne Early Warning Wing Twelve (now Carrier Airborne Early Warning Wing Atlantic); RVAW-120, the training squadron or "Rag;" VAW-121; VAW-122; and VAW-123 were established. The Navy continued to spawn VAW squadrons from VAW-12 detachments through 1969: VAW-124 (September 1, 1967); VAW-125 (October 1, 1968); and VAW-126 (April 1, 1969).

Another departure from Naval Air Station Norfolk worthy of mention occurred in October of 1965. Air Transport Squadron Twenty-Two (VR-22), predecessor of the famed VR-56 *Liftmasters,* a tenant command at the station since 1948, left for Naval Air Station Moffett Field at the southern end of San Francisco Bay, California. Upon their departure in October, VR-22 was under the command of Captain Charles D. Webb, who would also become the squadron's last commanding officer. VR-22 was disestablished at Moffett Field on April 30, 1967, after flying regularly scheduled cargo missions to Vietnam. Originally a utility transport squadron, VR-22 evolved from utility to fleet logistic support to flying global transport missions for the United States Air Force Military Airlift Command (MAC). In July of 1958, while still at Norfolk, VR-22 became a unit of MAC and, by the end of the year had flown two hundred Atlantic crossings. The squadron's C-118 Liftmasters were replaced by C-130E Hercules aircraft in the spring of 1964. The squadron's new Hercules planes were powerful turboprop cargo carriers. Carrying forty-five thousand pounds of payload, the Hercules could fly nonstop, transoceanic flights that assured the squadron a place in the global network. Between June 1966 and April 1967, just prior to disestablishment, VR-22 provided cargo and troop delivery to United States Forces in the Republic of Vietnam, supported Operation Deep Freeze in the Antarctic and airlifted the Gemini space capsule from Naha, Okinawa, back to Cape Canaveral, Florida.

On November 26, 1965, a new flag command was established at Norfolk under Rear Admiral William C. Abhau, making him the first commanding officer of the Atlantic Fleet Manned Spacecraft Recovery Force as well as the Chief of Naval Operations Representative, Manned Space Flight. The Atlantic Fleet's Manned Spacecraft Recovery Force organization started in the days of Project Mercury when it was part of the Destroyer Flotilla Four Staff. The command's rapid rise to independent status came from the increasing number of space shots, later moon shots, and associated problems with recovery of capsules plaguing the space program from its early days. The need for a separate recovery program was clear. Twenty-

Perhaps the best static aviation displays ever done at Naval Air Station Norfolk took place during the International Naval Review of 1957. The aircraft shown here were part of that exhibition.

The famous N3N Yellow Peril trainer was designed by Wright and built by the Naval Aircraft Factory in Philadelphia, Pennsylvania, in 1935. It was capable of operating as either a landplane or seaplane. The Yellow Peril was the same trainer that taught Navy pilots small field procedure which enabled them to operate effectively from aircraft carriers. It was still being used when this picture was taken at Norfolk for aviation indoctrination of midshipmen at the United States Naval Academy, Annapolis, Maryland. (Official United States Navy Photograph.)

The Consolidated PBY Catalina flying boat gained fame during World War II when it flew countless rescue missions, patrol flights, and bombing operations. On display at the aircraft exhibit of the International Naval Review, the Catalina was one of the many planes proposed for inclusion in the future National Air and Space Museum. Powered by two 1,200-horsepower engines, the plane had a range of more than 4,000 miles, and recorded more than 200 miles per hour top speed. Nearly 2,200 Catalinas were built between 1935 and 1957; only a few remained in Navy service at the time the picture was taken. (Official United States Navy Photograph.)

Although this experimental plane was never named, it was called the *Flying Pancake*. It, too, was proposed for inclusion in the National Air and Space Museum. Designated officially V-173, it was known as CV-XF5U-1, "CV" for its manufacturer, Chance-Vought. Designed by Charles H. Zimmerman, an aerospace research pioneer at NASA's Langley Research Center and strong proponent of the low-aspect-ratio wing (the association between the length of the wing compared to its width), this aircraft was used to test wing designs for jet planes of the future. The *Flying Pancake* (shown from both the front and starboard views) made its first flight in 1942 as a research vehicle. From data gathered during its short life came many of the concepts used on supersonic planes. Powered by two engines driving sixteen-foot propellers, the aircraft could get up to 425 miles per hour. The *Flying Pancake* was retired from service after 131 flight hours. (Official United States Navy Photographs.)

Rear Admiral C.D. Griffin, Commander Carrier Division Four (on right) poses beside a Grumman F9F-8T Cougar prior to a flight with Commander N.F. Waters, officer-in-charge of Fleet All-Weather Training Unit Detachment B (FAWTULANT "B"). The photograph was taken April 14, 1958, at Naval Air Station Oceana. FAWTULANT "B" came to Oceana in early 1955 to begin training pilots in instrument flying procedures. The new detachment was part of the FAWTULANT at Naval Air Station Key West, Florida. (Official United States Navy Photograph.)

Captain H.E. Vita, commanding officer of VAW-11 (July 14, 1961 to July 8, 1963), VAW-12's West Coast counterpart, flies a test hop in VAW-11's new WF-2 flight simulator, circa 1961. The squadron training officer, Lieutenant Commander Falvey McKee "Sandy" Sandidge (both photographs), offers some tips on operating the newly acquired simulator which was, at that time, used for procedure and instrument training of WF-2 pilots. The only other flight simulator, identical to this one, was located at VAW-12, at that time headquartered at Quonset Point. (Official United States Navy Photographs.)

one officers and forty-five enlisted personnel were headquartered at Naval Air Station Norfolk Hangar SP-71 with Abhau at the helm. All surface craft, fixed-wing aircraft and helicopters associated with spacecraft recovery were maintained at Norfolk. The air station's Space Training Unit evolved out of Project Mercury as well, adding yet another portion of the space program at Norfolk.

The passing of seaplanes at the end of 1963 was not the only aircraft retirement to end an era at Naval Air Station Norfolk. On July 5, 1967, Patrol Squadron Twenty-Four (VP-24) left Hampton Roads for Naval Air Station Patuxent River, Maryland, and at the same time transitioned from the SP-2H Neptune to the P-3A Orion. At the time, Patuxent River had become one of the East Coast centers of landbased antisubmarine warfare, with the Orion the aircraft of choice for the antisubmarine warfare community. Throughout the spring of 1967, VP-24 *Batmen* flight crews and ground support personnel trained for their transition to the far advanced Orion. The move to Maryland would be the sixth change of station for the *Batmen*. The squadron was homeported at Naval Air Station Floyd Bennett, New York (1945); Naval Air Station Atlantic City, New Jersey (1946); Naval Air Station Patuxent River, Maryland (1948); Naval Air Station Chincoteague, Virginia (1954); and Naval Air Station Norfolk (1959–1967). There were 350 officers and enlisted

The old and the new are dramatically contrasted in this shot of Commander Julian S. Lake in his MK IV full-pressure suit talking with Commander Frank Tallman, USNR, owner and pilot of the mint condition Nieuport 28 replica, vintage 1918, just prior to the start of the 1961 Bendix Trophy Race at Ontario, California. A McDonnell F4H-1 (F-4B) Phantom, the mainstay of Navy fighters at that time, is parked behind the Nieuport. Lake won the Bendix Trophy Race, the transcontinental speed competition, with an 869-mile-per-hour mean speed over 2,445.9 miles from Ontario Field, California, to Floyd Bennett Field, New York, in 2 hours and 48 minutes on May 24, 1961. Lake was commanding officer of Fighter Squadron Seventy-Four (VF-74) *Be-Devilers,* a Naval Air Station Oceana outfit, from March 1961 to May 1962. The *Be-Devilers* were the first Atlantic Fleet fighter squadron to accept the Phantom and one of the last two to replace their F-4S models for Grumman F-14A Tomcats. Lake later became the second commanding officer of the USS *John F. Kennedy* (CV-67) from September 3, 1969, to September 4, 1970, and retired with the rank of rear admiral. (Official United States Navy Photograph.)

personnel attached to the squadron in 1967, including commanding officer Commander A.S. Hibbs and his executive officer, Commander K.L. Geitz. The squadron's history, much of which took place in Norfolk, was rich, particularly in the years after the Second World War.

The *Batmen* of VP-24 were originally established as VB-104 at Naval Air Station Kaneohe, Territory of Hawaii, on April 10, 1943, and redesignated VPB-104 on October 1, 1944. In recognition of their daring raids on Japanese positions at Guadalcanal, Munda, and the Philippines, the squadron received two presidential citations for extraordinary heroism against enemy forces. Following the war, VP-24 assisted in testing and development of the Bat, the Navy's first air-to-surface guided missile. As a result, they got the nickname "bat squadron" and later, "*Batmen* of VP-24" was passed along. Work on the Bat missile also contributed to the squadron's famous "Bat girl" insignia, only the second official pinup girl insignia in Navy history, the other having belonged to Night Fighter Squadron One Hundred Three (VF(N)-103).[1] The *Batmen* would also be the first squadron equipped with the Petrel, another air-to-surface guided missile designed for use by patrol aircraft against shipping, on April 3, 1956. Their reputation as a missile squadron was assured with one operational assignment after another involving the latest in air-to-surface guided missile technology.

During the 1960s, VP-24 was a

A Grumman WF-2 "Willy Fudd," as she was affectionately called by naval aviators who flew her, bears the markings of VAW-11, the very first airborne early warning squadron in the Navy. This aircraft was later redesignated an E-1B Tracer, circa 1962.

On Friday, April 13, 1962, Naval Air Station Oceana was visited by President John F. Kennedy. Oceana happened to be the first stop for the president on his tour of Navy and Marine Corps installations in the Norfolk area. Accompanying President Kennedy on his visit were Vice President Lyndon Baines Johnson; Secretary of Defense Robert S. McNamara; Secretary of Commerce Luther B. Hodges; Chairman of the Joint Chiefs of Staff, General Lyman L. Lemnitzerk; and Commander of the Atlantic Fleet, Admiral Robert L. Dennison. Here, President Kennedy (center) confers with Dennison. (Official United States Navy Photograph.)

Utility Squadron Seven (VU-7) flew the Grumman US-2C Tracker aircraft shown here in flight, July 10, 1963. The US-2C was one of the sixty S-2Cs produced between 1954 and 1955, and modified for utility duties. (Photographer's Mate First Class (PH1) Clifford E. Wall, photographer. Official United States Navy Photograph.)

Norfolk, Virginia, heralded the arrival of Admiral of the Fleet, The Earl Mountbatten of Burma, K.G., Royal Navy (right), on May 24, 1965, at the naval air station. Here, Admiral Thomas H. Moorer, Commander-in-Chief, United States Atlantic Fleet (USCINCLANTFLT), himself a naval aviator, welcomes Mountbatten. Moorer became head of the Atlantic Fleet on April 30, 1965, and remained in that post until June 17, 1967. (Photographer's Mate Third Class (PH3) B.J. Flynn, photographer. Official United States Navy Photograph.)

Dependents were allowed to return to Cuba after cessation of the missile crisis. In this photograph, dependents board a Naval Air Transport Service aircraft for their return to Guantanamo on December 7, 1962, from Naval Air Station Norfolk. (Photographer's Mate Airman (PHAN) L. Smith, photographer. Official United States Navy Photograph.)

On June 27, 1960, this aerial photograph was taken of Naval Air Station Norfolk looking west. There was no Hampton Roads Bridge-Tunnel at that time. Granby Street snakes its way northwest, terminating at Ocean View. The Ocean View Golf Course is visible in the bottom center of the picture. The seaplane hangars are (center, right) across the inlet from the Assembly and Repair Department. The Grand Basin is visible, sans arch, northeast of the Assembly and Repair facility. The runway had not yet been extended in proximity of Hampton Boulevard. (Official United States Navy Photograph.)

member of Task Group Delta, a group which helped accelerate development of antisubmarine warfare (ASW) tactics, doctrine, and equipment in order to improve Atlantic Fleet readiness. With President John Fitzgerald Kennedy's October 23, 1962, remarks regarding the United States quarantine of shipping trade with Fidel Castro's Cuba, VP-24 deployed from Norfolk to Leeward Point Field, Guantanamo Bay, Cuba, on November 5, 1962. The squadron flew continuous surveillance missions and, perhaps most importantly, reported Communist Block shipping that entered Cuban waters. After the Cuban period, VP-24 deployed frequently to Keflavik, Iceland; Sigonella, Sicily; Guantanamo Bay, Cuba; Key West, Florida; and, in December of 1966, made a six-month split deployment to Rota, Spain. The *Batmen* of VP-24 enriched the fabric of naval aviation history at Naval Air Station Norfolk, carrying on a proud tradition of patrol aviation from the skies over Hampton Roads.

The air station continued to expand

Prelaunch preparations of a DSN-3 (DASH) remote control helicopter were photographed aboard the USS *Lind* (DD-703) while berthed at the destroyer-submarine piers, Naval Station Norfolk, Virginia, July 15, 1963. Drone antisubmarine helicopters (DASH) were phased out of service on July 1, 1971. More than seven hundred drones were manufactured between 1963 and 1971 at a cost in excess of $125,000 dollars each. Drones began deploying aboard ships, specifically destroyers, in 1963. On April 1, 1971, just months before the Navy ended the use of drones in antisubmarine warfare, it had established a DASH training unit at the Fleet Antiair Warfare Training Center at Dam Neck in Virginia Beach, Virginia. Consisting of twenty-five enlisted men and five officers, the unit hoped to assimilate the drones into the amphibious force. The commanding officer was Lieutenant Commander I.B. Anderson. Anderson's work with DASH units extended to reconnaissance equipment tests. (Official United States Navy Photograph.)

A McDonnell F4H-1 Phantom aircraft, Bureau Number 151477, later redesignated the F-4B Phantom II of Fighter Squadron Eighty-Four (VF-84) *Jolly Rogers* (then assigned to the USS *Independence* (CVA-62)) sits on the tarmac at Naval Air Station Oceana, circa 1964. Twenty-nine Navy and Marine Corps squadrons were flying this air superiority fighter by 1966. (Official United States Navy Photograph.)

Master Chief Aircrew Survival Equipmentman (PRCM) Forrest V. Miller, having donned a full pressure suit, was all set to enter the Naval Air Station Aviation Physiological Unit's new escape trainer prior to making a test run. Lieutenant C.C. Cole, USN (MSC), was officer-in-charge of the unit at the time—middle to late 1960s. (Official United States Navy Photograph.)

Less than one-tenth of one percent of the population is physically and academically qualified for flight training.

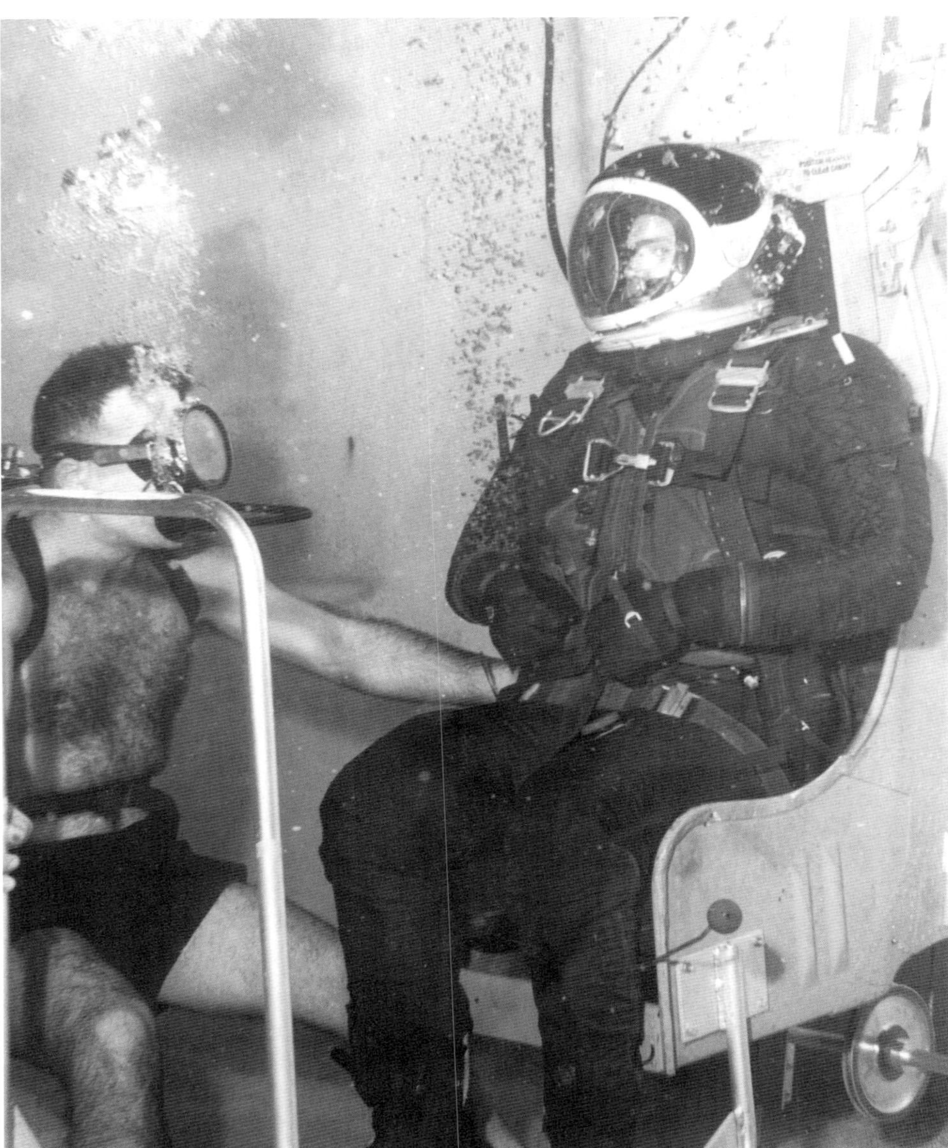

Hospital Corpsman First Class (HM1) Russell O'Day, provided underwater monitoring of Master Chief Aircrew Survival Equipmentman (PRCM) Forrest V. Miller (in full pressure suit). Topside, Miller was carefully monitored by Hospital Corpsman First Class (HM1) Harry L. Mitchell; Chief Aircrew Survival Equipmentman (PRC) Leonard A. Herold; Tradesman Third Class (TD3) Ernest S. Carner Jr. and, Chief Aircrew Survival Equipmentman Second Class (PR2) Robert L. Orozco, who maintained continuous communication poolside and monitored Miller's breathing rate and suit conditions during the run. The test was completed during the middle to late 1960s. (Official United States Navy Photograph.)

Commander Russell D. Kaulback navigates a Grumman TF-9J Cougar over Naval Air Station Oceana, October 11, 1966. Commander Kaulback had recently taken over as executive officer of Attack Squadron Forty-Three (VA-43). When VF-21 was redesignated an attack squadron on July 1, 1959, it became VA-43. VA-43 was redesignated VF-43 on June 1, 1973. The VF-43 *Challengers* were disestablished in 1994. (Official United States Navy Photograph.)

its number and diversity of aircraft in the 1970s from fixed-wing to rotors, a trend that has continued as naval aviation becomes increasingly driven by shifts in technology and multiple service mission. Perhaps one of the most important rotor-wing squadrons born at Norfolk, and one which would change the Navy's and world's perceptions of helicopter employment, was the establishment of Helicopter Mine Countermeasures Squadron Twelve (HM-12) *Sea Dragons* on April 1, 1971, as the first airborne mine countermeasures squadron in the world. Though the *Sea Dragons* had originally functioned as an operational fleet unit, Detachment 53 of Helicopter Combat Support Squadron Six (HC-6) *Chargers,* prior to their establishment as HM-12, the Navy decided on the basis of its intensive research and development of minesweeping weaponry, that airborne minesweeping was mission critical.

During the Second World War and, again, in the Korean Conflict, mines were a menace to shipping and military water traffic. The Vietnam Conflict proved no different. Harbors and navigable waterways in and around Vietnamese territory posed an absolute threat to ships. Just as in prior international conflicts, it was taking days for Navy ships to clear mines for invasion and combat support purposes. As Rear Admiral James A. Dare, commander of the Atlantic Fleet Mine Force during this period remarked, "the effort to sweep a mine field is almost exactly equivalent to a raid into enemy-held territory." When the Navy pronounced the establishment of the squadron, HM-12's course was set. Dare said it best:

"With the advent of HM-12 and the introduction of CH-53A Sea Stallion helicopters into mine warfare, the squadron will inject a dynamic, new and effective dimension into mine warfare and will greatly enhance the Navy's abilities to maintain the peace and freedom of the seas. The dedication of this new helicopter squadron to a unique naval warfare mission constitutes a significant expansion in the employment of helicopters by the Navy. Highly mobile and air transportable, the CH-53A (later the RH-53D) will provide the fleet with quick reaction mine countermeasures assistance anywhere in the world."

Naval Air Station Norfolk was the site of one the most impressive demonstrations of worldwide quick reaction mine countermeasures capability ever witnessed when HM-12 was called upon to participate in Operation Endsweep with only ten days notice of deployment in November 1972. The squadron was tasked to clear mines in thirteen harbors as well as coastal waters of the Democratic Republic of Vietnam. The first live mine was detonated on March 9, 1973, by HM-12 at Haiphong, which was completely cleared by June 20, 1973. The *Sea Dragons* then moved to Hon Gai and Cam Pha, clearing those ports by

Vocalist Rosa Lee; Airman (AN) M.A. Savastone, Public Affairs Office, Naval Air Station Norfolk; Actress Audrie Magee; Comedian George Jessel; Seaman Apprentice (SA) D.L. Chadwick, Public Affairs Office, Naval Air Station Norfolk; and Accordionist Ronald A. Richardello were photographed at the air station December 6, 1966. Lee, Magee, Jessel, and Richardello were here to entertain sailors as part of the USO show. (Chief Yeoman (YNC) V.O. Mills, photographer. Official United States Navy Photograph.)

June 27, 1973, before proceeding to Vinh, Quang Khe, Than Hoa, Dong Hoi, and Hon La, finishing mine countermeasures operations in those coastal areas by July 5. These were the only areas American mine countermeasures forces could clear since the North Vietnamese government abruptly refused to allow further minesweeping assistance in coastal reaches, and forbade any offer of United States Navy assistance in its inland waterways.

Upon reflection, Lieutenant Commander R.E. Berry Jr., a plankowner of HM-12, would be quoted as saying, "It [Haiphong effort] predicts the incursion of helicopters into new and varied tasks." Operation Endsweep was the first operation in history that helicopters towed sweeping gear in active minefields. Petty Officer Second Class Gary L. Fleck, a crewman aboard the CH-53As, was asked shortly after returning from overseas how difficult the operation had been for the *Sea Dragons*. Since the United States had not used contact mines, the traditional large metal ball-type anchored by a chain below the surface, and instead chose a mix of influence mines of magnetic and acoustic varieties, the operation was not difficult from the detonation and retrieval

The USO tour has come through Naval Air Station Norfolk many times over the years. On this occasion, December 5, 1966, comedian extraordinaire George Jessel (center) was in town. With him are (left to right) Lieutenant Commander J. Riding, Naval Air Station Public Affairs Officer; Seaman (SN) D.T. Flanigan, Public Affairs Office; and Chief Yeoman (YNC) V.O. Mills. (Official United States Navy Photograph.)

The Navy's Space Training Unit was established at Naval Air Station Norfolk November 26, 1965, as a new flag command under Rear Admiral William C. Abhau. The new command made Abhau the first commanding officer of Atlantic Fleet Manned Spacecraft Recovery Force and Chief of Naval Operations Representative, Manned Space Flight. The artwork shown here was a product of the Overhaul and Repair Department Decal Shop, which became known as the Naval Aviation Depot Norfolk. (Courtesy of the Naval Aviation Depot Norfolk.)

The Chief of Naval Operations, in disseminating the report of the Ad Hoc Committee on Astronautics, also known as the Connolly Board, approved its policy recommendations and enunciated organizational responsibilities in the Office of the Chief of Naval Operations on July 13, 1959. The most important portions of the report stated the Navy would use space to accomplish naval objectives, and that it would participate fully in space technology. Astronautics would be given high priority in the Navy's overall research and development programs as well. An Astronautics Division was established in the office of the Deputy Chief of Naval Operations for Air to support the deputy chief in his overall responsibility for directing the Navy astronautic program, including the formulation of plans, policies, and program requirements.

perspective. What Fleck noted was problematic was "the junks, sampan and schoals," in extraction areas.

The use of HM-12 in mine countermeasures operations continued successfully through the end of the 1970s. The squadron was called to the Suez Canal during Operation Nimbus Star in March 1974, and, again, in response to an inter-

Captain R.J. DePrez, commanding officer of Naval Air Station Norfolk, stands before the *Apollo 7* command module on October 25, 1968. The module was being deactivated at the air station's hangar LP-2 after returning from its eleven-day orbital flight. Helicopters from HS-5 aboard the USS *Essex* (CVS-9) deployed and recovered astronauts Walter M. Schirra, Don F. Eisele, and R. Walter Cunningham roughly 285 miles south of Bermuda, delivering them safely to the carrier. *Apollo 7* was the first manned flight of the Apollo program. (Official United States Navy Photograph.)

Less than two years after establishment, VAW-123 was returning from a major six-month deployment. Loved ones, prepared with welcoming home signs and smiles all around, eagerly await the squadron's arrival at Naval Air Station Norfolk in 1969. This homecoming stood in stark comparison to homecomings twenty-two years later and the aftermath of victory in the Persian Gulf War, especially for this squadron. Vietnam-era homecomings were normally affairs for family and close friends, and did not attract much public support. Public opinion of the Vietnam Conflict was negative, creating great tension for returning military members, some of which turned into open demonstrations and public unrest. Desert Storm homecomings extended the hand of welcome to all military returning home, especially the Navy in Hampton Roads. Celebrations were extravagant and well-attended by family, friends, general public, and the military establishment. (Courtesy of Carrier Airborne Early Warning Squadron One Hundred Twenty-Three.)

A Grumman E-2B Hawkeye waits for a company of well-ordered mallard ducks to pass. This photograph, circa 1969, shows the aircraft taxiing back to the SP hangars from Chambers Field. "SP" stands for seaplane, and "LP" initially stood for landplane. These original meanings have become less important over the years as subsequent inhabitants of the air station designate buildings according to whatever the prevailing system happens to be at the time. (Official United States Navy Photograph.)

Helicopter Mine Countermeasures Squadron Twelve (HM-12) *Sea Dragons* were established on April 1, 1971, at Naval Air Station Norfolk as the first airborne mine countermeasures squadron in the world. In the photograph shown here, Commander David W. Humphreys (third from left), the first commanding officer of the squadron, poses with executive officer, Lieutenant Commander Roger B. McPherson (fourth from left), and officials of the Sikorsky Aircraft Corporation: Wesley A. Kuhrt (far right), Sikorsky president whose son, Lieutenant (junior grade) Ronald W. Kuhrt was among HM-12's first officers; Robert Torok, programs director; Ray Maloney, marketing; and John W. D'Angelo, product support. Sikorsky manufactured the squadron's first aircraft, the CH-53A Sea Stallion (visible behind the men in the photograph). (Official United States Navy Photograph. Courtesy of Helicopter Mine Countermeasures Squadron Twelve.)

President Richard Milhous Nixon visited the USS *Saratoga* (CV-60) during a deployment in 1971. The enlisted sailor standing next to the president was a member of the VAW-123 *Screwtops* squadron. (Courtesy of Carrier Airborne Early Warning Squadron One Hundred Twenty-Three.)

Naval aviator and astronaut Walter M. "Wally" Schirra was approached by a stranger after one of his speaking engagements years ago. The stranger introduced himself saying, "I'm an ex-Air Force pilot." Schirra's quick reply was, "Oh? We have pilots in the Navy, too. We use them to dock our boats."

The Navy's *Blue Angels* have a long history of performing at the Naval Air Station Norfolk Azalea Festival Airshow. Between 1969 and 1973, the *Blue Angels* flew the McDonnell Douglas F-4J Phantom II aircraft, shown here at Norfolk circa 1970. It was not until December 10, 1973, that the squadron's designation was changed from Flight Demonstration Team to Flight Demonstration Squadron. The *Blue Angels* left their Phantom IIs and transitioned to the McDonnell Douglas A-4F Skyhawk aircraft. Commanding officer of the *Blue Angels* at that time was Commander (later Vice Admiral) Anthony A. Less. (Official United States Navy Photograph.)

Ely Hall, named for the famed civilian aviator Eugene B. Ely who gave birth to naval aviation at Hampton Roads in 1910, continues to serve as the Bachelor Officers' Quarters (BOQ) for Naval Air Station Norfolk, circa 1970s. The BOQ bears the name of naval aviation's most deserving pioneer. President Franklin Delano Roosevelt presented to Colonel Nathan D. Ely, United States Army (retired), Ely's father, a posthumous Distinguished Flying Cross on February 16, 1933, for his son's extraordinary achievement as a pioneer aviator and for his significant contibution as a civilian to the development of naval aviation when in 1910 and 1911, Eugene B. Ely demonstrated the feasibility of operating aircraft from ships. (Official United States Navy Photograph.)

On March 7, 1973, a C-9 Nightingale carrying four American prisoners of war (POWs) previously held in Vietnam was unable to land due to inclement weather and heavy fog. Nonetheless, well-wishers, friends, and family members had gathered at Naval Air Station Norfolk to greet the aviators. When word came that the aircraft diverted to Naval Air Station Oceana, an impromptu crowd consisting of a few from Norfolk, was on hand to welcome the men home, shown in the first photograph. (Official United States Navy Photograph.)

At approximately ten minutes after five the afternoon of March 7, the Nightingale transport touched down at Oceana carrying four former naval aviator POWs imprisioned by the North Vietnamese. Among the four men on the flight were Captain Allen Brady; Commander John Fellowes; Lieutenant Commander Michael Christian; and Commander Eugene "Red" McDaniel. McDaniel and the others received a warm welcome from those on hand at Oceana, but none was more precious than the reception awaiting these men from their own families. The excitement and relief of the POWs' return is evident in the outstretched arms of a wife rushing to embrace her aviator. (Official United States Navy Photograph.)

Vice Admiral Thomas F. Connolly, Vice Chief of Naval Operations for Air from November 1, 1966 to 1969 and an recognized naval aeronautics expert, killed Secretary of Defense Robert McNamara's attempt to navalize the Convair F-111B fighter. In May 1968, during U.S. Senate hearings on the aircraft in Washington, D.C., Senator John C. Stennis, chairman of the Armed Services Committee, singled out Connolly to give him an honest, personal opinion of the F-111B. Connolly responded: "Mr. Chairman, all the thrust in Christendom couldn't make a fighter out of that airplane." The result of his testimony was the end of any notion the Navy would ever outfit its carrier decks with the under-powered F-111B, and the beginning of the Grumman F-14 Tomcat. Naval Air Systems Command issued a contract to Grumman for development of the F-14A fighter and manufacture of six experimental aircraft on February 3, 1969. The F-14, intended as a high performance replacement for the F-4 Phantom and abortive F-111B, was developed with the variable-sweep wing and the ability to carry the Phoenix missile. Connolly, realizing his "honest, personal opinion" probably cost him his fourth star, went to work on the F-14 program and literally became its day-to-day manager. When it came time to put a Grumman "cat" name on the F-14, the decision was unanimous to call it a "Tomcat" in honor of Vice Admiral Connolly. The admiral passed away on May 24, 1997, at the age of 86, but he lives on in the aircraft that bears his name and the pilots who fly them.

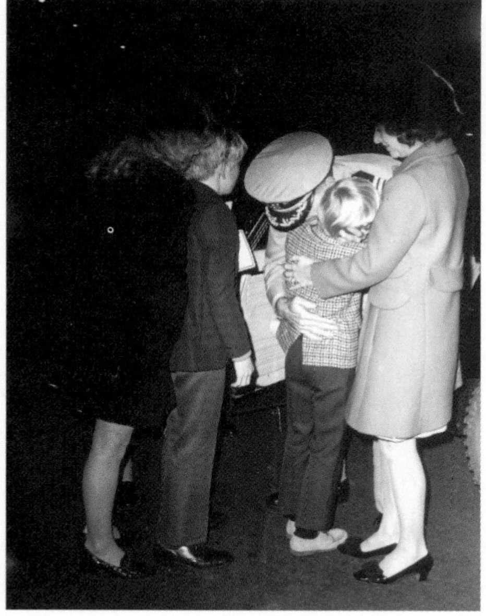

In the top photograph, Commander McDaniel addresses the crowd as his family looks on. Perhaps most poignant are the photographs of Commander Fellowes embracing his family for the assemblage (above), and again in a quieter moment before going home (left). (Official United States Navy Photographs.)

national incident involving the United States registered merchant ship *Neches* off the northern coast of the United Arab Republic of Egypt in late-August of 1975. The *Neches,* carrying electronic sensor equipment from Houston, Texas, to the Middle East hit a mine and sank. The United States agreed to clear the mines with a six helicopter detachment from HM-12, at that time operating from the deck of the USS *Inchon* (LPH-12). The *Sea Dragons* successfully swept thirty-five miles along Egypt's coast.

By the week of September 22, 1975, HM-12 had swept for Soviet mines in Port Said, the north entrance to the Suez Canal. The United States had previously swept the Suez fourteen months before HM-12's involvement using three surface minesweepers, but left in 1975 when it was decided safer to use helicopters for the same job. The Soviets did not clear their own mines because the Egyptians would not ask the Soviet government to clear the mines from the Suez or Egyptian territorial waters. The Egyptian government, then ruled by President Anwar Sadat, had expelled the Soviets from Egypt in 1972, thus clearing a path for the United States Agency for International Development to pay for HM-12's involvement in both opera-

A Grumman E-2C Hawkeye piloted by Commander J.J. George, executive officer of Carrier Airborne Early Warning Squadron 124 *Bear Aces,* is catapulted off the deck of the aircraft carrier USS *Theodore Roosevelt* (CVN-71) as the ship and its battle group got underway on deployment December 29, 1990. The *Bear Aces* were established on September 1, 1967, at Naval Air Station Norfolk and nicknamed the *Bullseye Hummers.* The squadron did not adopt the nickname *"Bear Aces"* until December 1980. The squadron had been handed immediate deployment orders to Keflavik, Iceland, to perform the airborne early warning missions usually flown by the United States Air Force E-3A AWACS aircraft which were, at that time, forward deployed to West Germany as a result of increasing tensions in Poland. This was the first operational deployment of an E-2 squadron to Iceland. As a result of five VAW-124 direct intercepts of Soviet Bear reconnaissance aircraft flying the North American run, the squadron acquired its present nickname, *Bear Aces.* (Courtesy of Carrier Airborne Early Warning Squadron One Hundred Twenty-Four.)

tions. It was not until 1978 that HM-12 became the H-53 Fleet Readiness Squadron (FRS) or "Rag," and spun off two new fleet squadrons: HM-14 *Vanguard* and HM-16 *Sea Hawks*. The *Sea Dragons* became responsible for replacement training of all CH-53E and MH-53E pilots, maintenance, and aircrew personnel in the Navy at that time.

Given the air station's strategic location to the fleet, its air squadrons and shore commands are geared toward personnel and logistics readiness for the Atlantic Fleet. Naval Air Station Norfolk is a fourth echelon command residing, unbeknownst to the public at large, on land owned by Naval Base Norfolk. In other words, the air station is the large tenant and its tenant commands, subtenants of the naval base. Primary support for the air station eminates from Commander Naval Base Norfolk, and aviation-related support is overseen by Commander Naval Air Force Atlantic Fleet (COMNAVAIRLANT). The air station includes nine departments and eleven special assistants who provide support to eighty-nine tenant commands, and sixteen nonresident commands as well as all Atlantic Fleet aviation-classified surface combatants. The current climate of military rightsizing has had its impacts on Naval Air Station Norfolk operations. With the loss of Naval Aviation Depot Norfolk, eighty-five buildings and two-and-a-half-million square feet of space had to be redesignated for other uses. Aside from the physical loss of the command, Naval Air Station Norfolk lost its only kindred spirit in the depot and the depot's history. The two commands shared their infancy, the growing pains, the hardships of war, and now the parting of history.

The first major test of the *Sea Dragons'* operational capability came in November 1972 during Operation Endsweep. The squadron was tasked to clear mines from thirteen harbors as well as coastal waters of North Vietnam. These mines had been laid by the United States to blockade the coastal areas and major ports of North Vietnam during the war. Mines laid by American aircraft were primarily magnetic and acoustic activated, or some combination thereof. The squadron had been made aware of the seeding process. With ten days notice, HM-12 moved its entire squadron operation to the Western Pacific as part of Task Force Seventy-Eight, loading their aircraft and equipment aboard the largest military transport in the free world, the leviathan Lockheed C-5A Galaxy aircraft. When the cease-fire agreement was finalized on January 27, 1973, in Paris, France, a terse directive was issued to the United States to immediately commence its removal of the mines. Though operation preparation had begun, the directive ushered the process along. In this photograph, Peter Jennings, now the ABC Evening News anchor, reports the first mine explosion by a mine countermeasures squadron, HM-12, in Haiphong Harbor, North Vietnam, on March 9, 1973, a Naval Air Station Norfolk based squadron. (Courtesy of Helicopter Mine Countermeasures Squadron Twelve.)

This 1970s period look at a Naval Air Station Norfolk airshow demonstrates the magnetic draw of static and aerobatic performances in years gone by. (Official United States Navy Photograph.)

The Flatley Family Legacy

Three generations of the Flatley family have graced naval aviation, thus providing an extraordinary legacy to Navy history. Starting with Vice Admiral James Henry "Jimmy" Flatley Jr. and continuing with his son, Rear Admiral James H. Flatley III and grandsons, Lieutenant Commander James H. "Seamus" Flatley IV and Lieutenant Commander Joseph Flatley, USNR, this family of naval aviators has left a permanent mark on their profession and Hampton Roads, the birthplace of naval aviation.

James Henry Flatley Jr. was born on June 17, 1906, at Green Bay, Wisconsin. He attended St. Norbert's College, West DePere, Wisconsin, before his appointment to the United States Naval Academy, Annapolis, Maryland, from his native state in 1925. Graduated and commissioned an ensign on June 6, 1929, he reported as a junior officer on board the USS *Saratoga* and, in April of 1930, reported for flight training at Naval Air Station Pensacola, Florida. Designated Naval Aviator No. 3806 on April 23, 1931, he joined Fighting Squadron Five, attached to Aircraft Squadrons, Battle Fleet, based on the USS *Lexington.* In June 1934, he was assigned to Patrol Squadron Four attached to Naval Air Station Pearl Harbor, Territory of Hawaii, and from June 1936 until October 1937, had consecutive duty with Fighting Squadrons Four and Six, based aboard the USS *Ranger* and USS *Enterprise,* respectively. In September 1937, he reported on board the USS *Omaha* to serve as her senior aviator in Mediterranean Squadron 40-T.

The F4B-1, a Boeing fighter, heads down the deck for takeoff. This fighter, developed in the late 1920s, was a popular airplane with Navy pilots during most of the 1930s and was standard for the period. The aircraft shown here, circa 1928, belonged to the famous *Red Ripper* squadron, designated VF-5 at the time. The squadron could trace its lineage to Hampton Roads, Virginia where it was established on February 1, 1927. The boar's head insignia was adapted from the design on bottles of Gordon gin. The literal interpretation of the insignia is "a horny bunch of two-balled bastards," so this rather colorful squadron adopted the pseudonym *Red Rippers*—it sounded much better and offended fewer people—in 1930 at the Chicago Air Races where they distinguished themselves with some of the best flight demonstrations ever witnessed. Perhaps the squadron's 1933 interpretation of this rather colorful insignia is preferable:

> **The wild boar is the ugliest-snouted, worst-tempered, fastest-moving creature in the whole Noah's Ark of nature, and is as full of tricks as a thirteen-spade bridge hand. He is the only animal that dares drink at the same pool with the tiger, he is as shifty as a pickerel in eel-grass. The boar's head is taken directly from the one that graces the label on the Gordon's Gin bottle. The scroll effect under the head is a string of sausage—the good line which all members of the squadron were to be adept at shooting.**

(Official United States Navy Photograph.)

In July 1939, Flatley returned to the United States for duty at Naval Air Station Pensacola, Florida, where he was a flight instructor at the Naval Air Advanced Training Command. Between December 1940 and September 1941, he was aide to the commanding officer of Naval Air Station Jacksonville, Florida, after which he was ordered to duty afloat as executive officer of Fighting Squadron Two, the Navy's famous *White Hat* squadron made up entirely of enlisted aviation pilots, based aboard the USS *Lexington,* and from April 1942, on board the USS *Yorktown* with VF-42. Flatley led VF-2 in the Battle of the Coral Sea.

After the Battle of Coral Sea, Flatley established and trained Fighter Squadron Ten, the famous VF-10 *Grim Reapers,* and in October 1942 the squadron reported on board the USS *Enterprise* (CV-6). They contributed to the Big E's days of glory when, alone among carriers, the *Enterprise* helped hold the battered line in the South Pacific. They participated in the Battles of Santa Cruz, Guadalcanal, and Rennel Island and even went ashore at Guadalcanal to aid hard-pressed Marines by operating their planes from Henderson Field when the fight looked darkest. For services as commanding officer of Fighting Squadron Ten, Flatley was awarded the Distinguished Flying Cross and Gold Star in lieu of the Second Distinguished Flying Cross. Before taking leave of the Reapers, Flatley would leave a final memo tacked to the squadron ready room board for his pilots to read. It went as follows:

Memo for the REAPERS

I can't find it in me to make a farewell speech. I'm afraid I'd get all choked up.

I want you to know that I take my leave of you with deep regret. No squadron commander, anywhere, has ever had a gang like you serving with him. I'm so darn proud and fond of every one of you that my heart's about to bust.

If I could have had the pick of the Navy for my relief, it would have been the "Killer."(1)

Take care of yourselves. Stick together and don't forget to respect that airplane. Every time you see a Jap, remember Leppla, Mead, Rhodes, Caldwell, Davis, Fulton, Barnes, Miller, Edwards, and Von Lehe.(2)

One parting word of advice—There

Lieutenant Commander James H. Flatley Jr. stands on the wing of his "Double Zero" F6F-3 Hellcat after making the first landing on the USS *Yorktown* (CV-10), May 6, 1943, in the Chesapeake Bay. (Courtesy of Mrs. James H. (Dorothy) Flatley Jr.)

is a definite tendency on the part of every one of you to throw caution to the wind every time you meet the enemy. We've been lucky as hell so far. But, it's dumb. We've spent hours and hours on tactics, designed not only to destroy, but all to protect ourselves. Keep that thought foremost in your minds. Rip 'em up and down, but do it smartly.

I trust our paths will cross in the near future. Meanwhile, keep your chins up and don't forget that little guy who called himself

REAPER LEADER

Lieutenant Commander Flatley would also not forget those who kept his *Reaper* aircraft flying. In a letter copied to USS *Enterprise* and Pacific Fleet, Flatley reserved high praise for all personnel responsible for the care and maintenance of his fighters. He penned, "The fighter pilots hereby express their appreciation for the excellence and conscientious care that is being taken of their planes. Needless to say," he continued, "it is a great consolation to all of us to know that we can depend on the guns firing and the aircraft getting us off and back again safely." The memorandum was dated December 17, 1942. His thanks was sincere, his love of the *Grim Reapers* unquestionned.

Flatley detached from command of VF-10 in February 1943 and returned to the United States. He had temporary duty with Fleet Air Command, West Coast, followed by duty fitting out Air Group Five, soon to be attached to the new USS *Yorktown*. Officially established at Naval Air Station Norfolk on February 15, 1943, Air Group Five included a mix of fighters, dive-bombers, and torpedo bombers.

While at Norfolk, the *Yorktown's* fighters, under the command of Lieutenant Commander Charles L. Crommelin, trained at Creeds and Oceana in the Grumman F6F-3 Hellcat. Flatley had assumed command of the air group upon commissioning of the *Yorktown* on April 7, 1943, and served in that command until September of that year. He would become responsible for the men and machines of Air Group Five which, in addition to thirty-six fighters, included another thirty-six bombers and eighteen torpedo bombers. Bombing Squadron Five (VB-5) was commanded at the time by Lieutenant Commander Robert M. Milner. The bomber was the infamous Curtiss SB2C Helldiver (otherwise known as "the Beast") and the torpedo bomber the proven TBF-1C Avenger which, like the Hellcat, was a Grumman aircraft. The Helldiver exhibited numerous performance problems for Air Group Five. Rear Admiral Patrick N.L. Bellinger worked feverishly as

Commander Air Force, Atlantic (COMAIRLANT) to have the Helldiver replaced, particularly when word was sent from the *Yorktown* that the SB2C was totally unsuited to carrier operations.

As for Flatley's torpedo squadron, it was commanded by Lieutenant Commander Richard Upson. Torpedo planes made good use of the Pungo auxiliary field for practice, according to COMAIRLANT records.

As an ace who would eventually accumulate ten victories, Jimmy Flatley was by far more interested in Crommelin's fighter squadron which had begun training with the Grumman F4F-4 Wildcat and ended up in the sleek Grumman F6F-3 Hellcat. Flatley's underlying message to his fighter pilots was safety first. As an intuitive yet learned pilot, Flatley would have occasion to lecture ready rooms of these young men on the virtues of finessing any aircraft but most especially the Hellcat, cautioning his brood not to overfly the airplane. Best warnings aside, accidents happened. Less than a week after reporting as Commander Carrier Air Group Five,(3) two of his Hellcat pilots were killed in a collision over the Great Dismal Swamp—a lesson learned and not forgotten.

In July of 1952, Flatley assumed command of the USS *Block Island* (CVE-106). During his command of the *Block Island,* the ship won the Battle Efficiency pennant for carriers of her class. Detached from command of the *Block Island* in July 1953, his next duty was as officer-in-charge of the Naval Aviation Safety Activity, Norfolk, Virginia—a facility upon which Flatley was destined to leave an indelible mark. As evidenced in his farewell message to the *Reapers,* aviation safety had always been Flatley's credo, so much so that he addressed issues of safety in a pointed lecture shortly after taking command, a lecture which set the tone for later establishment of the Naval Safety Center and much of the squadron-level safety procedures in place today. Flatley was aware of efforts by first Assistant Secretary of the Navy for Air, Dr. Edward P. Warner, to establish safety procedures for naval aviation, and he was keenly cognizant of the great number of accidents—most avoidable—from the late 1920s to the end of his career. The Naval Safety Center at Norfolk would bear his name but for the fact it had not been allocated in the budget for construction when Captain R.J. DePrez, commanding officer of Naval Air Station Norfolk, concurred with Commander Naval Air

Lieutenant Commander James H. Flatley Jr. was first told he had been picked as the first commanding officer of Fighter Squadron Ten (VF-10), destined to be the original *Grim Reapers,* while serving as executive officer of Fighter Squadron Forty-Two (VF-42) aboard the USS *Yorktown* (CV-5). During his return trip to San Diego, California, aboard a transport ship, Flatley worked on the details of his new position, one of which was what to call his new outfit. Flatley decided on the *Grim Reapers* which seemed to meet the approval of other transport passengers. The insignia was also his idea: a skeleton armed with a scythe. Stanley Johnston, a writer who was aboard the transport at the time and later wrote a book entitled *The Grim Reapers,* took a pencil and paper, made a rough outline of a skeleton, drew in a scythe held at full-cock, and gave the old boy a high-speed wing. Badly drawn as it was, squadron information makes it clear the general effect stood the test. All that was missing was the motto. After much deliberation, the two men decided on "Mow 'em Down" and sketched it at the bottom of their masterpiece. The skeleton was affectionately called "Moe" by the *Grim Reapers.* Over the years, the skeleton has been modified just a bit, losing his World War II leather flying cap. The scythe no longer drips blood, pleasing the weak at heart, and the motto has been removed from the bottom of the design. The *Grim Reapers* of VF-101, the F-14 Tomcat fleet replacement squadron at Naval Air Station Oceana, proudly sport their squadron insignia, a naval aviation tradition if there ever was one.

Force Atlantic Fleet, Vice Admiral Robert L. Townsend on July 16, 1970, that a suitable facility or building at Naval Air Station Norfolk be named for Vice Admiral Flatley. In the end, DePrez and Townsend agreed that the new complex of buildings comprising Fleet Airborne Electronics Training Unit, Atlantic be named the Flatley Center.

In June 1955, Flatley was ordered as commanding officer of the USS *Lake Champlain* (CVA-39), a "Long-Hull" *Essex*-class aircraft carrier which had undergone axial deck modernization in September 1952 under the Project 27A carrier conversion program.(4) This ship also won the Battle Efficiency pennant under his command. Detaching from

On October 29, 1953, Captain James Henry Flatley (later vice admiral) sent a letter home to the families of personnel reporting for duty at Naval Air Station Norfolk which said: "The strength and efficiency of this air station in these critical times in world history depend in large measure upon the morale and spirit of the crew. You and I share the responsibility for keeping that morale and spirit at the highest point." Family time has remained an important part of the spirit of the naval aviation community. Here, Fighter Squadron Twenty-One, redesignated Attack Squadron Forty-Three and, subsequently, VF-43 *Challengers,* enjoy a squadron Christmas party held December 21, 1957, on board Naval Air Station Oceana. (Official United States Navy Photograph.)

command of the *Lake Champlain,* he moved in July of the following year to the Office of the Chief of Naval Operations as head of the Special Weapons Plans Branch, Strategic Plans Division and, on October 21, 1957, became Director, Air Warfare Division. He was transferred to the retired list of the United States Navy effective June 2, 1958, and was advanced to the rank of vice admiral on the basis of combat awards.

Flatley's awards were impressive. In addition to the Navy Cross, the Distinguished Service Medal, the Legion of Merit with Combat "V", the Distinguished Flying Cross with two Gold Stars, the Bronze Star Medal and Commendation Ribbon, each with Combat "V", and the Presidential Unit Citation Ribbon with five stars, Vice Admiral Flatley wore numerous campaign awards. He died at the United States Naval Hospital, Bethesda, Maryland, on July 9, 1958, of brain cancer.

That is the story of Vice Admiral Flatley for the record. Flatley, the man, is the story no one ever reads about. As a lieutenant commander, Flatley would engage in some of the fiercest aerial combat in the history of naval aviation. And as "*Reaper* Leader" to his VF-10 *Grim Reapers,* Flatley exhibited the kind of courage and leadership style which set him apart from his contemporaries. In a memorandum to the *Grim Reapers,* he would pen, "In all of us is the desire to live. It surmounts every other desire. However, we all must die sooner or later. We are fighting now, not so much for our own lives, but for the lives of our entire nation, for our fathers and mothers, sisters and brothers. This is not a game. This is the most serious business of our lives."

"Jimmy" to his friends, Vice Admiral Flatley would move the Honorable Homer E. Capehart, United States Senator from Indiana and long-time friend, to comment for the *Congressional Record,* June 14, 1962:

"In the thirties, at a time when there was great complacency as regards U.S. military power, Jimmy Flatley was one of those whose vision extended beyond a limited horizon to see the potential of a balanced Navy which included as one of its major arms the aircraft carrier and its planes. But he was not content with vision alone. He spent some years in working with others developing a highly effective aircraft doctrine and tactics. Jimmy Flatley was a dedicated naval officer who spent his life making a major contribution to the naval power which has stood and continues to stand the United States in good stead."

Flatley's vision in the thirties culminated in the forties when he saw American carriers and their aircraft successfully defeat the enemy in the South Pacific.

Between the lines of records, combat, and time was also Flatley, the beloved husband and father. Capehart said it best when he quoted the first verse of the tenth chapter of Proverbs, "A wise son maketh a glad father." Flatley's wife, Dorothy, and four sons shared with him his love of country and his dedication to it, and Dorothy Flatley carried on the upbringing of their sons upon the vice admiral's death. As son Rear Admiral James H. Flatley III recounted in an interview, "[She] has had her fair share of worrying about the Flatley clan of naval aviators. First Dad, me, and two grandsons and a grandson-in-law, have been carrier aviators."

This woman of extraordinary strength shared her thoughts and eloquent and engaging commentary of her life in a letter dated August 29, 1994, a portion of which is shared here.

"July 1932 Our Meeting...

"[Vice Admiral Flatley's] military action is more in print than in my 86-year-old memory, but the memory of the man himself will always be close to my heart. I like to remember that handsome blue-blue-eyed, smiling, curly-haired blond wearing a blue sports jacket, standing a few feet from me at Caesar's Bar in Tijuana, where many naval aviators and their wives gathered on Wednesday and Saturday afternoons in the '30s before and after driving on to the [horse] races at Caliente. My hosts were the John Munns, who I was visiting in Coronado. In an aside to Toby Munn, I asked if he knew the person in the blue jacket who kept looking my way. Toby replied, 'Of course, I do. That's my friend, Jimmy Flatley. I'll bet he is wanting to meet you. How about it?' I was willing, so a few moments later, the man of my dreams stood before me. He was even the right height for my 5'2"—about four inches taller. In all my twenty-four years I had never felt the sensation of that meeting. Toby asked Jimmy to join us, so he went back to pick up his drink and we made space. My date for the day was on the other side of me. It turned out that he and Jimmy were classmates. Later on, Jimmy asked if he could take me to dinner and back to Coronado if it was all right with my date. So gracious as I tried to be, my date must have seen by then that he was becoming a third party, so he said he was joining some other friends. This was the beginning of six weeks of unforgettable courtship, then I had to return to Florida to fulfill my teaching contract. Jimmy's duty was at North Island in VF-5—*Red Ripper* squadron—a *Lexington* squadron.

"Married January 7, 1933...

"[The Flatleys] lived in Coronado after a [Flatley's] three-month fleet cruise, beginning in January—I stayed in S.D. [San Diego] with Leah Munn during the cruise. They had moved to S.D. after I left in the summer.

"Wives played tennis, bridge, had evening poker parties, had luncheons, suppers, shopped, played golf, read and wrote daily letters to our husbands, and I went house hunting, ending up with the same house in Coronado where we had courted, the Munn's house on the alley off 'D.'

"The day we met the Fleet, in the area of Long Beach, on March 10, 1933, there was an earthquake, but the ships came in without mishap and wives had found undamaged hotel rooms.

"That spring and summer I really learned what an outstanding young aviator I had married. This word came from squadronmates, his skipper, Gotch Dillon (Captain), and even Admiral Blakely. In my mind, then and always, Admiral and Mrs. Blakely were the ideal examples of great leadership from the top "Brass." Mrs. Blakely did not mind telling a fresh young wife what was expected of her, her duties, and the limits of her status in the Navy world. It was necessary to make formal calls and to leave our calling cards and to entertain by giving cocktail parties, luncheons, dinners, and to know that rank always had its privileges.

Shown here is one of two buildings nearing completion to house the Fleet Airborne Electronics Training Unit Atlantic (FAETULANT) facilities in the seaplane area at Naval Air Station Norfolk. Begun in March of 1956, one of the buildings was already complete when this photograph was taken August 9, 1956. Fleet Airborne Electronics Training Unit Atlantic, had been established on July 20, 1945, and headquartered at Naval Air Station Cape May, New Jersey, with five other detachments located at Quonset Point, Rhode Island; Grosse Ile, Michigan; Norfolk, Virginia; Sanford, Florida; and Edenton, North Carolina. In January of 1946, however, the command relocated to Naval Air Station Norfolk. Antisubmarine warfare training was the command's primary mission. On December 7, 1970, the FAETULANT complex was renamed the Flatley Center in honor of Vice Admiral James Henry Flatley Jr., famous naval aviator and former commanding officer of Naval Air Station Norfolk from October 1953 to June 1955. (Official United States Navy Photograph.)

"That summer of 1933 the National Air Races were held in Los Angeles. We attended because the services had been asked to exhibit some of their air power. The *Red Ripper* squadron was a part of this. Jimmy, Bill Arthur and Monty McCauley were a "stunt" wing of the squadron. I cannot remember whether they performed that day, but they did on many occasions. Son, Jim, did his share when his time came later on, and James IV made solo aerobatic feats that were above and beyond anything I've seen."

Dorothy McMurray Flatley's name is now synonymous with the annual award presented by the Association of Naval Aviation at their annual convention. Awards have been made in her honor since 1988.

The legacy does not end there, Dorothy Flatley would remark that "Jim wanted to follow in his dad's footsteps. I feel Seamus and Joe, also Kara [Jim's youngest daughter, a supply corps officer] felt the same inspiration, too. The service had been their way of life." Indeed, Rear Admiral James H. "Jim" Flatley III (retired), Naval Aviator No. V13295,(5) had a thirty-one year career in naval aviation.

Following his Naval Academy graduation and commissioning in 1956, Jim Flatley remained as company officer to assist in the plebe summer indoctrination of the Class of 1960. After proceeding on to flight training, Flatley was designated a naval aviator on October 9, 1957, and reported to his first fighter squadron, VF-33, in early 1958 to fly the Grumman F11F-1 Tiger. During this period, VF-33 called themselves the *Astronauts*.(6) Deployed aboard the USS *Intrepid* (CVA-11), Flatley completed three Mediterranean deployments, earning him his officer of the deck underway and landing signal officer qualifications during the first of these deployments, and working his way up the ladder during the remainder of his tour to become flight division leader and squadron department head.

Perhaps one of the most extraordinary facets of Rear Admiral Flatley's career was his period as a Navy test pilot. He proceeded to the United States Naval Test Pilot School for his first shore duty,

An F11F-1 Tiger of VF-33 makes a touch and go aboard the USS *Intrepid* (CVA-11), November 15, 1958. Rear Admiral James H. Flatley III was a member of the squadron at the time. (N.W. Kuykendall, photographer. Official United States Navy Photograph.)

graduating in November 1962, followed by assignment to the Carrier Suitability Branch of the Flight Test Division. For the next twenty-eight months, he participated in extensive testing of aircraft, aircraft systems, and stores in the aircraft carrier environment, and was, at least at one juncture, carrier qualified in thirteen different aircraft. He was the project pilot during development and delivery of the French Crusader, and for the unique carrier feasibility trials of the Lockheed C-130 Hercules, an aircraft he successfully landed on the deck of the USS *Forrestal* (CV-59).

His period of test piloting over for the time being, Flatley served as landing signal officer for Carrier Air Wing Three embarked on USS *Saratoga* (CV-60) for two additional Mediterranean deployments. Additionally, he served as safety officer, during which time Air Wing Three achieved the most favorable landing-to-accident ratio in the Atlantic Fleet. Rear Admiral Flatley, like his father, paid much-deserved attention to aviation safety, setting into motion many of the edicts of safety in place today.

From Carrier Air Wing Three, Flatley reported directly to Fighter Squadron 213 *Blacklions* in 1967, deploying twice to Vietnamese waters with the squadron aboard the USS *Kitty Hawk* (CV-63), spending a total of eighteen months under combat conditions. His efforts as safety officer and maintenance officer helped the squadron earn the Chief of Naval Operations Safety Award for eleven thousand accident-free operational and combat hours. Those eleven thousand hours brought VF-213's total accident-free hours to over twenty-five thousand, a record for a tactical air squadron at that stressful point in time in naval aviation.

When Jim Flatley finally stepped out of the cockpit for the first time in twelve years, he entered the Air Command and Staff College at Maxwell Air Force Base in August of 1969, and at the same time earned his master's degree in business administration from Auburn University (1970).

After a brief tour at Commander Fleet Air Norfolk and Fighter Squadron 101 *Grim Reapers,* Flatley reported to the Fighter Squadron 31 *Tomcatters* as executive officer in 1971. He subsequently assumed the commanding officer slot at VF-31 just as the squadron and the USS *Saratoga* sailed into combat waters for the first time in both the *Tomcatters'* and *Saratoga's* histories. During the ten-month deployment, the squadron flew over 2,200 combat sorties with no loss of crew or aircraft. The *Tomcatters* were awarded the Battle Efficiency "E" Award and the Chief of Naval Operations Safety Award for their performance on the cruise. Flatley would finish three Vietnam deployments with 350 combat

Captain James H. Flatley, commanding officer of the USS *Saratoga* (CV-60), is shown cutting the cake for his 1,500th carrier landing. He achieved this feat in a VF-31 *Tomcatter* aircraft, his old squadron, in 1980. James H. IV ("Seamus") (far left) was in the backseat of his father's F-4 Phantom for that landing. "Seamus" was on his third class (3/c) midshipman cruise aboard the *Saratoga* at that time. (Courtesy of Rear Admiral James H. Flatley III (retired)).

missions to his credit in addition to his many awards, including the Silver Star, two Distinguished Flying Crosses, the Bronze Star with Combat "V", numerous Air Medals with Combat "V", the Presidential Unit Commendation, the Navy Unit Commendation, and the Meritorius Unit Commendation. In addition, the Republic of Vietnam awarded Jim Flatley the Republic of Vietnam Distinguished Service Order Second Class, Gallantry Cross with Palm Unit Citation, and campaign ribbon.

Upon returning stateside, Flatley was ordered to Commander Naval Air Force Atlantic Fleet (COMNAVAIRLANT) as fighter training officer for the next eighteen months, a role which proved critical as the fleet began formal introduction of the Grumman F-14 Tomcat. Upon finishing his tour with COMNAVAIRLANT, Flatley assumed command of Carrier Air Wing Seven aboard the USS *Independence* (CV-62), and deployed on his seventh Mediterranean cruise via a major North Atlantic Treaty Organization (NATO) exercise in the North Atlantic. Returning to COMNAVAIRLANT as ships' training officer for a year, he participated in Class Two of the Senior Officer Ship's Material Readiness Course en route to command of the USS *Caloosahatchee* (AO-98). As commander of AO-98, Flatley was awarded the Legion of Merit for the high material and operational readiness attained by the thirty-year-old oiler.

Captain Flatley reported for his first tour in Washington, D.C., in 1978 as executive assistant and senior aide to the vice chief of naval operations (VCNO). He learned the whys and wherefores of life at the top in record time while providing the VCNO, Vice Admiral James R. Hogg, "an excellent sounding board on fleet operational and personnel issues." As of result of his outstanding performance, Flatley received the second of five Legions of Merit.

Though he was slated to assume command of the USS *America* (CV-66) upon leaving his Washington post, a short-notice requirement surfaced to detail a commanding officer to the USS *Saratoga*. Jim Flatley was the first to raise his hand. Taking leave of his executive assistant duties early, he headed for Mayport, Florida, with more than a small appreciation for the challenges ahead, gained during four earlier *Saratoga* deployments. Reporting aboard to find that the Physical Evaluation Board had declared the *Saratoga* materially unsafe to make the deployment scheduled prior to her entry into Ship's Life Extension Program (SLEP), as well as finding the daily unauthorized absence (UA) rate at 225, and the deserter count at 175, Captain Flatley set about to set the ship's company and physical condition right.

Five months later he deployed for the Mediterranean with a dedicated crew and a Commander-in-Chief United States Atlantic Fleet (CINCLANTFLT) material condition safety waiver based on the Engineering Department's demonstrated sound operating procedures and plant knowledge. At the conclusion of the deployment, the USS *Saratoga* and her crew were awarded the Admiral Arleigh A. Burke Award as the most improved ship in the Atlantic Fleet, and Captain Flatley was recognized for his contributions as commanding officer with the Navy League's coveted John Paul Jones Award for Inspirational Leadership. Later, Flatley would be instrumental in getting the carrier SLEP program off to a sound start, particularly in terms of resettling eight hundred young Navy families in the Philadelphia, Pennsylvania, area and formulating the arguments which helped win sea pay for sailors faced with supporting extended overhauls in harsh shipyard environments. His efforts associated with the *Saratoga* earned him, of course, his third Legion of Merit.

Perhaps one of the best outcomes of his time on the *Saratoga* was being frocked as a rear admiral. Jim Flatley, finally wearing flag rank, assumed command of the Navy's largest training center at Great Lakes in October of 1981. Much of what this naval aviator accomplished at Great Lakes is still evident today. He vigorously implemented many personnel development programs and dependent quality of life improvements while, at the same time, serving notice on the surrounding civilian community that the training center's massive numbers of young people needed a positive, safe, and supportive liberty environment to complement the intensive Navy indoctrination and training they were undergoing. Most impressively, he spent forty-five minutes personally counseling every one of the eighty-two thousand young sailors who graduated from the Recruit Training Command during his tour. His efforts and intense personal interest earned Rear Admiral Flatley much praise from the people of Chicago, Illinois, and earned him his fourth Legion of Merit.

Toward the end of his career, Rear Admiral Flatley assumed command of Carrier Group Eight and spent twenty-two of the next twenty-six months underway while serving successively as the Atlantic Fleet carrier workup commander for seven aircraft carriers, officer in tactical command for four battle group pre-deployment operational readiness evaluations (OREs), officer in tactical command as Commander Carrier Striking Forces Atlantic for two major NATO exercises in the Norwegian Sea, and Commander Task Force Sixty, and Commander Carrier Striking Forces South during a seven-month deployment to the Mediterranean. No aircraft were lost or seriously damaged during his twenty-six months as a group commander. His tour culminated in twenty-three years of sea duty in the carrier operational environment, including fifteen deployments, and more accident and incident-free carrier cockpit exposure than any other pilot in naval aviation history. It was at this time Rear Admiral Flatley was awarded his fifth Legion of Merit.

By 1985, Flatley had assumed his duties as director, Strike and Amphibious Warfare. He directed studies that brought economy and reason to the Fire Support Ship Study, the Airship proposal, and introduction of the first phase of the Integrated Strike Planning System (TAMPS) now in every deployed aircraft carrier. In 1986, he assumed duties as deputy director, Naval Warfare, and extended his influence further to encompass all major warfare areas and across all platforms. For this effort, and his entire naval career, Rear Admiral James H. Flatley III was awarded the Distinguished Service Medal. Today, Rear Admiral Flatley is chief executive officer of the state-owned Patriot's Point Naval and Maritime Museum in Mount Pleasant, South Carolina.

Rear Admiral Flatley's wife, Nancy, was the stabilizing force behind this great aviator, a fact supported by her eldest son, "Seamus," who commented, "I doubt my father could have had the career he did without the unwavering support of my mother. She did it all for all six of us kids, and she did it with such grace." Seamus remembered one occasion when his father was a department head and in Vietnam. "I guess she had had enough. She disappeared for awhile, leaving me in charge, but she came back and everything was like nothing ever happened. Of course," he said smiling, "we also straightened up quite a bit while she was gone."

When asked whether she thought her support was extraordinary, Nancy Flatley replied: "No, I think every Navy wife in my position would have done the same thing. Wives in my day did not work like they do today, so I think it is even tougher on the families to be together. Both spouses have to work hard at the relationship, and with the children." She was quick to add, "If I had it to do all over again, I wouldn't change a thing—the constant moving, the babies, the deployments. Jim and I have a life partnership. We have always known what's important."

To their credit, each of the third generation[7] of Flatleys in naval aviation—Lieutenant Commander James Henry "Seamus" Flatley IV[8] and Lieutenant Commander Joseph "Joe" Flatley,[9] USNR—has molded careers in and of their own making, each bringing his own personality, leadership skill, and flying ability to the job.

Lieutenant Commander Seamus Flatley, known his squadronmates by his call sign, "Flats," is the epitomé of the fighter pilot who has been tempered by the experience, understanding, and compassion for people that have made the Flatley name one to be respected.

Seamus Flatley's family has had a profound impact on his choices. Nancy Flatley remembers Seamus being about four years old when he first expressed an interest in flying. "Since I was knee high in knickers and living down on the north end [of Virginia Beach] watching F-4s fly by, I wanted to be an F-4 pilot," he remembers. "Then the F-14 came along and I knew I wanted to do that." He started planning early for his aviation career, and he knew it began with the United States Naval Academy. He graduated from the academy in 1983, and immediately went to work on well-planned personal goals.

In the course of his career, Seamus Flatley has gone the route of a fighter pilot where opportunities are competitive and, what a junior officer would call "a great deal," hard to come by. He has been an airshow pilot, commanding the F-14 Flight Demonstration Team, and an instructor pilot for the VF-101 *Grim Reapers,* the F-14 "Rag" and the very squadron his grandfather founded. Commander Steven C. Schlientz, former commanding officer of Fighter Squadron 103 *Sluggers,* remembers Seamus Flatley as a young lieutenant in 1989 when Schlientz was operations officer and Flatley, a first-tour lieutenant at VF-103. "Seamus started out working for me, and he worked so hard and was just such a phenomenal officer, I made him my assistant operations officer. When someone works as hard as he did, you make things happen for him. The talent he has is incredible. I would rank him among the top two or three of all time first-tour lieutenants I have ever seen.

Captain James H. "Jim" Flatley III, commanding officer, USS *Saratoga,* 1980. (Courtesy of Rear Admiral James H. Flatley III (retired)).

This Grumman F-14A Tomcat from VF-143 *Pukin' Dogs* was photographed above cloud cover, circa early 1980s. The F-14A was produced through the mid-1980s though its Pratt & Whitney TF30-P-414A turbofan engines were plagued with problems. The original engine configuration produced 10,875 pounds of military rated thrust, 17,077 pounds at full afterburner. The first flight of the F-14A was on December 21, 1970, and the first flight of the F-14B—the F-14A conversion—was September 12, 1973. Conversion kept the original F-14A airframe in service. The F-14A+, fitted with General Electric F110-GE-400 engines, first flew on November 14, 1987. The A+ designation was also changed to F-14B in 1991. A total of 633 F-14 aircraft were produced by Grumman Aerospace Corporation for the United States Navy, and an additional eighty F-14As were built for Iran. Seventy-nine of the eighty were delivered to Iran between 1976 and 1979, with one retained by Grumman after the Iranian revolution which deposed the Shah of Iran. (Official United States Navy Photograph. Courtesy of Fighter Squadron One Hundred Forty-Three *Pukin' Dogs*.)

He's an outstanding ground officer. If Seamus saw a problem come up he took care of it, and came back to me with the answer. He is a naturally gifted pilot." Lieutenant Commander Larry Slade, one of Flatley's contemporaries, shares that opinion: "Seamus has risen and fallen in this profession on his own merits. He is one of the hardest working aviators I have seen. He has personal goals, a work ethic to be admired."

Only once has he wavered in those goals. "It had been a bad year for me all around, wondering what to do for orders, what squadron I'd go to," Seamus paused. "I got shuffled around, which was not the way to treat an instructor pilot. Then there was Tailhook, downsizing. The Navy was not looking so fun to me, so I was seriously considering getting out until I realized all this is a cycle."

The turning point came when Flatley attended the change of command ceremony for Vice Admiral Anthony A. "Tony" Less, Commander Naval Air Force Atlantic Fleet. "Tony Less gave a great speech. I wrote him afterward and told him it had been a rough year but when I heard your speech, it took me back to why I am in the Navy, why I am an aviator, amongst lots of other things." Flatley asked for a copy of the speech and Less complied. "I hold that speech with me so when I get that [down] feeling I pull it out, read it, and feel good again."

Seamus swears now that he never really entertained the idea of getting out, remarking that he felt good about the fact he had never quit anything in his entire life, "except," he said with a smile, "the trumpet in fourth grade, and I vowed never to quit anything again. And I never have. You have to wonder if quitting the Navy was quitting the Navy or throwing your hands up in frustration at what was going on." Again smiling, he added, "j.o.'s [junior officers] always see things the way they really are."

Nancy Flatley has said, "I believe Seamus wants to get to a position to make the Navy work better. Jim [his father] worked to the top to do the same, to make a difference. Seamus sees how the system works and knows that to make changes for the good of people, you have to get to the top."

Gone are the silk scarf days of combat, detailed descriptives of pilot observations of the landscape, and ultimately, the feeling of being in the cockpit. When asked if he thought there were any challenges, or for that matter, excitement left to flying today's technologically-driven fighters, Seamus Flatley offered the following comments. "If a person stays in the cockpit long enough there will be enough excitement in a lifetime of flying to capture that thrill. There are moments," he added, "you just sit there flying off the boat, day in, day out. Pilots develop entrenched patterns. But, if you do it long enough, there will be excitement, like all the flying we did over Iraq and Bosnia."

And then there were the airshow problems he had. There were two instances during airshows, in particular, which could have easily ended tragically for him but did not. "That's where I think just in that three- to four-week span in 1992 where I've always believed my grandfather was my guardian angel. He takes care of me. He was there, no kidding." In the first instance, Seamus had engine trouble and put the Tomcat on the ground, sensing it was important that he not wait to finish the routine. "It was determined I needed a new engine," he explained, "so we pulled it out, and one of the Grumman reps comes up to show me the problem and says, 'Look, see that big bubbling area right here, where it's all brown. Looks like you probably had about thirty seconds' time on this engine before this would've burned through and gotten to your flight controls.'" He had known when to stop. Flatley had been maneuvering that day over a crowd of eighty thousand people. His aircrew's safety and that of those on the ground mattered the most. Then there was Cleveland. Flatley lost another engine during a performance and, without hesitation, he remarked, "He's looking after me."

Vice Admiral Flatley also looked out for the family, working tirelessly in the course of his career to improve family life for dependents of military members in his commands. His indomitable sense of the family's importance elevated the stature of wives, children, fathers, mothers, and extended family members in the eyes of the Navy. His efforts effectively boosted morale as sailors and their families became part of the information network, and part of the much greater Navy family. Vice Admiral Flatley's legacy of family was taken up by his son who, in turn, passed along the virtues of family to Seamus and Joe.

Bearing the Flatley name in today's Navy has never spared him nor brother Joe from people picking up on the history. "Even if they don't know me," Flatley noted, "some guys pick up on the name but, I take pride in the fact that name is well-remembered." He contin-

The *Fighting Omars* of Fighter Squadron Composite Twelve (VFC-12) are shown flying their McDonnell Douglas F/A-18 Hornet aircraft over Naval Air Station Oceana, 1994. The Kola Peninsula paint scheme and tail markings set the squadron apart. In their adversary mission, *Omar* instructors simulate threat aircraft and tactics that fighter crews might expect to encounter in actual combat. The squadron has taken over the Strike Fighter Air Combat Maneuvering or ACM Readiness Program (SFARP), an intensive three-week program encompassing ground and flight training. (Official United States Navy Photograph. Courtesy of Fighter Squadron Composite Twelve *Omars*.)

ued, "they [his father and grandfather] were leaders. You wonder if you are displaying the same leadership attributes because in my opinion, these are the two people I admired the most, and still do. If it [leadership skill] was successful for them, it should be successful for me. We all want to be successful."

The Flatley family commitment to naval aviation is clear. The commitment they have to each other equally impressive, especially when it would be so easy to lose touch by virtue of career changes, and moves.

Seamus and his wife, Christine, have three boys of their own, and Joe and his wife, Bridgette, have four—one boy and three girls. The best advice their father has given them regarding their own families is to spend more time with them whenever they can, perhaps because the admiral knows the pain of considerable separation from Seamus, Joe, and their siblings all too well.

When asked about his bond to his brothers and sisters, particularly brother Joe, Seamus Flatley replied: "Joe had to live in my shadow for a couple of years in high school, and Joe is a fine athlete," he added, "Joe's also a natural at aviation. I have to work at it. He is very well-respected in his air wing."

Joe Flatley has also been given the call sign "Flats" by fellow pilots. Joe remarked that there was one time both he and Seamus were up flying and they called each other on the radio, "Hey Flats, it's Flats." Joe is a seasoned adversary pilot, so the likelihood of him finding brother Seamus aloft becomes a distinct possibility. Joe works these days in the TAR (Training Active Reserve) program. "Family had everything to do with my decision to accept a TAR billet," Joe explained in an interview. "I wanted the time with Bridgette and our children. I could not do that deploying like I used to when I was regular Navy."

His role as an adversary pilot keeps Joe flying the F/A-18 Hornet, and gives him the fulfillment of teaching fleet pilots the ins and outs of aerial combat, a job never taken lightly by adversary pilots like Flatley. The survivability of the fighter pilot depends on his ability to keep abreast of enemy tactics, aircraft, and mental juxtapositioning that happens only in the heat of combat.

Seamus Flatley speaks candidly of his family and its place in naval aviation: "At no time have I ever felt pressure at this job because of my background, because I don't see it like that. There are times when I think I have to be careful of what I do because it might not reflect well. But if truth be known, it's probably motivation at times, motivation turned into a work ethic."

The similarities between the careers of Vice Admiral Flatley and son, Jim, were uncanny at times, and could have been daunting. But the Flatley legacy seems to rest steady but sure on the shoulders of this generation. Seamus Flatley reflects:

"Some guys pick up on the name, but I take pride in the fact that name is well remembered. They [his father and grandfather] were leaders. You wonder if you are displaying the same leadership attributes because...these are the two people I admired the most, and still do. If it [leadership skill] was successful for them, it should be successful for me. Dad never had the opportunity to watch his father's career unfold, as my grandfather died in 1958 and my father was only two years into the Navy himself. In my case, I have seen my father's career almost from the beginning, and have tried, despite the oft pressures of being a Flatley, to work hard and make a way for myself in naval aviation. I think I have done that. [Pause] At least I hope so."

It was not until called for an interview that Seamus Flatley started thinking about the number of years of service, culminating in himself and his brother, the Flatley family has invested in naval aviation. Clearly, the legacy itself is nearing seventy years of service and, as he phrased it, "In the history of naval aviation, there's been a Flatley in the cockpit continuously with the exception being the period of the Wright Brothers and Eugene Ely."

1. "Killer" was Lieutenant Commander William R. Kane.
2. Squadron members killed-in-action.
3. Following a month's temporary duty with Fleet Air, West Coast, Jimmy Flatley reported in October of 1943 as Director of Training on the staff of Commander Fleet Air, West Coast, transferring in July of 1944 to the staff of Task Force Fifty-Eight as operations officer for Admiral Marc A. Mitscher, Naval Aviator No. 33.

   In June 1945, Flatley returned again to duty on the staff of Commander, Fleet Air, West Coast, and served in that assignment until July 1945, after which he was assigned until September 1945 to the staff of Commander-in-Chief, United States Pacific Fleet as aviation plans officer. Flatley would be given temporary duty as liaison officer, Far Eastern Air Force, during the occupation of Japan. In October 1945, Flatley became director of training at the Naval Air Basic Training Command, Corpus Christi, Texas. He was a student at the Air War College, Maxwell Air Force Base, Montgomery, Alabama, commencing in July 1947 and lasting one year, then joined the staff of Commander, Air Force, Atlantic Fleet as assistant chief of staff for operations, plans and training. Flatley assumed command of Naval Air Station Olathe, Kansas, in July 1950.
4. Project 27A was originally approved by the Chief of Naval Operations on June 4, 1947, as part of a postwar aircraft carrier refurbishment plan. *Essex*-class carriers were modified to meet new operating requirements demanded by development of aircraft and weapons systems. The *Essex*-class carriers had to be able to operate aircraft up to 40,000 pounds, and included the installation of two H-8 catapults, strengthening the flight deck and clearing it of guns, increasing the elevator capacity and adding provisions for jet aircraft such as blast deflectors, increased fuel capacity and jet fuel mixers. Project 27A was amended on February 1, 1952, to include more powerful arresting gear, higher performance catapults and a replacement of the number three centerline elevator with a deck-edge type of greater capacity. Three *Essex*-class carriers incorporating these modifications were completed in 1954 under Project 27C, the "C" reflecting the addition of an axial as opposed to angled-deck conversion. Angled-deck conversion was introduced under Project 125 of the carrier improvement program in 1954.
5. The number of naval aviators increased dramatically as the United States was drawn into the Second World War. A good example of this occurred on June 25, 1940, when the Chief of Naval Operations promulgated plans for an expanded flight training program that called for the assignment of 150 students per month beginning July 1, and a regular increase to an entry rate of 300 per month within a year. Recognizing that the numeric aviator designation process would become next to impossible to maintain, the Chief of the Bureau of Aeronautics converted to an alphanumeric system of recording naval aviator designation and precedence. In terms of number, there were 2,203 naval officer pilots as of July 1, 1940, and 349 enlisted pilots but, by the end of World War II, this number had soared to 49,380 officer pilots and 439 enlisted pilots. On the Marine Corps side, in 1940 there were 304 officer pilots and 45 enlisted pilots, but by 1945, the numbers had jumped to 10,229 officers and 47 enlisted men in the cockpit.
6. The United States had entered the race to put a man in space and the Navy, Marine Corps and Air Force provided the pilots to the National Aeronautics and Space Administration program, formed in 1958 from vestiges of what had been the National Advisory Committee for Aeronautics, to fulfill that goal. Four of the seven men selected as prospective astronauts under Project Mercury, a basic program in the development of space exploration and manned orbital flight, were naval aviators: Lieutenant M.S. "Scott" Carpenter, and Lieutenant Commanders Walter M. Schirra and Alan B. Shepard of the Navy, and Lieutenant Colonel John H. Glenn, USMC.
7. The first third generation naval aviation family began with Rasmus "Chris" Christensen, Naval Aviator No. 1885, who began his naval aviation career as a member of the first Navy class for aviation mechanics started at Pensacola on August 30, 1915. He received his airman's certificate No. 5 upon completion of the course on December 4, 1916. "Chris" Christensen rose from a chief machinist's mate (aviation) (CMM(A)) to warrant machinist (aviation) and student naval aviator to be designated a naval aviator on December 14, 1918. Christensen was part of the crew of the famous NC-1 as she attempted the transatlantic crossing in 1919. He retired after thirty years of naval service and was placed on the retired list September 1, 1934. Christensen's son, Ernest E., became a naval aviator and rose to the rank of rear admiral. Rear Admiral Christensen's son, Ernest E. Jr., also became an active duty naval aviator.
8. Lieutenant Commander Seamus Flatley was assigned to Fighter Squadron 143 *Pukin' Dogs* at Naval Air Station Oceana, as the squadron's operations officer when he was interviewed in 1995.
9. Lieutenant Commander Joe Flatley, USNR, was assigned to VFA-203 *Blue Dolphins,* a McDonnell Douglas F/A-18 Hornet squadron at Naval Air Station Jacksonville, Florida, at the time he was interviewed.
10. Lieutenant Commander Larry Slade was assigned to VF-103 at the time he was interviewed.

Chapter 12: "Without Us, They Don't Fly"

When the first naval aviation detachment arrived at Pine Beach in 1917, it was accompanied, in short order, by blacksmiths, carpenters, machinists, and riggers who wore rates of seaman (aviation). These men became the nucleus of the facility which was later known as Naval Aviation Depot Norfolk, employer to over four thousand residents from Virginia Beach, Norfolk, Chesapeake, Portsmouth, Suffolk, Hampton, Newport News, and outlying cities like Elizabeth City and Moyock, North Carolina, prior to its disestablishment in September 1996. In this early period, military rates were trained to work on motor construction, wing and fabric manufacture, aerial bomb releases, and special air armament. The Navy even employed, as it does today, professional engineers to supervise engine and machine shops. Since these were the days of wood, canvas and wire airframes, master carpenters and smiths oversaw intricate wirework and joiner work. During its first weeks of operation, the naval air detachment had aircraft anchored off the beach but, as conditions improved, canvas hangars appeared. While aircrew and mechanics made do with makeshift canvas hangars, wooden buildings were being constructed along the road through the air base and its adjacent piers.

What had begun as a relatively small operation at Norfolk grew quickly and, by 1918, Naval Air Station Hampton Roads was born and with it the parent facility of the depot: the Construction and Repair Department. During the First World War, the air station had three primary duties: experimentation, anti-submarine patrols, and instruction of both student naval aviators and, of course, enlisted personnel in the construction and maintenance of seaplanes. The Mechanics' and Quartermasters' School trained upwards of one thousand men by the end of the war.

The Construction and Repair Department was renamed the Assembly and Repair Department in 1922. Though in the beginning personnel were mostly enlisted men, this would change with postwar growth. The first brick and concrete buildings on Naval Air Station Hampton Roads were built in 1930 for Assembly and Repair and the Supply Department. The first civilian employees, numbering about fifty, were hired the same year from a pool of eligible personnel at the Norfolk Navy Yard. The newly named Assembly and Repair Department would have a workforce of 786 consisting of both enlisted and civilian personnel by 1939. As war in Europe intensified, an extensive building expansion and land reclamation program was begun in 1940 under commanding officer of the naval air station, Captain Patrick N.L. Bellinger, and a good portion of this was complete prior to the United States' entry into the Second World War. The Assembly and Repair Department claimed over 8,600 men and women, military and civilian, among its ranks by the end of the Second World War. This would be the largest number of employees to work at the facility in its history.

The department was redesignated the Overhaul and Repair Department on July 22, 1948. Overhaul and repair facilities at Norfolk did not escape the effects of military downsizing in the post-World War II period. Attentions shifted once again to research, testing, and technological advancement. As has normally been the case between wars, increasing emphasis was placed on weapons of war:

When this picture was taken circa 1930, the Assembly and Repair Department comprised considerably less area with fewer facilities. V-52 and V-53 had not been built nor had V-60 or V-90. The latter two were constructed on what is water in the picture (to the right). The large homes in the lower center of this photograph are state houses from the 1907 Jamestown Exposition. (Official United States Navy Photograph.)

This Bellanca JE-1 was sent to the Assembly and Repair Department at Naval Air Station Norfolk for re-skinning. The only JE-1, typically a civilian nine-place transport, also called a "Senior Pacemaker," acquired by the Navy in 1938 was Bureau Number 0795. The picture was taken May 19, 1941. (Official United States Navy Photograph.)

An F4F Wildcat was returned from combat duty for maintenance at Norfolk. Its signage noted that the aircraft had a Japanese merchant ship and an Axis French ship to its credit. The young woman and sailor are paying close attention because the sign also called upon those at Overhaul and Repair to do a good job since "the performance by this plane and its pilot, and others, depends on the work done here. Congratulations, F4F Wildcat, and may you soon again return to 'business as usual'." Government censors had taped over any mention of the aircraft model and name in this 1944 photograph. (Courtesy of the Hampton Roads Naval Museum.)

aircraft and armament topping the list. And, of course, by 1948 the Navy had its first jet squadron qualified for fleet operation. Helicopters would also begin to have more of a presence in fleet amphibious operations.

Under the leadership of Captain G.A. Dussault, commanding officer of Naval Air Station Norfolk (February 1948 to June 1950) and Captain T.B. Haley, officer-in-charge of Overhaul and Repair, a new Integrated Aeronautic Program was initiated in accordance with Bureau of Aeronautics instruction. At the end of the 1940s, the Bureau of Aeronautics and Department of the Navy bought new combat aircraft at a cost ranging from one hundred thousand to over one million dollars, the larger patrol planes and jet aircraft costing closer to one million. Typical Navy combat aircraft averaged two hundred thousand dollars new. After a service tour of about eighteen months, aircraft were estimated to show definite indications of water and/or combat fatigue, or component aging in need of change or improvement. The Navy made the choices fairly simple: service, salvage or overhaul. There are limits to the life of all aircraft. Initially, the Bureau of Aeronautics had estimated the length of service—the envelope in which the aircraft could operate safely—for maintenance tracking. During the Second World War, Overhaul and Repair personnel employed a special reconditioning process since the aircraft had to be treated according to its life cycle and extreme combat fatigue. In stark contrast to today's sophisticated jet aircraft, there were only some thirty thousand to one hundred thousand parts in early World War II and postwar aircraft, dependent on the model.

The Overhaul and Repair Department at Norfolk was still competing, in many instances, with the aircraft manufacturer to overhaul a plane during the postwar period, even though it was clear at the time the Navy could do the most cost-effective rework on its own aircraft. The manufacturer was primarily concerned with the original design and airframe. Overhauling the aircraft presented an entirely different problem from manufacturing. As is still true today, combat aircraft used by the Navy consist of many valuable parts not made by aircraft manufacturers, otherwise known as government furnished equipment, parts the manufacturer is in no position to fix. Overhaul and Repair tooled parts for aircraft and proved itself

An assembly line of F6F Hellcats and TBF Avengers was captured on film, February 27, 1945. (Official United States Navy Photograph.)

capable of numerous aeronautical engineering and prototype developments.

The tradition of training military and civilian personnel grew stronger under Haley's command. Overhaul work at Norfolk provided enlisted mechanics and other ratings the opportunity to be trained in a comprehensive fleet maintenance facility. No school or combat setting could provide the same depth of experience. Rotation of enlisted and officer personnel in the facility brought forth new ideas, ideas drawn from the convergence of operational experience at squadron-level maintenance and the Overhaul and Repair protocol.

The Bureau of Aeronautics had just initiated the Integrated Aeronautic Program (IAP), a program with the goal to fly the best airplane in the best condition of readiness in the most efficient manner at the lowest possible cost. Overhaul and Repair was, of course, obligated to salvage, and to test aircraft, engines, accessories, and other related naval aeronautical equipment as directed by the bureau or its higher authority. The department was likewise tasked to complete limited manufacture of aircraft parts and assemblies, and maintenance and limited manufacture of tools and equipment used in performance of such work.

During the 1950s, once aircraft were repaired, overhauled and/or modified at the Overhaul and Repair Department, the aircraft was cleared by department Repair and Ground Check Division, then turned over to the Naval Air Station Flight Test Division, precursor of Naval Aviation Depot Norfolk's Flight Test Center. Flying reciprocating, jet, and multi-engine aircraft, pilots tested as many as twelve different Navy planes at any given time, averaging thirty-five flights per month. Accumulated flight time of individual pilots in the Flight Test Division ranged between 3,100 and 10,500 hours. After the preflight, division pilots assumed all responsibility for their aircraft, checking as they would today the airframe, controls, instruments, radios, and all other systems for malfunctions and discrepancies. The Flight Test Division mission centered around operations as much as testing Overhaul and Repair planes. Flight test of aircraft under Bureau of Aeronautics guardianship, flight test of special projects assigned to the Bureau of Aeronautics, operations of R4Q cargo transports, and training of foreign pilots in the Mutual Defense Assistance Program (MDAP) were also in the job description. Between October 1948 and December 1952, the Flight Test Division played a major role in the MDAP and, roughly half-way through the program, it would be joined by the Overhaul and Repair Department in this effort.

Assignment of the Overhaul and Repair Department with the MDAP came in early February 1950 when the Bureau of Aeronautics (1 BUAER dispatch 031844Z[1] February 1950) scheduled the induction of Grumman F6F Hellcat and Curtiss SB2C Helldiver aircraft for overhaul and preparation for delivery to France. This presented a completely new problem in making certain that aircraft would render all the service built into it—in other words, extend its service life. The Overhaul and Repair Department

Workers balance aircraft propellers in Shop 6422, Building LP-21, May 7, 1947. (Official United States Navy Photograph.)

An engine crankshaft in its balancing machine, January 12, 1950. (Official United States Navy Photograph.)

Aircraft final assembly continues in building V-60, February 27, 1950. Operations within these shops consisted of the progressive assembly of small planes by stages. Planes were inducted into the first stage and in chronological order underwent such assembly operations as installing the fuel system and landing gear; installing and checking part of the hydraulic systems; installing fixed equipment, electrical equipment and systems; installing fuel and lubricating systems; installing flight controls in the fuselage; and, clearing discrepancies from all preceding operations. Workers then proceeded to install instruments, engines, propellers, and water injection systems; ordnance equipment and systems; and electrical equipment and systems before clearing discrepancies again. After the second phase of installation and trouble-shooting protocol had been followed, and workers installed cowling, fairing, and fixed equipment; fitted the wings; installed and completed hydraulic systems, and cowling and fairing; completed installation of fixed equipment and flight controls; tested electronics equipment and systems; and, as a final stage of the operation, cleared all remaining discrepancies, installed the cowling, and inspected the covers. (Official United States Navy Photograph.)

instructed French personnel in logistics and future programs for maintenance and overhaul in order that aircraft would best serve the intent and purpose of the MDAP. A total of eighty-two aircraft were loaded aboard the French carrier *Dixmude,* which made three Atlantic crossings to complete the delivery. In addition to France, the MDAP also scheduled aircraft for delivery to Italy, and with numerous special modifications, model Beech JRB-6 Voyager airplanes from Naval Air Station Norfolk were sent to naval missions in Central and South America. Special modifications to the JRB-6 included installation of oxygen systems, special seats, additional radio equipment, and special markings.

The year Overhaul and Repair began preparing aircraft for the MDAP, the United States entered into the Korean Conflict. Suddenly, the overhaul and repair facility was thrown into high gear working on many aircraft types, including the Grumman F9F-2 Panther, North American AJ-1 Savage, Douglas JD-1 Invader, and the Martin P5M-1 Marlin and all subsequent model variations, one of the last of the great flying boats. The department would also begin work during and after the Korean Conflict on a project of far-reaching importance.

The United States Navy was engaged in the early 1950s in putting heavier, faster jet aircraft onto aircraft carriers. This presented a challenge; existing carriers were hardly configured to handle the newest breed of aircraft. Officer-in-charge of Overhaul and Repair at what proved to be a critical juncture in modern aircraft carrier development was Captain Sheldon W. Brown (1953-1955). Brown had had a career rife with experience. In 1938, as a junior lieutenant, he had been the structure overhaul officer of the old Assembly and Repair Department. A 1932 Naval Academy graduate, Brown also earned his naval aviator wings in 1935 at Pensacola, Florida. Brown was destined to play a vital role in guiding program development which would, in the end, be largely instrumental in providing aircraft carriers with greater striking potential and operational flexibility in addition to increasing safety of operations on the flight deck. As head of both the Overhaul and Repair Department and director of the Ship's Installation Division (SID) of the Bureau of Aeronautics, Brown became instrumental in development of the canted flight deck for carriers. Brown was called upon to work the SID post when it became clear there existed serious difficulties in adapting new jet aircraft types to the

There were only thirty-six of the Martin PBM-5A amphibians, shown here, ever built. The aircraft, its telltale retractable landing gear visible, was put into production in the post-Second-World-War period. At the time this photograph was taken in March 1950, the aircraft was undergoing repair work at Overhaul and Repair. (Official United States Navy Photograph.)

carrier environment. His technical and administrative skill coupled with years of experience led to development of true innovations such as not only the canted deck but also the steam catapult and the barricade emergency arrestment device.

By January 1954, the naval air station at Norfolk had completed the Overhaul and Repair Department's aviation accessories overhaul building, a one-story structure on the site of Old Chambers Field. The building was unique in that it signalled a major departure in construction policy on the air station. Traditionally, buildings had to be constructed for hangar space. The new aviation accessories overhaul facility was equipped, at least by standards of its day, with a dust-free ventilation system that enabled plant personnel to overhaul delicate instruments and electronic and electrical equipment at a fraction of the cost of buying new equipment. The original structure was concrete with glass block windows and featured a conveyorized production flow line.

At the end of the decade, the department was maintenancing the Douglas R5D-3 Skymaster, Grumman's F9F-2 Panther, F9F-6 Cougar and F11F-1 Tiger, Martin P5M-1 and -2 Marlin, and Vought F8U-1, -2, and -3 Crusader aircraft types, evidence that jets had taken their place in the fleet. Aircraft armament included guided missiles as well as guns. The rapid pace at which new aircraft were being turned out of aircraft factories nationwide becomes all the more obvious from the 1950s into the 1960s. In 1966 alone, Overhaul and Repair produced 596 fleet aircraft, 2,738 missiles and 1,547 engines. The facility fleet-tested, checked and repaired 27,300 components. Even in 1966, the department was one of largest employers in Hampton Roads, with total wages and materials payouts in excess of eighty-six million dollars.

On April 1, 1967, the Overhaul and Repair Department became the Naval Air Rework Facility (NARF). Seven of its original branches became NARF departments: administrative services, management control, weapons, engineering, quality assurance, production planning and control, and production engineering. The new NARF was servicing the Grumman A-6A Intruder, EA-6A Intruder (countermeasure), EA-6B Intruder (electronics, not yet called the Prowler), Convair F-111B (variable-sweep, twin-jet, definitively aborted by the Navy on February 3, 1969, when Naval Air Systems Command issued a contract to Grumman for development of the F-14A Tomcat fighter and manufacture of six experimental aircraft), Lockheed's P-3A Orion and SP-2 Neptune, and the Vought F-8E Crusader, as well as the J57, R2800, R3350, T56, and TF30 engines. The redesignated NARF Norfolk could boast 119 buildings, 6,000 civilian, and 76 military employees including commanding officer, Captain Chester A. Briggs. It should be noted that NARF was also the rework point for all versions of six missile types in the late-1960s, including the AIM-7 Sparrow, AIM-9 Sidewinder, AGM-53 Condor, AGM-62 Walleye, AIM-54 Phoenix, and RIM-X, a radar guided surface-to-air weapon.

Just as Overhaul and Repair underwent significant changes, including a change of name, the Chief of Naval Operations created Aircraft Intermediate Maintenance Departments (AIMDs) on May 15, 1967, intended to operate

On Armed Forces Day, May 17, 1952, the Overhaul and Repair Department exhibited this Pratt & Whitney reciprocating engine, just one example of their artisans' refurbishing work. (Official United States Navy Photograph.)

This hangar at the Overhaul and Repair Department at Naval Air Station Norfolk was chock full of the Navy's grandiose patrol aircraft, primarily the Martin P4M-1Q Mercator, when this picture was taken in 1950. The Mercator in the foreground is Bureau Number 124365, one of a dozen purchased by the Navy within Bureau Numbers 124362 to 124373. The aircraft was built in limited number for antisubmarine warfare, but ended up flying spy missions along the borders of America's Cold War enemies, primarily the Soviet Union, China, and North Korea. The first Mercator took to the air on September 20, 1946, and the last of the twenty-one bought by the Navy was delivered in September 1950. Powered by two Pratt & Whitney R-4360s, capable of 3,200 horsepower, and two Allison J-33s, 4,600-pound-thrust engines, the Mercator had an operating range of 2,000 miles and a ceiling of 17,000 feet. The Q-configuration, indicative of electronics countermeasure capability and designed by Lieutenant Robert L. Ashford, USNR, was installed in the P4M-1 and delivered to Patrol Unit/NAVCOMUNIT 32G in February and March 1951. The back-end installation, the object of the photograph shown here, was problematic, so work started almost immediately to rectify placement. Four APR-4s and four APR-9s were installed, each with self-contained tuning units and panoramic adaptor, in addition to improved intercom systems segregating the cockpit and forward stations in the Mercator from the surveillance operators and evaluator in the back of the plane. For safety-of-flight reasons, the evaluator could talk to one or all of his operators, and the pilot could override the system and be understood by all crewmembers. The Q-configured Mercator began replacing the Navy's aging fleet of PB4Y-2s by June 1951.

Electronic Countermeasures Squadron One (VQ-1), the first squadron of its type in the United States Navy, was established at Naval Air Station Iwakuni, Japan, on June 1, 1955. Lieutenant Commander Eugene R. Hall was its first commanding officer. The squadron flew Mercators. A Mercator, while on night patrol out of Iwakuni on August 22, 1956, Bureau Number 124362, reported that it was under attack by aircraft over international waters, 32 miles off the coast of Wenchow, China, and 180 miles north of Formosa, and was not heard from again. Carrier and land-based air and surface ships, searching for the plane, found wreckage, empty life rafts, and the bodies of two crewmembers. Two additional crewmen's bodies were eventually recovered by the Chinese and the other twelve members of the Mercator's crew initially listed as missingin action, but later declared dead. The first body recovered was that of an enlisted crewman named Jack A. Curtis.

The Mercator did not fair well under attack on June 16, 1959, by two North Korean MiG-15s. While flying a patrol mission over the Sea of Japan, the aircraft, Bureau Number 122209, was attacked fifty miles from the Korean demilitarized zone. During the attack, the Mercator sustained severe damage to its starboard engines and flight controls, and the tailgunner was seriously wounded. The pilot brought his aircraft down safely at Miho Air Force Base, Japan. (Official United States Navy Photograph.)

Captain Sheldon W. Brown was instrumental in the development of the canted deck for aircraft carriers. A native of Toledo, Ohio, Brown was assigned to the Bureau of Aeronautics in Washington, D.C., where he spent three years. He was credited during that time with assisting in the development of the canted deck, the high-capacity steam catapult, and the new barricade emergency arrestment device which was being installed on the newest carriers in the 1950s. Brown became officer-in-charge of the air station's Overhaul and Repair Department shortly before this picture was taken on October 24, 1953.

aboard all operational aircraft carriers except the carrier operating in concert with the Naval Air Training Command, Pensacola, Florida. Aircraft Intermediate Maintenance Departments assumed responsibility for maintenance afloat, a role formerly played by air wings and air group commanding officers.

This insignia did, indeed, belong to the world renowned *Blue Angels* squadron. The artwork was generated by the Decal Shop of the Overhaul and Repair Department. It appeared sometime during the winter of 1954–1955 when the squadron was flying the Grumman F9F-5 Cougar aircraft and began as a result of the aircraft performing fleur de lis aerobatic maneuver. The fleur de lis is reflected in the pattern superimposed on the pilot wings. As the premier flight demonstration team, the *Blue Angels* have been in business since 1946. The insignia shown here was incorporated very early in the squadron's history and shows the classic pinup girl of the period. (Courtesy of Naval Aviation Depot Norfolk.)

In the 1970s the Navy introduced the Grumman F-14A Tomcat and the McDonnell Douglas F/A-18 Hornet. NARF was designated the cognizant field activity (CFA) for the F-14 in addition to ongoing CFA/depot work on the A-6A Intruder and TF30 and J57 engines. The first F-14 aircraft repaired at NARF was flight-tested on July 8, 1974. The facility prototyped the Vought F-8J Crusader for a massive rewire program of the F-14 Tomcat by the end of the year.

The 1980s would bring state-of-the-art advancements in technology and the need to streamline the control and administration of all six Naval Air Rework Facilities. Thus, on March 31, 1987, the six NARFs became Naval Aviation Depots and with this change came the reorganization effort in which depot headquarters function moved from Naval Air Station Patuxent River, Maryland, to Commander Naval Air Systems Command, Code Air-43, in Washington, D.C.

Although operations at Naval Aviation Depot (NADEP) Norfolk ceased in September 1996, the facility continued to service the fleet with the same quality and efficiency, typical of the facility's long history of doing so, until the end. Command pride shows, and none was more proud, more enthusiastic, and conscientious of the collective quality of work turned out of a command than the civilian and military personnel associated with NADEP Norfolk. The quality of work reflected in every artisan's trade continued the tradition of excellence at the facility that had been its hallmark since 1917.

Captain Bruce A. Pieper became the twelfth commanding officer of NADEP Norfolk on July 17, 1992. A naval flight officer and "Top Gun" graduate, Pieper endured perhaps the most grueling command of NADEP Norfolk as the facility was subsequently targeted by the Defense Base Realignment and Closure Commission (BRAC) for closure. Pieper and his executive officer, Captain John

Commander J.P. Adams receives his check-off list from Chief Aviation Machinist's Mate (ADC) and Naval Aviation Pilot (AP) W.A. Wilkinson as he prepared for take off in an Grumman F9F Cougar jet in March 1957. Each type of aircraft tested by the division had a similar list of items to be checked out while the plane was airborne. Adams was an inspection group officer and Flight Test officer-in-charge at Overhaul and Repair when the picture was taken. Wilkinson belonged to the rare breed of naval aviation pilots, enlisted naval aviators, in the post-Second-World-War period. (Official United States Navy Photograph.)

Engine assembly shops, Building LP-20, June 1958. (Official United States Navy Photograph.)

C. Bucelato, wrestled with the possibilities of closure and worked with civilian and local congressional leadership to save the command from being listed for termination. Pieper's command encompassed over 84 specialty trades spread out in more than 90 buildings and 172 acres of the Naval Air Station Norfolk, making it the largest tenant command on the station and an integral part of the Hampton Roads megaport complex. It also remained, despite cutbacks, the largest employer in the city of Norfolk, and a viable industry force in the Commonwealth of Virginia. There were nine major departments at the depot, two of which had been devoted to engineering services.

The Naval Air Systems Command (NAVAIR) Engineering Support Office held ultimate responsibility for accomplishing engineering projects and coordinating engineering efforts related to the F-14 and A-6 programs, including avionics and propulsion systems, avionics support equipment and automatic test equipment. It was the Production Engineering Department of NADEP, however, that provided the mechanical, electrical, tooling and industrial engineering services for the activity related to prepping the aircraft for the work at hand. The latter also determined what plant facilities, equipment and tools were needed to maintain plant operations and meet those needs.

Naval Aviation Depot Norfolk in the 1990s provided Standard Depot Level Maintenance (SDLM), modification, and in-service repair/field modifications to the Grumman A-6E Intruder, KA-6D (tanker), EA-6B Prowler and F-14A, including its transformation into the F-14D Tomcat as well as most of the components associated with these platforms. Since Grumman Aerospace Corporation (now Northrop-Grumman) had ceased production of the F-14 Tomcat, the need for NADEP Norfolk's rework expertise had become critical to fleet fighter squadrons located at Naval Air Station Oceana, the East Coast's master jet base. The depot functioned as the only site for all F-14 Standard Depot Level Maintenance and shared some of its SDLM workload on the A-6 Intruder, as it was being phased out of use, with NADEP Alameda, California.

At the time of BRAC's 1993 decision to close NADEP Norfolk, roughly half of the F-14/A-6 tactical fleet was based in Hampton Roads. With subsequent transfer of Naval Air Station Miramar, California, to the United States Marine Corps, all of the Navy's F-14s—with the exception of squadrons stationed in Japan—were moved to Naval Air Station Oceana, doubling the Tomcat population of the only master jet base on the East Coast. Oceana also gained a significant percentage of Naval Air Station Cecil Field, Florida, F/A-18 Hornets. But, no NADEP Norfolk.

Depot level maintenance remained the primary mission of the facility, though artisans did perform modifications to the aircraft and components to improve structural and tactical performance, and increase reliability of the aircraft and its systems. According to facility records, there were several modifications ongoing within NADEP Norfolk critical to the tactical and structural performance of both the F-14 and A-6. The F-14 was in the process of being converted from the F-14A aircraft to the F-14D remanufacture configuration, and the depot had designed and developed an F-14A/B upgrade also in line with the program. The upgrade was designed to add air-to-ground strike capability to the aircraft mission. On the A-6E Intruder aircraft, NADEP Norfolk installed the new composite wing to replace aging metal wings. Composites is a term commonly used to describe aircraft structures which use chemical bonding as a principal means of fabrication and may involve both metallic and nonmetallic materials. If the A-6E had not been phased out of fleet use, composite wings would have added service life to the airframe. In addition to the composite

The Overhaul and Repair Department, Flight Test Branch (LP-97), and Transfer Group Ferry Line (LP-99) consisted of these two makeshift quonsets in 1958. (Official United States Navy Photograph.)

When this photograph was taken on January 28, 1959, Shop 6136, Building LP-20, housed part of the aircraft nose buildup operation. (Official United States Navy Photograph.)

wing program, NADEP Norfolk worked on the System Weapons Integration Program (SWIP), an upgrade package which included avionic and serviceability enhancements to the Intruder. Aside from the composite wings, the program encompassed a full range of safety and performance features to protect aircrew and support personnel. Fuel tanks were split to increase battle damage operability. Nickel-coated fabric was applied in wing construction to neutralize possible effects of lightning strike and prevent immoderate damage to the composite wings.(2)

NADEP Norfolk remained the maintenance engineering cognizant field activity for the F-14 and A-6 aircraft and their associated components for nearly twenty-five years. In this role, the depot oversaw all maintenance from organizational and intermediate to depot level of the aircraft. Naval Air Systems Command was nearing completion of its transfer of more design engineering and logistics management responsibilities to NADEP Norfolk when BRAC announced its 1993 closure list. Final phase of the transition should have been completed by the end of 1995.

In addition to the primary mission of Naval Aviation Depot Norfolk, the facility provided a host of services to customers all over Hampton Roads. These services were as varied as flight line depot repairs to a Grumman E-2C Hawkeye aircraft at Naval Air Station Norfolk to the plating of ship parts for the Norfolk Naval Shipyard, Portsmouth, Virginia, or conducting a laboratory oil analysis for the Elizabeth City Coast Guard Station.

Naval Aviation Depot Norfolk retained its fleet training function for nearly eighty years. It trained as many sailors in aviation maintenance as the Mechanics' and Quartermasters' School did in 1917; nearly one thousand enlisted personnel came through the program annually. NADEP Norfolk was considered the key training center on the East Coast, providing schooling necessary to refine the skills of fleet maintenance technicians and improve the quality of the aircraft repairs these personnel perform once they returned to their squadrons or ships. Areas of instruction included paint and finish of aircraft, corrosion control and treatment, hydraulic component repair, fiberglass and bonded structural repair, and weight and balance of aircraft. Training courses varied in length and included classroom and/or practical hands-on instruction.

In its history, the depot maintained its ability to execute unique repair and modification to aircraft. Some of Naval Aviation Depot Norfolk's modern-day accomplishments are worth mention as they were executed through the talents of innumerable artisans and engineers, men and women skilled at some of the hardest rework to ever enter the facility. On the A-6E(3) aircraft, NADEP Norfolk employees assumed the role of prime contractor after the Boeing Aircraft Corporation withdrew its agreement to finish installation of the new composite wing. The depot completed the installation package by designing the support fixtures to facilitate the modification—all without the benefit of a manufacturer technical data package on how to do it. Within one year of the start of the installation program, NADEP was producing aircraft at approximately the same rate as Grumman at the company's St. Augustine, Florida, facility.

Perhaps some of the most interesting modern-day fixes have come by way of crash-damaged F-14 aircraft. One of these, as it was explained and documented during research phase, was so badly damaged that NADEP personnel had to use major assemblies from two stricken F-14s to effect repairs. This effort required the separation of the aircraft at fuselage station 533. The 533 bulkhead had to be replaced and much of the cockpit area had to be rebuilt. During this repair, both engine inlets and nacelles were removed and replaced, respectively, and the center wing box beam was replaced. No other facility, commercial nor government, has duplicated this kind of fix.

Employees working on wiring harnesses in the aircraft pointed out the fact there are twenty-six miles of wiring in an A-6E Intruder. Even more interesting is the fact NADEP designed, manufactured and installed complete replacement wiring harnesses for several models of A-6 aircraft, up to and including complete aircraft rewires. A number of similar assemblies have been installed in the F-14.(4) Perhaps most fascinating would have to be the digitized test capability to support these rewired aircraft, also developed by NADEP personnel. This highly specialized capability consisted of test software, interface cabling design and manufacture, and all process documentation to support the production effort.

Because of recently discovered structural failure modes on the F-14 aircraft, NADEP Norfolk developed a new "Hole Quality Program." This program required the development and utilization of unique nondestructive inspection techniques—a roll scan—to evaluate hole drilling operations, especially in high-strength steels. These techniques are considered innovative because they allow detection of surface and subsurface microstructure material tempering which is the initiation point for microstructure material cracking in high-strength steels. Of course, there came with this process the need for classroom and practical training to educate depot artisans in proper drilling techniques and evaluation of the holes.

The Lockheed P2V Neptune aircraft skyrocketed into the annals of aviation history by establishing the nonfueling distance record. The record flight originated in Perth, Australia, and terminated at Columbus, Ohio. This record stood for many years, and the record setting aircraft, the *Truculent Turtle,* graced Naval Air Station Norfolk for approximately twenty years until 1977 when it was donated to the National Museum of Naval Aviation in Pensacola. NARF Norfolk reworked the P2V aircraft until fiscal year 1973. The P2V rework was then contracted out to make room for the newer aircraft in the inventory. The majority of P2V aircraft were phased out of the inventory, but the Navy retained five P2Vs to support the Atlantic Fleet Weapons Range. In August 1976, NARF once again became the rework facility for the Neptune. P2Vs were reworked and concurrently converted to drone carriers. Two additional Neptune aircraft were simply reworked, the last of which was Bureau Number 147969, shown here. With the departure of 147969, another chapter in naval aviation history was concluded. (Official United States Navy Photograph.)

Unique to Naval Aviation Depot Norfolk was a team of highly skilled mechanics, engineers and support personnel known as the Voyage Repair Team (VRT), which is now part of NADEP Jacksonville, Florida. This elite team repairs and reworks vital equipment aboard ship such as the catapults and arresting gear, fresnel landing systems, pilot's landing assist television, flight deck audio systems, flight deck lighting, and glide scope indicating systems. They also possess the only Landing System Calibration Facility (A400 Tester) in the world. Services via the VRT are provided to a wide variety of ships both Navy and United States Coast Guard. Approximately ninety percent of their work is done on ships in the Hampton Roads port. This includes the Naval Station piers, Norfolk Naval Shipyard, Newport News Shipbuilding and Drydock Company, Coast Guard Station Elizabeth City, North Carolina, and numerous other private ship repair yards such as Norfolk Shipbuilding and Drydock Corporation and Moon Engineering.

The VRT supervisor is Thomas "T-Bear" Cowden who once remarked, "We don't want just anybody on the team. Everyone here is cross-trained in every repair trade: electrical, mechanical, hydraulics... Our operation is a team effort. We know what has to be done. It is part of the training and we have a great deal of pride instilled by the result of our work. Sailors actually cheer when we get there [aboard ship] and get the job done." "When the USS *John F. Kennedy's* catapult and arresting gear went down during Desert Storm, we deployed to the carrier and made repairs while flight operations continued around us," noted Cowden.

The Voyage Repair Team is the only full-service team on the East Coast of the United States. Besides providing services in Hampton Roads, the team deploys all over the world to repair ships,(5) particularly aircraft carriers. It was no accident that the team kept a headquarters at Norfolk until 1995 when the VRT relocated its operation to Jacksonville. The VRT's work requires access to highly specialized tools and equipment. NADEP Norfolk was often the recipient of defective components from the catapult and arresting gear systems from aircraft carriers removed by the VRT for repair and/or remanufacture. This process, now subsumed by NADEP Jacksonville, includes stripping, blasting, machining, nondestructive inspection, coating applications, plating, and restoration of finishes. Equipment and components are easier to truck between the depot and the piers, only a matter of minutes or at most, a few hours, without the added burden of expensive transportation or supply system costs. NADEP Norfolk and VRT's operations was serendipitously located at the largest naval complex in the world. The work accomplished by the Voyage Repair Team falls directly under Commander Naval Air Force Atlantic Fleet which is headquartered in Norfolk. This co-location also minimized reaction time to problems requiring rapid response.

Perhaps one of the most impressive of Naval Aviation Depot Norfolk's facilities, and one which certainly demonstrated how far the repair/rework establishment had progressed over nearly eight decades, was the Materials Engineering Laboratory/Navy Standards Laboratory.(6) The laboratory can perform mass calibration to one tenth of one millionth of a gram (in molecules, of course). As J.C. Kelly and Fred Stokey, laboratory supervisors, would add, "we can measure the standard volt [of electricity] to a whole one points per million of direct voltage." The Materials Engineering Laboratory—-the top ranking Navy facility of its kind in the country, moved into a new ten million-dollar building, shared with metrology engineering, the Navy's only East Coast Standards Laboratory—in 1994. This laboratory and engineering facility matches any like it at the National Aeronautics and Space Administration (NASA) and has a reputation as one of the most sophisticated engineering laboratories on the East Coast, specializing in routine and unique analysis and problem solving. The Materials Engineering Laboratory has the capability of providing rapid—same day—turnaround testing services for a wide variety of aircraft fluids and materials such as greases, lubricating oils, anti-icing agents, fuels, hydraulics fluids, preservatives, and so forth, giving its customers at Naval Air Station Oceana, Naval Air Station

The one hundredth A-6A Intruder, Bureau Number 152893, produced by the Naval Air Rework Facility (NARF) departed Norfolk on March 18, 1968. (Left to right) Lieutenant Richard W. Schram and Lieutenant Commander Brian J. Gallagher of NARF Flight Test turn over the aircraft to Lieutenant (junior grade) Brad Betz and Lieutenant (junior grade) Roger Harreld of Attack Squadron 128. Lieutenant Commander James F. Roth (far right) of Flight Test congratulates Harreld. (Official United States Navy Photograph.)

Norfolk, Naval Station piers, Yorktown Weapons Station, Langley Air Force Base, Elizabeth City Coast Guard Station, and many others, timely answers to often critical inquiries.

It is interesting in the age of environmental conservation and recycling of fluids that the Materials Laboratory has evolved a process of extending the use of oils for longer periods of time. The laboratory currently performs quantitative analysis of additive packages and thermal oxidative stability testing of lubricating oils such as MIL-L-23699 and DOD-L-85734. This is in support of efforts to establish new operating criteria that can allow oils to be utilized for longer periods of time. As a direct consequence, the disposal rate of oil goes down, lessening the impact on the environment.

The laboratory has developed an impressive analytical microscopy facility that is capable of conducting detailed analysis of single fiber (both natural and synthetic) and minerals in addition to micro particle analysis and filaments. The Naval Safety Center uses the local Materials Engineering Laboratory support for immediate failure analysis of aircraft parts and components associated with aircraft accident investigations. Many of these parts and components must be evaluated immediately due to the rapid deterioration of some of the materials involved, such as magnesium, or volatile liquids. The laboratory does a considerable amount of mishap investigation work, testing large to minute pieces of airframe, fluids, aircrew gear, and instrumentation for stress, burn pattern, fatigue, and any number of other problems depending on the circumstances of each mishap.

There are innumerable services provided by the Materials Engineering Laboratory which are part of its prototype facilities including provision of rain erosion boots for aircraft radomes; special sealant repair kits for emergency fleet maintenance of local and deployed hardware; one-of-a-kind weld repairs to flight-critical components; small-scale production of out-of-production polymeric parts and components; and exotic plating, using gold and other alloys, of small, out-of-production parts such as electronic contacts, and special anticorrosion coatings for flight-critical parts. The Naval Criminal Investigative Service has used the services of the laboratory to investigate bogus materials usage by commercial ship repair companies. These services involve chemical, metallurgical, nondestructive and physical testing of a wide variety of materials and parts, many of which are deployment-critical.

At any given time in the early 1990s there were upwards of five hundred fleet operational aircraft in the confines of the Hampton Roads area. Though most of the area's naval aircraft eligible for what the facility dubbed its In-Service Repair (ISR) program are located at Naval Air Stations Norfolk and Oceana, the depot took into account service needs outside the immediate naval complex and sent teams to other air stations on the East Coast and deployed aircraft carriers. The ISR staff consisted of highly skilled artisans from all the aircraft trades, in addition to a group of planners and estimators with unique abilities in the repair of aircraft in the field.

Having an ISR program equates to minimal downtime for operational aircraft. The team can even provide navigational calibration and alignment, and weight and balance services to squadrons. Because the ISR program was available locally, its personnel had been tasked for repairs on all types of naval aircraft including the F-14, A-6 and E-2C aircraft, and SH-2F, SH-3G, CH-46, MH-53E, RH-53D and CH-53E helicopters. As part of ongoing improvements to the E-2C Hawkeye, ISR teams had been installing major wiring improvement modifications into the aircraft.

NADEP Norfolk supplied services to other countries and commands throughout its distinguished history. The ISR program was involved in the foreign military sale of twelve RH-53D helicopters to Israel, and they also supported carrier suitability testing by the French Air Force in more recent years.

Naval Aviation Depot Norfolk's environmental standards were high. In the future, the people of Hampton Roads will be thankful that history recorded acts of environmental consciousness. As a partner in "Save The Bay," NADEP Norfolk formed its own Chesapeake Bay Committee. The facility researched alternate paint stripping processes to reduce or eliminate the use of hazardous chemicals and it recovered materials such as chromic acid, cadmium, and precious metals. To reduce volatile organic compound (VOC) emissions, NADEP Norfolk replaced high VOC coatings, degreasers and freons with environmentally compliant materials where possible in applicable work spaces. For their outstanding efforts to protect the environs of the Chesapeake Bay and Hampton Roads, Naval Aviation Depot Norfolk won the Secretary of the Navy Environmental Quality Award for 1993 and 1994, and had been recognized by local and regional environmental groups

An A-6E Intruder undergoes maintenance, circa 1990, Naval Aviation Depot Norfolk. (Official United States Navy Photograph.)

for its ongoing efforts to improve an already aggressive protection and recycling program.

One aspect of naval aviation history that is often lost has to be the expanse of technology that goes into making naval aircraft take to the air safely, and Naval Aviation Depot Norfolk's story is truly the marriage of technology and practicality to commitment and blood, sweat and tears poured into every project entering the facility's hangar doors. History is clearly about people and the role they have played through time to ensure, in this case, a functional and safe naval air force. Naval Aviation Depot Norfolk picked up over a dozen major awards in less than a decade, all of them indicative of commitment to excellence. Employees of NADEP Norfolk were recipients of four consecutive Secretary of the Navy Environmental Quality Awards in 1991, 1992, 1993 and 1994; an American Lung Association Silver Award (1992), given for providing a clean indoor environment to employees; the Quality Improvement Prototype Award finalist (1992); 1991 PortFolio Environmental Award; Naval Personal Excellence Partnership of the Year Award (1991); Quality Improvement Prototype Award finalist (1991); City of Norfolk Exemplary Volunteer Programs Award (1990); President's Council for Management Improvement (PCMI) Management Excellence Award (1990); Secretary of the Navy Action Plus Excellence Award for Quality and Productivity, awarded for outstanding implementation of the principles of Total Quality Management philosophy (based on measurable and verifiable quality improvements and savings they had achieved as a result of implementing total quality management principles) (1989); Naval Air Systems Command Aviation Safety Award (1988); and, the United States Senate Productivity Award for Virginia (1988).

The heart of naval aviation is maintenance. The motto "without us, they don't fly," is true not only of Naval Aviation Depot Norfolk, but, remains the charge of all maintenance performed on the flight line, aboard ship, and in hangars at naval aviation facilities and aboard ships around the world. Squadron-level maintenance, sometimes aided by depot and manufacturer personnel, has had a profound impact on the operational readiness of fleet aircraft. Aviation maintenance personnel have been keeping naval aircraft flight worthy since naval aviation was in its infancy at Hampton Roads.

An unknown poet penned the following poem, one which most certainly captures the sentiment of every squadron commanding officer who ever looked to maintenance crew to keep his aircraft flying.

Remembering The Forgotten Mechanic

Through the history of world aviation, many names have come to fore
Great deeds of the past on our memory will last as they're joined by more and more—
When man first started to labor in his quest to conquer the sky,
He was designer, mechanic and pilot and he built a machine that would fly—
The pilot was everyone's hero, he was brave, he was bold, he was grand,
As he stood by his battered biplane with his goggles and helmet in hand—
But for each of these flying heroes, there were thousands little renowned
And these were the men who worked on the planes but kept their feet on the ground—
We all know the name of Lindbergh and we've read of his flight to fame
But think, if you can, of his maintenance man; can you remember his name?
And think of our wartime heroes and all the acclaim they got
Can you tell me the names of the crew chiefs? A thousand to one you cannot—
So when you see mighty jet aircraft as they mark their way through the air,
Remember the grease-stained man with the wrench in his hand;
He's the man who put them there.

Chapter 13: Birth of the Flattop

History has all but forgotten the USS *Birmingham* (CL-2), Eugene Barton Ely's chariot and his platform for giving birth to naval aviation on November 14, 1910. The *Birmingham* was launched on May 29, 1907, at the Fore River Shipbuilding Company, Quincy, Massachusetts. She was commissioned on April 11, 1908, with Commander B.T. Wallin, commanding officer. The *Birmingham* would serve the Atlantic Fleet until June 27, 1911, when she joined the reserve fleet in Boston, Massachusetts, on June 30, 1911. The ship would be brought back into service on several occasions, later serving in the First World War on patrol off the northeast coast of the United States until June 14, 1917, when she sailed to New York to escort the first American troop convoy to France. In later years, the *Birmingham* cruised the waters along Central America and northern South America until she returned to Philadelphia Navy Yard, Pennsylvania, for decommissioning on December 1, 1923. The *Birmingham,* harbinger of so much history, was sold for scrap on May 13, 1930. The *Birmingham's* place in naval aviation history rests in Ely's moment of triumph but is, nonetheless, important in all that was to come as pioneers of flight and architects of the aircraft carrier forged ahead, culminating in the christening and commissioning of the Navy's two newest nuclear aircraft carriers: USS *John C. Stennis* (CVN-74), christened November 11, 1993, at Newport News Shipbuilding, Newport News, Virginia, and commissioned December 9, 1995, at Pier 12, Naval Station Norfolk; and USS *Harry S. Truman* (CVN-75), christened September 7, 1996, at Newport News Shipbuilding, and commissioned July 25, 1998, at Pier 12.

The first aircraft carrier, the USS *Langley* (CV-1), has been called the Navy's floating laboratory, and rightly

The USS *Langley* (CV-1), the Navy's first aircraft carrier, was called the "Covered Wagon." Her unobstructed flight deck was built atop the main deck which, after conversion, also served as a hangar bay for aircraft repairs. While the ship was being constructed at Norfolk Navy Yard between 1919 and 1922, aeronautical engineers and draftsmen at the air station built a replica of her flight deck on old Chambers Field to train pilots for deck landings aboard the *Langley*. (Official United States Navy Photograph.)

The deck of the aircraft carrier, USS *Langley,* was bustling with activity. Boeing Pursuits were aboard the carrier in 1926. The Navy put the Pursuit through extensive testing at the National Advisory Committee on Aeronautics, Langley Field, Virginia.

The *Langley* used the image of a covered wagon canopy rising over the flight deck of the aircraft carrier as its command insignia.

The Vought O2U-2s on the hangar bay of the USS *Langley* were photographed about 1928. These aircraft had been assigned to the famed "Covered Wagon," and bear the conestoga wagon within the band located mid-fuselage on the O2U-2 Corsairs. The wagon was the insignia of the *Langley*. The O2U-2 model was produced in 1928, containing room for a pilot and observer. (Courtesy of Fighter Squadron Fourteen Tophatters.)

so. The *Langley* was the proving ground, the benchmark for all aircraft carriers to come. The carrier was named for Samuel Pierpont Langley, a distinguished American astronomer, physicist, and pioneer in the development of heavier-than-air aircraft. Langley, who devised the bolometer and many other scientific devices, was born in August of 1834, and died on February 27, 1906, at Aiken, South Carolina, and would never see the grand ship named in his honor. In retrospect one cannot escape the feeling that history thrust the weight of its greatest irony on the *Langley*. The date of Samuel Pierpont Langley's death, February 27th, appears at two critical junctures in the ship's history, her later conversion to a seaplane tender, completed on February 27, 1936, and what would be her tragic end, February 27, 1942.

Originally commissioned the USS *Jupiter* (AC-3), a coal collier, on April 7, 1913, at Vallejo, California, it was decommissioned on March 24, 1920, for conversion to the first aircraft carrier at Norfolk Navy Yard, Portsmouth, Virginia. The ship's name was changed to *Langley* on April 21, 1920, reclassified CV-1, and recommissioned March 20, 1922, with Commander Kenneth "Ken" Whiting, Naval Aviator No. 16, commanding. Aside from being the Navy's first carrier, the *Langley* was also the first electrically-driven ship in the fleet. For the next two years, the Navy's first aircraft carrier recorded many firsts.

On October 17, 1922, Lieutenant Commander Virgil Childers "Squash" Griffin, Naval Aviator No. 41, completed the first takeoff from a carrier deck. Griffin reported for duty with the aviation detachment aboard the ship in September of 1921. By March 1922, "Squash" Griffin had become head of the air department. Griffin would later become head of the air department on the USS *Lexington* (CV-2) at the time the carrier was fitted out in 1926 and, in 1928, would advance to commander, Scouting Wing, Aircraft Squadrons Battle Fleet and commanding officer, Scouting Squadron Two (B) or VS-2B. Griffin would come back to Norfolk, Virginia, as commanding officer of Patrol Wing Five in February 1939. A little over a week after Griffin's feat aboard the *Langley,* on October 26, 1922, the first landing on a carrier deck was made by Lieutenant Commander Godfrey deCourcelles Chevalier, Naval Aviator No. 7.

The *Langley* departed Hampton Roads for the West Coast to join the battle fleet in 1924. In April of 1925, two extraordinary events would occur aboard the pioneer carrier. On April 2, the use of flush-deck catapults to launch landplanes was demonstrated with a 400-horsepower Douglas DT-2 flown by Lieutenant Commander Charles Perry

Officers and enlisted personnel of Fighting Plane Squadron One (VF-1) posed for this photograph aboard the USS *Lexington*, June 20, 1928. Lieutenant Commander Gerald F. Bogan, squadron commander, sat seventh from the left in the second row (center). (Courtesy of the National Museum of Naval Aviation.)

"Charlie" Mason, Naval Aviator No. 52, with Lieutenant Braxton Rhodes, Naval Aviator No. 2916, his passenger, while the *Langley* was moored at her San Diego, California, pier. Mason's experiment with flush-deck catapult gear would later enable constructors to evolve the apparatus, making it better and safer for all Navy pilots. Just days after Mason's launch, on April 8, the first night landing was made on the *Langley* by Lieutenant Commander John Dale Price, Naval Aviator No. 2730, while the ship was at sea off the coast of San Diego. Though Price's night landing is considered the official "first" of its kind aboard a Navy aircraft carrier, his friend, Lieutenant Harold James "Hap" Brow, Naval Aviator No. 571, accidently landed aboard the *Langley* the evening of February 5 when his aircraft stalled in the middle of night approach practice. Brow, it is of some interest to note, led the squadron of Navy Martin bombers which participated in Billy Mitchell's bombing tests off the Virginia Capes in 1921.

The *Langley* completed conversion to a seaplane tender (AV-3) on February 27, 1937, at Mare Island Navy Yard, California. On February 27, 1942, the grand lady of naval aviation was sunk by her escorting destroyers about seventy-five miles south of Tjilatjap, Java, after a mortal attack by nine Japanese bombers.

After completion of the *Langley,* the Navy produced two additional aircraft carriers, the USS *Lexington* (CV-2) and the USS *Saratoga* (CV-3). The *Lexington* and *Saratoga* were constructed on the hulls of battle cruisers cancelled as a result of the Washington Naval Conference of 1922.(1) The "Lex" and "Sara," as they were affectionately known to aviators, had to be redesigned to carry larger aircraft. The *Lexington* was commissioned on December 14, 1927, at Quincy, Massachusetts, with Captain A.W. Marshall as her first commanding officer. Lieutenant Alfred Melville Pride, Naval Aviator No. 1119, made the first takeoff and landing aboard the *Lexington's* deck in a Vought UO-1 as the carrier navigated from the Fore River Plant to the Boston Navy Yard on January 5, 1928, marking the first fleet operations aboard the Navy's second aircraft carrier. Six days later, on January eleventh, Commander Marc A. Mitscher, Naval Aviator No. 33, also flying a UO-1, completed the first takeoff and landing aboard the *Saratoga*. Mitscher was air officer of the *Saratoga* from her date of commissioning, November 16, 1927; consequently he served under the legendary Harry E. Yarnell, first commanding officer of the *Saratoga*. A little over two weeks after Mitscher's landmark landing, the Navy's first dirigible shipboard operations occurred when the USS *Los Angeles* (ZR-3) made a successful landing aboard the *Saratoga* on January 27, 1928. The marrying of the *Saratoga* and *Los Angeles* was without a doubt a monumental achievement in Navy airship history, and a milestone in the colorful history of the *Saratoga*.

At 888 feet long, beams of 110 feet, displacement of 33,000 tons, and speed in excess of 33 knots, which was actually closer to 40, the identical *Lexington* and

A Vought O2U-2 Corsair belonging to Scouting Squadron Three (B) (VS-3B), takes off from the USS *Lexington* on February 28, 1929. (Official United States Navy Photograph.)

USS *Langley* was caught at anchor near Cristobal, March 7, 1930. (Official United States Navy Photograph.)

Saratoga were the pride of the American fleet. The only way historians can tell them apart in photographs is the striping on the superstructure: the *Saratoga* had a vertical stripe, the *Lexington* a horizontal band around the top of the superstructure.

In June 1928, the *Lexington* made passage from Los Angeles, California, to Honolulu, Territory of Hawaii, in 72 hours, 36 minutes, a distance of 2,226 miles, averaging a speed of 30.7 miles per hour. The *Lexington* had a power plant capable of 180,000-horsepower. This enormous power enabled the *Lexington* to supply Tacoma, Washington, with all the electricity it needed during an emergency which deprived the city of its electric power in January 1930.

Both carriers, like the *Langley*, ran under electric propulsion, their four propellers driven by twenty-two, five-hundred-horsepower electric motors geared to each. Generators provided 4,500 kilowatts for auxiliary power requirements. The *Lexington* and *Saratoga* were oil burning with boiler uptakes, eight-inch turrets, navigating bridge and masts offset from the flight deck, presenting an unusual appearance from a distance.

The interior of the two carriers had much the same configuration as modern-day American nuclear aircraft carriers, hangar bays for aircraft storage below deck, and elevators to transport airplanes between hangar decks and flying decks. Machine shops, administrative quarters and living spaces fell into other decks of the carriers, built to sail with a crew of 2,000 officers and men. The USS *Lexington* and USS *Saratoga* had about 2.3 acres of deck space for aircraft, and there were typically between seventy-five and one hundred planes aboard on a regular basis for experimentation, training, and operations.

Until 1934, the *Langley, Lexington,*

A VF-1B *High Hatter* F3B-1 aircraft deck launches from the USS *Saratoga* (CV-3), 1930.

and *Saratoga* were the only aircraft carriers in the fleet, serving both as defenders of democracy on the high seas, and experimental platforms for aeronautical engineers and physicists tinkering with their inventions. Perhaps the perfect example would be the innumerable tests conducted by National Advisory Committee for Aeronautics engineers and scientists on Norfolk-based carriers of the battle and scouting fleets in the 1920s and 1930s. One such test was the use of variable pitch propellers in exercises on August 8, 1933, using six Boeing F4B-4s from Fighter Squadron Three (VF-3) aboard the *Langley,* and one F4B-4 of Fighter Squadron One (VF-1) on the *Saratoga.* Fighting Three had previously tested variable pitch propellers on the *Langley,* thus leading to initial acceptance of the type by the Bureau of Aeronautics.

The USS *Ranger* (CV-4) was commissioned on June 4, 1934, distinctive from her predecessors as the first naval vessel originally designed from keel up as an aircraft carrier. Like her predecessors, the *Ranger* could carry nearly one hundred aircraft. Her first commanding officer was Captain Arthur LeRoy Bristol Jr., who later became a vice admiral. Constructed at Newport News Shipbuilding and Drydock Company, the *Ranger,* at 727 feet, with an 80-foot beam, mean draft of 19 feet, and displacing only 13,000 tons, was smaller than the *Saratoga* and *Lexington.* She was also unarmored, a factor which later limited the *Ranger's* participation in World War II to the Atlantic theater. That fact,

The starboard landing gear of this Boeing F3B-1, Bureau Number A7680, collapses upon landing aboard the USS *Saratoga,* 1930. The aircraft belonged to the VF-2B, a USS *Lexington*-based squadron by 1931. The aircraft sustained considerable fuselage and gear damage. This particular F3B-1 illustrates the elaborate paint schemes which existed on United States naval aircraft of the period. The rondelle (the star pattern enclosed in a circle) on the top wing was vintage September 1918 to May 1942, and the stripes inside the wing are section leader chevrons. Inside the section leader markings was the number of the aircraft in the squadron, in this case, a "3." Deck crews quickly converged on the aircraft, helping the pilot, believed to be an unlucky fellow by the name of Saboris, out of his severely damaged F3B-1.

A *High Hat* F2B-1's landing gear failed on landing aboard the USS *Saratoga,* 1930. The *High Hatters* were then designated VF-1B. The aircraft sustained major airframe and engine damage, and was in the process of being inspected for repair when this picture was taken.

A landing signal officer (LSO) aboard the USS *Saratoga* gives landing instruction to a Keystone-Loening OL-8A amphibian aircraft, 1930. Only twenty of the OL amphibians were configured for carrier operations. Note the tailhook visible just under the port landing gear.

Ensign Melvin N. Gough (fourth from left) was flying with the *High Hatters* when this photograph was taken aboard the USS *Saratoga,* 1930. The squadron had lost a pilot, hence the black armbands and silk ties on the swords. (Courtesy of William W. Gough, M.D.)

coupled with the carrier's comparatively slow-speed and aircraft-launching capability, influenced how the *Ranger* would be used during the war. Larger and faster aircraft carriers were fitted-out and sent to the Pacific theater.

The honor of landing the first aircraft aboard the *Ranger* went to none other than Admiral Ernest J. King, who would become Commander-in-Chief, United States Fleet, and Chief of Naval Operations during the Second World War. He was chief of the Bureau of Aeronautics at the Navy Department at the time of his record-making flight.

Based out of Naval Air Station Norfolk, the *Ranger* Air Group began a series of cross-country flights on January 14, 1935, to Hartford, Connecticut, and Buffalo, New York, to test the functioning of aircraft and special equipment in low temperatures. These tests were completed on the second of February.

The mighty *Ranger* would have many famous captains during her reign on the high seas, most of whom held significant positions during World War II, including John S. McCain, Deputy Chief of Naval Operations (Air); Patrick Neison Lynch Bellinger, Naval Aviator No. 8, Commander Air Force, Atlantic Fleet; William K. Harrill, Naval Aviator No. 2955; Ralph F. Wood, Naval Aviator No. 2924; Alfred E. Montgomery, commander of a task force in the Pacific theater; and, of course, Bristol.

Despite its smaller configuration, the *Ranger* was special, particularly to naval aviators who trained on her decks in the golden era of the 1930s before the outbreak of the Second World War. Pilots were challenged to learn the art of flying, and this was readily apparent in the remembrances of Captain James Arbes, Naval Aviator No. 5713, who recorded his memories of his time aboard the *Ranger,* memories now made timeless by their accuracy and by his marvelous sense of history and humor.

Arbes received his wings in August of 1938 at Pensacola, Florida. He reported out of flight school to Bombing Squadron Three (VB-3) *High Hats,* on September 24, 1938. He would recount many interesting, often hair-raising events in his flying days associated with the *Ranger*. One such even occurred on the night of November 17, 1938, during his first night flight as a member of the *High Hats,* stationed at Naval Air Station North Island flying the Vought SB2U Vindicator. Arbes had reported to the squadron fresh out of flight training and at the time had a total of about 420 hours, 60 of which were in the Vindicator.

On the night in question, there were five or six aviation cadets, all relatively new VB-3 pilots, involved in their first night familiarization flight, which consisted of about an hour of touch-and-go landings on the large mat at the north portion of the field. The landing area was lighted by flood lights and as far as Arbes could recall, the pilots had no radio contact with the tower. All traffic signals were given by signal light and the tower

The pointer dog first appeared on VS-2B aircraft in 1930, the same year these photographs were taken of squadron aircraft ashore detached, of course, from the USS *Saratoga*. This scouting squadron would become VB-4 and, eventually, VB-5 during the Second World War. The aircraft in both photographs are Vought O2U-2 Corsairs, distinguishable by the larger rudder, low-profile windscreens for both pilot and observer, and dihedral on the lower wing.

Below: Vought O2U-2 Corsairs belonging to VB-2B, then the Felix the Cat squadron, are shown crowding the flight deck of the USS *Saratoga* on May 20, 1930. Felix the Cat was first adapted as a Navy insignia in 1921 and picked up by VB-2B in 1927. Famous Felix is currently the insignia of Fighter Squadron Thirty-One *Tomcatters,* a squadron with an extensive history in Hampton Roads. (Charles S. Borjes, photographer. Courtesy of Kirn Library.)

The USS *Saratoga* was photographed leaving the Norfolk Navy Yard and passing the downtown Norfolk waterfront in the spring of 1930. (Charles S. Borjes, photographer. Courtesy of Kirn Library.)

Captain Kenneth "Ken" Whiting, Naval Aviator No. 16, commanded Naval Air Station Hampton Roads between June 1930 and 1932. Whiting would have quite a history at Norfolk as he was truly the father of the modern aircraft carrier. He commissioned the USS *Langley* into service on March 20, 1922, as executive officer of the Navy's first aircraft carrier. And, on October 18, 1922, he made the first catapult launch from the *Langley* flying a PT-1 aircraft. Whiting was assigned to the Bureau of Aeronautics in July of 1924, and put in charge of arresting gear development for the USS *Lexington* and USS *Saratoga,* then being converted from their original configurations, a battle-cruiser design. He served as executive officer of the *Saratoga* upon her commissioning, November 16, 1927, and less than two years later was assigned as chief of staff and aide to Commander Aircraft Squadrons, Battle Fleet. From this post, Whiting became commanding officer of the air station. This pioneer of naval aviation and architect of the aircraft carrier would become commanding officer of the USS *Langley* in 1933, and he fitted out the USS *Ranger* at Newport News Shipbuilding, remaining at the yard to work on plans and specifications for the USS *Yorktown* and USS *Enterprise* the same year. His love of aircraft carriers is evidenced by a string of command billets on America's earliest flattops. Ken Whiting was the Navy's expert on the subject. He became commanding officer of the USS *Saratoga* in 1934 before moving on to his role as Commander Aircraft Squadrons, Battle Fleet and commanding officer, Fleet Air Base, Pearl Harbor, Territory of Hawaii, in 1935. The last command held by Whiting with a flying requirement was as commanding officer of Patrol Wing Two in 1937, during which time he conducted numerous experiments in refueling aircraft from a submarine platform. He retired the first time on June 30, 1940, after serving as General Inspector of Naval Aircraft, Eastern Division, Third Naval District. Whiting would be recalled to active duty again during the Second World War and placed in command of Naval Air Station New York, otherwise known as Floyd Bennett Field. He died on active duty, April 24, 1943, and, as was his request, buried at the deepest point in Long Island Sound, New York—the 119-foot-point off Execution Light. (Official United States Navy Photograph.)

"One of the reasons I wanted to be a naval aviator when I was young had to be the F4B," remarked retired naval aviator Nicholas J. "Nick" Pope, as he pulled out a photograph of this F4B-4, taken August 30, 1931; "it's a classic." Indeed, the F4B epitomized the golden era of naval aviation. (Official United States Navy Photograph.)

The 14,500-ton USS *Ranger* was the first ship built as an aircraft carrier from the keel up. Its predecessors had all been skilled conversions. The *Ranger*'s keel was laid in September 1931, and the ship was commissioned three years later. (Official United States Navy Photograph.)

The Grumman F3F-2 aircraft of Marine Corps Fighter Squadron Two (VMF-2) photographed December 31, 1937, came in gear up. The Navy first contracted the Grumman Corporation to produce the aircraft in early 1937, and supplied them to Fighter Squadron Six (then designated VF-6M under the squadron designation system in use prior to July 1, 1937) aboard the USS *Enterprise,* and Marine Corps squadrons VMF-1 and VMF-2 in late 1937 and 1938. (Official United States Navy Photograph.)

The USS *Langley* (AV-3), by then relegated to a seaplane tender, is loaded with the equipment and personnel of VP-1 and VP-18 at Pearl Harbor, Territory of Hawaii, in this July 29, 1938, photograph. (Official United States Navy Photograph.)

was manned by a duty officer supplied by the squadron.

While Arbes was getting squared away in the cockpit, the plane captain told him there was an enlisted sailor, Seaman Second Class R.H. Kuckelman, from a utility squadron who needed flight time and wanted a ride. Arbes told the plane captain it was fine with him if the sailor was crazy enough to fly with him on his first night flight. Apparently, none of Arbes' chiding impressed the sailor who immediately jumped in the rear cockpit, checked out the intercom, and said he was ready to go.

"It was a black night with no moon but clear with a light westerly wind," Arbes would describe much later. His plane cleared Point Loma, one of the last plane groups to take off that night. Arbes climbed to one thousand feet then turned downwind, taking a comfortable interval on the plane ahead. Suddenly, as he was looking for the plane ahead, he saw the orange flotation gear in the light of the engine exhaust rising out of the left wing root, and at the same time the plane nosed down, turned to the left and was generally out of control. At nearly five hundred feet, the right flotation bag also inflated, which served to level off the wings and restore some modicum of elevator control.

"The rudder and aileron control remained almost entirely ineffective. The rudder pedals were banging on my feet and the stick was shaking, making it difficult to hang on to. Since the left bag inflated first this turned the plane toward the field and was headed right at the Officers' Club on the south shore of North Island," Arbes remembered, "The plane was coming down rapidly and was very nose heavy. I two-blocked the prop control and gave the engine full power which enabled me to bring up the nose and miss the Officers' Club. Fortunately, the hangar lights at the north side of the

The first aircraft carrier named USS *Enterprise* was photographed coming into her berth at Norfolk on January 4, 1939. The "Big E" had only been in service since May 12, 1938. (Charles S. Borjes, photographer. Courtesy of the Kirn Library.)

field provided a horizon, and I was able to land the plane wheels up on a small unlighted surfaced area used for field carrier landing practice."

Actually, Arbes thought he had lowered the landing gear, but in all the excitement forgot to activate the flap control which was required to lower the wheels. He later learned, had he lowered the gear, it was entirely possible that the additional drag would have prevented him from getting the nose up sufficiently to land the aircraft. He also might have wiped out the officers' club, himself, and the very brave sailor in the backseat.

When the Vindicator skidded to a stop, Arbes turned off the ignition, jumped out of the cockpit and checked to see how his last-minute passenger was doing. Kuckelman was hanging on to the plane with white clenched fingers, and the first words he was able to utter were, "What the hell happened, Mac?" Arbes shone his flashlight on what was called the "T" handle that activated the flotation gear located just in front of the passenger and noted that it had been pulled. He immediately asked Kuckelman if he had pulled it, and he replied, "No."

Arbes instructed Kuckelman to get out of the plane since it might catch fire. "I thought planes always caught fire when they crashed. He did, too. I stood there at the crash waving my flashlight hoping to be rescued and at the same time tried to find out how the 'T' handle was pulled." In the end, it turned out Kuckelman's radio cord slipped over the "T" handle when he leaned forward to close the rear canopy, and when he pulled back in his seat, the lever released the flotation device.

Across the field, Arbes could see his squadronmates making touch-and-go landings, so he continued waving his flashlight trying to attract attention. Within a few minutes, an old coupe drove up and what Arbes described as a "distinguished looking gentleman in civilian clothes accompanied by a teenaged boy" stopped to assess the pilot's predicament. The gentleman started questioning Arbes about the accident and, since he looked rather important, Arbes answered the man with "many 'Sirs.'" When the man appeared satisfied with his answers, he and the boy returned to their car and drove away. Arbes figured he still was not rescued, that is, until he heard the scream of sirens and saw the flashing lights of rescue vehicles. He later learned the gentleman who found him was none other than then-Vice Admiral Ernest J. King, who at that time was Commander Air Battle Force, Pacific Fleet. King would become Admiral King, Commander-in-Chief, United States Fleet. As for

The Doolittle Raid on Tokyo

On February 2, 1942, Norfolk sailors would witness a sight not soon forgotten: two North American B-25C Mitchell bombers craned aboard the deck of the USS *Hornet* (CV-8) pierside at Naval Station Norfolk. Within hours, the carrier was out in the Chesapeake Bay on one of the most top secret tests of the entire war, unbeknownst to anyone who had seen the bombers being craned aboard. If tests that day in the bay were successful, it would spell the beginning of a brilliant plan to bomb and strafe Japan in retribution for the enemy's attack on American military facilities, naval ships, and air stations at Pearl Harbor and outlying targets. The first question which needed an answer was whether a medium-range bomber carrying two thousand pounds of ordnance could make it off a pitching and rolling flight deck with five hundred feet or less to takeoff.

During the middle of the afternoon, one day out of Norfolk, the bombers were given the signal to takeoff. Both Mitchells took off with relative ease, much to the satisfaction of Captain Marc A. Mitscher, Naval Aviator No. 33 and commanding officer of the *Hornet,* and Captain Donald B. Duncan, Naval Aviator No. 2943, standing at Mitscher's side. This was the first sign the raid on Tokyo was destined for success.

The raid on Tokyo was conceived and tested in Hampton Roads. Aside from being a beautifully executed joint Army and Navy operation, the Tokyo strike in the spring of 1942 was a tremendous morale booster to American military forces in the Pacific theater. There are a number of accounts of how the Tokyo raid was conceived in Norfolk by Captain Francis S. Low, a submariner and operations officer for Commander-in-Chief, United States Fleet, Admiral Ernest J. King. In the early months of 1942, King and his counterparts in the Army heard President Roosevelt's message loud and clear: focus on mainland Japan and find a way to strike deep at the heart of the enemy.

Captain Low was in Norfolk on January 10, 1942, checking, ironically, on the progress of USS *Hornet,* built at Newport News Shipbuilding and Drydock Company and ready for its shakedown cruise in the Chesapeake Bay. Low's aircraft was leaving Norfolk to return to Washington, D.C., when the idea of launching Army bombers from an aircraft carrier deck came to him and, to be more accurate, the idea literally flew by. Low had seen Army twin-engine bombers making passes at the outline of a carrier deck painted on the airstrip at Naval Air Landing Field Fentress. He told Admiral King. The captain knew striking range for naval aircraft launched from a carrier was typically three hundred miles but, with the range of Army bombers, the Army could launch its aircraft from a Navy ship and bomb Japan. Low pointed out the fact that the B-25C Mitchell might be loaded aboard a carrier and successfully launched at the heart of Japan, hence the origin of the phrase "Raid on Tokyo." After meetings with General Henry H. "Hap" Arnold, Army Air Corps Chief of Staff, Low, and King, a plan was approved and the operation proceeded with test flights on the *Hornet*. Captain Marc A. Mitscher, commanding officer of the *Hornet,* along with Lieutenant Colonel James H. Doolittle of the United States Army, were among a handful of men to know of the future raid prior to the carrier's departure from Norfolk for the Pacific theater.

In less than three months, Lieutenant Colonel James H. Doolittle, of the United States Army, took off from the *Hornet* in the first of sixteen B-25C Mitchells on April 18, 1942, to bomb mainland Japanese targets with familiar names: Tokyo, Yokohama, Yokosuka, Kobe, and Nagoya. Doolittle and seventy-nine other officers and enlisted men launched from the *Hornet,* most of whom survived because they were able to ditch their aircraft near the Chinese coastline or in the Soviet Union. Of the eighty crewmen who risked their lives on the raid, eight would be taken captive, and three of these were executed by Japanese soldiers.

President Franklin Delano Roosevelt inadvertently named a future aircraft carrier, the USS *Shangri-La,* when he made his radio address announcing Doolittle's aircraft came from a fictitious island of Shangri-La, a surreal Tibetan location from James Hilton's novel *Lost Horizon*. The *Shangri-La* was constructed at Norfolk Naval Shipyard in Portsmouth, Virginia, in 1944. Josephine "Joe" Doolittle, Lieutenant Colonel Doolittle's wife, was the *Shangri-La's* sponsor, and Hilton would be on hand for the commissioning ceremonies in its honor. Japanese radio picked up Roosevelt's broadcast and, according to reports later in the war, were perplexed at the President's reference to the fictitious Shangri-La.

Lieutenant Colonel James H. "Jimmy" Doolittle, USA, wires a Japanese medal to the fin of a five-hundred-pound bomb which shortly thereafter was released over an enemy target. The ceremony took place on the deck of the USS *Hornet,* from which the Army B-25C Mitchell bombers took off April 18, 1942. (Official United States Navy Photograph.)

Cleared for takeoff from the deck of the USS *Hornet,* an Army B-25C goes on its way to take part in the first United States air raid on Japan, April 18, 1942. (Official United States Navy Photograph.)

Soaring off into a gray sky, a North American B-25C United States Army bomber heads for Japan in America's first attempt to bring the war home to the enemy. The attack, launched from the flight deck of the USS *Hornet,* was delivered at low altitude, and the airmen reported that every bomb was dropped on appointed target areas. First Japanese accounts admitted heavy damage, both from explosions and fires—the latter largely set by the supply of incendiaries carried by Doolittle's raiders, members of the 17th Army Air Force Air Group. (Official United States Navy Photograph.)

On February 20, 1942, this Consolidated XPB2Y-3 Coronado aircraft, Bureau Number 1638, was photographed on the deck of the USS *Ranger.* (Official United States Navy Photograph.)

Kuckelman, he still needed more flight time.

The most immediate result of Arbes' incident was an aircraft change which required a metal cup placed around the "T" handle so that nothing could get behind it to inadvertently activate the flotation devices. This was incorporated on the handle in the front cockpit as well as the rear.

The *Ranger* returned to Naval Station Norfolk by 1939. Arbes would recall an unusual event which occurred October 27, 1939, Navy Day. The air group was ordered aboard the *Ranger,* and the carrier was to sail under secret orders to be opened only when they were in open seas. War in Europe was already a fact of life. The squadron loaded all its gear aboard ship that day, and the next day flew its aircraft to the carrier. After landing, the senior officers and squadron commanders were summoned to the wardroom to learn what the secret orders were really all about. Commanding officer John G. Crommelin asked Arbes to attend the meeting because he was the squadron's navigator, and navigation might be involved. The squadron's orders were relatively straightforward: locate and embarrass the German tanker *Emmy Frederick,* which was refueling Axis submarines in the Gulf of Mexico.

"Off the Florida coast it was obvious we were running into a hurricane and our orders were changed to proceed to Guantanamo Bay, Cuba, around [its west end] to avoid the hurricane," Arbes recalled. When the ship finally arrived at Guantanamo Bay, the landing signal officers (LSOs) and squadron plane handling personnel were offloaded and proceeded to Carter Field on the west side of the bay. The *Ranger* put to sea, and the air group flew to Carter Field, coming in on paddles as the field had not been used since the First World War.

The LSOs had gone ahead of the squadron and staked out a clear landing area. There was absolutely nothing on the grass strip except "an old Cuban and his pig in a rundown shack at the west end of the field," Arbes remembered. "We actually spent two weeks [at the field]." In the end, once the squadron's mail finally caught up to them, it turned out the *Emmy Frederick* was scuttled by her crew a week before VB-3 ever left Norfolk.

Arbes would make at least two memorable emergency landings aboard the *Ranger* and he always felt it was good quality landing signal officers (LSOs) who made the difference. "I qualified on the *Saratoga* under the watchful eyes and directions of Lieutenant Jack Hoerner. On the *Ranger,* Lieutenant "Red" Welsh, with his assistant, Lieutenant Jimmy Vosseller, was the landing signal officer. "Jimmy," Arbes would recall years later, "moved up when Red was detached and replaced by Bunky Ottinger. During my over two hundred carrier landings on [the] *Saratoga, Yorktown,* and *Ranger* in the SB2U, not a plane was scratched or a tire blown thanks to the plane and those great LSOs."

Ranger squadrons patrolled the Atlantic on Neutrality Patrol during most of 1941. Arbes' squadron, designated Scouting Squadron Forty-One (VS-41) by March 15, 1941, took part in patrols aboard both the *Ranger* and *Yorktown* (CV-5). The carriers typically started the patrols around Bermuda and went out toward the Azores before heading north for a short distance. The last leg of the patrol took them back to Bermuda. The entire trip lasted about two weeks. An old British freighter was placed in the search track as bait while a British cruiser sat in wait for a German submarine to attack. The British guarded the patrol pilots' radio frequency, and the American Navy lay in wait to assist scouting the British warship's prey.

During Arbes' first patrol in early May 1941, many changes were taking place in the *Ranger's* air operations to adapt to the intense tempo of patrol work. By the time the squadron's first patrol was completed, the new flight schedule was working efficiently and effectively. In late May, VS-41 transferred briefly to the *Yorktown* which had arrived off Bermuda from the Pacific. Personnel aboard the *Yorktown* were not accustomed to *Ranger* operating procedures so,

A ball of flame and smoke rises from the signal bridge of the USS *Hornet* (CV-8) after a Japanese dive-bomber hit it in a suicide run. Note the Japanese dive and torpedo bombing planes at the right. The *Hornet* took mortal hits during the Battle of Santa Cruz Islands, October 26, 1942. The Japanese did not have a kamikaze pilot corps in 1942 but, nonetheless, enemy pilots took it upon themselves to sacrifice their lives crashing into American aircraft carriers. (Official United States Navy Photograph.)

as Arbes later noted, "We had to go through all the mistakes we made on the *Ranger* before *Yorktown* personnel would adapt to our recommendations."

By the summer of 1941, the executive officer of the VS-41 *High Hats* was Lieutenant W.S. "Bill" Harris, who was training officer in Squadron One (Primary Seaplanes) at Pensacola, Florida, when Arbes had gone through flight training in 1937 and 1938. Arbes remembered Harris as a very good friend, particularly since they served together in the squadron for three years.

"I vividly remember December 7, 1941," wrote Arbes. "We were aboard the *Ranger* proceeding north thru [*sic*] Mona Passage returning from escorting British troop ships to the South Atlantic. Shortly after lunch, I was enjoying a nap in my room when Bill came busting in all excited. He said the Japanese had bombed Pearl Harbor and it looked like war."

At first young Arbes did not think it could possibly be true, but, upon listening in the radio shack, his doubts were blown away by the reality of a world engulfed in world war. The *Ranger* was diverted to Trinidad on the way back to Norfolk to pick up mail, and it was at that point Arbes received orders sending him to Naval Air Station Opa-locka as an instructor pilot. Arbes detached from the *High Hatters* on December 10, 1941, and carried out his orders as written, despite his desire to stay with the squadron and join the fight. His time would come later.

The *Ranger* was followed in 1937 by the USS *Yorktown* (CV-5) and USS *Enterprise* (CV-6), sister ships at 751 feet, with 83-foot foot beams, 20,000-ton displacement, and an average underway speed of 32 knots. The USS *Enterprise* was placed in commission at Norfolk, Virginia, on May 12, 1938, Captain Newton H. White, Naval Aviator No. 2281, commanding officer. Two more carriers would follow: the USS *Wasp* (CV-7) in 1940, and USS *Hornet* (CV-8) in 1941. Both were similar to the *Yorktown* and *Enterprise*, though the *Hornet* was bigger by six thousand tons.

A great deal has changed but some ideas have endured with regard to the way American military strategists perceive the use of aircraft carriers. Firstly, the type of aircraft used aboard early aircraft carriers drove their design. Second, high speed and armament of the flattops was good, but pioneer carrier designers also wanted them equipped with maximum firepower: bombers and fighters.

Just prior to the outbreak of the Second World War, there were few other

The first USS *Hornet* was irreparably damaged at the Battle of Santa Cruz Islands. Old Glory still flies from the gaff of the superstructure after a Japanese dive-bomber crashed on the signal bridge of the carrier. (Official United States Navy Photograph.)

methods, aside from aerial observation, available to ascertain the strength, location and movements of enemy forces, and to maintain the information link. Reconnaissance squadrons provided these early aircraft carriers with their first forward look at the enemy and with an invaluable communications platform every bit as important to their battle groups as the Grumman E-2C Hawkeye is to the modern-day nuclear-powered aircraft carrier. Scouting squadrons were attached to every carrier to ensure successful missions. Many of these scouting squadrons doubled as bombing units since their aircraft were, on the average, able to carry about five hundred pounds of ordnance. Architects of carrier strategy also provided the carriers with protection in the event of attack; most of them were outfitted with an antiaircraft battery fire control system, and with fighter planes to maintain patrols and double as reconnaissance, much akin to the Grumman F-14 Tomcat and McDonnell Douglas F/A-18 Hornet protecting today's aircraft carrier battle groups. Heavy bombers and torpedo planes became the foundation of the carrier attack group, the Grumman A-6E Intruder their modern-day counterpart.

Aircraft carriers used landplane configuration early on, after repeated tests proved this was the optimal design for aircraft performance. Aboard ship, aircraft had shorter wings, and later, folding wings. Short takeoff runs and arrested landings aboard the *Langley* in Hampton Roads, and continuing with the *Hornet,* enabled aircraft designers and naval architects to fine-tune aircraft and aircraft carriers, marrying the two to the fleet's strike advantage. Even though the planes aboard the carriers were landplanes, they were still equipped with flotation. Flotation bags were placed in the wings and could be inflated automatically upon immersion or by manual control. Each plane had a life raft for the whole crew—be it a lone pilot or a pilot, radioman or gunner—who likewise were

Wreckage litters the flight deck of the USS *Hornet* as fire fighting crews try to extinguish flames set by the suicide run of a Japanese bomber pilot. (Official United States Navy Photograph.)

Taken aboard the USS *Independence* (CVL-22), April 30, 1943, this picture reveals some of the complicated mechanism of a flush-deck catapult. The machinery is located below the hangar deck. (Official United States Navy Photograph.)

equipped with personal life jackets, emergency rations, Very pistols and shells, and first aid kits.

The air department on the carriers controlled all aviation activities, including aircraft squadrons. The air department ran this operation from the superstructure which, as is true today, sat to the starboard side of the flight deck. The superstructure housed the bridge, pilot house, signal platforms, radio rooms, and support spaces. The officer in charge of the air department was called the air officer. He also had command over all activity in the hangar bays.

Aircraft carriers in this period began as part of carrier divisions of the battle force to train in fleet maneuvers. Essentially, carriers were part of other units afloat. Aircraft carrier tactics necessitated new applications of sea power which called for revisions to existing naval strategy. The United States Navy would take a couple of more decades before arriving at the CV (Carrier) concept in which the flattop was the center of its own battle group.

As described in a previous chapter, the Navy would experiment heavily with shipboard aircraft catapults in Hampton Roads prior to Pearl Harbor, commencing with tests aboard the USS *Langley*. The catapult launch found on fleet battleships at Norfolk was usually found atop the gun turret, aft of the quarterdeck. On cruisers, catapults were balanced horizontally on top of a tall cylinder, with the airplane perched on a small rectangular car atop the catapult structure. The catapult itself was a rugged latticework of box-girder-type which formed the foundation of the machinery. The girder was seventy feet long, nearly three to four feet wide and maybe the same depth; it was carried on a turntable. Two heavy steel tracks, extending the full length of the structure, carried the car, which was secured on the tracks by metal slippers. At the far end of the track was a buffer to stop the car at the end of its run. A heavy steel cable attached to the forward end of the car, and extended down between the tracks to the far end, where it disappeared into the structure around a large steel wheel, working platforms, guard rails, and control panel with an array of gauges, valves, levers, and wheels to operate the catapult.

Below deck was a different story. A system of steel cable and sheaves provided the mechanical means of converting short powerful strokes, similar to common rope and pulley systems. This rope got pulled and, most simply, moved the car at high speed along the track. In a normal operating situation, the driving force sent the aircraft off the end of the track at nearly seventy miles

This photograph shows a group in the combat information center (CIC) of an *Essex*-class aircraft carrier, November 19, 1943. From this room, the pilot fighting an air battle many miles distant from the ship got his direction towards the target, be it enemy aircraft or ships. Major changes had been ordered for *Essex*-class carriers on March 3, 1943, and installation of the combat information center, fighter director station, additional antiaircraft batteries, and a second flight deck catapult in lieu of one athwartships on the hangar deck soon followed. (Official United States Navy Photograph.)

an hour, certainly slow by today's standard.

Like modern-day naval aviators, those of yesteryear took "cat" shots pretty much the same. The pilot and aircrew placed their bodies firmly against the seat back, resting their heads on the seat head support. The pilot signaled when ready to go, the jolt of the catapult launch seizing his entire body. Even early catapults caused pilots the same anxiety as they do today. However, early pilots worried not about excessive force during a catapult but a weak one where there was not enough speed to sustain altitude and clear the ship's wake. The catapult officer aboard the first carriers made the ultimate decision to launch, and it was his responsibility to check the cat and remove the pin.

By December 7, 1941, the USS *Lexington,* USS *Saratoga,* and USS *Enterprise* had been moved from the East Coast to the Pacific Fleet to strengthen American naval presence in the Far East. The Navy's aircraft carriers were spared from any damage during the Japanese attack on Pearl Harbor since they were out to sea. The *Enterprise* saw its first action of World War II chasing down the Japanese task force that hit Pearl Harbor, pursuing the enemy from the middle of December 1941 to January 1942.

This *Enterprise* was the fifth naval vessel to be so named, the first being a 135-foot topsail schooner launched at Baltimore, Maryland, in 1798 shortly before the outbreak of the United States' undeclared war with France. Even before then, though, the name *Enterprise* had become somewhat a tradition. The fronticepiece of a hurriedly assembled suicide flotilla with which Benedict Arnold stopped the British advance along Lake Champlain in 1776 counted among its number a little armed sloop named *Enterprise*. More than half a century had passed since the name *Enterprise* was used when shipbuilders settled on *Enterprise* for the fighting lady of the Pacific, welcoming her to the ranks of the sea on October 3, 1936, at Newport News. Of the famed three sisters, *Yorktown, Hornet,* and *Enterprise,* the "Big E" was the sole survivor of the war.

America's entry into the Second World War thrust Hampton Roads into the forefront of wartime planning, training, and outfitting of aircraft carriers for battle in both the Atlantic and Pacific

The USS *Ranger,* built by Newport News Shipbuilding and Drydock Company, Newport News, Virginia, was the first ship in the United States Navy to be designed and constructed as an aircraft carrier. Perhaps the most colorful of this Atlantic-based carrier's many blows against German forces was her strike against enemy shipping off the coast of Norway in October 1943 when her planes sank in excess of forty thousand tons of shipping, including four merchant vessels, a tanker, and an oil barge. The *Ranger* would also play a decisive role in the invasion of North Africa in 1942 as part of the Western Naval Task Force engaged in Operation Torch. Additionally, the carrier ferried hundreds of United States Army fighter aircraft across the Atlantic. According to Navy records, the *Ranger* first launched sixty Curtiss P-40F Warhawks of the Army Air Force (AAF) to Accra, off the African Gold Coast, on May 10, 1942, from which point they were flown in a series of hops to Karachi, India, for operations with the Tenth Army Air Force. This was the first of five ferry trips made by the *Ranger* to deliver AAF fighters across the Atlantic, subsequent deliveries being made July 19, 1942; January 19, 1943; February 24, 1943, and this delivery of Lockheed P-38 Lightnings in April 1944. The famous *Ranger* was named after the flagship of Commodore John Paul Jones. (Official United States Navy Photograph.)

theaters of operation. Carrier air groups trained at Naval Air Station Norfolk and its surrounding auxiliary air stations and landing fields. Carrier crewmen, ship's company and flight deck personnel proved the adage, "it takes more than pilots and planes to make an aircraft carrier." Norfolk bustled with sailors who served aboard flattops, showing even in 1941 that the vast organization which comprised a carrier looked something like a small city afloat.

Personnel who handled aircraft on carrier decks were, interestingly enough, the ones called "airedales," not the aviators, as is the case today. Airedales during the Second World War, when the term originated, fueled, armed, positioned, and repaired airplanes aboard aircraft carriers. Like their modern-day counterparts, airedales wore jerseys to distinguish fuelers from plane handlers, fire fighters from corpsmen, catapult officers from wing folders. Plane handlers wore blue shirts and helmets. Fuelers and fire fighters donned red jerseys, while the arming control officer was distinguished by his white jersey and head gear. Green was worn by arresting gear personnel and photographers, brown by plane captains. Hospital corpsmen wore white and were distinguishable by the red cross on their helmets. Chief petty officers, the glue that bound the working parties together, could be found on the deck by looking for their distinctive black helmets. Wing folders and aircraft inspectors wore green jerseys but, to set them apart from arresting gear crew and photographers, had a black stripe down the center of their helmets.

Training at Hampton Roads enabled many of these crewmen to walk out on the deck of an aircraft carrier and safely launch and recover aircraft and, when conditions were not good, perform to the best of each crewmember's ability to protect the flight deck and the aircrews. During wartime, flight decks could be more dangerous, at bare minimum as hazardous, as meeting the enemy in mortal aerial combat. Intensive training in the waters of Hampton Roads, the Chesapeake Bay, and off the Virginia Capes resulted in some horrific accidents as young, inexperienced pilots practiced going to war. An out-of-control aircraft careening across the flight deck could kill and maim many men. A story from the USS *Hornet* during the Battle of

In the photograph shown here, Captain Gordon Rowe, commanding officer of CV-4, and the architect of the *Ranger's* raid on Nazi shipping off Bodo, Norway, in October of 1943, looks quizzically at a picture published in the English-language edition of the German magazine *Signal* in July 1943. The caption described the man pictured as Lieutenant Otto von Bulow who purportedly sank the American aircraft carrier USS *Ranger*. It read:

"A Man Whose Name Was In Everybody's Mouth. Lieutenant Otto von Bulow, holder of the Oak Leaves to the Knight's Insignia. This U-boat commander in addition to torpedoing four steamers caught and sank the American aircraft carrier *Ranger* on the same voyage with the result that he returned to his base somewhat later than expected. Little Henning, whose birthday it was, was naturally very proud of his father. He and all the children who had been invited to his party begged for the postponement of the celebration until the father came home. This was done and the joy later was all the greater."

The USS *Ranger* was very much afloat and perhaps the most formidable opponent of German forces in the Battle of the Atlantic. German propoganda made von Bulow a national hero, though he never came close to sinking the *Ranger*. The photograph was released to the public February 10, 1944. (Official United States Navy Photograph.)

Midway brings home this point.

The *Hornet* had already lost Torpedo Squadron Eight (VT-8), Lieutenant Commander John C. Waldron's outfit, early in the Battle of Midway (June 4, 1942), and while the fight raged on, continued to face more destruction, more death. One of the carrier's fighter pilots had taken on a Japanese Mitsubishi Zero astern of the *Hornet* and, as anxious gunners and flight deck personnel watched, their young naval aviator was shot up very badly by the enemy plane. This aviator had, in fact, been shot through both legs but, despite his personal agony, managed to get his aircraft on the deck. As his plane touched down on the *Hornet,* the pilot bounced his aircraft at least twice, finally catching the last arresting wire. In great pain, and obviously not able to completely control his fighter, the pilot inadvertently set off his machine guns, littering the flight deck with fifty-caliber bullets. Three Marine Corps gunners were killed instantly in gun mount number three, and many others were wounded. As one observer to this scene described it, "death is ubiquitous." Navy and Marine Corps gunners were yet another dimension of the flight deck, and they paid a heavy price standing their ground, particularly later in the war when the kamikaze threat became so great.

Then, as now, flying was controlled from the superstructure, the island mounted to the starboard side of the flight deck. Even in World War II, this air

A cascade of spray and smoke towers above the *Saar,* a new type of German merchant vessel, from a near hit during a raid by planes of the USS *Ranger* off Bodo, Norway, October 1943. When last seen, the *Saar* was down by the stern. (Official United States Navy Photograph.)

traffic control tower was chock-full of communications gear. The commanding officer of the carrier and his planes operations officer (air boss) operated from their perch in the island, and later in the war, those aboard *Essex*-class carriers could depend on a combat information center for up-to-the-minute information on aerial engagements.

Personnel on the flight deck actually made up a small percentage of crew on an aircraft carrier, which is also true today. During World War II, those who worked below the flight deck, especially those in the propulsion room, engineering spaces, ordnance, maintenance, food services, medical department, chaplain's office, and a host of equally important roles, were the majority aboard ship. Shore-based administrative, maintenance, and training commands also contributed immeasurably to the preparedness and performance of these fortresses at sea.

Back on deck a significant change was taking place. Admiral Ernest J. King, Commander-in-Chief, United States Fleet, ordered the removal of athwartship hangar deck catapults from the USSs *Wasp, Yorktown, Enterprise,* and *Hornet* on February 17, 1942, putting technicians at Naval Station Norfolk to work dismantling the system aboard the *Wasp* and *Hornet*. Originally, only the *Yorktown* and *Enterprise* had the two bow catapults on the flight deck and one athwartship on the hangar deck. When the Secretary of the Navy ordered the installation of hydropneumatic flush-deck catapults aboard carriers in his Bureau of Aeronautics request dated November 15, 1934, little did he anticipate the change in size, configuration, and speed of World War II-period naval aircraft. Athwartship catapults became impractical, and the space they occupied on the hangar deck could be used to store additional aircraft and armament.

The Navy lost the *Hornet* at the Battle of Santa Cruz Islands, October 26, 1942, six months after the carrier's participation in the Doolittle raid on Tokyo. The *Hornet* and *Enterprise* were making way off Santa Cruz with the battleship USS *South Dakota,* nine cruisers, and the requisite destroyers. The *Hornet* had been a target for Japanese aircraft since the Tokyo bombing, and it would be enemy planes from the Japanese carriers *Shokaku* and *Zuikaku* which finally found the American carrier and mortally wounded her. Despite a valiant defense by her own antiaircraft guns and embarked aircraft, enemy aircraft—twenty-seven was the official count—penetrated the carrier's air defenses. The *Hornet* was struck by two one-hundred-pound rounds, three five-hundred-pound bombs, and two torpedoes. Two flaming Japanese aircraft hit the *Hornet* as well, one near the stack and the other at the signal bridge. Every man within reasonable distance of these areas was killed instantly. Had it not been for over two hundred able-bodied sailors

A Grumman TBF Avenger, photographed May 1, 1943, is directed for catapulting by a landing signal officer aboard the USS *Independence*. His upraised arm and hand motion are signals for catapulting. (Official United States Navy Photograph.)

forming a fire brigade, the *Hornet* would have been abandoned almost immediately. The quick and certain action of these sailors saved the ship, at least temporarily.

The cruiser USS *Northampton* attached a tow line and tried to move the *Hornet* out of harm's way. The *Northampton* would have stood a reasonable chance of saving the *Hornet* had the Japanese not mounted yet another attack, the second more brutal than the first. The hull of the *Hornet* began to list dangerously close to the water, so much so that Captain Charles Perry "Charlie" Mason, Naval Aviator No. 52, ordered the *Hornet* abandoned. Squadrons from the *Hornet* flew to Guadalcanal but not before catching the Tokyo Express in the slot, seriously damaging two enemy cruisers and sinking two destroyers. Perhaps one of the most valiant efforts to save the ship, despite Mason's order to abandon her, was carried on by Commander Pat Creehan and his black gang who found it nearly impossible to give up on such a valiant ship. One hundred and twenty-nine men were killed in action aboard the *Hornet* during the two attacks.

The mighty *Hornet* was partly laid to rest in the sea by two destroyers in her screen but, it would take additional rounds from Japanese warships to finish her. The *Makigumo* and *Akigumo* moved in after dark and fired four torpedoes

Dramatic images like this one of a landing signal officer aboard a Pacific-based flattop show just how precarious the perch of deck crewmen on America's aircraft carriers could be in the heat of battle. During the Second World War many deck crewmen lost their lives in horrific fashion, including landing signal officers standing directly in the path of incoming aircraft. It took more than fleet feet to avoid disaster, it took the grace of God. The job of the landing signal officer remains much the same today—to direct Navy pilots in landing aboard the pitching, rolling deck of an aircraft carrier. This was—and is—hazardous duty. When directing landings in World War II, landing signalmen, pilots themselves, operated from a small platform on the flight deck. They stood, flags in hand, indicating by motion of the flags, the type of approach the pilot should make before coming to the flight deck. Planes passed incredibly close to landing signalmen. If a pilot was not quite on the mark, the landing signalman was in the most danger. One pilot and landing signalman, Lieutenant Frank L. Butters, of Boston, Massachusetts, recorded about twelve thousand aircraft he personally directed to the deck during his tour in the Pacific theater. (Official United States Navy Photograph.)

into the *Hornet* to send the ship to the bottom.

The first *Hornet* to do battle against the Japanese would lead her crew down a prophetic road. According to the ship's history held by Newport News Shipbuilding, a junior officer aboard the first *Hornet* (CV-8) decided one day to read the Bible from cover to cover. When he encountered Deuteronomy, the young officer's eyes fell upon a passage he enjoyed sharing with everyone aboard. From the twentieth chapter, seventh verse, the passage reads, "Moreover the Lord, thy God, will send the hornet among them until they that are left, and hide themselves from thee, be destroyed." Newport News Shipbuilding built another *Hornet* in less than a year. The USS *Hornet* (CV-12) was completed in 1943, but her crew would not soon forget the words of Deuteronomy.

Hampton Roads played a pivotal role in the first major amphibious assault of World War II, the invasion of North Africa in 1942. Starting many months in advance of the October 24, 1942, departure of the Operation Torch amphibious force, the Nansemond Hotel at Norfolk's Ocean View was home to the United States Atlantic Amphibious Force. When its ninety-nine ships departed Norfolk for the shores of North Africa, they included the USS *Ranger,* USS *Chenango* (CVE-28), USS *Sangamon* (CVE-26), USS *Santee* (CVE-29), and the USS *Suwannee* (CVE-27). The combined complement of aircraft aboard the carriers included 111 Grumman F4F Wildcats, 27 Eastern TBM-1 and Grumman TBF-1 Avengers, 36 Douglas SBD-1 Dauntlesses, 78 Curtiss P-40F Warhawk fighters aboard the *Chenango,* and four Army L-4 Piper Cub observation planes.

The date of the invasion was November 8, 1942, and surprisingly, the Western Naval Task Force departed Norfolk en masse and never encountered a German U-boat during the entire trip. The *Ranger* was the only large flattop available in the Atlantic Fleet to accompany the Operation Torch invasion force. The landing of troops was to take place at night. The Vichy French, driven to action by their Nazi German counterparts, opened fire on American naval forces with shore batteries, not fully grasping the scope of the invasion force amassed off the North African coast. The USS *Massachusetts* (BB-59), took out the *Jean Bart,* a French battleship, with her sixteen-inch guns and, in so doing, became the first ship to fire her guns in the invasion.

Air attacks from the *Ranger* commenced against Vichy French submarines and destroyers shortly after the battleships exchanged their first barrage. Wildcats from Oceana-based Fighter Squadron Nine aboard the *Ranger* strafed Vichy positions, and took on twenty-one aircraft without taking a loss to their own ranks. Sixteen inexperienced French fighter pilots ran into

The Story of the USS *Franklin*

The keel of the USS *Franklin* (CV-13) was laid at Newport News Shipbuilding and Drydock Company, Newport News, Virginia, on December 7, 1942, the first anniversary of the Japanese attack on Pearl Harbor. Ten months later, on October 14, 1943, the *Essex*-class carrier was launched, sponsored by Captain Mildred A. McAfee, USNR, director of the WAVES. The USS *Franklin* was the fifth ship of the United States to bear the name, the first dating back to a schooner in the fleet General George Washington fitted out in the ports of Massachusetts in the fall of 1775.

"Big Ben," as she was affectionately called, had been fitted out and, on the morning of January 31, 1944, was towed by tugs to the Norfolk Navy Yard in Portsmouth, Virginia. Amidst great fanfare, the *Franklin* was commissioned, with Captain James Marshall Shoemaker, Naval Aviator No. 2951, as its first commanding officer. Shoemaker was a familiar face in Norfolk. He had assumed command of Naval Air Station Norfolk on November 2, 1942, succeeding Rear Admiral Elliot Buckmaster in the post. Shoemaker remained commanding officer of the air station only two weeks, until November 14, 1942, because he was assigned as commandant of Naval Air Center Hampton Roads, a new and challenging role, but one he relished and did well. On May 24, 1943, Shoemaker assumed the additional duty as commanding officer of Naval Air Station Norfolk, relieving Captain Carleton C. Champion and retaining command of the center. He detached from both billets to take command of the USS *Franklin*.

Air Group Thirteen was created by Rear Admiral Calvin T. Durgin, Naval Aviator No. 2725, and pilots and aircrew were assembled in Norfolk to establish squadrons. Each prospective pilot was checked out aboard the USS *Charger* (CVE-30), the East Coast training carrier, and assigned to a command. Once the *Franklin* was completely fitted out, it was eased into Hampton Roads and the Chesapeake Bay on February 21, 1944. After trial runs, gunnery practice, system testing, and carrier qualifications for the pilots of Air Group Thirteen, consisting of Bombing Squadron Thirteen (VB-13), Fighter Squadron Thirteen (VF-13), and Torpedo Squadron Thirteen (VT-13), the carrier was ready for its shakedown cruise. The first takeoff from the deck of the USS *Franklin* was made by Commander Joseph "Joe" Taylor, air officer aboard the carrier. During one phase of its grueling workup schedule, the "Big Ben's" air group flew synchronized simulated amphibious attacks with the Army on King Island in the Chesapeake Bay, an exercise planned and executed under the watchful eye of Commander Charles C. "Sunshine" Howerton, the first commanding officer of Carrier Air Group Thirteen (CAG-13).

Upon completion of the shakedown cruise, repairs and loading, the carrier left Norfolk on May 5, 1944, for the Pacific theater via the Panama Canal. On her decks were Grumman F6F-3 Hellcats of Fighter Squadron Thirteen, then under the command of Lieutenant Commander Wilson M. Coleman, who relieved the squadron's first commanding officer, Lieutenant Commander Thomas B. Bradbury, on November 17, 1943; Douglas SBD-5 Dauntlesses of Bombing Squadron Thirteen under the command of Lieutenant Commander Richard Lucius "Dick" Kibbe, who later became commander of CAG-13; and Grumman TBF-1D Avengers of Torpedo Squadron Thirteen, commanded by Lieutenant Commander Lawrence F. French.

The *Franklin* underwent voyage repairs at San Diego, California, before making way for the Naval Station at Pearl Harbor, Territory of Hawaii, arriving on June 5, 1944. Shoemaker took the carrier into battle for the first time on June 29, 1944, when the *Franklin* became the flagship for Rear Admiral Ralph E. Davison's Task Group 38.4, under the auspices of Task Group Thirty-Eight, Third Fleet, commanded by Admiral William F. "Bull" Halsey Jr. Essentially, all Fifth Fleet assets were transferred to the Third Fleet under Halsey the first of June, redesignating the Task Force "38.4" as opposed to "58.4." The group consisted of the USS *Enterprise* (CV-6), USS *Belleau Wood* (CVL-24), and USS *San Jacinto* (CVL-30), escorted by the cruisers USS *Boston,* USS *Canberra,* USS *San Juan,* and destroyers. The first point of attack was the Bonin Island chain, six hundred miles to the south of Tokyo, Japan.

Roughly three hundred miles from the target of attack, the USS *Wasp* (CV-7), part of Task Force 38.1, launched twenty planes to raid a Japanese-held airfield. The fighters returned after successfully downing a dozen Japanese aircraft as the enemy attempted to take off from the field. Many other aircraft were reported damaged.

According to the ship's official history, Vice Admiral Marc A. Mitscher's Fast Carrier Task Force Thirty-Eight threw a Fourth of July party aboard all the ships before launching strikes from its four aircraft carriers the next day. Aircraft from the *Franklin* hit targets at Iwo Jima, Chichi Jima, and Ha Ha Jima, destroying Japanese gun positions, airfields, hangars, ground buildings, and aircraft. Torpedo planes struck enemy merchant shipping along the coastal areas of the Bonins and Volcano Islands. After completing its strikes on the Jimas, Task Group 38.4 headed south to sweep Guam in the Marianas chain where the *Franklin's* squadrons hit Rota and Guam, the latter being one of four major enemy air bases of which Saipan was perhaps the largest. The *Franklin* remained with its task force in the Marianas throughout most of July before steaming toward the Palau Islands, Yap, and Ulithi on the twenty-fifth of the month to join its two other task groups to comprise Task Force Thirty-Eight. Operations were highly successful at Palau Islands.

The *Franklin* participated in a number of engagements between July and the first of September, 1944, launching strikes as part of the Western Caroline Islands operation, Iwo Jima, Chichi Jima, Yap, Ulithi, and providing invasion support at Peleliu and Anguar Islands, Palau Islands and Leyte. During October the fighting became brutal. Though the carrier would later become renowned for the March 19, 1945, kamikaze attack which took so many lives, the *Franklin* had tangled with suicide planes on a number of significant occasions in October of 1944, with the result that three large gun mounts were fitted to her port side below the flight deck.

The *Franklin* sustained negligible damage as a result of a strafing by a Japanese kamikaze or suicide aircraft while launching strikes against Tainan, Island of Formosa, on October 12 and 13, 1944, and from three twin-engine enemy torpedo planes, one of which crashed just aft of the island structure. The Japanese torpedo plane went careening off the port five-inch gun director and slid across the flight deck into the sea from the starboard side. Many *Franklin* personnel on the flight deck were killed.

Suicide aircraft were the bane of more than one aircraft carrier in the Pacific theater of operations. The *Franklin* was constantly under attack by kamikazes. While her planes struck targets on Aparri, Manila, and Legaspi in the Philippine Islands, October 14–19, 1944, Japanese pilots took aim once again at "Big Ben." Three Japanese bombs caused minor damage to the ship on October 15, 1944, east of Luzon Island. One five-hundred-pound bomb penetrated the corner of the deck edge elevator and detonated just below the flight deck level, causing fragment damage and gasoline fires on the hangar deck. The second bomb detonated upon hitting the water, close to the port side of the carrier, and the third exploded to the starboard, knocking out the number thirteen forward forty millimeter gun platform.

The USS *Franklin* came through the Battle of Leyte Gulf, also called the Second Battle of the Philippine Sea, on October 24 and 25, 1944, without any damage, but her luck was about to change. During support operations for the amphibious assault at Leyte on the thirtieth of October, the *Franklin* was extensively damaged by three Japanese kamikazes east of Samar Island. The first kamikaze slid off the flight deck to port, causing minor gasoline fires that were quickly extinguished. The second aircraft carried a bomb load and crashed through the flight deck, igniting aircraft parked at the aft end of the flight and hangar decks. The bombs carried forward, detonating among the gassed aircraft in the forward hangar and igniting fires throughout the hangars. Fires spread rapidly to the second and third decks. Gas explosions occurred in the hangar, but all fires were extinguished in a little over two hours. Structural damage was extensive to the flight and galley decks as well as to the lower deck spaces. The *Franklin* was forced to retire under the protection of aircraft from Task Force Thirty-Eight and proceed to an advance base for minor repairs before returning stateside. The ship lost more than one hundred men as a result of the attack.

The month of October had been costly, in general, for the *Franklin* and its air wing. Commander Richard L. Kibbe had turned over command of Bombing Squadron Thirteen to become commanding officer of the air group aboard the *Franklin* on August 8, 1944. A commanding officer had to be found to take Kibbe's place because, unfortunately, his executive officer, Lieutenant Commander Carl Berman "Swede" Holmstrom, failed to return from a strike against enemy merchant shipping at Chichi Jima Harbor, Bonin Islands, on August 5, 1944, just three days before he was set to take over the squadron. Lieutenant Charles Allen "Chuck"

Smoke and flame entirely blanketed the USS *Franklin* in this distant view, taken on March 19, 1945, as the ship listed in the Inland Sea, less than sixty miles from the Japanese mainland. Blast after blast swept through the ship, yet when the smoke blew away, the ship could still be seen, fighting successfully to keep afloat. (Official United States Navy Photograph.)

Skinner, who had previously been executive officer of Bombing Squadron Eleven (VB-11), became commanding officer of VB-13 on October 1, 1944. In the interim, Lieutenant Rupert John "Rupe" Weber Jr. acted as commanding officer from August eighth until Skinner reported to the squadron. Upon Skinner's arrival, Weber became his executive officer. Weber failed to return to the *Franklin* after a strike on Formosa, October 12, 1944, and was later confirmed killed in action. His replacement as executive officer was Lieutenant Lloyd Nelson "Woodie" Wood, who flew more strikes than any other man in the squadron and lived to tell about it.

So many of VB-13's pilots and aircrew would not see another day. Fighting became increasingly fierce the closer American naval forces moved toward mainland Japan. After flying 1,342 combat sorties between July and October of 1944, the pilots of VB-13 had christened their wings with the blood of squadronmates and shipmates of the *Franklin,* such a high price to pay for liberation of Japanese-held territory. When pilots were lost, the pain ran deep among the other flyers. The men took the loss of Lieutenant John Henry Finrow, USNR, particularly hard. Finrow was a wing leader for the entire length of the squadron's first tour of combat operations. When he failed to return from leading an attack against the Japanese fleet on October 25, 1944, it was as if fate had snatched him away. It was Finrow's last mission of the deployment, and would have completed his second combat tour in the Pacific, his first having been with Bombing Squadron Ten (VB-10) aboard the USS *Enterprise.* Lieutenant (junior grade) Marshall D. Barnett, USNR, of Bombing Squadron Thirteen, was killed the day before Finrow while his squadron was attacking the Japanese Second Fleet in the Sulu Sea, Philippine Islands. Barnett was a poet, writing prophetically about his first aircraft carrier in a poem called *The Franklin,* written as he rode the ship to war.

Hungry for the ocean's surge,
  for white plumes across her bow;
Thirsting for a draught of oil,
  to snort, to roll, to plow;

Longing for the touch of men,
  someone to pull her hook;
Looking for the enemy;
  the devils are in her book;

Grim missionary of Peace,
  but she is mighty full of fight;
Sent out with tender touches,
  to set the world aright;

She doesn't believe in luck or omens;
  she is on God's side of this war;
She mothers red-blooded Americans
  who know what they're fighting for;

She's ready to die tomorrow,
  if dying she can turn the tide;
That men may live once more,
  where harmonious love abides;

We salute you, proud warrior of steel,
  with Mizpah we say adieu;
Our eyes will be on your actions;
  our prayers will be for your crew.

Highlighted by an area of flame, smoke spread a choking curtain over the stern of the *Essex*-class aircraft carrier USS *Franklin.* Behind the pall scores of courageous men risked their lives as they exerted every effort to save the ship. (Official United States Navy Photograph.)

On October 31, 1944, Vice Admiral Mitscher was relieved as head of Fast Carrier Task Force Thirty-Eight by Vice Admiral John S. "Slew" McCain, previously in charge of Task Group 38.1 of the Fast Carrier Task Force.

On November 7, 1944, Captain Leslie E. Gehres, became the carrier's second commanding officer. Gehres had been commissioned an ensign in the surface Navy in April 1918, and did not begin his aviation career until the early 1920s. As a pilot and flight operations officer for Fighter Squadron One on the USS *Langley*, USS *Lexington,* and USS *Saratoga* between October 1927 and December 1929, Gehres earned the respect and admiration of his squadronmates, the *High Hatters,* and ships' crews. He led the *Nine High Hats* stunt team at the National Air Races in 1927. Between June 1932 and July 1934, Gehres was executive officer of both Fighter Squadron Six aboard the USS *Saratoga,* and Fighter Squadron Five on the USS *Lexington*. As his experience grew, so did his assignments both aboard ship and with squadrons, culminating in his selection as commanding officer of the *Franklin* in 1944. From the ship's departure at Ulithi, eventually ending up at Puget Sound Navy Yard, Bremerton, Washington, Gehres commanded "Big Ben." Little did he know the fate which awaited his ship upon her return to the Pacific on March 13, 1945. When the *Franklin* joined Vice Admiral Marc A. Mitscher's Task Force Fifty-Eight (the designation on paper was once again under Fifth Fleet), the ship became, for the second time, Rear Admiral Ralph E. Davison's flagship and lead ship of Task Group 58.2.

The attack came early the morning of March 19, 1945, when a seven-plane enemy formation crept toward the *Franklin,* then located off Shikoku in close proximity to Kyushu. The first alert was sounded aboard ship at three minutes after seven, notifying ship's company and aircrews of Japanese aircraft sightings near the *Franklin*. Planes were still being launched from the *Franklin's* decks when watchers on the bridge caught their first glimpse of an enemy bomber as it streaked over the flight deck. Two bombs spun down toward the *Franklin* as the aircraft, not fifty feet above the deck, pulled up and climbed away. The Japanese pilot was pursued by Lieutenant (junior grade) Locke Trigg from the USS *Bataan* (CVL-29), and shot down after a twenty-mile chase.

The first bomb, a five-hundred-fifty-pound armor piercing round, exploded on the forward hangar deck, blasting a tremendous hole in the three-inch armor plate and setting fire to the heav-

Seething banks of smoke envelop the stern of the *Franklin* as flames raced through the carrier's interior. Men of the cruiser USS *Santa Fe* (right) watched in fascinated horror as they awaited the opportunity to lend a hand. Burning gasoline escaped out of the side of the *Franklin,* while a group of survivors clambered down a cargo net to the far left. (Official United States Navy Photograph.)

ily gassed and armed aircraft above and below decks. Planes already on the *Franklin's* full flight deck, some of which were Chance-Vought F4U-1Ds with Marine Fighter Squadron Two Hundred Fourteen *Black Sheep* pilots aboard, had been blown from the carrier like leaves in a windstorm. One eyewitness to the devastation noted that an entire ready room of night fighter pilots suffocated from smoke and fumes because they were located in the forward compartment just below the first explosion point. The second bomb struck aft, crashing through two decks and exploding on the third deck near the chief petty officers' quarters.

A column of black smoke poured from the forward elevator well and sheets of flame shot up from the forward starboard edge of the hangar deck. On the flight deck, airmen tried desperately to jettison aircraft before fire spread to them and set off more explosions. Smoke rose from the stern of the ship and little more than a minute passed before the sheets of fire spread over the heavily armed planes on the flight and hangar decks. Violent explosions set off a chain reaction of fires, each more horrific than the one before. The inferno was exacerbated by detonation of ready ammunition lockers which were filled with rockets and shells. Men died by the scores on the flight and hangar decks, and the gallery deck, sandwiched between these two decks, was a death trap. Over thirty tons of high explosives were on the aircraft alone, and countless tons were in the ship's magazines. Explosions continued well below deck in the engine room, by then so choked with smoke and fire, the crew had donned gas masks and rescue breathing equipment. Firefighters could not douse the *Franklin's* engine room conflagration; no amount of water could quell fires burning as fiercely as those on "Big Ben."

The *Franklin's* plight drew assistance from escort ships in the task force. The destroyer USS *Miller* ignored the inherent dangers of getting too close to the *Franklin* and brought water hoses to bear on uncontrollable fires on the carrier's hangar deck where forty thousand gallons of aviation fuel were feeding the flames. Into the spreading fire moved the *Franklin's* men, explosions of every type of ammunition around them. Seven large five-hundred-pound bombs and two smaller ones rolled about the flight deck so hot they seared flesh, yet the men of the *Franklin* rolled these bombs overboard. The crew removed ammunition lockers and more bombs, throwing them over the side also. The sound of exploding shells was deafening and smoke rose above the ship a mile high, advertising a crippled aircraft carrier to the enemy.

Gradually, as the crew of the *Franklin* restored some semblance of order, men on the flight and hangar decks halted the flames. Below them, men on the second and third decks, and those trapped on the aft hangar deck, made their way to safer areas of the ship.

Following Navy tradition, the cruiser USS *Santa Fe* risked its own destruction by moving alongside to within arm's length of the *Franklin* in order to fight the fires and to remove exhausted and injured crewmen. Bringing the cruiser in such close proximity to the carrier was a magnificent feat of seamanship on the part of the commanding officer and crew of the *Santa Fe*. (Official United States Navy Photograph.)

Dozens of crewmen had been blown over the side while others, hopelessly trapped, had leapt into the sea. For hours, small groups struggled on the fantail where they fought fires with every means at their disposal, jumping into the water only after they lost the battle with the fire. Sadly, everyone in the *Franklin's* hospital ward—doctors, corpsmen, and patients—died after what can only be described as a gallant, but futile fight against explosions, fire, and suffocation. Three hundred men were trapped in a compartment on the third deck, only to be led to safety more than three hours later. Groups of men, isolated by fires, fought raging infernos with their backs to the sea until finally overwhelmed.

At no time did Captain Leslie E. Gehres give the order to abandon ship, nor would he yield to Rear Admiral Ralph E. Davison, Task Group 58.2 commander whose flagship was the *Franklin,* nor Rear Admiral Gerald F. Bogan, aboard as an observer, to do so. When Davison and Bogan transferred to a destroyer, Gehres remained steadfast on the bridge of the *Franklin.* Gehres reasons were clear—he was not about to torpedo the *Franklin* with three hundred men trapped on the third deck. The practice at that time was typically to abandon ship and sink it with a torpedo, and, unfortunately, sign the death warrant for anyone trapped below deck. Gehres made a determined effort to save his ship and her trapped crew in what was perhaps one of the most heroic efforts of the *Franklin* saga.

There would be many acts of heroism that day, some which may never be known but to the dead who gave their lives for those of shipmates and ship. At half past eight in the morning, only two aft firerooms and the aft engine room were still operative, though these areas soon became intolerable from smoke and increasing heat. The USS *Santa Fe* came alongside about the same time, directing all her water hoses on the *Franklin's* flaming decks, and then began the task of moving the wounded to her decks. The *Franklin* had begun to list further and further into the water, and, at half past nine, as steam ceased to flow from the boilers, the ship lost steering control. Only fifty to sixty miles from Japan, the nearest any American surface warship had approached the mainland shore of the enemy in the war, the *Franklin* was dead in the water.

Preparations were already underway

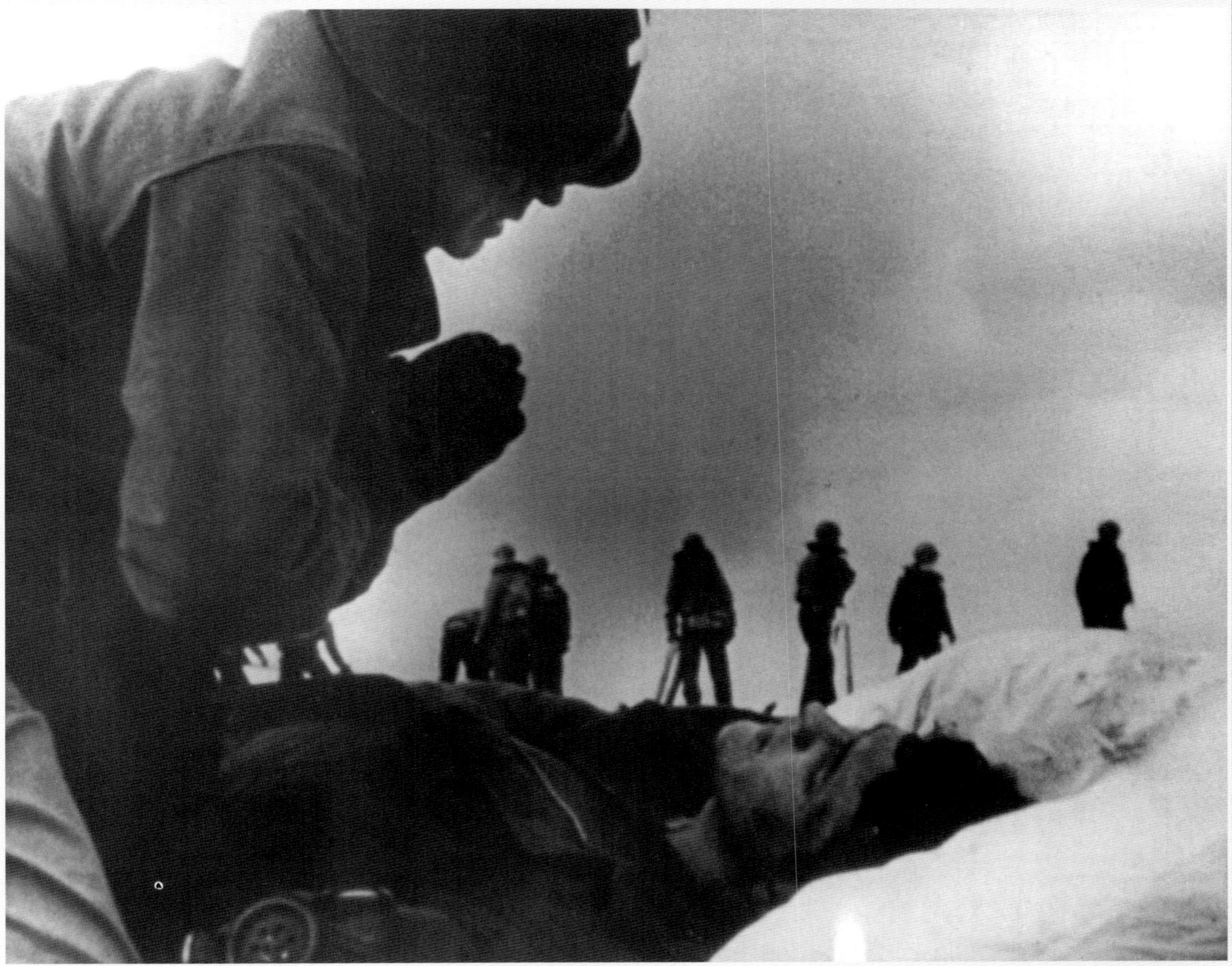

Gloved hands pressed together, Lieutenant Commander Joseph O'Callahan, of Boston, Massachusetts, the Roman Catholic Navy chaplain aboard the *Franklin,* administered last rites to a mortally wounded crewman on the deck of the burning carrier. O'Callahan was awarded the Medal of Honor for his acts of courage and valor above and beyond the call of duty, the first chaplain of any service so honored. (Official United States Navy Photograph.)

for the cruiser USS *Pittsburgh* to take the crippled aircraft carrier in tow, and the USS *Santa Fe,* unable to hold her position, backed away rapidly from the ship, snapping her lines. When the USS *Franklin* lay on a steady heading, drifting with the current, *Santa Fe* came in again. Boldly and with magnificent seamanship, her captain maneuvered the cruiser into actual contact with the gallery deck of the *Franklin* to evacuate the wounded, 832 of them to be exact. Destroyers of the force circled through the frigid waters, picking up *Franklin* survivors. This small group of warships, nearly immobile by virtue of the *Franklin's* situation, were in a precarious situation at best. The *Pittsburgh* was stopped while attempting to take the *Franklin* in tow. The *Santa Fe* was rescuing personnel alongside the burning ship. The five ships of Destroyer Division 104—the USS *Hunt,* USS *Hickox,* USS *Marshall,* USS *Miller,* and USS *Tingey*—steamed slowly in a circle around the heavy ships, picking up survivors as they went and prepared to defend the group against further attack. One of the survivors plucked from the sea by the USS *Tingey* was a young seaman second class by the name of Jonathan C. "Jack" Trout who, fifty years later, still vividly recalls that day's events. He wrote in a letter dated February 4, 1995:

"The letter from Reon [Reon G. Hillegass Jr.] was interesting and the list of lost men brought an end to a mystery about two men whose fate was in question.

"One man was burned over most of his body—his station was on the hangar deck—his name was easy to remember BLANKENSHIP [Warren Harding, (Aviation Machinist's Mate First Class)(AM1c)], and was often called on the speaker which helped his name stay with me.

"I saw him briefly after we were picked up. He was not conscious and in bad shape. I only knew his name and the list says he did not make it. The other name was of a man that was in the water with me and three others. We got together and hung on to a corner of the remains of a cork raft. I swam to him and pulled him back. His hands were burned and he said nothing. The other men said he was hit before while in the merchant marine in the North Atlantic. U.S. destroyers were picking up survivors in the water and we were 200 yards from a destroyer and all of a sudden they left us and waved to us as they steamed off. I later found out that all the destroyers were ordered to return to protect the carrier from further attack. COX, [Walter Ben,(Seaman Second Class)(Sea2c)] the man who kept drifting away, was now about twenty yards away and would not respond to our calls. There were no ships in sight. I could not swim the distance and pull him back. I had no life jacket and figured we all were equally doomed no matter where we were. Much later, I saw a ship on the horizon and I took off my shirt, threw it in the air to attract attention. It worked and they picked us up on the way to protect the carrier or whatever they were ordered to do.

"When I got aboard the destroyer, I collapsed and was carried to a bunk. The list shows three men with the name COX [Walter Ben, Sea2c] but, since I never knew his first name, I could not be sure of his fate."

Being less then one hundred miles from major Japanese air bases, it was considered only a matter of time before enemy bombers returned. Strangely, there would be false alarms but no attacks, save one. Explosions were dying back and hangar deck fires had subsided, so, by noon an attempt was underway to get back to the engineering spaces. Just after the *Santa Fe* cleared the ship's side of survivors, a Japanese Judy bomber slipped past the combat air patrol, came in on a fast glide-in run on the *Franklin,* and dropped a large bomb which exploded only two hundred yards off her starboard quarter. The enemy bomber was shot down within sight of a formidable screen of Navy fighters.

After the towing line to the USS *Pittsburgh* was finally connected shortly after two in the afternoon, the cruiser succeeded in getting the *Franklin* underway and headed south at three and a half knots. Meanwhile, firefighters slowly worked their way back to the engineering spaces, and, by seven that evening, most of the fires below decks were under control. By dawn the next day, the twentieth of March, "Big Ben" was going ahead at six knots, but still under tow, and roughly eighty-five miles from Japan. The night had been rough. After dark the Japanese were out in force, dropping flares on the horizon, looking for the *Franklin.* Instead, they encountered other task groups, and a continuous battle was fought ten miles away all night, one in which forty Japanese aircraft were shot down.

Shortly after dawn on March twentieth, firefighters were still searching for smoldering compartments, and engineers worked on the engines, trying to find a way to get up more steam. By ten in morning, the *Franklin* was churning ahead under her own power at fourteen knots with the added escort of two battle cruisers—USS *Alaska* and USS *Guam*—and two destroyers. At two-thirty that afternoon, enemy aircraft closed on the group and the battle cruisers moved in close to the wounded carrier. One more hit could have easily sent the *Franklin* to the bottom. Fighters on combat air patrol shot down most of the Japanese planes but through their screen came one bomber, for some reason undaunted by flak, until he got close on his run. The *Franklin's* few remaining antiaircraft gun mounts opened up with fast and accurate fire, surprising the Japanese pilot so much that he swerved his plane as he dropped the bomb, causing the explosive to miss the ship by little more than a hundred feet. This would not be the only attempt made by the Japanese to sink the *Franklin* as she limped across the Pacific to Pearl Harbor, but each time they made a play for the disabled carrier, fighters from a task group thirty miles away intercepted and destroyed the enemy aircraft before they could reach the *Franklin.*

As the *Franklin* worked her way toward Hawaii she gradually picked up speed and, by sunset, was steaming at better than twenty knots, 170 miles from Japan. By daybreak on March 21, 1945, the aircraft carrier was three hundred miles away, though enemy aircraft still tried to find her. That evening the carrier joined Task Group 58.2, which was retiring to Ulithi, and with the destroyers *Miller, Marshall,* and *Hunt* in her screen, the *Franklin* steamed as an independent unit. On the twenty-fourth of March, the *Franklin* dismissed her screening destroyers to take her place in the column of warships steaming into Ulithi lagoon, living proof of her captain's words, "a ship that will not be sunk cannot be sunk." Two days later, accompanied by two destroyer escorts, the *Franklin* and *Santa Fe* set course for Pearl Harbor, arriving there on April 3, 1945. Nine hundred and sixteen of her crew and attached air group had given their lives for their country; seven hundred and four men remained aboard as she came home.

Among those who lost their lives were twenty-two men of a Marine Corps detachment sailing with the *Franklin;* twenty-five Commander Carrier Division Two and Four officer and enlisted personnel; hundreds of men from Carrier Air Groups Thirteen and Five; thirty-six pilots and enlisted personnel from Major Pappy Boyington's famous VMF-214 *Black Sheep* squadron, including Second Lieutenants Clare R. Beeler, Robert L. Hugler, Ralph W. Husted, Dallas L.

A little over seven hundred men remained aboard the USS *Franklin* as crew members struggled to extinguish smoldering fires both above and below decks. The photograph taken here, March 19, 1945, shows the *Franklin* being towed by the USS *Pittsburgh.* (Official United States Navy Photograph.)

Hyatt, Herbert D. Scramuzza, Joseph E. Stout, Oscar D. Urbom, and Captains W.O. Chapman, Robert M. Jones, and Roger W. Conant; and thirty-four pilots and enlisted personnel from VMF-452, among them, Second Lieutenant Thomas D. Pace, USMC, and First Lieutenant Wallace Mattsfield, USMC. There are names and faces for all the dead of war. For these men, the war ended in the deep, dark churning water off the coast of Japan.

Following a five-day stay at Pearl Harbor, the *Franklin* steamed east on April ninth, passed through the Panama Canal on the seventeenth, and on April 28, 1945, she arrived off Gravesend Bay, New York. Two days later, the carrier the press called "the ship that wouldn't die," moved into the Brooklyn Navy Yard, where she was repaired. The crew moved ashore to barracks and prepared for rehabilitation leave, which was quickly forthcoming. Workers at the Brooklyn Navy Yard worked day and night, cutting away entire sections of the blasted decks of the *Franklin.* On June 30, 1945, Captain Gehres was relieved as commanding officer of the *Franklin* by Commander Clarence E. Dickinson.

The war came to an end on August 15, 1945, while the *Franklin* was still undergoing repairs. On Navy Day, October 27, 1945, thousands of visitors came aboard the *Franklin* at the Brooklyn Navy Yard, most of whom came to pay respects to a ship and her crew they never knew. The aircraft carrier's repairs were completed on June 15, 1946, and two days later she reported to the Atlantic reserve fleet for deactivation. The USS *Franklin* was placed out of commission on February 17, 1947, in the New York group of the reserve fleet.

To this day, survivors of the *Franklin* cling to their precious memories of heroism, death, and survival against the worst kind of odds. Reon Glessner Hillegass Jr., a seaman second class when the *Franklin* was hit, once told the author he just wants people to remember what happened that fateful day in March of 1945, a day in which the lives of 3,450 men were irrevocably changed. Hillegass underscored that war is a terrible, ugly process which has no niceties, no bands playing, no glory in the act of dying. The glory is in the fight, the camaraderie, the surviving. He handed over a copy of Edgar A. Guest's poem, *Navy Epic,* written about the *Franklin.*

You can tell it to them, sailor, in the years that are to be,
You were one aboard the *Franklin* in that epic of the sea.
You've a right to boast about it; you were one who saved "Big Ben."
One who lived to tell the story of her glorious fighting men.

You can tell it to them, sailor, with a touch of Yankee pride,
You were one of those aboard her when that good ship almost died.
One below, or was it topside? —oh, it doesn't matter where—
You were one to give the Navy added glory, all can share.

When the youngsters gather round you, as they will when you're ashore,
You've a stirring tale to give them that will live forevermore.
You can tell them of the *Franklin,* under Japanese attack,
With the dead and maimed upon her, but the living fighting back.

To American tradition; aye, to Yankee faith and pride,
And the glory of the Navy, spread the story far and wide!
You've a right to boast about it till your breath is running short;
How you brought the battered *Franklin,* flag still flying, into port!

On March 11, 1987, former President Ronald Reagan wrote eloquently of the USS *Franklin* and her crew.

"I am proud to send greetings to the crew of the aircraft carrier USS *Franklin* (CV-13), 'The Ship That Wouldn't Die,' as you gather in reunion.

"No one who knows the history of our beloved country and the price paid by those who have sacrificed for our liberty—no one who reveres names like the Alamo, or Old Ironsides, or Concord Bridge—will ever forget you men of the *Franklin* and the valor that was yours. Suffering repeated attacks and grievous casualties in the crucible that was the Pacific Theater in World War II, you made duty and courage your way of life as you contributed greatly to our victory.

"Your chaplain, Lieutenant Commander Joseph O'Callahan, S.J. (USNR), and Lieutenant (JG) Donald Gary received Medals of Honor for their valor; and, as the number of decorations the rest of you won indicates, they were by no means alone in heroism.

"Among those decorations were 808 Purple Hearts awarded posthumously. I take a moment with you to honor your shipmates who can no longer report for muster. They, and you, will be remembered by the generations of your countrymen. God bless you, and God bless America."

The launching of the USS *Shangri-La* (CV-38) on February 24, 1944, produced one of the largest crowds, estimated at over one hundred thousand people, in the history of wartime launchings at Norfolk Navy Yard. The *Shangri-La* was the first of three aircraft carriers built by the yard during World War II. The keel of the 27,100-ton carrier was laid on January 15, 1943. (Charles S. Borjes, photographer. Courtesy of Kirn Library.)

another Wildcat squadron, and, though the Americans shot down eight enemy planes, they also lost four of their own. The *Ranger's* Dauntless dive-bombers hit Casablanca targets along the waterfront and pressed the attack continuously to keep landing and transport craft safe from French aircraft. Interestingly enough, it was Curtiss SOC Seagull float-planes from light cruisers in the invasion force, and the USS *Massachusetts,* which broke up a French tank column by dropping depth charges fitted with jury-rigged impact fuses.

Some of the stories to emerge from the Torch invasion have been profoundly tragic and the one about to be told would have been, too, had it not been for a relatively benign outcome. On board the *Ranger* were four Army L-4 observation aircraft. On November the ninth, the *Ranger* launched three of its Army L-4 Piper Cubs, easy enough for the carrier to do since she was making good headway. Unfortunately, at least for the Army pilots, someone aboard the carrier forgot to inform the rest of the fleet that the little planes were friendly. Climbing to two thousand feet and headed for shore, the L-4s made good target practice for an American light cruiser which opened fire, scattering the Piper Cubs like moths. Two were forced down on land near the old fortification at Casablanca, their pilots held prisoner until someone turned friendly and decided to bail them out of deep trouble. The third pilot tried to stay on course, only to be shot down over the beach-head by overanxious American infantry. Although its pilot was wounded, he crashed his frail aircraft, and had the good fortune to be saved by American troops.

In attendance for the launching of the USS *Shangri-La* (left to right) were Colgate Darden, governor of Virginia; Captain J.E. Manch, the only Virginian to participate in the Doolittle Raid on Tokyo; Mrs. Josephine "Joe" Doolittle, the ship's sponsor; and Mary McClellan, flower girl. The aircraft carrier derived its name from the mysterious Shangri-La referenced by President Franklin D. Roosevelt in his radio broadcast after Lieutenant Colonel Jimmy H. Doolittle's famous air raid on Tokyo from the aircraft carrier *Hornet* on April 18, 1942. Roosevelt, knowing the Japanese were listening, suggested the B-25 bombers of the 17th Army Air Force Air Group which hit Tokyo came from the utopia of Shangri-La and not a Navy aircraft carrier 668 miles from the target. (Charles S. Borjes, photographer. Courtesy of Kirn Library.)

The *Jean Bart* recovered from its earlier beating by American forces and started engaging Allied forces once again. The *Ranger* deployed nine of her dive-bombers fitted with one-thousand-pound bombs and took two hits to sink it. A French submarine then fired four torpedoes at the *Ranger* and missed. Aircraft from the *Suwannee* sunk the French submarine, at that time erroneously identified as a German U-boat. The ferry carrier, *Chenango,* began launching its P-40Fs on the tenth of November.

Carriers played a vital role in the

Douglas SBD Dauntless aircraft take off from the USS *Enterprise* May 29, 1944. (Official United States Navy Photograph.)

invasion. These early carriers extended, much as they do today, the forward air power of the United States. Of the carriers participating in Operation Torch, forty-four aircraft were lost. Escort carriers were new conversions with new crew and aircrew, so most of those losses could be attributed to having so many inexperienced pilots in the air early in the war.

All of the escorts accompanying the *Ranger* would eventually end up in the Pacific theater fighting the Japanese. According to the ship's paper, *Bullhorn,* dated Navy Day, October 27, 1945, the *Ranger* would become the first aircraft carrier to cross the Arctic Circle and the first to raid German shipping in Norway.

Escort carriers were not available for combat in the mid-Atlantic until March of 1943, but, as with the North African invasion, when they did arrive on the scene, the results were dramatic. These scaled-down versions of *Essex*-class aircraft carriers were considered faster and more maneuverable against the Axis submarine menace in the Atlantic and, of course, Japanese submarines in the Pacific theater. Keeping sea lanes in the Atlantic open to Allied shipping became their primary mission. This meant hunting down German U-boats with well-coordinated attacks.

The USS *Long Island* (CVE-1), was the first escort carrier in United States Navy history. Commissioned at Newport News Shipbuilding and Drydock Company on June 2, 1941, the *Long Island* was commanded by Commander D. B. Duncan. Though originally designated AVG-1, this ship became as much an aircraft carrier as her larger counterparts, once conversion was completed at Newport News Shipbuilding. The shipyard set a record by converting the *Long Island* from the cargo ship *Mormacmail* to a flush-deck carrier in sixty-seven days. The first landing and takeoff, and catapult launch from the *Long Island,* were made by Lieutenant Commander W. D. Anderson, commanding officer of VS-201.

A latecomer in the Navy's air war was the Curtiss SB2C Helldiver, which entered the fight in November 1943. The aircraft first proved its effectiveness in the attack on Rabaul shipping and harbor defense. This photograph was taken August 22, 1944. (Official United States Navy Photograph.)

Convoys plying the high seas could breathe easier when accompanied by the escort carrier. The first to arrive in the Atlantic was the USS *Bogue* (CVE-9) in late-March 1943; she remained in the Atlantic throughout the war. At the end of 1943, the *Bogue* had been joined in the Atlantic by nine other escort carriers, including the USS *Card* (CVE-11), USS *Core* (CVE-13), USS *Block Island* (CVE-21), USS *Croatan* (CVE-25), USS *Santee* (CVE-29), USS *Charger* (CVE-30)(actually a permanent fixture in the Chesapeake Bay as the Atlantic Fleet training carrier), USS *Pybus* (CVE-34) (which joined the American fleet on July 31, and one week later, was turned over to the British who renamed *Pybus* the HMS *Emperor*), USS *Mission Bay* (CVE-59), and, finally, the USS *Guadalcanal* (CVE-60). Operating in hunter-killer groups made up of the escort carrier and four to six destroyers or other escort ships, these specially trained units became a submariner's worst nightmare. The *Bogue* ended the war with the highest number of submarine kills, recording seven German U-boats, one Japanese submarine, and two additional U-boat kills assisted by her own aircraft and other surface ships in *Bogue's* screen.

The *Card,* commanded by Captain Arnold J. Isbell, was second only to the *Bogue* in submarine kills, sinking eight German submarines, four of those in August of 1943 as part of a hunter-killer group with three World War One-period destroyers in her screen. An aircraft flown by Lieutenant (junior grade) Robert L. Stearns, of VC-9 aboard the *Card* spotted four surfaced U-boats in the process of refueling on October 4, 1943, during the ship's second cruise. Stearns attacked, and the *Card,* then eighty-three miles away, dispatched three additional planes to assist. Lieutenant Commander Howard M. Avery, commanding officer of VC-9, had experienced pilots at his disposal. The squadron, flying Grumman F4F-4 Wildcats and Grumman TBF-1C Avengers, had reported to the *Card* from the *Bogue*.

In the ensuing action, the largest submarine, a 1,600-ton replenishment U-boat or "milch cow," was sunk, and three others damaged before submersion. Later the same day, one of the previously damaged U-boats surfaced and was sunk by *Card* aircraft. On October 12, 1943, *Card* aircraft damaged a German supply submarine and, the next day, sunk another which was trying to rendezvous with yet another supply submarine. The *Card's* aircraft attacked a third U-boat but it escaped, at least until a week later when planes from the escort carrier *Core* sank her. The *Card* sank its eighth enemy submarine on October 31, 1943. Twenty-two members of VC-9 attached to the *Card* between September

A Sailor Boy Remembers

Reon Glessner Hillegass Jr. was a young eighteen-year-old from Norfolk, Virginia, whose greatest concern before he came of age was whether his school grades passed muster with his parents. He was raised in a devout Roman Catholic home. His mother was Mary Veronica Foley, an Irish Catholic, and his father, a German Reformist, which made for, as Hillegass has pointed out, "a great Christian family."

Upon graduation from high school, Reon wanted to join the fight and, with his parents' permission, enlisted in the Navy. He completed boot camp at Great Lakes Naval Training Station, Illinois, in the fall of 1944, and from there he and twenty-nine other seamen in his class, Company No. 1861, were sent to Shoemaker, California. In December of that year, Hillegass and his company boarded a first class Pullman train traveling north from Shoemaker to Seattle, Washington, and from there to Bremerton, Washington, where they went aboard the USS *Franklin* for the first time. The *Franklin* was being repaired after having been hit by a kamikaze plane off Leyte during the Second Battle of the Philippine Sea.

In an interview, Hillegass recalled the people and events starring in this fateful assignment that would shape his life:

"Shortly after reporting aboard, I, with twenty-nine others from my boot company from the Great Lakes Training Station were assigned to Pacific Beach for gunnery practice. We practiced on five-inch, forty millimeters, and twenties. After returning to the *Franklin,* it was not long before we put out to sea. We went down Puget Sound to the Pacific Ocean and south to San Francisco and under the Golden Gate Bridge to Alameda where we picked up Air Group Five and other planes which we ferried to Pearl Harbor. During this time, I met Father Joseph Timothy O'Callahan, the Catholic chaplain on our ship. He was a regular guy, good looking, well-educated and concerned with the well-being of every man on the ship. Needless to say, my brothers and I, from a very early age, were accomplished altar boys and this is probably the reason I got to know Father O'Callahan so well.

"Mass was held as far as I can remember, daily by Father, many times... on the ship focsle. I was almost always there because that is how I was raised. After a few times there were not people to serve the Mass and I automatically volunteered to serve. Father O'Callahan was most appreciative. We developed a friendship which I will treasure for the rest of my life.

"[Being a boot replacement], I was assigned to the task of mess cook, a task which I thoroughly enjoyed and an experience which I treasure and have benefited from every day of my life. During this time I became a friend of a very devout Jewish fellow by the name of Gindy. I don't know what his first name was, but he was always called Gindy and, much to my sorrow, years later I found that Gindy was truly his last name. He told me that he and his friends needed a better place to meet on Friday nights because the mess hall just wasn't the greatest place to hold their Jewish services. I told him I would talk to Father O'Callahan about his desires the next morning after Mass. The next day was Wednesday and, beginning on Friday and until the ship was hit on March 19, [1945], Gindy and his Jewish friends met in Father O'Callahan's office for their Friday services."

Hillegass would describe Father O'Callahan as a product of his time who

Seaman recruit Reon G. Hillegass Jr. was photographed at Great Lakes Naval Training Station, 1944. He was only a seaman second class when the USS *Franklin* was hit by kamikaze planes, March 19, 1945. (Courtesy of Reon G. Hillegass Jr.)

always had a good thought, a provoking sermon that was never too long. "During this time," Hillegass recounted, "one of the greatest evils in the world was communism, and Father O'Callahan always made it clear that if you were killed fighting the Japanese, you were killed fighting the dreaded communist philosophy and as a result, you would go to heaven. In essence, he was saying, 'don't be afraid to die, life is really very short, do your very best at your station and win.'" Just a week or so before the *Franklin* was hit, Father O'Callahan stressed what Hillegass remembered as his "theory of doing your duty, no matter what the cost, especially your life. On more than one occasion, I heard shipmates say, 'I wonder what he would do under the same conditions.'" As the crew of the *Franklin* would learn, Father O'Callahan practiced what he preached.

The events which followed have not always been easy for Hillegass to discuss. In the early morning hours of March 19, 1945, the USS *Franklin* earned her title, "The Ship That Wouldn't Die." The carrier was fifty miles off Kyushu, Japan, positioned for Carrier Air Group Thirteen aircraft to conduct air strikes against strategically important enemy targets. An undetected Japanese bomber made a low-level run at the *Franklin* at three minutes after seven that morning, dropping two five-hundred-pound bombs. After the initial round of explosions, more would follow until in excess of 300,000 pounds of ordnance stored aboard the *Franklin* exploded.

Seaman Second Class (Sea2c) Hillegass was one of three hundred men trapped on the third deck of the carrier in a compartment normally suited to no more than one hundred sailors. He was one of the lives commanding officer Gehres held so precious, one that he made a determined effort to save. Hillegass shared a special part of his story, one he has been particularly hesitant to discuss all these years—his story of survival aboard the inferno that was the *Franklin*.

"Of the twenty-nine that came aboard from boot camp with me, twenty-eight were killed that morning. The twenty-ninth, James J. "Red" Forrester was left one hundred percent disabled for the balance of his life and died in November of 1991. I am the only survivor today. My gun mount [Gun Mount Thirteen] captain was from Elizabeth City, North Carolina, and he told me shortly after seven in the morning to report to the galley. We had been at general quarters for thirty-six hours and we had bogey alerts continuously. As a result, I didn't want to go down three or more decks. Our quad forty mount was of a newer type and had been welded to the side of the ship. The magazine was in the lower part of the mount and this was my battle station. There were three of us in the lower magazine and we passed the ammunition up through slots to the decks of the gun mount. In the starboard bulkhead we had a vertical dogged hatch leading into the ship. Instructions were to keep the hatch dogged at all times. Also, adjacent to the hatch was the ship's incinerator. We took a vote among the three of us and voted to leave the vertical hatch undogged. Finally, the gun captain told me to report to the mess deck or receive a captain's mast. As a result, I reluctantly left and went to the third deck. Eleven minutes later, we were hit and everyone on the gun [twelve men] was killed instantly by the concussion of the simultaneous explosion of the incinerator."

At the time of the first explosion, Hillegass was carrying two gallons of hot coffee back to the gun mount, coffee he spilt on other sailors as they all hit the deck. He had only been below for about five to eight minutes. In that time, a Japanese bomber pilot had gotten lucky and hit an American carrier. Most of the *Franklin's* air group had blown up on the deck, and the survival of three hundred men was to hang in the balance, one man—Captain Leslie E. Gehres, the carrier's commanding officer—holding their fate in his hands.

Sailors ran forward and aft along galley deck corridors trying to escape internal explosions and heavy smoke. Hillegass knew the mess deck, for he mess cooked when he was not manning his battle station. He made his way to an adjacent mess hall with four hatches, three of which he secured and the fourth, with a wheel, he left slightly ajar. He continues his story:

"When sailors figured they could not get out, they started pouring into this relatively small mess area. The overboard discharge valve offered the only source of air. Here we were trapped in that compartment with little air. It was hopeless. We were going to die, the ship was blowing up like a firecracker, it had started to list. It was only a matter of time before she turned over in the water. And, you know, it was practice in those days to abandon ship and have one of our destroyers torpedo it. I can truthfully say, I sat at a table next to the overboard discharge valve thinking to myself that I had no problem with the ship turning over and sinking to the bottom because I knew when I died I was going to heaven. I believed in what I was fighting for, I believed I had fought hard, beat back the enemy, just as Father O'Callahan had said."

Three hours after Hillegass' ordeal began, it ended, thanks to the heroic act of Lieutenant (junior grade) Donald Gary, an engineering officer, who located an air shaft and, one by one, hand in hand, led sailors up six decks to safety. Donald Gary, according to Hillegass, "had worked his way through the enlisted ranks [to be an officer] and, aboard the *Franklin,* had been responsible for damage control. He knew the ship." The lieutenant bravely led three hundred men topside, found a ladder welded to the side of the carrier and, somehow, managed to get the men to the end of a catwalk near the blown-out gun mounts. It was at that time that Hillegass saw all the men in his mount—Number Thirteen—had been killed, in addition to those in Nine and Eleven.

Once free on deck, Hillegass climbed an antenna close to the cruiser USS *Santa Fe* which had pulled alongside the crippled carrier to take on survivors, and jumped over at the urging of none other than Merritt Bibb, his childhood friend from Norfolk, then a *Santa Fe* crewman. He and Bibb were neighbors when Hillegass was growing up on Thirty-eighth Street near Colley Avenue. Merritt's uncle, Edwin E. Bibb, operated the most respected lighting company in the city at that time. Today, Hillegass finds this rather ironic, since he would end up owning his own lighting company, Hillegass Lighting, on Military Highway in Chesapeake, Virginia.

For his actions that day, Gary was awarded the Medal of Honor, one of two awarded *Franklin* crewmembers for their gallantry of March 19, 1945. The other Medal of Honor went to Father Joseph Timothy O'Callahan, Lieutenant Commander, United States Navy, who, according to Hillegass, "practiced what he preached." O'Callahan not only gave last rites to the dead and dying, but also watered down bulkheads to keep stored ammunition from exploding below decks, and tossed ordnance over the side to prevent it from catching fire or detonating as a result of intense heat. "He wore his Congressional Medal of Honor only once—the day he received it—and never again," Hillegass recalls. "He was the first chaplain in history to receive this award, one which carried with it such deep emotions, he could not bring himself to wear it."

Hillegass would be one of only fourteen crewmen from the *Franklin* who did not immediately return home from the Pacific after the crucible of "Big Ben." Once he reached Pearl Harbor, Hillegass was transferred to the USS *Corregidor* (CVE-15), an escort carrier, as an aviation fueler. "It was great duty because we replenished other carriers within proximity of Pearl, and we came in every Friday night to port. We brought the *Corregidor* back to Norfolk in early 1946 for decommissioning, so I came home," he remarked with a smile. "It took me twenty years to talk about what happened on the *Franklin* because it was war and I thought everyone got hit that hard. Looking back, I know there was so much death because we had just secured to Condition Three and the men aboard ship were moving in large numbers toward the mess. It is fortunate for those of us who were trapped below deck that the *Franklin* took no hits below the waterline." He attributes the survivability of the *Franklin* to Newport News Shipbuilding. As he put it, "they make a good ship."

"The *Franklin* made it back to Pearl Harbor, the most heavily damaged ship in the Navy ever to make it to port under its own steam," Hillegass notes with pride. The ship was stricken from the Navy record and cut up for scrap in 1966 at Money Point, also known as Mill Dam Creek, in South Norfolk. Hillegass was joined by a handful of former crewmen, including Captain Leslie E. Gehres, to observe the start of the scrapping process. He went over and found the discharge valve and cover which served as the only source of air for three hundred trapped men for over three hours, and Hillegass has held on to this symbol of survival—human triumph—over death for nearly thirty years. Finally, on the occasion of the fiftieth anniversary of the *Franklin* saga, he presented this precious piece of history to the Patriot's Point Naval and Maritime Museum in Mount Pleasant, South Carolina, home to the world's finest aircraft carrier museum and memorial.

Hillegass tried to hold back his emotions as he spoke of the significance of March the nineteenth—the feast of Saint Joseph, father of the Holy Family, and the fact that back home in Norfolk it was only the wee hours of March eighteenth, and his parents had been out since early that evening for their usual St. Patrick's Day celebration with friends. He could not die on the feast of Saint Joseph, he could not put his father through the pain of losing a son. At that point, Hillegass would say that he was fortunate to have his faith. "No matter what religion anyone is, young people are missing an awful lot if they are ever tested under similar circumstances and do not have their faith. Despair feeds on lack of faith. I am forever thankful for my background."

"This ordeal shaped my life," Hillegass responded when asked what impact the *Franklin* incident left on a young eighteen-year-old sailor boy, "I vowed if I ever got back home, I was going back to school and getting my education. I did get my education and was an outstanding student, much to my father's relief. He had tried so hard before I went to war to get me educated." Hillegass ends his story, "I grew up that day, it changed my life forever. It made me a more determined person, more determined to take on a job and get it done, live my life like I want to live it, and enjoy myself at doing it all. I don't believe in messing around. Get the job done, and go on to the next one."

23, 1943, and November 10, 1943, were decorated or commended at Norfolk for their fierce attacks on enemy submarines.

Stories abound from both the *Bogue* and the *Card*. These escort carriers spearheaded the two most successful hunter-killer groups roving the Atlantic. Some of the names and faces have not faded into the past. Captain Arnold J. Isbell turned over command of the *Card* March 9, 1944, and it is today's Navy patrol aviation community which annually confers its highest award for excellence to the best Lockheed P-3C Orion squadron in the Atlantic Fleet named in honor of Isbell. Winners of this award can be especially proud to receive the Isbell Trophy; its namesake was one of the great architects of antisubmarine warfare in the Battle of the Atlantic.

The only escort carrier lost in the Battle of the Atlantic was the USS *Block Island* (CVE-21), sunk the evening of May 29, 1944, when the *U-549* came through an escort screen around the carrier and torpedoed her. The *Block Island* took three torpedo hits. One of her escort destroyers came to the rescue and sunk the German raider. Ably assisted by her destroyer screen, the *Block Island* took very few of her crew to the bottom. Ten men perished but 951 were saved, in large measure to the quick action of destroyer crews which rallied around the stricken carrier and saved countless lives.

Perhaps the most famous of all escort carrier commanders in the Atlantic was Captain Daniel B. Gallery, later promoted to rear admiral. Gallery, commanding officer of the USS *Guadalcanal,* brought the long-fought Battle of the Atlantic to the front page of newspapers across the country, if not the world.

The United States had not captured a submarine or boarded a ship since 1814. The British, of course, had captured the German submarine *U-110* in May of 1941, before the United States was in the war, but *U-110* sank on the way into port. During August of 1941, *U-570* was successfully cornered by the British, towed to port, and later used by the Royal Navy. After Gallery's *Guadalcanal* sunk the *U-515* in April of 1944, he was certain the Nazi submarine could have been captured if escort carriers had trained boarding parties in their screen.

Gallery set out to train his own boarding party, and, on the morning of June 4, 1944, off the Azores, one of his destroyers reported contact with a U-boat. They commenced an attack. Eventually, three destroyers and two General Motors FM-1 Wildcats from Composite Squadron Eight (VC-8) made repeated attacks on the *U-505.* Depth charges blew open the submarine's hull, leading the boat's crew to think she was going to sink. The *U-505* was brought to the surface and her sailors began abandoning ship. Before the U-boat's captain could set his own explosives and destroy *U-505,* the destroyer USS *Pillsbury* sent a boarding party over, seizing valuable papers, charts, code books, and, most importantly, disconnecting demolition charges belatedly set by *U-505's* captain and closing sea valves. Gallery had a prize of war. The *U-505* was towed back to Bermuda.

In early 1944, the Navy had announced it planned to build three 45,000-ton carriers, two to be completed in 1944, and the other in 1945. These would be CVBs, "B" standing for "battle." The Navy wanted them built bigger to accommodate larger aircraft types, and to improve the armor plating and compartmentation of the ship. Though not finished before the end of the war, these carriers would become formidable representatives of American diplomacy in the Cold War period. The USS *Midway* (CVB-41), USS *Franklin D. Roosevelt* (CVB-42), and USS *Coral Sea* (CVB-43) were marvels of aircraft carrier

Pilots of Torpedo Squadron Fifty-One (VT-51) return to the USS *San Jacinto* (CVL-30) after a strike on the Japanese carrier fleet during the Battle of Leyte Gulf, October 25, 1944. A Grumman TBF-1 Avenger is in the background. Former President of the United States George Bush, flew with VT-51 off the *San Jacinto.* The commanding officer of the squadron was Lieutenant Commander Donald J. Melvin, USNR. Torpedo Squadron Fifty-One was established as Composite Squadron Fifty-One on September 22, 1943, at Norfolk. On November eighth of that year, VC-51 was redesignated VT-51, and Melvin was its first commanding officer. Squadron pilots initially trained in Douglas SBD-5 Dauntlesses and Grumman TBF-1 Avengers, later settling on the TBF-1. On April 8, 1944, training and carrier qualifications on the new *San Jacinto* over, the squadron departed Norfolk for the Pacific theater. (Official United States Navy Photograph.)

technology in their time. The USS *Midway,* the first of her class, would be commissioned at Newport News Shipbuilding and Drydock Company on September 10, 1945, with Captain Joseph F. Bolger, her first commanding officer.

It was not until August 10, 1944, that the composition of carrier air groups shifted to reflect the kamikaze threat to the aircraft carrier, and the need for night fighter and photographic reconnaissance aircraft the closer the American fleet moved toward Japan and her outer islands. Carrier decks were filled with fifty-four fighters (VFs), twenty-four bombers (VBs), and eighteen torpedo aircraft (VTs), with a provision for four night fighters and two photographic reconnaissance planes included in the fighter group. Just a few months later, it became clear this configuration was also obsolete. The USS *Santee* (CVE-29) and USS *Suwannee* (CVE-27) were struck by kamikazes on October 25, 1944, in early morning Japanese suicide raids on their task group.

Joseph "Bolo" Cavanaugh was an aerial gunner assigned to Torpedo Squadron Twenty-Seven (VT-27) aboard the *Suwannee.* Cavanaugh was only

Ensign Falvey McKee Sandidge was photographed in the cockpit of his Chance-Vought F4U-1D Corsair aboard the USS *Shangri-La* while the carrier engaged in training exercises in the Chesapeake Bay late 1944. He was a pilot with the VF-85 *Sky Pirates.* (Official United States Navy Photograph.)

Grumman's Best Customer—Navy Ace Alexander Vraciu

One of the most engaging and colorful personalities to emerge in the course of completing this work was Commander Alexander "Alex" Vraciu, now retired and living in Danville, California. Born in East Chicago, Indiana, Vraciu won a scholarship to DePauw University and, sensing a war looming on the horizon, obtained a private pilot's license under the government's Civilian Pilot Training program during the summer between his junior and senior years at DePauw. Following graduation in 1941, Vraciu started naval flight training at Pensacola, Florida, just prior to the Japanese attack on Pearl Harbor, and earned his wings of gold in August of 1942.

With what he would recall as a great shortage of aircraft and aircraft carriers in the early phase of the war, he was ultimately given the opportunity to carrier qualify on the USS *Wolverine* (IX-64), a converted Great Lakes steamer. He qualified on eight straight passes in a Grumman F4F Wildcat fighter. His first taste of combat came flying the Grumman F6F Hellcat off carriers, learning what he called his deadly trade for five months as wingman to Medal of Honor winner Lieutenant Commander Edward H. "Butch" O'Hare, commanding officer of Fighting Squadron Three (VF-3), later redesignated Fighting Squadron Six (VF-6).

While flying section lead in Lieutenant Commander O'Hare's division, Vraciu shot down his first enemy aircraft, a Japanese Mitsubishi Zero fighter, at Wake Island in October 1943. He then got a reconnaissance Betty two-engine bomber at Tarawa, and on January 29, 1944, qualified as an "ace"(1) after downing three more Bettys over Kwajalein. The last of these was destroyed after a long, low-level pursuit with only one gun firing parttime at the Betty which he noted was jinking and turning in. Alex Vraciu would see his next major combat during a Task Force Fifty-Eight (TF-58) strike at Truk, February 16, 1944. Fighting Squadron Six was carrier-based on the USS *Intrepid* (CV-11). The best account of his aerial combat at Truk came to the author from Vraciu himself.

"The two-day operation began at dawn with a new experience for carrier fighter pilots—a fighter sweep by seventy-two Hellcats, with no bombers to protect. Three divisions of Fighting Squadron Six took off from the *Intrepid* at 0640 to rendezvous with the remainder of the task force fighters, with the prime mission of destruction of enemy aircraft airborne over Truk Atoll and its Moen, Eten, and Param Island airfields.

"We approached Truk on a heading of 239 degrees at 1,000 feet until approximately forty-five miles out, then climbed for our assigned, intermediate altitude. Arriving over the atoll at 13,000 feet, just before sunrise, we began circling over Moen Island. Enemy planes could be seen on the field, including two Bettys taking off. Antiaircraft fire had already commenced and had found the level range of our flight, although the bursts were off to both sides. Our flight leader began spiralling down preparatory to initiating a strafing attack on the Moen airfield, with my section at the tail end of this flight.

"Remembering my first skipper's (Butch O'Hare) wise advice of always looking back over my shoulder before commencing the dive, I rubbernecked once again before pushing over myself. Our first ten fighters were already well into their runs when I spotted a group of enemy fighters about two to three thousand feet above and on the port side starting a highside run on our flight. The Zeke enemy leader's guns already could be seen firing at us. I quickly tallyhoed, and turned my section into the attack, getting bursts at the leader and causing him to break off his attack and head downward.Enemy planes appeared to be all around us.

"Maintaining our speed, we pulled up in a steep chandelle and aileron-rolled down on a Zeke trying to stay on our tail. The Zeke pulled up into a climbing turn and spun out at the top. We started to jump him, but I had to let him dive on down when other Zekes seemed to be preparing to strike from above. By scissoring with another friendly Hellcat, we soon worked all the Zekes down to our level and below. From here on, the picture changed completely as we were able to press home the attack. We noticed that the Japanese pilots were not reluctant to attack, but once they were countered, they would dive steeply for the deck or a cloud.

"The Hellcat can definitely outmaneuver the Zero at speeds of 250 knots or better, so we began to follow them down. I was able to follow three planes in this manner, two being Zeros and one a Rufe, setting them all afire. All hit the water inside Truk Atoll. While climbing back for altitude after the last attack, I noted another Zero skirting a not-too-thick cloud, so I began a pass at him. He promptly headed for a thicker cloud, and after playing cat-and-mouse with him for several minutes, I climbed into the sun, letting him think I had retired. When I came down on him for the last time, from five o'clock above, he never knew what hit him. His wing tank and cockpit exploded.

"A later, afternoon hop for us produced no additional air-to-air activity. We returned to the role of escorting a bomber and torpedo strike against enemy shipping attempting to escape to the north. Our flight principally strafed a listing cruiser dead in the water. That evening *Intrepid* was torpedoed by enemy air action, forcing our withdrawal from the combat zone."

When Fighter Squadron Six was returned to the United States after its second carrier torpedoing, Vraciu—ever the consummate fighter pilot—requested he be returned to combat duty. As he put it, "The Pacific war was warming up and all good fighter pilots naturally want to be where the action is." The Navy assigned the ace to Fighter Squadron Sixteen (VF-16), nicknamed the *Airedales,* aboard the USS *Lexington* (CV-16), where he added two more Zeros at the second Truk raid on April 29, 1944. His twelfth kill, another Betty snooper, was shot down north of Saipan on the twelfth of June. Vraciu would note that Bettys became his obsession after being told that it was a versatile Betty bomber that had shot down Butch O'Hare on a strange night encounter. On June fourteenth, participating in a strike against enemy shipping in the harbor, Vraciu sunk a large enemy merchant ship with a direct hit on its stern.

Then-Lieutenant (junior grade) Alex Vraciu naturally associated his most successful combat flight with the opportunity afforded his squadron at what became known as the great Marianas "Turkey Shoot." As he would later remark, "not many fighter pilots get a once-in-a-lifetime occasion like this." Vraciu's account of the Marianas "Turkey Shoot" remains a priceless record of brutal aerial combat conditions over Saipan. It is told here, in his own words.

"As part of the American task force protecting the Saipan operation, we were expecting an attack by over four hundred Japanese carrier planes on the morning of June 19, 1944. Bogeys were picked up on radar approaching in several large groups, and carrier fighter

Lieutenant (junior grade) Alexander "Alex" Vraciu of Fighter Squadron Sixteen, aboard the USS *Lexington,* on June 19, 1944, following the Marianas "Turkey Shoot." He holds aloft six fingers to indicate his enemy kills. (Courtesy of Commander Alexander Vraciu, USN (retired).)

aircraft were scrambled to supplement the combat air patrol already aloft. I was part of a standby group of twelve fighters launched from the Lex [USS *Lexington* (CV-16)]. As we were climbing for altitude at full military power, I heard Sapphire Base, *Lexington's* Fighter Director Officer (FDO) saying, 'Vector 270, climb to angels 25, pronto.' Fighter Squadron Sixteen skipper, [Lieutenant Commander] Paul Buie, was leading our three divisions of four planes each. I led the second division of F6F Hellcats.

"Overhead, converging contrails of fighters from other carriers could be seen heading in the same direction. After awhile, the skipper, who was riding behind a new engine, began to pull ahead steadily until out of sight. We had seen his wingman, Lieutenant (junior grade) W.C.B. Birkholm, drop out. The full-power climb was too much for his engine and his propeller froze, causing him to ditch in the water. Luckily, he was picked up about twelve hours later by a destroyer.

"My engine was throwing an increasing film of oil on my windshield, forcing me to ease back slightly on the throttle. My division stayed with me, and two other planes joined us. When I found that my tired engine would not go into high blower, our top altitude became 20,000 feet. This limitation was reported to the Sapphire Base FDO. All the way up, my wingman, Ensign Homer W. Brockmeyer, kept insistently pointing toward my wing. Thinking he had spotted the enemy, I attempted to turn over the lead to him, but he would only shake his head negatively. Not being able to comprehend what he meant, I finally shook him off to concentrate on the immediate task at hand. Later, I found out that my wings were not fully locked—the red safety barrel locks were showing—hence, Brock's frantic pointing. Apparently, it was all over before our group reached this particular wave of attacking aircraft, and I was ordered to return my group to orbit over the task force at 20,000 feet.

"We had barely returned to our station when the FDO directed us to vector 265 degrees. There was something in his voice that indicated that he had a good one on the string. The bogeys were seventy-five miles away when reported, and we headed out hopeful of meeting them halfway. I saw two other groups of Hellcats converging from the starboard side—four in one group, and three in the other. About twenty-five miles away, I tallyhoed three bogeys and closed toward them. In the back of my mind, I figured there's got to be more than three

Vraciu exits the cockpit of his F6F-3 Hellcat marked with all nineteen of his kills. The VF-16 squadron insignia is visible forward of the windscreen. This photograph was taken aboard the *Lexington,* June 1944. (Courtesy of Commander Alexander Vraciu, USN (retired).)

planes, remembering the seriousness in the fighter director's voice. Spot-gazing intently, I suddenly picked out a large, rambling mass of at least fifty planes 2,000 feet below on the port side. My adrenalin flow hit high C. They were about thirty-five miles from our ships and heading in fast. I remember quickly thinking that this could develop into a once-in-a-lifetime, fighter pilot's dream. Then, a little puzzled and suspicious, I looked about for the fighter cover that normally would be overhead, but there did not seem to be a top cover. By this time, we were in a perfect position for a high-side run. Giving a slight rock of my wings, I began a run on the nearest, inboard straggler—a Judy dive-bomber.

"Peripherally, I was conscious of another Hellcat seeming to have designs on that [same] Judy, [and since] he was too close for comfort, almost blindsided, I aborted my run. There were enough cookies on this plate for everyone, I was thinking. I streaked underneath the formation, getting a good look at the planes for the first time. They were Judys, Jills, and Zeros. I radioed an amplified report.

"After pulling up and over, I picked out another Judy on the edge of the formation. It was doing some mild maneuvering and the rear-gunner was squirting away as I came down from the stern. I worked in close, and gave him a burst. He caught fire quickly and headed down to the sea, trailing a long plume of smoke. I pulled up again and found two more Judys flying a loose wing. I came in from the rear, sending one down burning. Dipping the Hellcat's wing, I slid over on the one slightly ahead, and got it on the same pass. It caught fire, also, and I could see the rear-gunner still peppering away at me as he disappeared in an increasing sharp arc downward. For a split second I almost felt sorry for the little bastard. That made three down, and we were now getting close to the fleet. The enemy planes had been pretty well chopped down, but a substantial number still remained. It did not look like we would score a grand slam. I reported this information back to base.

"The sky appeared to be full of smoke and pieces of planes, and we were trying to ride herd on the remaining attacking planes to keep them from scattering. Another meatball [Japanese aircraft] broke formation up ahead, and I slid over onto his tail, again working in close because of my oil-smeared windshield. I gave him a short burst, but it was enough—it went right into the sweet spot at the root of his wing tanks. The pilot or control cables must have been hit, because the burning plane twisted crazily out of control.

"In spite of our efforts, the Jills were now beginning to descend to begin their torpedo runs and the remaining Judys were at the point of peeling off to go down with their bombs. I headed for a group of three Judys in a long column. By the time I had reached the tail-ender, we were almost over our outer destroyer screen, but still fairly high. The first Judy was about to begin his dive, and as he started to nose over, I noticed a black puff beside him in the sky. Our five-inchers were beginning to open up. Foolishly, maybe, I overtook the nearest one. It seemed that I scarcely touched the gun trigger and his engine started coming to pieces. The Judy started smoking, then torching alternately off and on, as it disappeared below. The next one was about one-fifth of the way down in his dive—appearing to be trying for one of the destroyers—before I caught up with him. This time a short burst produced astonishing results—he blew up with a tremendous explosion right in front of my face. I must have hit his bomb, I guess. I had seen planes blow up before, but never like this. I yanked up sharply to avoid the scattered pieces and flying hot stuff, then radioed, 'Splash number six. There's one more ahead and he's diving on a BB [battleship]. But I don't think he'll make it.'

"Hardly had the words left my mouth than the Judy caught a direct hit that removed it immediately as a factor to be worried about in the war. He had run into a solid curtain of steel from the battle wagon. Looking around, only Hellcats seemed to be in the sky. Glancing backward from where we had come, in a pattern thirty-five miles long, there were only flaming oil slicks on the water."

Vraciu added that he used only 360 rounds of ammunition that morning and required less than eight minutes to shoot down the six dive-bombers. He tallied one more enemy aircraft, a Zeke, to his total kills the next day while flying escort for bomber and torpedo planes on a record, long-range strike against the Japanese fleet at the First Battle of the Philippine Sea, making him the Navy's leading ace for a four-month period at that stage of the war.

Air Group Sixteen was returned to the United States after the Philippine Sea engagement but, as he had done before, Vraciu requested he be sent back into combat. Unfortunately, he would be shot down on December 14, 1944, by antiaircraft fire on his second mission while strafing near Clark Field, Luzon, Philippines. He parachuted to safety and spent the next five weeks with the USAFFE guerrillas, a resistance force made up of stranded American and Philippine regular troops in northern Luzon, and was given the honorary rank of brevet major while with the group. During the final weeks of his high adventure with the guerrillas, Vraciu found himself in command of 180 men, dodging Japanese troops to meet General Douglas A. MacArthur's advancing friendly forces. He marched into an American camp no worse for wear, sporting a Luger pistol and carrying a Japanese sword. Soon thereafter, he was returned to the United States to stay.

The indefatigable Vraciu survived service on six aircraft carriers (two of which were torpedoed), two ditchings, and two parachute jumps, to become known as "Grumman's Best Customer." He would have nothing short of his highest praise for the Grumman F6F Hellcat which was designed to do combat with the Mitsubishi Zero, a formidable opponent in the early months of the Second World War. As he put it, "the Hellcat gave us not only the speed, range, and climb to compete successfully against the Zero, but it could dictate the rules of combat. It had a rugged dependability, a solid and stable gunnery platform, and distinctly was more of a pussycat than a Hellcat in its carrier operations. What better success could be attributed to the F6F than to acknowledge its kill-to-loss ratio of nineteen-to-one." From January 1944 to the end of the war, sixty percent of the Grumman F6F-3 Hellcats were powered by R-2800-10W engines, in which water injection boosted emergency power to 2,200-horsepower and by April all aircraft in the fleet were so powered. The last of the 4,402 F6F-3s was delivered to the Navy by April 21, 1944, and the improved F6F-5 started making its appearance. Though there were no major changes to the F6F-5, there had been progressive changes to the F6F-3 and F6F-3N models. Features of the F6F-5 included the R-2800-10W engine, a flat frontal windshield, strengthened canopy, red instrument lighting, increased armor, stronger tail, and racks for two one-thousand-pound bombs and six five-inch rockets. At the end of its production run, some of these F6F-5s had two twenty-millimeter cannon installed to replace the inboard fifty caliber guns. This was what was known as the mixed battery configuration.

Vraciu's experience with the Hellcat was shared by just about all Navy pilots who ever flew the aircraft. The Marianas "Turkey Shoot" was the crowning moment for Vraciu and the Hellcat. Three hundred American carrier fighters, all but five of them Hellcats, fought enemy aircraft over the skies of Guam. The engagement lasted for perhaps eight hours, the Americans losing only twenty-three aircraft. Of the 373 Japanese aircraft sent into battle, only 130 returned to their bases. Between ground and air losses of aircraft, the Japanese lost 315 planes on June 19, 1944.

In the end, Alex Vraciu was the Navy's one-time leading ace, having shot down nineteen enemy aircraft and destroying twenty-one more on the ground. During the last few months of the war he would serve as a test pilot at the Naval Air Test Center, Patuxent River, Maryland, helping to evaluate tactical performances of American and enemy aircraft. As a commander, Vraciu commanded his own squadron, Fighter Squadron Fifty-One (VF-51) *Striking Eagles*. While commanding officer of VF-51, Vraciu recorded the best individual score at the Second Annual Naval Air Weapons Meet, April 5, 1957, reaffirming the steady hand and sharp eye that made him one the greatest fighter pilots in the Second World War.

1. Five kills.

seventeen years old at the time he enlisted in the Navy in September 1942 and joined the squadron. When the *Suwannee* left for the Pacific theater shortly after completing Operation Torch, the invasion of North Africa, Cavanaugh went with her. The USS *Suwannee* was involved in the famed engagement of American escort carriers and what remained of Japanese Vice Admiral Takeo Kurita's fleet, October 25, 1944. Even today, Cavanaugh can recall with great accuracy the precise time the kamikaze attack came the morning of the twenty-fifth, "thirty seconds after the *Santee* was hit at quarter to eight, we were hit. We were the second escort carrier to be hit by kamikazes. Two hundred and twelve men on the *Suwannee* died in the Battle of Leyte Gulf, seventy-eight were buried in one night. When we took her [the ship] back to port for repairs, there was one pipefitter who outright refused to come aboard because

A Japanese aircraft falls into the sea near the escort carrier USS *Kitkun Bay* (CVE-71) in heavy fighting off Saipan, June 18, 1944. The battle for the Marianas was a fiercely fought contest, perhaps bringing home more than ever the saga of the escort carrier, fighting for survival against kamikazes and a host of enemy efforts to halt the encroachment of Allied forces closer to mainland Japan. (Official United States Navy Photograph.)

the ship stank with the smell of seared flesh."

The *Suwannee* made the last landing of American forces in Balikpapen, Borneo, and holds the distinction of being one of the few ships that entered Nagasaki, Japan, within weeks after the second atomic bomb was exploded. When the smoke cleared, the *Suwannee* had supported more troop landings with her aircraft than any other aircraft carrier built. That, coupled with the fact that she was in the Pacific combat area during the Second World War longer than any other carrier, made this ship particularly remarkable. As Cavanaugh remembered, "We crossed the equator fifty-four times; crossed the 180th meridian date line twelve times and lost six days of our lives but took 'em back later; and crossed the 180th meridian date line and the equator the same time as the sun, thus becoming a charter member of the Order of the Purple Porpoise. And who else had the distinction of sinking an American tug boat? The tug struck our port screw and sank. No lives were lost." Crewmen on the *Suwannee* also became members of what was known as the West of Tokyo Missionary Society, an elite organization comprised of those who traveled west of Tokyo longitude on a combat mission.

According to official Navy records, the *Suwannee* holds the record for being underway while under constant combat at eighty-five days. The USS *Essex* has the record for time underway, the *Suwannee* coming in second, but the *Essex* was not consistently under combat conditions. Included in the *Suwannee's* combat time were three of the costliest missions in naval history: New Georgia in the Solomons, Tarawa, and Leyte Gulf. After she was hit by kamikazes on October 25, 1944, the *Suwannee* also established a record for being repaired in the shortest period of time. Her rapid turnaround time in the yards was reported throughout the country by national news services.

Suwannee's squadrons played a pivotal role in breaking the back of Japanese air power. Composite Squadron Twenty-Seven (VC-27) was in large part responsible for securing the Solomon Islands during critical air and ground support operations like Munda, Rabaul, and Bougainville. Composite Squadron Forty (VC-40) flew over three thousand sorties and ten thousand hours with only thirty aircraft in one single operation—Okinawa. Composite Squadron Sixty (VC-60) played a significant role in the

Ace of Aces

David McCampbell was born in Bessemer, Alabama, on January 16, 1910, son of Andrew Jackson and LaValle Perry McCampbell. He attended Staunton Military Academy in Virginia, and went for one year to Georgia Institute of Technology, Atlanta, Georgia, before his appointment to the United States Naval Academy by Senator Park Trammell of Florida in 1929.(1) As a midshipman, McCampbell qualified as an expert rifleman and was active in athletics, primarily baseball and swimming. He was an Amateur Athletic Union (AAU) Diving Champion, mid-Atlantic states in 1931, and Eastern Intercollegiate Diving Champion in 1932. Upon graduation on June 1, 1933, due to congressional legislation limiting commissions in the United States Navy that year, he was honorably discharged from the service and the same day was commissioned an ensign in the United States Naval Reserve.

During the following year while on inactive status in the naval reserve, he was employed by a construction company in Alabama, and as an assembly mechanic with the Douglas Aircraft Company. On June 14, 1934, McCampbell was transferred from the naval reserve force to the regular Navy and subsequently commissioned an ensign to rank from May 29, 1934. Through subsequent advancement McCampbell attained the rank of captain.

Upon recall to active duty, David McCampbell was assigned to the cruiser USS *Portland* in June 1934, and in July 1936, took a billet as an aircraft gunnery observer with Scouting Squadron Eleven, the aviation unit assigned to the cruiser. He was detached in June 1937 to report to Naval Air Station Pensacola, Florida, for flight training, and after the normal course of training, designated Naval Aviator No. 5612 on April 23, 1938. For two years thereafter, he served with Fighting Squadron Four, based on the USS *Ranger,* and in May 1940 he was dispatched to Norfolk, Virginia, for duty with the USS *Wasp* Air Group. McCampbell subsequently served as landing signal officer aboard the *Wasp* early in the Second World War until the carrier was lost in enemy action in the South Pacific on September 15, 1942.

During his period aboard the *Wasp,* the carrier rescued the crew of the schooner *George E. Klenck,* which was foundering in heavy gales off Cape Hatteras, North Carolina, in March of 1941. He also participated in scattered actions in the Pacific to keep supply lines open to Guadalcanal following the Battle of the Eastern Solomons in August 1942. After his return to the United States, McCampbell had consecutive duty at naval air stations in Jacksonville and Melbourne, Florida, from November 1942 through August 1943.

After fitting out Fighting Squadron Fifteen (VF-15), McCampbell commanded that squadron from September 1, 1943, until February 8, 1944, at which time he was relieved by Lieutenant Commander Charles W. Brewer. Lieutenant Commander McCampbell assumed command of Air Group Fifteen, based on the second USS *Hornet* (CV-12), on February 9, 1944, taking over from Commander William M. Drane. The *Hornet* transported the air group to the Pacific theater of operations. For all intents and purposes, the *Hornet* was Air Group Fifteen's carrier, her pilots were there upon the ship's commissioning and, no doubt, felt privileged and proud to take her into battle. Edwin P. Hoyt would write in *McCampbell's Heroes* (Van Nostrand Reinhold Company, 1983), "the fighter pilots of Air Group Fifteen were hard-flying, hard-drinking young men who liked to party as well as they liked to be in the air. The most notable event at Pungo, they said, was the squadron party held after the commissioning of the USS *Hornet,* 'their carrier,' which began at the Navy officers' club in Portsmouth, and ended a number of hours later in the general store at Pungo."

The squadron would join the USS *Essex* (CV-9) upon rendezvous with Task Group 38.3. In addition to his duties as air group commander of the "Fabled Fifteen," he became the Navy's highest scoring pilot with a total of thirty-four airborne enemy aircraft destroyed—the greatest number ever shot down by an American pilot during a single tour of combat duty, and the greatest number ever scored by any American Navy fighter pilot in history. His feat of destroying nine in one flight was unequalled in the annals of combat aviation. He was also credited with the destruction of twenty grounded planes.

Lieutenant David McCampbell (right), landing signal officer, takes his hat off to Pilot Officer Smith (left), Royal Air Force, for successfully landing his Spitfire on the USS *Wasp,* May 10, 1942. The *Wasp,* on special ferry duty out of Glasgow, Scotland, had previously launched forty-seven Spitfires of the Royal Air Force to Malta. When the same operation was repeated starting May ninth, Winston Churchill sent the message, "Who says a *Wasp* cannot sting twice?" (Official United States Navy Photograph. Courtesy of the National Museum of Naval Aviation.)

Commander David McCampbell is pictured here with his plane captain, Chet Owens, in November 1944. Note his Hellcat is adorned with all thirty-four of his kills, making him the leading Navy ace in history. (Official United States Navy Photograph. Courtesy of the National Museum of Naval Aviation.)

Under McCampbell's leadership, Air Group Fifteen fought from the central to the far western Pacific, participating in campaigns and attacks in the Marianas, Iwo Jima, Palaus, Philippines, Formosa, and the Nansei Shotos. The group also took part in the First Battle of the Philippine Sea, when Task Force Fifty-Eight, under command of Vice Admiral Marc A. Mitscher, Naval Aviator No. 33, conducted the now famous Marianas "Turkey Shoot," and destroyed over four hundred enemy aircraft in one battle. McCampbell's group would continue its famed exploits up to and including the Battle of Leyte Gulf.

After seven months and more than twenty thousand hours of combat operations, Air Group Fifteen was returned to the United States for a rest period. The "Fabled Fifteen" destroyed more enemy aircraft—315 airborne and 348 grounded—and sank more Japanese shipping—296,500 tons sunk and over half a million tons damaged or probably sunk—than any other air group in the Pacific theater of the war. Among the major combat ships sunk was the battleship *Musashi* (a 64,000-ton sister ship to the *Yamato*), three aircraft carriers, and a heavy cruiser. Additional ships damaged included three battleships, a carrier, five heavy cruisers, four light cruisers and nineteen destroyers.

For his brilliant record in command of Air Group Fifteen, McCampbell was awarded the Medal of Honor, the Navy Cross, the Legion of Merit with Combat "V", the Silver Star,(2) the Distinguished Flying Cross with two Gold Stars in lieu of the second and third similar award, and the Air Medal. The Medal of Honor citation reads, in part:

"For conspicuous gallantry and intrepidity at the risk of his life above and beyond the call of duty as Commander Air Group Fifteen during combat against enemy Japanese aerial forces in the First and Second Battles of the Philippine Sea...(He) led his fighter planes against a force of eighty Japanese carrier-based aircraft bearing down on our fleet on June 19, 1944...(and) personally destroyed seven hostile planes during this single engagement in which the outnumbering attack force was utterly routed and virtually annihilated. During a major fleet engagement with the enemy on October 24, Commander McCampbell, assisted by but one plane, intercepted and daringly attacked a formation of sixty hostile landbased [air]craft approaching our forces... (and) shot down nine Japanese planes and, completely disorganizing the enemy group, forced the remainder

Commander David McCampbell, Commanding Officer of Carrier Air Group Fifteen, and fellow officers are pictured aboard the USS *Essex* in 1944. The officers are identified only as (left to right) Heil, Miller, McCampbell, Lynch, Maness, and Bruninghouse. (Official United States Navy Photograph. Courtesy of the National Museum of Naval Aviation.)

to abandon the attack before a single aircraft could reach the fleet."

The Navy Cross wording would only emphasize all the more the great prowess of this legendary naval aviator,

"For distinguishing himself by extraordinary heroism and skill in operations against the enemy in the vicinity of Luzon, Philippine Islands, while serving as target coordinator for the combined aircraft of three task groups on October 25, 1944. His coolness, quick thinking, superior judgment and outstanding leadership resulted in the sinking of one medium aircraft carrier, one light cruiser, two destroyers, and the damaging of one battleship. By his outstanding performance not only was the maximum damage inflicted on the enemy but our own losses were kept at a minimum."

McCampbell was king of the calculated risk. He was as skilled a tactician as he was a pilot. His personal decorations speak to his enormous success. The Silver Star citation was presented to McCampbell for his heroic exploits in aerial combat on September 12, 1944, in the central Philippine Islands. He led his fighter group into battle, inflicting much damage and destruction to Japanese forces. Commander McCampbell personally engaged and destroyed four enemy airplanes in aerial combat and, in the face of antiaircraft fire, strafed and caused serious damage to an enemy merchant ship. The Legion of Merit stated that while attached to the USS *Essex* during action against Japanese forces in the Philippine Islands November 11–14, 1944, McCampbell directed the operations of several attack groups during this period, ultimately destroying a large enemy troop convoy.

McCampbell holds three Distinguished Flying Cross citations, all of which address the heroism of this Hellcat pilot. His first flying cross was awarded for heroism while commander of an air group in operations against the Japanese at Marcus Island on May 19, 1944. Early in the attack of heavily fortified enemy fortifications on Marcus, McCampbell's aircraft was hit by antiaircraft fire which seriously damaged the aft fuselage and controls, and set fire to the auxiliary fuel tank. Despite heavy damage to his own aircraft, Commander McCampbell remained to direct operations of his group until all ammunition was expended, then led his pilots back to the carrier. For the second citation, awarded for action against enemy forces on June 13, 1944, McCampbell led components of his group in an outstanding attack against a Japanese convoy in the vicinity of the Marianas Islands, resulting in the destruction of upwards of fifty thousand tons of enemy merchant shipping, at least one enemy destroyer, and three escort vessels, and damage to numerous others. In the third action for which he won the Distinguished Flying Cross, McCampbell was recognized as pilot of a carrier-based fighter plane on September 13, 1944, when, as leader of a fighter sweep assigned to a mission against the enemy in the central Philippines, he did engage and destroy in aerial combat three enemy planes and, in the face of antiaircraft fire, destroy two more aircraft on the ground on a strafing run.

From March 1945 through January 1947, Commander McCampbell was on duty at Naval Air Station Norfolk, Virginia, as chief of staff to Commander Fleet Air Quonset Point, and as Commander Carrier Air Groups Hampton Roads, Virginia. He was next assigned to the Armed Forces Staff College at Norfolk, first as a student, and later as a member of the staff in the intelligence division. After attending language school at Anacostia, McCampbell was sent to Buenos Aires, Argentina, as the senior naval aviation advisor to the Argentine Navy where he remained from October 1948 to January 1951.

In February 1951, McCampbell joined the USS *Franklin D. Roosevelt* (CVB-42) as executive officer, and from March 1952 until July 1953 was planning officer on the staff of Commander Aircraft Atlantic, headquartered at Naval Air Station Norfolk. He assumed command of the Naval Air Technical Training Center at Jacksonville, Florida, in 1953 and a year later became flight test coordinator, Naval Air Test Center, Patuxent River, Maryland.

By June of 1956, McCampbell joined the staff of Commander Sixth Fleet in the Mediterranean Sea, and in January 1958 was detached for duty as commanding officer of the USS *Severn* (AO-61). He commanded the USS *Bon Homme Richard* (CV-31) from February 1959 until May 1960, when he was assigned to the Joint Staff Office, Joint Chiefs of Staff, Washington, D.C. He later served briefly in the Bureau of Naval Personnel, Navy Department, and in September 1962 became Assistant Deputy Chief of Staff for Operations to the Commander-in-Chief, Continental Defense Command, with headquarters at Colorado Springs, Colorado. He remained there until relieved of active duty pending his retirement, effective July 1, 1964.

In addition to the Medal of Honor, Navy Cross, Silver Star Medal, Legion of Merit with Combat "V", Distinguished Flying Cross with two Gold Stars, and the Air Medal, Captain McCampbell has the Joint Services Commendation Medal; the Presidential Unit Citation awarded to Carrier Air Group Fifteen aboard the USS *Essex;* the American Defense Service Medal with bronze "A"; Asiatic-Pacific Campaign Medal with seven engagement stars; European-African-Middle Eastern Campaign Medal with one star; American Campaign Medal; World War II Victory Medal; National Defense Service Medal; and the Philippine Liberation ribbon with two stars. He also possesses the Navy Expert Rifleman's Medal.

It can be said that Captain David McCampbell lived his life to the fullest, contributed immeasurably to the fighting spirit of naval aviation, and to this work. In a letter to the author dated September 17, 1994, Captain McCampbell wrote, "I think you have chosen a very worthwhile subject to write about." Although McCampbell was referring to the story of naval aviation, his story too is a "worthwhile subject." In conversation with McCampbell, as with so many others he was most excited when questions focused on his days homeported in Norfolk as a landing signal officer on the *Wasp* and, of course, his tremendous accomplishments as the Navy's ultimate fighter pilot—the "Ace of Aces." He died in 1996.

1. McCampbell, an Alabama native son, was appointed by Trammell, who was born in Macon County, Alabama, on April 9, 1876, and moved to Lakeland, Florida, with his parents in his youth. Trammell was the twenty-first governor of Florida (1913–1917) and a United States senator from March 4, 1917, to the day he died on May 8, 1936, in Washington, D.C. McCampbell could not have been appointed by a more influential senator at that time, at least as far as the Navy was concerned. Trammell served on the Senate's Committee on Naval Affairs in the Seventy-third and Seventy-fourth Congresses.
2. The Silver Star is second only to the Medal of Honor as a military decoration for heroism.

landings at Leyte Gulf and, against great odds, prevented many kamikaze aircraft from sinking American ships. Cavanaugh eventually spent a total of forty-two months in the South Pacific fighting the Japanese from the back of a TBM Avenger. The back of his flying cap bears to this day three Japanese flags representing his three kills in aerial combat. Cavanaugh has said he often thinks of how our carrier forces would respond to similar fighting conditions if they existed in the world today as they did with such ferocity in the crucible that was the war in the Pacific, "freedom is something you have to fight for," his words choked with emotion. Though he would never want to go through it again, Cavanaugh, in his own words, "would not take a million dollars to trade the experience."

American aircraft carriers such as the USS *Franklin* (CV-13) and other flattops in Task Group Fifty-Eight off the coast of Kyushu, Japan, were exposed to kamikazes using conventional bombs and Baka flying bombs—the infamous

Ensign Falvey McKee "Sandy" Sandidge Jr. flew the F4U-1D Corsair off the USS *Shangri-La* the latter part of the war in the Pacific. Sandidge trained with VF-85 at Norfolk and aboard the *Shangri-La* in the Chesapeake Bay until the squadron was split into two divisions—one devoted to a fighter mission (VF-85), and the other a bombing fighting outfit (VBF-85). Commanding officer of VF-85 was Lieutenant Commander Warren W. Ford. Though essentially part and parcel of the same squadron, VBF-85 had its own commanding officer, Lieutenant Commander Stockton B. Strong. Strong's executive officer was Lieutenant Commander John "Tex" O'Neill. Both divisions of the *Sky Pirates* flew the same aircraft, the F4U-1D Corsair. Sandidge flew with Bombing Fighting Eighty-Five. The squadron left Norfolk aboard the *Shangri-La* in mid-January 1945 for the Pacific theater and saw their first real action off the ship during an attack on Okino Daito Shima, April 25, 1945. (Official United States Navy Photograph.)

Pilots of VF/VBF-85 *Sky Pirates* from aboard the USS *Shangri-La* posed ashore in Marine Corps Fighter Squadron One Hundred Twenty-Two (VMF-122) aircraft with the squadron's telltale insignia "Big Bad Wolf" flipping the bird and piloting a whiskey bottle made up like a dive-bomber. This was an authorized squadron insignia during the war. The Navy pilot is Lieutenant Bayard Webster, of VBF-85 *Sky Pirates,* 1945. (Official United States Navy Photograph.)

human guided missile used by the Japanese late in the war. The attacks on the flattops required more fighters, resulting in all *Essex*-class air groups adding nineteen fighters. This brought the total number of fighters to seventy-three, and dropped the number of bomber and torpedo aircraft to fifteen each. There were two squadrons of thirty-six aircraft, plus one fighter set aside for the air group commanding officer, and including four night fighters, designated VF(N)s; two photographic reconnaissance planes, designated VF(P)s; and two evacuation aircraft, dubbed VF(E)s. Marine Corps fighter squadrons were also added to *Essex*-class carriers in December 1944, as were bombing fighting squadrons or VBFs.

Ship repair such as that of the *Suwannee* was not the only activity put in fast forward. The USS *Bennington* (CV-20), a 20,000-ton flattop, was launched at Brooklyn Navy Yard on Saturday, February 26, 1944. Building aircraft carriers before the war took twenty-three months, but during the war this time was cut to fourteen months—the *Bennington* a perfect example. The carrier was built in drydock and was the first to be constructed in its entirety at the Brooklyn Navy Yard. Authorized on December 15, 1941, just days after the Japanese struck Pearl Harbor, her keel was not laid until December 15, 1942.

Two days prior to her launch at Brooklyn in 1944, the same day the echo of bombs hitting Tokyo reverberated across the Pacific theater, the USS *Shangri-La* (CV-38) plied the seas out of the Norfolk Navy Yard, Portsmouth, Virginia. *Shangri-La,* her name born of a moment's ad-libbing by President Franklin Delano Roosevelt in his radio address after Doolittle's Raid on Tokyo, became a full-fledged portent of Japan's defeat. Josephine Doolittle, known simply as "Joe" to family and friends, commissioned the ship as its sponsor with the traditional bottle of champagne across the bow. She was joined on the platform by her famous husband, Jimmy Doolittle, architect of the 1942 Raid on Tokyo. The *Shangri-La* and her air wing, Carrier Air Group Eighty-Five (CAG-85) trained off the Virginia Capes for several months before detaching on January 25, 1945, en route to the Pacific theater. The ship's commanding officer was Captain James D. Barner, who shared the spotlight with Vice Admiral John S. McCain, since the *Shangri-La* was his flagship.

On July 18, 1945, off Tokyo, two hundred dive-bombers from Task Force Thirty-Eight using 1,000-pound bombs battered the 32,720-ton Japanese battleship, *Nagato,* while the pride of the enemy navy was secured to her berth at Yokosuka Naval Base, Tokyo Harbor, Japan. Navy pilots believed her sunk, one of the last two Japanese battleships. While carrier-based aircraft struck the *Nagato,* 1,500 additional British and American planes went after Tokyo. Commander Wallace A. Sherrill, of Boston, Massachusetts, commander of McCain's carrier flagship air group, directed the attack on the *Nagato,* an air wing which had trained long and hard in Hampton Roads waters for action in the Pacific. The successful attack on the *Nagato,* nemesis of the American fleet at the Second Battle of the Philippine Sea, was a great coup for the pilots aboard the *Shangri-La*. When all was said and done, the *Nagato* was finished, her eight sixteen-inch guns and secondary battery of eighteen five-and-a-half-inch guns silenced forever.

Chapter 14: The Price of Peace

After the war and roughly six months after her commissioning on September 10, 1945, the USS *Midway* (CVB-41) embarked on one of the great explorations in post-World War II history—Operation Frostbite. With elements of Air Group Seventy-Four aboard, and accompanied by three destroyers, the *Midway* left Norfolk under the flag of Rear Admiral John H. Cassady to conduct cold weather tests in Daris Strait. In the period from March 7 to 22, 1946, these units operated as a carrier task force off the coast of Labrador and above the Arctic Circle conducting flight operations with World War II-type aircraft, newer Grumman F8F Bearcats, Ryan FR-1 Fireball jets, and the Sikorsky HNS-1 helicopter. The Ryan FR-1 was the Navy's first experience with a jet aircraft but, for all intents and purposes, it looked like a propeller-driven aircraft. Ryan was the only manufacturer who grasped the importance of designing an aircraft configured for conventional aircraft carrier decks. Jet aircraft then on the drawing board were too heavy and fast for existing carrier takeoff and landing devices. Though new catapult and arresting gear was in research and development—and larger carriers were being constructed—the American fleet had to move carefully into the jet age. The Fireball, the apotheosis of compromise, was powered by one 1,350-horsepower Wright R-1820-72W radial engine, and one 1,600-pound static thrust General Electric J31 turbojet mounted under the rear fuselage. Operation Frostbite would record the first use of propeller-driven and jet-propelled aircraft flying from the same carrier deck.

The *Midway, Roosevelt,* and *Coral Sea* became the workhorses of the fleet—platforms for great experimentation—in the postwar period. Marine Lieutenant Colonel Marion E. Carl, the celebrated World War II ace-turned-test-pilot, flying a Lockheed P-80A Shooting Star jet aircraft, made two catapult launches, four free takeoffs, and five arrested landings aboard the USS *Franklin D. Roosevelt* (CVB-42) on November 11, 1946, as part of ongoing investigations of the carrier suitability of jets begun June 29, 1945. Carl's Shooting Star was fitted with an arresting hook, the only one of three P-

Members of VA-3A *Black Panthers* were photographed aboard the *Kearsarge* at Guantanamo Bay, Cuba, August 1947. Members of the squadron included (back row, left to right): Harry Allen, Mac McNaughton, Howard Howser, Tex Hogan, Urey Patrick, John "Jawn" Farley, Heber Badger, Bill Wilson, Chris "Chico" Due, Grover Jones, "Baby Face" Floyd, Bill Parks, and Bill Swain. The front row included (left to right): John Smerdon, Robbie Robertson, Pat Patterson, "Swede" Munson, George Eiswald, James L. "Jim" Holloway, Roy Agnew, "MHO" Henderson, Shel Corner, Tony Ill, Bob Kibler, and Mac McMahon. The *Black Panthers* were redesignated VA-3A on November 15, 1946, and flew off the *Kearsarge* at that time. Lieutenant Commander Heber J. Badger was commanding officer of the squadron. Lieutenant James L. Holloway was Badger's executive officer. They are standing in front of a Curtiss SB2C-5 Helldiver. (Courtesy of Attack Squadron Thirty-Five.)

Lieutenant James L. Holloway of VA-3A *Black Panthers* takes off in squadronmate Ensign Chris "Chico" Due's Curtiss SB2C-5 Helldiver aboard the USS *Kearsarge* (CV-33), April 1947. (Courtesy of Attack Squadron Thirty-Five.)

Below left: The USS *Midway* (CVB-41) arrives from its Mediterranean cruise March 11, 1948. (Courtesy of the Kirn Library.)

80As to be equipped for shipboard use by the Navy. The Navy obtained these three aircraft from the United States Air Force and gave them bureau numbers 29667, 29668, and 29689 (Carl's aircraft). However, no unique Navy designation had been given these aircraft as was the case with planes like the R4D-5 Skytrain transport, otherwise known as a C-47 Dakota to the Army and Air Force who used them.

At the end of 1946, the Navy ordered the USS *Philippine Sea* (CV-47), then on her shakedown cruise in the Atlantic Ocean, to head back to port at Naval Station Norfolk. Once again pierside, the *Philippine Sea* was loaded down with six R4D-5 transports on December 31, 1946, and directed to take these aircraft, along with two Convair OY-1 Sentinels (liaison aircraft which flew aboard later), to the Antarctic as part of Operation Highjump. Manufactured by the Douglas Aircraft Company, the R4D-5 was powered by two 1,200-horsepower Pratt & Whitney R-1830-92s, and was by far the largest aircraft to have ever taken off from a flattop in 1946. With a wingspan of ninety-five feet, a length of sixty-three feet, three inches, and a height of seventeen feet, the Skytrain left quite an impression on anyone who saw six of her kind sitting on the flight deck of the *Philippine Sea*. En route to the continent, the aircraft were fitted with skis, which made takeoff from the carrier all the more difficult—and dangerous. The wheels of the aircraft's standard landing gear cleared the skis by only three inches. The wheels could not be removed and the skis put back in place

Lieutenant James L. Holloway (later vice admiral) of VA-34 *Black Panthers* strides across the flight deck of the USS *Kearsarge* with "the mob" after a flight. In typical aviator fashion, "the mob" communicated the mission with plenty of hand language. The squadron was redesignated VA-34 on August 7, 1948, and a short time later this picture was taken of Holloway and his squadron mates. (Courtesy of Attack Squadron Thirty-Five.)

Lieutenant James L. Holloway turns up Lieutenant Commander Heber Badger's "Scarface One" aircraft, a Curtiss SB2C-5 Helldiver, for deck launch off the *Kearsarge*. Chief Aviation Radioman (ACRM) Buck was in the rear seat. Taken during the squadron's May to September 1948 Mediterranean cruise, this picture is classic for the period. (Courtesy of Attack Squadron Thirty-Five.)

A VA-34 *Black Panther* SB2C-5, No. 311, Bureau Number 83236, crashed over the bow of the USS *Kearsarge* on August 13, 1948, due to engine failure. The pilot wsa Lieutenant J.C. Quillen, who can be seen on the right struggling to clear the sinking aircraft. (Courtesy of Attack Squadron Thirty-Five.)

Lieutenant Commander Heber J. Badger, commanding officer of the *Black Panthers,* was photographed in the cockpit of "Scarface One" during air operations off Malta, 1948. (Courtesy of Attack Squadron Thirty-Five.)

The Grumman F6F-5 Hellcat, Bureau Number 94032, and North American SNJ-5 Texan, Bureau Number 85062, in this image were photographed at Naval Auxiliary Air Station Oceana in 1951. (Official United States Navy Photograph.)

until the R4D-5s reached the airstrip at Little America.

The *Philippine Sea* launched the first of her six R4D-5 aircraft off the coast of Little America, Antarctica, on January 29, 1947. This was not only the first aircraft off but also the first carrier take-off for an R4D-5 Skytrain. The aircraft was piloted by Commander William M. Hawkes, and carried Rear Admiral Richard Evelyn "Dick" Byrd Jr., Naval Aviator No. 608, as a passenger. Beginning December 24, 1946, six Martin PBM Mariners based on seaplane tenders operated in open seas around the continent of Antarctica, and from February ninth, the six R4D-5s operated ashore from the airstrip at Little America. Together, these aircraft accounted for 650 hours of photographic mapping of the continent, covering 1,500,000 square miles of the interior, and 5,500 miles of coastline or, as Navy records indicate, the equivalent of about half the area of the United States and its entire coastline—Atlantic, Pacific, and Gulf Coasts combined. Air operations as part of Operation Highjump ended in the Antarctic on March 4, 1947.

Under the Navy's Project 27A, *Essex*-class aircraft carriers were modified to meet new operating requirements resulting from advances in aircraft and weapon designs. Aircraft carriers needed to be able to accommodate aircraft up to forty thousand pounds and, as a result, two H-8 hydropneumatic catapults were installed on *Essex*-class flattops, and flight decks and elevators were reinforced to support the weight and dimensions of new aircraft. Under Project 27A, initiated June 4, 1947, carriers were also equipped with jet blast deflector shields, an essential element on all aircraft carriers today but, in those days, a particularly important piece of equipment on wooden flight decks. The USS *Oriskany* (CV-34) was the first to undergo conversion in October 1947.

The first all-jet squadron, Fighter Squadron Seventeen (A) (VF-17A), was

The USS *Franklin D. Roosevelt* (CVB-42), a *Midway*-class aircraft carrier, leaves Norfolk for a Mediterranean deployment September 13, 1948. The *Roosevelt* had already made a significant contribution to naval aviation history when, on the morning of July 19, 1946, an McDonnell XFD-1 Phantom jet was craned aboard the carrier at its Norfolk berth. On July 21, 1946, while at sea off the Virginia Capes, Lieutenant Commander James J. Davidson flew the Navy's very first jet aircraft from the deck of a carrier, the *Roosevelt*. The XFD-1 was later redesignated the FH-1 Phantom, the first of which were delivered to Fighter Squadron 17A in 1947. During the late-1940s, the *Roosevelt* was configured to accommodate specially fitted P2V-3C Neptunes as part of a program to provide overseas nuclear strike capability via an aircraft carrier. The Neptunes were configured to carry atomic warheads. By the early 1950s, the *Roosevelt* would also carry the nuclear capable AJ-1 Savage which operated successfully from her decks in the Mediterranean Sea. (Charles S. Borjes, photographer. Courtesy of Kirn Library.)

outfitted with the McDonnell FH-1 Phantom, July 23, 1947. The XFD-1 Phantom prototype had first landed aboard an aircraft carrier—USS *Franklin D. Roosevelt*—on July 21, 1946, becoming the first all-jet aircraft to fly from the deck of an American aircraft carrier. The Phantom's pilot, Lieutenant Commander James J. Davidson, made several successful landings and takeoffs from the deck of the *Roosevelt*. With completion of carrier qualifications aboard the USS *Saipan* (CVL-48), May 5, 1948, VF-17A took its sixteen FH-1 Phantoms into the history books by also becoming the first carrier-qualified jet squadron in the Navy. In three days of operations, all squadron pilots, in addition to Commander Air Group Seven, qualified with a minimum of eight takeoffs and landings apiece. Fighter Squadron Seventeen (A)'s Phantom was but the first of the famed Phantom series and had a short-lived career.

The Navy began experimenting with large aircraft aboard its battle aircraft carriers (CVBs) in the late 1940s, and, on April 27, 1948, the first carrier launchings of two Lockheed P2V-2 Neptunes, piloted by Commander Thomas D. Davies and Lieutenant Commander J.P. Wheatley made jet-assisted takeoffs (JATOs) from the deck of the USS *Coral Sea* (CVB-43) just off Norfolk. The aircraft had been brought out to the carrier by barges and craned aboard ship. Jet-assisted takeoff bottles abetted all specially fitted Neptune and Skytrain aircraft in leaving aircraft carrier decks in those days.

A P2V-3C Neptune piloted by Captain John T. Hayward, commanding officer of Composite Squadron Five (VC-5)—a Norfolk-based squadron—

Lieutenant (junior grade) Falvey McKee Sandidge Jr. (left) celebrates having made the three thousandth catapult shot from the *Roosevelt*. The picture was taken January 5, 1948, aboard the *Roosevelt*. Lieutenant (junior grade) R.J. Mattus looks on. Note the squadron patches on both lieutenants' flight jackets: Sandidge has the insignia of VF/VBF-85 *Sky Pirates* on his right shoulder and a VF-3A *Tomcatters* patch on his right chest. The *Tomcatters,* otherwise known by their famous Felix, were redesignated VF-3A on November 15, 1946, only to be redesignated VF-31 on August 7, 1948. This photograph was snapped while the squadron was aboard the *Roosevelt* flying the Grumman F8F-1 Bearcat. Mattus has the insignia of Patrol Bombing Squadron One Hundred Sixteen (VPB-116) on his jacket. (Official United States Navy Photograph.)

There have been four squadrons designated Fighter Squadron Forty-One (VF-41). The current squadron by this designation traces its traditions to June 1, 1945, when it was established as Fighter Squadron 75A at Naval Air Station Chincoteague, Virginia. The squadron's first commanding officer was Lieutenant Robert H. Anderson, acting, until the arrival of Lieutenant Commander Theodore S. Gay, on June 6, 1945. The squadron's primary purpose was training replacement pilots for the Pacific theater. Those who would be flying the Chance-Vought F4U-4 Corsair used the Chincoteague base as a place for learning the finesse the aircraft for combat operations. On August 1, 1945, VF-75A was redesignated VF-75, and Gay retained command of the squadron.

The squadron, still flying the Corsair, was moved to Naval Air Station Norfolk in 1947. The designation was changed from VF-75 to VF-3B, and on September 30, 1948, became VF-41, with Lieutenant Commander J.P. Adams, as commanding officer. Lieutenant O.J. Donahoe was Adams' executive officer. It seems all too rare to find the roster of one of the earliest groupings of squadron officers, many of them coming and going too quickly to be recorded in histories—and memory. The officers of the original postwar VF-41 *Black Aces,* shown here, were (first row, left to right): Adams and O.J. Donahoe; (second row, left to right): Lieutenant David L. Thompson, Lieutenant Jay Arnold Jr., Lieutenant Louis A. Farber, Lieutenant (junior grade) John D. Hicks, Lieutenant (junior grade) E.H. Loftin, Lieutenant (junior grade) E.C. Hoskins, USNR, Lieutenant (junior grade) Falvey McKee "Sandy" Sandidge Jr.; (third row, left to right): Lieutenant (junior grade) D.H. Williams, Ensign T.A. Crawford, USNR, Ensign C.W. Parr, Ensign W.J. Whitney, Ensign A.B. Morris Jr., Ensign H. "Nick" Noesen, Ensign R.I. "Ricky" Roy; (fourth row, left to right): Ensign F.A. "Dan" Dandrea, Ensign E.E. Riley, Ensign D. Howard, Ensign H. Urban Jr., Ensign Richard I. "Dick" Van Allen, USNR, Ensign R.H. "Hap" Spradlin, USNR, and Ensign N.K. Donahoe. The *Black Aces* were embarked on USS *Franklin D. Roosevelt* post-war, making deployments aboard the *Roosevelt* and USS *Midway* (CVB-41) before moving to a new homebase at Naval Air Station Jacksonville, Florida, in January 1949. The *Black Aces* would be disestablished shortly thereafter only to be resurrected again on September 1, 1950, at Naval Auxiliary Air Station Oceana, Virginia. Today's *Black Aces* can officially claim their history as of September 1, 1950. (Official United States Navy Photograph.)

Commander Thomas Robinson eased this Lockheed P2V-3C Neptune off the deck of the USS *Franklin D. Roosevelt* on February 7, 1950. Jet-assisted takeoff (JATO) rockets created the smoke down the flight deck. Robinson's flight was part of a Navy effort to demonstrate carrier long-range attack capability. The *Roosevelt* was steaming off the coast of Jacksonville, Florida, when Robinson and his crew took off on their 5,060-mile flight that took 25 hours, 59 minutes. (Official United States Navy Photograph.)

launched from the *Coral Sea* in proximity to the Virginia Capes with a ten-thousand-pound-load dummy nuclear device on March 7, 1949. Hayward flew his aircraft to the West Coast, dropped the payload at sea, and flew back home again in 23 hours, covering nearly 4,500 miles. His flight was followed on the fifth of October by another P2V-3 Neptune piloted by Commander Frederick L. Ashworth, executive officer of VC-5, who took off from the USS *Midway* at sea off Norfolk and flew to the Panama Canal, then northward over Corpus Christi, Texas, and on to Naval Air Station San Diego, California, completing a 4,800-mile nonstop, nonrefueling flight in 25 hours, 40 minutes, extending the record set by Hayward. Yet another P2V-3C Neptune flown by Commander Thomas Robinson took off from the USS *Franklin D. Roosevelt* as she steamed off Jacksonville, Florida, flew over Charleston, South Carolina, the Bahamas, the Panama Canal, up the coast of Central America, and over Mexico, to land the next day at Municipal Airport, San Francisco, California. The flight exceeded all previous records, covering 5,060 miles in 25 hours, 59 minutes—the longest flight ever made from the deck of an aircraft carrier as of February 7, 1950.

These were exciting accomplishments, exciting times to be in naval aviation, every bit as important as those first tentative moments when the radio operator on the USS *Birmingham* broadcast the message, "Ely just gone," to the world. Maneuvering an aircraft the size of a Neptune or Skytrain from the deck of an aircraft carrier must have felt just a bit like taking a leap of faith from a speck in the ocean.

Experimentation with heavy aircraft aboard carriers continued into the 1950s, and on April 21, 1950, Captain Hayward, flew the Navy's first nuclear bomber, the North American AJ-1 Savage from the deck of the *Coral Sea*. By the end of August, VC-5 pilots had completed carrier qualifications in the Savage. By far the heaviest aircraft ever launched from a carrier at that time was a P2V-3C, piloted by Lieutenant Commander R.C. Starkey, of VC-6, who took off from the *Coral Sea* on the same date as Hayward launched in the AJ-1. Starkey's Neptune lifted off with a gross weight of 74,668 pounds.

Where naval aviation lost its luster after World War II did not take place on the flight deck of an aircraft carrier; it happened in the hallowed halls of Washington, D.C. By 1949, naval aviators were hearing the word "unification,"

Grumman F9F Panthers of Fighter Squadron Thirty-One *Tomcatters* are maneuvered for catapulting from the USS *Leyte* (CV-32) for a strike on Korea, November 17, 1950. (Official United States Navy Photograph.)

and no one welcomed it. Unification of American military defense forces quickly pitted the newly created Air Force against naval aviation, and had the Air Force's leadership prevailed, naval aviation would have been relegated to shore-based antisubmarine and escort duty. The aircraft carrier-concept was in deep jeopardy.

The fight which ensued in Congress caused the resignation of Assistant Secretary of the Navy for Air John Nicholas Brown on February 11, 1949. Brown vehemently protested the appalling treatment of naval aviation both in its funding and stature in the Defense Department. Secretary of Defense James V. Forrestal, a former naval aviator and the very first man to hold his title on a presidential cabinet, provided little assistance in the political power plays behind closed doors. Forrestal was replaced in March 1949 by Louis Johnson, a man already known to agree with the Air Force's consolidation plan. Johnson is also the defense secretary who cancelled the first aircraft carrier to be named the *United States* (CVA-58), which had been authorized by Congress but could still be quashed by the Secretary of Defense. Newport News Shipbuilding and Drydock Company had already laid the keel of the *United States*. Even the Secretary of the Navy John L. Sullivan was caught totally unaware of the carrier's cancellation. Sullivan resigned immediately after he heard the news. He was hurriedly replaced by Francis P. Matthews, a man who knew nothing of the Navy, a fact he readily admitted to the American press.

Secretary of Defense Johnson was engineering the demise of naval aviation by budgetary stangulation. No one but a handful of top aides in the Pentagon knew that Johnson and then Air Force Secretary Stuart Symington had a major conflict of interest by virtue of their personal investment in the Convair B-36 intercontinental bomber procurement program. With the resignation of Sullivan and the cancellation of the *United States*, the Navy redoubled its efforts against the B-36, an aircraft that survived the controversy but was never the performer it was touted to be by its champions in Congress. Air Force growth, especially in the form of cash flow, was increasing while ernstwhile Navy admirals watched their budgets dwindle away.

In the spring of 1949, Vice Admiral Felix B. Stump, Naval Aviator No. 2734 and Commander Naval Air Force Atlantic Fleet, played host to senators and congressmen who visited Norfolk and eyed flight operations aboard aircraft carriers off the Virginia Capes. Stump was aided in this effort by Fleet Admiral William Frederick "Bull" Halsey Jr. and Admiral William H.P. Blandy, Commander-in-Chief, United States Atlantic Fleet. Stump, Halsey, Blandy and others were lobbying congressional support for naval aviation and, as a result, their doing so became known as the Revolt of the Admirals.

Those taking part in the Revolt of the Admirals paid a heavy price. Modern-day naval aviators owe a great debt to the strength of leadership and character exhibited by aviation and non-aviation admirals in 1949. Chief of Naval Operations Admiral Louis Denfeld was forced to resign. Vice Admiral Gerald F. Bogan, former Commander Fleet Air Norfolk and Commander Naval Air Force Atlantic Fleet (February 1946 to December 1948), was denied his retirement with four stars. The venerable Admiral Arleigh A. Burke, then a captain, nearly got caught in the cross fire. Leading the fight for naval aviation, however, was Captain John G. Crommelin who exposed the attempts of Johnson, Matthews, and Symington to unify the military establishment at the expense of naval aviation. Though he was reprimanded by his superiors, Crommelin eventually retired as a rear admiral.

Crommelin and the others knew the seriousness of their claims firsthand. As of June 30, 1950, naval aviation was at its all-time lowest point. Carrier forces consisted of three battle, four fleet, four light, and four escort types, while aircraft on hand numbered only 14,095, and pilots on active duty totalled only 9,418. This was not postwar downsizing, it was fallout from the battle raging in the hallowed halls of Washington, D.C. Since the United States was nearing war in Korea, naval aviation should have been expanding, not shrinking.

The spread of communism on the

Ordnance crewmen make a final check of an F4U-4 Corsair's armament aboard the USS *Sicily* (CVE-18) prior to a strike on Korea, November 16, 1950. (Official United States Navy Photograph.)

The USS *Coral Sea* (CVB-43) had its ship's Christmas party at Norfolk City Arena on both December 2 and 3, 1952, because there were simply too many sailors to fit all of them in the room for one night. The photograph here was taken on the first night, December 2, 1952. (Courtesy of the Kirn Library.)

European continent was only the first front of Soviet aggression after the Second World War. When North Korea invaded South Korea over the Thirty-Eighth Parallel on June 27, 1950, President Harry S. Truman ordered the United States Seventh Fleet into action to prevent the Red Chinese, the primary architects of North Korean aggression, from moving into Hong Kong and outlying reaches of China's mainland. In the Atlantic Fleet, the only aircraft carriers at Truman's disposal were the *Midway, Roosevelt,* and *Coral Sea.* The USS *Leyte* (CV-32) and light carriers *Bataan* (CVL-29), *Cabot* (CVL-28), *Saipan* (CVL-48), and *Wright* (CVL-49), and escort carriers *Mindoro* (CVE-120) and *Palau* (CVE-122) were also ported on the East Coast. There were no big attack carriers on the West Coast. The Navy had been reduced in strength to an all-time low when the Korean crisis once again enveloped the country in the flames of war. With four fleet, four light, and two escort carriers, 14,095 aircraft, and only 9,418 active duty pilots on hand, the Navy and its Marine Corps brethren had to call heavily upon the reserves.

Initial strikes against Yalu River bridges at Sinuiju by aircraft of Carrier Task Force Seventy-Seven met enemy opposition in the form of MiG-15s. This was the first recorded aerial engagement of Navy jet aircraft with enemy MiGs. Lieutenant Commander W.T. "Tom" Amen, commanding officer of VF-111 aboard the USS *Philippine Sea,* flew his Grumman F9F-2 Panther jet into history when he scored one kill and became the first Navy pilot to shoot down a jet aircraft. The date was November 9, 1950, almost forty years to the day after Eugene B. Ely's flight in Hampton Roads.

As the Navy scrambled its fast carrier forces, additional escort carriers joined the fight overseas. The USS *Bataan* carried Marine Corps Fighter Squadron Two Hundred Twelve (VMF-212) aboard when she embarked with United States naval forces in the Sea of Japan on December 17, 1950, to protect the evacuation of United Nations troops from Hungnam and other coastal ports. The *Bataan* was actually pressed into service after dropping off replacement aircraft to Japan, and VMF-212 had been one of the squadrons forced to withdraw from its airfield in North Korea near Yonpo ten days earlier.

With the coming of a new year, the Navy established its first heavy attack wings. Heavy Attack Wing One was in operation out of Naval Air Station Norfolk, Virginia, effective February 1, 1951, and Captain Robert Goldthwaite, Naval Aviator No. 3364, served as its first commander. Composite Squadron Five (VC-5) became the first squadron assigned to the Heavy Attack Wing.

Of the numerous events which took place in 1951, two involving the USS *Essex* in combat off the east coast of Korea would hold great significance for the naval aviation community. The *Essex* joined Carrier Task Force Seventy-Seven on the twenty-third of August, launching aircraft from Air Group Five under intense combat conditions. This World War II veteran and namesake to a whole class of aircraft carriers became the very first postwar conversion of her period

A Grumman F9F-2 Panther of VF-123 was photographed aboard an *Essex*-class carrier (note the wooden deck) sometime between February 1953 and mid-1956. The aircraft was flown by Lieutenant Commander R.E. Kuntz, a former *Pukin' Dog.* Fighter Squadron One Hundred Forty-Three, stationed at Naval Air Station Oceana, is a lineal descendant of Fighter Squadron One Hundred Twenty-Three. Reserve Fighter Squadron Eight Hundred Seventy-One was called to active duty on July 20, 1950, only to be redesignated VF-123 on February 4, 1953. A little over five years later, on April 12, 1958, VF-123 was redesignated VF-53. VF-53 was later redesignated VF-143 on June 20, 1962. (Official United States Navy Photograph.)

carrier to go into combat. Two days later, McDonnell F2H Banshees and Grumman F9F-2 Panthers from the *Essex* provided fighter escort for B-29s on a high-altitude bombing mission against the marshalling yards at Rashin in extreme northeast Korea.

Within two years' time, the Navy would have British-engineered steam catapults and angled flight decks. Colin Campbell Mitchell, a Scotsman, conducted the earliest research and development on catapults and arresting gear for the Royal Navy starting about 1928. Not until after the Second World War was Mitchell afforded the opportunity to return to his work on steam catapults. Rear Admiral D.K. "Danny" Weitzenfeld, since retired, a young aeronautical engineering duty officer at the time of Mitchell's highly successful demonstrations of the steam catapult for the United States Navy in 1952, wrote in the Naval Aviation Museum's publication *Foundation* in the spring of 1985 that "[we] would have no modern aircraft carriers such as the *Nimitz, Vinson, Washington,* and *Lincoln* in the 1980s and 1990s," without Colin Campbell Mitchell's steam catapult. Weitzenfeld noted that the most outstanding feature of Mitchell's catapult was his method of braking the shuttle and piston. Weitzenfeld remarked that in hydropneumatic catapults [the H-8 type used during World War II, for example] the "5,000 pound shuttle was braked to a stop by a fifty-foot hydraulic pneumatic [hydropneumatic] system."

This was not the case with Mitchell's design which called for the same braking action to be performed by a five-foot water brake. It was Weitzenfeld's observation that Mitchell's catapult gave a peak-to-mean ratio of 1.2-to-1 plus forty-five additional feet of power stroke. While the British worked to perfect steam catapults, their American counterparts at the Naval Aircraft Factory turned to research and development on powder catapults.

When the HMS *Perseus* arrived at Philadelphia on January 20, 1952, to

The USS *Midway* (CVB-41) is pictured as she returns from deployment December 27, 1954, to Norfolk Naval Station. The *Midway* was the first in her class. At 45,000 tons and 968 feet in length, she was a behemoth carrier that could boast her size as much as an armored flight deck (quite a departure from World War II wooden flight decks) and highly compartmentized lower deck design. She would be joined in her class by the USS *Franklin D. Roosevelt* and the USS *Coral Sea* (CVB-43). In February 1955, the *Midway* left Norfolk to become the first carrier of her class to serve the Pacific Fleet. (Charles S. Borjes, photographer. Courtesy of the Kirn Library.)

Tales of Swordsmen, Corsairs, and a Medal of Honor Winner

When we ask ourselves, "where are the heroes?" a look into the faces of the young men and women we catapult off our aircraft carrier decks is as good a place as any to begin the quest. That is kind of how it all started for Ensign Jesse L. Brown, the first African American to complete the Navy's basic flight training program for pilot qualification,(1) and his wingman, Lieutenant (junior grade) Thomas Jerome Hudner Jr., an incredibly courageous young man from Massachusetts. At the outbreak of the Korean Conflict, Fighter Squadron Thirty-Two (VF-32) *Swordsmen,* Brown and Hudner's unit, were flying the Chance-Vought F4U-4 Corsair from the deck of the USS *Leyte* (CV-32). From October 1950 to January 1951, VF-32 participated in strikes against Korean targets including Wonsan Harbor, Puckchong, Chonjin, and Chosin Reservoir.

Perhaps the most moving incident of the entire Korean Conflict would occur on December 4, 1950, during a strike against the Chosin Reservoir in which Brown and Hudner participated. Ensign Brown was flying an armed reconnaissance mission as section leader when he took hits at low altitude from antiaircraft fire, probably ground troops, and trailed smoke as his Corsair was forced down in North Korean-held territory. *Swordsmen* aircraft maneuvered immediately to circle Brown and protect him from enemy troops moving in on the crash site. Brown managed to wave to his squadronmates from the wreckage to indicate he was still alive and needed help. His Corsair was on fire and the flames had begun creeping toward the cockpit. Brown was helplessly pinned.

Hudner was aware of the extreme danger in landing on rough mountainous terrain but he also could not abandon his wingman. If he landed his aircraft near Brown, Hudner would have scant hope of escape or little chance of survival in subzero temperatures. Those were the possibilities. Hudner put his Corsair down skillfully in a wheels-up landing in the presence of enemy troops. With his bare hands, Hudner packed the fuselage of Brown's plane with snow to keep the flames away from the pilot while he struggled to pull Brown free. Unsuccessful in this and refusing to give up, he returned to his crashed plane and radioed other airborne aircraft, requesting that a helicopter be dispatched with an axe and fire extinguisher. Hudner remained by Brown's side waiting for the rescue helicopter despite continuing danger from North Korean and Chinese troops.

A Marine Corps helicopter pilot answered Hudner's call for help. The rescue pilot and Hudner renewed a desperate but futile battle against time, cold, and flames to extricate Brown from his burning aircraft. Brown's legs were hopelessly pinned by a pinched fuselage and while Hudner and the Marine Corps pilot tried to free him, Brown died of his wounds. Five miles behind enemy lines and facing the possibility of capture themselves, Hudner and his Marine rescue pilot were compelled to depart the area immediately. To prevent the enemy from getting to Brown and his aircraft, the next day the Navy dropped napalm on the plane, thereby preventing the North Koreans from desecrating the site. For his courage and perseverance, Lieutenant (junior grade) Hudner received the Medal of Honor, and Ensign Brown, a posthumous Distinguished Flying Cross. Heroes can be your wingman, a squadronmate, and they can also be that line chief or a twenty year old petty officer who, faced with a crisis or call to action, makes a split-second decision to meet the challenge with, as Hudner's Medal of Honor citation reads, "valiant action and selfless devotion to a shipmate" which exemplifies the highest traditions of the United States naval service. Hudner was only the fourth Corsair pilot, and the only carrier pilot during the Korean Conflict, bestowed the Medal of Honor.

Midshipman Jesse L. Brown, circa 1947. (Courtesy of the National Museum of Naval Aviation.)

Ensign Jesse L. Brown, circa 1950, in the cockpit of his Chance-Vought F4U-4 Corsair of Fighter Squadron Thirty-Two *Swordsmen*. (Official United States Navy Photograph.)

1. Ensign Oscar Wayman Holmes entered the Navy during World War II as a qualified pilot. He completed flight instructor training on June 30, 1943, at which time he was designated a naval aviator, thus becoming the first African American to wear the wings of gold though the Navy did not actually know Holmes was black at the time he was commissioned an ensign in 1942. Even though the Navy subsequently "knew" Holmes was African American, his peers and superior officers did not segregate him from white officer quarters.
2. The tactical call sign of a squadron is its official fleet communication, such as radio, identification.

Lieutenant (junior grade) Thomas J. Hudner Jr. receives his Medal of Honor from President Harry S. Truman on April 13, 1951. (Courtesy of the National Museum of Naval Aviation.)

The Overhaul and Repair Department Decal Shop at Naval Air Station Norfolk generated the artwork and subsequent insignia for Operation Deep Freeze in 1955. This black line artwork is all that remains of the original Task Force Forty-Three art but, fortunately, not the end of this wonderful, quite colorful, special operation insignia. Operation Deep Freeze patches still appear on the flight jackets of naval aviators. It was on November 14, 1955, that the flagship of Rear Admiral George Dufek, Commander Task Force Forty-Three, sailed from Norfolk for New Zealand to rendezvous with Operation Deep Freeze escort ships for the southward trip to Antarctica.

The USS *Bennington* (CVA-20) is shown underway on deployment April 4, 1958. The aircraft on the deck nearest the elevator is a North American FJ Fury. (Official United States Navy Photograph.)

calibrate the dead load of its XBS-1 catapult, American designers took notice. Following tests of Mitchell's steam catapult conducted at the Philadelphia Naval Shipyard, the *Perseus* came to Naval Station Norfolk on February eleventh, secured at the carrier piers and conducted all of its catapult tests pierside. From February 12 to 15, 1952, HMS *Perseus* launched American naval aircraft from its steam catapults while the ship sat tied to the pier. The first aircraft launched was a Douglas F3D-1 Skyknight which, according to Weitzenfeld, "launched ten knots downwind. The same aircraft using the H-8 hydraulic catapult would have needed twenty-eight to thirty knots headwind." The launch of this F3D-1 was also historically significant in light of one remark exclaimed by Commander Naval Air Force Atlantic Fleet, Vice Admiral John J. Ballentine, Naval Aviator No. 2878, who, while watching the tests in the company of Weitzenfeld, Lieutenant Russ Reiserer, and his staff, said, "I want that steam catapult." Ballentine called the Navy Department in Washington, D.C., immediately upon return to his office.

Other aircraft tested at Norfolk included the Grumman F9F-2 Panther and the McDonnell F2H-2 Banshee. The Navy adopted the steam catapult effective April 28, 1952, for its carriers, dispensing with the idea of powder catapults after witnessing the tremendous success of Mitchell's BS-1 steam catapult. The BS-1 was later redesignated the C-11.

American engineers were being encouraged by the Bureau of Aeronautics to build upon Mitchell's original design, customizing each catapult configuration to meet the needs of the United States' fleet of aircraft carriers. The first step was clearly to obtain permission from the British to use Mitchell's original drawings and calculations. Under the direction of Captain Sheldon W. Brown, (see Chapter Twelve), primary architect of negotiations with the British and later a main player in American development of the canted or angled flight deck, Commander Richard Tunnell, James Scholl, and Captain Emerson Fawkes, the United States Navy obtained permission from the British to use the C-11 steam catapult designed by Mitchell with the intention of building them here in the United States.

The USS *Hancock* (CV-19) was the first aircraft carrier equipped with a steam catapult. Commander H.J.

In this poignant moment, the crew of the USS *Bennington* spells out the name of the sunken battleship USS *Arizona* as the carrier passes directly by the future memorial on May 31, 1958. The *Arizona* memorial was under construction at the time, a lasting remembrance of those who died in the surprise Japanese attack on Pearl Harbor December 7, 1941. (Official United States Navy Photograph.)

Air operations aboard the USS *Bennington* were caught on film June 13, 1958. Note the mix of aircraft: propeller-driven and jet aircraft shared the flight deck. The largest aircraft on the deck in the photograph are the four North American AJ-2 carrier-based nuclear strike planes. The aircraft in the foreground, Bureau Number 134044, gives the clearest view of the size of the aircraft in proportion to other planes on the *Bennington*. The engines on the AJ-2 were upgraded for more power to two 2,400-horsepower Pratt & Whitney R-2800-48 engines with 4,600 pounds of thrust provided by an Allison J33-A-10 turbojet mounted in the tail. There were only four squadrons left flying the AJ-2 in 1958, the year the picture was taken. (Official United States Navy Photograph.)

A Grumman WF-2 or "Willy Fudd" was photographed revving up for a launch on the starboard catapult of the USS *Bennington* (CVS-20) on July 8, 1959. (Official United States Navy Photograph.)

Crewmembers of the USS *Saratoga* (CVA-60) and USS *Essex* (CVA-9) spell out "Hello America" on their respective flight decks en route from Gibraltar to Mayport, Florida, February 24, 1960. (Official United States Navy Photograph.)

Jackson, piloting a Grumman S2F-1 Tracker, catapulted from the *Hancock,* June 1, 1954, in the first operational test of the C-11 steam catapult. Work aboard the *Hancock,* dubbed Operation Steam, took place on the West Coast and ended February 18, 1955. The great success of *Hancock's* tests resulted in blanket approval of the C-11-1 (-1 with American modifications), for use aboard all Navy aircraft carriers. The Navy has since improved upon Mitchell's original steam catapult a few times over, and American carriers are now equipped with four steam catapults, C-13-1s with a launch stroke of three hundred and ten feet.

Between May 26 and 29, 1952, the Bureau of Aeronautics approved feasibility tests of the angled deck concept, demonstrating its use on a simulated angled deck aboard the USS *Midway* by Naval Air Test Center (NATC) and Atlantic Fleet pilots flying both jet and propeller-driven aircraft. The keel-laying of the USS *Forrestal* (CV-59)(1) on July 14, 1952, at Newport News Shipbuilding and Drydock Company, heralded the arrival

The USS *Bennington* (CVS-20) had transited to the Pacific Ocean when one of its C-1A Trader aircraft was photographed towing a target, November 12, 1966. The Trader was typically a carrier on board delivery cargo transport aircraft but, the one shown here belonged to the antisubmarine warfare support activity aboard the ship, Antisubmarine Squadron Thirty-Eight (VS-38), established as reserve squadron VC-892 on July 20, 1950, and later redesignated VS-38, an active fleet unit, on February 4, 1953. (Official United States Navy Photograph.)

of the 59,000-ton aircraft carrier designed with an angled flight deck as well as the latest in catapult and arresting technology. In ceremonies held at the Newport News shipyard, Deputy Secretary of Defense William C. Foster concluded his remarks by saying to his many listeners, "And now let us in our hearts echo the prayer that from these beginnings an historic ship may rise successfully; that she will render service to the nation consonant with that rendered by the man whose name she bears; and, that she will carry to the far ends of the earth our championship of peace."

By January 12, 1953, the Navy was ready to test its first angled deck carrier, the USS *Antietam* (CVA-36). To kick off initiation tests aboard the *Antietam,* Captain S.G. Mitchell, the ship's commanding officer, landed a North American SNJ Texan aboard her new angled deck. Six aircraft types would make landings, touch-and-go runs, night landings, and takeoffs over a span of four days.

Nearly seven months after success with the *Antietam,* the armistice agreement was signed at Panmunjom at 0112 hours Korean time, July 27, 1953, thus ending thirty-seven months of conflict and death on the Korean peninsula. The attention of American naval forces was turned directly toward the hostile Soviet Union. This meant naval aviators faced the shadow of communism that had crept so quietly throughout disadvantaged countries, through China, and the Far East, and thrust angrily into wartorn Europe head on. The mask was removed, the enemy came out in the open. Changes had to be made to carrier forces to combat the Soviet submarine threat.

Six attack carriers (CVAs) were redesignated submarine hunters (CVSs) effective as of August 8, 1953, just days after the cease-fire in Korea. A little over two months later, on November sixteenth, the Douglas XF4D-1 Skyray successfully completed carrier trials aboard the USS *Coral Sea* off the Virginia Capes. Production F4D-1s flew with 14,500-pound static thrust Pratt & Whitney J57-P-2 engines with afterburner. This carrier-based interceptor was not delivered to a fleet squadron until April 16, 1956, because of power and performance problems encountered in the aircraft's production. When it did reach a fleet squadron, Composite Squadron Three (VC-3), these problems had been resolved to the satisfaction of the manufacturer and the Navy.

In the tradition of grand ship christenings held at Newport News Shipbuilding and Drydock Company, this one in the chill of December 11, 1954, wind off the waters of Hampton Roads, the USS *Forrestal*—the first of her class—was launched. The newest and largest of the Navy's aircraft carriers was named in honor of James Vincent Forrestal, Naval Aviator No. 154, and the nation's first Secretary of Defense (September 1947 to March 1949). Years before the fresnel lens, popularly known as the "meatball," Experimental Squadron Three (VX-3) began operational evaluation of a mirror landing system installed on the USS *Bennington* (CVA-20). The squadron's commanding officer, Commander R.G. Dose, flying a North American FJ-3 Fury, made the first

The USS *America* (CV-66) was photographed underway in the Atlantic Ocean, May 14, 1970. A Carrier Airborne Early Warning Squadron One Hundred Twenty-Four *Bullseye Hummer* is shown turning up for a catapult shot. (Photographer's Mate Third Class (PH3) L.H. Lafeir, photographer. Official United States Navy Photograph.)

landing aboard the *Bennington* using this device August 22, 1955. Two days later, Lieutenant Commander H.C. MacKnight made the first night landing in a Grumman F9F-8 Cougar, guided by this system. Since the tests were successful, the Bureau of Aeronautics decided to have the mirror system installed on all its aircraft carriers.

In early 1955, Captain George J. Dufek formed Task Force Forty-Three, thus activating a plan of magnanimous scope to build facilities, airstrips, and deliver supplies in support of United States participation in International Geophysical Year 1957–1958 in the Antarctic. By February 1, 1955, Dufek had Operation Deep Freeze well underway. Dufek's flotilla sailed from Naval Station Norfolk for New Zealand to rendezvous with ships of Task Force Forty-Three and proceed to Antarctica.

Dufek's operation to the south was not the only major news concerning aircraft carriers in February of 1955. By the sixth, the USS *Midway* had arrived on station with Carrier Task Force Seventy-Seven for operations in the China Seas. The *Midway* had made its way from the Atlantic to Pacific around the Cape of Good Hope, and marked the first operations of her class in the Western Pacific.

When the USS *Forrestal* was commissioned on October 1, 1955, it signaled the coming of a new Navy, a stronger naval aviation service ready to meet the challenges of the Cold War. Captain R. L. Johnson was the first commanding officer of the *Forrestal*. First air operations were conducted aboard ship on January 3, 1956, when Commander R.L. Werner, commanding officer, Air Task Group 181,[2] and Commander W.M. Harnish, commanding officer of Fighter Squadron Twenty-One (VF-21), piloting North American FJ-3 Furies, were the first to land aboard and be catapulted from the bow of the *Forrestal*. Fighter Squadron Twenty-One was redesignated VA-43 on July 1, 1959, and VF-43 on June 1, 1973, thereafter becoming known as the *Challengers,* a Naval Air Station Oceana adversary squadron.

From the Hampton Roads perspective, the aircraft carriers were as rich an environment as ever for experiments with lasting and, in some case, lofty proportions. Attack Squadron Eighty-Three (VA-83) *Rampagers*, equipped with the Vought F7U-3M Cutlass and the Sparrow I missile, left Norfolk on the USS *Intrepid* (CVS-11) for duty in the Mediterranean Sea March 12, 1956, marking the cruise as the first deployment overseas of a naval missile squadron. The Sidewinder missile would not be deployed overseas with a fleet squadron until July 14 of that year, and when it was deployed, the Sidewinder travelled with VA-46 and its Grumman F9F-8 Cougars aboard the Norfolk-based carrier USS *Randolph* (CV-15) for opera-

Lieutenant Robert I. "Gull" Randall is shown shortly after returning from a hop in a VF-101 *Grim Reaper* F-4J Phantom, October 28, 1973. Randall was the first former Vietnamese Conflict prisoner of war from an East Coast fighter squadron to return to flying after his repatriation to the United States. (Official United States Navy Photograph.)

tions with the Sixth Fleet in the Mediterranean.

Hampton Roads, with the world's greatest natural harbor, was home to the International Naval Review, the first held in American waters since the Jamestown Exposition of 1907. It was during this particular naval review that the United States' supercarrier, USS *Saratoga* (CVA-60) (second of the *Forrestal*-class), sailed alongside ships from seventeen countries, a good many of them reminiscent of the Age of Sail. More than one hundred naval vessels participated in the review, held from June 8, 1957, and lasting just a little under two weeks. Sixty of these were from the United States Navy, and consisted of every type of ship from minesweepers to the *Saratoga,* all participants with their foreign counterparts in what review planners called the "Freedom of the Seas" sail.

The International Naval Review was as much a show of North Atlantic Treaty Organization unity in the face of the Cold War with the Soviet Union as it was a display of friendly cooperation amongst the Atlantic treaty allies. Admiral Arleigh A. Burke was the Chief of Naval Operations during this critical juncture in the Navy's development of its aircraft carriers, nuclear submarines, and naval weaponry. He had stated quite clearly at the time of the review in Hampton Roads, "the more a potential aggressor must worry about our wide-ranging carriers, our jet fighters and attack planes, and our guided missiles, all on the move about his extensive coastlines, the less effort he can devote to our stationary military bases, our industries, and our cities."

The USS *Ranger* (CVA-61) soon followed *Saratoga* when, on September 29, 1956, this third ship of the *Forrestal*-class, was launched at Newport News Shipbuilding and Drydock Company and christened by the wife of the legendary Admiral Arthur W. Radford.(3) Commissioned August 10, 1957, this was the second aircraft carrier and seventh ship of the United States Navy to bear the name *Ranger*. The *Forrestal, Saratoga,* and *Ranger,* in addition to three carriers still under construction at that time, represented the world's newest carriers to incorporate the latest advances in carrier construction and equipment. These carriers now carried on their decks the Vought F8U Crusader, which had only recently set the world's speed record in excess of one thousand miles per hour; and, perhaps most interesting of the lot, the Douglas A3D-1 Skywarrior, a high-speed bomber with a combat radius of 1,500 miles.

The workhorse of the fleet was, however, still perched on carrier flight decks awaiting its next mission. The Douglas AD-1 Skyraider and all subsequent variations was produced by its manufacturer, Douglas Aircraft Company of El Segundo, California. The Skyraider first entered the fleet on March 18, 1945, and was flown by pilots of Attack Squadron Three (B)(VA-3B) and Attack Squadron Four (B)(VA-4B) from the deck of the USS *Sicily* (CVE-118), two weeks prior to the United States' invasion of Okinawa. Though production of the Skyraider was curtailed after the war ended, postwar manufacture continued and Fighter Squadron Nineteen (A) (VF-19A) received the first of the postwar-manufactured aircraft in 1946.

Though originally designed to carry about one thousand pounds of armament, the Korean Conflict saw the Skyraider carrying anywhere from four to eight thousand pounds of ordnance into combat. The aircraft saw its first missions over Korean targets July 3, 1950, flying from the deck of the USS *Valley Forge* (CV-45). Carrying the brunt of the air war in Korea for the Navy and Marine Corps, it effectively earned its

Elements of Carrier Air Wing Seventeen aboard the USS *Saratoga* (CV-60), including VF-74 *Be-Devilers* and VF-103 *Sluggers* flying the Grumman F-14B Tomcat; VFA-81 and VFA-83 flying the McDonnell Douglas F/A-18C Hornet; VA-35 *Black Panthers* with their Grumman A-6E Intruder; VAW-125 *Tigertails* flying the Grumman E-2C Hawkeye; VS-30 flying the Lockheed S-3B Viking; VAQ-132 with the Grumman EA-6B (ICAP-II) Prowler; and, HS-15 flying the SH-60F and HH-60H Seahawk helicopters, experience the fury of the North Atlantic during Operation Falcon Brave, February, 1992. (Courtesy of Fighter Squadron Seventy-Four.)

"workhorse of the fleet" nickname.

The Skyraider's twenty-eight variations covered a multitude of missions, including atomic bombing, day and night attack, antisubmarine search and kill, radar countermeasures, and airborne early warning. Unique configurations of the Skyraider included a two-thousand-pound-capacity cargo plane, six-seater personnel transport, four-litter ambulance, and long-range bomber. All variations were powered by a Wright R-3350-26W reciprocating engine which turned 2,700-horsepower, and each aircraft had an Aero products four-bladed, thirteen-and-a-half-foot steel propeller. The AD-4 set an all time single-load carrying mark in May 1953 when it went up over Dallas, Texas, with a total useful load of 14,941 pounds, including 10,500 pounds of bombs. This exceeded the aircraft's basic weight of 10,546 pounds by more than 3,000 pounds. Regarded as the most versatile combat aircraft of its day, the Skyraider still holds the international load carrying record for aircraft with one reciprocating engine.

The aircraft fell prey not to enemy fire but to what was then dubbed the midget atom bomber, the McDonnell Douglas A4D-1 Skyhawk, produced for McDonnell Douglas Corporation by its newly acquired Douglas Aircraft Company at El Segundo and Long Beach, California, plants. The Navy received its last Skyraider from Douglas in 1957 after twelve continuous years of production of the aircraft once called "the world's most powerful single-engine, propeller-driven airplane."

By 1957, the Skyhawk held the world speed record of 695.163 miles per hour over a five hundred kilometer closed course. America's smallest combat aircraft, the Skyhawk began its service to fleet squadrons in 1956. Less than half the size of all its contemporaries on the flight deck, this highly maneuverable attack jet had no folding wings, yet could carry atomic bombs, rockets, guided missiles, machine guns, and other weapons of war of much larger and heavier aircraft. The Skyhawk was redesignated the A-4 with changes to the aircraft designation system effective September 18, 1962.

Just as the Skyraider was being laid to rest by its manufacturer, and the *Forrestal* entered service, the Navy issued a contract dated November 15, 1957, for

Captain John P. Gay (left) passed command of the aircraft carrier USS *John F. Kennedy* (CV-67) to Captain Timothy R. Beard (right) on March 7, 1992. (Jim Walker, photographer. Courtesy of Kirn Library.)

what was to become both the world's largest ship and the first nuclear-powered aircraft carrier, the USS *Enterprise* (CVAN-65). Newport News Shipbuilding and Drydock Company won the contract and laid her keel on February 4, 1958. The *Enterprise* was built with eight reactors generating over 200,000-horsepower. With a speed in excess of 30 knots, overall length of 1,101 feet, 2 inches, and extreme breadth of the flight deck measuring 252 feet, the Navy's first nuclear attack aircraft carrier would be a formidable opponent on the high seas. From keel to mast top, the *Enterprise* equals the height of a twenty-three story building. Including its air group, the ship was originally configured to carry 4,600 men.

As the first ship of her kind in the world, the "Big E" challenged her designers and those who pieced the mighty ship together. All four of the ship's propellers are 5 blades each, measuring 21 feet in height, and weighing 64,500 pounds each. By completion, the *Enterprise* would expend 60,923 tons of structural steel, 3,400,000 pounds of weld metal, and 3,014,266 pounds of aluminum in her construction, and in the process, would use an additional 625 miles of electrical cable. Today's computer-aided design techniques save countless hours particularly when one considers that *Enterprise* designers generated 16,100 drawings and 2,400 miles of blueprints.

Chief Warrant Officer Fourth Class Edward A. Bremer (retired) spent the latter part of his naval career aboard the *Enterprise* at Newport News Shipbuilding. His first job was inspector of certification pressurizer heaters for the number three reactor department. "I believe the number three plant was the first to go critical," he recalled. "I was assigned to the *Enterprise* when she was commissioned, and met Admiral Hyman J. Rickover, the father of the atomic sub. He had a lot to do with the start-up of quality control and [our] quality inspection department. I believe to this day there has never been a nuclear accident, thanks to the procedures of Newport News Shipyard's Atomic Power Division and [its] Submarine Reactor Propulsion Department."

The *Enterprise* was christened on September 24, 1960, and commissioned November 25, 1961, with Captain Vincent P. DePoix as her first commanding officer. The first air operations aboard the *Enterprise* were recorded when Commander George Talley made an arrested landing and catapult launch January 17, 1962, in an F8U Crusader. Record keepers did not count the three VRC-40 TF Traders that had taken off from the "Big E" on October 30, 1961, to carry dignitaries to the mainland after observing the carrier's sea trials. Commander Talley's flights were significant because they marked the start of the carrier's regular fleet operations.

Perhaps one of the star pupils of the nuclear Navy was Vice Admiral John T. Hayward, Deputy Chief of Naval Operations for Development, the same Hayward who pioneered the use of nuclear bombers in the fleet in the 1950s at Norfolk. In a move clearly designed to centralize and strengthen the Navy's research and development program, providing more direct access for technical control and program guidance over the Operational Development Force in the Office of the Chief of Naval Operations, the Operational Test and Evaluation Force (COMOPTEVFOR) was created May 15, 1959. This command is now headquartered adjacent to United States Atlantic Command, Norfolk, Virginia. The mission of the force has been revised and broadened to include testing and evaluation, including a comprehensive oversight of what transpires in the Navy's experimental squadrons at selected sites across the country, and units afloat. The existence of the Operational Test and Evaluation Force is essential to the technological advancement of instruments, airframes, and equipment utilized on a daily basis aboard aircraft carriers as well as in helicopter mine countermeasures, patrol aviation, and aviation submarine tracking squadrons.

Commencing with Commander Alan B. Shepard's landmark flight as the first American into space May 5, 1961, aircraft carriers began playing a role that put flattops in the limelight of the race for space. The USS *Lake Champlain* (CVS-39) dutifully carried Commander Shepard home after he splashed down in the Atlantic in his *Freedom 7* capsule. Following on the heels of Shepard's famous flight was the July 21, 1961, space flight of Captain Virgil I. "Gus" Grissom, USAF, only the second American in space, who completed his flight down the Atlantic Missile Range. A premature blowoff of the hatch cover caused flooding of the capsule, making its recovery impossible. Grissom was picked up unharmed by a helicopter from the USS *Randolph* (CV-15).

Within a few months of Shepard and Grissom's flights, astronauts received their own breast insignia. The new design displayed a shooting star superimposed on the traditional aviator wings of the astronaut's respective service. In ceremonies held December 6, 1961, Shepard and Grissom were the first astronauts to be winged.

Lieutenant Colonel John H. Glenn, USMC, launched in the Mercury craft, *Friendship 7,* February 20, 1962, leaving Cape Canaveral via an Atlas rocket. Glenn completed three turns around the earth, becoming the first to complete a manned orbital flight. He was recovered

The *Kennedy:* Goodwill Ambassador of the Fleet

President John Fitzgerald Kennedy once said, "Any man who may be asked in this century what he did to make his life worthwhile, I think can respond with a good deal of pride and satisfaction, 'I served in the United States Navy.'" Today, as we turn toward a new century, those words carry us across the threshold of time and place with a renewed sense of pride in the projection of American naval power worldwide. The legacy of our thirty-fifth president of the United States in carrier aviation resides in the USS *John F. Kennedy* (CV-67) and in the crew who brings her to life. When Caroline Kennedy was nine years old, she christened the carrier in ceremonies held at Newport News Shipbuilding and Drydock Company. This future ambassador to the world, dubbed "Big John" by her crew, had its keel laid one month shy of the first anniversary of President Kennedy's death, November 22, 1963. When she was finally commissioned September 7, 1968, it was a grand affair, drawing an awestruck crowd which gathered on the starboard side of Pier 8, Newport News Shipbuilding. Guest speaker at the ship's ceremony was Robert S. McNamara, President Kennedy's former Secretary of Defense, who said:

"Somewhat over a year ago many of us here witnessed the hand of a child bestow the name of her father on this great steel ship. It is a name that puts one in mind of the sea. For the man who bore it loved the sea and sailed with valor. A ship I think is like a man's life. The man whose name is born by this vessel never turned away from those perils [of life or the sea]. His whole life was monogrammed with courage. He sailed his course in too brief a time. Not in too brief a time for him. For he loved life with a fullness few men achieve. For our hearts were quickened, and our hopes were spurred and our spirits moved by this man. And for a bright blazing moment his youth made us all feel young with him. And then the moment was gone. And we, all of us, lost something in ourselves. Of no man, I think—no matter how great—can we say that he alone turned the tides of history. For history is like the sea, intracable, horizonless, in eternal movement. But there are men whose very course across the sea of history alters the course of other men. There are men in history who sail by so noble a heading that other men, looking on, fix their compass to the same course and follow afterwards. And so it is with us. For though brief was his voyage, we who knew him will never again be the same men. And it

The USS *John F. Kennedy* (CV-67) was photographed for its twenty-fifth anniversary in 1993, Carrier Air Wing Three (CVW-3) riding her decks. (Official United States Navy Photograph.)

is not only for us few, but for multitudes of others the globe around."

In retrospect of its more than twenty-five years of service to the Atlantic Fleet, the *Kennedy* has lived up to the speech McNamara delivered September 7, 1968, perhaps moreso than anyone listening to speeches and admiring the ship could have ever envisioned that crisp fall day in Hampton Roads. The *Kennedy* has been the ambassador to the world her namesake would have wanted this great ship to be. When McNamara addressed the global impact of Kennedy, he compared his impact to the mission of the carrier:

"We saw in him the emodiment of a new hope, that reason and civility, and sanity might prevail. That the rigidities of extremism might give way to the realities of accommodation.

"That prejudice be less persuasive, and bigotry less contagious.

"That human diversity be accepted not simply as a fact, but as a value.

"That the arts be promoted, and the life of the mind made to flourish."

"That American endeavor, in whatever form, be always stamped with the hallmark of excellence.

"And, most fundamental of all, that a peace be forged—forged not in the furnace of mutual hatred, but on the anvil of mutual interest."

This mutual interest of which McNamara spoke could be forged only in light of a peace that carried with it reasonable expectations, not peace born of perfection or the expectation of a perfect world. As he so befittingly phrased it, "That is the hope that millions saw in this man. And that is the course to be charted, a course whose destination was the fulfillment of all those daring dreams. We dreamed those dreams with him. And those dreams have not died. Our world is married as it is with the scars of human folly, yet bears the mark of his wisdom. He passed this way, and his path bears yet the imprint of his passing."

In his final words to the masses gathered to watch the *Kennedy* commissioned, McNamara said, "And now USS *John F. Kennedy,* duly commissioned, will go forth to sail the sea he loved. It now begins an odyssey whose final landfall we cannot foresee. For there is an unfathomable poignancy about the sea. It is—like life itself—beyond our power to predict." In the last speech of his life, President Kennedy reminded us, and McNamara drew upon it in closing, that the world is a dangerous and uncertain place. "No one expects our lives to be easy. Not in this decade. Not in this country," McNamara continued, "The life of this ship may not prove to be easy, but may it always mirror the life of him for whom it is named."

He ended his eloquently delivered speech with these words:

"May it sail with integrity.
May it sail with his valor.
May it sail with his true greatness."

The first commanding officer of the *Kennedy* was Captain Earl P. Yates who officially reported aboard his newly commissioned carrier at ten minutes to three the afternoon of September 7, 1968. Yates held his post through September 3, 1969. In the 1970s, the *Kennedy* deployed several times to the Mediterranean Sea. The first time was in response to a deteriorating situation in the troubled Middle East. The ship's fourth Mediterranean cruise included her first visit to a North Atlantic port, Edinburgh, Scotland. In 1978 alone, the ship recorded 31,568 flight hours and 12,438 arrested landings. The *Kennedy* then underwent a year-long major overhaul that ended in 1979. On its ninth deployment, nearly two years later, the *Kennedy* made her first trip to the Indian Ocean. When the *Kennedy* transited the Suez Canal on that deployment, she hosted the first visit aboard an American naval ship by a Somali head of state, and achieved her 150,000th arrested landing.

Between 1982 and 1983, the *Kennedy* received numerous accolades and answered the call for support as a result of escalating tensions in Beirut, Lebanon. It was in 1982 that the ship won its eighth Battle Efficiency or Battle "E" award, and a fourth Golden Anchor retention award. Near the end of that year, as diplomatic solutions in Beirut began to crumble, the *Kennedy* was called to action. During this period, the ship won a ninth Battle "E," the Silver Anchor award for retention of personnel in the Navy, the Flatley Award for safety, and the Battenburg Cup as the best ship in the Atlantic Fleet.

The *Kennedy* spent the better part of the winter of 1984 in drydock at Norfolk Naval Shipyard for complex overhaul. In 1985, she received a fifth Golden Anchor retention award, and several departmental efficiency awards. While in the shipyard, the *Kennedy* was also given the first Department of Defense Phoenix Award, signifying a level of maintenance excellence above all other Department of Defense components worldwide. The ship served as the centerpiece of a vast naval armada during the International Naval Review in honor of the one-hundredth anniversary and rededication of the Statue of Liberty in July 1986. She departed for the Mediterranean in August, returning in March 1987.

After a brief stint in the shipyard, the *Kennedy* visited Boston, Massachusetts, and then Portland, Maine, marking the first visit of an aircraft carrier to that city. The carrier's flight deck crew

Caroline Kennedy Schlossberg (left foreground) and her husband, Edwin Schlossberg (center), converse with Leanne Carol Less (right foreground), wife of Vice Admiral Anthony A. Less, Commander Naval Air Force Atlantic Fleet (standing directly behind Mr. Schlossberg), aboard the *Kennedy,* September 5, 1993. (Courtesy of Commander Kevin Michael Wensing.)

trapped their 200,000th aircraft in November 1987. The twelfth major deployment of the *Kennedy* came in August of 1988 when the ship departed Norfolk, Virginia, for the Mediterranean Sea. This turned out to be a history-making episode not only for the ship but also naval aviation as a whole. On January 4, 1989, while conducting routine operations in international waters, Grumman F-14A Tomcats from the ship's embarked air wing shot down two Libyan MiG-23 aircraft that were approaching the battle group in a hostile manner.

Nearly five years later, in the spring of 1989, the *Kennedy* entered Norfolk Naval Shipyard for a short industrial period. The ship then spent the remainder of the year honing its battle readiness in preparation for yet another deployment. The ship made scheduled visits to Fort Lauderdale, Florida, and Portland, Maine, the *Kennedy's* second trip to the state. With the coming of a new year, the United States would again be challenged to keep its commitment to maintain the balance of power, to keep peace. After spending the first half of 1990 participating in a wide array of fleet exercises, the *Kennedy* paid a port visit to New York City for Fleet Week '90, and to Boston for the Fourth of July. With sounds of celebration still reverberating throughout the ship, the *Kennedy* was soon to become embroiled in war.

In August, with just four days' notice, the *Kennedy* deployed with her ship's company and air wing of five thousand men and eighty aircraft in support of Operation Desert Shield. Entering the Red Sea in September 1990, the *Kennedy* became the flagship of Commander, Red Sea Battle Force. When the ship's air wing, Carrier Air Wing Three (CVW-3), began Operation Desert Storm on January 16, 1991, its aircraft were at the forefront of attacks on Iraqi military positions. "Big John" launched 114 strikes and 2,895 sorties with CVW-3 aircrews flying 11,263 combat hours and delivering more than three and a half million pounds of ordnance in the conflict. After the cease-fire, the ship transited the Suez Canal for the fourth time in seven months and headed for home: Naval Station Norfolk, Virginia. When she arrived in Norfolk on March 28, 1991, the *Kennedy* was welcomed by the greatest homecoming celebration and outpouring of public support since the end of World War II.

The *Kennedy* entered a four-month shipyard restricted availability period at Norfolk Naval Shipyard after its return from Desert Storm. The carrier departed the yards in Portsmouth at the end of September with its refurbished engineering and flight deck systems and for the first time, was equipped to handle the McDonnell Douglas F/A-18 Hornet aircraft to replace the aging Ling-Temco-Vought A-7E Corsair IIs that had flown

The ship's seal is based on the coat of arms of the Kennedy and Fitzgerald families. These ancient symbols represent the stability that stems from tradition. Modern symbols have been incorporated to show the progress that stems from innovation. Both stability and progress were characteristic of the policies of President John Fitzgerald Kennedy, and both are essential to the continued accomplishment of the ship's mission. The black shield with three gold helmets is the traditional coat of arms of the O'Kennedy of the Ormonde. The helmets represent the original Gaelic word for Kennedy, "Ceinneide," which means helmeted head. The red and white borders are the colors of Fitzgerald of Desmond. Above the shield is the single helmet, crowned with a wreath of the Kennedy colors, black and gold, and flanked by the red and white mantel in Fitzgerald colors, symbolic of courage.

The crest of the coat of arms is a malled forearm, holding a sheaf of arrows and framed by olive branches, symbolizing power and peace, as do the eagle's claws in the presidential seal. The bottlenosed dolphins holding the banner at the bottom are traditional symbols of the sea and sailors. They represent our freedom to roam the seas, freedom essential to progress in the world community. Dolphins are friends of man but deadly enemies of aggressors, attacking only when provoked.

The shamrock-shaped banner symbolizes good luck, President Kennedy's Irish ancestry, and our ties with Ireland. Written on larger versions of the ship's banner in Latin is the Kennedy's motto, *"Date Nolite Rogare,"* which means "Give, be unwilling to ask." The phrase represents the spirit of President Kennedy's inaugural address and specifically that famous line: "Ask not what your country can do for you, ask what you can do for your country."

The wings are symbols not only of the *Kennedy's* air power, but also of progress and the freedom to roam the skies. Stars, representing the fifty states, surround the shield. A fifty-first star, the topmost in the seal, represents the high state of readiness sought by the ship. In years that the carrier earns the coveted Navy Battle Efficiency Award, this top star will be gold in color. The ship's seal was designed by the ship's first commanding officer, Captain Earl P. Yates.

on their last deployment from the *Kennedy*. The last deployment of the *Kennedy* itself prior to entering the Philadelphia Naval Shipyard for a two-year comprehensive overhaul in September of 1993 was the carrier's 1992–1993 Mediterranean Sea cruise. The ship conducted operations in the Adriatic Sea in support of the United Nations relief effort in the former Yugoslavia. This marked the *Kennedy's* fourteenth deployment to the Mediterranean.

Upon returning to Norfolk, the USS *John F. Kennedy* celebrated its silver anniversary with a gala evening shipboard featuring a visit by Caroline Kennedy Schlossberg and her husband, Edwin Schlossberg, on September 5, 1993. Captain J.R. Hutchison, the nineteenth commanding officer of the *Kennedy,* hosted an evening punctuated by the appearance of distinguished political, civilian, and military guests, including Vice Chief of Naval Operations Admiral Stanley R. Arthur, a featured speaker.

The feelings which stirred aboard the "Big John" that night were electric, emotional. Celebrating the *Kennedy's* twenty-fifth anniversary was both going back in time looking at the great history of the ship, and contemplation of the future of naval aviation, the continued projection of American naval power overseas via the aircraft carrier. Caroline Kennedy Schlossberg greeted a small group of journalists that night in the admiral's quarters, the same quarters so beautifully accentuated with wood paneling and paintings provided by the Kennedy family. Her gracious manner was reminiscent of images of her mother standing beside her father, the strength in her handshake projecting the confidence and vigor of Jack Kennedy. When Caroline Kennedy Schlossberg later addressed the guests in the hangar bay, everyone listened. The words of a now mature and confident Caroline echoed over the assemblage:

"I am honored to be here this evening to share the celebration of this anniversary with you. I remember so well how I practiced and practiced for the christening with a bowling pin in the basement. I remember how nervous I was since I didn't know how hard to swing the champagne bottle, since the bowling pin had never broken no matter how hard or soft I swung.

"At the christening I was given a beautiful vanity set, a picture of the *Blue Angels* that hung on my wall in Hyannis Port and a scroll signed by every one of the crew. My cousins and I used to unscroll it in our living room in Hyannis Port to see how long 5,000 names really was.

"Growing up it always meant so much to my brother and me to know this ship, and all of you, were bringing my father's name and memory around the world. We were so proud whenever we would read of "Big John" in the newspapers being in the Mediterranean, in Desert Storm, in the Adriatic or in New York Harbor. We would always say a special prayer for this ship and her crew.

"Of all the memorials to my father, I know this is the one of which he would be most proud. His courage, dedication to our country, his love of the sea, and the Navy are all kept alive here. That is why I think my brother and I always feel a special connection with my father whenever we come aboard.

"On behalf of my mother, my brother and my whole family, I want to thank you for honoring my father with your extraordinary service and let you know how proud we are of the *John F. Kennedy* and all who have served on this ship over the last twenty-five years."

As a conventional carrier, the life expectancy of the *Kennedy* in a nuclear Navy has led to discussions of viability, length of service and refurbishing cost. After completing its service life extension in Philadelphia in late 1995, the *Kennedy* was sent to its new home at Mayport, Florida. Perhaps McNamara was right when he said, "A ship I think is like a man's life. For a ship must put to sea, and brave such perils as await it there." The USS *John F. Kennedy,* like the man for whom she is named, will bear the future with the same dignity and courage which are the defining characteristics of our thirty-fifth president of the United States, and of the United States Navy.

Aircraft carrier construction requires lifts of several-hundred-ton modules. Here, a giant Newport News Shipbuilding gantry crane prepares to lower the island house of the USS *John C. Stennis* (CVN-74) into place, 1993. The USS *John C. Stennis* was commissioned on December 9, 1995, at Naval Station Norfolk before a crowd in excess of seventeen thousand. Her first commanding officer was Captain Robert C. Klosterman. (Courtesy of Newport News Shipbuilding.)

Christening a Flattop

These days, American nuclear aircraft carriers are christened at one place and one place only: Newport News Shipbuilding and Drydock Company, a shipyard which has launched twenty-eight flattops since 1933. With completion of CVN-76, the USS *Ronald Reagan,* the total comes to twenty-nine. The yard has built every conventional and nuclear-powered carrier in the fleet since the USS *Enterprise*. The tradition of ship christening runs deep to the very soul of the company and the pride every individual who works there harbors for the Navy's aircraft carriers. The artisans of Newport News Shipbuilding stand proud on christening day alongside each new queen of the sea.

According to Lyn Lyon in the Newport News Shipbuilding public relations office, letters are received on a regular basis from former employees as well as active duty and retired Navy personnel who have worked or served aboard the nation's aircraft carriers. These letters become a part of the ship's file, marked with the hull number of the aircraft carrier assigned by the shipyard. Their extensive files provide a rich source of historical information on the christening process.

Historically, the ritual of ship christening goes back four thousand years. The practice of using wine or champagne to toast new ships can be traced almost as far back in time. Though champagne has been the most popular means of christening ships in the twentieth century, during Prohibition (1919–1933) the use of holy water became common. The great airship USS *Los Angeles* (ZR-3) was christened with holy water from the River Jordan.

Ship christenings in the days of the Vikings were hardly an occasion everyone would have been happy to attend. The Vikings christened their ships by spilling blood and by human sacrifice, and, as if that were not enough, their high priests held incantations to appease the gods. The Greeks and Romans later used water as a token of purification in blessing ships and crews, officers, passengers, and cargo.

The Middle Ages redefined the method of ship christening. New ships were surrounded by religious shrines. Wine, a suitable substitute for blood sacrifice, appeared in the Middle Ages and was offered as the vessel hit the water. During the Tudor era, christening ceremonies took place after the ship was in the water. The event was marked by the fanfare of trumpets, and the king's lieutenant would appear and be seated in a lavishly decorated chair on the ship's poop deck. He was then presented with a goblet made of precious metal and filled to the brim with red wine. After a cursory sip of wine, he whispered the ship's name, wishing it good luck on the voyage. Spilling the wine on the deck, the lieutenant marked the four points of the compass and drank to the king's health. As a finale, he tossed the goblet over the side and departed the ship. Many of the spectators went over the side along with the goblet, hoping, no doubt, to retrieve the gold cup.

It became increasingly expensive to use gold cups in the christening of ships so, in the interest of economy, beginning in 1690 a bottle was used in place of the cup. Champagne had become widely known about that time and gradually it, rather than wine, was used to christen ships.

Perhaps of interest today is how women became sponsors of ships. The ceremony of christening a British ship was performed by a male member of the royal family or a dockyard commissioner until 1811 when George IV introduced the first female sponsor of a ship. There were quite a few accidents recorded by the first women to christen ships. One sponsor's aim was so bad she hit a spectator who was injured and sued for damages. The British admiralty then directed that in the future, the bottle be secured to the stem of the ship by a lanyard. Despite the initial accident or two, for over a century and a half now, women have christened ships. Newport News Shipbuilding has broken that tradition only once, when a fifteen-year-old boy christened a cargo ship in 1916.

As has already been noted, champagne was not always the beverage of choice to christen ships, particularly at Newport News Shipbuilding where ten ships were baptized with nonalcoholic beverages ranging from grape juice to waters from the seven seas. There were also occasions other than Prohibition in which the ship's owner or sponsor substituted a liquid deemed more in keeping with the name of the vessel or its particular namesake. Obviously, the range of concoctions varied greatly. Newport News Shipbuilding has devoted a great deal of attention to the champagne bottle itself. The bottle is enclosed in a slotted aluminum casing made in the shipyard and covered with a crocheted cotton sleeve. The coverings prevent fragments of glass from flying out and possibly injuring bystanders. The champagne bottle is kept in an insulated bag at room temperature to ensure good fizz and splash. If the weather is cold, an electric heater is provided to keep the bag warm. And, to be sure nothing is left to chance, a spare bottle is within reach as a backup to the original.

The christening of the USS *John C. Stennis* (CVN-74) on November 11, 1993, was a rare glimpse into the pomp and circumstance surrounding an aircraft carrier's right of passage into the American fleet. Here, ship's sponsor Margaret Stennis Womble, daughter of retired Mississippi Senator John C. Stennis, is cracking the bottle of champagne over the flattop's bow while Vice President of the United States Al Gore and Chief of Naval Operations Admiral Frank B. Kelso look on. (Courtesy of Commander Naval Air Force Atlantic Fleet Public Affairs Office.)

Senator John C. Stennis is shown here at Newport News Shipbuilding taking part in the July 1976 christening of the guided missile cruiser USS *Mississippi.* (Courtesy of Newport News Shipbuilding.)

some 166 miles east of Grand Turk Island in the Bahamas by the destroyer USS *Noa,* and then delivered by helicopter to the *Randolph.*

Of course, as in Grissom's recovery, not all splashdowns went smoothly. Lieutenant Commander M. Scott Carpenter, in *Aurora 7,* was launched into orbit from Cape Canaveral on May 24, 1962, on the second manned orbital flight. Upon finishing three orbits he returned to earth, landing in the Atlantic some two hundred miles from the planned splashdown point. Carpenter was located by a persistent Navy P2V-7 Neptune, ably assisted by a rescue team dropped from an Air Force RC-54 aircraft. After spending nearly three hours in the Atlantic Ocean, Carpenter was rescued and taken by helicopter to the USS *Intrepid* (CVS-11). His capsule was later recovered by the destroyer USS *John R. Pierce.*

Aircraft carriers continued to recover space capsules and astronauts throughout the 1960s and early 1970s. The process ended on a rather historic note July 24, 1975, with the last at-sea recovery of the Apollo spacecraft used in the Apollo-Soyuz mission. This crew consisted of Thomas Stafford, Vance Brand, and Donald "Deke" Slayton. Astronauts in the Mercury, Gemini, and Apollo programs would gladly admit they lived to tell the tale in some cases due to the professionalism and persistence of countless naval aviators, carrier crews, and sailors aboard surface combatants.

Newport News Shipbuilding and Drydock Company has constructed every Navy aircraft carrier since the *Enterprise*. The USS *America* (CV-66) was launched from Newport News Shipbuilding on February 1, 1964, and commissioned January 23, 1965. It was followed by the USS *John F. Kennedy* (CV-67), christened May 27, 1967 (see *Kennedy* sidebar, page 316). The *America* and *Kennedy* are conventionally-powered ships, and slightly smaller than the *Enterprise* in terms of length, beam, and displacement.(4)

Aircraft carriers have been called to hot spots all over the world since the cease-fire in Korea. The uncertain nature of governments, large and small, all over the world have made the role of the aircraft carrier the fastest means of checking the imbalance of power, or so it is hoped when crisis situations have arisen. Perhaps the classic example involved simultaneous hot spots in Lebanon and Taiwan during late summer of 1958. While aircraft from the USSs *Essex* and *Saratoga* flew cover from long range, and the Sixth Fleet stood on ready alert, amphibious units landed eighteen thousand Marines on the beach near Beirut to support the Lebanese government and protect American lives. As the situation eased, the *Essex* withdrew with four of her destroyers, departing the Sixth Fleet and making a rapid transit of the Suez Canal en route to the Seventh Fleet sitting off Taiwan, where tensions were at an all time high.

When word was received on January 23, 1968, that the USS *Pueblo*(5) had been captured by a North Korean patrol boat, a task group composed of the carrier USS *Enterprise* and her screen was ordered to reverse course in the East China Sea and turn northward to the Sea of Japan, where the task force operated in the vicinity of South Korea for nearly a month. When a North Korean aircraft shot down an unarmed EC-121 propeller-driven Constellation on a routine reconnaissance patrol over the Sea of Japan April 14, 1969, its entire thirty-one man crew was killed. In response to North Korean aggression, the United States activated Task Force Seventy-One to protect such flights over international waters in the future. The task force consisted of the aircraft carriers *Enterprise,* USS *Ticonderoga* (CVA-14), USS *Ranger* (CVA-61), and USS *Hornet* (CVS-12) with each flattops' respective cruiser and destroyer screens.

Fires aboard contained environments like aircraft carriers can be devastating, but this need not be the case with improved firefighting equipment and proper training of the ship's company and air wing personnel. A new, major development in aircraft carrier fire prevention was recorded May 26, 1969, when the USS *Franklin D. Roosevelt* (CVA-42) put to sea from Norfolk Naval Shipyard after an eleven-month overhaul which included installation of a deck edge, and a spray system utilizing the sea water-compatible, firefighting chemical called "light water." Before installation of this revolutionary fire prevention system, fires aboard aircraft carriers had resulted in horrific outcomes with great loss of life. A fire aboard the *Enterprise* on January 14, 1968, resulting from detonation of an MK-32 Zuni rocket warhead that became overheated by the exhaust of an aircraft starting unit, took the lives of 27 men, injured another 344, and completely destroyed 15 aircraft.

In another 1969 milestone, the Navy first instituted a hands-off arrested landing device using the AN/SPN-42 automatic carrier landing system on an aircraft carrier on June 24, 1969, aboard the USS *Saratoga* (CVA-60). The aircraft, a McDonnell F-4 Phantom II, was flown by Lieutenant Dean Smith and Lieutenant (junior grade) James Sherlock of Fighter Squadron One Hundred Three (VF-103) *Sluggers*. The AN/SPN-42 was the outgrowth of the SPN-10, which was first tested in 1957 but fell short of fleet requirements.

In response to unrest in the Middle East as a result of the Jordanian crisis in which Palestinian terrorists attempted to unseat the monarchy in Amman September 25, 1970, the United States scrambled three attack aircraft carriers, the USS *John F. Kennedy,* USS *Saratoga,* and USS *Independence* (CVA-62) in the Mediterranean, followed by seven additional Navy ships, including the amphibious carrier USS *Guam* (LPH-9) two days later. The Sixth Fleet was later strengthened to some fifty-five ships which served as a standby force in the event United States military protection was required in the evacuation of Americans, and as counterbalance to the former Soviet Union's Mediterranean fleet.

By the 1980s, Hampton Roads witnessed the creation of a totally new class of aircraft carrier bearing the name of the first ship of the group, USS *Nimitz* (CVN-68). Christening of the *Nimitz* took place on May 13, 1972, followed by commissioning ceremonies three years later, on May 3, 1975. The *Nimitz* has been making headlines since leaving the pier that day at Newport News Shipbuilding. The *Nimitz* became famous for the August 19, 1981, shoot-down of two Libyan SU-22 Fitter aircraft. The Libyans took on two Grumman F-14 Tomcats from the Fighting Forty-One *Black Aces* on their routine combat air patrol (CAP) covering the *Nimitz*.

Carrier Airborne Early Warning Squadron One Hundred Twenty-Four *Bear Aces* were flying CAP control from their Grumman E-2C Hawkeye radar aircraft. The *Nimitz,* for its part, was participating in routine Sixth Fleet missile firing exercises in international waters of the Mediterranean Sea, including the Gulf of Sidra, Momar Kaddafi's Line of Death abutting Libyan national waters, the day prior to the shoot-down. The Libyans had already brushed close to American naval forces in the Mediterranean that day. Fighters from the *Nimitz* and the USS *Forrestal* had spent the better part of their day escorting Libyan aircraft out of the exercise range.

On the morning of the nineteenth, two Fitters were picked up by *Black Ace* Tomcats sixty miles south of the *Nimitz,* too close for comfort. As the Tomcats closed, one of the SU-22s fired what was assumed to be a Soviet-made Atoll missile from its wing station. The Tomcats, piloted by Commander Henry M. Kleeman and his radar intercept officer, Lieutenant David J. Venlet, and Kleeman's wingman, Lieutenant Lawrence M. Muscyznski and his radar intercept officer, Lieutenant James P. Anderson, engaged the Fitters and shot down both with AIM-9L Sidewinder missiles. According to the rules of engagement, this was self-defense. Sixth Fleet exercises continued without further incident, though the Libyans did keep patrols up to keep an eye on the American fleet. The F-14/E-2C team had worked in concert to protect the aircraft carrier. The *Nimitz* was fortunate that the choreography worked so well.

The USS *Dwight D. Eisenhower* (CVN-69) soon followed the *Nimitz*. The "Ike" was christened October 11, 1975, and commissioned two years later on October 18, 1977. The USS *Carl Vinson* (CVN-70) was christened March 15, 1980, and commmissioned into service two years later. Others would follow in two- and three-year intervals: the USS *Theodore Roosevelt* (CVN-71), christened October 27, 1984, and commissioned October 25, 1986; USS *Abraham Lincoln* (CVN-72), assigned to the West Coast, christened February 13, 1988, and commissioned November 11, 1989; USS *George Washington* (CVN-73), christened July 21, 1990, and commissioned July 4, 1992; USS *John C. Stennis* (CVN-74), christened November 11, 1993, and commissioned December 9, 1995; and USS *Harry S. Truman* (CVN-75), christened September 7, 1996, and commissioned July 25, 1998.

The *George Washington* was the sixth of the *Nimitz*-class nuclear aircraft carriers built by Newport News Shipbuilding and Drydock Company. Like all of its predecessors and successors, the aircraft carrier battle group is the Navy's principle tool in peacetime diplomacy, crisis control, and warfighting. As the center of its own battle group of four to six additional ships, the nuclear aircraft carrier can conduct sustained combat air operations anywhere in the world, anytime. The rapid response capability of America's carriers has been demonstrated time and again as these giant warfighting platforms have been used to conduct retaliatory strikes, support land battles, protect the battle group or other friendly shipping, implement a sea or air blockade, or simply provide a visible deterrent to aggressors, a show of indisputable strength, a source of power amidst crisis.

Two aircraft carriers, the USS *Independence,* a West Coast carrier, and USS *Dwight D. Eisenhower,* Norfolk-based, were the first coalition forces to respond to Iraq's invasion of Kuwait on August 2, 1990, making their way to the region within five days of the aggression. As Desert Shield operations unfolded, war with Iraq became certain. When the air war against Iraq began the evening of January 16, 1991, there were six carrier battle groups in the Persian Gulf and Red Sea poised to strike at Saddam Hussein's forces in the desert, including Norfolk-based aircraft carriers USS *Theodore Roosevelt,* USS *John F. Kennedy,* USS *America,* and the Mayport, Florida, based USS *Saratoga*. The other two carriers were West Coast homeported, USS *Midway* and USS *Ranger*. The Navy flew in excess of 18,100 fixed-wing aircraft sorties from its six carriers operating around the Arabian peninsula. Each carrier, with its seventy-five aircraft air wings, presented a formidable threat to the Iraqis. Fleet air wing composition consisted of Grumman F-14 Tomcats for fleet air defense and strike; McDonnell Douglas F/A-18 Hornets flying strike and strike escort; Grumman A-6E Intruders and Ling-Timco-Vought A-7 Corsair IIs for strike; KA-6 and KS-3 tankers; Grumman EA-6Bs Prowlers for electronic jamming; Grumman E-2C Hawkeyes flying airborne early warning; SH-3 helicopters to perform search and rescue; Lockheed S-3S Vikings flying antisubmarine patrol and strike; and Grumman C-2 Greyhounds to support battle group logistical requirements. During the war itself, lasting from January 16, 1991, to February 28, 1991, six carrier battle groups flew 4,855 theater strikes against Iraqi positions, accounting for the majority of sorties flown in Desert Storm.

The USS *John C. Stennis* has taken its place in the lineage of carriers begun the day of Ely's flight and is an excellent example of the metamorphasis of an aircraft carrier from keel laying to commissioning. The modern *Nimitz*-class supercarrier takes five years and forty million man hours to build from keel to delivery. While the *Stennis* is preceded in her class by six other carri-

"Where Are the Aircraft Carriers and Tomahawks?"

Naval aviation is more than fixed-wing and rotor aircraft. It is missiles and missile technology. The command structure of Cruise Missile Support Activity, Atlantic Fleet, or CMSA, developed between 1979 and 1981, carving itself a critical niche in the United States Atlantic Command. This history is as much about the evolution of cruise missile technology leading up to and including recent strides made with the Tomahawk, as the activity itself. The Tomahawk has become the pinnacle of modern weaponry, the tip of the sword of every chief executive of the United States since President James Earl "Jimmy" Carter. When presidents of the United States face world crises, they no longer ask simply, "Where are the aircraft carriers?" but "Where are the aircraft carriers and Tomahawks?"

The United States Navy has been involved in guided missile research and development since the spring of 1917 when, at the behest of the Naval Consulting Board, the Secretary of the Navy allocated fifty thousand dollars toward experimental work on aerial torpedoes. Aerial torpedoes came in the form of automatically-controlled aircraft or aerial machines rigged to carry high explosives. The exact date of this apportionment was April 14, 1917. Automatically-controlled aircraft were nothing new in 1917. Then-Lieutenant (junior grade) Patrick Bellinger, flight-tested Dr. Elmer Ambrose Sperry's gyroscopic stabilizer or automatic pilot on August 30, 1913, in a Curtiss C-2 flying boat at Hammondsport, New York.

Sperry's son, Lawrence Burst "Gyro" Sperry, later Naval Aviator No. 345, was present for the engineering trials. Lawrence Sperry was nothing short of brilliant, adding immeasurably to our understanding of aerial warfare and proving through practical trial and error the merits of gyrostabilized aircraft in flight. In large measure due to Lawrence Sperry's work, the Navy Department issued contracts to the Sperrys to develop a bombsight, the forerunner of the turn and bank indicator, gyro compass and the aerial torpedo, precursor of the guided missile. Elmer Sperry had already contributed to invention of the automatic pilot, gyrostabilized bombsights, flight instruments and catapults. Between 1896 and 1915, the elder Sperry had evolved the gyroscope and in 1915 was able to adapt the device for the Navy to use aboard ship. His interest in aircraft led to his research and development of a gravitad to use on aircraft in 1911, the same year "Spuds" Ellyson became Naval Aviator No. 1.

Elmer Sperry and his son joined forces with Peter Cooper Hewitt in 1916 to develop this aerial torpedo or pilotless aircraft. Hewitt was the inventor of the mercury vapor lamp and contributed, in large part, to the development of the vacuum tube. The result of their collaboration was a string of wonderful inventions, including the gyroscopic stabilizer (essentially a directive gyroscope), aneroid barometer to regulate altitude (an instrument for distance gearing), and servomotors for control of rudders and ailerons. Basically, if all of these devices could be installed in an aircraft and catapulted, the aircraft would fly a predetermined distance and, after going that distance, drop its ordnance or dive into the ground.

The Navy provided the Sperrys and Hewitt five N-9L aircraft with which to test their equipment. By the time a Navy N-9L flying bomb was tested on November 21, 1917, at Amityville, Long Island, New York, the Navy already had its aerial torpedo project well in place. An unmanned flying bomb-type aircraft was successfully launched and flown for one thousand yards at the Sperry Flying Field, Copiague, Long Island, New York, March sixth of the following year.

Elmer A. Sperry was a brilliant instrument and component designer. His flying bomb project might very well be the first in a long line of antecedents of the Tomahawk cruise missile. He had some encouragement from Rear Admiral Ralph Earle, Chief of the Bureau of Ordnance, who wanted to end the war quickly for the United States. Earle was of the opinion that if the Allies could destroy German home bases and submarine pens, the enemy would capitulate even faster. Sperry's flying bomb seemed to be the answer. The admiral wanted very much to launch these flying bombs against German bases at Wilhelmshaven, Cuxhaven, and Helgoland, all submarine hideaways.

Powers-that-be higher than Earle ended any notion of using a flying bomb to eliminate enemy U-boat bases. The main reason for doing so was the tentative nature of the airframe used as the flying bomb, not the idea itself. A pilotless Curtiss N-9L training aircraft, converted to automatic pilot, launched at Copiague, Long Island, and flew its prescribed course with great success, although it should be duly noted the distance device failed to land the N-9L at a preset range of 14,500 yards. The N-9L was last seen over Naval Air Station Bay Shore at an altitude of four thousand feet, October 17, 1918, flying an eastward heading. In all probability, the N-9L crashed at sea.

The Navy continued to press the development of the flying bomb even after the armistice was signed on November 11, 1918, and eventually it would be the Navy which took over research and development of the flying bomb from Sperry and Hewitt. During the early 1920s, the Navy worked on similar projects based on their own research of the Witteman-Lewis aircraft and Carl L. Norden's gyrostabilizers. Quickly, the Navy went from Norden to radio-control-type devices, but it would be 1936 before the service truly embarked on research and development of target drones and pilotless aircraft with any consistency.

It came as no surprise that the Navy could launch an aircraft via radio control by 1924, for the Naval Research Laboratory recorded successful radio control of a Curtiss F-5L at Hampton Roads on April 15, 1923. This aircraft was found to adequately demonstrate radio control at a range of up to ten miles and it should be noted that this also included takeoff and landing of the aircraft. A little over a year later, September 15, 1924, an N-9L seaplane equipped with radio control and without benefit of a human pilot, was flown on a forty-minute flight at the Naval Proving Grounds, Dahlgren, Virginia. Even though the N-9L sank from damage sustained during a rough landing, the test certainly established the practicability of radio-controlled aircraft or unmanned vehicles.

Guided missiles like the Tomahawk have much in common not only with these early experiments with radio control but also with attack drones developed at the end of the 1930s. Lieutenant Commander D. S. Fahrney, later a rear admiral, was tasked in 1936 to develop a radio-controlled target aircraft. The result was an assault drone used in the Second World War, forerunner of modern missiles like the Tomahawk. In order to develop his radio-controlled target aircraft, Fahrney went back to the books. He first researched all the documents from the Naval Research Laboratory dating back to the First World War and early features of flying bombs developed at that time.

What he found was an eye opener. The experience of the Naval Research Laboratory during the First World War had resulted in the guided missile. Elmer A. Sperry, renowned inventor of field stabilization and radio control, had developed the guided missile as well. During the last decade of the nineteenth century, and the first years of our own century, Americans saw perhaps the greatest convergence of events laying the foundation for guided missile technology as we know it today. First, there was Marconi's wireless transmission in 1896 and the first successful flights of aircraft designed and built by Orville and Wilbur Wright in 1903. Following the Wright Brothers' flight at Kill Devil Hills, North Carolina, aircraft began a rapid ascent to the pinnacle of technology, combining airframe and engine advances with electronic impulses as America moved closer to the war in Europe.

The first American use of a drone target aircraft in antiaircraft exercises occurred on August 24, 1938, when the USS *Ranger* fired upon a radio-controlled JH-1 making a simulated horizontal bombing attack on the fleet. This did, in effect, show the long-distance capability of aircraft or aircraft-like unmanned vehicles to eliminate hostile targets. A little over three weeks later, on September fourteenth, the Navy launched a radio-controlled N2C-2 target drone against the battleship USS *Utah* in a test firing of the ship's antiaircraft battery. Proponents of guided missiles, be they past or present, consider this the first demonstration of an air-to-surface missile.

Two months prior to the United States' entry in the Second World War, on October 8, 1941, an organizational provision was made for guided missiles in the fleet with the institution of "Special Project Dog" in Utility Squadron Five (VJ-5), a Naval Air Station Cape May, New Jersey, outfit, to test and operate radio-controlled offensive weapons, and to train personnel in their use. Utility Squadron Five was directed to develop radio-controlled fighter aircraft, an aerial ram or torpedo as it were, to be flown into enemy bomber formations and explode. During the Second World War, there would be a succession of bright, progressive young officers who commanded the squadron: Lieutenants Earl R. Eastwold and Thomas D. Harris in 1943, and later, commanding officers of the Utility Wing headquartered at Norfolk.

By June 17, 1942, and six months into the war, the National Defense Research Committee, through the sponsorship of the Bureau of Ordnance, announced the development of the Pelican, an antisubmarine guided missile. The Pelican was essentially a glide bomb which honed in on the radar beam refracted by its target. Two months later, on August 12, 1942, the Navy would have yet another success when it demonstrated the effectiveness of the radio-proximity fuse against aircraft by destroying three radio-controlled drones with four proximity bursts fired from the five-inch guns of the USS *Cleveland* (CL-55), then operating in the lower Chesapeake Bay. The demonstration quickly led to mass production of the radio-proximity fuse, and with good reason—it was a wholly effective device which completely eradicated the target.

Between the Second World War and the early 1970s, the guided missile program grew by leaps and bounds. The Chief of Naval Operations standardized the terminology effective August 14, 1946 —at least within the Navy—to the degree he directed that the term "guided missiles" be used for all types as such developed by the Navy. However, the old terminology, "special weapons ordnance device" (SWOD) and the phrase, "pilotless aircraft," seemed to stick for a time despite a broad-brush effort to rectify all the verbage and call them guided missiles.

The Regulus cruise missile (SSM-N-8) program was begun in 1947 by the Navy and the Chance-Vought Aircraft Corporation. The Regulus was capable of delivering three-thousand-pound forty to fifty kiloton W5 or twenty-eight-thousand pound one to two megaton W27 thermonuclear warhead within a range of five hundred nautical miles from a submarine, heavy cruiser, and aircraft carrier platform. Though the Regulus is rarely mentioned in the historical chronology of cruise missile development, the Regulus was a critical step in the evolution of cruise missile technology, and one which had a direct impact on the future development of the Polaris, Poseidon and Trident ballistic missiles, and the Tomahawk, its sophisticated cruise missile successor.

Guided Missiles Service Unit Number 211 was established at the Naval Mine Depot, Yorktown, Virginia, on April 1, 1952, as the first of six planned Terrier units. The Terrier was among the first post-World War II surface-to-air guided missiles. The school consisted, at least initially, of students who had gone through Guided Missiles Training Unit Number Two at the Consolidated Vultee Aircraft Corporation in San Diego, California. In order to better provide fleet officers and enlisted personnel with corporate knowledge of the operation, maintenance, and control of surface and submarine-launched guided missiles, the Naval Guided Missile School was established at Fleet Air Defense Training Center, Dam Neck, Virginia, on July first of the same year. At the same time, the Navy also established the Naval Air Guided Missile School for advanced training at Naval Air Technical Training Center, Naval Air Station Jacksonville, Florida.

The Naval Aircraft Factory, long on the cutting edge of aeronautic technology and equipment, was renamed the Naval Air Engineering Facility (Ships Installation) on April 26, 1955, and tasked with a broader spectrum mission to include research, engineering, design, development, and limited manufacturing of devices and equipment for

The Navy deployed the Regulus I guided cruise missile aboard its first two diesel-powered nuclear deterrent patrol submarines: USS *Tunny* (SSG-282) and USS *Barbero* (SSG-317) in 1959. Eventually, the *Tunny* and *Barbero* were joined by three additional diesel-powered nuclear deterrent submarines: USS *Grayback* (SSG-774), USS *Growler* (SSG-577), and the nuclear-powered USS *Halibut* (SSGN-587). The *Tunny* (SSG-282) was commissioned on March 6, 1953, and outfitted at Mare Island Naval Shipyard to launch the Regulus I surface-to-air missile for testing purposes but, eventually, routine patrol operations. The *Grayback* test-fired the first Regulus II off the coast of California on September 16, 1958. The Navy ended its nuclear deterrent patrols in 1964.

A Tomahawk cruise missile is launched from the battleship USS *New Jersey* (BB-62), circa 1992. The USS *Wisconsin* (BB-64) and USS *Missouri* (BB-63) fired Tomahawks during the Persian Gulf War, though these ships were not, by far, the only platform to fire the missile at hostile targets. Desert Storm was the first combat test of the Tomahawk missile, but it was also the first time an aerial assault came from both cruise missiles and fleet aircraft in a carefully orchestrated tactical strike on enemy targets. According to CMSA personnel, two varieties of Tomahawks were among the 290 or so that were fired into Iraq and occupied Kuwait—the TLAM-C, a conventional land-attack missile, and the TLAM-D, a submunition version of the Tomahawk. (Official United States Navy Photograph. Courtesy of the Cruise Missile Support Activity.)

launching and recovering aircraft and guided missiles. The redesignation of the facility was, in itself, a sad day. The name Naval Aircraft Factory had become celebrated in the annals of naval aviation history.

The Navy's Guided Missiles Division was transferred in its whole from the Deputy Chief of Naval Operations for Air to the newly created Deputy Chief of Naval Operations for Development under the direction of Vice Admiral John T. Hayward on May 5, 1959. The Navy Department was in a state of reorganization and streamlining to reflect the incorporation of new technologies and weaponry such as the development of cruise missiles. It would take the Navy nearly twenty-five years to establish a cruise missile project office to manage the technology.

A Cruise Missile Project Office was established at the Naval Air Systems Command April 16, 1973, with a clear directive to develop both tactical and strategic versions of the cruise missile. A little over two years later, on September 26, 1975, the Chief of Naval Operations (CNO) approved the popular name Tomahawk for the Navy's Sea Launched Cruise Missile (SLCM) and, that same year, McDonnell Douglas Missile Systems Company won the contract to develop the guidance system for the Navy's newest strike weapon. The first Terrain Contour Matching (TERCOM) Guidance Test Vehicle was flown on February 11, 1976, using a modified Navy Firebee drone. This TERCOM technology was then used in the Tomahawk cruise missile.

Great strides would be made in Tomahawk technology between 1976 and 1980. The Navy launched the first fully-guided Tomahawk cruise missile over the White Sands Missile Range in New Mexico on June 5, 1976, thus beginning a series of platform tests necessary to adjudge the viability of the missile in a broad spectrum of naval warfare environments. The missile flew for sixty-one minutes after it was released from the wing of a Grumman A-6 Intruder aircraft from the Pacific

Missile Test Center at an altitude of 11,500 feet. Not only was this the first flight in the platform series test but the first functional application of the test vehicle's capability to perform navigation, guidance updates, and low-terrain following maneuvers, and the first test flight utilizing a turbofan engine. Turbojets had been used in previous tests. The day after successful tests at White Sands, an Intruder aircraft successfully test-fired the tactical version of the Tomahawk cruise missile using the Terrain Contour Matching Navigation System.

Designed as a long-range weapon system with strategic and tactical application, the Tomahawk can be launched from tactical and strategic aircraft, surface combatants, submarines and land platforms. It was not until February 2, 1978, however, that the Tomahawk was successfully deployed from a submarine, the USS *Barb* (SSN-596), and flew a fully-guided land attack test flight which terminated at Edwards Air Force Base, California. This was the first launch of the Tomahawk from a submarine. This test was followed a little over a year later, February 14, 1979, by a Tomahawk launch from the nuclear-powered attack submarine USS *Guitarro* (SSN-665) off the California coast, and it was shortly thereafter that elements of what is now known as the Cruise Missile Support Activity were enjoined as a command within the Atlantic Fleet. The Guitarro test was the first of three submarine launches and flight tests of the Tomahawk conducted between February and June which demonstrated the missile's over-the-horizon capability to search for, locate, and conduct simulated attacks on a target ship deployed at sea. Aircraft carriers were also employed to test Tomahawk IIs, on November 22, 1980, while suitability tests of the medium-range air-to-surface missile were finished. In 1982, McDonnell Douglas became the dual-source producer of the Tomahawk all-up-round which included logistics support and depot maintenance of the warhead.

McDonnell Douglas began production of the Tomahawk missile at its Titusville, Florida, plant in October of 1983, and continued to manufacture the missile until the contract was sold to Hughes Aircraft in 1994. Five years after McDonnell Douglas began full-scale manufacture of the cruise missile, the company received its first Block III upgrade contract for the Tomahawk Conventional Land Attack Missile. The Tomahawk uses two navigational modes, the previously-mentioned Terrain-Contour Matching (TERCOM), and Digital Scene-Matching Area Correlation (DSMAC). In addition to four variants of the Tomahawk, there is also the Block III missile and a new, more advanced, Block IV. The Nuclear Land-Attack Tomahawk (BGM-109A) or TLAM-N, Conventional Land-Attack Tomahawk (BGM-109C), known as a TLAM-C, and Submunition Land-Attack Tomahawk (BGM-109D), the TLAM-D, are land-attack variants, while the Conventional Ship-Attack Tomahawk (BGM-109B) or TASM is strictly anti-ship. The TASM variant has been dropped from Navy inventory. The Block III variant is an improvement upon the standard TLAM, adding a sophisticated global positioning system; time-of-arrival software; insensitive munitions/extended range feature; and, of course, a much-improved engine. Block IV Tomahawks contain a dual-mission sensor, capable of performing both antiship and land-attack missions.

During Desert Storm, the combined firepower of sixteen-inch guns and Tomahawk cruise missiles, primarily of the TLAM-C variety, aboard the USS *Missouri* (BB-63) and USS *Wisconsin* (BB-64) helped bring a swift end to the Persian Gulf conflict. Tomahawks were also fired from a wide array of cruisers, destroyers, and submarines. The first Tomahawk strike of the Persian Gulf War came the evening of January 17, 1991, when the USS *San Jacinto* (CG-56) in the Red Sea, and the USS *Bunker Hill* (CG-52) in the Persian Gulf, opened up on targets in Iraq. This was the first use of the Tomahawk missile in wartime. At war's end some 288 Tomahawk missiles had been fired at Iraq or Iraqi-held positions. Most of these missiles were of the TLAM-C variety. Tomahawk missiles fired in Operation Desert Storm could not provide real-time bomb damage assessment. New forward-looking sensors and data link will allow for bomb damage assessment and thus increase the utility of the weapon system. Military planners can use this information to plan coordinated strikes, thus increasing the battle commander's flexibility on the battlefield.

Cruise Missile Support Activity, United States Atlantic Command.

"Ain't Miss B. Havin"

The *Bear Aces* of Carrier Airborne Early Warning Squadron One Hundred Twenty-Four (VAW-124) have two insignia, the first being a design approved by the office of the Chief of Naval Operations while the second, affectionately called "Molly" by successive generations of squadron members, is an unofficial insignia with an interesting history. Established on September 1, 1967, the squadron adopted the first insignia to reflect their tactical callsign—*Bullseye Hummers*. This insignia has remained in use alongside the unofficial-but-ever-popular "Molly" since December 1980.

The squadron earned the nickname *Bear Aces* after a successful deployment at the end of 1980, beginning of 1981, to Keflavik, Iceland, to run intercepts on Soviet Bear reconnaissance aircraft. The *Bullseye Hummers* had to run intercepts on at least five Bear aircraft to be considered an "ace" squadron. By the end of the deployment, VAW-124 had achieved that end as a Bear ace squadron, hence the name *"Bear Aces."* The *Bear Aces* favored the "Molly" insignia until the squadron was informed in 1994 that it could no longer use the female figure as part of its unit design. Though not the first Navy squadron insignia to bear the female form, it may be the last. Current guidelines covered in Chief of Naval Operations instruction prohibit the use of female images on Navy and Marine Corps squadron insignia.

During Desert Storm, Carrier Air Wing Eight aircraft, flying combat hops from the USS *Theodore Roosevelt* (CVN-71), were transformed into warbirds, complete with beautifully executed nose art. A competition was held aboard the carrier to judge the best nose art and *"Miss B. Havin,"* the VAW-124 entry, won. Photographs of the nose art are all that remain.

When the time came for the air wing's return home, the artwork had to be removed from the nose of every aircraft so as not to offend anyone. Examples of the artwork were hard to come by and, consequently, to publish in such a public forum as a book. Naval aviators were afraid of the repercussions of publicizing what was, indeed, an art form driven by the tensions of war, a personal release as it were from endless hours of combat missions and round-the-clock shipboard operations. Airmen spent many long hours preparing some of the best nose art on military aircraft seen since the end of World War II. Gunshy of public opinion, the aircraft were stripped of their art before anyone could question it—or admire the craftsmenship.

It took "Molly" nearly fifteen years to become politically incorrect, Carrier Air Wing Eight nose art even less, which either says something of how silly we have suddenly become over issues that really are not issues at all, or that "Molly" and those like her belonged to another era when young men went to war and needed a hopeful reminder of who and what they were fighting for.

"Molly" raised issues no one is yet prepared to answer. The public should care less about a squadron insignia and more about the people who wear them. The publicity generated as a result of military "Mollys" outweighs informative and positive images of our fighting men—and women—to the degree the American public understands little of their service, sacrifice, traditions, and quality of life.

The widow of Admiral John Henry "Jack" Towers, Naval Aviator No. 3, once said of her husband and his time that Towers brought with him to the profession his best qualities as well as his foibles, and these two were interwoven into the fabric of his time and place. Successive generations of naval aviators

The *Bullseye Hummers* adopted their "Bear Aces" nickname and unofficial "Molly" insignia in early 1981 after scoring intercepts of five Soviet Bear aircraft while deployed on special assignment to Keflavik, Iceland.

Left: Carrier Airborne Early Warning Squadron One Hundred Twenty-Four (VAW-124) uses this artwork as its official squadron insignia. From their establishment in 1967 to early 1981, the squadron was known as the *Bullseye Hummers*.

have brought with them an inextricable sense of youth, of fearlessness, of compassion, of daily discovery, of those same personal foibles which make each of them unique, that forged their wings, and compelled them to fly into harm's way to defend this country in every time, in every corner of the world since 1911. Military "Mollys" find their way into our permanent memory in the twists and turns of history and though sometimes we can delight in their humor, these snippets of our culture should make us think even harder of how they got there in the first place.

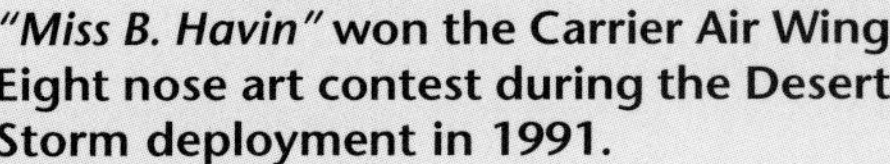

***"Miss B. Havin"* won the Carrier Air Wing Eight nose art contest during the Desert Storm deployment in 1991.**

ers—the *Nimitz, Dwight D. Eisenhower, Carl Vinson, Theodore Roosevelt, Abraham Lincoln,* and *George Washington*—technological advancements between construction of each carrier make one vary from the others. These magnificent nuclear marvels are 47,000 tons of structural steel and about 1,000,000 pounds of aluminum. Modular construction is used to piece together the ship much like toy building blocks. Through the use of three-dimensional computer imagery, engineers view the complex structures and systems of ships such as the *Stennis,* thereby getting an accurate assessment of how various ship systems interact with hull components long before this building block process is actually begun. Once units are welded together, they form a module or superlift weighing upwards of nine hundred tons. There can be as many as 170 superlifts in an aircraft carrier like the Stennis.

As the modules and superlifts come together, shipyard employees add major piping, electrical components, machinery, equipment, and heating and air conditioning systems. A superlift lowered into the drydock to form the ship already has many of its final working systems installed. Outfitting of smaller systems continues throughout the ship as the hull begins to take shape. Though small and large systems are tested repeatedly pierside, the Navy took the *Stennis* on sea trials which began in late-1995 and continued through June of 1996, thus testing the new carrier under operational conditions and stresses.

In sea trials off the Virginia Capes, the *Stennis* demonstrated her speed and maneuverability. The *Stennis'* top speed is in excess of thirty knots and this, of course, was tested by running the propulsion system at one hundred percent of its capacity to assess the ship's actual maximum speeds forward and astern. Like her sister ships, the *Stennis* is powered by two nuclear reactors that can operate for twenty years without refueling. The carrier, as planned, can be operational for about fifty years and, once delivered to the Navy after trials, can carry over eighty combat aircraft. Four, two-inch diameter arresting wires on the deck bring an airplane going 150 miles per hour to a stop in less than 400 feet.

Nimitz-class carriers tower twenty stories above the waterline and are 1,092 feet long—nearly as long as the Empire State Building in New York City is tall. The flight deck alone encompasses four-and-a-half acres. Four bronze propellers, each 21 feet across and weighing 66,220 pounds, are fitted to each ship in this class. Steering is accomplished by two rudders, each twenty-nine feet by twenty-two feet, and weighing twenty-three tons. Four high-speed aircraft elevators, each the size of two average city lots, bring airplanes to the flight deck from the hangar bay.

Operational nuclear aircraft carriers today are home to about 6,000 sailors and airmen. Typically, the ship stores enough food and supplies to operate for ninety days without replenishment. Approximately 18,150 meals are served daily. The distillation plant provides four hundred thousand gallons of fresh water from sea water daily, enough to supply two thousand homes in Hampton Roads. In materials, the ship is proliferated with nearly thirty thousand light fixtures; two thousand telephones; fourteen thousand pillowcases, and twenty-eight thousand sheets; and nine hundred miles of cable and wiring.

Newport News Shipbuilding and Drydock Company is the only shipyard in the United States contracted to build America's fleet of nuclear aircraft carriers. The USS *Harry S. Truman* (CVN-75) joined the fleet in July 1998, and construction moves forward on the USS *Ronald Reagan* (CVN-76). Former President Ronald Reagan was an advocate of "peace through strength," of which there is no better example than an American nuclear-powered carrier wielding the weight of its forward-deployed air wing in seas all over the world.

In the broad scope of aircraft carrier history, while Kenneth Whiting is the undisputed father of the aircraft carrier, Senator John C. Stennis of Mississippi was the father of America's modern Navy and, most especially, its aircraft carriers. Quoting this oft-quoted champion of the aircraft carrier, "[the] mission to maintain decisive naval power for our global interests will remain as imperative for the future as the past. Our global interests and overseas dependence grows, not lessens, with each passing year. We must always remember that when the chips are down and shots are fired, it will be the modern-day naval patriots who will risk their lives, man the ships, and fire the guns."

"Of Sun-Split Clouds...and Burning Blue Sky"

My husband once described to me the sensation of flight, the vividness of the sky's blue and the clouds split by a brilliant sun. "I climbed through the clouds. My world was white mixed with delicate shades of gray. Breaking out on top, the gray gave way to azure blue and the glint of gold from a blazing sun struck the cockpit. Below was a bed of pure white clouds." The selection of images for the color section was an effort to show some of the most compelling photography and art in the possible light, and to bring visual perspective to the sun-split clouds and burning blue sky that aviators experience in flight.

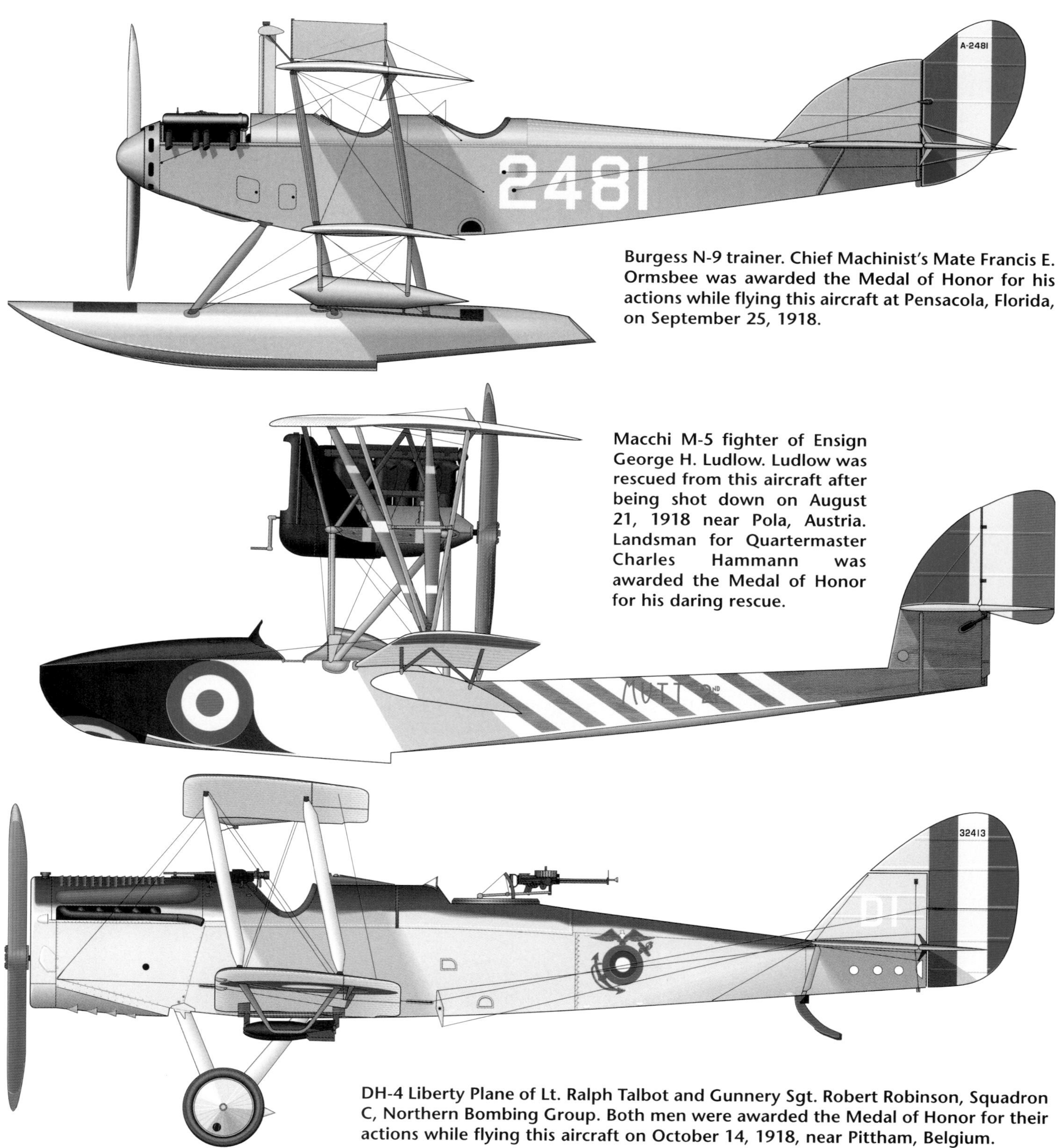

Burgess N-9 trainer. Chief Machinist's Mate Francis E. Ormsbee was awarded the Medal of Honor for his actions while flying this aircraft at Pensacola, Florida, on September 25, 1918.

Macchi M-5 fighter of Ensign George H. Ludlow. Ludlow was rescued from this aircraft after being shot down on August 21, 1918 near Pola, Austria. Landsman for Quartermaster Charles Hammann was awarded the Medal of Honor for his daring rescue.

DH-4 Liberty Plane of Lt. Ralph Talbot and Gunnery Sgt. Robert Robinson, Squadron C, Northern Bombing Group. Both men were awarded the Medal of Honor for their actions while flying this aircraft on October 14, 1918, near Pittham, Belgium.

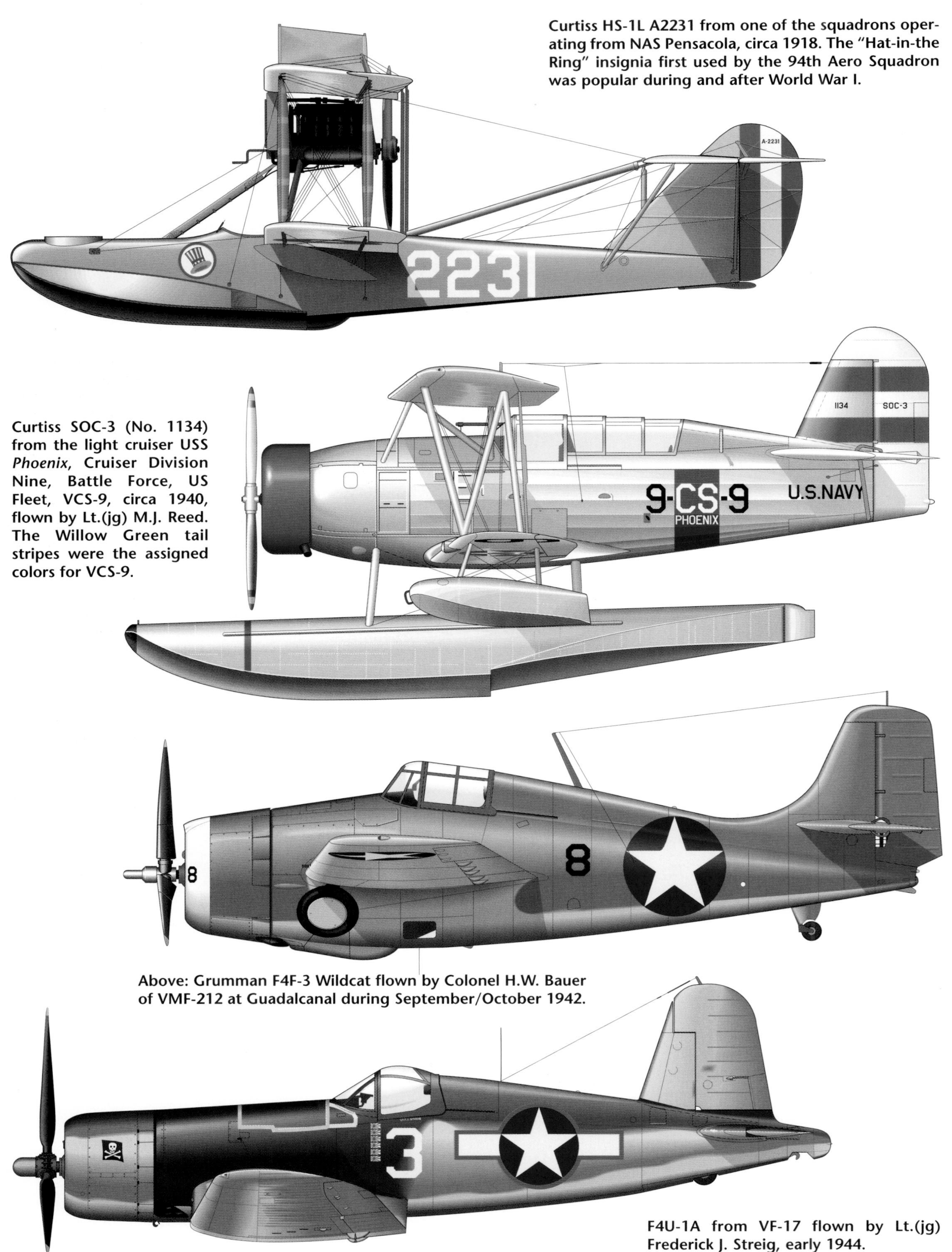

Curtiss HS-1L A2231 from one of the squadrons operating from NAS Pensacola, circa 1918. The "Hat-in-the Ring" insignia first used by the 94th Aero Squadron was popular during and after World War I.

Curtiss SOC-3 (No. 1134) from the light cruiser USS *Phoenix*, Cruiser Division Nine, Battle Force, US Fleet, VCS-9, circa 1940, flown by Lt.(jg) M.J. Reed. The Willow Green tail stripes were the assigned colors for VCS-9.

Above: Grumman F4F-3 Wildcat flown by Colonel H.W. Bauer of VMF-212 at Guadalcanal during September/October 1942.

F4U-1A from VF-17 flown by Lt.(jg) Frederick J. Streig, early 1944.

Wings of Gold—Navy Pilot Wings.

Above and below left: On February 9, 1929, Congress authorized the President of the United States to award in the name of Congress gold medals to Commander John H. Towers for "conceiving, organizing, and commanding the first transatlantic flight" and to officers and crew members of the Navy flying boat NC-4 who crossed the Atlantic with him. The NC-4 medal was designed by Catherine G. Barton. The medal has a gull volant over waves on the obverse. The inscription reads: "First Transatlantic Flight United States Navy May 1919." The reverse names those to whom the medal was awarded with the words: "Presented by the President of the United States in the name of Congress." The medals were inscribed: "Newfoundland, NC-4, Portugal." The large gold NC-4 medal was not designed to be worn. A bronze miniature, as large as the Navy's full-sized medals, was authorized by Congress on April 25, 1935.

Famous "Felix the Cat" has been a naval aviation icon since 1921 when an outfit known as Combat Squadron Four used this feisty feline for the first time. When the squadron was disestablished in 1922, Felix was adopted by a continuous string of fighter and bombing squadrons, all meeting their end well before lucky Felix. On July 1, 1935, VF-1B was established and picked up on the Felix insignia. Fighting One (B) would be redesignated on several occasions, the first occurring on July 1, 1937, when the unit became known as Fighter Squadron Six (VF-6). VF-6 was redesignated Fighter Squadron Three (VF-3) on July 15, 1943, and, subsequently, VF-3B on November 15, 1946. Felix followed his lucky lot of naval aviators through one more redesignation on August 7, 1948, when VF-3B became known as Fighter Squadron Thirty-One (VF-31), now the famous *Tomcatter* squadron.

Right: The Distinguished Flying Cross was established by Congress on July 2, 1926, as an award to any person who, serving with the Army Air Corps, including National Guard and reserve units, or with the Navy, Marine Corps, or Coast Guard, after April 6, 1917, distinguished himself by "heroism or extraordinary achievement while participating in an aerial flight." The medal was designed by Elizabeth Will and Arthur E. DuBois.

This poster was produced to recruit WAVES during World War II.

The Walt Disney Company designed and produced much of the great World War II insignia artwork for the United States military. Navy commands, especially aviation units, were proliferated with Disney artists' renderings of cartoon caricatures, serpents smashing Axis submarines, and eight-legged creatures handling vital communications. The insignia shown here is an original Disney cartoon cell designed for the United States Naval Communication Station Norfolk shortly after the United States entered the war. This colorful, somewhat whimsical octopus sounds the alarm, answers the phone, takes dictation and messages, sends message traffic, and even types—quite a job for a seagoing creature. A modified version of this insignia is used today by the Naval Computer and Telecommunications Area Master Station LANT Message Center.

Lieutenant Commander James H. Flatley Jr. was first told he had been picked as the first commanding officer of Fighter Squadron Ten (VF-10), destined to be the original *Grim Reapers,* while serving as executive officer of Fighter Squadron Forty-Two (VF-42) aboard the USS *Yorktown* (CV-5). During his return trip to San Diego, California, aboard a transport ship, Flatley worked on the details of his new position, one of which was what to call his new outfit. Flatley decided on the *Grim Reapers* which seemed to meet the approval of other transport passengers. The insignia was also his idea: a skeleton armed with a scythe. Stanley Johnston, a writer who was aboard the transport at the time and later wrote a book entitled *The Grim Reapers,* took a pencil and paper, made a rough outline of a skeleton, drew in a scythe held at full-cock, and gave the old boy a high-speed wing. Badly drawn as it was, squadron information makes it clear the general effect stood the test. All that was missing was the motto. After much deliberation, the two men decided on "Mow 'em Down" and sketched it at the bottom of their masterpiece. The skeleton was affectionately called "Moe" by the *Grim Reapers.* Over the years, the skeleton has been modified just a bit, losing his World War II leather flying cap. The scythe no longer drips blood, pleasing the weak at heart, and the motto has been removed from the bottom of the design. The *Grim Reapers* of VF-101, the F-14 Tomcat fleet replacement squadron at Naval Air Station Oceana, proudly sport their squadron insignia, a naval aviation tradition if there ever was one.

Fighter Squadron Thirty-Three changed their tactical call sign from the *Tarsiers* to *Starfighters* in early 1981, though the new insignia did not appear until late 1987. The *Tarsier* never quite went away, however, since it held the longest history with the squadron. Both versions are shown here. The *Tarsier* call sign and insignia evolved from the time of the squadron's establishment on October 12, 1948, and continued thus until Fighting Thirty-Three was disestablished in 1993 during an initial drawdown of F-14 Tomcat squadrons at Naval Air Station Oceana. The tarsier, as a matter of explanation, looks somewhat like a monkey-type squirrel with some characteristics so much its own the animal has been assigned to genus *Tarasius.* This small nocturnal East Indian mammal is actually related to the lemur, hence the enormous pair of goggle eyes. The squadron adapted their insignia from this nimble beast, accentuating his teeth as large fangs, and making the little fellow's eyes look quite ferocious.

The insignia formerly worn by the *Sunday Punchers* of Attack Squadron Seventy-Five (VA-75) was a scrappy little boy wearing boxing gloves and riding a bomb. The design was completed after the Second World War, and approved for use on June 25, 1947, for the squadron, then designated VA-7A. This original insignia was intended to project fighting spirit so the boy's facial expression was one of fierce determination. Squadron literature indicated the insignia shown here, a bomb coming through a boxing glove placed over a pair of aviator wings, is symbolic of the haymaker punch, a knockout punch. The design was initially approved by the Bureau of Aeronautics for Bombing Squadron Eighteen (VB-18) but, of course, the boy with boxing gloves replaced it in 1947. The insignia as it is displayed here, the same as the one used in 1945, reappeared with modifications around 1970.

The ship's seal is based on the coat of arms of the Kennedy and Fitzgerald families. These ancient symbols represent the stability that stems from tradition. Modern symbols have been incorporated to show the progress that stems from innovation. Both stability and progress were characteristic of the policies of President John Fitzgerald Kennedy, and both are essential to the continued accomplishment of the ship's mission. The black shield with three gold helmets is the traditional coat of arms of the O'Kennedy of the Ormonde. The helmets represent the original Gaelic word for Kennedy, "Ceinneide," which means helmeted head. The red and white borders are the colors of Fitzgerald of Desmond. Above the shield is the single helmet, crowned with a wreath of the Kennedy colors, black and gold, and flanked by the red and white mantel in Fitzgerald colors, symbolic of courage.

The crest of the coat of arms is a malled forearm, holding a sheaf of arrows and framed by olive branches, symbolizing power and peace, as do the eagle's claws in the presidential seal. The bottlenosed dolphins holding the banner at the bottom are traditional symbols of the sea and sailors. They represent our freedom to roam the seas, freedom essential to progress in the world community. Dolphins are friends of man but deadly enemies of aggressors, attacking only when provoked.

The shamrock-shaped banner symbolizes good luck, President Kennedy's Irish ancestry, and our ties with Ireland. Written on larger versions of the ship's banner in Latin is the Kennedy's motto, "*Date Nolite Rogare,*" which means "Give, be unwilling to ask." The phrase represents the spirit of President Kennedy's inaugural address and specifically that famous line: "Ask not what your country can do for you, ask what you can do for your country."

The wings are symbols not only of the *Kennedy's* air power, but also of progress and the freedom to roam the skies. Stars, representing the fifty states, surround the shield. A fifty-first star, the topmost in the seal, represents the high state of readiness sought by the ship. In years that the carrier earns the coveted Navy Battle Efficiency Award, this top star will be gold in color. The ship's seal was designed by the ship's first commanding officer, Captain Earl P. Yates.

The USS *John F. Kennedy* (CV-67) was photographed for its twenty-fifth anniversary in 1993, Carrier Air Wing Three (CVW-3) riding her decks. (Official United States Navy Photograph.)

The VF-5 boar's head insignia was adapted from the design on bottles of Gordon gin. The literal interpretation of the insignia is "a horny bunch of two-balled bastards," so this rather colorful squadron adopted the pseudonym *Red Rippers*—it sounded much better and offended fewer people—in 1930 at the Chicago Air Races where they distinguished themselves with some of the best flight demonstrations ever witnessed. Perhaps the squadron's 1933 interpretation of this rather colorful insignia is preferable:

"The wild boar is the ugliest-snouted, worst-tempered, fastest-moving creature in the whole Noah's Ark of nature, and is as full of tricks as a thirteen-spade bridge hand. He is the only animal that dares drink at the same pool with the tiger, he is as shifty as a pickerel in eel-grass. The boar's head is taken directly from the one that graces the label on the Gordon's Gin bottle. The scroll effect under the head is a string of sausage—the good line which all members of the squadron were to be adept at shooting."

Between 1951 and 1964, the Navy established a series of nuclear strike squadrons dubbed heavy attack squadrons or VAHs. The very first of these were the ever so cool, *Smokin' Cats* of VAH-1, whose insignia shown here dates to the redesignation of the squadron September 1, 1964, upon assignment of the North American RA-5C Vigilante aircraft as a reconnaissance attack squadron, RVAH-1. The squadron was originally established November 1, 1955. The *Smokin' Cats* artwork was screened at the defunct Naval Aviation Depot Norfolk. As VAH-1, the *Cats* were the first to take delivery of the Douglas A3D-1 Skywarrior, later redesignated the A-3A, an aircraft designed specifically for nuclear payload. The squadron was disestablished on January 29, 1971.

In terms of squadron lineage, VAH-11 was actually older than VAH-1, but since it did not become a heavy attack unit until after the *Smokin' Cats,* VAH-11 received its higher designation. Established as VC-8 on December 3, 1951, the squadron was redesignated VAH-11 on November 1, 1955, and subsequently, RVAH-11, June 1, 1966. The squadron was disestablished on June 1, 1975.

The backbone of the carrier airborne early warning aircraft was captured in formation in 1962. Clockwise from the top: Douglas AE-1E Skyraider; Grumman WF-2 Willy Fudd (an E-1B Tracer); Douglas A-1J Skyraider; and, lastly, the Grumman S-2A Tracker.

During the Vietnamese Conflict, helicopters were an essential part of the war on the ground as well as providing critical support, rigged as gunships, for fast river patrol boats. Soldiers and sailors called them everything from "copters," "choppers," and "whirlybirds" to "jolly greens" and "jolly green giants." Here, United States Marines rush out of a Boeing H-46 Sea Knight helicopter during a vertical assault against the Viet Cong in Operation Jackstay, an attack involving 1,200 Marines in the treacherous Rung Sat Zone located thirty-five miles from Saigon, South Vietnam. During the war, the H-46 Sea Knight helicopter was used for transport of soldiers and Marines, vertical replenishment, medical evacuations, and search and rescue operations. (Courtesy of Commander Naval Air Force Atlantic Fleet.)

In the post-World War II era, the Patrol Squadron Twenty-Four *Batmen* participated in testing and development of the Navy's first air-to-surface guided missile. The Bat was the first generation radar guided bomb with a glide ratio of five-to-one. The device could glide one mile for every one thousand feet of altitude. From this capability, the squadron developed its insignia (shown here) and nickname, the *Batmen*. The Bat capability is represented by the "Bat girl," the mining mission by a parachuting mine, and the antisubmarine warfare mission by a periscope. These symbols are superimposed over a Navy sword to depict readiness to defend the nation. The insignia is unique in that it was for many years one of only two authorized active duty squadron insignia displaying the female form, the other having belonged to the original Night Fighter Squadron One Hundred Three (VF(N)-103). With the loss of the VF(N)-103 pinup girl, a figure looking very much like a "bat girl," VP-24's insignia became the only authorized insignia bearing the female form. Reliable sources say that the model for the original squadron insignia was the very beautiful and talented Denise Darcel. With changes in the rules and regulations governing insignia, VP-24 was forced by 1995 to alter their historic and attractive logo to the one shown here, the bat hovering over the conning tower of a submarine. The squadron has since been disestablished.

Carrier Airborne Early Warning Squadron One Hundred Twenty (VAW-120) was established as RVAW-120 on July 1, 1967, at Naval Air Station Norfolk. The greyhawk in the open book (first insignia) was the first design used by RVAW-120, the fleet airborne early warning replacement squadron or "Rag" around the time of its establishment. The *Greyhawks* retained this insignia even after the squadron was redesignated VAW-120 on May 1, 1983. The new insignia, also shown here, and the one still considered the official squadron logo by the guidelines established by the Chief of Naval Operations (OPNAV), was instituted in the late 1980s.

The insignia of Helicopter Mine Countermeasures Squadron Twelve used the symbols of the flying sea dragon clenching the lightning bolt and grasping a contact mine. Created in 1971, this insignia remained with the squadron until it was disestablished on September 30, 1994. The lightning bolt's use in naval warfare insignia typically represents electronics, in this case the detonation of mines via electronic devices. The contact mine is the most universally recognized waterborne mine, thus the squadron adapted it to their insignia. The squadron's nickname was the *Sea Dragons*. At the time of its disestablishment, the squadron was flying the MH-53E Sea Dragon which purposely bore the name of this pioneering airborne mine countermeasures squadron.

The *Dragon Slayers* of HS-11 were established June 27, 1957, and became famous as the squadron which plucked the astronauts of *Gemini 7* from the Atlantic Ocean, December 18, 1965. Helicopter Anti-Submarine Squadron Eleven recovered Lt. Col. Frank Borman, USAF, and Commander James A. Lovell, USN, in the western Atlantic, 250 mile north of Grand Turk Island, and delivered them to the USS *Wasp* (CVS-18). During the fourteen day flight of *Gemini 7,* astronauts Borman and Lovell carried out many experiments in space, and set the record for manned space flight. The *Dragon Slayers* played a critical role in the successful conclusion of the space flight. The squadron later became a member of Carrier Air Wing One (CVW-1), established in 1934 and the Navy's oldest air wing, aboard the USS *America* (CV-66). Today, the *Dragon Slayers* are homeported at Naval Air Station Jacksonville, Florida, flying the SH-60F Seahawk helicopter.

The VAW-123 *Screwtops,* also known as the *Cyclops,* squadron insignia is a large cyclop's eye in the center of a blue swirl. The insignia is known worldwide as a direct reflection of the aircraft's mission as the "eye" of the fleet. The dome insignia, seen here in a photograph taken of *Screwtop 603,* a Grumman E-2C Hawkeye aircraft, flying over the Virginia Capes in 1992, clearly demonstrates why it is known as the largest military unit insignia in the world. Applying the aircraft insignia to the top of the radar dome is no easy task. Ground crew personnel are suspended from the hangar ceiling to paint the insignia, a job which is painstakingly undertaken and quite literally exhausting. Fortunately, the dome remains in good enough condition that the paint work only has to be done once in awhile. Touch ups are performed in the interim. (Courtesy of Carrier Airborne Early Warning Squadron One Hundred Twenty Three.)

Aircraft Intermediate Maintenance Department (AIMD) at Naval Air Station Norfolk is an integral part of fleet aviation maintenance, providing noninvasive analysis and actual repair of airframes and engines, and aircraft support equipment for squadrons and aircraft carriers stationed at Norfolk. The AIMD Norfolk insignia bears the motto, "Always Prepared," on its banner, and the word, "Support," in the center signifying, of course, support as its major mission.

The Chief of Naval Operations approved the popularly known Naval Air Station Norfolk beaver the week of October 16, 1953. The design portrays a pair of aviator's wings held by a busy sailor-beaver against the background of Naval Air Station Norfolk and Willoughby Spit. This snappy escutcheon bears the Latin motto, *"Naves sustinemus,"* translated, "We support the ships." To get the new insignia, a contest was held in early 1953 at the air station with a twenty-five dollar bond awarded to the winner who best depicted the station's mission. Aviation Structural Mechanic Third Class (AM3) Richard J. Nichol designed the winning entry. His rendering was modified by Illustrator Draftsman First Class (DM1) R.A. Genders of the Naval Aviation Safety Activity Norfolk to comply with existing Department of Defense rules and regulations governing base insignia. The sailor-beaver holding the wings overhead symbolizes support of the fleet and shore naval aviation activities. The double circle frame has the words, "Naval Air Station • Norfolk • Virginia." A cloud background completes the design.

Uniform regulations provided for a breast insignia for Navy and Marine Corps personnel qualified as Flight Officers as of August 24, 1968. The new wings (above) replaced the old Naval Observer wings (top) effective December 31 of that year.

Aboard the USS *Essex,* McCampbell, an ace four times over with twenty enemy planes to his credit, sits in the cockpit of *Minsi III,* a Grumman F6F Hellcat. This is a National Archives color photograph 806K2181, 1944. (Courtesy of the National Museum of Naval Aviation.)

The Decal Shop: Where Art Captured Essence

The decal shop at Naval Aviation Depot Norfolk produced outstanding command insignia over the years, but none moreso interesting than some of the facility's own. The decal shop can claim a hand in designing many squadron and Navy insignia, genuine pieces of art which were carefully drawn and screened by shop artisans. The walls, cabinets, and tables throughout the decal shop were covered in squadron and aviation command designs—and dope on the floor. The decal shop spaces were once used as the dope shop, then part of aircraft wing assembly. Workers would stretch fine muslin cloth over wing frames, then spray the cloth with the dope. After the dope hardened, what had been soft cloth turned into beautiful seaplane wings. Dried dope was caked throughout the decal shop in patterns indicating where each stage of preparation and assembly actually occurred. No one knew this history quite like John Parker, who came to the decal shop in 1949 as a graphics art mechanic, and who retired in 1994 after forty-five years of devoted, painstaking work, as its manager. Parker designed important and memorable insignia for countless commands.

The artistry and ingenuity of past naval aviation insignia speak for themselves. Having combed the shop and watched the actual screening process before the shop ceased operation, it was nearly impossible to not be in awe of the patience and skill of shop artisans. The experience was a delight. Gerald R. "Gerry" Jean, in the decal shop since 1974, was the last graphics artisan in the department and an expert in military

decal history and design. When asked his personal favorite among the many done by the shop, Jean remarked, "Carrier Air Wing Seventeen is probably my favorite. It had eleven colors in the screen. Very nice." The first insignia Jean ever screened for the decal shop was the Chief of Naval Education and Training Support. Perhaps one of the oldest decals made at the shop was the image of Naval Air Station Norfolk's infamous beaver wearing mechanics clothes and holding a wrench and a pair of naval aviator wings. The decal was used by Overhaul and Repair Department inspectors to approve work done in the shops.

The decal shop had screened many insignia over the years for commands not located in Hampton Roads. The best of example of these was the United States Navy Test Pilot School, Naval Air Station Patuxent River, Maryland, one of the oldest in the shop collection, and the Naval Aviation Depot Corporation, Naval Air Systems Command. The test pilot school insignia carries the Douglas F4D Skyray, a short-range carrier-based interceptor fighter developed by Douglas Aircraft Company for the Navy in the early 1950s, in the center of the crest.

S.H.O.P. SAFE HEALTHY OPERATING PROCESS
NAVAL AVIATION DEPOT
NORFOLK, VIRGINIA
PLANT
SERVICES
650
DEPARTMENT

NARF NORFOLK
F-14 TOMCAT
DEPOT LEVEL MAINTENANCE

F-14A
EA-6A
KA-6D
PMA(F)-224
NAVAIRSYSCOM DETACHMENT
NORFOLK
A-6E

F.O.D. PREVENTION
EVERYONE'S RESPONSIBILITY

NAVAL AVIATION DEPOT NORFOLK, VA.
POSITIVE TOOL CONTROL
"THE TIDEWATER INDUSTRIAL TIGER"

CVW
17

UNITED STATES NAVY
CHIEF OF NAVAL EDUCATION AND TRAINING SUPPORT

NAVAL AIR STATION
NORFOLK, VIRGINIA
O&R
OVERHAULED
BY O&R DEPT.
DATE

U.S.N.T.P.S.

A Grumman F9F-2 Panther jet sits on the deck edge elevator of the USS *Franklin D. Roosevelt* (CVB-42), circa 1950. (Courtesy of the National Archives.)

Originally adopted in 1948, the flaming devil head insignia quickly became famous worldwide as the symbol of Fighter Squadron Ten (A) (VF-10A) *Be-Devilers.* Designed by Ensign John P. Humphries, the first emblem displayed a blue flaming devil head on a white background. The *Be-Devilers* were redesignated Fighter Squadron Ninety-Two on August 12, 1948, and it was not until January 15, 1950, that the *Be-Devilers* became Fighter Squadron Seventy-Four. At the time of Fighter Squadron Seventy-Four *Be-Devilers* disestablishment in April 1994, the fierce red flaming devil head peered through the cross-hairs at the enemy, thus instilling dread in all who encountered the *Be-Devilers* of Fighter Squadron Seventy-Four.

Commander Michael C. Vogt (later captain), commanding officer of Attack Squadron Sixty-Five *Fighting Tigers,* catches an "OK" three-wire on the USS *Abraham Lincoln* (CVN-72) after returning from a flight on February 9, 1990, which pushed him over the 4,000-hour mark in the venerable A-6E Intruder. On his way to achieving this aviation milestone, Commander Vogt had completed over nine deployments and 1,170 carrier landings on eight different carriers. (Official United States Navy Photograph.)

An A-6E SWIP Intruder of Attack Squadron Thirty-Four (VA-34) *Blue Blasters* prepares to launch from the USS *George Washington* (CVN-73), 1993. (Photographer's Mate Third Class (PH3) Raymond M. Connors, photographer. Official United States Navy Photograph.)

The USS *America* (CV-66) was commissioned on January 23, 1965, and her symbol is as historic as the name she bears, her "Don't Tread On Me," banner taken from the famed 1775 Culpeper Flag. The minutemen of Culpeper County, Virginia, carried the flag into battle with the British as early as 1775, as a symbol of their patriotism and honor. The America ended her long and honorable service to the fleet on August 9, 1996.

The USS *Saratoga* (CVA/CV-60) was commissioned on April 14, 1956, the sixth ship of the United States Navy to bear the name; Captain R.J. Stroh, its first commanding officer. The carrier was redesignated CV-60 on June 30, 1972. On August 20, 1994, the grand lady of the Atlantic Fleet was decommissioned, having served as the oldest aircraft carrier in the Navy. The crest of CV-60 incorporated some of the elements of her World War II predecessor (CV-3), namely the fighting rooster. The crown and trident symbolized the victor at sea, the *"Invictus Gallus Gladiator,"* translated as "the one who never loses."

The insignia of disestablished Attacked Squadron Thirty-Four *Blue Blasters* was designed in 1966 by cartoonist Roy Crane, the originator of the Buzz Sawyer comic strip. The noted cartoonist created a unique, if somewhat sinister, emblem by combining elements from the two previous insignias of Fighter Squadron Twenty, nicknamed *Jokers Coming Through.* New pilots in the squadron were called "Jokers," hence the sobriquet. One of these early designs had depicted bomb blasts on a blue background, thus the name *Blue Blasters.* The other was Fighting Twenty's version which included a skull with the words "Fighting Twenty" for teeth and paddles in the hands of a skeleton landing signal officer (LSO) for eyes. This "roger ball" signal represented a smooth, professional approach to an aircraft carrier's flight deck in the earliest days of naval aviation.

Carrier Air Wing Three (CVW-3) remains the second oldest air wing in the Navy. Established on July 1, 1938, CVW-3 was aboard the first aircraft carrier to bear the name USS *Saratoga* (CV-3). From 1981 to 1993, CVW-3 flew from the decks of the USS *John F. Kennedy* (CV-67). Since that time, the air wing has embarked aboard the USS *Dwight D. Eisenhower* (CVN-69). The insignia shown here was used by the air wing in the 1970s and 1980s, but is no longer in use. Controversy arose over the causcasian versus African-American hand in the design and, as a direct consequence, it was changed to an African-American hand for awhile. When controversy swung in the other direction, the hand design was dropped altogether in favor of bright colored lightning bolts shooting from a carrier, the number "3" superimposed over the rainbow design.

Attack Squadron Thirty-Six was established March 1, 1987, at Naval Air Station Oceana, to form the second A-6E Intruder squadron assigned to Carrier Air Wing Eight (CVW-8) aboard the USS *Theodore Roosevelt* (CVN-71), and disestablished April 1, 1994. Commander Mark J. Himler was the last commanding officer of the *Roadrunners*. When the squadron was established, plans had been hatched to designate the squadron VA-153 and adopt the traditions of the first *Blue Tail Flies*. When the time came for designation, the squadron decided to follow the traditions of the first VA-36 Roadrunners, an A-4 Skyhawk outfit disestablished in 1970. The squadron was not permitted to use the famous Roadrunner of cartoon fame under guidelines established by the Office of the Chief of Naval Operations which governs the approval of squadron insignia. Rules now applied to squadron insignia forbid the use of animals doing human acts or cartoons (the mainstay of vintage insignia), and female images on unit artwork. Instead of settling for a whimpy design, the squadron selected a realistic roadrunner choking the life out of a rattlesnake, hence the *Roadrunner* nickname came alive despite the guidelines.

The USS *Theodore Roosevelt* (CVN-71) transited to Norfolk Naval Shipyard, spring 1994, down the Eastern Branch of the Elizabeth River in front of Town Point Park. The World Trade Center and financial district are in plain view to the right, while the National Maritime Center, NAUTICUS, sits to the left, nearly obscured by the superstructure of the carrier. (Official United States Navy Photograph.)

Vice President of the United States Al Gore addresses the crowd at the christening of the USS *John C. Stennis* on November 11, 1993, Newport News Shipbuilding and Drydock Company, Newport News, Virginia. (Courtesy of Commander Naval Air Force Atlantic Fleet Public Affairs.)

The USS *John C. Stennis* (CVN-74) is shown shifting berths at Newport News Shipbuilding November 13, 1993. (Courtesy Commander Naval Air Force Atlantic Fleet Public Affairs.)

Fighter Squadron Eighty-Four *Jolly Roger* F-14s are shown here flying formation in 1994. (Courtesy of Fighter Squadron Eighty-Four.)

The Norfolk-based aircraft carrier USS *Dwight D. Eisenhower* (CVN-69) was photographed in 1994 with her embarked air wing, Carrier Air Wing Three (CVW-3), aboard. The carrier departed Naval Station Norfolk on October 20, 1994, for the Persian Gulf and Operation Southern Watch. From the Persian Gulf, the *Eisenhower* headed for the Adriatic Sea and Operation Deny Flight. On Friday, April 14, 1995, the *Eisenhower* Joint Task Group returned to Norfolk after what has been described as a landmark, perhaps historical, cruise in which 415 women sailed with 4,560 male counterparts in the ship's and air wing's personnel complement. (Official United States Navy Photograph. Courtesy of Commander Naval Air Force Atlantic Fleet Public Affairs Office.)

The premier carrier-based airborne early warning aircraft serving the American fleet is the Grumman E-2C Hawkeye. The E-2C Hawkeye, in service with the United States Navy and several foreign governments, is the latest airborne early warning command and control aircraft built by the Grumman Aerospace Corporation, now known as Northrop-Grumman. This advanced version—the result of what Grumman has dubbed a more progressive airframe, propulsion, and systems development over the past twenty years—represents the state-of-the-art in airborne early warning command and control (AEWCC). The E-2C's ability to detect targets over land and over water at long ranges, coupled with high reliability, provides the AEWCC capability needed for operations through the 1990s and into the twenty-first century. The all-weather carrier and shore-based system is primarily designed for air defense. Secondary mission capabilities include surface surveillance, strike control, search and rescue, air traffic control, and communications relay. The crew consists of a pilot, copilot, combat information center officer (CICO) also doubling as the mission commander, air control officer (ACO), and radar operator (RO). Control capability is tripled since the three operators can work independently on the modes, including sensor display, data retrieval, and automatic control. The Hawkeye has two Allison T56-A-425A turboprop engines, 4,910 ESHP. Here, a VAW-124 *Bear Ace* Hawkeye, AJ 602, flies over the Virginia Capes operating area. This photograph was taken by a photographer dangling precariously out the open bay of a Grumman C-2A Greyhound aircraft in 1994. (Courtesy of Carrier Airborne Early Warning Squadron One Hundred Twenty-Four.)

The USS *George Washington* (CVN-73) was the Navy's newest operational nuclear-powered aircraft carrier when this photograph was taken. The USS *John C. Stennis* (CVN-74) was in its precommissioning phase at Newport News Shipbuilding and Drydock Company at the time. The *Washington* made her maiden deployment in 1994. Aircraft carriers like the *Washington* contain nearly thirty thousand lighting fixtures; more than nine hundred miles of wiring and cable; in excess of sixty thousand tons of structural steel; and require a stack of technical manuals as high as the Washington Monument to operate. The Washington Monument is 555 feet high. (Official United States Navy Photograph. Courtesy of Commander Naval Air Force Atlantic Fleet Public Affairs Office.)

The newest aircraft carrier, USS *John C. Stennis,* makes a high speed turn during rudder checks conducted as part of a highly successful Builder's Sea Trials, October 3–6, 1995, off the Virginia Capes. (Chief Photographer's Mate (Air Warfare) (PHC(AW)) Tom Hensley, photographer. Official United States Navy Photograph.)

The USS *John C. Stennis* (CVN-74) command seal was produced from the combined efforts of several members of the ship's company working in concert with the Stennis Center for Public Service, the John C. Stennis Space Center, and the United States Senate Historian. The seal implies peace through strength, just as Senator John C. Stennis was referred to as an "unwavering advocate of peace through strength" by former President Ronald Reagan when the ship's name was announced in June 1988. The circular shape signifies the *Nimitz*-class aircraft carrier's unique capability to circle the world without refueling while providing forward presence from the sea.

The predominant colors are red, white, blue and gold, the same as the United States of America and United States Navy. The four gold bands and eight ties denote John C. Stennis' four decades (41 years) in the Senate and the eight presidents he served with, from President Harry S. Truman to President Ronald Wilson Reagan. The seven stars in the blue border represent his seven terms in the Senate and characterize USS *John C. Stennis* as the seventh *Nimitz*-class aircraft carrier. The red and white stripes inside the blue border represent the national flag and the American people USS *John C. Stennis* serves. They also honor the courage and sacrifice of our country's armed forces.

The eagle and shield is a representation of the gilt eagle and shield overlooking the Old Senate Chamber, which Senator Stennis' dedicated efforts helped to restore. The shield represents the United States of America, the country USS *John C. Stennis* and her air wing serves and protects. The twenty stars represent our twentieth state, Mississippi, the home of John C. Stennis. The three arrows in the eagle's talons symbolize the ship and air wing's awesome ability to project power. They also represent Senator John C. Stennis' over three decades on both the Senate Armed Services Committee (37 years) and the Appropriations Committee (33 years), where he oversaw the country's military capabilities and earned the title "Father of America's modern Navy." The burst of light emanating from the shield, representative of the emergence of a new nation in the United States Senate seal, portrays the birth of over twenty-five major naval aviation programs under Senator Stennis' leadership, including all aircraft carriers from USS *Forrestal* (CV-59) to USS *Harry S. Truman* (CVN-75), and aircraft from the F-4 Phantom to the F/A-18 Hornet. The eagle is representative of John C. Stennis' stature in the Senate, where he was respected and admired as a "soaring eagle" by his colleagues. The eagle also embodies independence and strength, and depicts the constant readiness of USS *John C. Stennis* and her air wing to preserve, protect, and defend freedom.

The carrier on the seal, cutting an impressive swath in the sea, exemplifies Senator Stennis' philosophy of "Look Ahead." Embodied in the ship are the principles of honor, courage, and commitment, principles that John Cornelius Stennis constantly upheld in his long service to America, and values the ship's crew uphold in their service. The carrier's path also evokes Stennis' pledge to "plow a straight furrow right down to the end of my row," just as the ship will steer a steady course to complete all missions in the preservation and defense of freedom.

In accordance with tradition, the seal, after selection by the ship's crew, was submitted to Mrs. Margaret Stennis Womble, the ship's sponsor and daughter of Senator Stennis, and to Mrs. John Hampton Stennis, the matron of honor and wife of Senator Stennis' son, for their approval. They approved the design in February 1995.

Epilogue: "Wings of Valor, Wings of Gold"

Naval aviation has a set of traditions all its own which bespeaks of the camaraderie, bravery and history of those who belonged and still belong to this time-honored profession. Time and again, young men, and now women, have given their lives for their country. Gone but not forgotten are the innumerable squadrons and personalities which brought Navy and Marine Corps aviation to life, and though they are no longer with us, their names and faces will be remembered for having built the framework that carried naval aviation into the next century. Numerous commands have met with disestablishment since 1990. In just one year's time, 1994, thirty-seven naval aviation squadrons met with disestablishment, the largest number on record for one year since the year prior to the outbreak of war in Korea. Many stand out in memory and will most certainly never be forgotten, but naval aviation, perhaps most especially its history, is fighting for its life. The Eugene Elys and Paul Bakers of naval aviation deserve to have their names, faces, and contributions preserved for this and every generation to follow.

World needs and increased emphasis on doing more with less is an issue which will continue to test the strength of carrier aviation. The forward projection of naval air power that has been the hallmark of the United States Navy since the grim days of World War II will face new challenges in the twenty-first century, and whether naval aviation adjusts to these challenges and meets them head on is certainly up to the people who wear the wings of gold.

When Commander Naval Air Force Atlantic Fleet Vice Admiral Anthony A. Less(1) retired from active duty on March 18, 1994, in ceremonies held aboard the aircraft carrier USS *George Washington,* he expressed what wearing the wings of gold meant to him, the "wings of which I will forever be proud":

"What are these gold wings of Naval Aviation?

"What is the strength and stamina behind their luster?

"And what, over the years, have they meant to me?

"Perhaps it begins with love for the assignments, the diverse experiences, the places we go. Maybe it's the nostalgia of the early morning fog off Pensacola Bay, or sunrise reflecting off Jacksonville's St. Johns River, or the desert wind stirring

An A-6E Intruder, located at Naval Air Station Oceana, gets checked out on the flight line by squadron personnel on September 16, 1985. (Official United States Navy Photograph.)

Lieutenant Gregory E. Glaros (right center) of Attack Squadron Thirty-Five (VA-35) *Black Panthers* receives medals for Gulf War combat from Vice Admiral Anthony A. Less, Commander Naval Air Force Atlantic Fleet, 1991. (Paul Aiken, photographer. Courtesy of the Kirn Library.)

Attack Squadron Thirty-Four A-6E Intruders were painted in D-Day colors to commemorate the fiftieth anniversary of the June 6, 1944, invasion of Europe. Aircraft were first painted in this tell-tale black-and-white-stripe pattern for D-Day to keep them from being shot down by Allied forces on invasion day. The *Blue Blasters* were deployed aboard the USS *George Washington* (CVN-73) at the time this photograph was taken in June 1994. (Official United States Navy Photograph.)

the evening air at Miramar or North Island, or the hazy sultriness of a summer sunset at Hampton Roads.

"More likely, it's the pungent odor of jet fuel, the hammer of a steam catapult, the pounding of another plane catching a wire, or the distinctive sound of jet engines in afterburner, straining on the catapult with ocean spray and fresh clean air waiting to lift it toward the sky.

"It was the exhilaration of soloing in a T-34B at Saufley Field, the immense feeling of accomplishment the first time I felt the jerk on my harness as the tail-hook of my T-28 snagged the arresting gear.

"Unfortunately, it was comprehension of the unforgiving nature of the profession, hammered home early as I saw a fellow student lose his life, falling prey to an approach-turn stall.

"It's the clear memory of squadron men and women who work so hard. It's the dog-tired plane captain crossing in front of my airplane, hauling another load of tie-down chains at the end of his 12-hour shift.

"It's the image of a father and carrier sailor, standing proudly, right here on Pier 12 in Norfolk, saying goodbye to his wife and small children before shoving off on a lengthy deployment. And it's the hugs of joy upon his return.

"It's the dedication of a wingman who guarded my life with his. It is a bond of trust between wingmen. It's the almost indescribable feeling of coming over-the-top of a loop in delta formation, working my scan between far horizon, gauges and the mirrors—confidence that number 2,3, 4, 5, and 6 would always be there.

"There are the hundreds of fantastic squadronmates with whom I have flown. It's my Line Chief, Chief Petty Officer Jim Randall, and my Line Petty Officer, Mac McKeon, when I was a Line Division Officer, who taught me so much about working with young sailors.

"It's the recollection of a young Tomcat pilot in the middle of the Indian Ocean, at night, with no divert field closer than 1,000 miles, who made nine attempts to land aboard. And it's heroes like Tom Sobiak, now commanding

This low port view of a *Tophatter* F-14 Tomcat shows the aircraft loaded with its AIM-9E Sidewinders, AIM-7M Sparrows, and bombs instead of its standard AIM-54C Phoenix long-range radar-guided missile. The Tomcat has scored kills at launch ranges of over 110 miles with the Phoenix. Direct hits have repeatedly been scored on widely separated, multiple target drones simulating cruise missiles. The F-14 is fitted with the M-61 cannon, a 20mm gun, which fires 6,000 rounds a minute. The F-14 platform can carry an impressive array of bombs, including the Mark 82, 83, and 84 general purpose bombs; GBU-10 and -16 laser guided bombs; and the MK-20 Rockeye cluster munitions bomb. The photograph was taken about 1994. (Official United States Navy Photograph.)

Grumman A-6E Intruders from four Naval Air Station Oceana squadrons fly over the Wright Brothers Memorial at Kill Devil Hills, North Carolina, during a demonstration flight in August 1994. The squadrons shown here represented the last of a breed—the A-6E Intruder, Attack Squadron Forty-Two (VA-42) *Green Pawns* (which changed its squadron name to *Thunderbolts* before disestablishment on September 30, 1994) (top left); Attack Squadron Thirty-Five (VA-35) *Black Panthers,* disestablished January 31, 1995 (bottom left); Attack Squadron Eighty-Five (VA-85) *Black Falcons,* disestablished September 29, 1994 (bottom right); and Attack Squadron Seventy-Five (VA-75) *Sunday Punchers,* disestablished in 1997. (Official United States Navy Photograph.)

This photograph received world attention in January 1995. It shows Fighter Squadron Eighty-Four *Jolly Rogers* F-14B Tomcats making a bombing run on the practice range at Vieques Island, Puerto Rico. (Official United States Navy Photograph.)

officer of VF-124, in the back seat with that young pilot, who, after hearing him express fading confidence, slapped the pilot's helmet with his kneeboard, refusing to let him quit. After refueling, they make it aboard.

"There's the memory of wise words from a CAG, carrier air group commander, who told me, 'Don't worry, Tony. There are those who have had these nights, and those who are gonna have them!'

"It's the reward of watching that fearful Tomcat pilot becoming an LSO and one the wing's top ten pilots.

"I will always remember that these wings reflect not only the light of this bright noonday sun. They also proudly radiate the talent, the dedication, and the courage of thousands of patriots who served and continue to serve, to keep this great nation of ours free.

"For the rewarding memories they evoke, the heroic achievements they symbolize, and most of all, for all the dedicated people they represent, these are the wings of which I will forever be proud."

In Memory of Major General Marion E. Carl, USMC
(November 1, 1915–June 28, 1998)

The words most often used to describe Marion E. Carl—hero, humility, and humor—followed the man his whole life. The tall, lean and always smiling aviator never smiled more fully than when flying or in the company of his bride, Edna, a former Powers model, their two children and their families. A love affair that lasted well-over fifty years, Marion and Edna Carl were the picture-perfect wartime couple. When most pilots came down with the newly-wed jitters on their tours of duty, perhaps hesitant to take chances in the air, Carl aggressively pursued the enemy, becoming the first Marine Corps ace as a result of actions of August 1942. As his friend Joseph R. Rees would say, "Marion knew where fear belonged," and it obviously was not in the cockpit of his fighter plane.

Flying from the deck of the USS *Long Island* on August 20, 1942, then Captain Carl and eighteen VMF-223 pilots landed their Grumman F4F-4 Wildcats on the captured Japanese airstrip at Guadalcanal in the Solomon Islands. On the twenty-fourth, fourteen Wildcats took off from the airstrip to take on a flight of fifteen Mitsubishi Zeros flying cover for Nakajima Kate dive-bombers from the Japanese carrier *Ryujo*. The enemy flight would be joined by roughly twenty Mitsubishi Betty bombers from Rabaul just north of Henderson Field. When describing that day, Carl once said: "I glanced down and saw a formation of Japanese bombers. I rolled into an overhead pass and splashed one bomber. Then, of course, things fell apart. My division split up and I lost contact with the other three pilots, but we kept hammering away at the bombers. I dropped a second bomber in another overhead run and shot a Zero off [Technical Sergeant John] Lindley's tail. As the flight drifted closer to Henderson, I claimed another bomber that was confirmed a bit later. These four kills [added to the Zero he shot down at Midway] made me an ace—the first in Marine Corps history—but that thought didn't occur to me at the time." By the time World War II ended, Carl would have eighteen-and-a-half victories, the majority of them earned in the Marines' push to take Guadalcanal, and continuing in the early phases of the "island hopping" campaign through the Solomons.

As Marine Corps squadrons switched over to the Chance-Vought F4U Corsair, Carl would have the opportunity to fly alongside America's penultimate hero, Colonel Charles A. Lindbergh, during this period.

In this photograph, taken on Vella Lavella on January 5, 1944, by Technical Sergeant D.Q. White, USMC, Marine ace Major Marion E. Carl had recently run his score of Japanese victories to eighteen-and-a-half, which made him the number four Marine Corps ace at that time. Only Major Joseph J. Foss, Major Gregory "Pappy" Boyington (both with 26), First Lieutenant Kenneth A. Walsh (20), and Lieutenant Colonel John Lucian Smith (19) had better records. Major Carl was on his second tour of duty in the South Pacific, by far the theater of war which defined the projection of power—and the future—of Navy and Marine Corps aviation. Carl shot down one plane during the Battle of Midway, fifteen-and-a-half during the fighting on Guadalcanal, and two as commanding officer of VMF-223, earned within a month prior to this picture being taken. Carl was not just the Marine Corps' first ace of World War II; he was the first Marine Corps ace in history. (Official Department of Defense Photograph.)

Lindbergh, though denied entry into the Army Air Corps for obvious reasons of age and danger, was a consultant to several aircraft companies. In this capacity, the famed aviator managed to convince the Marines that he needed combat flight time in the Corsair to evaluate its performance. In the end, he flew with several Marine Corps squadrons. Carl observed of Lindbergh that the aviator was a good pilot, but he took too long pre-flighting his Corsair before the mission started. But Carl would also remark on several occasions that Lindbergh had lived to be an older and wiser pilot because he was cautious, something he said all the young Marine pilots could certainly have learned from Lindbergh.

After the Second World War, Carl became a military test pilot. On November 11, 1946, Lieutenant Colonel Carl, piloting a Lockheed P-80A Shooting Star, made two catapults, four free takeoffs, and five arrested landings aboard the USS *Franklin D. Roosevelt.* Carl's test flights in the seat of the P-80A were part of an extensive investigation of the carrier suitability of jet aircraft which had begun on June 29, 1945—before the end of World War II—with delivery of the P-80A to Naval Air Station Patuxent River, Maryland. The following year, on August 25, 1947, Carl set a new world's speed record of 650.796 miles per hour in the Douglas D-558-1 Skystreak at Muroc Field, now Edwards Air Force Base, in California. Nearly four years later, Carl piloted the Douglas D-558-2 Skyrocket to a new altitude record of 83,235 feet over Muroc.

A restless and much younger generation began to fill the ranks of Naval and Marine Corps aviation in the years prior to Vietnam, and aging aviators akin to Carl were at a loss to understand the mores of a generation he believed was far removed from the patriotic spirit which defined his own. Regardless, when duty called once more, Carl returned to combat during the Vietnam Conflict, commanding the Second Marine Air Wing. He retired in 1973 with 13,000 flight hours, and an impressive record of military decorations, including a Navy Cross with two gold stars, the Legion of Merit with three gold stars, the Distinguished Flying Cross with four gold stars, and the Air Medal with thirteen gold stars.

The Douglas D-558-1 Skystreak was first flown on April 14, 1947, by a Douglas test pilot who, in August of that year, managed to push the aircraft to a speed of Mach 0.85. This record was succeeded the same month by back-to-back world speed records of 640 miles per hour and 650.796 miles per hour set, respectively, by two military test pilots, one of whom—Major Marion E. Carl—hit the highest mark for speed on August 25, 1947. The Skystreak was outfitted with the most powerful turbo-jet engine obtainable in the United States at that time: the General Electric TG-180. Because the aircraft was constructed with magnesium alloy for enhanced aerodynamics in relation to the actual structure of the airframe, the D-558-1 incorporated enough structural durability to sustain the speed of sound and an ultimate G-force load of eighteen. Four years later, flying the D-558-2 swept-wing model, a civilian pilot achieved a speed record of 1,238 miles per hour, while Major Carl set an altitude record of 83,235 feet. (Official United States Navy Photograph.)

Retired Major General Marion E. Carl, 82, famed World War II ace and postwar test pilot, remembered by his contemporaries and historians as the "Chuck Yeager of the Marine Corps," was gunned down in his home during a botched burglary on June 28, 1998, by a nineteen-year-old too young to know who Carl was. Those who loved and knew him best gathered in Oregon to bid him farewell at his funeral on July 6. Longtime friend and Marine Corps retired Brigadier General Joseph Jacob Foss, a Medal of Honor recipient, remembered his first flight with Carl in 1940. Foss was a cadet; Carl was an instructor at Pensacola's training command. "He did everything with that airplane that an airplane could possibly do for one-and-a-half hours. I was green," recalled Foss. "And from that day on, I respected him as the number one pilot in the world. If young folks would set their eyes on people like that, we wouldn't have punks like the one who ended his life."

Carl possessed a boundless knowledge in the cockpit, but he also knew how to have a good time out of one, too. At his funeral service, Colonel Hap Langstaff, of Sacramento, California, took mourners back to the days when both men were stationed in Washington, D.C., in 1959. Carl yearned to go hunting in Eastern Oregon. The two men would climb into a T-28 on Friday afternoons after work, flying all night to make Oregon, and buzzing a narrow dirt road to clear the cattle off before landing on a ranch. "We always got deer," Langstaff remarked. "Back in Washington, D.C., Marion had difficulty explaining how cow manure got on the landing gear." According to newspaper accounts of the service, as the laughter died away, Langstaff's voice broke with emotion as he turned to the flag-draped casket and, with a sharp salute, said: "I'm going to miss you, Marion."

Carl was buried at Arlington National Cemetery in his beloved Marine Corps dress blue uniform bearing a crisp set of ribbons signifying his many decorations. In the pocket over his heart, Edna had tucked his favorite photographs of her, their children and two grandchildren. Major General Marion E. Carl bore with him always humility, integrity, and loyalty, exemplifying the famed saying from Iwo Jima, "Uncommon valor is a common virtue."

Endnotes

Chapter 2

1. Glenn H. Curtiss started teaching Callan to fly in 1911 at his Hammondsport, New York, flying complex and in 1912, Callan received his Aero Club of America license No. 102. Callan was employed by the Curtiss Aeroplane Company as a pilot, flight instructor, superintendent of training schools, foreign representative to Italy and England, and as a demonstrator, test pilot and salesman for flying boats. He enrolled in the Naval Reserve Flying Corps on February 20, 1917, as a lieutenant and designated Naval Aviator No. 1442. During World War I, he commanded all United States Naval Air Forces in Italy. "Lanny" went on to win the Navy Cross for his wartime exploits. Callan was the Navy liaison officer to the Italian Schneider Cup team at Baltimore in 1925 and in Norfolk in 1926. Before he retired from active duty on May 1, 1948, Callan oversaw foreign observers of the Navy's atomic bomb tests at Bikini in August of 1946. He was hospitalized at the Naval Hospital, Bethesda, Maryland, in 1947 for undisclosed ailments. He retired from active duty on May 1, 1948, and died October 8, 1958, of liver cancer.
2. We can credit Curtiss and Ely for coining the phrases "black shoe" and "brown shoe" used to this day to distinguish surface navy from aviation service. The distinction came, of course, from the way the two services dressed. Naval officers in the surface fleet wear black shoes but aviators have always worn brown. The earliest "brown shoe" can be traced to 1910 and the feet of Eugene B. Ely, a pioneer aviator who never donned a naval uniform but who perhaps did more to advance naval aviation in its infancy than he was ever credited.

Chapter 4

1. The Massachusetts Institute of Technology (MIT) at Cambridge, Massachusetts, with its naval air detachment, was the main ground school for the Naval Reserve Flying Corps. The school was established on July 23, 1917, under the command of Lieutenant (junior grade) Edward Hyslop "Mac" McKitterick, Naval Aviator No. 39. The last students to attend the MIT ground school graduated on January 18, 1919. The detachment was deactivated shortly thereafter.
2. Chambers was awarded the medal of the Aeronautical Society for the year 1912 and cited for "his unusual achievements in being the first to demonstrate the usefulness of the aeroplane in navies, in developing a practical catapult for the launching of aeroplanes from ships, in assisting in the practical solution of the hydroaeroplane by the production in association with others of the flying boat, in having been instrumental in the introduction into our halls of Congress of bills for a National Aerodynamic Laboratory, and a Competitive Test, and through his perseverence and able efforts in advancing the progress of Aeronautics in many other channels."
3. Oman possessed the command presence of a seasoned operations officer at sea and, though Mustin had command at sea experience as commanding officer of the USS *Mississippi,* his forté was decidedly as an executive and administrator. His skills were prized by a Navy which needed his ingenuity and insight, and Mustin's considerable aptitude for design, to develop naval aviation.

Chapter 5

1. Building V-4 at the former Naval Aviation Depot Norfolk was constructed in 1915, making it the final vestige of what had been part of the original Naval Air Station Hampton Roads.
2. This site, once the Old Chambers Field and occupied today by the Naval Air Station Norfolk Heloport, is entirely landfill.
3. For the purpose of aircraft identification in photographs, on February 8, 1918, the national aircraft insignia changed. The white star design was replaced with concentric circles of red and blue around white. The order of red, white, and blue vertical bands on the rudder were reversed, placing the red nearest the rudder post. This change would not last long. By 1919, the Secretary of the Navy ordered naval aircraft back to the 1917 insignia pattern, with blue once again nearest the rudder post.
4. The Bureau of Yards and Docks authorized removal of the hangar in 1929. The hangar was reconstructed at Lakehurst in 1931.
5. The fact that Hoyt held two aviator numbers was not all that unusual in the designation process of LTA and HTA pilots. Pilots were permitted to qualify in both airships and fixed-wing aircraft in the early years of naval aviation.
6. After successful trials of the British-built dirigible *R-34* in July 1919, the British were contracted to build a rigid dirigible for the United States Navy at a cost of $2 million. The *R-38,* later given the United States designation *ZR-2,* was completed in her hangar at Cardigan, England, located near Howden air station in June 1921. At 699 feet long, 85 feet abeam and powered by six 350-horsepower engines, with a capacity of 2.7 million cubic feet of hydrogen, the *R-38* had a theoretical ceiling of twenty-five thousand feet. Hoyt was part of the American Navy crew which went to England in August 1921 to transfer of the airship to the United States. On August 23, General E.M. Maitland, head of British balloon forces and commandant at Howden, took the *R-38* up for final tests of rudder and control surfaces. The airship was 2,500 feet above the town of Hull and the Humber River when several girders snapped and the envelope split, breaking the *R-38* into two sections. Men, equipment and pieces of flaming airship plummeted into the Humber. The cause of the disaster was determined to be "ripe" gas cells, meaning that oxygen had seeped into the hydrogen, making it more explosive than dynamite. The seventeen United States Navy men who were aboard the *R-38* had not been authorized to be on the flight by the British Admiralty. The only American survivor was Rigger T.O. Walker. Lieutenant Richard Evelyn Byrd, Naval Aviator No. 608, had been selected as navigator for the *ZR-2* and should have been aboard the fateful flight, but the day of the crash, he missed his train back to the airfield and arrived just in time to see the airship go aloft.
7. Fractional numbers were assigned in an attempt to establish the chronological sequence of the naval aviator's designation.
8. Though the F-5L as built from a British design, the Felixstowe F-5, it should be noted that the Felixstowe series of flying boats—the F-2A, F-3, and F-5—were in turn derived from the Curtiss H-12. Commander John Cyril Porte of the Royal Navy spearheaded the effort that evolved the F-2A from the H-12, the most significant changes being to the hull in an effort to improve its strength, seaworthiness, and takeoff characteristics. The "L" in F-5L indicated powered by the Liberty engine.

Chapter 6

1. Remarks by Robert Underwood Johnson, United States Ambassador to Italy, were found in his papers located at the University of Delaware Library, Newark, Delaware, Robert Underwood Johnson Papers, Special Collections Department.
2. The United States Army Quartermaster Intermediate Depot was located on property now part of Norfolk International Terminals on Hampton Boulevard, Norfolk, Virginia. An historic monument marks the spot of the *Roma* disaster.
3. The *R-38,* otherwise known as "the Flying Lemon," was *ZR-2.*
4. The nucleus of training for crews destined to serve aboard the USSs *Shenandoah* and *Los Angeles,* underway at Naval Air Station Hampton Roads since July 1, 1922, was ended by March 15, 1923, when the dirigible ground school opened at its new location at Naval Air Station Lakehurst, New Jersey. Captain Anton Heinan, a lighter-than-air expert formerly of the German Navy, was commanding officer of the dirigible ground school at Lakehurst.
5. Rosendahl was considered an experienced mooring and navigation officer. A subsequent court of inquiry convened to investigate the *Shenandoah* disaster found no fault with his heroic performance. Rosendahl's *Shenandoah* log book notes that he had 174 hours and 41 minutes accounting for sixteen flights of various duration towing targets, scouting with the fleet, and mooring to the USS *Patoka* on trips between Newport, Rhode Island, and Hampton Roads, Virginia, between July 13 and 30, 1925.
6. Rear Admiral Moffett was the first to bear the title "naval aviation observer," in accordance with a provision of the law establishing the Bureau of Aeronautics that its chief and at least seventy percent of its officers be either pilots or observers. The Bureau of Aeronautics defined the functions and qualifications of naval aviation observers and recommended a course of study for their training. Upon its approval by the Bureau of Navigation, Moffett reported for training and on June 17, 1922, qualified as the first naval aviation observer.
7. Rosendahl was mooring officer and navigator of the *Los Angeles* from November 25, 1924, at which time he moored the airship for her christening in Washington, D.C., through May of 1925, when he went aboard the USS *Patoka* to moor the "Pride of the Navy," June 3, 1925. From the *Los Angeles,* Rosendahl went to the *Shenandoah*. During October and November, he was drawn into the Court of Inquiry convened in Washington, D.C., to find a cause of the *Shenandoah* disaster. He assumed the role of executive officer of the *Los Angeles* on March 9, 1926, where he accumulated thirty-eight hours and thirty minutes of flight time on twelve local flights around Lakehurst that ranged from forty-one minutes to seven hours, fifty-seven minutes in duration. On May 10, 1926, Rosendahl became commanding officer of the *Los Angeles,* where he remained until May 9, 1929.
8. He was relieved as commanding officer on June 22, 1932, after commanding forty of *Akron's* seventy-three total flights.
9. The First Naval District was headquartered at Quonset Point, Rhode Island, and at various periods of its history included naval air bases at Ayer, Beverly, Hyannis, Martha's Vineyard, Nantucket Island, New Bedford, Otis Field at Camp Edwards, Salem, and Squantum, Massachusetts; Bar Harbor, Brunswick, Casco Bay, Lewiston, Rockland, and Sanford, Maine; Charlestown, Torpedo Station at Newport, and Westerly, Rhode Island; Groton, Connecticut; and a lighter-than-air base at South Weymouth, Massachusetts.
10. Blimp Squadron Fourteen (ZP-14) made a record-setting transatlantic flight from Weeksville, North Carolina, to Port Lyautey, French Morocco, on May 1, 1945. ZP-14 arrived at Port Lyautey to take part in antisubmarine operations around the Straits of Gibraltar. The crossing of the Atlantic Ocean from Weeksville was completed in a total elapsed time of seventy-seven hours, of which sixty-two were in actual flight. The Bermuda-Azores leg of the crossing was the longest over-water flight made by a nonrigid airship: 1,881 nautical miles in twenty-nine-and-a-half hours.
11. The first blimp to arrive at Fortaleza was *K-84,* belonging to Blimp Squadron Forty-One (ZP-41).
12. The last flight of a Navy airship occurred on August 31, 1962, at Naval Air Station Lakehurst. Though the Navy's airship program had been disestablished in 1961, two blimps had been kept around as airborne aerodynamic laboratories in the development of vertical (short) take-off and landing (VSTOL) aircraft and antisubmarine search systems. The pilots on the last flight were Commanders W.D. Ashe and R. Shannon. Along for the ride were Vice Admiral Charles E. Rosendahl and Captain Fred N. Klein, both retired.

Chapter 7

1. The Navy received a license to operate an air station from Anacostia, an Army field, effective November 1, 1917. Anacostia was established as a naval air station on December 18, 1918, and on January 1, 1919, commissioned for seaplane test and administrative flights. The entire base was transferred to the Navy under an agreement approved September 26, 1935. The last flight from the field was on December 8, 1961. Naval Air Station Anacostia was disestablished on January 1, 1962. Lieutenant William Ellwood "Gink" Doherty, Naval Aviator No. 430, was the first to command the Navy portion of the air station in its pre-commissioning period. Doherty came to Anacostia from Naval Air Station Hampton Roads. There is some controversy regarding who holds title as first commanding officer of the air station. For many years, Doherty claimed to have been first commanding officer, but that was before Anacostia was commissioned. George Dominic Murray, Naval Aviator No. 22, who also claims the honor, and rightfully so, was the first commanding officer of the commissioned naval air station.
2. Some naval aviators were never assigned numbers although they were designated naval aviators before some of those with numbers below 2,000. Others with numbers above 2,000 should actually have had lower ones, but so often the numbers did not marry up to the order of designation dates. The first 2,000 naval aviator numbers do include some who were not among the first 2,000, and do not include some who deserved to be recognized in that group. There is actually no way to be sure if the roster of 00 aviators is complete unless families reveal the naval aviator's information to researchers for verification. Stillwell should have been entitled to a number between 727 and 849 since he was designated a heavier-than-air pilot on July 22, 1918.
3. Miami served as a seaplane training and patrol station. Construction of its facilities began in October 1917. The commission date of the station is uncertain, and the air station closed on May 28, 1920. Marc Andrew "Pete" Mitscher, Naval Aviator No. 33, was

commanding officer in March 1918, but it is not known whether he was the first. A Marine Flying Field was established at Miami on a tract adjacent to the naval air station in March 1918.

4. Naval Base Norfolk was the headquarters for the Commandant of the Fifth Naval District. The Navy's association with its civilian neighbors had been limited primarily to coastal reaches around naval installations prior to the establishment of the naval district system in 1910. The United States and its parochial possessions were divided into fourteen (later fifteen) naval districts for the purpose of better organization of coastal defenses and resource mobilization. The Fifth Naval District encompassed the Commonwealth of Virginia, the states of West Virginia and Maryland, and sixteen counties in North Carolina. When it was first demarcated in 1910, the district only took into account seven counties in North Carolina, but with subsequent expansion south, the total area of Fifth Naval District coverage was roughly 116,000 square miles. The commandant of the district was tasked with coordination of all shore activities within the district in support of combatant naval forces. During the height of World War II, the district included air bases at Chincoteague, Creeds, Fentress, Franklin, Monogram in Suffolk, Norfolk, Oceana and Pungo, Virginia; and Elizabeth City, Harvey Point, Manteo and Weeksville in Elizabeth City, North Carolina. On September 30, 1980, the Fifth Naval District was vitiated after the Navy realigned its combatant and shore activities structure.
5. The Fourth Naval District, headquartered at Cape May, New Jersey, included air stations at Atlantic City and Wildwood, New Jersey; and New Cumberland at Harrisburg and Willow Grove, Pennsylvania.
6. The *O.B. Jennings* was a 10,000-ton tanker owned by Standard Oil Company. The tanker's captain was George Nordstrom. She was sunk by the German submarine, *U-140,* sixty miles southeast of Cape Henry on August 4, 1918. The tanker had a full gun crew and was returning empty from its Plymouth, England, to Newport News, Virginia, run. The *O.B. Jennings'* gun crew manned one four-inch deck gun after Nordstrom spotted the first *U-140* torpedo. This torpedo struck the tanker, but did not sink her. The *O.B. Jennings* engaged the U-boat in a running gun battle for nearly an hour before the submarine's gunners finished her off. Second Steward James H. Scott was the *O.B. Jennings'* only fatality. Captain Nordstrom switched clothes with Scott to prevent his capture by the U-boat crew. Nordstrom and his men climbed into three lifeboats which were subsequently searched by the crew of the surfaced *U-140.* The Germans were looking for the captain and when they could not find him, they took Second Officer Rene Bastin as prisoner, leaving everyone else behind. Bastin was not seen again. The USS *Hull* had responded to the *O.B. Jennings'* distress call, arriving after the U-boat had left the area. The *Hull* took in two lifeboats while the Italian steamer, *Umbria,* picked up Nordstrom and the men in his lifeboat. The *Umbria* dropped the lifeboat near the shore at Currituck Beach and they rowed ashore.
7. The *Mirlo* could not have been shelled by a German submarine as Vorys' dispatch stated. The *U-117* was the only German U-boat operating on the East Coast of the United States at that time, and has been estimated to have been some eighty miles north when the *Mirlo* struck the mine. The *U-117* had seeded Wimble Shoals off the coast of North Carolina with mines in early August 1918 before heading north to do more of the same as well as target merchant ships bound for Europe. The *Mirlo,* a British tanker of 6,679-tons and a crew complement of fifty-two, had a full load of gasoline she had picked up in New Orleans, Louisiana, on August 10, before heading across the Gulf of Mexico, through the Florida Keys and northeast toward Norfolk. As *Mirlo* passed Cape Hatteras on August 16, Captain W.R. Williams, her master, made the decision to head in the direction of Wimble Shoals. The *Mirlo* struck a mine near the Wimble Shoals Light Buoy. Captain Williams ordered the lifeboats readied as he nursed his crippled ship toward the beach. A second explosion of the gasoline forced Williams to lower the lifeboats. One lifeboat of sixteen crewmen capsized as it was being lowered, dumping these men into the sea. They clung helplessly to the overturned lifeboat. Two other lifeboats, one with Captain Williams and sixteen crewmen, and the other with nineteen merchant seamen, moved as quickly as possible away from the *Mirlo* and the growing sea of fire forming around the sinking ship. A third explosion split the *Mirlo* in half, enveloping the crewmen clinging to the capsized lifeboat in flames. The *Mirlo* slipped beneath the sea, but the fire traveled over the water as it was fed by the gushing gasoline from the ship's hold. Only six men still clung to the lifeboat, ten died in the flames and never resurfaced. Lifesavers from the Chicamacomico Coast Guard Station moved in to save the six crewmen and the group of nineteen crew who drifted near the sea of fire in their disabled surfboat, also the smallest of the lifeboats lowered by the *Mirlo.* The wind blew flames at this small boat and seared the flesh of the nineteen men and set fire to their boat. The men's clothing was completely gone, leaving them naked and blackened by the fire which had licked their flesh. Lifesavers led by Captain John Allen Midgett located the disabled surfboat near nightfall. Forty-two of *Mirlo's* fifty-two crewmen survived. Midgett and his lifesavers performed an incredibly courageous and selfless act in saving the *Mirlo* crew. These intrepid lifesavers, themselves burned in the rescue, recovered and returned to their duties.
8. The United States Navy seaplane base at Porto Corsini, Italy, was commissioned a naval air station on July 24, 1918, and closed on December 31, 1918. The first commanding officer of the Naval Air Station Porto Corsini was Willis Bradley Haviland, Naval Aviator No. 577.
9. Two additional Medals of Honor were awarded for naval aviation-related incidents during World War I. Ship's Fitter First Class Patrick McGunigal, born on May 30, 1876, in Hubbard, Ohio, was attached to the USS *Huntington.* On the morning of September 17, 1917, the *Huntington* was passing through the war zone and had just dispatched a kite balloon aloft with Lieutenant (junior grade) Henry Willets "Susie" Hoyt, Naval Aviator No. 545, aboard as an observer. The balloon was about 400 feet in the air when the temperature suddenly dropped, causing the balloon to descend 200 feet, at which point it was struck by a severe squall. As the crew hauled the balloon down, it struck the water so hard that Hoyt became entangled in the lines and submerged underwater in the balloon's basket. Hoyt's predicament looked pretty grim until McGunigal dove in, untangled Hoyt, and got a line around him so the near-drowned observer could be hauled onto the *Huntington's* deck. McGunigal was safely brought aboard behind Hoyt.

The other Medal of Honor went to Chief Machinist's Mate Frances Edward Ormsbee Jr., born April 30, 1892, and a native of Providence, Rhode Island. On the morning of September 25, 1918, Ormsbee was up flying with Ensign John Auguste Jova, Naval Aviator No. 429, when Ormsbee saw an N-9, Bureau Number A2422, flown by Ensign Thomas C. McCarthy, Naval Aviator No. 1221, go into a spin at 1,000 feet and crash into Pensacola Bay about three-quarters of a mile to his right. The time was 9:55 a.m. Ormsbee and Jova went to the aid of the N-9's crew. Ormsbee managed to pull Radio Gunner Paul B. Parsons from the wreckage, then made repeated dives into the bay to rescue McCarthy, but to no avail. Ensign McCarthy drowned. Ormsbee later became a Naval Aviation Pilot (NAP).

Chapter 8

1. "Gobs" were enlisted men who worked on aircraft, and not always while the aircraft was on the ground. Enlisted mechanics often and knowingly climbed into the cockpits of naval aircraft they knew were poorly designed. "Gobs" went up to test engines and serve as flight engineers. Placing flight engineers on big flying boats to check fuel, temperature, and power plants made long patrols possible. It was not uncommon for an enlisted mechanic to climb out on a motor to work on or replace a spark plug with a seaplane at 200 feet or more nor was it unusual for "gobs" to put out in-flight fires at 2,000 feet.
2. "Groundhogs" or "hogs" were primarily naval aviation officers who did not wear the wings of gold. Most "hogs" were engineering officers who supervised the repair and maintenance of power plants, wings, and hulls, but there were also others who specialized in communications, administration, supply, and religious services. A few naval aviators crossed-over into "hog" territory such as Ensign Frederick Elmer King, Naval Aviator No. 245, who conducted extensive radio work at Naval Air Station Hampton Roads.

Chapter 9

1. The Langley detachment of twenty-seven naval aviators was put through their preliminary flight phase in Curtiss JN-4 Jennies. Near the end of the training syllabus, the detachment flew Dayton-Wright DH-4 aircraft to master formation flying skills. Both aircraft, the JN-4 and DH-4, were procured from the United States Army for Navy use.
2. The squadron designation process was a complex ordeal in the mid to late 1920s. Heavier-than-air squadrons had their class designation, in this example a utility squadron "VJ," followed by a second part called its identification number. The final part of the squadron designation used an assignment letter, in this case "B" for Battle Fleet. Feher's utility squadron, VJ-1B, was assigned to the USS *Aroostook* (CM-3) as part of Aircraft Squadrons, Battle Fleet. VJ-1B was known to have been assigned to the *Aroostook* in August 1928, its pilots flying an assortment of NB-1, OL-3, OL-6, OL-8, T2D-1, and PN-12 aircraft.
3. "F" in a squadron's assignment letters indicated Fleet Base Force. VJ-2F was assigned to Commander Aircraft, Base Force, and was a flag unit flying five PM-2 aircraft in 1934. By 1937, VJ-2F was reassigned within the Base Force flag structure to the USS *Wright* (as well as the USS *Riegel*) where the squadron flew JF-1, J2F-1, and RD-3 aircraft.
4. This was an "artificial" test environment. The torpedoes were "dummies" and the "hits" based on the Mk VII's trajectory to target which included important information such as direction and progression of the torpedoes.
5. Shoemaker later advanced to captain and commanded Naval Air Station Norfolk.

Chapter 10

1. General Order 161 made significant changes to the squadron designation system in 1928. These changes were amended on September 28, 1929, to include two new squadron designations which did not appear in the previous year's General Order. General Order 179 (series 1921), the amendment to General Order 161, listed scouting and bombing squadrons.
2. Congressional members and War Department representatives acknowledged as early as mid-1941 that if the United States was drawn into the war in Europe, there would be a manpower shortage in all the military branches, particularly Navy shore-based operations. The Navy's Bureau of Aeronautics proposed using women to fill the manpower requirements of fleet installations and recommended to senior Navy officials that legislation be put before Congress immediately. Navy hierarchy did not show any interest in the idea until after the Japanese attacked Pearl Harbor on December 7, 1941. The Bureau of Aeronautics advocated and embraced the concept of a women's reserve force within the Navy when the service's leadership proposed only an auxiliary or less than full military status for its women members. The Bureau of Aeronautics proposal prevailed and the the enabling legislation (H.R. 6807) in the House appeared in March 1942 along with an identical Navy bill in the Senate. The Women's Naval Reserve was established by law on July 30, 1942, as P.L. 689. The acronym WAVES stands for Women Accepted for Volunteer Emergency Service. Mildred McAfee, the first director of the Women's Naval Reserve, did not particularly want an acronym used. She favored Women's Naval Reserve. The WAVES program existed from 1942 to 1972 at which time its women members were given the option of joining the regular Navy or the Naval Reserve program. Women could join the regular Navy after World War II when specific billets were opened for them. Greta von Sothen is one example of a woman who chose the latter opportunity.
3. Naval Amphibious Base Little Creek, though located on lands which were once part of Princess Anne County, now merged with the city of Virginia Beach, does not have a Virginia Beach address. The amphibious base is a continuation of Norfolk and its address reflects this often overlooked fact.

Chapter 11

1. During the latter part of World War II, numerous designation modifications and additions were made to the Secretary of the Navy's confidential letter (SC) A3-1/VV Serial 0104540 of January 2, 1943, Naval Aircraft Squadrons, Designation and Renumbering of, issued as Navy Department Bulletin C-19 and dated January 15, 1943, effective March 1, 1943. Night fighter squadrons were among those added to the designation list.
2. The "MS" in VP-MS-1 indicated Medium Patrol Squadron (seaplane). An "ML" meant Medium Patrol Squadron (landplane).
3. Though it was formally disestablished on September 30, 1994, HM-12 remained in operation until November 30, 1994.

Chapter 12

1. Zulu time is based on the Prime Meridian. The meridian line is an imaginary line which runs from the

North Pole to the South Pole. By international convention, this line runs through the primary transit instrument at the Royal Observatory at Greenwich, England. This is known as "initial meridian." All longitude is calculated both east and west from this meridian up to 180°. All countries adopted a universal day, called a Mean Solar Day, beginning at the mean midnight at Greenwich and counted on a twenty-four hour clock. Nautical and astronomical days everywhere begin at mean midnight. These criteria date back to the International Meridian Conference held in Washington, D.C., in 1884.

2. Composites have a history that has evolved from basic fiberglass to the advanced type used today. The oldest composite designs were the reinforced plastic materials such as fiberglass. Composite designs such as sandwiches of honeycomb bonded to thin skins have been in use for approximately twenty-five years. The honeycomb cores and skins are usually metals such as aluminum alloy or titanium, but some nonmetallic materials such as resin impregnated textiles were also used. Since the early 1980s, the use of stiffer fibers such as boron and graphite in the resin binder became a popular design option among aircraft manufacturers. Additionally, the fabrication techniques have derived to alter the direction and ply thickness of continuous fibers to control the flexibility and ultimate strength of the cured assembly. The newer series of graphite and boron composites are referred to as advanced composites.

   To demonstrate the importance of composites to fleet operation, one only need damage the surface area or leading edge of an F-14 or A-6 aircraft. The F-14 Tomcat utilizes 218 bonded panels, including flight controls, intake walls, fairings, stress panels, and engine doors fabricated from aluminum honeycomb with aluminum or titanium alloy skins. The F-14 horizontal stabilizer skins are maunufactured from a boron composite material. The radome is an epoxy fiberglass design.

   The new wing on over 150 A-6E Intruders was manufactured from graphite/epoxy composite material with titanium alloy fittings. The A-6E and EA-6B Prowler utilizes dozens of flight control and other bonded panels fabricated from aluminum honeycomb with aluminum alloy skins. NADEP Norfolk developed repair, and in most cases, remanufacturing capabilities for all of the composite parts on the F-14 and A-6 aircraft especially since the original manufacturer, Grumman, had discontinued making them. In fact, as Grumman Aerospace Corporation began downsizing its own operation at its Bethpage Plant on Long Island, New York, NADEP Norfolk provided the manufacturer the use of its autoclaves. Norfolk's facility kept the typical composite set up consisting of the autoclaves, cold storage equipment, clean rooms, vacuum blankets, and specialized hand tools that had been in-house manufactured or acquired over time. Bonded structures requiring autoclave processing were limited to sixteen feet in length by the autoclave size but most aircraft sections did not exceed that dimension. Repair of composites is a capability which coexists with conventional and advanced metal working ability to deal with the broad spectrum of fabrication techniques found on modern naval aircraft. Items like the center wing section on an A-6E Intruder are not removable and therefore, must be repaired in the context of the entire aircraft.

   Many of the bonded panels on the F-14 Tomcat have extremely high-load carrying requirements in supersonic flight and the bonding integrity of these panels after rework or remanufacture are correspondingly critical. The Naval Air Systems Command recently instituted extremely stringent certification requirements for activities which perform this work. The certification requirements demand a twelve to eighteen month series of destructive tests which verify the ultimate bond strength of successive batches of production samples. The bond strength requirements must be demonstrated in the temperature range of -67 to +350 degrees Fahrenheit. Many of the panels on operational F-14 aircraft have experienced severe delamination and corrosion in service and NADEP Norfolk had to completely remanufacture the degraded items because, of course, the original manufacturer is no longer producing them. The depot remanufactured virtually hundreds of panels to satisfy critical fleet requirements in the absence of any other alternative. Naval Aviation Depot Norfolk was the only facility qualified to work on the F-14's bonded titanium intake walls.

   The Tomcat's nose and main landing gear require periodic regeneration of a composite collar lining which serves as a bearing surface. NADEP Norfolk developed a unique fabrication technique to complete the work over a period of time. In addition, the facility had also perfected its ability to repair and remanufacture advanced composites. NADEP Norfolk first honed its skills on composite molding and layup of carbon fiber components in order to fabricate hot bondform tools which support F-14 components during autoclave curing cycles.

   Inclusive in the composite program was the nondestructive inspection (NDI) department. NDI technicians used a real time x-ray chamber for immediate detection of moisture intrusion and internal corrosion of metal bonded structures. This instrument permits viewing of x-ray images on a television-type monitor without a need for photographic development of films. The scanning mechanism of the x-ray chamber is programmable and can easily follow complex curves. In addition, NADEP Norfolk used portable C-scan ultrasonic machines to develop an NDI footprint, for instance, of every A-6E wing which could later be used for comparison of delamination areas or other discrepancies. This technique was also utilized to identify delamination of F-14 metal bonded structures. The C-scan technique develops a color relief map of the scanned area which is recorded as a computer disk file and can be filed indefinitely for analytical purposes. A transportable C-scan machine using fluid coupling and robotic scanning mechanisms was acquired and made operational in 1993. Given the level of expertise required in composite work, the depot trained nearly a dozen engineers on finite element analysis and design applications of composites. The facility maintained several materials engineers with specialized knowledge of composite materials and bonding techniques, including one with a doctoral degree in the subject area.

3. The A-6 aircraft presented one problem at least the manufacturer, Grumman Aerospace Corporation, did not believe could be repaired without separation of the airframe. Naval Aviation Depot Norfolk was able to develop a process for replacement of the A-6 fuselage station 227 and 285 bulkheads without having to cause separation.

4. Remanufacture of an F-14 Tomcat from an A to D configuration is a massive change that includes a total aircraft rewire, major structural modification (5,000-hour Time Compliance Requirements or TCR) installa-

tions, and installation and testing of an entirely new avionics system—including the AN/APG-71 radar system, General Electric F110 engines, Naval Aircrew Common Ejection Seats (NACES) seats, and OBOGs oxygen generation system. In support of this program, a number of new processes were developed or established internally such as titanium line brazing, F-14D boresight capability, and avionics bench testing of over one hundred different components. This effort also included the replacement of all airframe wiring which is the same as the A-6, approximately twenty-six miles, and testing all wiring harnesses.

5. The personnel of the Voyage Repair Team account for in excess of 100,000 man-hours per year.
6. The Navy Standards Laboratory at Norfolk was formed in 1993 through the consolidation of the calibration functions and capabilities of the Washington Primary Navy Standards Laboratory East with those of the depot. This consolidation resulted in the formation of a Navy Primary Standards Laboratory for the East Coast, located in Hampton Roads. The rationale for the decision was based on the fact NADEP Norfolk was not only centrally located on the eastern seaboard, but co-located with the majority of the East Coast operational fleet, the new megaport at Norfolk. The Materials Engineering Laboratory facility happened at the same time, thus allowing materials engineering to share their new sixty-thousand-square-foot building with the standards lab. The Navy Standards Laboratory at Norfolk calibrates precision standards for hundreds of other military and contractor metrology laboratories, and provides a common reference of traceability to the National Institute of Standards and Technology. The laboratory provides measurement services and engineering expertise in virtually every parameter which can be measured, including physical and mechanical measurements, electrical and electronic measurements, and electro-optics. Scientists and engineers maintain unique capabilities such as wind tunnel laser velocimetry, Josephson Junction Array technology for DC voltage calibration, and high-energy laser measurement capability.
7. The laboratory initiated a surface analysis development program almost ten years ago. The program protocol has been applied to routine failure analysis and process development efforts. Evidence of the surface analysis development program is realized in the analytical depth the scientists and technicians are able to pursue to develop cause and effect data associated with aircraft component failure and processing deficiencies, a skill critical to the fleet.

Chapter 13

1. The Washington Naval Conference resulted in a treaty limiting naval armament. The treaty was signed by representatives of France, Great Britain, Italy, Japan, and the United States. Provisions of the treaty established the tonnage ratio at 5-5-3 for capital ships of Great Britain, the United States, and Japan, respectively, and slightly less for France and Italy. The same ratio was applied to aircraft carrier tonnage, set at 135,000-135,000-81,000 tons. The treaty also limited any new aircraft carriers to 27,000 tons with a provision that if the total carrier tonnage were not exceeded, nations could build two carriers of not more than 33,000 tons each or obtain them by converting existing or partially-constructed ships which would otherwise be scrapped by the treaty.

Chapter 14

1. The Navy changed the designation of aircraft carriers on October 1, 1952, at which time CVs and CVBs became CVAs, "A" representing "attack." Consequently, the *Midway* was redesignated CVA-41, and the *Forrestal,* CVA-59.
2. Air Task Groups were formed after the Korean Conflict in response to lessons learned from combat operations aboard *Essex*-class carriers. Operations planners discovered that five squadrons could not be operated effectively in combat so they withdrew one squadron from each carrier about to deploy, beginning in 1951. ATGs were never commissioned air groups aboard the carriers but continued to operate in informal fashion until 1959.
3. Admiral Arthur William Radford (1896–1973) completed naval flight training at Pensacola, Florida, in 1920, though Radford had been a shipboard officer since 1916. After receiving his wings, he embarked on the adventure that was naval aviation in the 1920s and 1930s. During World War II, Radford was promoted to rear admiral and placed in charge of Carrier Division Eleven before returning to Washington, D.C., to work in the office of the Chief of Naval Operations. Radford was appointed vice chief of naval operatons for air in January 1946, and a little over three years later, was engaged in the Revolt of the Admirals along with his friends Arleigh A. Burke and Forrest Sherman, among others, who fought unification of America's military establishment and reduction of the Navy as an independent branch of the service. Radford survived the Revolt of the Admirals and was subsequently selected by President Dwight D. Eisenhower as chairman of the Joint Chiefs of Staff in 1953 and reappointed in 1955. Radford did not retire from the Navy until 1957.
4. The *Kennedy,* though even smaller than the *America* with its 1,040-foot length, 128-foot, 6-inch beam, displaces at 81,119 tons, compared to the *America* at 79,166 tons.
5. Eighty-two crewmen survived boarding by the North Koreans. The crew was held captive for exactly eleven months, charged with spying. Since neither Moscow or Peking intervened, North Korean President Kim Il Sung became a demigod in the eyes of his people. The *Pueblo* crew was released only after the United States government apologized for conducting espionage in North Korean waters, promising never to do so again. In a move unprecedented in the realm of international law, the United States labeled the apology document, containing an espionage confession, false before signing it—hence, admitting no fault and no espionage.

Epilogue

1. Vice Admiral Less was Commander Naval Air Force Atlantic Fleet from August 6, 1991, to March 18, 1994. At the time of his retirement, Less had been on active duty for nearly thirty-four years.

Bibliography

Primary Sources

Unpublished Manuscripts

Bellinger, Vice Admiral Patrick Neison Lynch, "The Gooney Bird," (no date).

Lewis, Henry P. (1967), "The Story of Flight A 1917–1919 and Recollections of Its Members."

----------(no date), "Golden Eagle # 200."

Government Documents

There were hundreds of government documents and personnel records, aviation log books, aircraft historical cards, command histories, and personal and official papers and correspondence used in the compilation of this volume. Individual archives and libraries named in the acknowledgments conscientiously aided me in my quest to present as complete a story of naval aviation as possible, providing me with treasure troves of information. Below are examples of those resources:

Congressional Record, Proceedings and Debates of the 76th Congress, Second Session (1939). Inclusive of radio address on American neutrality by Major Al Williams. Washington, D.C.: U.S. Government Printing Office.

Deputy Chief of Naval Operations (Air). Aviation Shore Establishments, 1911–1945.

National Archives, Military Reference Branch, Washington, D.C. The archives in Washington, D.C. contain the log books of the Naval Air Station Hampton Roads, Virginia, for the periods ascribed forthwith, January 7, 1918–July 31, 1918; November 1, 1919–December 31, 1920; January 1, 1921–December 31, 1921; January 1, 1922–December 31, 1922; February 1, 1923–December 31, 1923; December 1, 1924–December 31, 1924; and January 1, 1925–July 31, 1925.

Naval Air Station, Norfolk, Virginia (1979, April 23). Official Transfer Ceremony of the Kawanishi H8K2 Emily Flying Boat to the Museum of Maritime Science, Tokyo, Japan, with remarks by Vice Admiral Forrest S. Petersen, Commander, Naval Air Systems Command, Washington, D.C.

-----------(1970, December 7). Dedication of Flatley Center with remarks by Vice Admiral Robert L. Townsend, Commander Naval Air Force, U.S. Atlantic Fleet.

United States Government Printing Office (1947). Building The Navy's Bases in World War II: History of the Bureau of Yards and Docks and the Civil Engineering Corps 1940–1946. Washington, D.C.: United States Government Printing Office.

United States Naval Aviation, 1910–1970, 2nd Edition. (1970). Washington, D.C.: NAVAIR 00-80P-1.

United States Navy Bureau of Aeronautics (1928). Rigid Airship Manual 1927. Washington, D.C.: U.S. Government Printing Office

Interviews

Hundreds of interviews and exchanges of correspondence went into the aggregation of this book. Persons named below contributed the most significant information. Talks the author considered less than a formal interview are denoted as conversations. All conversations and interviews were conducted by the author unless otherwise noted. Interviewees and correspondents are listed alphabetically: Commander Martin R. "Marty" Allard; Vice Admiral Richard C. Allen (retired) and his wife, Peggy; William J. Armstrong Ph.D. (conversation); Admiral Stanley R. Arthur (retired) (conversations); Frank Ault (conversation); Virginia Massenberg Barnes; Commander Martin P. Bricker; Joseph "Bolo" Cavanaugh; Stephen D. Chalker; Commander Rudy R. Costanzo; Thomas D. Crouch; Walter C. Diehl; Captain E. Lee Duckworth; Stephen Ewing (conversation); Dorothy Flatley; Rear Admiral James H. Flatley III (retired); Lieutenant Commander James H. Flatley IV; Admiral Whitey Fleightner (retired); Janie Forbes; Captain Daniel J. Franken; Rear Admiral Jack A. Garrow (retired); William W. Gough, M.D.; Lyle and Mary Kay Heldenbrand; Reon G. Hillegass; Thomas C. Hise; Rear Admiral Alfred C. "Bud" Holmes (retired); Gerald Jean; Vice Admiral Anthony A. Less (retired); Captain David McCampbell (retired and deceased); Captain J.B. McKamey (retired); Lieutenant General Dennis J. Murphy, USMC (retired); Samuel B. Murphey; John Parker; Commander Gerald C. Peebles (retired); Commander Thomas J. "Sparky" Sparks; Colonel Theodore Argyres Petras, USMC (retired); Captain Bruce Peiper; Captain Nicholas J. Pope (retired); Henry Proescher; Kenneth S. Reightler Sr.; Caroline Kennedy Schlossberg; Captain Robert "Whiskey Bob" Schmidt; William L. Skliar; Captain Dale O. "Snort" Snodgrass, Lieutenant Commander Greta von Sothen (retired); Commander Alexander Vraciu (retired); David White; Alice Williams (conversation).

Published Sources

Books

Aero Club of America (1907). *Navigating the Air: A Scientific Statement of the Progress of Aeronautical Science up to the Present Time.* New York, New York: Doubleday, Page and Company.

Barker, Ralph (1981). *The Schneider Trophy Races.* Shrewsbury, England: Airlife Publishing Limited.

Bertrand, Kenneth J. (1971). *Americans In Antarctica 1775–1948.* New York, New York: American Geographical Society.

Blackburn, John Thomas (1989). *The Jolly Rogers.* New York, New York: Orion Books.

Buchanan, A.R. (Ed.)(1946). *The Navy's Air War.* The Aviation History Unit OP-519B, Deputy Chief of Naval Operations (Air) with Foreward by Admiral Marc A. Mitscher. New York, New York: Harper and Brothers Publishers.

Burgess, Charles P. (1927). *Airship Design.* New York, New York: Ronald Press Company.

Cooper, Josephine L. (1993). *Pioneer Pilot—Based on Walter Lees' Journals.* San Marino, California: Converse Publishing.

Davis, Arthur Kyle (Ed.)(1924). *Virginia War History in Newspaper Clippings, Volume II.* Richmond, Virginia: Virginia War History Commission.

-----------(1923). *Virginians of Distinguished Service of the World War, Volume I.* Richmond, Virginia: Virginia War History Commission.

Durkota, Alan (1998). *Medal of Honor, Volume 1: Aviators of World War One.* Stratford, Connecticut: Flying Machines Press.

Dwiggins, Don (1966). *The Air Devils: The Story of Balloonists, Barnstormers, and Stunt Pilots.* Philadelphia, Pennsylvania: J.B. Lippincott Company.

Gablehouse, Charles (1967). *Helicopters and Autogiros.* Philadelphia, Pennsylvania: J.B. Lippincott Company.

Hearne, R.P. (1916). *Zeppelins and Super-Zeppelins.* London, England: John Lane.

Hollenbach, Commander Robert C., USN, et al. (1967). *United States Naval Reserve Training Command Golden Anniversary 1916–1966.* Marceline, Missouri: Walsworth Publishing Company, Inc.

Holm, Major General Jeanne, USAF (retired)(1982). *Women in the Military: An Unfinished Revolution.* Novato, California: Presidio.

James, Derek N., A.M.R.Ae.S. (1981). *Schneider Trophy Aircraft 1913–1931.* London, England: Putnam and Company.

William T. Larkins (1988). *U.S. Navy Aircraft 1921–1941/U.S. Marine Corps Aircraft 1914–1959.* New York, New York: Orion Books.

Layman, R.D. (1979). *To Ascend from a Floating Base: Shipboard Aeronautics and Aviation, 1783–1914.* Cranbury, New Jersey: Associated University Presses, Inc.

Melhorn, Charles M. (1974). *Two-Block Fox: The Rise of the Aircraft Carrier, 1911–1929.* Annapolis, Maryland: Naval Institute Press.

Munson, Kenneth (1971). *Flying Boats and Seaplanes Since 1910.* New York, New York: Macmillan.

-----------(1969). *Pioneer Aircraft 1903–14.* New York, New York: Macmillan.

Paine, Ralph D. (1925). *The First Yale Unit (1917–1920).* Two volumes. Cambridge: Riverside Press.

Presidential Commission on the Assignment of Women in the Armed Forces (1992). *Women in Combat.* Washington, D.C., and New York, New York: Brassey's, A Maxwell Macmillan Company.

Robinson, Douglas H. & Charles L. Keller (1982). *"Up Ship!" : A History of the U.S. Navy's Rigid Airships 1919–1935.* Annapolis, Maryland: Naval Institute Press.

Roseberry, Cecil R. (1972). *Glenn Curtiss: Pioneer of Flight.* Garden City, New York: Doubleday.

Schoeni, Arthur L. (1978). *Vought: Six Decades of Aviation History.* Texas: Aviation Quarterly Publishers.

Swanborough, Gordon and Peter M. Bowers (1968). *United States Navy Aircraft Since 1911.* Annapolis, Maryland: Naval Institute Press.

WAVES National (1990). *Navy Women 1908–1988.* Volume 1 and Volume 2. No location: WAVES National.

Williams, Al (1940). *Airpower.* New York, New York: Coward-McCann.

Articles

Armstrong, William J., Ph.D. (1978, June). "Aircraft Go to Sea: A Brief History of Aviation in the U.S. Navy," *Aerospace Historian,* (25) 2.

Chambers, Captain Washington Irving Chambers (1986, Reprint). "The First Year," United States Naval Institute *Proceedings* Supplement. Original article appeared in the November 1912 issue of *Proceedings.*

Grosvenor, Gilbert (1943, June). "Insignia of the United States Armed Forces," *National Geographic,* (83) 6.

Haley, Lieutenant Commander M.F., Division Officer (Ed.) (1953, May 15). *Injun Overhaul,* (1) 14, a publication of the Power Plant Division of the Overhaul and Repair Department.

Hardie, George Jr. (1961, Spring). "The Birth of Naval Aviation," *American Aviation Historical Society Journal,* (6) 1.

"Sixth Fleet F-14s Down Libyan Su-22s." (1981 August 24). *Aviation Week & Space Technology.*

Small, Dorothy L. (1954, October). "Catapults Come of Age," United States Naval Institute *Proceedings,* (80) 10.

Squires, J. Duane (1937, July). "Aeronautics in the Civil War," *American Historical Review,* (42).

Valenteen, Bill (1968, September). "Naval Air Rework Facilities: Naval Air Station Norfolk," *Digest of U.S. Naval Aviation Weapons Systems,* (2) 3, NAVAIR 08-1-504.

Miscellaneous

Armstrong, William J., Ph.D. (1986, February 18, document sent via Naval Air Systems Command), "U.S. Naval Aviation Training 1911–1922."

Index

O

P

The Author

Amy Waters Yarsinske received her B.A. degrees in Economics and English from Randolph-Macon Woman's College and Master of Planning degree from the University of Virginia School of Architecture. Amy is a well-known and respected author and journalist, as well as president of AWY & Associates, an entity which encompasses her entrepreneurial interests in the fields of book writing, speechwriting, and urban planning practice. Though her professional and community affiliations are extensive, Amy is a past president of the Norfolk Historical Society and the Norfolk Historical Foundation, an organization she co-founded, a member of the Rotary Club of Norfolk, the American Planning Association and its Virginia Chapter, the Navy League of the United States and the organization's Hampton Roads Chapter, the Association of Naval Aviation and its Hampton Roads Squadron, and an alumnus of the prestigious CIVIC Senior Leadership Institute. Amy, a Norfolk native, is the author of more than a dozen books and many journalism pieces pertaining to regional and national history, historical biography, military and aviation history, and non-fiction subject matter. She and her husband, Raymond, a naval flight officer, have three children, ages 7, 4, and 1.

More Quality Aviation History Books from Flying Machines Press

In a Now Forgotten Sky
The 31st Fighter Group in WW2

By Dennis Kucera
$49.95, ISBN 0-9637110-9-1

- The story of the 31st Fighter Group, the highest-scoring fighter group in the Mediterranean Theater of Operations, is traced from its origins in the 1st Pursuit Group in WWI to the jets of today, with the focus on the 31st's dramatic role in North Africa, Italy, and over the *Reich* in WW2. The 31st was one of only two American fighter groups to fly the famous Spitfire.
- Full of personal anecdotes and air combat.
- 450 photos, most from private collections of the 31st F.G.
- 8 color pages illustrating 8 Spitfires and 8 P-51 Mustangs in profile plus color photos of post-war jets flown by the 31st F.G.
- Hard-bound, 8.5-inch by 11-inch format, 418 pages.

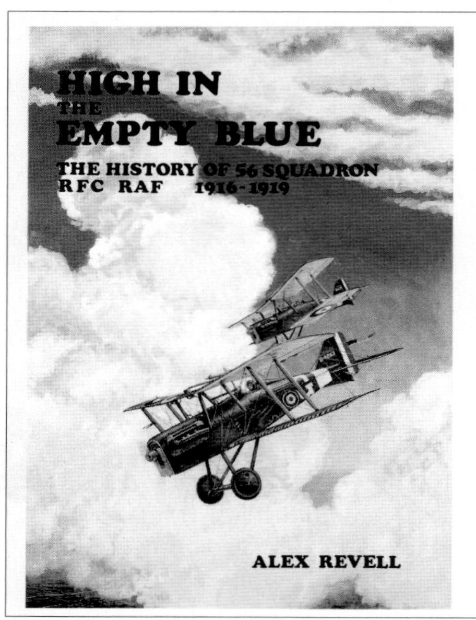

High in the Empty Blue
The History of 56 Squadron RFC/RAF 1916–1919

By Alex Revell
$49.95, ISBN 0-9637110-3-2

- The complete history of 56 Squadron RFC/RAF, Britain's premier WWI fighter squadron in 225,000 words.
- Full of personal anecdotes and air combat.
- 430 photos, 30 documents and drawings.
- 8 pages of color showing 17 aircraft.
- SE5 and SE5a scale drawings to both 1/48 and 1/72 scales.
- 21 appendices list all squadron personnel, aircraft, victories, casualties, etc.
- Hard-bound, 8.5-inch by 11-inch format, 450 pages.

French Aircraft of the First World War

by Dr. James Davilla and Arthur Soltan
$89.95, ISBN 0-9637110-4-0

- The first and only complete coverage of these important warplanes.
- 983 rare black and white photographs.
- 185 3-views scale drawings; 130 to 1/72 scale, 50 to 1/144 scale, and 5 to non-standard scales.
- 25 pages of color plates illustrating 61 aircraft.
- Two full-page color paintings and 8 color photos of museum aircraft bring the total to 30 pages of color.
- Approximately 300,000 words of text, including lists of all types used in every *escadrille,* extensive operational details, and order of battle information never previously available.
- Hard-bound, large 9-inch by 12-inch page format, 652 pages.

More Quality Aviation History Books from Flying Machines Press

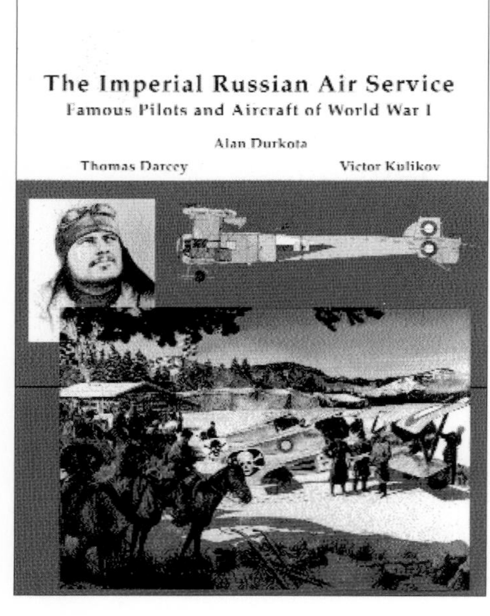

The Imperial Russian Air Service

Famous Pilots and Aircraft of World War I

by Alan Durkota, Tom Darcey, and Victor Kulikov
$79.95, ISBN 0-9637110-2-4

- The first comprehensive coverage of the Russian Air Service in WWI.
- 615 rare photos, 20 drawings and maps.
- Scale drawings of 40 aircraft (30 at 1/48 scale, 10 at 1/72 scale).
- 48 pages of color illustrating 85 aircraft, including many aces' aircraft, supported by detailed captions, plus aviators and awards.
- Detailed biography of each Russian ace.
- Biography of each foreign ace who served in Russia.
- Famous Russian designers Sikorsky and Grigorovich and their aircraft.
- Key Russian manufacturers Anatra, Dux, and Lebed and their aircraft.
- Overview of army and naval aviation and EVK.
- Distinguished Russian aviators, first women combat pilots, etc.
- Appendices cover lighter-than-air aviation, Russian awards, pilot victory lists, aircraft flown by aces.
- Hard-bound, large 9-inch by 12-inch page format, 560 pages.

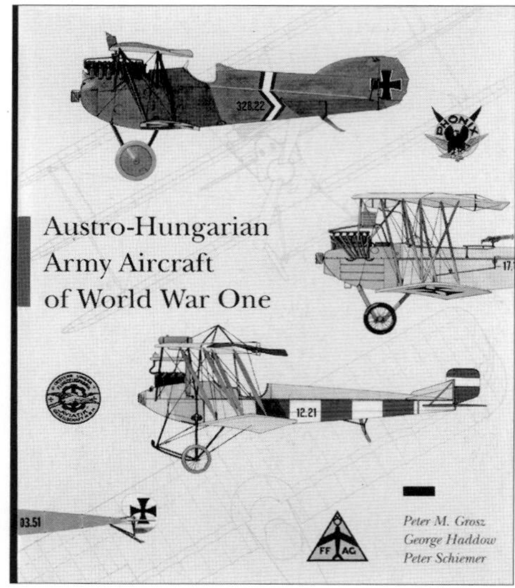

Austro-Hungarian Army Aircraft of World War One

by Grosz, Haddow, and Schiemer
$84.95, ISBN 0-9637110-0-8

- The standard reference on these rare and exotic warplanes.
- 903 rare photos and 25 drawings.
- 102 3-views (62 in 1/48 scale, 40 in 1/72 scale).
- 26 pages of color illustrating 56 aircraft supported by full captions.
- Full coverage of German aircraft purchased by Austria-Hungary.
- Coverage of WWI Austro-Hungarian helicopters!
- Hard-bound, large 10-inch by 12-inch page format, 570 pages.

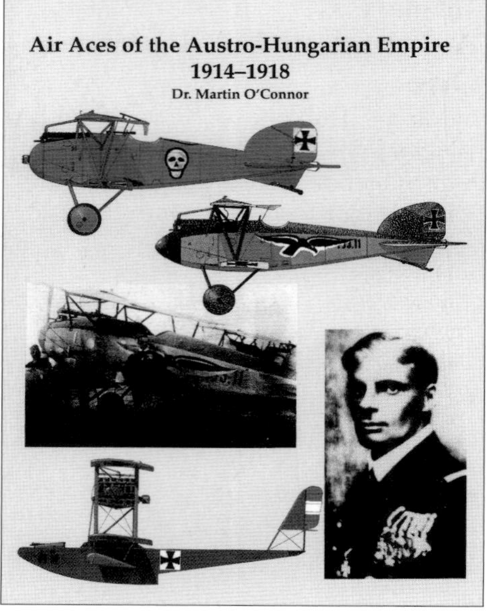

Air Aces of the Austro-Hungarian Empire 1914–1918

by Dr. Martin O'Connor
$49.95, ISBN 0-9637110-1-6

- The standard work on these courageous airmen, with biographies of all 49 WWI Austro-Hungarian air aces.
- 240 rare photos.
- 16 pages of color profiles showing 50 aces' aircraft with full captions.
- Hard-bound, 8.5-inch by 11-inch format, 336 pages.